OXFORD PAPERBACK REFERENCE

A Concise Companion to the
Jewish Religion

Dr Louis Jacobs CBE is Rabbi of the New London
Synagogue and Goldsmid Visiting Professor at
University College London. He is the author of many
books and hundreds of learned articles on Judaism,
Talmud, Jewish Mysticism, and general Jewish
thought.

Oxford Paperback Reference

*forthcoming

A Concise Companion to the
Jewish
Religion

Louis Jacobs

OXFORD

UNIVERSITY PRESS

Great Clarendon Street, Oxford OX2 6DP

Oxford University Press is a department of the University of Oxford.
It furthers the University's objective of excellence in research, scholarship,
and education by publishing worldwide in

Oxford New York

Athens Auckland Bangkok Bogotá Bombay Buenos Aires Calcutta
Cape Town Chennai Dar es Salaam Delhi Florence Hong Kong Istanbul
Karachi Kuala Lumpur Madrid Melbourne Mexico City Mumbai
Nairobi Paris São Paulo Singapore Taipei Tokyo Toronto Warsaw

and associated companies in Berlin Ibadan

Oxford is a registered trade mark of Oxford University Press
in the UK and in certain other countries

First published 1995 as The Jewish Religion: A Companion
This abridged and updated edition published as an
Oxford University Press paperback 1999

British Library Cataloguing in Publication Data

Data available

Library of Congress Cataloging in Publication Data

Data available

ISBN 0-19-280088-4

1 3 5 7 10 8 6 4 2

Typeset by Market House Books Ltd
Printed in Great Britain
on acid-free paper by
Cox & Wyman Ltd
Reading, Berkshire

Contents

For my grandson

Abraham Peter Jacobs

Preface

This *Companion to the Jewish Religion* is a concise version of *The Jewish Religion: A Companion*, published by OUP in 1995. All the entries in the larger work have been included in this one, but many of the elaborations have been omitted in order to produce a much more compact volume. As in its predecessor, the conventional Jewish method of dating has been followed: BCE ('Before the Common Era') for BC and CE ('the Common Era') for AD. Thus 586 BCE = 586 BC and 70 CE = 70 AD. I am grateful to Hilary O'Shea of OUP for suggesting that I compile the larger volume and to Angus Phillips of OUP for suggesting that I compile this shorter but still sufficiently comprehensive volume.

A

Aaron Brother of Moses; Aaron together with his sister *Miriam, features in the Bible among the three leaders of the Israelites from Egyptian bondage: 'For I brought thee up out of the land of Egypt, and redeemed thee out of the house of servants; and I sent before thee Moses, Aaron, and Miriam' (Micah 6: 4). Aaron and his sons were consecrated to be the *priests in the sanctuary (Leviticus 9). On the basis of this and other biblical passages, the descendants of Aaron are held to be the priestly cast, although there has been much discussion among modern scholars on the actual historical development of the Aaronic priesthood.

Abba Aramaic equivalent of the Hebrew *Av* ('Father') with Imma (Hebrew *Em*) for 'Mother'. There is thus no support for the view that these are terms of endearment like 'Daddy' and 'Mummy' and that Jesus was using Abba in this sense (Mark 14: 36). In modern Hebrew these two are the usual forms of address to parents.

Abbaye and Rava Two fourth-century Babylonian teachers whose debates in matters of Jewish law appear frequently in the Babylonian Talmud; so much so that from the Middle Ages the term 'the debates of Abbaye and Rava' was used as a synonym for Talmudic dialectics as a whole.

Abortion There is no actual prohibition in the Bible against aborting a foetus. Nevertheless, in the unanimously accepted Jewish consensus, abortion is a very serious offence, though foeticide is not treated as homicide.

Abraham First of the three *patri-archs of the Jewish people, father of *Isaac and grandfather of *Jacob. The story of Abraham is told in the book of Genesis (11: 27–25: 18). Critical scholarship sees in this account a welding-together of different traditions, and the migrations of Abraham as a later attempt at mirroring the journeys of the children of Israel towards the land of Israel in order to provide a theological scheme in which later events are anticipated through the divine promise to Abraham and his seed. The suggestion made by nineteenth-century scholars that Abraham is not an historical figure at all has been abandoned by the majority of contemporary scholars who detect behind the stories and myths a real historical figure living in approximately the eighteenth century BCE. In the Jewish tradition, Abraham is the father *par excellence* of the Jews and Judaism. God's covenant with Abraham was given its expression in the rite of *circumcision (Genesis 17). The circumcision rite of Jewish male children is called 'entry into the covenant of Abraham our father', and the name of the rite itself is the *berit*, the 'covenant'. But the idea of Abraham as the 'father' of the Jews is not understood only in terms of physical parenthood. Abraham is the spiritual father of all who are converted to Judaism. At the *conversion ceremony, the convert is given a Hebrew name and is called a 'child of Abraham our father'.

Abravanel, Isaac Don Isaac Abravanel, prominent statesman in Portugal and later in Spain, Jewish philosopher, and biblical exegete, born Lisbon, 1437, died Venice, 1508. Abravanel objected to the attempt by thinkers such as Maimonides to draw up lists of *principles of faith. These thinkers, he declares, thought of the Torah as a science operating with certain axioms or principles from which everything else can be derived, whereas the God-given Torah is complete in itself with every detail of its precepts a principle and none more important or more axiomatic than the others.

Abudarham, David Pupil of *Jacob ben Asher, who compiled in Seville in 1340 an influential commentary to the *liturgy, every detail of which he expounds on the basis of traditional teachings but with original ideas of his own.

Adam and Eve The first parents of the human race, whose story is told in the opening chapters of the book of Genesis. There is no doubt that until the nineteenth century Adam and Eve were held to be historical figures, but with the discovery of the great age of the earth and of human civilization many modern Jews have tended either to read the story as a myth expressing important ideas about the human condition in non-historical form or to identify Adam with prehistoric man in general.

Adam, Fall of While it is incorrect to say that post-biblical Judaism attaches no special significance to Adam's fall or knows nothing of *original sin, it is certainly true that, with the exception of the Kabbalah, the fall does not occupy an important place in Jewish theology. There are many interpretations of Adam's sin and of the tree of knowledge from which he ate after having been forbidden by God so to do. Opinions range from that which understands the knowledge of good and evil as having a sexual connotation to that according to which the tree was no different from any other tree and was simply set aside as a test of obedience. In the Talmud there is a view that it was not a tree but wheat from which

Adam and Eve ate, since an infant only acquires the knowledge that enables it to speak when it has begun to eat bread. Another view in the Talmud is that it was the vine from which Adam and Eve ate, since so many of the troubles of the world result from drinking wine. No apple!

Adam Kadmon Primordial man, a term used in the Kabbalah to denote the stage of the divine unfolding which provides the link between *En Sof and the *Sefirot.

'Adon Olam' 'Lord of the universe', the title, after the opening words, of a popular hymn of uncertain authorship. In many liturgies this hymn forms the beginning of the daily morning services and the closing hymn on the Sabbath and festival services. Because the final stanza reads: 'My soul into His hand divine | Do I commend: I will not fear, | My body with it I resign, | I dread no evil: God is near', this hymn is often recited as part of the night prayers before retiring to sleep and, where possible, on the deathbed after the *confession. A number of melodies with which to chant the hymn have become universally popular among Jews. 'Adon Olam' is built around the idea that God rules before and after His creation of the world and will reign for ever. He is, was, and will be through all eternity. Another stanza reads: 'And at the end of days shall He | The dreaded one, still reign alone, | Who was, who is, and still will be | Unchanged upon his glorious throne.' Since the hymn is poetry, not a statement about *eschatology, this stanza is not usually interpreted to mean that at 'the end of days' no creatures will exist, only God alone.

Adoption Although legal adoption was recognized in the ancient Near East as far back as the Code of Hammurabi around 1700 BCE, there is no clear evidence that this institution existed in ancient Israelite law. Pharaoh's daughter adopted Moses as her son (Exodus 2: 10) but this is stated in the context of Egyptian norms. Similarly, the statement in the book of Esther (2: 7) that Mordecai took his orphaned cousin Esther to be his daughter may be intended to reflect conditions in the Persian Empire. The Talmudic Rabbis rely on the biblical stories of Pharaoh's daughter and Esther to teach that if anyone brings up an orphan in his household, Scripture considers it as if he had actually given birth to the child; but nowhere in Talmudic law is real legal adoption recognized, despite the fact that the Romans certainly knew of it. There is nothing in Jewish law to prevent the drawing-up of new legislation in such matters and the Adoption of Children law of 1960 in the State of Israel empowers a court to grant an adoption order for children under the age of 18. However, an adopted child is not treated as a natural child in every respect. If a couple adopt a boy and a girl unrelated to one another the laws of consanguinity do not apply and, when they grow up, they are free to marry, the fact that they are brother and sister by adoption being irrelevant.

Adret, Solomon Ibn Spanish Rabbi, theologian, and Kabbalist (1235–1310), known, after the initial letters of his Hebrew name, as Rashba. Adret was one of the most outstanding scholars of medieval Jewry. During the fierce debates on the question of the study of *philosophy, Adret steered a middle course, discouraging this study ('What did the Greeks know of God?') and yet, in a ban he pronounced in Barcelona (1305), he declared it forbidden only to those under the age of 25.

Afikoman This word of uncertain etymology but of Greek origin means 'dessert' and is now used to denote the piece of unleavened bread, *matzah, eaten at the end of the *Seder on the

first night of *Passover. It is customary not to eat anything else after the *afikoman* in order for the taste of *matzah* to remain in the mouth all night. There is a folk-belief that if a piece of the *afikoman* is kept in the house after Passover the house will not be visited by burglars during the year.

Age Respect for the aged is an important principle in Judaism. 'Thou shalt rise up before the hoary head and honour the face of the old man, and thou shalt fear thy God: I am the Lord' (Leviticus 19: 32). This is understood in the Talmud to mean that whenever an old man or woman passes by one should rise to one's feet as a token of respect.

In most Jewish communities there is a special old-age home (*moshav zekenim*) in which the old people are adequately cared for. The thirteenth-century biblical exegete *Bahya, Ibn Asher, commenting on the verse (Exodus 20: 12): 'Honour thy father and thy mother, that thy days may be long upon the land which the Lord thy God giveth thee', remarks that it is undoubtedly true that care of aged parents can be a severe burden but in return the Torah promises longevity to those who shoulder the burden. A Talmudic saying has it that if the young tell you to build and the aged to destroy, listen to the aged; for the construction of the young is destruction, but the destruction of the aged is construction.

Aggadah The aspect of Jewish, especially Talmudic, literature that embraces all non-legal topics. Aggadah treats of Jewish history, ethics, philosophy, folklore, medicine, astronomy, popular proverbs, pious tales, and so forth. Aggadah is thus best defined as including any subject of relevance to Judaism that is not embraced by the term *Halakhah, the legal side of Judaism.

Agnosticism A term coined by T. H. Huxley to denote that attitude which, unlike theism (conviction that God exists) and *atheism (conviction that God does not exist), maintains that it cannot be known whether or not God exists. Judaism, as a monotheistic religion, obviously rejects the agnostic attitude as it does that of atheism. This is not to say, however, that there are no unexplored areas in matters of *belief.

Agunah A woman bound or 'chained' either to a missing husband or to one who refuses to *divorce her. In Jewish law the State cannot intervene to grant a couple a divorce. The only way a married woman can become free to remarry is by obtaining a release from her husband by his death or by him delivering to her, of his own free will, the *get, the bill of divorce. From early Rabbinic times efforts have been made to help the agunah obtain release from the tragic situation in which she is prevented from marrying another by a husband who is no husband.

Ahad Ha-Am 'One of the People', penname of Asher Ginsberg (1856–1927), Hebrew essayist and Zionist thinker. For Ginsberg, *Zionism was important not only because it sought to provide a physical homeland for the Jewish people but because this homeland had the potential of becoming a spiritual centre for world Jewry.

Akedah 'Binding of Isaac', the account in the book of Genesis (22: 1–19) of *Abraham, at the command of God, taking his son, *Isaac, to be offered as a sacrifice on Mount Moriah. Abraham *binds* his son (hence 'the Binding of Isaac') to the altar and is ready to perform the dreadful deed when an angel appears to tell him to stay his hand and to promise him that his seed will increase. There is no reference to this episode anywhere else in the Bible. Nor does it feature very prominently in post-biblical Jewish literature until the third century CE. Some biblical scholars, Jews included, have read the story as a protest against human sacrifice, the significant point being that the angel intervenes to prevent the murder as an obscene act that God, unlike the pagan deities, hates and could never really have intended. But in traditional Jewish thought, the *Akedah* is used as a paradigm for Jewish *martyrdom; the Jewish people are ready at all times to give up life itself for the sake of the sanctification of the divine name (*Kiddush Ha-Shem).

Akiba, Rabbi Foremost teacher of the Torah who lived in the second half of the first century and the first half of the second century CE. As is the case with so many of the *Tannaim and Amoraim, it is has proved difficult for historians to disentangle the facts of Akiba's life from the pious legends with which it is surrounded. The statement, for example, that Akiba was an ignoramus (*am ha-aretz) until, at the age of 40, he was encouraged by his wife to study the Torah for forty years, after which he taught for forty years, is obviously far too neat to be anything but legendary, and was presumably intended to place Akiba among the great teachers who wore the mantle of Moses who lived to be 120. The same applies to the dialogues Akiba is supposed to have engaged in with Turnus Rufus, the Roman Governor of Palestine, though these might reflect early Rabbinic associations with the Gentile authorities and the kind of queries Roman nobles might have addressed to the Rabbis.

Albo, Joseph Spanish philosopher (fifteenth century), author of *Sefer Ha-Ikkarim* (*Book of the Principles*), an eclectic work based on the ideas of earlier teachers such as his own mentor, Hasdai *Crescas, but important as the last great system of medieval Jewish philosophy. In this work, part *theology, part

*apologetics, Albo sets out the principles of the Jewish religion by which Judaism differs from other religions, especially Christianity.

Alfasi, Isaac Alfasi (1013–1103) lived for most of his life in Fez in Morocco (hence the name Alfasi, 'from Fez' or the Rif, 'Rabbi Yitzhak Fesi') and was the author of one of the great *Codes of Law, the *Sefer Ha-Halakhot* (*The Book of the Laws*). By the time of Alfasi the Babylonian Talmud had become the supreme source of Jewish Law, but the Talmud is not a Code; rather, it is a corpus of the discussions by the Rabbis on numerous questions, most of them of law. Alfasi's method was to give the basic debates in matters of law in the original form in which they appear in the Talmud but omitting all the elaborate discussions, stating simply, in his own words, at the end of each passage: 'This is the law'.

Allegory The method of scriptural interpretation in which persons and events mentioned in the Bible are understood not in a literal sense but as referring to stages in the religious life of the Jews. *Philo, the greatest of the allegorists, understands, for example, the command to Abraham to obey Sarah and send away his handmaiden Hagar (Genesis 21: 10) to mean that in order to achieve perfection a man has to obey the voice of reason and banish the passions that control his life.

Alphabet, Hebrew The Hebrew alphabet has twenty-two letters, five of which have a slightly different form when they occur at the end of a word to close the word. The letters are shown in the table above:

These letters are all consonants, to which the vowels have to be added in order to form words. In the *Sefer Torah, for instance, only the consonants are written, the reader supplying the

The Hebrew Alphabet					
alef	א	= 1	*ayin*	ע	= 70
bet	ב	= 2	*pey*	פ	= 80
gimel	ג	= 3	*tzade*	צ	= 90
dalet	ד	= 4	*kof*	ק	= 100
hey	ה	= 5	*resh*	ר	= 200
vav	ו	= 6	*shin*	ש	= 300
zayin	ז	= 7	*tav*	ת	= 400
het	ח	= 8			
tet	ט	= 9	The five final letters		
yod	י	= 10	are:		
kaf	כ	= 20	*kaf*	ך	
lamed	ל	= 30	*mem*	ם	
mem	מ	= 40	*nun*	ן	
nun	נ	= 50	*pey*	ף	
samekh	ס	= 60	*tzade*	ץ	

vowels. The vowels and the signs by which they are recorded are:
patah (–) = a as in hat.
segol (∵) = e as in let.
hirek (.) = i as in lit.
kibbutz (ֻ) = u as in bull.
kametz, short (ָ) = o as in top.
kametz, long (ָ) = a as in yard (sign the same for both short and long).
tzere (..) = e as in they.
shurek (ּו) = long u as in flute.
holem (ֹ) = long o as in role.

Amalek The name of a tribe that attacked the Israelites in the wilderness (Exodus 17: 8–16; Deuteronomy 25: 17–19), whose memory was to be 'blotted out'. In the later Jewish tradition the actual identity of this tribe is unknown but Amalek becomes the symbol of wanton cruelty and murderous intent. The Jewish moralists speak of the need to eradicate the Amalek residing in the human heart—that is, aggressive tendencies in general.

Amen The liturgical response now used not only in Judaism but also in *Christianity and *Islam. The word has the same Hebrew root as *emunah* ('faith') and is also connected with the word *emet* meaning *'truth'. The idea expressed is of firm trust, acceptance, and reliability. Amen is found in a variety of contexts in the Bible (Numbers 5: 22; Deuteronomy 27: 15; 16, 17, 18, 19, 20, 21, 22, 23, 24, 25, 26; 1 Kings 1: 36; Isaiah 65: 16; Jeremiah 11: 5; 28: 6; 1 Chronicles 16: 36; Nehemiah 5: 13; 8: 6; Psalms 41: 14; 72: 19; 89: 52; 106: 48). Louis Ginzberg has translated Amen as 'So be it' or 'So shall it be' and has described it as 'perhaps the most widely known word in human speech'. A late second-century teacher in the Talmud takes the initial letters of Amen to represent *el melekh neeman*, 'God, Faithful King'.

Am Ha-Aretz An ignoramus, in contradistinction to the *Talmid Hakham*, the scholar. The term, meaning literally 'the people of the land', is found in the Bible (e.g. in Genesis 23: 12-13), perhaps referring to the governing body of the people, the Parliament. In post-biblical times the 'people of the land' were the farmers and agricultural labourers and later still the term was applied to the individual in the sense of the ignorant man, by much the same process as in the development of the English words 'peasant' and 'commoner'.

Amos The first of the literary prophets who lived, according to the biblical book which bears his name, during the reigns of King Uzziah in Judah and Jeroboam in Israel, in the Northern Kingdom, in the eighth century BCE. Amos came from the village of Tekoa in the Southern Kingdom of Judah and he is described (Amos 7: 14) as 'a herdman and a dresser of sycamore trees', which probably means that he was a kind of gentleman farmer. Because of his occupation, Amos uses in his prophetic utterances similes taken from agricultural and farming life. Students of the prophetic books have seen this phenomenon of a prophet expressing himself in language drawn from his own personal status and type of life as showing that however

*prophecy is to be understood, it does not mean that in his experience of the divine and the inspiration to which it gives rise, the personality of the prophet is taken over or obliterated. When Amos says (Amos 7: 14): 'I was no prophet, neither was I a prophet's son', he is not declaring that his father was not a prophet but that he had never belonged among the 'sons of the prophets', the guild of prophetic disciples. Like other prophets, Amos claims to have been called by God to prophesy without having either prepared himself for the experience or even desired it.

Amulet Heb. *kamea*, a magical charm to protect from harm the one who possesses it or wears it. Despite the strong biblical opposition to magic and *divination, white magic in the form of the amulet was tolerated by the Talmudic Rabbis, who allowed a tried amulet (one written by an expert in the art, which had worked successfully on three different occasions) to be carried even on the Sabbath when carrying objects in the public domain is normally forbidden.

Angels Supernatural beings who perform various functions at God's behest. The Hebrew word *malakh* comes from a root meaning 'to send' and is used both in the ordinary sense of a messenger and in the sense of an angel 'sent' by God.

References to angels are found throughout the Bible but with the exception of Gabriel (Daniel 8: 16; 9: 21) and Michael (Daniel 10: 13; 12: 1) in the late book of Daniel, the angels in the Bible have no name. When Manoah asks the angel to tell him his name, the angel replies that it is secret (Judges 13: 17–18).

Among many modern Jews, belief in the existence of angels is very peripheral. Even when those parts of the liturgy referring to angels are still maintained, they are understood more as sublime poetry than as theological statements. However, there are comparatively few outright denials of the actual existence of angels and some Jews, even today, look upon belief in angels as an important part of the religious life.

Anger Most of the rules and regulations of Judaism have to do with actions rather than with character traits. Emotional states cannot be made subject to categorical injunctions. The standard Code of Jewish law, the *Shulhan Arukh*, offers no guidance on when and why not it is permissible to fly into a rage. There are many expressions, however, in the non-legal sources—the moralistic literature, for example—where it is stated again and again that anger is an ugly emotion and has to be avoided; but the appeal here is to character-cultivation and it is acknowledged that individual temperament is involved.

Animals, Attitudes to There is no single theological view in Judaism on the purpose of the animal creation *Saadiah Gaon, discussing why God created animals, gives three possible reasons. The first is that God simply willed it so and it is not for man to try to fathom the divine will. Secondly, it may be that God created the wondrous animal kingdom in all its variety so that His wisdom could be revealed to man. Thirdly, it may be that animals have been created for man's benefit. Maimonides (*Guide of the Perplexed*, 3. 13), on the other hand, does not consider the question of why God created animals a significant one, since we must eventually fall back on the idea that it is God's will, as it is with everything else in creation. Maimonides refuses to interpret the creation narrative in Genesis (Genesis 1: 26–8) as implying that animals, sun, moon, and stars were created solely for man. True, argues Mai-

monides, the Genesis account states that man can rule over the animals but this in no way implies that God created them for this specific purpose. Maimonides (*Guide of the Perplexed*, 3. 17) also ridicules the notion that animals will be recompensed in the Hereafter for the sufferings they have to undergo on earth. This view is held by Saadiah but Maimonides believes it to be foreign to Judaism. The Rabbinic literature was not composed by systematic theologians like Saadiah and Maimonides. In this literature there are teachings about animals which do seem to imply that everything in creation, including animals, exists for the sake of human beings.

Animals, Cruelty to While Judaism does not advocate *vegetarianism and permits the killing of animals for human use, causing unnecessary pain to animals is strictly forbidden, whether by biblical *law, according to some teachers in the Talmud, or by Rabbinic law, according to others. The Talmud urges a man to feed the animals in his care before he himself sits down to eat. Some teachers explain the existence of the law of *shehitah, the killing of animals in a special way, on the grounds that this method causes the least pain to the animal. The biblical injunctions against taking the young from the nest before sending away the mother bird (Deuteronomy 22: 6–7) and against slaughtering an animal and its young on the same day (Leviticus 22: 28) have been similarly explained. This would certainly seem to be the reason for the prohibition against muzzling an ox when it treads the corn (Deuteronomy 25: 4). While *hunting animals for food is permitted, many authorities frown on hunting for sport.

Annihilation of Selfhood The mystical state in which the ego, confronted by the divine, especially in prayer, loses its separate identity; Heb. *bittul ha-yesh*. The doctrine of self-annihilation is prominent in *Hasidism in general but is stressed particularly in the *Habad group. In cultivation of this attitude some Hasidim would try never to use the 'I' pronoun in conversation. *Bittul ha-yesh* has strong affinities with the *unio mystica* in general mystical theology and it is therefore incorrect to say, as some scholars do, that in Judaism the gulf between God and human beings is so vast that no version of the religion teaches the possibility of the soul of the mystic being absorbed in the divine.

Antediluvians The men before the *Flood who lived to fabulous ages (Genesis 5). According to Maimonides, it was only particular individuals who lived to these great ages but *Nahmanides considers this view to be untenable; all men of those generations lived to a great age and it was only the deterioration of the atmosphere after the Flood that brought about a gradual shortening of human life. Some students of the Bible have suggested that the numbers of 'years' are really those of 'months' but the Hebrew word *shanah* used here always means a 'year' in the Bible and a different word is used for 'month'.

Anti-Semitism Hatred of Jews or unreasonable prejudice against them; a term coined in 1875 but with the reality behind it going back virtually to the beginnings of Judaism itself and culminating in the Nazi persecution of the Jews and the *Holocaust in which six million Jews perished. Anti-Semitism has assumed various forms. Greek and Latin authors ridiculed the Jewish religion and the Jews who adhered to it either because the Jews were 'atheists' in refusing to acknowledge the Greek and Roman deities, or because they thought of themselves as superior.

The cause of anti-Semitism is a question much discussed in modern times.

If the phenomenon is due to prejudice, how does the prejudice arise? Opinions have varied from simple dislike of the unfamiliar to the objection to Jews foisting their religious values on the non-Jewish world with a resulting conflict of conscience for the betrayal of these values. It would be too much to say that anti-Semitism has disappeared in civilized society today but, once its horrific consequences in the Holocaust have been perceived, very few decent men and women view it as anything but an aberration.

Apocrypha The books produced by Jewish writers during the period of the Second *Temple but not included in the Bible as part of sacred Scripture, as they are in Catholicism but not in the Protestant Church. The books of the Apocrypha are: the first book of Esdras; the second book of Esdras; Tobit; Judith; the rest of the chapters of the book of Esther; the Wisdom of Solomon; Ben Sira (Ecclesiasticus); Baruch; a letter of Jeremiah; the Song of the Three; Daniel and Susanna; Daniel, Bel, and the Snake; The Prayer of Manasseh; the first book of the Maccabees; the second book of the Maccabees.

Apologetics, Jewish The systematic defence of the Jewish religion against its detractors from within and without. Numerous examples of apologetics are found in the Rabbinic literature in which the Jewish sages frequently engage in controversy with heretics or with pagan philosophers and rulers. The Rabbis often use the ministering *angels as an apologetic device. The angels are made to ask God why He shows favour to Israel and why He allows Rabbi Akiba, who had devoted himself to the study and teaching of the Torah, to be tortured to death by the Romans. Usually God is made to give an explanation but in the instance of Rabbi Akiba, all that God says is: 'Be silent. This is how it has entered My thought.' In the history of Jewish apologetics, both these types of response are prominent: those matters capable of a reasonable explanation are elaborated on, while there is always an acknowledgement that some matters are beyond human comprehension and must be left to faith.

Aramaic A sister language of Hebrew (from Aram, the ancient name of the country now Syria). The Bible contains some portions in Aramaic. The language of scholarship in *Palestine in the Mishnaic period was Hebrew and the Mishnah itself is in Hebrew, but the language of the common people was Aramaic. In the post-Mishnaic period (from the beginning of the third century CE) the scholars used both Hebrew and Aramaic in their debates and discussions so that both the Palestinian *Talmud and the Babylonian Talmud are in Aramaic (the former in the Western dialect of Aramaic, the latter in the Eastern dialect) with a strong mixture of Hebrew, especially for legal maxims and similar formulations. As an important legal document, the *ketubah is in Aramaic, the language the people knew and understood. To the present day, in *Orthodox Judaism, the original Aramaic form is retained in the ketubah.

Architecture From the earliest times Jews were influenced by the various architectural styles used by the surrounding peoples, so that no specifically Jewish architectural style ever developed. But Jewish teaching has always been in favour of sound building techniques for aesthetic reasons and for reasons of safety and security.

Even with regard to the construction of a *synagogue there is nothing like official regulations. Often synagogues in Islamic lands were built in a similar style to mosques and, in Christian lands, synagogues were frequently built on the pattern of churches, though not, of course, with any cruciform pattern. Many synagogues in the nineteenth century were built in a mixture of Gothic and oriental styles; the latter apparently because this was felt appropriate for a religion which came originally from the East. In modern times there has been considerable experimentation in synagogue building, though some feel that the newly built synagogues have occasionally substituted the novel for the numinous.

Aristotle Renowned fourth-century BCE Greek philosopher. In the Middle Ages, when Greek thought in its Arabic garb had penetrated the circles of the Jewish philosophers, Aristotle is quoted and his opinions discussed.

Ark, Biblical The chest containing the two *tablets of stone on which the *Decalogue was inscribed. The account is given in the book of Exodus (25: 10–22) of Moses being commanded by God to instruct the people to make an Ark (aron) into which the 'testimony' (understood as the two tablets on the basis of other passages in the Bible) was placed. The Ark was a chest of acacia wood overlaid inside and outside with pure gold, its length 21/2 cubits, its width 11/2 cubits, and its height a 11/2 cubits. On top of the Ark there was a cover of pure gold to which were affixed two golden figures with outstretched wings, the *cherubim. Four golden rings were attached to the Ark into which two staves of acacia wood were placed so that the Ark could be carried from place to place.

In Solomon's *Temple the Ark was placed in a special shrine (the 'holy of holies') but the cherubim figures were no longer attached to it, being placed on the floor of the shrine (2 Kings 6 and 8: 6). Some time during the First Temple period, the Ark is said mysteriously to have disappeared and there was no Ark in the holy of holies in the Second Temple.

Ark, Noah See FLOOD.

Ark, Synagogue Following the pattern of the biblical *Ark, every *synagogue has an Ark containing the Scrolls of the Torah (*Sefer Torah). In Talmudic times the Ark was a portable chest, like the biblical Ark, and was also used as a stand upon which the Scroll was placed for the reading of the *Torah. In post-Talmudic times down to the present day, the Ark is a built-in cupboard at the eastern wall of the synagogue, covered by a curtain.

Arrogance A sense of brazen superiority or sheer effrontery; Heb. *azut*. In Ethics of the Fathers (5. 20) it is said: 'The arrogant [*az panim*, lit. "brazen faced"] is destined for Gehinna but the shamefaced is destined for Gan Eden' (see HEAVEN and HELL).

Art It has been said that while the Greeks taught the holiness of beauty, the Hebrews taught the beauty of holiness. This is an unfortunate generalization, although it is true to say that the ancient Hebrews did see holiness as beautiful. It would be way off the mark to say, however, that Jews have been indifferent to the creation of beautiful things.

Artificial Insemination The question of whether Judaism permits artificial insemination has been much discussed in the *Responsa of twentieth-century Rabbis. There are two kinds of artificial insemination: (a) where the semen is the husband's, AIH; (b) where the semen is from a donor other than the husband, AID. AIH is generally allowed. Orthodox Rabbis frown on AID. Many Reform Rabbis adopt a more lenient stance and permit AID, especially where the woman is single, though here the question of allowing a child to be brought up without ever knowing the identity of his natural father is not easily dismissed.

Asceticism Self-denial for a religious purpose; Heb. *perishut*, 'separation' from worldly things. As in other religions there are ascetic trends in Judaism. As we might have expected, the Talmud contains statements both in favour of asceticism and against the tendency.

Ashkenazim Jews whose ancestors lived in the Middle Ages in Germany and the surrounding countries, as distinct from those with a Spanish or oriental ancestry, the *Sephardim. The name Ashkenaz in the Bible (Genesis 10: 3) was identified in the Middle Ages with Germany, hence Ashkenazim, 'Germans'. There are no doctrinal divisions between Ashkenazim and Sephardim but each community preserves its own traditions.

Ashmedai King of the *demons, as this strange figure is described in the Talmud, where he is provided with a consort, Igrat, 'queen of the demons'. Ashmedai, in Jewish folklore, is not identified with the Devil or *Satan but is rather like Shakespeare's Puck, a mischievous prankster but not evil.

As If The philosophical theory of Hans Vaihinger (1852–1933) according to which ideas, the truth of which cannot be determined, can still be of value when treated *as if* they are true. The nearest approach to this theory in the Jewish tradition is the ancient Rabbinic attempt to heighten certain concepts by treating these as if they represented concepts of greater significance.

Astrology The belief that human destiny is determined, or at least affected by, the stars and planets in the ascendancy when a person is born. The majority of Jews today are not much affected by astrological beliefs one way or the other, although in Yiddish parlance the expression *mazal tov* for 'good luck' is still used, more as a convention than as a matter of belief.

Atheism The attitude that affirms there is no God. Until the Middle Ages, when the philosophers, Jewish, Christian, and Muslim, who in response to atheistic attacks sought to prove by rational argument the existence of God, theoretical atheism was unknown. When the Psalmist (Psalms 14: 1) castigates the fool for saying in his heart there is no God, he is thinking of practical atheism: that, so far as human conduct is concerned, God does not matter, that God is unconcerned about whether or not human beings practise justice and righteousness. It goes without saying that Judaism, which stands or falls on the belief in the existence of God, is totally incompatible with atheism, though Jewish *secularism does try to preserve Jewish *values and even some Jewish rituals together with an atheistic attitude.

Authority That by which the beliefs and practices of Judaism are sanctioned.

In traditional Jewish thought, the ultimate authority is the God-given Torah as interpreted by the Talmudic Rabbis, so that the Talmud, as the sole authentic interpreter of the biblical text, became, in one sense, more authoritative than the bare text itself. *Reform Judaism in the early nineteenth century rejected the authority of the Talmud, but, especially after the *Holocaust in the twentieth century, came to pay greater heed to Talmudic teachings and to Rabbinic law, at least where these are not seen as contrary to the modern spirit.

Autopsies The dissection of corpses in order to discover the cause of death. Whether autopsies are allowed in Judaism has been much discussed in recent years. There are two possible objections to autopsies according to

*Orthodoxy (*Reform Judaism is usually more permissive): 1. It is forbidden to mutilate a corpse. 2. It is forbidden to enjoy any benefit from a corpse. But against these objections is the principle that the saving of *life overrides most prohibitions of the Torah, so that logically autopsies should be allowed since they help to increase medical knowledge of benefit to mankind in the saving of many persons who would otherwise die.

Av, Ninth of The ninth day of the month of Av (*tisha be-av*), the fast day commemorating the destruction of the *Temple and other calamities in Jewish history. Tisha Be-Av is treated with greater severity than the minor *fast days in that it begins at sunset of the previous night and on it are forbidden not only eating and drinking but also marital relations, bathing, and the wearing of leather shoes.

Voices have been raised, even in the Orthodox camp, to the effect that following the establishment of the State of Israel there is no longer any need to fast on Tisha Be-Av and given the repopulation of its cities it is unfitting, and might even seem ungrateful, to pray for the rebuilding of Jerusalem. These voices are now mute but many Jews have altered the phrase in the special Tisha Be-Av prayer, 'the city that is desolate', to read 'the city that was desolate'.

'Avinu Malkenu' 'Our Father our King', a prayer attributed in the Talmud to Rabbi *Akiba and recited during the penitential season from *Rosh Ha-Shanah to *Yom Kippur and on fast days. God is referred to as both the stern King and the loving Father and is entreated to show mercy to His people.

Azazel The place, according to the Jewish tradition, to which the scapegoat was taken on *Yom Kippur in Temple times. In some ancient legends Azazel is connected with one of the fallen angels in the book of Genesis (6: 1–4). These and similar fanciful ideas remain purely in the realm of speculation and have no relevance to Jewish theology of any variety.

Azikri, Eleazar Safed Kabbalist (1533–1600), author of *Sefer Haredim (The Book of the God-fearers)*, in which the *precepts are given an original classification corresponding to the various organs and limbs of the body with which they are carried out.

Azulai, Hayyim Yosef David Jerusalem Kabbalist, bibliographer, Talmudist, and traveller (1724–1806), especially known for his *Shem Ha-Gedolim*, a bibliographical and biographical lexicon of Rabbinic authors and their works. His travel diary is also well known. Azulai (called, after the initial letters of his name, *Hida*) has good claim to the title of first modern Jewish bibliographer, even though he often has an uncritical approach to his sources.

B

Baal Shem Tov 'Master of the Good Name', the title given to Israel ben Eliezer (1698–1760), founder of the Hasidic movement (*Hasidism). The title (often abbreviated to Besht, after its initial letters) refers to the use, as in the *Kabbalah, of various combinations of divine names ('*names of God') in order to effect miraculous cures. Like other miracle-workers of the time, the Besht was first known as a practitioner of white magic but this aspect of his life is usually played down by the Hasidim, who prefer his role as spiritual master and guide to predominate. The Besht stressed the divine immanence, contemplation of which is bound to fill the heart with religious joy and enthusiasm.

Baal Teshuvah Repentant sinner, literally 'one who returns' from his evil ways. That a sinner is to be encouraged to return to God and repent of his sins is stressed by the Talmudic Rabbis, following the biblical teachings about *sin and repentance.

In times when conversions to other religions were not unknown among Jews, the name *baal teshuvah* was given especially to a convert to Christianity or Islam who had returned to the Jewish fold.

In the second half of the twentieth century, there has emerged a strong *baal teshuvah* movement in which the name is given to those, especially young persons, formerly estranged from or ignorant of full Jewish observance, who have now returned to the fully *Orthodox way of life. The name *baal teshuvah* has here lost its original meaning, which bordered on the pejorative, to denote something of a status symbol.

Babylon The country between the rivers Tigris and Euphrates, now Iraq, to which the Jews were exiled by Nebuchadnezzar after the destruction of the First *Temple and by the rivers of which the exiles refused to sing 'the Lord's song in a strange land' (Psalms 137).

Under the early third-century teachers *Rav and Samuel, Babylon became a centre of Jewish learning, a keen rivalry existing between the Babylonian and Palestinian scholars. The Babylonian Talmud became more authoritative than the Palestinian under the influence of the *Geonim, who looked upon themselves as the heirs of the Talmudic sages.

Baeck, Leo German Reform Rabbi, preacher and thinker (1873–1956). Baeck was deported by the Nazis to the Theresienstadt concentration camp where his great courage in the face of adversity was an encouragement to the other inmates. Baeck was a renowned preacher but it was said of him that he never used the personal pronoun 'I' in his sermons. This fondness for objectivity and abstract thought is evidenced in all Baeck's works, making them difficult reading despite the importance and wide influence of his ideas. In Baeck's major work *The Essence of Judaism*, Judaism is described in strongly ethical, albeit God-inspired and God-directed, terms.

Bahir 'Brightness', the earliest book of the Kabbalah, of unknown authorship, which first appeared in southern France at the end of the thirteenth century and in which the doctrine of the *Sefirot is adumbrated. Like its successor, the Zohar, the Bahir is a pseudepigraphic work, sayings being attributed in it to various *Tannaim and Amoraim who could not have been the actual authors.

Bahya, Ibn Asher Thirteenth-century Spanish biblical exegete and Kabbalist, author of a commentary to the Pentateuch written in the year 1291. Bahya was a disciple of Solomon Ibn *Adret, whose Kabbalistic ideas as well as those of Adret's teacher, *Nahmanides, are expressed more or less openly in his commentary.

Bahya, Ibn Pakudah Spanish philosopher of the eleventh century. Bahya's *Duties of the Heart* is a treatise of morals and religion, translated into *Yiddish, sure evidence of the work's popularity among ordinary devout Jews, although the opening section on the unity of God is strictly philosophical and written for thinkers. In this section Bahya stresses that the nature of God cannot be apprehended by the human mind.

Balaam The heathen soothsayer and prophet whose story is told in the book of Numbers (22: 1–24: 25). This strange biblical passage, giving rise to a number of problems, has been widely discussed by Jewish commentators throughout the ages. How Balaam's curses could have been effective and why it was necessary for God to turn them into blessings, for example, troubled Jewish thinkers, who generally treat the topic as part of the wider problem regarding the efficacy of *blessings and curses. Another problem, that of Balaam's talking ass, for long an object of ridicule by foes of the Bible, has been considered by Jewish exegetes; the more miraculously inclined among them see no reason why God should not have endowed an ass temporarily with the power of speech, while the rationalists interpret the whole episode as having taken place in

a dream, or suggest that Balaam imagined the noises made by the ass to be human speech.

Bare Head It would be difficult to find a more trivial matter that was the source of greater controversy in Jewish life than the question of whether or not it is permitted for males to pray with uncovered head. From the very few references in the Talmud it would appear that only men noted for their piety covered their heads, not only for prayer but at all times, out of respect for God 'on high', that is, above their head. As late as the eighteenth century *Elijah, Gaon of Vilna could write (note to the *Shulhan Arukh, Orah Hayyim*, 8) that according to the strict law there is no need to pray with covered head and that to cover the head is no more than an act of piety. For all that, especially in reaction to Christian worship, it became the universal practice among the *Orthodox to cover the head (either with a hat or with the *yarmulka) at all times. Certainly, it is now unheard of for worshippers in an Orthodox synagogue to have their head uncovered. In the early days of *Reform Judaism it was often the practice to pray with bared head even in the synagogue but this is rare nowadays, and some Reform Jews have adopted the Orthodox practice of wearing a head-covering at all times.

Bar Kochba General in Judaea who led a great revolt against Roman dominion (d. 135 CE). Letters written by Bar Kochba (and the coins he struck during his early successes against Rome) have been discovered. From these we learn that the real name of this leader was Simeon bar Kasivah. The name Bar Kochba ('son of the star') was evidently given to him later on the basis of the verse in the oracles of *Balaam (Numbers 24: 17): 'There shall step forth a star out of Jacob', said to be a forecast of the brave warrior who will arise to save the Jewish people from its oppressors.

Bar Mitzvah 'Son of commandment', a boy who has reached, at the age of 13, his religious majority, that is, the age at which he is responsible for his actions and hence obliged to keep the *precepts of the Torah. The word 'bar' ('son') means in this context 'belonging to', associated with the precepts. In the older tradition there was no special initiatory rite for the new status of *bar mitzvah*. When he reached the age of 13 a boy simply lost his status as a minor not responsible enough to carry out any religious duties and became, in law, a responsible adult, although, according to some authorities, God did not hold him to be fully responsible until he reached the age of 20. In the Middle Ages, especially in German communities, the transition was marked by special ceremonies. The boy was called up to read the *Torah; he began to put on the *tefillin*; and a party was held in his honour at which he delivered a learned discourse, displaying his learning or, in some cases, his lack of it. In Western lands, much has been made (some Rabbis hold, too much) of the Bar Mitzvah ceremonies.

Bat Kol 'Daughter of a voice', an echo, the term given in the Talmudic literature and Jewish mystical thought to a communication from heaven, the lowest form of direct divine *inspiration. In modern Jewish thought, even among the *Orthodox, claims to have heard a Bat Kol would be treated with extreme suspicion and dismissed as chicanery or hallucination.

Bat Mitzvah 'Daughter of the commandment', the status of religious obligation to keep the *precepts which a girl attains at the age of 12 as a boy becomes *Bar Mitzvah at the age of 13. While a boy marks his religious majority by putting on the *tefillin* and by being called up to the reading of the *Torah, until recent times there were no special ceremonies for the Bat Mitzvah. With the greater trends towards equality of the sexes, ceremonies such as special prayers and a party have been introduced in many communities. In *Reform and *Conservative Judaism the girl reads a portion in the synagogue just as a boy does on his Bar Mitzvah but the *Orthodox object, in any event, to *women reading the Torah.

Beard The verse: 'Ye shall not round the corners of your heads, neither shalt thou mar the corners of thy beard' (Leviticus 19: 27) is understood by the Talmudic Rabbis not to mean that it is wrong for a man to be clean-shaven, but only that facial hair must not be removed with a razor. *Reform Jews do not consider the prohibition on shaving with a razor still to be binding.

Belief Heb. *emunah*. In the Bible and the Rabbinic literature this term denotes 'belief in', that is, trust in God and in His Torah, but in the Middle Ages the term is more generally used to denote 'belief that' God exists and that the *dogmas of Judaism are true. Although the emphasis in Judaism is on action, there are principles of *faith in which the Jew is expected to believe. Lack of belief is considered sinful, though *Crescas and others have discussed how anyone can be blamed for something beyond his control. Some later teachers have suggested that all unbelief is only in the category of unwitting sin (see ATHEISM and EPIKOROS).

Belz Name of a small town in Galicia and of the Hasidic dynasty founded there by Rabbi Shalom Rokeah (1779–1855). Shalom was succeeded as both the Rebbe and the town Rabbi of Belz by his son, Joshua, who was in turn succeeded by his son, Issachar Dov, succeeded by his son, Aaron (1880–1957) who escaped the *Holocaust to set up his 'court' in Tel Aviv. When Aaron died, his nephew, Issachar Dov II, was a little boy, but the Belzer Hasidim adopted him as the rightful Belzer Rebbe, which post he still occupies.

Benedictions Blessings in which thanks are offered to God for spiritual and physical benefits He has bestowed. The benediction (Heb. *berakhah*) begins with the words: 'Blessed art Thou, O Lord our God, King of the universe, who . . .' and then goes on to state the particular matter for which the benediction is recited; for example, over wine: 'Blessed art Thou, O Lord our God, King of the universe, who creates the fruit of the vine'; over *tefillin*: 'Blessed art Thou, O Lord our God, King of the universe, who hath sanctified us with His commandments and hath commanded us to put on *tefillin*.'

Ben Sira The name of the ancient author (second century BCE) and of his book, also called Ecclesiasticus, one of the books of the *Apocrypha. The book was written originally in Hebrew but translated into Greek by Ben Sira's grandson. Although the Talmudic Rabbis had a somewhat ambivalent attitude towards this work and the other books of the Apocrypha, a number of quotations from the book are found in the Talmud.

Beruriah Wife of Rabbi *Meir. She is reported to have been a woman very learned in the Torah, although the few details about her in the Talmud and the *Midrash are vague and belong largely to legend. Naturally, in modern Jewish *feminism the figure of Beruriah occupies a prominent place, especially in her role as scholar.

Bet Din 'House of Law', that is, court of law, composed of three judges learned in the law. According to the Talmud, a court had to be composed of

three fully ordained *Rabbis but since Semikhah, *ordination, was reserved for the Jews in the Holy Land, the courts of the *Diaspora, in *Babylon and other lands, operated by the legal fiction that they functioned on behalf of the Palestinians. Most authorities hold that a Bet Din has to be composed of three males but some medieval French teachers ruled that a woman could serve as a judge (witness *Deborah), an opinion followed by *Reform and *Conservative Jews, who have women judges as they have women Rabbis.

The main functions of the Bet Din are to decide in matters of civil law; to supervise the *divorce proceedings; to see that *conversion to Judaism is carried out in accordance with the law; and, in many communities, to give a seal of approval that foodstuffs are *kosher, that is, that they have been prepared in such a manner that people who buy them will not offend against the *dietary laws.

Bible The collection of books constituting sacred literature, which Christians refer to as the Old Testament to distinguish it from the New Testament. The Hebrew Bible is divided into three: 1. *Torah (the five books of Moses, the *Pentateuch); 2. *Neviim* (*Prophets', embracing the books of the literary prophets and the historical books); 3. *Ketuvim* ('Writings', the books of the Hagiographa). After the initial letters of these words, the Bible is called the *Tanakh.* Jewish tradition sees these three divisions as composed under different degrees of *inspiration. The Torah, as the very word of God, is seen as possessing the highest degree of inspiration; the prophets as having the degree of prophecy, that is, the word of God mediated through the personality of the prophet; and the Hagiographa as composed under the lower degree of inspiration known as the *Holy Spirit. But for all practical purposes no distinction is made between one part of the Bible and another so far as its *authority is concerned.

The books of the Bible are:

Torah

Genesis, Exodus, Leviticus, Numbers, Deuteronomy.

Prophets

Joshua, Judges, Samuel, Kings (known as the 'early prophets').

Isaiah, Jeremiah, Ezekiel, the Twelve Prophets (the 'later prophets') (the Twelve are Hosea, Joel, Amos, Obadiah, Jonah, Micah, Nahum, Habakkuk, Zephaniah, Haggai, Zechariah, and Malachi).

Hagiographa

Psalms, Proverbs, Job, Song of Songs, Ruth, Ecclesiastes, Lamentations, Esther, Chronicles, Daniel, Ezra, and Nehemiah.

In the later Jewish tradition there are said to be twenty-four books of the Bible. This number is arrived at by counting the Twelve as a single book and Ezra and Nehemiah as a single book, thus:

1. Genesis; 2. Exodus; 3. Leviticus; 4. Numbers; 5. Deuteronomy; 6. Joshua; 7. Judges; 8. Samuel; 9. Kings; 10. Isaiah; 11. Jeremiah; 12. Ezekiel; 13. The Twelve; 14. Psalms; 15. Proverbs; 16. Job; 17. Song of Songs; 18. Ruth; 19. Ecclesiastes; 20. Lamentations; 21. Esther; 22. Chronicles; 23. Daniel; 24. Ezra and Nehemiah.

From the historical point of view, there was no actual official body to determine which books of the Bible belonged there and which did not. The Pentateuch was accepted as the sacred Torah from the earliest times, the Prophets somewhat later, and the books of the Hagiographa later still. In effect it was by a kind of mysterious consensus among the Jewish people that these twenty-four books and no others came to be held as *the* Bible. The practical consequence is that, for Jews, the authority of the Bible depends on how the Bible has been interpreted by the sages of Israel. This is why a naked biblicism, in which the biblical text is examined for direct guidance, is foreign to the Jewish tradition.

Who wrote the various books of the Bible? A distinction has to be drawn between the claims of authorship made in the books themselves and the understanding of later generations. In the Pentateuch itself, for instance, there is no statement that all five books were written by Moses or in the book of Psalms that all the Psalms were written by David, yet the tradition developed that the five books are the books of Moses and the whole book of Psalms the Psalms of David. This question of authorship was only scientifically examined with the rise of *biblical criticism. The ancient Rabbis made many references to the authors of the various books, yet in doing so they were not stating any dogma but simply referring to the general views of their day.

Biblical Criticism The close examination by modern biblical scholars of the composition, authorship, and text of the biblical books. The 'lower criticism' or textual criticism seeks to discover the original text as this left the hands of the final editors. The 'higher criticism' seeks to discover how the books were compiled, their sources, whether oral or written, and the process by which they came to assume their present form. The text handed down from generation to generation is known as the Masoretic Text, after the *Masorah, the traditional form of the text. But, while the Masoretic Text is very reliable, great care having been taken in its transmission, the evidence of early versions such as the *Septuagint, which contain variant readings, shows that before the Masoretic Text had been established, readings which differ from it had been widely known, and modern scholars are certainly not averse to suggesting their own emendations of the text where these seem plausible. The higher criticism seeks to detect, by noting anachronisms, for example, the sources behind the particular books.

All this activity has presented a considerable challenge to traditional views. Reform and Conservative Jewish scholars usually accept the results of biblical criticism and acknowledge that it demands a revision of traditional views, without necessarily affecting the view of the Bible as inspired. Many Orthodox scholars still reject all biblical criticism in the belief that its untraditional opinions constitute *heresy but a few hold that its findings can be accepted for all the books of the Bible except the Pentateuch, which, they affirm, as the very word of God, cannot be subjected to critical examination as if it were a book produced by human authors. Hardly any Orthodox scholar will say otherwise than that the doctrine of 'Torah from Heaven' implies that the whole of the Pentateuch is a unified, not a composite, text, communicated directly by God to His faithful servant Moses.

Bimah The elevated platform in the *synagogue at which the *reading of the Torah takes place. The bimah has steps on its two sides so that those called to the reading ascend at the side nearest to them and descend, after their portion has been read, by the steps at the other side; the principle is that one should ascend for the reading of God's words by the swiftest route and leave, as if reluctant to depart, by the longest route.

Bioethics The branch of ethics concerned with the preservation of human life; sometimes referred to as medical ethics, since many of the issues arise as a result of advances in modern medicine. Among the questions considered in Jewish bioethics are: preference for medical treatment; *abortion; *autopsies; *birth-control; withholding treatment from the terminally ill (see EUTHANASIA); *genetic engineering; cosmetic surgery; organ transplants, and *artificial insemination. These and similar questions are discussed at length in the *Responsa of contemporary Orthodox Rabbis on the basis of the *Halakhah, the Jewish legal system, in which new situations, unenvisaged in the classical sources of the *Talmud and the *Codes, are discussed by means of analogy. The questions are rarely discussed on the basis of general ethical principles since, for the Orthodox, these have no standing when they are in conflict with the Halakhic norms.

Birth-Control The prevention of the birth of unwanted children either by total abstinence from sexual relations or by engaging in them in a way that frustrates conception.

The objection to artificial contraception is on the grounds of what the Talmud terms 'wasting seed', that is the emission of semen which, if deposited in the womb, could have resulted in the birth of a child. This does not mean that sexual relations are forbidden unless they can lead to a birth. There is no objection whatsoever to sex where conception is impossible, for instance, where the wife is already pregnant or where she is beyond the childbearing age. In these instances, the semen is not actively destroyed, whereas the use of artificial methods of contraception positively destroys the seed. This is the Orthodox position, equating contraception by artificial means with *masturbation. Many authorities advocate the contraceptive pill as the most favoured method of birth control and, since this does not involve 'waste of seed' as defined above, some would permit the use of the pill on grounds other than danger to life.

Birthdays In recent times birthday

celebrations have become the norm among many Jews. Even if this practice was copied from the non-Jewish world, it is held that there is no harm in it since questions of doctrine are in no way involved. In some synagogues, Orthodox as well as Reform, special prayers of thanksgiving are recited for someone reaching the age of 70 or 80 or at his 'second *Bar Miztvah' when he reaches the age of 83! It is customary to greet an elderly man or woman on their birthday with the wish: 'May you live to be 120' (the age at which Moses died; Deuteronomy 34: 7).

Blasphemy Reviling God; Heb. *birkat ha-shem*, literally 'blessing [euphemism for "cursing"] the Name [of God]'. The one guilty of this offence is called a *megaddef* ('blasphemer'). In the two main passages in the Bible (Leviticus 24: 10–23 and 1 Kings 21: 8–13) the penalty for this offence is stoning to death. It is, however, none too clear what exactly is involved in the offence. Does it mean to insult God, or does it mean to curse God? According to the Gospels of Matthew (26: 63–6) and Mark (14: 53 64) Jesus was tried by the *Sanhedrin on a charge of blasphemy, but New Testament scholars have puzzled over both the question of the historicity of the event and the precise nature of the offence.

To insult the Torah or Moses, the other prophets, or the sages of Israel is also held to be a serious offence but this is, at the most, an extension of the original blasphemy law and is not covered by the death penalty, even in theory. In Christian Europe the Church, on the other hand, extended the law of blasphemy to cover any denial of God or denigration of the Christian religion, and Islam regarded it as covering any attack on the personality of Muhammad, as in the Salman Rushdie case. The whole subject is more than a little obscure so far as Jewish law is concerned and there is hardly any evidence that

trials for blasphemy took place among Jews in post-biblical times.

Blessings and Curses The invocation to God to bestow goodness and happiness (the blessing) or to visit evil and suffering (the curse) upon others. There is no doubt that in both the Bible and the Rabbinic literature the belief was strongly held that the word of blessing and curse possessed power so that, unless there was direct divine intervention, it would automatically take effect.

To this day parents bless their children on the eve of the Sabbaths and festivals, and teachers their pupils. The usual form of blessing for boys (based on Genesis 48: 20) is: 'God make thee as Ephraim and Manasseh'; for girls: 'God make thee as Sarah, Rebecca, Rachel, and Leah.'

Blood Libel The calumny that Jews murder Christian children in order to use their blood for ritual purposes such as the baking of *matzah for *Passover. The accusation is an amalgam of pagan notions of human sacrifice and ignorance about the nature of the Jewish religion and its utter abhorrence of consuming blood, wedded, in Christian Europe, to the alleged desecration of the Host by Jews. As the legend developed Jews were said to use Christian blood for all kinds of bizarre rituals and magical practices, for anointing Rabbis, for curing eye ailments, in stopping menstrual blood, removing bodily odours, and warding off the evil eye.

The whole sorry history of this absurd libel with its tragic consequences has been told many times. Perhaps the final word on the subject so far as Jews are concerned is the remark by *Ahad Ha-Am that Jews can obtain a melancholy satisfaction from blood libel. Every Jew knows that there is no basis whatsoever in the calumny and yet it was believed by so many. The conclusion to be drawn, he observes, is that if such a widespread belief about Jews and Judaism is really nonsensical, Jews, lacking in confidence, should not be too ready, when they meet with *anti-Semitism, to say to themselves that there is no smoke without fire. In the blood libel there was so much smoke without even the tiniest spark of real fire.

Books Although Jewish *literature embraces many fields, Jewish books, until modern times and the rise of Jewish *secularism, were complied chiefly to further the aim of *study of the Torah and were looked upon as religious works to be treated with a special respect and regard. There are references to books in the Bible and the Bible itself is a collection of books produced over a long period. Originally books were compiled in the form of scrolls written on parchment. Under Roman influence, the codex form was introduced and this was the norm in works compiled in the Middle Ages. These handwritten books were costly because of the shortage of paper and the scarcity of skilful copyists. With the invention of *printing the Jewish book came into its own, thousands of copies being produced of the ancient texts, together with numerous original works.

Buber, Martin Existentialist Jewish philosopher, educationist, and Zionist thinker, born Vienna, 1878, died Jerusalem, 1965. Buber's main contribution to philosophy is the distinction, made in his justly famous philosophical poem *I and Thou*, between the *I–It* relationship and the *I–Thou*. In the former man relates to others and to things in an objective, detached manner, as when the physical scientist examines his data and the social scientist the life of a community. In the latter relationship, man meets others as those to whom he says 'Thou'. That is to say, his approach to the other is as person to person, where the other is not a thing to be manipulated or even to be used for the satisfaction of his benevolent instincts, but a fellow creature with whom one can engage in dialogue, a favourite Buberian word. On the religious level, according to Buber, man cannot talk *about* God but can only encounter Him, not only in the dialogue of prayer but also by encountering the divine Thou behind all particular Thous.

C

Cain and Abel The two sons of *Adam and Eve (Genesis 4). Cain is a tiller of the soil and Abel a keeper of sheep. (The suggestion that the narrative contains echoes of a conflict between the settled farmers and the nomadic shepherds has no evidence to support it, since there is no record of such a conflict in ancient Israelite society.) Cain brings an offering to the Lord from the fruit of the soil and Abel from the choicest of the firstlings of his flock. God rejects Cain's offering but accepts Abel's. When Cain and Abel are in the field Cain attacks Abel and kills him, whereupon God condemns Cain to a life of wandering and puts a mark on him, as a sign that he is protected and no one must kill him. (The expression 'the brand of Cain' for a murderer is based on a misunderstanding. Cain was not 'branded' in order to mark him as a murderer but rather to protect him from himself becoming a victim of murder.)

Calendar The Jewish religious year with its feasts and fasts. Whatever its origins (the question of which is extremely complicated) the Jewish calendar, from at least the beginning of the present era, was a lunar calendar. The very word for 'month', *hodesh*, means 'that which is renewed' and refers to the waning and waxing of the moon; hence the biblical name *Rosh Hodesh, the 'head of the month', for the beginning of the month, observed as a festival in biblical times (I Samuel 20: 24).

The problem at the heart of the Jewish calendar is that while it is lunar, there is a need to bring it into relationship with the solar year. This is because the months are to be counted from the month in which the Exodus from Egypt took place (Exodus 12: 2) and yet the festival of *Passover, celebrating the Exodus, is said (Deuteronomy 16: 1) to fall in the month Aviv ('ripening' of the corn); Passover must fall in spring. Since the lunar year is shorter than the solar, something had to be done to prevent Passover moving through the solar year so as to fall in other than the spring month. The method adopted was to intercalate the lunar year, that is, to add an extra lunar month to seven years in a cycle of nineteen lunar years. (The leap years, the years which have an additional month, are the third, sixth, eighth, eleventh, fourteenth, seventeenth, and nineteenth of the nineteen-year cycle, the beginning of the cycle being established by tradition.)

The names of the months of Babylonian origin, as we now have them, are found only in late books of the Bible such as the book of *Esther. These names, used universally by Jews, are, counting from the first month, the month in which Passover falls: Nisan, Iyyar, Sivan, Tammuz, Av, Elul, Tishri, Marheshvan, Kislev, Tevet, Shevat, Adar. In a leap year the added month is always the one before Nisan and is called Adar Sheni, 'Second Adar'. See APPENDIX I: THE JEWISH CALENDAR.

Candles Candles of wax or tallow took the place of lamps used in various Jewish *rituals such as the *Sabbath lights; in the *Havdalah ceremony; and the *Hanukkah lights. A *synagogue had to be well lit and pious folk used to denote candles for the purpose. Now most synagogues use electric lights, but in some two candles are placed before the Cantor at the reading-desk.

Cannibalism The natural human revulsion against consuming the flesh of other human beings and the fact that examples of it in practice are only very rarely found, explains, perhaps, why the topic is virtually ignored in the Jewish sources. In the much-discussed cases of human beings saving their lives by eating the flesh of their dead companions, Judaism would permit the practice on the grounds that only three prohibitions (those of murder, incest or adultery, and idolatry) demand that life be sacrificed rather than offend against them.

Cantillation

Cantillation The mode of chanting for the *reading of the Torah and the other Scriptures in the synagogue and the system of musical notation for this. Scripture was not simply declaimed in the synagogue, but chanted. In post-Talmudic times various systems of notation were developed, one of which became standard; that is to say, there eventually arose a universally accepted system of musical notation with special signs for the different notes. All communities follow this system, although the actual form of the melodies is not the same in all communities. The *Ashkenazi melodies, for instance, are in a different mode from the *Sephardic, the latter having distinct traces of Arabic musical styles.

The signs for the various notes are called *neginot* ('melodies') or *teemim* ('flavours', i.e. giving flavour to the words). These notes have a double purpose. In the first instance they serve as punctuation similar to the full stop, colon, semi-colon, and comma in English, these not being shown in the original Hebrew. The notes also serve as a commentary to the text.

*Reform Jews tended to give up the whole method of cantillation, preferring to follow the practice in Protestant churches of declaiming Scripture, in the belief that this was more decorous in Western society. But, as part of a definite swing towards greater tradi-

tionalism, many Reform congregations have reintroduced the old system of cantillation.

Cantor The prayer leader in the synagogue. In Rabbinic times, many people were unfamiliar with the prayers, and so in public worship a man well versed in the *liturgy would recite the prayers aloud with the congregation responding to his benedictions with *Amen, this being considered as if they themselves had offered the prayers. Even after the wide dissemination of the *Prayer Book, the institution of the prayer leader was continued, so that the prayers were then recited by both the congregation and the reader.

A number of modern Cantors have been very gifted musically, some being also expert composers whose liturgical compositions were collected and used by Cantors all over the world. With the invention of the gramophone, there was a proliferation of Cantorial records and, later, tapes, enjoyed by Jews in their own homes.

Capital Punishment The Bible prescribes the death penalty for a large number of offences including religious offences such as idol worship and the profaning of the Sabbath. But the question of capital punishment in actual practice in ancient Jewish society is extremely complicated.

According to the Mishnah (*Sanhedrin* 1: 4) the death penalty could only be inflicted, after a trial, by a *Sanhedrin composed of twenty-three judges and there were four different types of death penalty (*Sanhedrin* 7: 1): stoning, burning, slaying (by the sword), and strangling. A bare reading of these and the other accounts in the tractate would seem to suggest a vast proliferation of the death penalty. Yet, throughout the Talmudic literature, this whole subject is viewed with unease, so much so that according to the rules stated in that literature the death penalty could hardly ever have been imposed. For instance, it is ruled that two witnesses are required to testify not only that they witnessed the act for which the criminal has been charged but that they had warned him beforehand that if he carried out the act he would be executed, and he had to accept the warning, stating his willingness to commit the act despite his awareness of its consequences. The criminal's own confession is not accepted as evidence. Moreover, circumstantial evidence is not admitted. The extreme case is referred to of a man running after another man with a drawn sword, the victim being found slain by that sword and no one else being present who could have done the deed: what greater evidence of his guilt could there be? It has to be appreciated, however, that practically all this material comes from a time when the right to impose the death penalty had been taken away from the Jewish courts by the Roman authorities. According to one report in the Talmud (*Sanhedrin* 41a) the power of the Jewish courts to impose the death penalty ceased around the year 30 BCE; according to another report (*Sanhedrin* 52b) it could only have been imposed while the Temple stood and must have come to an end not later than 70 CE when the Temple was destroyed.

This means that, although earlier traditions may be present in the Mishnaic formulations, the whole topic, including the restrictions, is treated in the Mishnah and the Talmud in a purely theoretical way. It is hard to believe that when the courts did impose the death penalty they could only do so when the conditions mentioned above obtained. Who would commit a murder in the presence of two witnesses when these had solemnly warned him that if he persisted they would testify against him to have him executed for his crime? In the State of Israel capital punishment was entirely abolished ex-

cept for treason committed in time of war.

Celibacy It is a high religious obligation to marry and have children (see PROCREATION, MARRIAGE, and BIRTH-CONTROL), so that the question of whether it is religiously proper to be celibate is really a question of whether there are circumstances when the religious injunction of procreation can be set aside. In practice, throughout the ages, only a very few scholars remained unmarried and there are only a very few instances of a community seeing no objection to appointing a bachelor as its Rabbi (but this is not entirely unknown). The weight of the tradition is against the celibate life even for the most dedicated students of the Torah. With the possible exception of the *Essenes, there has never been anything like a religious order of celibates in Judaism.

Censorship The control of Jewish books to make sure that they do not contain material considered by those exercising the control to be injurious to religion and morals or harmful to the reputation of the Jewish people.

In considering the question of censorship in Judaism, it must first be noted that there has never been anything like a universally recognized body of Rabbis responsible for controlling the kind of literature that Jews produce. This is not to say that individual Rabbis never sought to ban certain books but their power to do so was limited by the willingness of authors, publishers, and readers to obey the dictates of these Rabbis.

The censorship that did exist was of two kinds—external and internal. External censorship was exercised by governmental bodies who ordered the excision from Jewish publications of passages held to be attacks on *Gentiles or on the Christian faith. The Jewish authorities, too, anticipated this type of intervention by themselves deleting or altering such 'dangerous' passages.

Internal censorship was imposed by Rabbis who had the necessary power over books believed to contain heretical or immoral ideas. It is consequently quite incorrect for Jewish apologists to maintain that Judaism knows nothing of the censorship or burning of books. However, apologists are probably correct when they point to the fact that Jews, compared with the adherents of Christianity and Islam, have been rather less tempted to condemn works compiled by other Jews. Especially after the burning of books by the Nazis, most Jews have acquired a horror at the notion of burning books; cold comfort perhaps, but a measure of comfort nevertheless. Certainly most modern Jews have been influenced by the idea of religious *tolerance that has emerged in Western society through the writings of Milton, *Spinoza, John Locke, John Stuart Mill, and other thinkers in the liberal mode. See also HEREM.

Chariot The vehicle seen by the prophet *Ezekiel (Ezekiel 1), representing, in Jewish *mysticism, the realms on high into which the soul of the mystic is transported. The Hebrew for 'chariot' is *Merkavah*, and the Rabbinic name for this type of mystic gnosis is *Maaseh Merkavah* ('the Work of the Chariot'), as distinct from speculation on the theme of the divine creation, which is called *Maaseh Bereshit* ('the Work of Creation'). The mystics who attempted this ascent of soul are known as the *yoredey Merkavah*, the literal meaning of which is: 'those who *descend* the Chariot', possibly because the 'ascent' is through the depths of the mystic's psyche, or, perhaps, simply because one goes down into a chariot in order to ride in it rather like one who goes into a car today. In any event, the usual term in English is 'Riders of the Chariot'.

Charity Alms-giving and care for the poor; Heb. *tzedakah*. This word in the Bible denotes 'righteousness' in general but in post-biblical Judaism it is used to denote charity, as if to suggest, according to many exponents of the idea, that there should be no condescension in alms-giving. The poor are not to be patronized but given the assistance they need because they have a just claim on the wealthy. The Jerusalem Talmud records that in ancient Palestine a poor man when asking for help would say to his would-be benefactor: 'Acquire merit for yourself', as if to say: 'I am doing you a favour.' In a popular Jewish tale, when a rich man excuses the small size of his donation by protesting that he is unable to afford to give more generously because he has been obliged to pay his son's gambling debts, the poor man retorts: 'If your son wants to gamble let him do so with his own money, not with mine.'

There are grades of charity obligation with regard to precedence. The general rule is that the prior obligation is to the poor of one's own family, then to the poor of one's own town, and then to the poor of other towns. The poor of the land of Israel take precedence over the poor of other places. In many Jewish communities there was a special fund for the relief of poverty in the Holy Land. Other charitable organizations in Jewish communities provided dowries for poor brides; hospices for the sick, the aged, and the infirm; and money for those who required interest-free loans.

All the powerful appeals to give generously to charity are directed chiefly to individuals. There was nothing like a welfare state in former times when the classical sources were formulated. The State of Israel is a fully developed welfare state and yet here and in other advanced countries there is still room for private donations; moreover, the complementary ideal of benevolence is highly personal and cannot be relegated to governmental bodies. Although our whole social system is very different from that which obtained when the sources were compiled, Jews have followed the implication in those sources that charity and benevolence are among the highest values of the religion. One of the distinguishing features of the Jewish people, according to the ancient Rabbis, is that they are generous and compassionate.

Cherubim The winged creatures mentioned frequently in the Bible; Heb *keruvim*, the etymology of which is uncertain. In a Midrashic source the folk etymology is given according to which the singular form *keruv* means *ke-ravya*, 'like a young child', hence the depiction in art and literature of the cherubim as baby angels.

In the Bible God sets the cherubim at the entrance of the *Garden of Eden, after the expulsion of *Adam and Eve, to guard the way to the Tree of Life (Genesis 3: 24). Two cherubim overlaid with gold with outstretched wings were placed facing one another on the cover of the *Ark in the Tabernacle (Exodus 25: 18–20) and figures of cherubim were embroidered on the veil and the curtains of the Tabernacle (Exodus 26: 1, 31). In Solomon's Temple the two gilded cherubim were not attached to the Ark, as in the Tabernacle, but were placed as figures each 10 cubits high in front of the Ark (1 Kings 6: 27–8).

The whole matter of the cherubim was a source of puzzlement and embarrassment to the Jewish teachers. The Jewish philosophers, in particular, tried to rationalize the subject. In Philo's discourse on the cherubim these represent two aspects of God, His goodness and His authority. For Maimonides the cherubim represent a species of the angelic hosts. In Maimonides' scheme there are ten grades of *angels, and the cherubim belong to the ninth degree. Angels are seen by Maimonides as the various spiritual forces God uses for the control of the universe. The angels adjacent to the Ark represent the operation of these spiritual forces in the revelation of the Torah and are a symbolic representation of the dogma that the Torah is from heaven. There were two cherubim on the Ark because had there been only one it might have been confused with a representation of the One God (Maimonides, *Guide of the Perplexed*, 3. 45).

Chess Playing chess has long been a popular pursuit among Jews, although most scholars reject the notion that there are references to the game in the Talmud. Chess was favoured even by staid Rabbis who considered games to be a waste of time which would be better spent on the study of the Torah, since the game stimulated the mind and honed it for that very study. Thus most authorities permitted the playing of chess even on the Sabbath, provided, of course, that the game was not played for money. Some pious folk had a special silver chess set for use on the Sabbath. The association of chess with keenness of mind is no doubt behind the legend that the wise King Solomon played chess.

Children and Parents From biblical times onwards children are considered to be God's greatest gift. The first precept of the Torah is to engage in *procreation. A common Jewish blessing is: 'May you enjoy *naches* [Yiddish: satisfaction and pleasure] from your children.' Jewish parents have always claimed pre-eminence in their care for children and while no doubt the boast is often a vain one, the claim is not entirely without justification. And for children, the fifth commandment: 'Honour thy father and thy mother' (Exodus 20: 12) is a key text. Yet the Freudian insight into the conflict between parents and children is echoed in many a Jewish source. It is noteworthy that, apart from the general injunction to *love the neighbour, there is no special command for children to love their parents, only to pay them the respect due to them, which is construed by the Jerusalem Talmud as the simple payment of a debt to those who brought the children into the world.

Choirs When the *sacrifices were offered in the *Temple they were accompanied by the Levites playing musical instruments and singing psalms but the institution of a choir assisting the *Cantor in synagogal worship is not found before the early seventeenth century in Italy, where it was almost certainly introduced under Renaissance influence. There is a choir, nowadays, in most of the larger Western synagogues. *Hasidism tended to view the institution of the choir with distaste both because it seemed to be a copy of Christian forms of worship and because it was altogether too formal and lacking in spontaneous fervour.

Chosen People The idea that the people of Israel, later called the Jews, have been given a special role to play in the divine scheme is pervasive in the Bible and in all subsequent Jewish thought. There has been a rich variety of interpretation of this idea throughout the history of Judaism since, it has to be acknowledged, the whole doctrine appears, at first glance, to be in conflict with the belief in the One God whose care and providence extends equally, if it can be expressed in this way, to all human beings He has created in His image. Historically speaking, the doctrine that God has chosen Israel emerged out of the growing realization among generations of the Hebrew people, the Israelites and later the Jews, that among all the peoples around them they were the only monotheists.

The average Jew takes pride in his conviction that he belongs to a people with a special role to play in God's world. Rarely has such pride gone be-

yond the harmless boasting most people engage in with regard to the particular group to which they belong, their nation, their religion, their country, even their club or football team. And virtually all Jewish teachers stress that the choice of the Jews is not for privilege but for service. (Kaplan once retorted that to be chosen to serve is itself the greatest privilege.) In the best Jewish thought, the election of Israel is by God and for God and for the fulfilment of His plan for all mankind (see AMOS). And the doctrine was never racist. There is nothing like a pure Jewish race and *conversion to Judaism is possible, based on the idea that anyone who joins voluntarily the Jewish people and embraces the Jewish religion is a 'child of Abraham' and hence a full member of the Chosen People.

Christianity In its very earliest days, Christianity was seen by the Jewish teachers as a Jewish heresy; its adherents were Jews who believed in the divinity of Christ. But when Christianity spread and became a world religion, with numerous converts from the *Gentile world, it became a rival religion to Judaism. Christians were then seen as Gentiles not because they were Christians but because, in the main, they were, in fact, Gentiles (i.e. not Jewish).

In modern times there has been far greater co-operation between Jews and Christians; many Jews welcoming Jewish–Christian dialogues in which the aim of each side is to understand the position of the other, and even learn from it, without in any way moving from its own. Some Jews believe that Judaism and Christianity have so much in common that it is permissible to speak of a Jewish Christian tradition. But there is the strongest opposition on the part of all Jews, Orthodox, Conservative, and Reform, to the attempts by Christian missionary groups to convert Jews to Christianity. The Jews for Jesus movement is very much a fringe phenomenon and has justly been condemned by all faithful Jews as trying to introduce Christianity to Jews through the back door, so to speak. On the scholarly level, there have been Jewish investigations into the Jewish background of Christianity but in a purely objective way with the theological questions seen as irrelevant to scholarship. It would certainly be incorrect to say that the suspicions of the two religions of one another are a thing of the past. What can be said is that, in an age of greater religious tolerance, there has been a growing realization that the two have enough in common to enable them to work in harmony for human betterment.

Chronicles, Book of The biblical book dealing with the history of the people of Israel; Heb. *divrey ha-yamim*, lit. 'the accounts of the days', the usual biblical term for an historical account, although it is impossible to tell whether this title is the author's own or was given later. In current editions, Chronicles is divided into two, 1 and 2 Chronicles, but originally it was a single book, later included into the third section of the *Bible, the Hagiographa or Sacred Writings, and hence held to be of a lower order of inspiration than the other historical books, *Samuel and *Kings, which belong to the Prophets. According to the passage in the Talmud on the authorship of the various biblical books, Chronicles was compiled by *Ezra with additions by *Nehemiah. Modern biblical research tends to accept this connection and maintains that the three books of Chronicles, Ezra, and Nehemiah were originally a single book but that Chronicles in the form we now have is a separate and reworked account.

Chutzpah Arrogance, impudence; a Talmudic word that made its way into *Yiddish from which it was adopted

into American slang and has now entered the English language and is recorded in the *Oxford English Dictionary* as an English word. It comes from a root meaning 'to peel' and hence 'to be bare'; chutzpah means barefacedness, sheer cheek. The classical definition of chutzpah is given in the story of the boy who killed his parents and then threw himself on the mercy of the court on the grounds that he was an orphan.

Circumcision The removal of the foreskin in order to make manifest the 'sign in the flesh' of the *covenant made with *Abraham and hence called in Hebrew *berit milah*, 'covenant of circumcision' or, in everyday parlance, simply 'the Brit'. The covenant of circumcision is first recorded in the book of Genesis (17: 9–13), where Abraham is instructed to circumcise all his male descendants, just as he himself had been circumcised, as a sign of the covenant God had made with him and through him with them: 'Thus shall My covenant be marked in your flesh as an everlasting pact.' Here as well as in the book of Leviticus (12: 1–3) the age of circumcision is stated to be when a boy is eight days old. The Jewish tradition understands this to mean that while the ideal is for the child to be circumcised at this age, the rite is valid even if carried out later. If the child shows signs of jaundice, for example, it is the practice to postpone the circumcision until the doctor declares him to be fit enough for the operation. An adult whose parents did not have him circumcised is obliged to have the operation carried out as soon as possible and must not remain uncircumcised. A male convert (see CONVERSION) must be circumcised before he becomes a member of the covenant but for one born a Jew the rite is an initiation not into Judaism, but only into the covenant, since Jewish status is established by birth. A boy born of a Jewish mother is automatically Jewish, whether or not he has been circumcised.

In the early days of the *Reform movement, some of the Reformers advocated the abolition of circumcision, protesting that the rite was too particularistic and too cruel to be retained since the Reformers did not believe that it had divine sanction. The Reform leader, Abraham Geiger, notoriously described circumcision in a private reference as 'a barbaric, bloody act, which fills the father with fear'. But today all faithful Jews, Reform, Conservative, and Orthodox, do have their sons circumcised, among other reasons because contemporary Reform Jews are less suspicious of particularism than were their nineteenth-century predecessors at a time when the call of the age was so strongly universalistic. Although in more recent years a few voices have been raised in opposition to circumcision because of the alleged harmful psychological effect it may have on the infant, very few Jews take this objection sufficiently seriously even to think of abolishing a rite of such importance to Judaism.

Cleanliness The Talmudic Rabbis understand the verse: 'Ye shall not make yourselves abominable' (Leviticus 11: 43) as forbidding anything from which normal people recoil in disgust—eating from dirty plates, for example, or eating rotten food, or leaving the body unwashed. Passing water and movement of the bowels must be attended to as soon as the need becomes urgent and there are even instructions in the Talmud about wiping thoroughly afterwards.

Codes, Alphabetical A mode of expounding the Bible by means of various codes in which one Hebrew letter is substituted for another so that a word can have, in addition to its plain meaning, one or more hidden meanings depending on the code used. This kind of code is found especially in the Kabbalah (see GEMATRIA) and in the writing of *amulets where, to avoid writing the actual divine names, these were written in code. The codes are based on various arrangements of the letters of the Hebrew alphabet on the lines of the following illustration in the English alphabet:

ABCDEFGHIJKLMNOPQRSTUVWXYZ
ZYXWVUTSRQPONMLKJIHGFEDCBA

The word CAT can be written in code as XZG. This is known as the AT BASH code, *alef* (the first letter of the Hebrew alphabet) being represented by *tav* (the final letter); *bet* (the second letter) by *shin* (the penultimate letter), and so on. These codes were used in private communications as well, though they were obviously fairly easy to crack.

Codes of Law The Talmud is the ultimate *authority in Jewish *law but the Talmud is not itself a Code of Law. Besides containing much non-legal material, the Talmud, even in its legal portions, which constitute by far its major part, is generally concerned with theoretical discussion and debate rather than with practical decisions. For practical Jewish religious life, rules and regulations are required to be culled from the Talmud, a very difficult task considering the purely theoretical thrust of the work, and then presented in systematic fashion in a Code. When Codes were drawn up in post-Talmudic times, their authority was not based on the opinions of their compilers. Whatever authority they enjoyed was due to their correct assessment of the relevant Talmudic passages. This means that it was possible for the Codes to disagree with one another, since there can be various understandings of what the Talmud is saying and the decisions to be drawn from this gigantic work. Moreover, new conditions often obtained after a Code had been compiled. The whole of the *Responsa literature consists of questions and answers on topics for which there is direct guidance neither in the Talmud nor in earlier Codes. Later codifiers were obliged to take these into consideration when drawing up a fresh and more comprehensive Code of their own, and so the process has continued down to the present day, at least, in *Orthodox Judaism, of codification, Responsa, and further codification. In the sixteenth century Safed Joseph *Karo compiled his *Shulhan Arukh ('Arranged Table'), as if to say here is all the spiritual food the Jew requires for his practical life. Karo's Code was widely disseminated, being produced after the invention of printing, but, as has been noted, it is weighted in favour of the Sephardic practices.

To redress the balance, the Polish Rabbi Moses *Isserles, known, after the abbreviation of his name, as the Rema, produced glosses to the Shulhan Arukh: 'the Tablecloth', as it was called, to cover Karo's table so that Ashkenazim as well as Sephardim could enjoy the spiritual repast. The Shulhan Arukh, now comprising Karo's original text together with Isserles' glosses, became the standard Code for the majority of Orthodox Jews, the Sephardim relying on the original text of Karo and the Ashkenazim on the glosses of Isserles, since the two were now set side by side in the same work. Conservative Rabbis have begun to produce their own Codes and even contemporary Reform is no longer as hostile as Reform used to be to the codification of Jewish law.

Cohen, Hermann German Jewish philosopher (1842–1918). Cohen, the son of a Cantor, received a traditional Jewish education and studied for a time at the Breslau Jewish Theological Seminary with the intention of becoming a Rabbi, but he gave up this plan to study philosophy at the universities of Breslau and Berlin, receiving a doctorate from the University of Halle. Cohen's place in the history of general philosophy is as the founder of the Marburg school of neo-Kantianisne, in which the general Kantian position is subjected to critique and a reworking.

Cohen's thought is universalistic in scope, for all his insistence that God has a special relationship with the Jewish people. The sufferings of the Jews, far from being evidence that God has rejected them, is evidence of His love for them since God loves those who suffer. Yet Cohen's understanding of the doctrine of the *Messiah is in universalistic terms. The attempts by various communities to achieve better human conditions will lead eventually to the emergence of a world in which the ideal will triumph of social justice for all human beings. Cohen's opposition to *Zionism was based on his universalistic, Messianic thought, which he saw as frustrated by a particularistic movement like Zionism.

Communism When considering communism from the Jewish point of view, a distinction must be drawn between the political theory, developed by Karl *Marx, of a classless society based on common ownership of the means of production, and the practice of Communism in societies such as that of Soviet Russia after the Russian revolution. In the latter, where all religion is seen as opium for the masses, God is dethroned, and Judaism is subject to considerable restraint, there is obviously no room for any kind of Jewish acceptance. But the idea in itself of common ownership is not necessarily at variance with the ideals and practices of Judaism.

A prominent Rabbi once remarked that Communism would be a good thing if controlled by Rabbis; a very dubious proposition, but one can see his meaning. What is wrong with Communism is the dictatorship to which it seems inevitably to lead, which overrides the needs and opinions of individual human beings created in the image of God and results, indeed, in rejection of God Himself.

Community The Hebrew word *tzibbur* (from a root meaning 'to gather') is used both for the Jewish people as a whole and for a particular group of Jews organized as a community.

Strife and contention were no strangers to the Jewish community (see CONTROVERSIES). Wherever there are two Jews, the wry saying has it, there are three different opinions. All the more reason why the Jewish teachers, often not averse to a good dose of controversy themselves, repeatedly stressed the importance of communal harmony and cohesion, especially when the community was attacked from without. In Rabbinic and medieval times, the Jew who was disloyal to his community or who deserted it when it was in trouble or, worst of all, who sought to curry favour with the governmental authorities by pointing to the faults of its members so as to endanger their lives, was treated as an outcast. Within the community the danger was ever present of powerful leaders taking unfair advantage of the other members or seeking to lord it over them.

Compassion Fellow feeling, the emotion of caring concern; in post-biblical Hebrew *raḥamanut*, interestingly from the word *reḥem*, 'womb', originating in the idea of either motherly love or sibling love (coming from the same womb); in biblical Hebrew *raḥamim*.

In Jewish teaching compassion is among the highest of virtues, as its opposite, cruelty, is among the worst of vices. The prophet Jeremiah speaks of the people from the north country who 'lay hold on bow and spear, they are cruel, and have no compassion' (Jeremiah 6: 23). The people of *Amalek, in particular, are singled out in the Jewish tradition as perpetrators of wanton cruelty and an uncompassionate Jew is called an Amalekite.

Competition Jewish law accepts the principle that commercial activities are, in the nature of the case, competitive but draws the line between fair and unfair competition. The key biblical text is: 'Thou shalt not remove thy neighbour's landmarks' (Deuteronomy 19: 14). In the context this refers to a man moving the marker between his and his neighbour's field so that he takes to himself some of his neighbour's land. In Rabbinic law this is applied to every attempt to encroach, unfairly, on a neighbour's property or his means of earning a living. The operative word here is 'unfair' and the sources discuss at length how this is to be defined.

Confession In Judaism (see SIN AND REPENTANCE) a penitent sinner must give verbal expression to his remorse: he must confess his sin before God pardons him. Strictly speaking, the confession is acceptable even in the bare formulation: 'I have sinned', but more elaborate forms have been compiled and used. Maimonides (*Teshuvah*, ch. 1–2) holds that the more the sinner confesses at length the better, but gives as the basic form: 'O God! I have sinned, I have committed iniquity, I have transgressed before Thee by doing such-and-such. Behold now I am sorry for what I have done and am ashamed and I shall never do it again.'

Conservative Judaism The form of the Jewish religion that occupies the middle ground between *Orthodox and *Reform Judaism, with its centre in the United States, where it is the largest of the three movements, and with adherents in other parts of the world. The main institution for the training of Conservative Rabbis is the Jewish Theological Seminary in New York, with branches in Los Angeles and Jerusalem.

Conservative Judaism, published as a quarterly in New York, is the house organ of the movement. Conservative Rabbis are organized in the Rabbinical Assembly of Conservative Rabbis, the RAC, which meets annually in conference, publishing the proceedings in *Proceedings of the Rabbinical Assembly*.

The two key thinkers of Conservative Judaism are Zachariah *Frankel and Solomon *Schechter; the former describes his religious position as that of 'positive historic Judaism', the latter stresses the idea of 'Catholic Israel', that the ultimate seat of *authority in Judaism resides in the consensus of the Jewish people as a whole on the meaning of Judaism.

The attitudes of Frankel and Schechter were by no means novel in Europe in the nineteenth and twentieth centuries, where it became obvious to many thinking, observing Jews that, in the light of modern historical investigation into the Bible and the classical sources of Judaism, a reappraisal was required of the whole idea of *revelation. For these Jews, the too-neat picture of the doctrine 'the Torah is from Heaven', as presented in Orthodoxy, was unacceptable, since historical research has demonstrated the developing nature of the Jewish religion as it came into contact, throughout its history, with various and differing systems of thought. On the other hand, these Jews saw Reform as too ready to accommodate Judaism to the *Zeitgeist* and to abandon practices and doctrines hallowed by tradition, especially in Reform's indifference, if not hostility, to the system of Jewish law, the *Halakhah. The attitude of such Jews was articulated in Frankel's maxim: positive historic Judaism—'positive' in its acceptance of the tradition and the Halakhah, 'historic' in that it conceived of these in dynamic rather than in static terms. Schechter spelled it out further in his writings. Since, ultimately, as historical research has demonstrated, the dual process of acceptance and adaptation of ideas in conformity with the spirit of the religion was determined by the way Jews actually lived their religion, the Judaism of tradition is Judaism, although expressed in different ways in different times. On this view, the Jew can have an open mind on the question of origins. He may come to the conclusion, as the Bible critics argue, that some of the institutions of Judaism such as the Sabbath and the *dietary laws originated in primitive taboos. It is not origins that matter but what the institutions actually became in the Jews' long quest to discover the will of God.

Despite wide divergencies and pluralistic tendencies, all Conservative congregations agree in affirming the basic institutions of traditional Judaism—observance of the Sabbath and the festivals, the dietary laws, circumcision, daily prayer, marriage and divorce, *conversion in accordance with Jewish law, the centrality of Hebrew in the synagogue service, and, above all, the study of the Torah as a high religious obligation.

Contemplation The great emphasis placed in Judaism on the *study of the Torah, involving reflection, discussion, and debate, especially on the niceties of Talmudic and post-Talmudic legal topics, towards which practically all intellectual efforts were directed, was bound to result in a degree of indifference to religious contemplation of the more mystical kind. The medieval philosophers, represented particularly in this context by Maimonides, did, however, see contemplation of the wondrous world in which God is manifest as a high religious value.

Controversies There have been numerous controversies in the history of Judaism. In the Middle Ages for example, the Jewish world, after the death of Maimonides in the early thirteenth century, was divided over the vexed question of whether the philosophical approach to Judaism was legitimate. 'What did the Greeks know about God?' the anti-Maimonists roundly declared; to which the Maimonists retorted that even if *Joshua himself were to come down from heaven to forbid the study of philosophy he would not be heeded, so much had philosophy become part of their very being. The great divide in the nineteenth century was between *Reform and *Orthodox Judaism. The central issue, at first, was the comparatively minor matter of changes in the liturgy but eventually at stake was the doctrine of the immutability of the Torah. If the Torah is God's will, can it ever be 'reformed'? However, apart from Samson Raphael *Hirsch, who described the differences between Orthodoxy and Reform as akin to those between Protestantism and Roman Catholicism, no one thought of Reform and Orthodoxy as two separate religious denominations.

Conversion Something of a convention has emerged in which a convert to Judaism is described in English as a proselyte, while a Jew converted to another religion is referred to as a convert. In Hebrew, too, different terms are used: *ger* for the proselyte and *meshumad* (from a root meaning of 'to destroy') for the convert to another religion.

There are two requirements for admission into the Jewish fold: circumcision (for a male) and immersion in the ritual bath, the *mikveh, for both males and females. The applicant is interviewed by a court, *Bet Din, of three (nowadays usually composed of three Rabbis) who first test his or her sincerity and willingness to keep the *precepts. In fact, the practice is for the court first to discourage the applicant and only to permit entrance into Judaism when the applicant is determined to be admitted. The acceptance of the precepts is un-

derstood by Orthodoxy to mean that the proselyte must give an undertaking to keep all the rules and regulations of Orthodox Judaism, which often means that the probationary period can last for a year or even longer. *Reform Judaism is less strict, insisting only on compliance with those rules that Reform itself does not reject. Conservative Judaism follows the same procedures as Orthodoxy but usually with a lesser demand of total acceptance. Many Reform Rabbis did not always insist on circumcision for male proselytes or on immersion for male and female proselytes, but in contemporary Reform some, though by no means all, Rabbis tend to adopt the traditional requirements.

After acceptance, the proselyte is given a Hebrew name and is called son or daughter of our father *Abraham: 'Moshe ben Avraham Avinu' or 'Ruth bat Avraham Avinu'. The tradition is very insistent that the proselyte be made welcome, treated with great love, and never taunted with his or her pre-Jewish conduct.

Cordovero, Moses Safed Kabbalist (1522–70) whose family probably came from Cordoba in Spain. Cordovero was a disciple of Joseph *Karo in Talmudic and Halakhic studies and of his brother-in-law, Solomon Alkabetz, in the Kabbalah, in which subject he soon became the acknowledged master of all the Safed Kabbalists. Cordovero's literary output was amazing. The Kabbalists were fond of saying that he wrote by 'conjuration of the pen', that is, by means of magic power in which the pen seemed to write effortlessly and automatically. Cordovero wrote his *magnum opus*, the *Pardes Rimmonim* ('Orchard of Pomegranates') at the age of 27!

Corporal Punishment Flogging as a judicial punishment is mentioned in the book of Deuteronomy (25: 2–3) where it is stated that 'if the guilty person is to be flogged' he must be given forty stripes and no more. This whole procedure is known as *malkut* ('flogging'). But such flogging could only be administered by an ordained court, and *ordination was limited to courts in the Holy Land. However, as with *capital punishment, what the law took away with one hand it gave with the other. On the basis of the Talmudic statement (*Sanhedrin* 46a) that, where it is required by circumstances, a court can avail itself of extra legal remedies and can flog offenders, a 'Rabbinic' flogging was introduced, known as *makkat mardut* ('flogging for rebellion'), to be exercised at the discretion of the court, even a non-ordained court.

Corporal punishment was also practised in schools, following the biblical injunction: 'Do not withhold discipline from a child; If you beat him with a rod he will not die. Beat him with a rod and you will save him from the grave' (Proverbs 23: 13-14). Fathers would beat their sons and teachers their pupils, often with great severity, in spite of the fact that the Talmud advises that discipline in the school should only be carried out by means of a light strap; a shoelace is the illustration given. The cruelty of schoolteachers, especially the incompetents, became a byword in many communities.

With few exceptions, the modern educational theory, 'children should be seen and not hurt', is followed and corporal punishment is discouraged, although it would be too much to claim that it is completely unknown.

Corpse A dead body is considered in the Bible to be a source of ritual contamination. Anyone who came into contact with a corpse or a grave in which a corpse lay buried became contaminated and was forbidden to enter the Sanctuary until he had undergone the rites of purification by the ashes of the *red heifer (Numbers 19). A priest, *Kohen, was forbidden to come into contact with a corpse other than of one of his near relatives (Leviticus 21: 1-4).

Respect for a corpse is another matter. The Talmud compares a corpse to a Scroll of the Torah, a *Sefer Torah, that has been destroyed; meaning, presumably, that, while the person was alive he carried out the precepts of the Torah with the body, now lifeless, and hence the body, like the scroll, must be buried with reverence. Thus a corpse must not be left unattended before the funeral (see DEATH and BURIAL) and must be ritually cleansed and dressed in special white shrouds. It is forbidden to enjoy any benefit from a corpse or to make use of a grave or shrouds.

Cosmology Strictly speaking, there has never been in the history of Jewish thought a Jewish cosmology in the sense of a specifically Jewish way of understanding how the universe is constructed. Judging by the classical sources of Judaism, the preoccupation of the Jews was with the God of the cosmos, not with the cosmos itself. Jews simply adopted or accepted the cosmologies of the various civilizations in which they lived. They were interested in natural phenomena but chiefly as pointers to God whose glory fills the universe, as when the Psalmist pronounces: 'The heavens declare the glory of God, and the firmament showeth forth His handiwork' (Psalms 19: 2).

Covenant A pact or contract of mutual obligation, especially between God and Israel; Heb. *berit*. In the Bible (Genesis 9: 8 17) God, after the Deluge, establishes His covenant with Noah and his offspring and with every living thing upon the earth, promising never again to bring a flood to destroy the earth. The *rainbow in the sky is made to be the sign of this covenant. To this universal covenant is added the special covenant made with *Abraham (Genesis 15: 7-21). Since this was established, as the passage states, by Abraham passing through the pieces of animals that had been cut up, the term for it, in the Jewish tradition, is 'the covenant between the pieces'. *Circumcision, known particularly as the *berit*, is made the sign of the further covenant with Abraham (Genesis 17). A further covenant is made with Israel at *Sinai (Exodus 19: 5; 24: 1–8), in which God promises that Israel will be His special people if they will keep His commandments. At the entrance to the Promised Land, Moses repeats that God has made a covenant with the people and all their offspring (Deuteronomy 29: 9–14). Modern scholarship has succeeded in drawing parallels between God's covenant with Israel and the Hittite procedures in which a vassal king promises to be faithful to his overlord in return for the latter's protection. The parallel is too close to be accidental but the biblical covenant is unique in that it is between the God of all the earth and a particular people.

Creation That God is the Creator of the universe is accepted as a basic belief in the Jewish religion but the precise meaning of this doctrine has been disputed. The discussion revolves around the meaning of the Hebrew word *bara* in the very first verse of the Bible (Genesis 1: 1): 'In the beginning God created [*bara*] the heaven and the earth.' While this word is used throughout the Bible for God's creative activity alone (the word is never used of human creativity), it does not necessarily imply that He created the world out of nothing (*creatio ex nihilo*). Abraham *Ibn Ezra, in his commentary to the Pentateuch, points to the use of this word, in the same narrative, of the creation of man (verse 27), even though man is said, in Genesis 2: 7, to have been formed from the dust of the earth. The earliest reference to *creatio ex nihilo* is found in a book of the late second–early first century CE, 2 Maccabees (7: 28). But, contrary to this view, the Wisdom of Solomon (11: 17) speaks of God creating the universe 'out of formless matter'. *Gersonides (*Wars of the Lord*, 6) similarly accepts the notion, going back to Plato, that God created the universe out of a 'hylic substance'. For all the variety of opinions on this subject, the standard view did eventually become that of creation out of nothing. In reply to the stock objection that it is impossible for something to come out of nothing, the tradition generally replies that God cannot be bound by what seems possible or impossible to the human mind.

Cremation The disposal of a corpse by reducing it to ashes. While cremation was known in the ancient world, the universal Jewish practice, until the late nineteenth century when cremation became popular, was to bury the dead in the ground or in mausoleums (see DEATH AND BURIAL). In modern times, Reform Judaism has little objection to cremation, although it normally favours burial. Orthodox and, to a very large extent, Conservative Judaism frown severely on cremation. Orthodox Rabbis have been especially virulent in their opposition to the practice.

Some Orthodox Rabbis do not permit burial in the Jewish cemetery of the ashes of one who has been cremated, but others do allow it. It has long been the practice in the Orthodox community of Great Britain to permit this practice provided the ashes are placed in a normal coffin.

Crescas, Hasdai Spanish Jewish philosopher (d. 1412). Crescas, communal leader of the Aragonian Jewish communities, was one of the most influential personalities of Spanish Jewry, in particular in his efforts to prevent Jews from being lured away from Judaism in the wake of Christian persecution. His own son was killed during a persecution in 1391. Crescas devoted much of his effort to defending Judaism against theological attacks by Christians and to offering a critique of the popular philosophical trends. His work in Spanish (later translated into Hebrew), *Refutation of the Principal Dogmas of the Christian Religion*, came to occupy a prominent place in Jewish–Christian polemic.

Cripples Priests afflicted with physical deformities were barred from officiating in the Temple: 'Whoever hath a blemish, he shall not approach: a blind man, or a lame, or he that hath any thing maimed, or any thing too long, or a man that is broken-footed, or broken handed, or crook-backed, or a dwarf, or that hath his eye overspread, or is scabbed, or scurvey, or hath his stones crushed' (Leviticus 21: 18–20). The usual explanation is that the dignity of the sacred spot is impaired if those who officiate there are deformed. Whether the disqualification applies to a *Cantor, who leads the prayers in the *synagogue, was discussed in the Middle Ages. The German authority, Rabbi Meir of Rothenburg (d. 1293), was asked whether a cripple can act as the Reader in the synagogue. The Rabbi replies that no conclusions can be drawn from the disqualification of a cripple from service in the Temple. Apart from in the Temple, he observes, God wishes particularly to be served by the physically deformed. A human king uses only whole vessels whereas the King of kings prefers to use broken vessels. The Rabbi quotes the verse: 'A broken and contrite heart, O God, Thou wilt not despise' (Psalms 51: 19). The man broken in body has the broken heart that God wants.

Cruelty *Compassion is high among Jewish virtues while its opposite, cruelty, is prominent among the vices. *Amalek was later understood to be the symbol of wanton cruelty. To utter cruel words is a serious offence; it is wrong to taunt, for instance, a reformed criminal with his past misdeeds or to suggest to one who suffers that it is because he has sinned, or to call a man a bastard or other insulting names. The Italian scholar *Luzzatto understands the Hebrew word for the cruel, *akhzar*, as a compound standing for *akh*, 'only' and *zar*, 'stranger'. Only a stranger to others, only one who lacks the fellow feeling to put himself into another's place, will behave cruelly.

Customs Rituals, ceremonies, and practices adopted by particular Jewish communities or by the Jewish people as a whole. Originally, the term *minhag*, 'custom' (from a root meaning 'to follow', i.e. that which people follow) referred to a practice about which the law was unclear, perhaps where certain details were the subject of debate by the legal authorities. When it was observed that the people followed a particular interpretation the practice of the people was decisive and acquired full legal status. But in the Middle Ages, especially in Germany, the people followed certain practices for which there was no support in the law; sometimes, such practices were adopted from the customs of the peoples among whom Jews resided. At times, the Rabbinic authorities were suspicious of this kind of folk-custom, but when it became too deeply rooted to be eradicated, even this type of custom was incorporated into Jewish law and a new Jewish interpretation provided so as to render it innocuous.

Cycles The notion, found in early Kabbalistic works, that history proceeds in series of thousands of years. The doctrine runs that our world will last for 6,000 years after which there will be a 'Sabbath' of 1,000 years. After this, the cycle will begin afresh and continue until 49,000 years have elapsed, after which there will be a great Jubilee of 1,000 years. In some versions, after the great Jubilee, the whole process will begin once again.

Damages Compensation imposed by the court for injury to a person or to property. Included in the command to *love the neighbour is the obligation not to harm a neighbour or a neighbour's property. This is taken for granted in all the sources of Jewish law, which discuss mainly the nature of the compensation to be imposed by the court in particular cases. The Talmud expresses admiration for saintly folk who take the utmost care not to injure others or damage the property of others. The '*saints of old', it was said, would bury any pieces of broken glass they had in their possession so deep in the ground that it would be impossible for the plough to bring them up again to cause damage.

Dance Dancing as a form of religious celebration is referred to in a number of biblical passages. After the deliverance at the Red Sea, Miriam leads the women in a dance of glory (Exodus 15: 20). The fact that, in the narrative of the golden calf, the people are said to have danced (Exodus 32: 19) demonstrates that dancing was a customary form of celebration in an idolatrous context, as does the dancing of the priests of Baal when challenged by *Elijah (1 Kings 18: 26). When the *Ark was returned to the city of David, the king 'whirled with all his might before the Lord' (2 Samuel 6: 14). In the light of this it is surprising that, so far as we can tell from the sources, biblical and Talmudic, religious dancing, unlike the playing of musical instruments by the *Levites, had no part in the services in the *Temple, probably because of the idolatrous associations. A vestige of the ancient practice was, however, preserved in the *Water-Drawing Ceremony on the festival of *Tabernacles, when, the Mishnah (*Sukkah* 5: 4) states, 'Men of piety and good works used to dance before them with burning torches in their hands, singing songs and praises.'

Dancing plays no part in the service in the *synagogue, except for the late custom of dancing with the Scrolls of the Torah on the festival of Rejoicing in the Law (*Simhat Torah).

In *Hasidism the ancient religious dance comes to its own again. The dance as a form of worship occupies a prominent role in the movement whose favourite text in this connection is: 'All my bones shall say, Lord, who is like unto Thee?' (Psalms 35: 10). The Hasidim say that in the dance one foot at least is nearer to heaven than to earth. The usual form of the Hasidic dance is in a circle, with the hands of each Hasid on the shoulders of his neighbour. In the circle there is no beginning and end, no higher and lower, so that the dance expresses that all are equal members of the fraternity.

Daniel The biblical hero, living in the sixth century BCE in Babylon, where his people had been exiled, and whose story is told in the book of Daniel. The first six chapters of the book of Daniel tell of how Daniel and his companions, Hananiah, Mishael, and Azariah, were faithful to their religion despite the allurements and threats they were offered to forsake it. The second part of the book contains the visions of the future seen by Daniel, and their interpretation. Part of the book is in Hebrew but most of it is in *Aramaic.

The stories in the book of Daniel are among the best known in the Bible: the three young men cast into the fiery furnace for refusing to bow to the image of the king but emerging unscathed (ch. 3); King Belshazzar and the writing on the wall, which only Daniel can interpret (ch. 5); and Daniel in the lions' den (ch. 6).

The visions of Daniel were believed to contain hints of the time when the *Messiah will come but generally the Rabbis discouraged attempts to discover from the book the time of the advent of the Messiah, since it might lead to loss of faith if the date said to be predicted came and went without the anticipated event happening.

David The second king of Israel (tenth century BCE) whose story is told in the biblical book of *Samuel and whose descendants reigned successively for the four centuries until the Babylonian exile. At the end of the book of *Ruth, David's ancestry is traced back to this Moabite heroine. The narrative in the book of Samuel tells how the prophet Samuel was ordered by God to anoint David as king after the first king, Saul, had been rejected by God. David, in his youth, defeated the giant Goliath in a battle against the Philistines and eventually he was given the hand of Saul's daughter. In a different version in the book of Samuel, David came to Saul's attention because of his prowess as a musician in dispelling Saul's melancholy. David became the friend of Jonathan, Saul's son and heir, but this caused Saul to be jealous of David, who had to flee for his life and remained a fugitive until the death of Saul and Jonathan in battle. David first became king over Judah and then king over all Israel and he reigned for forty years. David resolved to build a *Temple in Jerusalem, the 'City of David', but, as a man of war, he was told by the prophet Nathan that he could not be the builder of the Temple (1 Chronicles 22: 8). The Temple was built by David's son and successor, King *Solomon. David was attracted to Bathsheba, wife of Uriah, and he ordered Uriah to be sent to the

battle-front where he was killed. For this Nathan, in the famous parable of the poor man and his ewe lamb, caused David to pronounce sentence of death upon himself (2 Samuel 12).

These are the bare bones of the biblical narratives about the life of David. The question posed in modern scholarship is: what proportion of all these sometimes contradictory stories are historical since, outside the Bible, there are no references anywhere to David? It has proved impossible to disentangle fact from legend in sources produced over a long period of time, although hardly any scholars go so far as to suggest that David is a purely legendary figure.

In the Jewish tradition, God's promise to David that his kingdom will endure for ever means that the future *Messiah will be a scion of David. Even in the New Testament, *Jesus, as the Messiah, is called 'son of David'.

Reform Jews, believing in a Messianic age rather than in the coming of a personal Messiah, generally treat the traditions about the Messiah as the son of David as belonging not to Jewish *dogma but to poetic fancy.

Dead Sea Scrolls Documents found in 1947 around *Qumran, near the Dead Sea in the Judaean Desert. The Jewish sect to which these documents belonged has been identified by some scholars with the *Essenes. The sect had its own solar calendar instead of the normal lunar *calendar, it had a monastic social order; great emphasis was placed on the life of purity; and, most startling of all, it was completely opposed to the Jerusalem *Temple which it termed an abomination. The scrolls of the biblical books found in Qumran, some complete, others only as fragments, resemble very closely the Masoretic Text but differ from it occasionally.

The Qumran material has rightly been investigated with the utmost care by scholars fascinated by discoveries which throw fresh light on Judaism in the centuries before the destruction of the Temple, on the text of the biblical books, and on the methods of scriptural exegesis in the period when the method later known as the Midrashic began to emerge. Since their discovery the Dead Sea Scrolls have been the subject of much debate among scholars, some of whom even declared that, despite the date of the jars in which they were found, clearly second century BCE, the Scrolls themselves were medieval and of *Karaite origin. This view is no longer held by the experts, who none the less have quarrelled vehemently over the details. It is all very exciting stuff but, it has to be said, of hardly any relevance to contemporary Jewish religion since it was known, long before the discoveries, that there are variant readings in the Bible and that in the period before the destruction of the Temple in 70 CE there was a proliferation of Jewish sects.

Death and Burial The Jewish religion encourages neither a morbid preoccupation with death nor any refusal to acknowledge the fact of human mortality. Judaism teaches that life on earth is a divine gift to be cherished in itself not only as a prelude to the *World to Come. Death is seen as a tragic, though inevitable, event.

There are no special 'last rites' in Judaism but a dying person is required, if his state permits it, to recite the *Shema and make *confession of his sins. After it has been ascertained that death has taken place, the eyes of the corpse are closed, by his sons if possible, on the basis of the verse which speaks of the death of the patriarch, *Jacob: 'And Joseph shall put his hand upon thine eyes' (Genesis 46: 4). The corpse is then taken from the bed and placed on the floor, care being taken that it remains decently covered.

In early times, the Talmud relates,

families would compete with one another to dress the corpse in splendid, costly garments, and people were in danger of becoming impoverished through the heavy funeral expenses. Rabban *Gamaliel, prince of his people, therefore left instructions in his will that he be buried in simple linen shrouds and this custom was followed. The shrouds are, nowadays, made of muslin, cotton, or linen. The usual items of the shrouds are: a headdress; trousers; a chemise; an upper garment known as a kittel (this is worn by pious Jews during the *Yom Kippur services as a symbol of purity and as a reminder of death); a belt or girdle; and a wrapping sheet. Men are clothed in addition with the *tallit, the prayer shawl they wore while alive, although it is the custom to remove one of the fringes to render the tallit unfit for use; otherwise the deceased is mocked since he is no longer capable of carrying out the precepts.

The coffin should be a plain wooden casket. The Jewish tradition frowns on elaborate caskets for the dead for the same reason that it objects to the use of costly shrouds. In death all are equal and ostentation is out of place. In the State of Israel the old custom is still preserved of not using a coffin at all, the dead being buried directly in the ground.

The funeral itself is simple in form. The body is escorted to the cemetery where the prayer acknowledging God's justice is recited.

After the funeral service in the cemetery, pallbearers bring the body to the grave, stopping seven times on the way to represent the seven 'vanities' mentioned in the book of *Ecclesiastes. The coffin is lowered into the grave and first the immediate relatives and then all those present shovel the earth into the grave. All then return to the hall of the cemetery where the mourners recite the *Kaddish.

The mourners return to their home

after the funeral to observe the *shivah* ('seven'), the seven days of mourning, where they sit on low stools and where they are visited by their friends and offered words of comfort and consolation. The psychological effect has often been noted. Where the grief is shared and where it is not kept bottled up but given expression in concrete forms, the burden becomes a little lighter and utter despair is overcome.

Death, Angel of The angel sent by God to bring about death, Heb. *malakh ha-mavet*. There are no references in the Bible to a specific angel of death but the concept is found frequently in Rabbinic literature and in Jewish folklore. In the latter, for instance, the practice of pouring out all the water in pots and so forth when a death occurs is said to be based on the belief that the Angel of Death dips his sword in the water and poisons it. Maimonides (*Guide of the Perplexed*, 3. 22) demythologizes the concept, understanding it as the life-denying, evil force that lurks in the human psyche. Maimonides quotes with much approval the Talmudic saying (tractate *Bava Batra* 16a) that *Satan, the evil inclination (see YETZER HA-TOV AND YETER HA-RA) and the Angel of Death are one and the same. In Yiddish slang a man with destructive tendencies or one who is always running down others is called an Angel of Death.

Deborah The female prophet and leader whose story is told in the book of *Judges 4 and 5. Deborah's famous song of triumph is recited as the *Haftarah on the Sabbath when the Song of Moses (Exodus 15) forms part of the Torah reading for the day The name *devorah* means 'bee' in Hebrew and it is difficult to know why she should have been called by such a curious name. According to one opinion in the Talmud, this was not her real name but was given to her because, like a busy bee, she took pride in calling attention to

her worth, calling herself, in her song, 'a mother in Israel'. In the Middle Ages there was considerable discussion on whether a woman can serve as a judge. Some of the French authorities argue that a woman can obviously serve as a judge, witness Deborah: 'She used to sit under the Palm of Deborah. . . . and the Israelites would come to her for judgement' (Judges 4: 5). Others argue that the case of Deborah is exceptional, either because she acted only in an emergency capacity by special dispensation or because both parties in the dispute agreed to abide by her decisions.

Decalogue The ten words, better known as the Ten Commandments, given by God to the people of Israel at *Sinai, as recorded in the book of Exodus (20: 1–14) and in the book of Deuteronomy (5: 6–18). The two versions are very similar but there a few differences such as '*Remember* the Sabbath' in Exodus and '*Keep* the Sabbath' in Deuteronomy. The discrepancies between the two versions are explained by the critics on the grounds that Exodus and Deuteronomy are two separate sources and by *Ibn Ezra on the ground that the Deuteronomic version is reported speech which is not necessarily exact. The accepted Jewish numbering of the items in the Decalogue is:

1. I am the Lord thy God;
2. Thou shalt have no other gods;
3. Do not take the Name of the Lord in vain;
4. Remember and keep the Sabbath;
5. Honour thy father and mother;
6. Thou shalt not murder;
7. Thou shalt not commit adultery;
8. Thou shalt not steal;
9. Thou shalt not bear false witness;
10. Thou shalt not covet.

The Decalogue was inscribed on two tablets of stone (Exodus 31: 18; 32: 15–16). In art these are usually depicted as two oblongs joined together with a copula on each. The copula, the invention of Christian artists, has been adopted in Jewish representations, although it is certainly unknown in any of the Jewish sources. As a matter of fact, the two tablets themselves do not appear at all as a specific Jewish symbol until around the year 1300 and were copied from the representation in Christian illuminated manuscripts. The older Jewish symbol for the Torah was not the Decalogue but the seven-branched candelabrum, the *Menorah, the symbol of spiritual light. In the Midrashim various suggestions are put forward regarding the arrangement of the words on the tablets. Some say that the two were separate tablets on each of which all ten of the commandments were written, but others see them as having the first five commandments on one stone, the second five on the other.

Democracy A democratic form of society was unknown before the modern period but the Jewish *community in the Middle Ages came close to this form in that the communal leaders were elected by a majority vote of those who paid taxes for the upkeep of the community. The poorer people, who made no contribution, did not evidently have a vote and had no representatives in the governing body. It is, consequently, futile to try to read modern democratic ideals into Jewish sources produced under different social structures. Yet majority rule was the norm even in these sources with regard to the decisions of judges and also in connection with communal enactments. The State of Israel is a democracy and the majority of communal bodies and synagogues are today organized on democratic lines. The general principle here is that any form of society favoured by the members is allowed according to Jewish teaching. A majority can, if it so wishes, vote to give its minorities the right to be represented, all of which means that mod-

ern democratic principles, albeit new in human society, can be and are adopted in Jewish life without this involving any real departure from the tradition.

Demons Supernatural, malevolent beings with the power to cause hurt to humans. (See MAGIC AND SUPERSTITION.) Belief in demons, though not very pronounced in Jewish life and thought, is still prevalent, in a semi-comical way, at the level of folklore. Even some of the learned feel compelled to accept, perhaps not too seriously, belief in demons because this belief is implied in the Talmud in many places. Needless to say, sophisticated Jewish thinkers who did believe in the existence of demons did not think of these as little devils with forked tails breathing fire but as spiritual forces which God has unleashed in the world for purposes of His own, or as harmful psychological processes which take place in the human mind.

Dessler, E. E. Religious thinker and prominent figure in the *Musar movement (1881–1954). Dessler was born in Homel in Russia where he received a traditional Jewish education leading to his Rabbinic ordination, *Semikhah. After trying his hand, unsuccessfully, in business, Dessler obtained a Rabbinic position in the East End of London. He was later instrumental in establishing in the town of Gateshead a Kolel, an institution in which married men with families are supported by patrons of learning while they devote themselves entirely to advanced Talmudic studies on the Lithuanian pattern; an institution now popular everywhere in the ultra-Orthodox world, but, at that time, unheard of in England.

Deuteronomy, Book of The fifth book of the *Pentateuch in which Moses delivers his final addresses to his people, reminding them of the events of their wanderings in the wilderness for forty years after the Exodus from

Egypt and repeating and elaborating on the laws given to them. The older Hebrew name for the book is *Mishneh Torah* ('Repetition of the Law'), rendered in Greek as *Deuteronomion* and in the Latin Bible as *Deuteronomium*, hence the present English title, Deuteronomy. All this is based on the *Septuagint rendering of the word 'Torah' as *nomos*, 'law' rather than 'doctrine'. The other Hebrew name for the book is *Devarim*, 'Words', after the opening verse: 'These are the words which Moses spoke unto all Israel.'

According to the tradition all five books of the Pentateuch were written by Moses at the 'dictation' of God and are really a single book. The Talmudic Rabbis (see BIBLICAL CRITICISM) found difficulties in the last eight verses of the book dealing with Moses' death. How could Moses have written the account of his own death after this had taken place? One Rabbi holds that Moses did write these eight verses, none the less, but with tears in his eyes while another Rabbi holds that these verses were added, after Moses' death, by Moses' disciple, *Joshua. Abraham *Ibn Ezra hints that all the last twelve verses, from the verse which describes Moses' ascent to the mount on which he died, must have been added later since, as Ibn Ezra says, 'once Moses ascended he did not return [to write the account]'. In the Middle Ages other voices were heard occasionally to suggest that there are some few post-Mosaic additions in the book but, until the rise of modern biblical criticism, the traditional view was that Moses is the divinely inspired author of, at least, by far the major part of Deuteronomy.

*Spinoza relies on Ibn Ezra's comments to suggest that the whole of the Pentateuch was compiled much later than Moses, although it is obvious that Ibn Ezra himself refers only to a small number of post-Mosaic additions and certainly would have repudiated Spinoza's radical departure from the traditional view.

If the critical view is correct, what significance does this have for the Jewish religion? Reform and Conservative Jews hold that the question of the Mosaic authorship of Deuteronomy (and of the other four books of the Pentateuch) is purely a matter of scholarly investigation and has no significance for the Jewish religion. What matters, they hold, is the teachings of Deuteronomy—its affirmation that there is only one God; that a great aim is the love of God; that man should have a passion for justice; that the Jewish people has no future unless it obeys God's word. As for the laws, produced, on the critical view, in response to particular conditions which no longer obtain, Reform Judaism does not consider all the Pentateuchal laws to be permanently binding in any event, while Conservative Judaism locates the authority of the laws in the way these have been interpreted and developed in the Jewish tradition, not in the bare biblical text (see CONSERVATIVE JUDAISM).

Devekut Attachment to God, having God always in the mind, an ideal especially advocated in *Hasidism but found, too, in earlier Jewish writings. The term *devekut*, from the root *davak*, 'to cleave', denotes chiefly this constant being with God but sometimes also denotes the ecstatic state produced by such communion.

Dialogue Discussions and conversations between two parties holding different views on some matters of high significance but who believe that it is fruitful for them to talk to one another and thus come fairly to understand why the other sincerely holds to his opinion, as well as to assist one another in the furtherance of the aims they have in common. Dialogue on the contemporary scene usually refers to discussions between Jews and Christians, hence the term Christian–Jewish dialogue.

Diaspora The communities of Jews dispersed in countries outside *Palestine; Heb. Golah or Galut ('Exile'). Originally, the term denoted the community formed by the Jews exiled to *Babylon after the destruction of the First *Temple in 586 BCE. The book of *Ezekiel begins with the words: 'In the thirtieth year, on the fifth day of the fourth month, when I was in the community of exiles [ha-golah] by the Chebar Canal.' The book of *Esther (2: 5) speaks of 'the group that was carried into exile [ha-golah] along with King Jeconiah of Judah which had been driven into exile by King Nebuchadnezzar of Babylon'. After the destruction of the Second Temple in 70 CE, the Diaspora consisted mainly of the communities of Babylon, Egypt, Rome, and other parts of Europe. At the present day the Diaspora consists of all the Jewish communities outside the State of Israel, the most prominent of which is the American community, which has a Jewish population larger than that of Israel.

As the name 'Exile' implies, Diaspora Jews, while often quite content to remain such, never completely gave up the hope that one day they would return 'home'. It was this hope, kept alive in many of the prayers and ceremonies, that paved the way for *Zionism and the establishment of the State of Israel. Ben Gurion, the first Prime Minister of Israel, went so far as to say that eventually the Diaspora will fade away entirely; the Diaspora Jews will either become so assimilated as to lose their Jewish identity or they will bid farewell to the Diaspora by emigrating to Israel. Very few Jews accepted this negative view, arguing that, as in the past, the Diaspora has its own specific contributions to make.

Dietary Laws The rules and regulations governing which items of food are forbidden and which permitted. The word kosher (kasher in the Sephardi and modern Hebrew pronunciation) means simply 'right' or 'fit', as in the verse: 'The thing seems right [kasher] in the eyes of the king' (Esther 8: 5) and originally had no special association with the dietary laws. (In American slang, derived from the Yiddish, a kosher business deal means one that is perfectly above-board.) But the term kosher is now used particularly for food that is permitted and the abstract noun kashrut is used as a synonym for the observance of these laws. Another biblical verse states: 'Ye shall be holy men unto Me; therefore ye shall not eat any flesh that is torn [terefah] of beasts in the field' (Exodus 22: 30). This term, terefah, often abbreviated to tref, was extended to include any food forbidden by the dietary laws. Thus, in current parlance, the observance of kashrut involves eating only kosher food and rejecting terefah food.

From two biblical passages (Leviticus 11 and Deuteronomy 14: 3–21) the following rules are extracted regarding which animals, birds, and fishes are kosher and which terefah.

Only animals which have cloven hooves and which chew the cud are permitted. The pig does have cloven hooves but does not chew the cud and is, consequently, forbidden. In the course of time, Jews came to have an aversion to the pig in particular, especially after Jews, in the period of the *Maccabees, were ready to give their lives rather than eat pig-meat when ordered by tyrants to do so as an expression of disloyalty to the Jewish religion as a whole. Many a Jew today, otherwise not too observant of the dietary laws, will still refuse steadfastly to eat swine-flesh. It might be remarked, however, it is only eating of the pig that is forbidden. Surprising though this may seem at first glance, there is no objection, in Jewish law, to a Jew having a pigskin wallet. The passage in Deuteronomy (14:

4–5) gives a list of the animals which chew the cud and have cloven hooves and are thus kosher: oxen, sheep, goats, deer, gazelles, roebuck, wild goats, ibex, antelopes, and mountain sheep. It is interesting to note that whale-meat and whale-oil are forbidden not because the whale is a forbidden fish but because the whale is a mammal which, obviously, does not have cloven hooves and does not chew the cud.

With regard to birds, the Bible gives a list of the forbidden birds, implying that all others are kosher. But since the exact identity of the birds mentioned is uncertain, it is the practice only to eat birds which are known by tradition to be kosher, such as chickens, turkeys, ducks, geese, and pigeons. The eggs of forbidden birds are terefah, but quails' eggs are permitted since the quail is a kosher bird (see Numbers 12: 31–2).

Nowhere in the whole of the Bible is there any reference to a particular fish, only to fish in general. In the two passages dealing with the dietary laws it is stated that only fish which have fins and scales are kosher.

Worms, frogs, eels, and all shellfish such as crabs and prawns are not kosher.

As noted above, the Bible forbids the eating of the meat of an animal torn (terefah) by wild beasts and it also forbids (Deuteronomy 14: 21) the meat of an animal that has died of its own accord, called nevelah, a carcass. The Rabbinic understanding of these two terms is that any animal that has not been killed in the manner known as *shehitah is treated as nevelah and any animal that has serious defects in its vital organs is treated as a terefah, so that its meat is forbidden even if it has been killed in the proper manner. This applies to birds as well as to animals. There is a vast literature on how to determine which type of organic disease renders an animal or bird terefah. Observant Jews, for instance, will bring to a Rabbi a chicken which seems to have some defect when it is opened up. After an examination, the Rabbi will declare it to be either kosher or terefah.

The strict prohibition of blood in the Bible (Leviticus 7: 26–27; 17: 10–14) is the basis for the laws governing the preparation of the meat of animals and birds for food. The usual practice is first to soak the meat in cold water for half an hour and then to salt it thoroughly and leave it covered in salt on a draining board so that as much as possible of the blood is drained off. An alternative method is to roast the meat over a naked flame. In many communities, nowadays, the butcher attends to this process, relieving his customers from having to do it themselves. The blood of fishes is permitted so there is no process of 'salting' for fish.

The biblical text repeats three times the prohibition of 'seething a kid in its mother's milk' (Exodus 23: 19; 34: 26; Deuteronomy 14: 21). This might originally have been intended to prohibit an act of such callousness or to ban any attempt at influencing nature by some kind of sympathetic magic, but in the Rabbinic tradition the prohibition means that no meat of any animal may be cooked in any milk (the 'kid' and the milk of the 'mother' referring only to the type of the forbidden mixture, i.e. the milk and meat of animals like a 'kid' and its 'mother'). As for the threefold repetition, this is said to forbid the initial cooking-together of meat and milk; to forbid the eating of meat and milk cooked together; and to forbid any benefit from the mixture: by selling it, for example, to a non-Jew to whom these laws do not apply.

Discipleship The acceptance by a person of another as master, tutor, and spiritual guide. The two chief examples of discipleship in the Bible are those of *Joshua and Moses (Exodus 33: 11; Numbers 12: 28; 27: 12–22; Deuteronomy 34: 9) and *Elisha and Elijah (1 Kings 19: 19–21; 2 Kings 2). The 'sons of the prophets' mentioned in the biblical nar-rative of Elisha (2 Kings 2: 3–11; 4: 1; 38) appear to have been a guild of aspirants to prophecy who gathered around prophets to be instructed in the art. The word 'son' (ben) should be under-stood in the sense of a close pupil and the Hebrew is best translated as 'disci-ples of the prophets'. Elisha's special disciple and retainer, Gehazi, is not viewed with complete favour in the narrative because of his interference in the master's affairs (2 Kings 4).

The Talmudic Rabbis, with the study of the Torah as their highest value, at-tached the greatest significance to disci-pleship. In the opening section of Ethics of the Fathers, the chain of tra-dition from Moses to Joshua and down to the Men of the *Great Synagogue is first recorded and these are then quoted as advising: 'Raise many disci-ples.' The Talmud contains numerous admonitions to teachers to impart their knowledge of the Torah to their disci-ples and to disciples to pay great re-spect to their masters.

In *Hasidism, in particular, disciple-ship is given the utmost priority. By definition, the Hasid is a follower of a particular Rebbe, the *Zaddik, whose approach to Judaism he tries to follow in every detail. In the earlier period of the Hasidic movement, it was the disci-ple of the master, not, as later, the son, who became the master's successor in the leadership of a particular group. The story has often been told of the disciple of *Dov Baer, the Maggid of Mezhirech, who declared that he did not journey to the master in order to learn Torah from him but to witness how the master tied his shoelaces.

Disinterestedness The mystical ideal of detachment from personal striving and ambition, also called equa-nimity. The Hasidic doctrine of *anni-hilation of selfhood comes very close to the ideal of disinterestedness. Disinter-estedness has its origin in Western thought in the Stoic doctrine of ataraxy, the absence of passion. This originally non-religious ideal had an ef-fect on the ascetic tendencies in early Christianity and, later, influenced the Sufi movement in Islam. Under the influence of Sufism, the doctrine ap-pears in *Bahya, Ibn Pakudah's Duties of the Heart (v. 2, 5). Bahya describes ten principles by means of which believers can draw near to God's service free from the taint of self-interest. As the sixth of these principles, Bahya notes: 'It should be all the same to him whether others praise him or denigrate him.'

Disputations Debates between rep-resentatives of the Jewish and Christian religions in the Middle Ages in which Jews were compelled to engage with the aim of persuading them that Chris-tianity not Judaism is the true religion. Three of these disputations, unlike the others, have been placed on record, though it is not too easy to determine what actually happened since, natu-rally, each side presents itself in its ac-count in the most favourable light. In all three the main spokesman for *Christianity was a converted Jew, anx-ious to defend his conversion to the dominant faith. The Jewish representa-tives were forced into a defence of their religion that was bound to result in a denigration of Christianity and in this they risked their own lives and the lives of their co-religionists.

Divination The practice of forecast-ing the future, especially by magical means (see MAGIC AND SUPERSTITION). A biblical text seems to condemn every form of divination: 'Let no one be found among you who consigns his son or daughter to the fire, or who is an augur, a soothsayer, a diviner, a sor-cerer, one who casts spells, or one who consults ghosts or familiar spirits, or one who inquires of the dead. . . . But you must be wholehearted with the

Lord your God' (Deuteronomy 18: 10–13). The famous French commentator, *Rashi, understands the last verse to mean that the man of faith should so rely on God's providence that he should have no urge to know what the future will bring, safely leaving his destiny in God's hand. Yet there are references in the Bible to apparently approved methods of divination. Joseph used a silver goblet for the purpose of divination (Genesis 44: 5), though this was said of Joseph in his capacity as ruler in Egypt, the land of magical practices. Eliezer, Abraham's servant, when he was sent to find a wife for Isaac, practised divination in order to know which maiden would be the one God had chosen.

Divorce Jewish divorce procedures are based on the Rabbinic understanding of Deuteronomy (24: 1–2): 'When a man hath taken a wife, and married her, and it come to pass that she find no favour in his eyes, because he hath found some uncleanness in her, then let him write her a bill of divorcement, and give it into her hand, and send her out of his house: And when she is departed out of his house, she may go and be another man's wife.' In the Rabbinic scheme, the 'bill of divorcement' is a document, known as the *get, in which it is stated that A hereby divorces his wife B and she is now permitted to marry whomsoever she pleases. The get is not a mere formal document of intent, but is the instrument through which the divorce is effected.

The most significant difference between the Jewish religious law of *marriage and divorce, and the law in this area in Western societies, is that the State or the court in Jewish law have the power neither to create a marriage bond nor to sever it. Both these actions can only be achieved by the two persons concerned. Even when the Jewish court, the *Bet Din, does supervise the writing and delivery of the get, this is only for the purpose of seeing that

the procedures are carried out correctly.

It has to be appreciated that, while a man obviously cannot marry a woman without her consent, it is she who is married to him not he to her, since, in the polygamous system which obtained until the ban on polygamy by Rabbenu *Gershom of Mayyence in the eleventh century, a man could have more than one wife. The husband is bound to his wife with regard to loving her, caring for her, and supporting her, but not in the sense that he cannot henceforth take another wife. The wife, on the other hand, from the time of her marriage, has bound herself entirely to this particular man and if, while still married to him, she has sexual relations with another man, it constitutes adultery. Thus, in traditional Jewish law, it is the husband who divorces his wife, not the wife her husband.

Throughout the history of the Jewish divorce-laws various measures were introduced by Rabbinic authorities to prevent abuse by the husband of the rights the law gives him. The most important of these measures was the institution of the *ketubah, the marriage settlement; this is a sum, determined by husband and wife when they marry, to be claimed by the wife from her husband's estate when he dies or from the husband himself when he divorces her. Thus, even though the wife's consent is not required for the divorce to be valid, there is the greatest check against hasty divorce by the husband since, when he divorces his wife, he is obliged to pay her the amount stated in the ketubah and this settlement is, naturally, enforceable by the courts.

The statement above of the purely legal position must not be taken to mean that there is no stigma attached to divorce in Judaism. On the moral and religious level a divorce should be resorted to only as a last option where the marriage has irretrievably broken down. The prophet states that God

Himself testifies against the man who breaks faith with the wife of his youth (Malachi 2: 14–15), upon which the Talmud (*Gittin* 90b) comments that the very altar of God sheds tears over the man who divorces his first wife. Nevertheless, if both husband and wife believe that they cannot continue to live together as man and wife, there is no objection to divorce by mutual consent, although the Rabbinic courts will usually try to bring about a reconciliation where this is possible.

Doctors The statement in the Mishnah (*Kiddushin* 4: 14), in the context of the kind of trade and occupation a father should train his son to pursue, that 'the best of doctors will go to hell', was not taken seriously in practice by subsequent Jewish teachers, many of whom were themselves skilled physicians, and who argued that the Mishnah denigrates only unscrupulous and unskilled healers.

In Jewish law, the opinion of a skilled physician is relied upon even in matters affecting the Jewish religion: when, for instance, a doctor advises strongly that a sick person should eat and not fast on *Yom Kippur, or where he urges that the Sabbath be profaned in order to care adequately for a dangerously sick person.

Dogmas In the eighteenth century, Moses *Mendelssohn and his followers tended to imply that Judaism does not, in the manner of the Christian Church, lay down that there are certain beliefs which a Jew must hold in order to be counted among the faithful. Judaism, on this view, is not a revealed religion at all but a revealed law. (The logical fallacy that to speak of a 'revealed law' is itself the formulation of a dogma is ignored.) Beliefs such as that in the immortality of the soul and belief in God are true, on this view, because reason tells us so, not because these and similar beliefs are expressed in any form

of a Jewish catechism. This view, 'the dogma of dogmalessness', as it is called by Solomon *Schechter in a celebrated essay, is far too sweeping. That areas of dogma are the subject of considerable discussion; that, for instance, there have been many debates around Maimonides' *principles of the faith; that, in Judaism, a bare belief in a dogma or doctrine without any attempt to abide by its consequences is valueless, cannot be taken to mean that Judaism has no fixed beliefs of any kind. If that were so, it is hard to see how Judaism itself can be defined at all.

Dogs Rabbinic attitudes to dogs are somewhat ambiguous. On the one hand, it is permitted and even advisable to have guard dogs where there is danger of attack (a Midrash states that God gave Cain a dog to protect him in his wanderings) but, on the other hand, there are stern warnings against a Jew keeping a vicious dog in his house. The earliest reference to keeping dogs as pets is found in a German work of the fifteenth century, although, in the apocryphal book of Tobit, it is said that the hero had a dog.

Dov Baer of Lubavitch Hasidic master (1773–1827), successor to his father, R. *Shneur Zalman of Liady, in the leadership of the intellectual tendency in *Hasidism known as *Habad. He is also known as Dov Baer of Lubavitch (the Russian town where he settled) and as the Middle Rebbe, that is, the master who came in the middle between his predecessor and his successor as Habad leaders. By all accounts, Dov Baer was a genuine mystic (his valet reported that he would not infrequently go into a trancelike state in which he was totally unaware of his surroundings) but was also a capable organizer who drew up plans for a farming enterprise through which his followers would be able to earn an honest living while having sufficient time to devote to *contemplation.

Dov Baer of Mezhirech Hasidic master (d. 1772), leader, theoretician, and organizer of *Hasidism after the death of Israel *Baal Shem Tov. Although Dov Baer was a competent Talmudist he was never a town Rabbi, occupying only the secondary Rabbinic position of 'Maggid' (the word means 'preacher') in the towns of Rovno and Mezhirech in Volhynia, and is hence known by the Hasidim either as 'the Mezhirecher Maggid' or as 'the Rebbe, Reb Baer'. Dov Baer only got to know the Baal Shem Tov during the last two years of the latter's life and while he quotes, very occasionally, sayings of the Baal Shem Tov, he never refers to him as 'my teacher'. Dov Baer is therefore more correctly to be seen as an original thinker with his own emphasis on what it is that Hasidism teaches.

Dreams In the Bible there is evident throughout a belief that dreams can contain revelations from on high, as in the dreams of *Jacob, *Joseph, and Pharaoh in the book of Genesis. The prophetic vision, the Bible states (Numbers 12: 6), comes in a dream. A Rabbinic saying has it that a dream is a sixtieth of prophecy. Maimonides (*Guide of the Perplexed*, 3. 36–8) develops his theory that in the dream the imaginative faculty is awakened, without which prophecy is impossible.

Dress There are three biblical laws regarding dress: that fringes (*tzitzit) are to be attached to the corners of garments (Numbers 15: 37–41); that a garment containing a mixture of wool and flax (*shaatnez) is not to be worn (Deuteronomy 22: 11); and that a man must not wear a woman's apparel or a woman a man's (Deuteronomy 22: 5). The reason given for the last prohibition is either that this might lead to men and women gaining entrance in

disguise into companies of the opposite sex for immoral purposes, or else because of the need to distinguish clearly between male and female in God's creation.

The Rabbis generally discouraged the wearing of ostentatious or loud garments. It is nowadays a distinguishing feature of the ultra-Orthodox that the menfolk wear dark jackets and coats and black hats, except on the Sabbath when some wear white or golden robes. Women were urged to be especially modest in their clothing, wearing ankle-length dresses with sleeves reaching to the wrist and with the head entirely covered by a *sheitel or a kerchief.

Dubnow, Simon Russian Jewish historian (1860–1941). Dubnow wrote his great *World History of the Jewish People* in Russian but it was published in German translation in ten volumes in Berlin (1925–9) and subsequently in Hebrew. Inevitably, Dubnow's thought with regard to Jewish history has been compared with that of the other famous modern Jewish historian, *Graetz. It has been said, perhaps too simplistically, that while Graetz sees the thrust of Jewish history chiefly in terms of great men and their ideas, Dubnow sees Jewish history as the expression of the rich and varied life lived by the Jewish people as a whole, not only its great heroes.

Dybbuk Sometimes spelled *dibbuk*, the soul of a person pursued by *demons that has found temporary security in the body of a living person. References to evil spirits entering human bodies are frequent in early Jewish literature but the notion of the *dybbuk* is not found until the sixteenth–seventeenth centuries where it appears in the writings of the Kabbalist Hayyim *Vital. Tales of *dybbuk* possession are numerous among Oriental and Eastern European Jews. In the usual version of these stories, a sinner dies and the demons or destructive angels hurry to bring him before the judgement throne. In order to escape for a time he can enter the body of a living person if that person has committed some sin, albeit of a minor nature, at the time. The *dybbuk* (from the root *davak*, 'to cleave', see DE-VEKUT) generally overtakes, to some extent, the personality of the one whose body it has entered, speaking in a strangled, muffled tone as if from a vast distance. In the ceremony of *exorcism a holy man orders the *dybbuk* to leave the body in which it has found lodging.

Dynastic Succession The transfer of power and authority from father to son throughout the generations. Jewish history knows of royal dynasties, especially the dynasty of King *David from whom all the kings of Judah were descended in direct succession. The *Messiah is thought of as a descendant of David who will reign as the legitimate scion of this royal house. The dynasties of the Maccabees and of Herod were viewed somewhat ambiguously by the later Rabbis. The Princes in Palestine during the first two centuries CE claimed descent from *Hillel: Rabban *Gamaliel I; his son, Simeon ben Gamaliel; Rabban Gamaliel II; his son, Simeon ben Gamaliel II; and his son, Rabbi *Judah the Prince.

In later *Hasidism, dynasties of Rebbes proliferated. During the nineteenth century, the comparison between the Rebbe and a king was taken almost literally, in the use of the term 'the Rebbe's court', for instance. There were often dynastic rivalries as to which son would inherit his father's 'throne' and much 'palace' intrigue. It was certainly not unknown for the sons of a Rebbe, when he died, to set themselves up as Rebbes in their own right, each claiming to be the true heir of the departed saint. And there were a number of instances of the Hasidim appointing a regent where the heir apparent was too young to assume office when his father died.

E

Ecclesiastes Biblical book, one of the Five Scrolls (Megillot) in the third section of the *Bible, the Hagiographa; Heb. name, Kohelet (usually translated as 'Preacher'). The opening verse of the book: 'The words of Kohelet, the son of David, king in Jerusalem' were understood in the Jewish tradition to mean that the author was none other than King Solomon but modern biblical scholarship is unanimous in holding that the book was compiled at a much later date, although opinions differ as to when and by whom the book was actually composed. The Talmud (Shabbat 30b) states that, at first, the sages wished to hide the work (i.e. they refused to endow it with the sanctity of sacred Scripture) because some of its statements contradict the Torah and are even self-contradictory. Eventually, however, the book was accepted as a biblical book on the grounds that it begins and ends with 'the fear of heaven'. In other words, for all the book's scepticism and pessimism about the human condition, the teaching which shines through is: 'Fear God and keep His commandments' (12: 13).

Ecology Concern with the preservation of the planet, especially acute in the twentieth century. The proliferation of vast industries; the successful fight against disease, creating the danger of overpopulation; the use of nuclear energy; building activities on a scale unimagined in the past; the risk of global warming or the greenhouse effect, as it is called: all these factors contribute to anxiety about the ecological state of the world. The classical Jewish sources, coming from a time when the problem was hardly a serious one, cannot offer any kind of direct guidance. The argument, on the basis of the verse: 'And replenish the earth, and subdue it; and have dominion over the fish of the sea, and over the fowl of the air, and over every living thing that creepeth upon the earth' (Genesis 1: 28), that, from the beginning, Judaism was opposed to ecological concerns, is extremely faulty. When this verse was written, there was no problem of ecology. On the contrary, at that time, man's problem was how to master the environment. This is quite apart from the fact that Jewish interpretations of the verse have never understood it to mean that man's right and duty to conquer nature is unlimited.

Economics In economic matters Jews have generally adapted themselves to whichever economic system was in vogue in the particular country in which they resided. There has never emerged anything like a specifically Jewish form of economics. This is not to suggest that Judaism has nothing to say on the subject. The principles of social justice and compassion are repeatedly stressed in the Bible, the Talmud, and the moralistic literature. But the problem today is how these principles can best be applied in the conditions that obtain in the age of capitalism—organized labour, the machine, and advertising on the widest scale, even if one does not go so far as to dub our society a rat race. While all Jews accept the principles, how they are to be realized is a matter on which men and women of goodwill differ profoundly. It is consequently futile to invoke Judaism in any direct fashion in trying to cope with economic problems.

Ecstasy Intense exaltation of spirit at

the nearness of God, in which the worshipper transcends his self in wonder. Ecstasy is closely associated with *devekut*, the ideal stressed in particular in *Hasidism. Since there is a marked reluctance on the part of Jewish mystics to record their most intimate religious experiences, very few accounts of ecstasy are found in the literature of Jewish worship. At a lower level, Hasidism speaks frequently of the state of *hitlahavut* (from *lahav*, 'flame'), the state of burning enthusiasm during prayer in which the soul of the worshipper reaches out to God in yearning.

Ecumenism The attempt by religious groupings with divergent views to discuss the things they have in common and work together for the furtherance of these things. On the Jewish–Christian scene the old antagonism of the *disputations has largely yielded to greater co-operation in *dialogue.

Education In Rabbinic Judaism, *study of the Torah is the highest of Jewish values, for men at least (see WOMEN). The need to study made education at every level a divine imperative. During the past two thousand years, Jewish communities saw it as a prime aim to establish elementary schools and, in the larger cities, Yeshivot (see YESHIVAH), at which young men engaged in advanced Jewish learning. In many communities, people would gather in study-groups, the members of which would meet regularly to study, at a less advanced level, the more basic texts of Bible, Talmud, and Codes. In addition, many Jews devoted a good deal of their leisure time to studying on their own, helped by the standard commentators. The past should not be idealized. Not every Jew was educated. Indeed, the constant refrain of the Jewish moralists, that everyone must devote time to study, suggests that the injunction was often needed. It remains true that parents would scrimp and save in order

for their children to be given a sound education. No one could be elected to high office in the Jewish *community unless he possessed a considerable degree of learning.

Eighteen Benedictions The series of benedictions recited thrice daily; Heb. Shemoneh Esreh ('Eighteen'), later also known as the Amidah ('Standing Prayer') because, while reciting it, the worshipper has to stand in respect. There is considerable confusion regarding the history of the Eighteen Benedictions. In some Talmudic sources they are attributed to the Men of the *Great Synagogue, in others to Rabban *Gamaliel II. To the original eighteen, the benediction directed against the sectarians (*minim*) was added, so that there are now nineteen benedictions. Similarly, the term Eighteen Benedictions is used for the Sabbath and festival Amidah, even though this only has seven benedictions.

The Amidah is in three parts. There are three benedictions of praise at the beginning, three of thanks at the end, and thirteen in the middle. The idea behind this form is that a petitioner to a king first praises the king, then states his request, and finally thanks the king for granting him an audience. The nineteen benedictions, each ending with: 'Blessed art Thou, O Lord Who . . .', are:

1. 'Fathers', praising God for choosing the patriarchs, Abraham, Isaac, and Jacob.
2. A benediction referring to the *resurrection.
3. Praise of God's holiness.
4. Prayer for wisdom and knowledge.
5. Prayer for repentance.
6. Prayer for pardon of sin.
7. Prayer for redemption from personal troubles.
8. Prayer for healing.
9. Prayer for sustenance.

10. Prayer for redemption of the Jewish people.
11. Prayer for the restoration of true judges.
12. Prayer for the downfall of the sectarians.
13. Prayer for the righteous.
14. Prayer for God to dwell in the rebuilt Jerusalem.
15. Prayer for the coming of the *Messiah, son of David.
16. A prayer for all prayers to be heard and answered.
17. Prayer for the restoration of the Divine Glory to the rebuilt Temple.
18. Thanksgiving.
19. Prayer for Peace.

Electricity The Hebrew word *ḥashmal*, used in Ezekiel's vision of the *Chariot (Ezekiel 1: 4, 27), is usually translated as 'amber' or 'electrum' and may be based on the recognition by the ancients that rubbing amber produces sparks. This word is, in fact, used for 'electricity' in modern Hebrew. Israeli children are astonished to find, as they think, that the prophet knew of electricity! Once this mysterious power was discovered and harnessed to cater to human needs, a host of problems became acute in connection with Jewish religious law. With regard to the Sabbath, for instance, on which the law forbids kindling fire (Exodus 35: 3), the question arose of whether this meant that it was wrong to switch on an electric light on the Sabbath.

Eliezer, Rabbi Rabbi Eliezer ben Hyrcanus (c. 40–120 CE), one of the five most distinguished disciples of Rabban Johanan ben *Zakkai, later to become one of the leading Rabbinic figures of his day and teacher of Rabbi *Akiba. The Mishnah records around 300 laws in the name of Rabbi Eliezer. The difficulty to be faced in attempting to reconstruct the life of Rabbi Eliezer is that he is, like all the other early Rabbinic figures,

a hero of Jewish legend, from which it is far from easy to disentangle the facts.

Elijah The ninth-century BCE prophet active during the reign of King Ahab and Ahaziah as told in the book of *Kings (1 Kings 17–19; 21; 2 Kings 1–2). In Elijah's confrontation with the prophets of Baal (1 Kings 18) the prophet presents to the people his famous either/or: 'How long will you waver between two opinions? If the Lord is God, follow Him; and if Baal, follow him!' Elijah, even in the Bible, is a mysterious figure, whose sudden appearance is announced without preamble and without the name of his father or any other details of his early life: 'Elijah the Tishbite, an inhabitant of Gilead, said to Ahab, "As the Lord lives, the God of Israel whom I serve, there will be no dew or rain except at my bidding"' (1 Kings 17: 1). In the book of Malachi (3: 24), Elijah is the figure who will reappear on the great judgement day of the future; on the basis of this, Elijah, who did not die but was taken up to heaven in a chariot of fire (2 Kings 2), becomes, in later Jewish thought, the herald of the *Messiah.

In the Talmudic period, it was believed that Elijah frequently returns to earth to teach and converse with certain Rabbis of special merit. Two later Midrashim, *The Great Teaching of Elijah* and *The Lesser Teaching of Elijah*, purport to be the record of these discourses of Elijah and the Talmudic Rabbis.

Elijah, Gaon of Vilna Famed Rabbinic scholar (1720–97). Elijah lived for most of his life in the Lithuanian town of Vilna, his renown being such that he was given, even in his lifetime, the title Gaon (see GEONIM). Judaism knows nothing of hermits but Elijah came closest to the hermit ideal, although he did marry at the age of 18 and had a family. Secluded in his study for most of the day and night, he engaged unceasingly in profound investigation into all the classical Jewish texts. He occupied no official Rabbinic position but was supported very generously by the Vilna community.

The Gaon believed that it was essential for a Jewish scholar to have sufficient knowledge of secular subjects such as mathematics, astronomy, botany, and zoology, to be able to understand the many Talmudic passages which take such knowledge for granted. Secular learning, however, was for the Gaon only a means to the supreme task of 'toiling in the Torah', as the Rabbis call this intense activity.

The Gaon is one of the three key figures belonging to the transitional period from medievalism to modernity in Jewish life and thought (the other two are the *Baal Shem Tov and Moses *Mendelssohn). The *Haskalah movement, founded by Mendelssohn, sought, mistakenly, to claim the Gaon for themselves. To be sure, the Gaon was a critical scholar, in the limited sense referred to above, but he was far removed from any attitude of broad tolerance towards views which diverged from the traditional path.

Although the Gaon took little part in communal affairs, he led the opposition to the Hasidic movement, convinced that the Hasidic doctrine of *panentheism, that everything is in God, is a heretical doctrine. It is not going too far to say that the Gaon persecuted the Hasidim, placing their leaders under the ban (see HEREM).

Elisha Successor to the prophet *Elijah (1 Kings 19: 19–21). The story of Elisha and the *miracles he performed is told is the book of *Kings (2 Kings 2–6). Elisha, more than any other prophet, is the prototype of the holy man of God endowed with the power to alter the ordinary course of nature. In *Hasidism, Elisha is the biblical forerunner of the miracle-working Hasidic saint,

the *Zaddik. On the other hand, there is a tendency in medieval Jewish *philosophy to rationalize Elisha's miracles; for example, it is said that the child Elisha revived from the dead (2 Kings 4: 32–7) was not really dead but in a coma in which he appeared to have died.

Elul The twelfth and final month of the Jewish year (see CALENDAR), the month of spiritual preparation for the coming New Year. At the end of the daily service during Elul the ram's horn, the *shofar, is sounded as a call to repentance, and Psalm 27 is read. Devout Jews are especially punctilious in their religious observances during this month.

Emancipation The recognition in Western societies that Jews are entitled to equal rights together with other citizens of the State, beginning with the State Constitution in Virginia in the USA in 1776 and the aftermath of the French Revolution and continuing during the nineteenth century. The Emancipation is often and rightly seen as the emergence of Jewry from the *Ghetto in order to play its full part in Western society. The Emancipation led to the formation of the *Haskalah movement, the main aim of which was to demonstrate that Jews could and should remain true to their own religion and culture while accepting Western mores and values. The problem was rarely quite as simple as that. Some Jews found the strain of living in two worlds too great to bear and they became totally assimilated in the surrounding culture. The Reform movement sought to deal with the problem by 'reforming' the system, adapting it so as to remove those features the Reformers saw to be at variance with what the Emancipation demanded. The Orthodox German thinker, Samson Raphael *Hirsch, sought to deal with the problem by developing his idea of 'Torah and the Way of the Land', that is, the combination of the traditional learning and way of life with the new values. Yet Hirsch saw fit to remark that if the Emancipation were to result in wholesale defection from Judaism and its values, it would have been better for it not to have taken place at all.

Emden, Jacob Renowned Talmudist and polemicist (1697–1776). Emden lived for most of his life in Altona, Hamburg, where he occupied no official Rabbinic position, earning his living by printing books, especially his own, including his Prayer Book (known as the 'Jacob Emden Siddur'), his collection of Responsa, his autobiography (very unusual for a Rabbi), and his valuable notes to the Talmud.

Enoch In the list of the generations from Adam (Genesis 5), Enoch belongs to the seventh generation. Unlike the other antediluvians mentioned in the passage, who reached the age of over 900, Enoch lived 'only' 365 years (the connection of this number with that of the days in the solar year has often been noted). The narrative does not say that Enoch died but, mysteriously, that 'he walked with God, and then he was no more, for God took him' (Genesis 5: 23), on the basis of which later Jewish legend considers Enoch to have been taken up to heaven, while still alive, to become an angel.

En Sof 'Without Limit', the Kabbalistic name for God as He is in Himself, utterly beyond all human comprehension. In the Kabbalah, God as He is in Himself produces, by a process of emanation, the ten *Sefirot, the powers or potencies in the Godhead through which En Sof becomes manifest in creation. Since En Sof is beyond all comprehension, It (the impersonal pronoun is usually preferred by implication, though Hebrew does not have any impersonal pronouns) cannot be spoken of

at all. True to this idea, the Zohar rarely speaks of En Sof and some early Kabbalists boldly remark that En Sof is only referred to in the Bible itself by hint. The God of whom the Bible speaks is God in manifestation.

Envy The state of being jealous or of being distressed at the success of others. Envy sours the life of its possessor. In Ethics of the Fathers (4. 21) the maxim occurs: 'Envy, lust and ambition drive a man out of the world.' Basing themselves on the Talmudic saying: 'The envy of scribes increases wisdom', many of the Jewish moralists, however, do not decry every kind of envy. To be envious of those who are intellectually superior or those more advanced in spiritual matters is held by the moralists to be no vice but, on the contrary, to act as a powerful spur to the living of the good life. Yet, in *Hasidism, the serene mind accepts its intellectual and spiritual limits, refusing to succumb to any pangs of envy, not even of those who have reached higher rungs on the ladder of perfection.

Epikoros An atheist or unbeliever in the Torah. The name *epikoros* is obviously derived from that of Epicurus, yet the term is used in the Rabbinic literature without reference to Epicurus. *Josephus, on the other hand, does apply the term to the followers of Epicurus, writing that: 'the Epicureans exclude Providence from human life and refuse to believe that God governs its affairs or that the universe is directed by a blessed and immortal Being to the end that the whole of it may endure, but say that the world runs by its own movement without knowing a guide or another's care' (*Antiquities* 10. 11. 7). The term has thus had a chequered history but in the Middle Ages and onwards it was used in various senses and eventually became a general term of opprobrium to denote anyone guilty of entertaining heretical opinions.

Equity The practice of righteousness in a civil dispute even where there is no strict legal obligation to be righteous. In Rabbinic teaching the requirement to go 'beyond the line of the law' is based on the biblical injunction to 'do what is good and right in the sight of the Lord' (Deuteronomy 12: 28). *Nahmanides understands this requirement as being in itself part of the law. That is to say, every person has an obligation to go beyond the line of the law, different from the law only in that the law is categorical and binding upon all, whereas when and when not to go beyond the letter of the law depends on the particular person and situation.

Eruv 'Mixing' or 'mingling', a legal device by means of which two areas or periods are mixed or combined in order to provide a relaxation of the Sabbath and festival laws; plural *eruvin*. There are three different types of *eruv*.

1. The *Eruv* of Limits or Boundaries
According to the *Halakhah, a person is allowed to walk any distance he wishes on the Sabbath and festivals provided he keeps within the town boundaries. In addition he is allowed to walk 2,000 cubits (rather more than half a mile) on all sides outside the town boundaries. This extra area is known as the 'Sabbath boundary'. Now, supposing a person wishes to walk beyond the 2,000 cubits in one direction, say, to the east of the town. The device permitting him to do this is the '*eruv* of boundaries'. Before the Sabbath (or the festival) he places a small amount of food at the eastern boundary, that is, at the end of the 2,000 cubits, and this becomes his domicile from which he now has a 2,000-cubit boundary at that spot. He is now able to walk on the Sabbath through the town itself and a further 4,000 cubits, 2,000 to his *eruv* and a further 2,000 to the east. But, since his domicile is now to the east, he has forfeited his right to walk to the west be-

yond the actual limits of the town. The *eruv* thus 'mingles' the two areas so that they are treated as a single area.

2. The *Eruv* of Courtyards
This applies only on the Sabbath when it is not permitted to carry objects from a private domain into a public domain. (On the festivals carrying is permitted.) Where houses surround a courtyard it is not permitted to carry objects from the houses into the courtyard unless, before the Sabbath, the *eruv* 'mingles' them so that the whole courtyard and its houses are treated as a single private domain in which it is permitted to carry.

3. The *Eruv* for Cooking
Although cooking and baking are forbidden on the Sabbath, they are permitted on a festival, provided the food is intended to be eaten on the festival. It is forbidden to cook on the festival for the following weekday. The question arises whether, when a festival falls on Friday, the eve of the Sabbath, it is permitted to cook on the festival for the Sabbath. By the device of the *eruv* it is permitted. The procedure is to set aside, on the day before the festival, two simple cooked dishes, say a boiled egg and a small piece of fish or a piece of bread. This is the *eruv*, in that it 'mingles' the festival with the weekday which precedes it and the principle then obtains that just as the two dishes are the beginning of the preparations for the coming Sabbath, all cooking on the festival is merely a continuation of the process begun on the weekday. The dishes prepared are eaten on the Sabbath.

Reform Jews are generally critical of the whole institution of the *eruv* and none of the three types of *eruv* is known at all in Reform Judaism. Many Conservative Jews are in agreement with the Orthodox in the matter of the *eruv*.

Esau The son of Isaac and twin brother of Jacob (Genesis 35, 36). Esau is identified with Edom (Genesis 36: 1) and, on the critical view (see BIBLICAL CRITICISM), the Esau–Jacob narratives reflect the conflict between the Israelites and the neighbouring people of Edom. In the later Rabbinic period, Edom is identified with *Rome and the narratives are read as a foretelling of the love–hate relationship between Rome and the Jewish people. Later still Edom (Rome) is identified in Jewish literature with the Christian Church, the narratives now being read as reflecting the rivalry between the two religions of Christianity and Judaism.

Eschatology The doctrine of the 'last things'. The actual term eschatology is found only in Christian theology but the themes embraced by the term—the doctrine of the *Messiah, the *resurrection of the dead, the immortality of the *soul, the *World to Come, *heaven and hell—are discussed in detail in the classical Jewish sources, albeit in a non-systematic way. Throughout the ages Jewish thinkers have reflected on what is to happen in the world of the future but much of this reflection is more in the nature of speculation than dogmatic formulation (see DOGMAS). It is, therefore, hazardous to speak of an official Jewish eschatological scheme.

According to the commonly held view, at a time in the not too distant future there will be a series of wars and catastrophes, 'the birth pangs of the Messiah', after which *Elijah will come to herald the advent of the Messiah. The Messiah will succeed in rebuilding Jerusalem and the Temple, where the sacrificial system will be reestablished. Warfare, hatred, and enmity will cease and a new era will be ushered in during which all mankind will acknowledge that God is the sole Ruler and the Jewish people will study the Torah and observe its precepts in a spirit of total dedication. Human beings in the Messianic age will live for a very long time but, eventually, all will return to the dust to await the resurrection of the dead. The resurrected dead will be judged in a great Day of Judgement after which those declared righteous will live on in a new earth and will enjoy the unimaginable bliss of the nearness of God. In the language of the Rabbis they will 'bask in the radiance of the *Shekhinah'. The souls of those who have died before the advent of the Messiah as well as the souls of those who died afterwards will enjoy the nearness of God in heaven but the less righteous will first be punished in hell. All souls will await the resurrection when they will be reunited with the bodies they formerly occupied.

Essenes A Jewish sect which flourished at the end of the Second Temple period, from the second century BCE. *Philo, *Josephus, and the Roman author Pliny all make mention of this sect but while references to the other two sects of this period, the *Pharisees and the *Sadducees, are frequent in the Talmudic literature, there is no mention of the Essenes anywhere in this literature, unless the references to the 'pious men of old', hasidim ha-rishonim, are to the Essenes. (A number of modern scholars, in fact, understand the name Essenes to be a Greek form of the word Hasidim.) The community that produced the *Dead Sea Scrolls seems to have been a community of Essenes or one with some association with the Essenes. Probably because there is no clear reference to them in the Rabbinic literature, the Essenes are not mentioned at all in later Jewish religious literature and they have had no direct influence on the development of the Jewish religion.

Esther Heroine and, according to tradition, author of the book of Esther, the *Megillah read on the festival of

*Purim. The book tells how Esther is chosen by King Ahasuerus to be his queen and how she and her cousin, *Mordecai, succeed in foiling Haman's plot to destroy the Jews. Esther in Jewish life and thought is the valiant woman who risks her life to save her people. She is not described in the book of Esther as beautiful, as are other biblical heroines, and one Rabbi, rather ungallantly, remarked that she had a sallow complexion and was only attractive because 'a thread of grace' was extended to her from on high.

Esther, Fast of Minor fastday held on 13 Adar, the day before *Purim, so called because it is stated in the book of Esther that Esther and her people fasted in order to avert Haman's decree. The fast is not mentioned anywhere in the Talmud. The earliest reference to it is in the eighth century CE. Because of its comparatively late origin, the Codes treat this fast less stringently than the other minor fasts (see CALENDAR).

Ethics The philosophy and systematic treatment of the theory of moral conduct The actual term ethics is not found in the Jewish sources, since classical Jewish thinking is organic rather than systematic. The practice of justice, for example, is advocated uncompromisingly in every variety of Judaism but there is hardly to be found in Jewish thought anything like a Socratic analysis of the nature of justice.

A significant anecdote is told in the Jerusalem Talmud. The Mishnah rules that if a company of Jews is attacked by heathen, they may save their lives by handing over one of their company if the heathen have specified that man by name, in other words, if they have declared that they have no wish simply to kill any member of the company, only that particular man. Rabbi Joshua ben Levi, following the Mishnaic rule, saved the lives of the citizens of the town in which he resided by handing over a man specified by name, whereupon *Elijah, a regular visitor to Rabbi Joshua ben Levi, visited him no more. After the Rabbi had fasted for many days, Elijah did appear to him and reproached him for his conduct. The Rabbi defended his act by appealing to the unambiguous ruling of the Mishnah. 'Yes,' retorted Elijah, 'but is that a teaching suitable for saints?' In this anecdote it is implied that a saint should have his own ethical code which he is expected to obey even where both logic and the law sees his actions as extreme. They are extreme, it is implied, but a saint is bound to be extreme by his very vocation.

Ethics of the Fathers A treatise, compiled not later than the end of the second century CE, containing Rabbinic maxims of various kinds. In reality this treatise is not a separate work at all but a tractate of the Mishnah. Its original name is *Avot*, 'Fathers', so-called because its sayings are those of successive generations of Jewish teachers, the 'fathers' of Rabbinic Judaism. In current editions of the Mishnah, *Avot* belongs in the order of the Mishnah known as Nezikin, but the association with this order, which deals with jurisprudence, is far from clear. It has been suggested that originally *Avot* was an appendix at the end of the whole Mishnah corpus, since it is in the nature of a summary of the teachings of the Mishnaic 'fathers'. The treatise was often published as a work on its own and was given the full name, *Pirkey Avot*, 'Chapters of the Fathers'. The name Ethics of the Fathers is not of Jewish origin but was given by Christian writers who found the book attractive and read it as a series of ethical maxims. The truth is, however, that while the book does contain such maxims, it is not an ethical treatise in the strict sense, its main thrust being to provide a series of statements of the basic ideas of each particular teacher mentioned.

Ethics of the Fathers has been extremely popular throughout the history of Jewish learning and piety, receiving a number of commentaries from prominent Jewish teachers, each of whom used the book as a vehicle for his own ideas and so, in a sense, continued the theme of the book itself. Ethics of the Fathers is in Hebrew, like the rest of the Mishnah, with one or two Aramaic sayings but it has been translated into many other languages.

Etiquette Correct behaviour, good manners; Heb. *derekh eretz*, 'the Way of the Earth', that is, how people on earth ought to conduct themselves. The term 'the Way of the Earth' suggests that the rules of decent, courteous conduct are not specifically Jewish but belong to humanity as a whole and are appreciated by all human beings without the need for them to be revealed as the precepts of the Torah are revealed to Israel.

Etrog See TABERNACLES.

Eulogies Funeral orations in which the praises of the departed are sung (in the older Jewish tradition literally 'sung', in a special mourning chant); Heb. *hesped*. There are references to eulogies in the Bible; the two best known are Abraham's lament over Sarah (Genesis 23: 2) and David's lament over Saul and Jonathan (2 Samuel 1: 12). The Talmud (*Moed Katan* 21b) gives a list of eulogies over famous Rabbis from which it appears that eulogies were in poetic form. The Talmud has a lengthy discussion (*Sanhedrin* 46b–47a) on whether the eulogy is in honour of the dead or of the living. The practical difference here is seen where the deceased left in his will that he was not to be eulogized. If the eulogy is out of respect for the living, the man's instructions can be disregarded since the honour being paid is not to him but to his family. The conclusion is that the eulogy is to pay respect to the dead, so that if such an instruction in made it must be heeded. One hears, occasionally, of prominent scholars who, out of humility, left instruction that no eulogies were to be recited over them.

Euthanasia Taking the life, at his request, of a person suffering from an extremely painful and terminal illness who will die very soon even if nature is allowed to take its course. Jewish law strongly condemns any act that shortens life and treats the killing of a person whom the doctors say will die in any event to be an act of murder. Positive euthanasia is thus ruled out. Switching off the life-support machine is rather more debatable. For one thing, a person who has suffered brain-death and has only a vegetable form of existence through the machine is held, by many authorities, to be actually dead so that the question of killing him does not arise. Furthermore, it has been argued, when the machine is switched off, the person dies because nature takes its course and there is no positive act of shortening life.

Evil Eye The ability to bring about evil results by a malicious gaze. In most cultures the belief is prevalent that some human beings have the power of sending destructive rays, so to speak, in order to cause harm to those of whom they are envious or otherwise dislike. The concept of the evil eye seems to have come about in stages in Jewish thought. Originally, in the Mishnah, for example, the 'evil eye' simply denoted that its possessor could not bear with equanimity the good fortune of others. In this sense the term is used in contrast to the 'good eye', the possessor of which enjoys seeing others happy and successful. But, especially in the Babylonian Talmud, the notion developed that some persons do have this kind of baneful power and there are a number of superstitious practices to ward off the harmful effects of the evil eye, for example spitting out three times when a person seems to be at risk. Even today some people, when praising others, will add: 'let it be without the evil eye' (in the Yiddish form, *kenenhora*), meaning I do not intend my praise to suggest that I am enviously casting a malevolent glance.

Evolution The theory, associated especially with Charles Darwin, that all living creatures have evolved, from the lowest forms, over an immense period of time, by a process of natural selection. In the science versus religion debates in the nineteenth century, Darwinism was rejected by some Christian theologians on two grounds. First, it was in conflict with the *creation narrative in the first chapter of Genesis, in which God is said to have created the world in six days. Secondly, and more significantly, the idea that species have evolved by natural processes appears to be in conflict with the whole doctrine of God as the Creator. Jewish theologians remained, at first, very much on the periphery of the discussion but later on thinking Jews were bound to react to the new challenges which affected the Jewish religion as they did the Christian religion. No official Jewish response has emerged. Indeed, it is doubtful whether one can speak of an official Jewish view in such matters (see DOGMAS).

Reform and Conservative Jews find no difficulty in the theory of evolution since they reject, in any event, the idea that the Bible is the inerrant word of God and hold that the human authors of the Bible, though divinely inspired, had only the science of their day.

Exilarch Head of the Jewish community in *Babylon. The origins of the office are obscure but there is clear evidence that the exilarchs, traditionally descended from King David, functioned virtually as Jewish kings under the Per-

sian rulers in Babylon in Talmudic times and under the Islamic rulers in the period of the *Geonim. The exilarch had his own police force and prisons. He regulated the economic life of the Jewish community by imposing strict market controls. Throughout the period of the exilarchs there was often rivalry between the holders of the office and the Rabbinic scholars, though it was not unknown for an exilarch to be himself a distinguished scholar.

Exile The banishment of the Jewish people from their homeland and the state of mind produced by this; Heb. *Galut*. Especially after the destruction of the Second Temple in 70 CE, Jews began to see the Galut as a catastrophic punishment for their sins. In the additional prayer recited on festivals the phrase occurs: 'because of our sins we have been exiled from our land and removed far from our country'. Tensions inevitably developed between the idea that Jews in the *Diaspora are in exile and the desire for Jews to accommodate themselves to the life of the countries in which they reside. On the theological level, exile is interpreted as remoteness from God so that, in some religious sources, redemption from exile means not alone the salvation of the Jews from oppression and persecution, but the restoration, in the individual soul, of the harmony and bliss that are the fruit of nearness to God. This emphasis is particularly strong in *Hasidism.

Existentialism The intensely personal philosophy in which the individual responds not to a philosophical system, which he surveys from the outside, but to what is true for him. In religious existentialism, the believer adopts monotheism not because his reason has demonstrated that there is a God but, as Kierkegaard puts it, by a 'leap of faith'. *Heschel's suggestion that Judaism substitutes a 'leap of action' for the 'leap of faith' sounds good but is unhelpful from the philosophical point of view in that it ignores the question of belief upon which, presumably, the action is founded. The two best-known Jewish religious existentialists are Martin *Buber and Franz *Rosenzweig. These two have been followed, rather too blindly, by a number of contemporary Jewish religious thinkers whose attitude has not unfairly been dubbed 'Kierkegaard with a *yarmulka'.

Exodus, Book of The second book of the Pentateuch, called Exodus, after the Greek, meaning 'the Departure' (from Egypt) and in Hebrew *Shemot*, 'the names of' (the Children of Israel), after the book's opening words. The book of Exodus tells of the sojourn of the Children of Israel in Egypt where they were enslaved by Pharaoh and afflicted by his taskmasters; the birth of Moses and his election by God to entreat Pharaoh to let the people go; the ten plagues visited on Pharaoh; the actual exodus of the people from Egypt; the crossing of the Red Sea and Moses' song of deliverance; the theophany at Sinai and the *Decalogue; the Code of law given to the people; the episode of the *golden calf, and the detailed instructions for erecting the *Tabernacle. The traditional Jewish view is that the book, like the rest of the Pentateuch, was written down by Moses at the dictation of God, forming the Torah of Moses. *Biblical criticism sees the book, again like the Pentateuch as a whole, to be a composite work produced at different times in Israel's history.

Exorcism The driving out of a *dybbuk, demons, or evil spirits. The belief that a holy man can order the expulsion of evil spirits that have invaded a place or the body of a person is ancient. It is referred to in Josephus, the New Testament, and the Talmud. Some commentators see a form of exorcism in David playing the harp to drive out Saul's evil spirit (1 Samuel 18: 10). In Jewish folklore there are numerous tales of exorcism by saintly persons. There is, however, no actual rite of exorcism in Judaism. The whole notion of exorcism, bound up as it is with *magic and superstition, is found only very rarely in contemporary Jewish life, but instances do occur.

Eybeschitz, Jonathan Talmudist, Kabbalist, preacher, and Rabbi (d. 1764). Eybeschitz's fame as a Talmudist rests chiefly on his *Urim ve-Thummim*, a work of keen analysis of legal concepts in the form of a commentary to the *Shulḥan Arukh, Ḥoshen Mishpat*. In his early career Eyebeschitz was the head of a *Yeshivah and a preacher in Prague, where he was on friendly terms with Christian prelates with whom he discussed and debated theological question. Many of his sermons were collected in his *Yaarat Devash*, a work that provided generations of Jewish preachers with sermonic material.

Ezekiel The priest who was exiled in 597 BCE to Babylon, where he began to prophesy. Dwelling beside the Chebar canal, he saw the vision of the *Chariot as told in the opening chapter of the book of Ezekiel and thus his prophetic vision contradicts the idea that *prophecy is limited to those who reside in the Holy Land. The Talmudic Rabbis compare the vision of the Throne of God seen by *Isaiah with Ezekiel's vision of the same throne carried on the chariot. Ezekiel, say the Rabbis, can be compared to a villager who, unfamiliar with the sight, waxes eloquent after he has seen the king. Isaiah's account is less elaborate and more subdued since he can be compared to the townsman for whom the sight of the king is not so rare that he is moved to share his experience with others at great length.

Ezra The biblical leader of the exiles who had returned to Jerusalem in

458 BCE. Ezra's associate was *Nehemiah and the story of these two leaders is told in the books of Ezra and Nehemiah. He is described in the book of Ezra (7: 6, 11) as a scribe and is known in the Jewish tradition (which gives each of the biblical heroes his own particular appellation) as Ezra the Scribe. As told in the book of Ezra (chs. 9 and 10) Ezra fought against the marriage of Jews with foreign women, evicting these men and their children from the community.

In the Rabbinic sources, Ezra is placed alongside Moses as the great teacher of the Torah. *Spinoza, a pioneer of *biblical criticism, suggested that Ezra was the actual compiler of the Torah of Moses, the Pentateuch—a view that is obviously at variance with the tradition, although the Rabbis do speak of Ezra placing dots over certain letters in the Pentateuch because he was uncertain whether the words over which the dots were placed belonged to the original Torah.

Faith The Hebrew word for 'faith', *emunah*, is used in the Bible and Talmud to denote trust in God (see BELIEF). The Talmud (*Makkot* 24a), for instance, observes that the prophet Habakkuk based the whole of the Torah on one principle, when he said: 'But the righteous shall live by faith' (Habakkuk 2: 4). This observation suggests that the whole Torah is based on trust in God, from which everything else in the Torah follows. It was not until the medieval period, when the Jewish thinkers were obliged to confront atheistic opinions (see ATHEISM), that these thinkers used the term 'faith' to denote belief in the existence of God, though the meaning of trust in God was not abandoned. The Jewish sources in the earlier biblical and Talmudic period addressed themselves to the central problem in their day, trust in God, whereas medieval and modern Jewish thinkers grappled with the problem of the very existence of God, so that before discussing the need for trust in God they sought to demonstrate that there is a God in whom to trust. Faith now acquires a cognitive connotation, involving assent to certain propositions such as that God exists, and lack of faith implies a rejection of these propositions.

Faith-Healing The cure of disease by methods that invoke religious belief either as a complement to natural methods or as a substitute for them. Judaism is obviously opposed to this kind of healing where it belongs to the practices and beliefs of another religion: in the name of Jesus, for example, or as part of a Christian service. The question of the legitimacy of recourse to faith-healing from the Jewish point of view arises where this is undertaken in the name of God. Traditionally, Judaism has viewed with suspicion supposedly supernatural intervention to cure human ills because this might be associated with *magic and superstition.

Falashas A tribe of black Jews in Ethiopia, many of whom have now emigrated to Israel. The name 'Falashas', meaning 'strangers', is pejorative and is never used by the Beta Israel ('House of Israel') as these Ethiopian Jews call themselves.

Fame Judaism does not normally encourage an attitude of contempt and disdain for fame and renown achieved by legitimate means. Fame is the spur to achievement. Yet a well-known statement in the Talmud (*Eruvin* 13b) warns: 'Whoever runs after fame, fame runs away from him. But whoever runs away from fame, fame runs after him.' In a delightful Hasidic tale, a man protested to a Hasidic master that while he had always followed the Talmudic advice to run away from fame, fame somehow did not run after him. Why was this? The master replied: 'Your trouble is that you are always looking behind you to see if fame is running after you!'

Family Judaism attaches great importance to the family. In the Bible (Genesis 10) the whole human race is presented as a family of nations and even the most obscure and trivial family relationships of the patriarchs are recorded in detail (see e.g. Genesis 22: 20–4; 26). The family both circumscribes and broadens the horizons of its members, each individual having a dual role: as a person in his or her own right and as father or mother, son or daughter, brother or sister, husband or wife, with the extended relationships of grandparents, grandchildren, uncles, aunts, nephews, nieces, cousins, parents-in-law, children-in-law, step-parents and stepchildren.

These family relationships are carefully graded in the Jewish tradition. The *mourning rites, for example, to be observed when a near relative dies, are limited to the seven nearest relatives—father, mother, son, daughter, brother, sister, husband, wife. Of these seven, the mourning period for a parent extends for a whole year, while for the other five for one month. Similarly with regard to *charity, the nearer a relative the greater the obligation to assist him or her when in need. Poor parents take precedence over other relatives, closer members of the family over more distant relatives, and members of the family over strangers.

Yet individual needs and rights are safeguarded by the tradition. While, for instance, the fifth commandment: 'Honour thy father and thy mother' is binding upon children, *Isserles rules that if a father objects to his son marrying the woman of his choice, the father's wishes can be disregarded (see CHILDREN AND PARENTS).

Fanaticism Excess of zeal in religious matters, especially when directed against others. Judaism, like most other religions, has had to face the problem of how to achieve a balance between complete, uncompromising loyalty, pursued with enthusiasm and utter conviction, and unbridled zeal, the possessor of which ignores some of the values of the religion itself. The problem is to distinguish between religious zeal and fanaticism.

Fast Days The days in the Jewish *calendar set aside for fasting by the whole community. In addition to the major fasts of *Yom Kippur and the Ninth of *Av, there are three minor fasts commemorating events connected with the downfall of Jerusalem and the destruction of the *Temple in ancient times. These are the fasts of 10 *Tevet, the 17 *Tammuz, and the Fast of *Gedaliah on 3 Tishri.

In addition to these three there is another public fast day on the day before *Purim known as the Fast of *Esther. Curiously enough, this fast day is observed by the Ethiopian Jews (see FALASHAS) but while the Shulḥan Arukh does refer to the Fast of Esther as obligatory, it allows certain relaxations. The Fast of the *First-Born on the eve of Passover is much later and is treated in even more lenient fashion.

Fatherhood of God It is often said that Judaism speaks of God as the Father of all human beings who consequently are all brothers and sisters. This idea is often described as the doctrine of the Fatherhood of God and the Brotherhood of Man. The fact is, however, that this formulation is modern and highly apologetical. There is much discussion on the whole question of *universalism and particularism in Judaism (and see CHOSEN PEOPLE) but this particular formulation finds no support in the Jewish sources. The Bible does not speak directly anywhere of God as Father but the idea is found by implication in the verse: 'Ye are the children of the Lord your God' (Deuteronomy 14: 1). Since 'ye' are His children it follows that He is 'your' Father. But the 'ye' in the verse refers to the people of Israel. The intimate relationship described in father–children terms is reserved for God's relationship to Israel, not for mankind as a whole.

Feinstein, Moshe Rabbi, teacher, and foremost authority in Jewish law (1895–1986). Feinstein was born in Russia and received his Talmudic education in the Yeshivot of Lithuania. He was Rabbi of the town of Luban in Russia from 1921 until 1937, at which date he emigrated to the USA where he served as the head of the Yeshivah Tiferet Yerushalayim in New York. Feinstein followed the methods of keen analysis of legal concepts as taught in the Yeshivot of Lithuania, with the emphasis on legal theory rather than on its application in practice. He published commentaries in this vein on a number of Talmudic tractates. But Feinstein's fame rests chiefly on his collections of *Responsa under the name *Iggerot Moshe*, 'Letters of Moses'. His decisions in these Responsa are widely held to be authoritative for the whole world of Orthodoxy.

Feminism The movement to obtain equal rights and opportunities for women in Jewish religious life. Following on from the general feminist movement in the 1960s, voices of Jewish men as well as women began to be raised, especially in the USA, that Judaism is too male-oriented. The Jewish woman is at a disadvantage, for instance, in matters of *divorce and a woman cannot be counted in the quorum required for communal prayer, the *minyan. The claims of Jewish feminism in these and similar areas of practice have been acceded to in Reform Judaism and, with some exceptions, in Conservative Judaism. Orthodoxy rejects any departure from the tradition in this area, although some Orthodox Rabbis see no objection to women coming together for services conducted by them in a separate women's minyan.

With the rise of Jewish feminism, the question began to be debated whether women could be ordained as *Rabbis. There is little Halakhic objection to having women serve as Rabbis since, traditionally, the Rabbi's function is to render decisions in Jewish law and, if a woman is competent to do so, there appears to be no reason why she should not exercise this function. Reform Judaism ordained women as Rabbis and accepted women as *Cantors in the 1970s and the majority of Conservatives soon

followed suit. Orthodoxy and some Conservative congregations accept women neither as Rabbis nor as Cantors.

Festivals The festivals of the Jewish year are treated under the separate headings: *Passover, *Pentecost, *Tabernacles, *Rosh Ha-Shanah, *Yom Kippur, *Hanukkah, *Purim, and the New Year for Trees. The last three are minor festivals compared with the first five, Hanukkah and Purim dating from ancient times, New Year for Trees being introduced as a festival at a much later date. Essentially, there are five major festivals and two minor in the sense that the major festivals are biblically ordained, the minor festivals only by Rabbinic law.

In connection with forbidden work, a distinction is drawn between the *Sabbath on the one hand and the major festivals on the other, with a further distinction between the major and the minor festivals. On the Sabbath all work is forbidden but on the major festivals (with the exception of Yom Kippur which is treated on a par with the Sabbath) work required for the preparation of food is permitted.

Fire The Bible explicitly forbids kindling a fire on the Sabbath (Exodus 35: 3). At the *Havdalah ceremony at the termination of the Sabbath, when fire can again be kindled, a special benediction is recited over a lighted candle, praising God for the gift of fire.

Fire is used frequently as a symbol of the divine, based on the verse: 'For the Lord your God is a consuming fire' (Deuteronomy 4: 24), which a Rabbinic comment understands to mean that man must strive to come near to God but not too near. In the narrative of the theophany at Sinai, the verse states that God descended upon the mount in fire (Exodus 19: 16), expressing the numinous quality of fire. Another Rabbinic comment has it that the Torah, given at Sinai, is compared to fire because, like fire, the Torah is freely available to all.

First-Born, Fast of The fast on 14 Nisan, the day before *Passover. The earliest reference to the first-born fasting on the eve of Passover is in the post-Talmudic tractate *Soferim* (ch. 21). This fast is said to commemorate the deliverance of the first-born Israelites when the Egyptian first-born were slain and is therefore unique as a fast not of mourning or penance but of thanksgiving. Traditionally, the completion of a Talmudic tractate in study is an occasion for a 'religious meal' in which it is a religious obligation to participate. This obligation overrides the need to fast on this day, which is an unusual fast in any event. It is consequently the well-nigh universal custom that a Talmudic scholar arranges to complete the study of a Talmudic tractate on this day after which the celebratory meal (usually just drinks and cakes) is partaken of by the first-born and this releases him from the obligation to fast.

First-Born, Redemption of The ceremony at which the first-born male child is symbolically purchased from a priest; Heb. *Pidyon Ha-Ben*, 'Redemption of the Son'.

The reason given in Exodus 13 for the redemption of the first-born is that when Pharaoh refused to let the people go God slew every first-born in Egypt, taking the first-born Israelites to Himself, and they have therefore to be redeemed. Many scholars have noted that in ancient societies the first-born son served as a priest and this may be the origin of the redemption law. There has also been read into the rite the idea that by dedicating the first-born to God's service the whole family is set on the right course.

Reform Judaism has generally abandoned rites associated with the ancient priesthood and many Reform Jews do not observe the ceremony of Pidyon

Ha-Ben, but others do. Some feminists (see FEMINISM) have sought to introduce a parallel ceremony for a first-born girl.

Fish It is somewhat surprising that while there are many references to fish and fishing in the Bible there are no names for particular fish. According to the *dietary laws only fish that have fins and scales may be eaten: 'These you may eat, of all that are in the waters. Everything in the waters that has fins and scales' (Leviticus 11: 9–11).

From Talmudic times it became the custom to eat fish on the Sabbath. One reason given for this preference is that in the creation narrative in the first chapter of Genesis three are blessed after they had been created: the Sabbath, fish, and human beings.

Flattery In the Jewish tradition flattery as a real vice applies only to any attempt to win the favour of a wrongdoer by justifying his evil deeds or by lauding him and paying him respect. The medieval authors refer especially in this connection to the verse: 'But what I see in the prophets of Jerusalem is something horrifying: adultery and false dealing. They encourage evildoers, so that no one turns back from his wickedness' (Jeremiah 23: 14). It is the encouragement of wrongdoing that is chiefly condemned. Insincere praise of a neighbour or praising a neighbour for virtues he does not possess or simply 'buttering him up' is not forbidden by the strict letter of the law. Nevertheless the moralists frown on such activities as well, but much depends in this grey area on the aim and purpose of the flattery and on its social effects.

Flood The deluge in which God destroyed all mankind (with the exception of *Noah and his family) because of their evil deeds, as told in the book of Genesis (6: 9–9: 28). The mythical nature of the Flood narrative has often been noted, especially in the account of the animals coming in two by two into Noah's Ark, which is not a huge ship but a comparatively small, box-like structure. Moreover, parallels to the Flood story are found in ancient Babylonian myths, especially in the *Gilgamish Epic* in which the gods decide to destroy mankind because people are disturbing them by making too much noise! Orthodox Judaism, stressing that the whole of the *Pentateuch is the very word of God, accepts the narrative as factually true in all its details. Even on the critical view (see BIBLICAL CRITICISM) that the Genesis narrative is mythical and that there is more than one account combined in the present form of the narrative, the critics readily note the vast difference between the monotheistic account of the Torah and the polytheistic Babylonian account.

Folklore The notions, tales, fancies, legends, proverbs, *magic and superstition, which stem from the people rather than the learned circles, although the Jewish teachers often have recourse to these. There is a good deal of folklore in the Bible and the Talmud and some of the folk-customs eventually found their way into the *Codes. The folklore of the Jews is obviously indebted to folk-beliefs current in the various civilizations in which Jews lived. These were taken over, often in their original vocabulary, but generally given a Jewish slant.

Forgiveness The Mishnah (*Bava Kama* 8: 7), after describing the amount to be paid in compensation by an attacker to his victim, draws on the story of Abimelech's taking Sarah, Abraham's wife, and then returning her to him (Genesis 20) to declare that monetary compensation is not enough. The attacker must beg forgiveness.

This is the general Jewish attitude in which justice and mercy are combined; justice in that the victim is entitled to compensation, mercy in that once the wrong has been redressed the victim should forgive and forget.

Frankel, Zechariah Rabbi, theologian, and historian of the Talmudic period (1801–73). Frankel studied Talmud in his native Prague under Rabbi Bezalel Ronsberg and philosophy, natural science, and philology in Budapest. His combination of traditional and general learning equipped Frankel to become one of the leading lights of the *Jüdische Wissenschaft movement in which the tools of modern historical criticism were used to explore the development of the classical sources of Judaism. Frankel became principal of the Jewish Theological Seminary in Breslau in 1854. In 1871 he founded the learned journal *Monatsschrift für Geschichte und Wissenschaft des Judenthum*, the foremost organ of modern Jewish scholarship.

The Breslau school, as Frankel and his associates came to be called, played an important role in its insistence that while freedom to investigate the origins of Jewish beliefs and institutions is granted and must be granted, this does not affect the need for strict observance of the *precepts, since such observance belongs to the living religion, as accepted in a kind of mystical consensus by the Jewish people, and this is independent of origins. Frankel coined the expression 'positive-historical' for his approach to Judaism; 'historical' because it acknowledges that Judaism did not simply drop down from heaven ready-made, so to speak, but has had a history; 'positive', because, whatever the origins, this is what the religion has come to be under the guidance of God.

Frankists The followers of Jacob Frank (1726–91) in Podolia, south-east Poland, who formed themselves into a Shabbetean sect (see SHABBETAI ZEVI). Frank, a charismatic figure but also, by all accounts, something of a charlatan and bold adventurer, boasted of his ignorance of the Talmud, claiming that the true, higher Torah is found only in the Zohar; hence the name Zoharists by which the sect was known in the eighteenth century. The name Frankists was not given them until the early nineteenth century, after Frank's death. The Frankists conformed outwardly to the *Halakhah, the legal side of Judaism, but in secret believed it essential to disobey the law. They even went so far as to indulge in orgies at which the sexual prohibitions of adultery and incest were cast aside.

Fraud The key text against fraudulent dealing is: 'Do not wrong one another' (Leviticus 25: 14), upon which text is based the Rabbinic term *onaah*, 'wronging', a term embracing any action by which unfair advantage is taken of another. The Talmud thus observes that there are two kinds of wronging: 1. wronging in monetary matters; 2. wronging with words. The first denotes chiefly an unfair overcharge on the part of the seller or undercharge on the part of the buyer in commercial transactions.

Wronging with words applies to misleading statements and insults. Examples given in the Talmud are: taunting a sinner with his past misdeeds; taunting a convert to Judaism from idolatry with his pagan background; and suggesting to a person who suffers that he has only himself to blame for his sufferings which are the result of his sinfulness. In their conviction that words can hurt severely, the Rabbis declare that the sin of wronging with words is greater than the sin of wronging in monetary matters.

Free Will That human beings have free will is axiomatic in Judaism. As many Jewish teachers have said, unless a man is able freely to choose, how can he be commanded in the Torah to do good and not evil? Robot-like creatures

with no will of their own cannot be issued with commands, not the kind of commands of the Torah at any rate.

For this reason, Jewish law is not binding on those such as minors or imbeciles who are not fully aware of what they are doing. According to Jewish law, acts done under compulsion, such as when a heathen forces a Jew to transgress the precepts of the Torah, are in no way culpable. Accidental homicide, for instance, is held to be culpable but only where there is a degree of negligence, failure to take proper care being considered itself to be the result of an unsound will. An imbecile whose powers of distinguishing between right and wrong are weak and inadequate is not guilty even if he commits 'intentional' murder.

Friendship The two extreme examples of friendship in the Bible are to be found in the story of *David and Jonathan (1 Samuel 20) and the story of *Ruth and Naomi (Ruth 1). In both these stories one of the friends (Jonathan and Ruth) is ready to sacrifice everything out of loyalty to the bond of friendship. In both instances the friendship is between persons of the same sex. No doubt this is because close friendships between men and women were exceedingly rare, on the grounds of sexual morality, so that 'friendship' between a man and a woman was expressed in *marriage.

Fundamentalism The attitude towards the sacred texts of a religion in which these are taken literally and treated as infallible. Jewish fundamentalism can be defined as that attitude in which all notions of historical development are rejected. For Jewish fundamentalists there can be no acknowledgement of any human element in the Bible as understood by the Rabbinic tradition.

G

Gamaliel, Rabban The name and title of six holders of the office of Nasi, Prince, in Palestine during the first five centuries CE. The title Rabban, 'Our Master', was used to distinguish the Nasi from other *Rabbis. The office of Nasi was primarily one of religious authority but the Nasi also played an occasional political role in representing the Jewish community to the Roman authorities. Since practically all the references to the office are in sources compiled later and are far from being contemporary records, it is difficult to know for certain how the office came about and the precise way in which the affairs of the Nasi were conducted. From the later sources (Talmudic and Midrashic) it appears that the first Nasi was Rabban Johanan ben *Zakkai, a disciple of *Hillel, after whom Rabban Gamaliel, a grandson of Hillel, served as Nasi; the office then became a hereditary one held by Gamaliel's descendants.

A list of princes until the end of the Mishnaic period, that is, until the beginning of the third century CE, can now be given:

1. Rabban Gamaliel the Elder (Gamaliel I), first half of the first century.
2. Rabban Simeon ben Gamaliel (Simeon ben Gamaliel I), son of (1).
3. Rabban Gamaliel of Yabneh (Gamaliel II), son of (2).
4. Rabban Simeon ben Gamaliel (Simeon ben Gamaliel II), son of (3).
5. Rabbi *Judah the Prince, editor of the Mishnah, son of (4).
6. Rabban Gamaliel (Gamaliel III) son of (5).

Gambling That there are no references to gambling in the Bible can hardly lead to the conclusion that this activity, found in all cultures both ancient and modern, was unknown in the biblical period; although it can be concluded that gambling was not widespread enough to constitute a social evil, otherwise its condemnation would have been recorded somewhere in the biblical records.

Whenever gambling got out of hand, the Jewish moralists condemned it as a frivolous pursuit (almost everything was a frivolous pursuit for some of the moralists) and, especially, because it could easily lead to impoverishment and destroy family life.

Games and Sport Jews, like all other people, played many kinds of games and engaged in sporting activities. Especially popular were card games, ball games, dominoes, *chess, archery, athletics, and swimming. From time to time, however, the Jewish moralists voiced a number of objections to overindulgence in games and *sport on the grounds that these are a waste of time that could be better spent on the study of the Torah.

Garden of Eden Heb. *Gan Eden* (Eden is a place-name but the word means 'fruitful'), the abode of *Adam and Eve before they were driven out as a result of their sin (Genesis 2, 3). The prophet *Ezekiel refers to Eden as the Garden of God (Ezekiel 28: 13). From the description in Genesis it is obvious that the Garden of Eden is situated on earth. But during the Rabbinic period, Gan Eden and its opposite *Gehinnom were names given to the places, respectively, of reward and punishment of the soul after the death of the body (see HEAVEN AND HELL).

Gedaliah, Fast of A minor fast on 3 Tishri to commemorate the murder of Gedaliah ben Ahikam, the Governor of Judah appointed by Nebuchadnezzar after the exile of the majority of the population to Babylon, as told in the Bible (Jeremiah 40: 5–41; 2 Kings 25: 22–6). Had Gedaliah not been killed the people remaining in the Holy Land might have rebuilt it but when Gedaliah was killed, they fled to Egypt.

Gehinnom Abbreviated form of *Gey Ben Hinnom*, 'Valley of Ben Hinnom', a place where children were burned in fire in the worship of *Molech (2 Kings 23: 10). Because of the association with burning in fire the name Gehinnom (or, from the Greek, Gehenna) became the name in post-biblical Judaism (and in the New Testament) for the place of torment of the wicked after death. Thus Gehinnom and its opposite Gan Eden are synonymous with *heaven and hell.

Geiger, Abraham Reform Rabbi and scholar (1810–74). Geiger, born in Frankfurt, received the traditional Talmudic education of his day and later studied at various German universities and was thus well equipped to become one of the pioneers of the *Jüdische Wissenschaft movement, in which the historical–critical method was employed to uncover the sources of Judaism and the way in which the religion developed. After occupying various Rabbinic positions (serving in Breslau as an Orthodox Rabbi where he met with determined opposition on the part of the Orthodox), Geiger became the Director of the Hochschule in Berlin, a position he occupied until his death. Geiger was strongly opposed to the neo-Orthodoxy of S. R. *Hirsch, a friend of his youth, and to the conservative philosophy of Zechariah *Frankel, but he was less radical in his Reform stance than S. *Holdheim, whose ideas seemed to Geiger to destroy continuity with the Jewish past.

Gemara 'Teaching', synonymous with Talmud. The term *gemara* originally meant a unit of teaching, a text upon which commentary was made. The term is often used in this sense in the Talmud. When, however, Christian polemicists claimed that the Talmud contains anti-Christian statements (see DISPUTATIONS), the printers, anxious to avoid any banning of the Talmud, substituted for this allegedly 'guilty' word the 'innocent' term Gemara (see CENSORSHIP). Thus, nowadays, the study of the Talmud is called the study of the Gemara.

Gematria The exegetical method by which a word is equated with a different word because the two words have the same numerical value. Gematria is derived from the Greek and its resemblance to the word geometry had often been noted, but scholars are now uncertain about this etymology.

Genealogy From biblical times pride was taken in tracing ancestry back to prominent families (see DYNASTIC SUCCESSION, FAMILY). In modern times many Jews are fond of working out their family trees. In some circles advice on this exercise virtually amounts to an industry of its own.

Generosity Jews have always placed the generous disposition high among the virtues. The ancient Rabbis observe that *compassion and generosity are among the distinguishing marks of the Jewish people (see CHARITY). It would be absurd to pretend that there have never been ungenerous Jews but it is true to say that generosity has always been upheld as an ideal among all sections of Jewry.

Genesis, Book of The first of the five books of Moses, the *Pentateuch.

The name Genesis is from the Greek, meaning 'origin' (i.e. of the universe). The usual Hebrew name for the book is *Bereshit* 'In the beginning', after the opening word. The book tells of the history of the world and mankind from the earliest beginnings down to the patriarchs, Abraham, Isaac, and Jacob, and Jacob's son, *Joseph, who became ruler in the land of Egypt where he received Jacob and his family. The story is taken further in the book of *Exodus, which tells of the sojourn of the children of Israel in Egypt and their eventual redemption from Egyptian bondage.

On the traditional view, the book of Genesis, like the Pentateuch as a whole, was conveyed by God to Moses and thus constitutes the infallible word of God. *Biblical criticism, on the other hand, sees the Pentateuch as a composite work, the parts of which were produced at various stages in the history of ancient Israel. The *creation narrative in Genesis is, if taken literally, at variance with modern scientific theories regarding the vast age of the earth and the origin of species through *evolution. Orthodox Judaism still maintains the correctness of the traditional view, but Reform and Conservative Judaism generally accept the critical view, or, at least, some version of it, and believe that the acceptance of this view need not affect the sacredness of the Pentateuch as a divinely inspired work, while acknowledging that the older doctrine of direct, verbal inspiration has to be abandoned in the light of the new knowledge.

Genetic Engineering The possibility of experimenting on human embryos in order to remove genetic defects and increase human fertility is still a new science, and no consensus has so far emerged as to its advisability. It can be said, however, that hardly any Jewish authorities have dismissed the whole project as an illegal tampering with nature. Judaism generally believes that God has created an unfinished world which it is the task of human beings to bring to greater perfection.

Genizah 'Hiding away', the storing of sacred Hebrew texts that are no longer capable of being used; also, 'hiding place'. The usual custom is to bury sacred books in the cemetery, not to destroy them directly, even when they can no longer be used because the writing has faded. In some communities, however, they were placed in a special room to be either buried later or simply left there untouched. The most famous genizah was situated in an attic in the Ben Ezra synagogue in Cairo. Much of the material of the Cairo genizah was brought to Cambridge by Solomon *Schechter at the end of the nineteenth century and is now studied by scholars in the Taylor Schechter Institute under the directorship of Dr Stefan Reif. This genizah contains a wealth of material from medieval times and has succeeded in enriching knowledge of the Jewish medieval world.

Gentiles Persons who are not Jews. Precisely because Judaism centres on a particular people (see CHOSEN PEOPLE) the tendency has been to define all non-Jews as belonging to the 'nations' of the world. The Hebrew for 'nation' is *goy* (a term used, incidentally, in the Bible for the Israelites as well), hence an individual Gentile is referred to as a goy and a number of Gentiles or Gentiles in general as goyyim. Originally the term goy was used simply as a designation and had none of the pejorative meanings it later often assumed.

The key text for Jewish–Gentile relationships is Leviticus 20: 23: 'You shall not follow the practices of the nations [*ḥukkot ha-goy*] that I am driving out before you. For it is because they did all these things that I abhorred them.' A second verse with the same import is: 'You shall not copy the practices of the land of Egypt where you dwelt, or of the land of Canaan to which I am leading you, nor shall you follow their laws' (Leviticus 18: 3). In the context, 'the practices of the nations' (*hukkot ha-goy*) refer to the sexual offences listed in Leviticus 18 and 20 but this was extended in the Rabbinic literature to practices prevalent in Roman Palestine in the first two centuries of the Common Era which were held to be 'un-Jewish'; the Rabbinic Midrash known as the Sifra gives the revealing illustrations of attendance at 'theatres, circuses, and arenas', or of stabbing an animal to death.

In the nineteenth century, a century that witnessed the *Emancipation of the Jews in Europe and the rise of Reform Judaism, great tension surrounded the concept of *hukkot ha-goy*. No Jews thought of adopting forms of worship associated with Christian dogma but Reform generally tended to play down the differences between Jewish and Christian worship where doctrinal issues were not involved, such as the use of the *organ in the synagogue service.

Geography Geographical details are imparted only indirectly in the Bible, for instance in the verse: 'I will set a sign among them, and send from them survivors to the nations: to Tarshish, Pul, and Lud—that draw the bow—to Tubal, Javan, and the distant coasts, that have never heard My fame nor beheld My glory. They shall declare My glory among the nations' (Isaiah 66: 19). In the table of the nations (Genesis 10) the geographical area in which the seventy nations live covers the whole of Arabia, Syria, and Asia Minor and extends as far as Greece, but, of course, there is no mention of the Far East. Similarly, the numerous geographical references in the Talmud are incidental to the information conveyed. In the Middle Ages, a number of Jewish travellers brought back accounts of life in

distant lands and these, supplemented by legends such as that of the Lost Ten *Tribes residing on the other side of the River Sambation, contributed to the medieval Jewish picture of the world, which from the tenth century was known by Jewish thinkers to be a globe (and see COSMOLOGY).

Geonim Plural of Gaon, the heads of the two great colleges of Sura and Pumbedita in Babylonia from the seventh to the eleventh centuries, though a minor Gaonite flourished also in the land of Israel and, after the tenth century, in Baghdad. The word Gaon means 'excellency' or 'pride', based on the verse: 'For the Lord has restored the pride of Jacob' (Nehemiah 2: 3.).

The Geonim looked upon themselves as the legitimate successors to the Babylonian teachers of the Talmudic period and it was largely owing to them that, for purposes of Jewish *law, the Babylonian Talmud—'our Talmud' as the Geonim called it—came to enjoy greater *authority than the Palestinian Talmud. It was said of the Geonim that all their words were 'words of tradition'.

Gershom of Mayyence Prominent German Jewish leader and legal authority (960–1028), also known as Rabbenu ('Our Master') Gershom and as 'Light of the Exile'. The great French commentator, *Rashi, remarked that all French and German scholars are the disciples of Gershom's disciples.

There are a number of communal enactments attributed to Gershom, although some scholars believe that these were only fathered on him later. In any event each of these is known as the 'the *herem* (ban) of Rabbenu Gershom'. One forbids a postman opening a letter to read its contents. But the two most famous of the bans are that on a man having more than one wife at the same time and that on divorcing a wife against her will. The latter was introduced to prevent a man who wished to take a second wife divorcing his first wife whether or not she agreed to the *divorce. The ban of Rabbenu Gershom was only binding on Ashkenazi Jews since Gershom, as an Ashkenazi leader, had no power to impose his rulings upon Sephardi Jews.

Gersonides Levi ben Gershom (1288–1344) of Provence, Talmudist, philosopher, and astronomer. Gersonides wrote a lengthy commentary on the Bible in which his general methodology is to give a list of 'advantages' to be gained from the biblical narratives, that is, the moral lessons to be derived from them. His philosophical approach in this work and particularly in his *Wars of the Lord* follows the rationalistic mode of Aristotelian philosophy in its Arabic garb. He understands, for instance, the fall of the walls of Jericho (Joshua 6) to have been caused by the weakening of the walls by the tramping foot of the priests and the blowing of the trumpets. Gersonides' principle is that the Torah does not oblige us to accept things that are contrary to reason. In his *Wars of the Lord*, Gersonides understands the doctrine of *creation as meaning not that God created the world 'out of nothing' but rather that he created it out of a formless substance.

Gestures Gestures and special posture in prayer are known in Judaism as in other religions from the earliest period. The biblical record refers to bending the knees (1 Kings 8: 54; Isaiah 45: 23); prostration on the face (Exodus 34: 8; Psalms 29: 2); the spreading of the hands heavenwards (1 Kings 8: 23; Isaiah 1: 15); and, possibly, the placing of the face between the knees (1 Kings 18: 42). In the Talmud bowing the head and body is advocated at the beginning and end of the *Eighteen Benedictions and this is now the standard practice. Of Rabbi *Akiba it is said that he would cut short his prayers in public but when he prayed alone he would bow and prostrate himself so much that he would begin his prayers in one corner and finish them in another corner. The practice of *swaying during prayer and the study of the Torah is frequently mentioned. In *Hasidism in particular there was a tendency to move the body vigorously during prayer, to the scandal of the staid Rabbinic opponents of the movement. Some of the early Hasidim used to turn somersaults in their prayers rather like their contemporaries, the Shakers in America. Part of the aim of this exercise was for it to symbolize the doctrine of *annihilation of selfhood. The self was overturned, as it were, seeking nothing for itself and desiring only the glory of God. In present-day Orthodoxy, except among the Hasidim, there is considerable restraint in the matter of gesture. Reform Judaism looks askance on bodily movement in prayer as indecorous by Western standards, although many young Reform Jews are attracted to the wilder types of enthusiasm favoured by the Hasidim.

Get The bill of *divorce given by the husband to the wife in order to dissolve the marriage. Just as a Jewish marriage is established by the delivery of the ring together with the declaration of marriage in the presence of two witnesses, an instrument, the *get*, is required to be given before the marriage can be dissolved. Thus the *get* is not merely a record of dissolution of the marriage but the means of dissolution. There are many rules about the *get*, especially that it be written specifically for this particular husband and wife whose names have to be recorded with complete accuracy. The word *get* means a document and is used in the Talmud for other types of document, but the term generally denotes the bill of divorce.

Ghetto The part of a town in which Jews were segregated from the rest of its citizens. The name is derived from the foundry, known as the ghetto, in Venice, where, by papal decree, the Jews were forced to live. The name ghetto was used for all such places of segregation; the ghetto in Germany was called the *Judengasse*. With the Emancipation of the Jews the ghettos were abolished, although Jews still tended to live in certain Jewish districts for purposes of convenience—proximity to the synagogue, stores providing kosher food, and Hebrew schools for the children.

God The Supreme Being, Creator of the world and all its creatures. Judaism stands or falls on belief in God. In the philosophical formulation of Maimonides (*Yesodey Ha-Torah*, 1. 1–3) with which the master's great Code opens:

'It is the basis of all foundations and the pillar on which all wisdom rests to know that there is a Prime Being who brought into being everything that exists and that all creatures in heaven and earth and between them only enjoy existence by virtue of His existence. If it could be imagined that He did not exist, then nothing else could have existed. But if it could be imagined that all beings other than He did not exist, He alone would still exist and He would not suffer cessation in their cessation. For all beings need Him but He, blessed be He, needs not a single one of them. It follows that His true nature is unlike the nature of any of them [i.e. His is necessary being, whereas theirs is contingent].'

God as a Person

The term 'a personal God' is not found in the classical Jewish sources, although the biblical anthropomorphisms in which God is described certainly suggest that, for the biblical authors, God meets human beings, as *Buber puts it, in the life of dialogue in which person addresses person. 'The Lord would speak to Moses face to face, as one man speaks to another' (Exodus 33: 11). But Jewish naturalists such as Mordecai *Kaplan, under the influence of scientism, believe that God can no longer be described in personal terms at all. God, on this view, is not a being or a person but the name people have given to the 'force that makes for righteousness', the principle in the universe which guarantees that righteousness will ultimately win out. This naturalistic understanding is not only a complete reversal of the traditional view but is less coherent in that it fails to explain how this affirmation that there is such a force in the universe can be 'cashed', as the linguistic analysts would say. As William Temple puts it, when God is described as a 'He' the meaning is that He is not an It. He is more than a 'He', not less. God can only be described, if spoken of at all, in human terms but that is because we are obliged to describe God in terms of the highest that we know and this is in terms of the human personality, always with the qualification that He is infinitely more than anything we can say of Him. Since Hebrew has no neuter gender, the biblical writers use the masculine 'He' when speaking of God and this term has persisted. Feminists believe that God should be spoken of, too, as a 'She' but both 'He' and 'She', when used of God, are only a poor attempt to describe that which is beyond description and to define that which is utterly beyond all definition.

God and Evil

While Maimonides can hold that God is described as 'good' in the Bible only on the analogy of human conduct, not that His essential nature, of which nothing can be known, can be described as 'good', it is postulated in all the Jewish sources that God desires the good for His creatures and urges them to struggle against evil. The biblical and Rabbinic authors are concerned, however, with the human struggle against evil and when the problem of evil is discussed it is generally, as in the books of *Ecclesiastes and *Job and in many a passage in the Rabbinic literature, in the context of why the righteous suffer and the wicked prosper. The abstract problem of why the benevolent Creator should have created evil and suffering in the first place is not touched upon until the age of the medieval thinkers. As the problem has often been expressed: theistic faith, in its traditional version, asserts three propositions: 1. God is wholly good; 2. evil is real; 3. God is omnipotent. The problem is how these three propositions can all be maintained at the same time. For if God can prevent evil and does not choose to do so, He cannot be good and if, on the other hand, He wishes to prevent evil but cannot do so, He cannot be omnipotent. One of these three propositions would seem to demand some qualification. The problem is severe and has been presented in modern times in a particularly acute form as a result of the *Holocaust in which six million Jews perished at the hands of the Nazis.

No representative Jewish thinker has sought to grapple with the problem by denying the second proposition, that evil is real. Even if it be postulated that the existence of evil is an illusion, the illusion is itself evil. Nor does it help to argue, as some Jewish thinkers have argued, that evil is only a negation, the absence of the good, since this is in itself an evil. Nor have Jewish thinkers believed that the first proposition can be qualified, even if some, like Maimonides, refrain from ascribing goodness to God's essential nature. From the human angle, at least, God is good and hates evil. The only way out for the traditional theist would seem to be to qualify in some way the doctrine of divine omnipotence. This is the famous free-will defence. God cannot do the absurd. If He is to grant free will to His creatures, the world must be the arena in which free will can be exercised and this involves the creation of a world that provides for the conflict between good and evil and hence the existence of evil. Some thinkers see no logical contradiction between God making man free and yet always seeing to it that he chooses the good. But if God always saw to it that man freely chooses the good, there would be no value in the choice.

This is how the majority of Jewish thinkers have tried to cope with the problem, although they usually add to the equation that by choosing the good, man makes it his own and so can enjoy it as his own creative achievement for all eternity (see HEAVEN AND HELL, WORLD TO COME). The world is seen, in Keats's famous phrase, as 'a vale of soul-making'. Jews can have no quarrel with F. R. Tennant's analysis of why there must inevitably be evil in a world in which moral values can be realized. For the world to be a theatre of the moral life there must be a regular operation of natural forces, there must a law-abidingness in the universe. A topsy-turvy world in which anything can happen or a fairy-tale world in which the ugly brute always turns into a prince would not be the requisite background for the emergence of moral qualities.

Tennant's discussion, and that of John Hicks who pursues a similar line, is helpful; but the average theist protests, granted that a degree of evil is necessary, why so much? Is the Holocaust a price worth paying for the world to be a moral theatre? The majority of believing Jews hold that there is no solution to the problem of evil capable of being grasped by the human mind in this life.

Gog and Magog The peoples who will wage war against the Jews before the advent of the *Messiah. These two names appear in the vision of the prophet *Ezekiel (Ezekiel 38, 39) where

Gog is the ruler of the country of Magog. Gog will lead his people in war against the land of Israel but will be defeated and God alone will reign supreme. Since Ezekiel prophesied in *exile about the return of the Jewish people to its land, it is possible that he was thinking of contemporary events. Attempts have been made to identify Gog and Magog with nations whom the prophet may have thought to pose a threat in the immediate future to the Jews who were to return to the land. On the other hand, as a number of biblical scholars understand it, the prophet himself may have had in mind events in the remote future as part of his apocalyptic vision. In subsequent Jewish *eschatology, both Gog and Magog are understood to be persons and the 'wars of Gog and Magog' become part of the whole eschatological scheme. As with regard to Jewish eschatology as a whole, there is a considerable degree of uncertainty about what is said to happen at the 'end of days'; the picture is really an amalgam of various folk-beliefs, some of them contradictory.

Golden Calf

The calf fashioned out of gold worshipped by the Israelites in the wilderness. The narrative of the golden calf is found in the book of *Exodus (32: 1–33: 23) where it is told how the people, seeing that Moses had tarried in his descent from Mount *Sinai, stripped off the golden ornaments from their womenfolk, and persuaded *Aaron, Moses' brother, to make for them a calf who would lead them in Moses' stead. When Moses came down from the mount and saw the people dancing before the calf, he shattered the two *tablets of stone containing the *Decalogue which he had brought down with him, destroyed the calf, and forced the people to drink the water into which its fragments had been scattered.

In subsequent Jewish literature the 'sin of the calf' becomes the prototype of national apostasy and idolatrous worship.

Jewish and Christian preachers often use the golden-calf narrative to call attention to the sin of greed and the unbridled pursuit of wealth. But this idea that an unworthy pursuit of wealth is to worship the golden calf is, of course, homiletical. Later Midrashim, noting that the women were extremely reluctant to give their ornaments for the making of the calf, state that women are more steadfast in faith than men. As a reward for their loyalty the women were given Rosh Hodesh, the New Moon day, as a special festival for women. Some pious Jewish women are still known to abstain from work on Rosh Hodesh.

It is traditional, when the golden-calf narrative is read from the Scroll in the synagogue, to chant it in softer voice than is usual in the *reading of the Torah in order to express the embarrassment of the congregation at the sin of their ancestors.

Golem

A creature made out of clay into which life has been injected by magical means.

The golem legend reached the city of Prague not earlier than the year 1730 where the famous *Maharal of Prague was said to have created a golem in order to protect the Jews of Prague from pogroms. When the golem began to get out of hand, the Maharal took the divine name from his forehead and restored the golem to his dust which is now supposed to reside in an attic in the Altneuschul. For the benefit of tourists, shops in Prague now sell models of the golem which closely resemble the figure of the Frankenstein monster.

Grace Before and After Meals

The special benedictions with a wording of their own recited before and after partaking of a meal. *Benedictions are recited before and after enjoying any food or drink, but the

Rabbis introduced special forms for a full meal.

The following is the traditional procedure, still observed by all religious Jews, although Reform Judaism has modified some of the regulations, having, for instance, a shorter form of grace after meals worded more in accordance with Reform theory.

The first step is the ritual washing of the *hands. Then the grace before meals is recited, ideally over a whole loaf: 'Blessed art Thou, O Lord our God, King of the universe, who has brought forth bread from the earth.' The bread is broken, dipped in salt, and distributed to the participants.

The form of grace after meals goes back to early Talmudic times and consists of four parts: 1. a benediction in which God is thanked for providing all His creatures with their food (for 'food' here the word *mazon*, 'sustenance', is used, hence grace after meals in Hebrew is *birkat ha-mazon*) 'benediction over food'; 2. thanksgiving for the land of Israel; 3. a prayer for the city of Jerusalem and its rebuilding; 4. a hymn of general praise and various petitions, some of which were added in post-Talmudic times. In one of these, guests at the table recite a special prayer for their host and hostess.

Graetz, Heinrich German Jewish historian (1817–91). Graetz received a traditional Jewish education in his youth but read widely in private works of general learning and early on was obliged to grapple with the problem of religious belief arising out of the conflict in his mind between traditional beliefs and the new ideas. Graetz was assisted in his struggle by the famous neo-Orthodox Rabbi Samson Raphael *Hirsch. Hirsch became Graetz's mentor for a time but eventually the two became estranged, partly because Hirsch was dissatisfied with Graetz's standards of Jewish observance but mainly because Graetz's historical approach to Judaism was not to the Orthodox master's dogmatic taste.

Graetz's fame rests on his monumental *History of the Jews*. Drawing on sources in many languages and building on the researches of the Jüdische Wissenschaft school, Graetz surveys in the work Jewish history from the earliest times down to his own day, presenting it all in systematic fashion together, in the original German edition, with learned footnotes in which he gives his sources. Graetz emerges as an objective historian but one with a profound belief in God and in the contribution of the Jewish people in realizing the divine will. Graetz's emphasis, and here he differs from the later Jewish historian, *Dubnow, is on Jewish spirituality as expressed in literary sources and on the spiritual strivings of the Jewish people as the essential feature of their political and social life. There is very little social history in the work and hardly any use of archival material.

Despite the legitimate criticisms by later scholars of Graetz's *History*, the book retains its importance as a pioneering work of modern Jewish historiography and for the proud advocacy of the importance of Judaism to the world at large. In the memoir of Graetz contributed by Dr Phillip Bloch to the English translation of the *History of the Jews*, the anecdote is told of a meeting between Graetz and the great Leopold *Zunz. Graetz was introduced as a scholar who was about to publish a Jewish history. 'Another history of the Jews?' Zunz pointedly asked. 'Another history,' was Graetz's retort, 'but this time a *Jewish* history.'

Gratitude In the ethical literature of Judaism, gratitude is a great virtue, ingratitude a great vice. It is not that there is any actual precept to express gratitude for favours done. To be grateful is rather seen as what is involved in being a decent human being for which no precept is required. A key text for the principle of gratitude is: 'You shall not abhor an Egyptian, for you were a stranger in his land' (Deuteronomy 23: 8), as if to say, despite the bondage to which the Egyptians subjected the children of Israel, the latter must never forget that, after all, at first, they were offered hospitality in the land of Egypt and for this they should be eternally grateful. A text quoted by the Jewish moralists against ingratitude is: 'Whoso rewardeth evil for good, evil shall not depart from his house' (Proverbs 17: 13).

Great Synagogue, Men of

The body of sages said to have flourished during the early days of the Second *Temple. Many modern scholars, Jewish and non-Jewish, tend to see the references to the Men of the Great Synagogue as allusions not to a body that existed only at a particular time but to an ongoing activity extending over the first two centuries of the Second Temple. In any event, references in the Rabbinic literature to the Men of the Great Synagogue can be taken to mean that ideas, rules, and prayers, seen to be pre-Rabbinic but post-biblical, were often fathered on them.

Greetings

The best-known Jewish greeting is: 'Shalom alekhem' ('Peace to you') to which the reply is: 'Alekhem Shalom', 'To you be peace'. In modern Hebrew the form is usually simply Shalom. Greetings are known as *sheilat shalom* ('asking peace' or 'requesting welfare'), after the biblical verse (Exodus 18: 7): 'Moses went out to meet his father-in-law; he bowed low and kissed him; each asked after the other's welfare.' Since Shalom is said to be a divine name, this form of greeting is not used in the communal bath-house where people are naked. On the Sabbath people greet one another with: 'Good Sabbath' and on a festival with: 'Good Yom Tov'. In modern Israel the usual greeting for the Sabbath is 'Shabbat Shalom' and on a festival, 'Hag Sameah', 'A joyous festival'. '*Mazal tov' (literally 'A good star') is the standard form of congratulation. The greeting to one embarking on a journey by ship or plane is 'Nesiah tovah', 'A good journey'. Every community has its own form of greetings for special occasions in addition to the above. For instance, English Jews greet a person who has lost a near relative with: 'I wish you long life', a form found nowhere else in the Jewish world.

Habad The movement and tendency within *Hasidism which places particular emphasis on the role of the intellect in the life of religion. Habad (often spelled Chabad in English) is an acronym formed from the initial letters of the three Hebrew words: *Ḥokhmah, Binah, Daat,* standing, respectively, for Wisdom, Understanding, and Knowledge; in this context these refer to the three unfoldings of the divine mind taught in the Kabbalistic doctrine of the *Sefirot.

The founder of the Habad tendency, *Shneur Zalman of Liady (1745–1813), became a foremost disciple of *Dov Baer, the Maggid of Mezhirech (d. 1772), disciple of the *Baal Shem Tov and organizer of the developing Hasidic movement. Shneur Zalman evidently owes many of his specific ideas to the Maggid and his son, known as Abraham the Angel; ideas to which Shneur Zalman gave systematic form. Although an offshoot of Hasidism, Habad is essentially a movement of its own, looked at with a degree of indifference and, on occasion, hostility, by the other Hasidic masters who, while admiring Shneur Zalman himself, believed that the Habad understanding of Hasidism is too intellectually orientated and too close to philosophy for comfort. Shneur Zalman's successor in the leadership of the Habad group was his son, *Dov Baer of *Lubavitch (1773–1827). Dov Baer was succeeded by his son-in-law and nephew, Menahem Mendel of Lubavitch (1787–1866). Menahem Mendel's descendants served in the main as successive masters of the Lubavitch dynasty but a few established Habad schools of their own in opposition to Lubavitch, although their followers were eventually absorbed in Lubavitch.

Habad theology involves a radical interpretation of the Kabbalistic ideas of the famed sixteenth-century Safed mystic, Isaac *Luria, known as the Ari. In the Lurianic Kabbalah, the first step in the divine creative process is a withdrawal or contraction of the *En Sof, the Infinite ground of being, God as He is in Himself, 'from Himself into Himself'. This act of divine limitation is known as Tzimtzum. As a result of the Tztimtzum an 'empty space' is left into which the light of En Sof then streams forth eventually to produce, through a further series of contractions, the Sefirot and through these all the worlds on high and the material world experienced by the senses.

The basic problem is how the Tzimtzum and especially the 'empty space' are to be understood. The Kabbalists generally understand the 'empty space' in other than spatial terms, as a metaphor for that which is other than God, very few entertaining the bizarre notion that there really is a kind of immense circular hole in En Sof into which the universe has emerged. But even if the Tztimtzum is understood in more sophisticated terms to denote spiritual processes in the divine realm taking place outside space and time, humans do have the experience of space and time and the physical world certainly seems real enough. Since this is so, the problem the doctrine of Tzimtzum was intended to solve, how there can be a universe apart and separate from the limitless and infinite En Sof, still remains as obdurate as ever. In Habad thought the extremely radical solution is that, from the point of view of ultimate reality, there is no universe. The universe and the creatures who inhabit the universe only appear to enjoy existence. From our point of view, the world is indeed real, but not from God's point of view, as the Habad thinkers put it.

Habakkuk A prophet whose date is uncertain, although a number of scholars draw the conclusion from the book that bears his name that he prophesied towards the end of the seventh or at the beginning of the sixth century BCE. The unusual name of the prophet has been connected with an Assyrian word meaning 'fragrant herb'.

The book of Habakkuk is the eighth in the book of the Twelve Prophets (see BIBLE) and consists of two chapters of prophetic narration and a third chapter in the form of a psalm. Habakkuk boldly challenges God on why the wicked seem to prosper while the righteous are victimized, but he affirms that God's justice will eventually triumph. Habakkuk's declaration, 'the righteous shall live by his faith' (2: 4) is described in the Talmud (*Makkot* 24a) as a statement upon which all the precepts of the Torah are based.

'Had Gadya' 'One kid'; the song, printed in the final pages of the Passover *Haggadah, with which the *Seder ends. 'Had Gadya' is in *Aramaic, in a form that lends itself easily to the jingling melodies in which it is sung. Some use the tune of 'Three Blind Mice'. The doggerel resembles in form such nursery rhymes as 'This is the House that Jack Built'. 'Had Gadya' begins with: 'One kid, one kid, that father bought for two *zuzim*' and then goes on to tell of the cat that ate the kid, the dog that bit the cat, the stick that beat the dog, and so on until the final stanza: 'Then came the Holy One, blessed be He, and smote the angel of death, who slew the slaughterer, who slaughtered the ox, that drank the water, that quenched the fire, that burned the stick, that beat the dog, that bit the cat, that ate the kid, that father bought for two *zuzim*. One kid, one kid.'

The song first appeared in the Middle Ages and was adopted by Ashkenazi Jews as what they evidently considered to be a suitable ending to the Seder, probably in order to keep the children happy and awake during the long service.

Hafetz Hayyim Israel Meir Kagan (1838–1933), Talmudic and Rabbinic scholar, ethical and religious teacher, venerated by Jews all over the world, especially those in the Lithuanian tradition, for his saintliness and learning. Israel Meir (his original surname was not Kagan but Poupko) is universally known by the title of his first book directed against the evils of slander and malicious gossip. He published this work anonymously, its title taken from the verses: 'What is he that delighteth in life [*he-hafetz hayyim*], and loveth many days that he may see good? Keep thy tongue from evil, and thy lips from speaking guile' (Psalms 34: 13–14). Reform and Conservative Jews, while recognizing that the Hafetz Hayyim's simplistic approach and fundamentalism were not for them (this applied, to a large extent, to the neo-Orthodox as well), never attacked him and still saw him as a saintly figure, whose integrity, practical wisdom, and deep piety made him a model of traditional Jewish living at its best.

Haftarah The 'termination', the prophetic reading which follows the *reading of the Torah. When the practice arose of adding a reading from the prophets after the reading of the Torah in the synagogue is uncertain. A popular view, which goes back to David *Abudarham, is that in a time of persecution, perhaps that of Antiochus in the days of the *Maccabees, when a decree was issued against the reading of the Torah in public, readings from the prophets, not covered by the decree, were substituted. The practice is, in any event, ancient, seemingly referred to in the *New Testament's reference (Acts

13: 15) to the reading of the law and the prophets in the synagogue.

Haggadah 'The telling', the book containing the passages dealing with the theme of the Exodus, recited at the Passover *Seder. The reading of the Haggadah is based on the verse: 'You shall tell your son on that day: it is because of what the Lord did for me when I came forth out of Egypt' (Exodus 13: 8). Although the Talmud mentions some features of the 'telling' by the father at the Seder, no formal Haggadah was produced until the Middle Ages, when the current form was established in essence and became universally accepted. The Haggadah now contains passages from early and late sources dealing with the Exodus, instructions for the conduct of the Seder, psalms and other songs of praise, *grace before and after meals, concluding in the Ashkenazi version with a number of table songs (see 'HAD GADYA'). It has been estimated that no fewer than 2,000 different editions of the Haggadah have been published. No other Jewish sacred book has enjoyed such popularity.

Haggai Prophet after the return of the people from the Babylonian exile at the time of the process of rebuilding the Temple. Although details of Haggai's life are not given in the book that bears his name, the date of his prophecies is clearly implied. The prophecies in this little book of only two chapters were delivered in the year 520 BCE. This does not mean, however, that the book itself, which is the tenth in the book of the Twelve Prophets (see BIBLE), was composed at that date or that it was necessarily composed by the prophet himself. In the Rabbinic tradition, Haggai, together with *Zechariah and *Malachi, are the last of the prophets. After them, the Holy Spirit ceased in Israel. Thus these three are often described as the last of the great prophets. The name Haggai seems to be associated with the Hebrew word ḥag, 'festival'; perhaps the name means 'one born on a festival'. The prophet urges the people, who had delayed for too long, to continue to build the Temple, whose glory in the future will exceed the glory of Solomon's Temple.

To illustrate his message, Haggai (2: 11) puts a question to the *priests regarding the laws of ritual contamination. This question and whether or not the priests gave the correct ruling is discussed at length in the Talmud and it is probably on the basis of this that the Talmud attributes to Haggai a number of other rulings and so turns him into a legal authority as well as a prophet (see HALAKHAH).

Hai Gaon Head of the college of Pumbedita at the end of the Geonic period (see GEONIM) (939–1038). Hai served in the Gaonite of Pumbedita together with his father, *Sherira Gaon. When Sherira died, Hai was inducted formally into the office with the pomp and ceremony typical of the institution. It is reported that there was read in the Babylonian synagogues the narrative of *Solomon's succession to the throne of *David (1 Kings 2: 10–12), adapted to the occasion: 'And Sherira slept with his fathers . . . And Hai sat upon the throne of Sherira his father; and his kingdom was established firmly.' Hai was the son-in-law of the Gaon of Sura, Samuel Ibn Hofni, whose rationalism in Bible interpretation was not to Hai's taste.

As a theologian of note, Hai was among the earliest Jewish thinkers to discuss, in a Responsum, the vexed question of how to reconcile God's foreknowledge with human freedom, a problem of concern to the Arabic thinkers in Hai's day. In another Responsum, Hai reacts to Islamic fatalism when he considers the idea that every man has a life-span fixed beforehand. When a man is murdered, Hai was asked, does this mean that even had he not been slain, he would have died, in any event, at that particular moment? Hai replies that we simply do not know. We can either suppose that if he had not been murdered he would have died at that moment in any event, or we can suppose that if he had not been murdered he would have lived on until a later date. But, it might be objected, supposing a murderer killed a large number of persons on the same day, is it plausible to suggest that they would all have died in any event on the same day? 'Why not?' replies Hai. Experience shows us that a large number of people do sometimes die at the same time, when, for example, a building collapses or when a ship goes down and all the passengers are drowned. But if the victim of a murder would have died in any event, Hai asks, why is the murderer punished for his crime? Hai replies that it is the act of murder that constitutes the crime. The murderer deserves to be punished for the evil act that was his and his alone.

This Responsum has been quoted at length to demonstrate Hai's theological approach, one in which he is thoroughly familiar with the Islamic thought of his day (he knew Arabic and some of his writings are in this language) but proudly defends Judaism against its critics.

Halakhah The legal side of Judaism, in contradistinction to *Aggadah; the latter embracing all the non-legal ideas. In the earliest Rabbinic period, the term Halakhah (from the root *halakh*, 'to go' or 'to walk') was confined to a particular ruling or decision. But, subsequently, while the original meaning was retained, the term Halakhah was also and chiefly used for the whole system. The Halakhah came to denote that aspect of Judaism which is concerned with Jewish *law as a whole; the rules and regulations by which the Jew 'walks' through life.

In every version of Orthodox Judaism,

the Halakhah in its traditional form is sacrosanct as the sole guide for the application of the law to Jewish life. Some Orthodox scholars, fully aware of the findings of modern scholarship, tend to draw a distinction between theory and practice. The scholar can and should have an open mind on the question of how the Halakhah has come to be, while following scrupulously the demands of the Halakhah in practice. The one is a matter of pure scholarship, the other of religion in action. To take an illustration from the Hebrew language, a scholar may investigate the origin and development of Hebrew as a Semitic language but his researches will in no way affect his use of Hebrew in prayer and worship since this language and no other, whatever its origins and development, became the 'sacred tongue'. Reform Judaism, from the beginning, had a far lesser appreciation of the role of the Halakhah in Judaism, preferring to see the religion more in terms of the prophetic thrust in the direction of ethical monotheism. In more recent years, however, Reform has acquired a new respect for the Halakhah, at least in those areas, such as in synagogal life, where many Reform Jews wish to follow the traditional norms where these are not in conflict with Reform ideology. Conservative Judaism adopts a middle-of-the-road stance, accepting the traditional Halakhah in broad terms but feeling free to allow historical considerations to have a voice in Halakhic application.

Halitzah 'Taking off' the shoe, the rite by means of which a widow whose husband has died without issue is released from the bond of levirate *marriage. In the book of Deuteronomy (25: 5–10) the law is promulgated that the widow of a childless man is obliged to marry his brother but if the levir ('brother-in-law') refuses to marry her he has to undergo the rite of Halitzah: 'But if the man does not want to marry his brother's widow, his brother's widow shall appear before the elders in the gate and declare, "My husband's brother refuses to establish a name in Israel for his brother; he will not perform the duty of a levir." The elders of his town shall then summon him and talk to him. If he insists, saying, "I do not want to marry her", his brother's widow shall go up to him in the presence of the elders, pull [from the root ḥalatz, hence the name Halitzah] the shoe off his foot, spit in his face, and make this declaration: "Thus shall be done to the man who will not build up his brother's house!"' (Verses 7–9.)

Reform Judaism in the nineteenth century rejected the requirements of either levirate marriage or Halitzah, although Reform Rabbis have been known to participate in the rite if the widow feels herself bound by conscience not to remarry without Halitzah.

Hallel 'Praise', the joyous recital of Psalms 113–18 during the morning service on festivals. Hallel is not recited on the solemn judgement days of *Rosh Ha-Shanah and *Yom Kippur. Nor is it recited on *Purim, either because the miracle of Purim took place outside the Holy Land or because the reading of the *Megillah on Purim takes the place of Hallel. Hallel is recited on *Hanukkah.

The Talmudic sages frowned on any recital of Hallel on days when it has not been ordained, probably on the principle that it is unfitting to sing God's praises when the mood of the day is not one of particular joy.

Hallelujah 'Praise ye Yah'. The current English form is from the transliteration of the letter 'yod' as 'J'. A more correct transliteration is Halleluyah and this is, in fact, how the word is universally pronounced. The word occurs twenty-three times in the book of

Psalms but is not found in the Bible outside this book. Hallelujah has become, like 'Amen', a liturgical expression in Christian as well as in Jewish hymnody. Numerous musical compositions have been created around this word, the best known, of course, being the Hallelujah Chorus in Handel's *Messiah*.

Haman See PURIM.

Ḥametz 'Leaven', in contradistinction to *matzah*, 'unleavened bread'. As recorded in the book of Exodus, chapter 12, no leaven must be eaten during the 'feast of unleavened bread', *ḥag ha-matzot*.

On the night preceding the festival (the night belonging to the following day of 14 Nisan) the house is searched for ḥametz and any found is removed from the house. In addition, a declaration is made that any ḥametz that may have been overlooked is rendered null and void. This declaration and the whole procedure of searching for the ḥametz is found in all editions of the Passover *Haggadah.

Hands, Washing of The ritual washing of the hands on various occasions In Temple times there were elaborate rules in connection with ritual impurity. If a person had been rendered impure through having come into contact, say, with a dead rodent, he contaminated sacred food such as the tithe given to the *priests, which must then not be eaten. The way in which contamination of this kind could be removed was through immersion in a ritual bath (see MIKVEH). But the sages imposed in certain circumstances the minor form of contamination known as 'hand contamination', in which only the hands, not the whole body, were contaminated and for this to be removed total immersion was not required, only the ritual washing of the hands. Since there was a good deal of priest's tithe in ancient Palestine which could easily come into contact with the hands, the sages eventually ordained that the hands of every Jew, not only the hands of a priest, must be washed ritually before meals.

The Talmud also refers to washing the hands after meals but here the reason given is that people used to eat with their hands and a certain salt added to food in those days might cause injury to the eyes if it came into contact with them. The French authorities in the Middle Ages argued that this hygienic reason no longer obtains, since this kind of salt is no longer used. Many observant Jews follow this line of thinking and do not wash the hands after the meal, not as a ritual in any event.

Hannah Biblical heroine, mother of the prophet *Samuel. Hannah's story is related in the first two chapters of the book of 1 Samuel. Here it is told how Hannah, who was barren, prayed to God to give her a son whom she promised to give to the Lord. Her prayer was answered and when the boy Samuel was 2 years old she brought him to the High Priest, Eli, to serve in the Sanctuary.

The Talmud (*Berakhot* 31a–b) considers the story of Hannah and her prayer to be the supreme biblical model for how individual prayers are to be offered. The story of Hannah was chosen as the *Haftarah for the first day of *Rosh Ha-Shanah.

Hanukkah 'Dedication', the minor winter festival that begins on the twenty-fifth day of Kislev and lasts for eight days, to celebrate the victory of the *Maccabees over the forces of Antiochus after a three-year battle in the second century BCE, as related in the two apocryphal books, 1 and 2 Maccabees. In the well-known Talmudic legend (*Shabbat* 21b) the Maccabees, when they rededicated the *Temple, found only a small jar of oil, sealed

with the High Priest's seal, for the kindling of the *menorah, the candelabrum. This jar contained sufficient oil for only one night but, by a miracle, it lasted for eight nights until fresh, uncontaminated oil could be produced. There are thus two separate ideas behind the celebration of Hanukkah: 1. the victory of the Maccabees; 2. the miracle of the oil.

According to Jewish practice, based on Talmudic sources, lights are to be kindled in each Jewish house during the eight nights of Hanukkah. These lights are kindled in a special eight-branched candelabrum which used to be called a menorah (although the menorah in the Temple had only seven branches) but is more usually called, nowadays, a Hanukkiyah.

The Hanukkah lights are kindled during the service in the synagogue as well as in private homes. In the State of Israel (nowadays, in other countries as well on occasion) huge, electrically operated menorahs are placed in public squares and on prominent buildings.

Hasidism The revivalist movement founded by Israel *Baal Shem Tov (in abbreviated form, the Besht) in eighteenth-century Podolia (south-eastern Poland), later extending to the whole of Eastern Europe and beyond. There are adherents of Hasidism (Hasidim) today in the State of Israel, the USA, England, France, and many other countries.

Hasidism is less a movement with ideas of its own than one in which ideas found in the classical Jewish sources, especially the Kabbalah, are given new life and fresh emphasis. The task of discovering in what this emphasis consists is rendered difficult because each of the early masters has his own interpretation of Hasidic doctrine.

There is a lifestyle common to all Hasidim but with variations according to the patterns and traditions of particular dynasties. All Hasidim wear a girdle for prayer to divide the upper part of the body from the lower. The majority of Hasidim wear on the Sabbath the squat fur-trimmed hat known as the *streimel but the Hasidim of Ger substitute for the streimel the tall fur hat known as the spodik, while the Hasidim of Lubavitch wear neither. Some Hasidim wear white socks on the Sabbath as a symbol of purity; others allow only the most distinguished Hasidim to wear white socks; and others do not know of the custom at all (see DRESS). All Hasidim usually sport beards and cultivate long ear-locks, *peot, but some Hasidim have straight, others 'corkscrew', peot.

When a Hasid pays his regular visit to the Rebbe's court, he presents a written petition, the kvittel, to the *Rebbe, in which he requests the Rebbe to pray for his needs and those of his family to be satisfied. In return the Hasid donates a sum of money known as a pidyon ('redemption'). The Rebbe uses the moneys he receives from the pidyon and from collections made in the various towns not only for his own use and the upkeep of his court but also, perhaps primarily, for charitable purposes, the wealthier Hasidim contributing in this way to the maintenance of their poor associates.

At the sacred meal on the Sabbath the Hasidim sit in awesome silence around the Rebbe's 'Tish' (table) until he gives them the sign to sing the traditional Sabbath songs. Some Rebbes are themselves gifted composers, others have Hasidim who compose melodies which then form the repertoire for all the Hasidim of the particular group and, often, for other Hasidim as well. After the Rebbe has tasted a little from the dish placed before him, the 'leftovers' (shirayim) are distributed among the Hasidim in the belief that to eat of the food that has been blessed by the Rebbe brings material and spiritual blessings. At the Tish the Rebbe delivers a discourse on the Torah portion of the week read in the synagogue. The majority of Hasidic works consist in the main of the Rebbe's discourses which were recorded, after the Sabbath, by Hasidim who retained the Rebbe's ideas in their memory.

Haskalah 'Enlightenment', the movement which originated in eighteenth-century Germany with the aim of broadening the intellectual and social horizons of the Jews to enable them to take their place in Western society. The term Haskalah, in medieval Jewish literature, is from the Hebrew word sekhel, 'the intellect', but, as here applied, refers to the attitude of attraction to general knowledge, secular learning, and Western culture. The followers of the Haskalah movement were called Maskilim.

The first major contribution of the Haskalah to modernization was the translation of the Bible into German by Mendelssohn, provided with a Hebrew commentary by a number of his associates called the Biur (Commentary). Through the translation, Jews, familiar with the Hebrew of the Bible, acquired a fair knowledge of the German language. Through the Commentary, they were introduced to a new approach to the Bible since the Commentary departed radically from the fanciful homiletical style, popular for centuries, in favour of what they felt was the plain meaning of the biblical text.

From Germany the Haskalah spread to Galicia and later to Russia. In these countries the Jews were far more deeply immersed in the traditional Jewish learning and far more observant of Jewish practices than their German co-religionists and had little reason to feel culturally inferior to their Polish or Russian neighbours. Nevertheless, the Haskalah ideal proved extremely attractive to a number of thoughtful Jews in the Galician towns of Lemberg and Brody. The Reform movement had its origin in the German Haskalah as did the neo-Orthodoxy of Samson

Raphael *Hirsch. After the Haskalah, there was no longer any need to argue that a Jew could be loyal to his religion without ignoring the values of Western society. Zionism can be said to be a more Jewish version of the Haskalah and, of course, the State of Israel is a modern state in which the liberal values of the West are accepted without reservation.

The final verdict on the Haskalah has not yet been given. For all their attacks on some aspects of the traditional way of life, the Maskilim were, in the main, religious men who wished to further the cause of Judaism in the new environment. They saw their struggle as directed against what they considered to be the superstitious and reactionary elements in the tradition, not against the tradition itself and certainly not against the Jewish religion. Despite their espousal of secular learning, the Maskilim were remote from secularism. It is going too far to see the Haskalah as a religious movement, but the religious motivation was rarely absent from their thinking and activities.

Havdalah 'Division', the ceremony performed at the termination of Sabbaths and festivals to mark the division between the sacred day and the ordinary days of the week. The ceremony is performed in the synagogue at the end of the evening service and especially in the home. A cup of wine is taken in the right hand and the benediction is recited: 'Blessed art Thou, O Lord our God, King of the universe, who createst the fruit of the vine.' (If wine is not available, the benediction can be recited over other liquids but not over water.) Then the Havdalah benediction is recited: 'Blessed art Thou, O Lord our God, King of the universe, who makest a distinction [hamavdil] between holy and profane, between light and darkness, between Israel and other peoples, between the seventh day and the six working days. Blessed art Thou, O Lord, who makest a distinction between holy and profane.' These two benedictions alone form the Havdalah ceremony at the termination of a festival. At the termination of the Sabbath two further benedictions are recited, one over sweet-smelling spices, the other over a plaited candle. Over the spices the benediction is: 'Blessed art Thou, O Lord our God, King of the universe, who createst various kinds of spices.' Over the candle, the benediction is: 'Blessed art Thou, O Lord our God, King of the universe, who createst the lights of the fire.'

Health Jewish teaching advocates strongly that proper care be taken for the health of mind and body, since life is God's precious gift. The Talmud forbids a scholar to reside in a town in which there is no physician to care for the health of its citizens (see DOCTORS) and the Talmud contains much advice on how a person is to keep in good health. Maimonides, himself a physician, devotes a section of his great Code to the subject in which he adds to the Talmudic prescriptions hygienic measures deriving from his own experience and the medical knowledge of his day.

The body must be bathed regularly and the bodily functions attended to as soon as they become necessary. To withhold evacuation of the bowels and passing water is considered sinful. Washing the *hands before meals is a ritualistic prescription but the hands are also to be washed after visiting the privy and after touching parts of the body that are usually covered. Over and above the *dietary laws, some of which themselves have occasionally been understood on hygienic grounds, there are rules which prohibit the eating of food that may cause ill health. Nowadays, as a result of researches into the harm that is caused by smoking cigarettes, many Rabbis frown upon smoking (see TOBACCO). Alcohol is nowhere proscribed as such but caution must be exercised not only to avoid drunkenness but also to ensure that imbibing alcoholic beverages should not cause mental or physical ill health. Taking drugs, unless prescribed by the doctor, is certainly frowned upon for this and for other sound reasons. Regular exercise is advocated for the purpose of keeping the body strong and healthy.

Naturally, it is generally acknowledged, some of the regulations found in this context in the ancient sources are not necessarily sound and may be positively harmful in the light of medical advances. But the principle of health-preservation still holds good, although it is the voice of the contemporary physician that should be heeded rather than any appeal to ancient sources.

Heaven and Hell The places in which, respectively, the righteous are rewarded after death and the wicked punished. The usual terms in Jewish literature are the *Garden of Eden for heaven and *Gehinnom for hell. The Hebrew word *shamayyim* means either the sky, the firmament, as in the first verse of Genesis, or God, as in the Rabbinic expression: 'the fear of heaven'. In the earlier literature, the term never refers to the location of souls after the death of the body. The medieval thinkers generally demythologize the statements in the Talmudic literature about heaven and hell, interpreting them in terms of purely spiritual bliss and spiritual torment.

The heaven of the Jewish mystics is similarly all spiritual. According to the Zohar (i. 90b–91a) when the righteous depart from the world their souls ascend and God prepares for them a garment woven from the good deeds they performed while on earth and the great banquet of the future is the feasting of the righteous on divine mysteries never before revealed (Zohar, i. 135b). In this vein the eighteenth-century mystic Moses Hayyim *Luzzatto begins his work of moral perfection,

The Path of the Upright: 'Our Sages have taught us that man was created only to find delight in the Lord, and to bask in the radiance of His Shekhinah for this is the true delight and a pleasure far greater than every imaginable pleasure. But the real place for such delight is the World to Come, which has been created for that very purpose. The present world is only a path to that goal.'

Hebrew The language spoken and written by the ancient Israelites and, in various forms, throughout the history of the Jewish religion. The *Bible (the 'Old Testament') is in Hebrew with the exception of parts of the books of *Ezra and *Daniel, a single verse in *Jeremiah, and two words in the *Pentateuch. These are in the sister language of Hebrew, Aramaic. Both Hebrew and Aramaic belong to the Semitic branch of languages. Scholars have detected various forms of Hebrew in the Bible itself; the poetic portions, for example, preserve traces of archaic Hebrew case-endings and have other distinguishing features. A more or less successful attempt was made by the *Haskalah to produce poetry, novels, and other 'secular' writings in Hebrew. This paved the way for the development of Hebrew as a modern language spoken now in the State of Israel and all over the Jewish world, and called Ivrit ('Hebrew'). This name, Ivrit, is not new. It is found in the Mishnah (*Gittin* 9: 8) and has been described as 'Hebrew reborn' but is, in many ways, a new language. In Ivrit, numerous new words and forms have been introduced into the language, many of them adaptations from earlier Hebrew forms and many based on European languages. Maimonides (*Guide of the Perplexed*, 3. 8) writes that Hebrew is called 'the sacred tongue' because it contains no words with which to designate the male and female genitals, the sex act itself, sperm, urine, or excrement, for all of which euphemisms are used. *Nahmanides (commentary to Exodus 30. 13), as a Kabbalist, finds Maimonides' reason unconvincing. The reason why Hebrew is called 'the sacred tongue', says Nahmanides, is because God spoke in this language to His prophets and created the world by means of the letters of this language. One imagines that for the majority of Jews today, Hebrew is the 'sacred tongue' because, whatever its origin, it is in this language and in no other that the classical works of the Jewish religion have been written. For Jews, the Hebrew language is not intrinsically sacred, as Nahmanides and the mystics would have it, nor is it sacred in the sense of 'pure', as Maimonides would have it. It is sacred because of its association with all that Judaism holds sacred.

Height Height as a symbol for the spiritual is found very frequently in Judaism as it is in all cultures. It seems that early on in the history of the human race, the sublime was thought of as spiritually rather than spatially transcendent. In the Bible, God is often said to reside in heaven, the firmament above the earth (Genesis 1: 8), but it is hard to believe that this was taken literally even though the older spatial connotation is reserved in the language used (see COSMOLOGIES), as when, for instance, the prophet *Isaiah says that he saw the Lord 'sitting on a throne, high and lifted up, and his train filled the temple' (Isaiah 6: 1). Similarly, when Deutero-Isaiah (Isaiah 66: 1) declares: 'Thus saith the Lord, the heaven is my throne, and the earth is my footstool', the 'throne' on high is as little to be taken literally as the 'footstool' on earth. Particularly significant in this connection is the Psalmist's declaration (Psalms 113: 4–6): 'The Lord is high above all nations, and His glory above the heavens. Who is like unto the Lord our God, that dwelleth on high; that looketh down so low upon the heavens and the earth?' As Edwyn Bevan has noted, the first chapter of Genesis demolishes in a single phrase in the first verse, any idea of God as coinciding with the sky: 'In the beginning God created the heavens'. If God created the heavens, He must have existed in almighty power before there was any heaven there at all. No doubt many Jews did, and still do, like many non-Jewish believers, think of God as somehow located 'up there', but ordinary folk as well as the thinkers generally qualify this by, consciously or unconsciously, treating height in this connection as a metaphor.

Hellenism Greek culture, which spread from the end of the fourth century BCE to influence Jews in the land of Israel and in the *Diaspora, to some features of which many Jews became increasingly attracted and to some of which they reacted with hostility in the name of their religion. The *Maccabees fought against the armies of Antiochus in his attempt to introduce Greek culture to the detriment of Judaism but it was Jewish Hellenizers who encouraged the tyrant in the first place. Hellenism in the Greek and later the Roman period in Palestine made heavy inroads into the life of the Jews. Buildings, public highways, bath-houses, and markets all followed the Hellenistic pattern. It is highly revealing that the highest court in the land became known by the Greek name, Sanhedrin.

The Greek-speaking Jews of Alexandria, whose greatest representative is *Philo, produced the *Septuagint, the translation of the Bible into Greek. In Philo the two cultures, Judaism and Hellenism, met and, for the first time, an attempt was made to interpret, or at least to defend, the religion, in the light of Greek thought. The conflict between the Maimonists and anti-Maimonists in the Middle Ages over the desirability of studying Greek *philosophy contained many echoes of the earlier struggle between Judaism and

Hellenism. Those who favoured the study of philosophy justified their stance by referring to the legend, known already to Philo, that Alexander the Great was a disciple of Socrates, who travelled with him when he came to the land of Israel. There Socrates sat at the feet of Jewish sages who taught him all he came to know, so that Greek philosophy is, in fact, Jewish philosophy.

Herem A ban imposed on an individual to separate him from the other members of the community. In the Middle Ages, among the offences for which the *herem* was invoked were: disobedience to court orders; refusal to pay damages; insulting an official of the court; reviling scholars; and preventing the community from discharging its duties. The *herem* was thus an effective method of maintaining communal cohesion and authority. There are rare instances of a *herem* imposed on an individual for his heretical views, of which the best-known instance is the ban on *Spinoza by the court in Amsterdam. The ban on polygamy attributed to Rabbenu *Gershom of Mayyence became known as the *herem* of Rabbenu Gershom, although there is no evidence that this enactment took the form of a *herem*.

In modern times the whole institution of the *herem* has largely fallen into desuetude. On the threshold of the modern period, Moses *Mendelssohn, on grounds of religious tolerance, expressed his opposition to the right of the Rabbis to impose the *herem*. In many European communities, the governments declared the imposition of the *herem* to be illegal and Jews obeyed the laws of the countries in which they resided. Excessive resort to the *herem* was, in any event, self-defeating. When *herem* met with counter-*herem*, it often happened that so many people were under the ban that it became totally unenforceable, nothing more than an expression of strong disapproval. The sporadic attempts, nowadays, to impose a *herem* are treated as something of a joke.

Heresy The holding of beliefs contrary to the Jewish religion. Any attempt to study the phenomenon of heresy in Judaism has to take note of the differences in this matter between Judaism and the Christian Church. The various councils of the Church met in order to define Christian doctrine, any departure from which was seen as heresy. In Judaism, on the other hand, while there are Jewish *dogmas, there has never been any officially accepted formulation of these, no meeting, say, of authoritative Rabbis, to decide what it is that Judaism teaches in matters of faith. It is no accident that Maimonides, who drew up his thirteen *principles of the Jewish religion, was the first noted Jewish thinker to attempt a systematic treatment of the various types of heresy. Ironically, Maimonides himself was accused of heresy because of his declaration that anyone who believes that God is corporeal is a heretic! What actually happened in the history of Judaism was that a kind of consensus emerged among the faithful that there are limits in matters of faith, broad to be sure, to step beyond which is heretical.

Hermeneutics The science of biblical exegesis by the early Talmudic Rabbis in accordance with certain rules. The idea behind the system is that the full implications of the biblical laws can only be ascertained by a close scrutiny of the text for which the hermeneutic principles provide the key.

The employment of seven hermeneutical principles is attributed in the sources to *Hillel. But the formulation of thirteen principles by the first- to second-century teacher, Rabbi *Ishmael, is the usually accepted formulation, appearing in the standard Prayer Book as part of the morning service. This inclusion in the Prayer Book is based on the idea that every Jew, in addition to his prayers, should study each day something of the Torah, which the rules provide in capsule form, although it cannot be imagined that the average worshipper has an inkling of what he is saying when he recites these difficult rules.

Hertz, Joseph Herman Orthodox Rabbi, communal leader, and author (1872–1946). Hertz was born in Romania but emigrated when young to America where he studied, obtaining his Ph.D. degree from Columbia University. He was the first Rabbinic graduate of the Jewish Theological Seminary. Later he was greatly influenced by Solomon *Schechter's ideas on the desirability of allowing the Jewish tradition to be open to the findings of modern scholarship. Hertz served first as a Rabbi in Syracuse, New York State, and later as Rabbi in South Africa, where he was a powerful advocate of human rights. In 1913 Hertz was appointed Chief Rabbi of the United Hebrew congregations of the British Empire, a post he occupied for the rest of his life. Among his many political activities, Hertz, a deeply committed Zionist, was instrumental in frustrating the efforts of some leaders of the Anglo-Jewish community to prevent the Balfour Declaration being issued.

Hertz's best-known and most influential work is his *Pentateuch and Haftorahs*, written in collaboration with other Anglo-Jewish scholars. In the book, Hertz is prepared to accept the theory of *evolution; sees no dogma involved in the suggestion that the second part of Isaiah was composed by an unknown prophet during the exile; and quotes an opinion that the plague of darkness in Egypt was caused by a partial eclipse of the sun. Yet his attitude towards *biblical criticism proper is very one-sided. With great zest he sets up supposedly critical views in order to demolish them, so that his work has to be seen more as a exercise in apologetics than as one of objective scholarship. Reform Rabbis saw the work as too Orthodox, Orthodox Rabbis as too Reform. But Hertz was disturbed neither by critics of the Pentateuch nor by his own critics and went on his way undaunted.

Herzl, Theodor Foremost leader of political *Zionism (1860–1904). Herzl belonged to a fairly assimilated Jewish family in Vienna. He took a law degree at the university but earned his living as a playwright and particularly as a successful journalist on the *Neue Freie Presse*. The story has often been told of how Herzl, reporting for his paper in Paris on the Dreyfus Affair, in which the thoroughly assimilated Captain Dreyfus, in an anti-Semitic plot, was falsely accused of treason, came to realize that the *Emancipation of the Jews, far from solving the Jewish problem, only aggravated it by creating severe tensions between the Jews and their neighbours in European society. In Herzl's view, the Jews had to consider themselves to be not only a religious body but also a nation capable of developing its own political institutions in a land of its own.

Herzl gave expression to his views in 1896 with the publication of *Judenstaat* ('Jewish State'). He eventually came to appreciate that the creation of such a Jewish State could be feasible only in Palestine, the traditional homeland of the Jewish people. Herzl has been described as a 'practical dreamer' and it is true that, with considerable organizing ability, he worked for the practical realization of his aim, succeeding in winning many Jews to co-operate with him in, at the time, a seemingly impossible task. The first Zionist Congress was held in Basle in 1897 at which the World Zionist Organization was founded and Herzl elected as its President. In 1902

Herzl published his utopian vision of the Jewish State, the *Altneuland* ('Old New Land'). Herzl died, at the early age of 44, in Vienna, where he was buried. In 1949 Herzl's remains were taken to Jerusalem where they were buried on a hill, now called Mount Herzl. More than any other thinker and politician, Herzl was indirectly responsible for the emergence of the State of Israel and is acknowledged to be the State's true founder.

Herzog, Isaac Outstanding Rabbinic leader (1888–1959). Herzog was born in Lomza, Poland, but was brought up in Paris and lived later in Leeds, the cities in which his father served as a Rabbi. Unusually for his time in Orthodox circles, Herzog was largely self-educated. It is said that at the age of 16 he succeeded in completing the study of the whole of the Talmud. Herzog also studied general subjects, obtaining the D.Litt. degree from London University for a thesis on 'The Dyeing of Purple in Ancient Israel'. After serving as Chief Rabbi in Ireland, Herzog was elected, in 1936, Ashkenazi Chief Rabbi of Palestine, succeeding Rabbi Abraham Isaac *Kook.

Heschel, Abraham Joshua Religious philosopher (1907–72). Heschel was descended on both his father's and mother's side from a long line of Hasidic *Zaddikim. Heschel himself seemed destined to occupy the role of a Hasidic Rebbe but, while intensely loyal to Hasidism, he preferred, at an early age, to follow in the path of modern philosophy and scholarship, leaving his native Poland to study in Berlin at the university and at the Jewish Hochschule für die Wissenschaft des Judenthums. He was deported by the Nazis in 1938 but eventually escaped to London and was later invited to occupy a Chair at the Hebrew Union College in Cincinnati, the main institution for the training of Reform Rabbis. Heschel was not really at home in a Reform seminary and in 1946 he was appointed to the Chair of Jewish Ethics and Mysticism at the Conservative Jewish Theological Seminary in New York, a position he occupied for the rest of his life.

Heschel was a prolific author. All his works have a strong mystical tinge, owing much to his Hasidic background. In his book on the Hebrew *prophets (*Die Prophetie*), published in English as *The Prophets* (New York, 1962), Heschel broke new ground in biblical studies in seeing the prophets as participants in the divine pathos; an idea criticized by some thinkers as too anthropomorphic.

Heschel, in his Hebrew work on the doctrine 'the Torah is from heaven' and in his other works, develops the idea that the Torah, while it should not be understood in any fundamentalistic way—that God literally delivered all the precepts to Moses at Sinai—is, none the less, the record of the divine will.

High Priest Chief among the 'priests who officiated in the *Temple; Heb. *kohen gadol*, lit. 'great priest'. The High Priest was distinguished from ordinary priests in a number of respects. Based on Exodus 28, the Talmudic sources state that every priest, while performing the Temple service, had to wear four garments: a tunic, a girdle, a turban, and breeches reaching from the hips to the thighs. These four were worn by the High Priest as well but in addition he wore four further garments. These were: the *ephod*, a kind of apron, worn from behind with a sash in front around his middle; the *meil*, a coat reaching from his neck to his feet with bells and pomegranate-shaped adornments at its hem; the *hoshen*, a breastplate to which were affixed twelve precious stones containing the engraved names of the twelve tribes; and the *tzitz*, a gold forehead piece on which were engraved the words: 'Holy to the Lord.' With the destruction of the Temple, the office of High Priest vanished entirely from Jewish life.

Hillel Foremost teacher in Palestine in the first century BCE. Together with *Shammai, Hillel is mentioned in the first chapter of Ethics of the Fathers as the last of the 'Pairs' (see ZUGOT), the five sets of two spiritual heads in succession until the leadership of the people was in the hands of Hillel's descendants, of the house of Rabban *Gamaliel. A number of Hillel's descendants were also named Hillel, of whom the best-known is the fourth-century Hillel to whom is attributed the fixing of the *calendar.

Hirsch, Samson Raphael German Rabbi and religious thinker (1808–88). Hirsch was born in Hamburg where he received a general as well as a traditional Jewish education. His teacher in Hamburg was Isaac Bernays and in Mannheim Rabbi Jakob Ettlinger, the most distinguished Talmudist in German Jewry. Both these teachers were men of a comparatively broad outlook. Influenced by them, Hirsch saw his life's task as being to demonstrate that traditional Judaism is fully compatible with Western culture. Hirsch studied classical languages, history, and philosophy for a short time at the University of Bonn but he did not take a university degree. Abraham *Geiger was a fellow-student of Hirsch at Bonn but later their paths diverged, Geiger becoming leader of the Reform movement to which Hirsch was relentlessly opposed. In 1830 Hirsch was appointed Rabbi of Oldenburg and in 1846 he was appointed District Rabbi of Moravia, living in the town of Nikolsburg. A small number of Orthodox families in Frankfurt-on-Main, disturbed by the assimilated tendencies of the general Jewish community, invited Hirsch to become their Rabbi in 1851. This new Orthodox community flourished under Hirsch's guidance.

Hirsch believed that the only way to preserve the Orthodoxy of his community was to obtain permission from the German authorities to establish a separatist organization. To further this aim, Hirsch argued that the differences between Orthodoxy and Reform were akin to those between Catholicism and Protestantism in Christianity: two religious attitudes that could not exist side by side. Hirsch's community soon became the model for communities ready to be both open to general culture and strict in adherence to Orthodox practices, hence the term neo-Orthodoxy by which this tendency is known. In a real sense, Hirsch was a child of the *Haskalah but his 'enlightenment' had a far greater thrust in the direction of Orthodox Jewish beliefs and observances. In his early work *The Nineteen Letters of Ben Uziel*, Hirsch typically remarked that it would have been better for the Jews not to have been emancipated if the price they had to pay was assimilation.

The statement in Ethics of the Fathers (2. 2) of Rabban *Gamaliel III: 'Torah is good together with *derekh eretz*', formed the basis of Hirsch's understanding of Judaism for modern Jews. In the context, *derekh eretz* (literally, 'the way of the earth') refers to a worldly occupation. But Hirsch develops the concept to embrace Western culture. This is the 'way of the world' which has to be combined with the study and the practice of the Torah. Hirsch states that *derekh eretz* refers not only to ways of earning a living but also to the social order that prevails on earth, the mores and considerations of courtesy and propriety arising from social living and things pertinent to good breeding and general education. Hence Hirsch speaks of the ideal Jew as the 'Israel-Man', that is, the Jew who is proudly Jewish, a believer in the eternal values and precepts of the Torah as divinely ordained, and is, at the same time, a cultured 'man', a human being belonging to the modern world.

History With the exception of *Josephus, it was not until the sixteenth century that scholars emerged to study the Jewish religion historically. Even then, David Ganz had to justify his historical approach by quoting the verse: 'Remember the days of old' (Deuteronomy 32: 7) and when Azariah de Rossi dared to examine Jewish history with reference to the Greek and Roman authors, Joseph *Karo sought, unsuccessfully, to have his book banned for its rejection of some Talmudic statements about the past as pure legend. The historical study of Judaism by historical-critical methods did not, in fact, begin until the rise of the *Jüdische Wissenschaft movement in the early nineteenth century when *Zunz, *Krochmal, *Rapoport, and *Frankel pioneered the critical approach to the classical Jewish sources, followed by *Graetz, *Dubnow, and many others.

From the religious point of view, the new historical approach to the Jewish religion has created problems. To study Judaism historically, rather than simply to chronicle the Jewish past, results inevitably in a degree of relativism. If it can be shown that Judaism has had a history, has responded to external conditions in various ways, this seems to strike a blow at the traditional view in which Judaism is seen as a static body of divine truth conveyed without change from age to age. Instead of reading the religion of the Bible with Talmudic eyes and the Talmud with medieval eyes, the historians tried to see each period with its own particular stresses, hopes, and fears. Reform and Conservative Judaism have largely accepted without qualification the historical approach and have sought to understand Judaism in the light of the new knowledge. Orthodox Jews, with some exceptions at the extreme right, have also been prepared to accept this approach with regard to the Talmud and even, to some extent, to the rest of the Bible with the exception of the

*Pentateuch, the Torah. Here, for Orthodoxy, all *biblical criticism is still taboo.

Holdheim, Samuel German Reform leader (1806–60). Holdheim received a thorough traditional Jewish education in his native Poland where he was looked upon as an infant as a Talmudic prodigy; he later supplemented his early knowledge by his reading of general literature and his studies in the University of Prague. Together with Abraham *Geiger, Holdheim provided much of the intellectual vigour for the Reform movement, although Geiger, for all his radicalism, did not see eye to eye with some of Holdheim's excesses. For Holdheim, the Jewish religion contained in the past two elements: the universalistic–ethical monotheism and the doctrine of the immortality of the soul, and the nationalistic–the rituals such as the sacrificial system in Temple times and institutions such as the *dietary laws.

From 1847 Holdheim was the Rabbi of the Berlin Reform Temple, in which the most extreme reforms were introduced. Hebrew was largely eliminated from the prayers, Sunday services were eventually substituted for the Sabbath services, on the grounds that in Western society many Jews had to earn their living by working on the Sabbath, and intermarriage between Jews and Gentiles was not discouraged. Holdheim's extremism was not viewed with favour in Germany, apart from in his own congregation, but found an echo in the USA version of radical Reform towards the end of the nineteenth century.

Holiness The Hebrew word for 'holiness', *kedushah*, conveys the twin ideas of separation *from* and dedication *to* something and hence holiness as a religious ideal refers to the attitude and state of mind in which certain activities and thoughts are rejected in order to come closer to God. The concept is found in a general sense in two biblical verses. At the theophany at *Sinai, the ideal of holiness is expressed in the words: 'And ye shall be unto Me a kingdom of priests, and a holy nation' (Exodus 19: 6). The introductory verse to the Holiness Code (as it is called by modern scholars) states: 'Speak unto all the congregation of the children of Israel, And say unto them: Ye shall be holy; for I the Lord your God am holy' (Leviticus 19: 2). In the first verse, Israel is to be separate from other nations as a holy nation dedicated to God. In the second verse, the plain meaning would seem to be: separate yourselves from the illicit practices mentioned later in the Holiness Code in order to be holy because God is holy.

Holocaust The destruction of six million Jews by the Nazis during World War II. It is not known who coined the English name 'Holocaust' for this, the most terrible event in all Jewish history. In all probability the term, meaning a 'burnt-offering', was used because of the crematoria in which the bodies of the victims were burned. The Hebrew terms are *Shoah* ('Catastrophe') and *Ḥurban* ('Destruction', obviously based on the term used in the tradition for the destruction of the *Temple). It is unnecessary to spend any time discussing the pernicious view of revisionist 'historians' that the Holocaust never took place. This final insult to those who perished is too absurd to require refutation. Sober historians have documented all the details of the Holocaust.

It is generally acknowledged in contemporary theological discussion that, while the daunting problem of how *God, the all-good and all-powerful, can tolerate evil in His creation has always been the most stubborn the theist has to face, the problem as it confronts twentieth-century man is so acute as to render banal most of the earlier attempts at a solution.

For many sensitive Jews there is the strongest distaste for even considering the problem. Haunted by feelings of guilt at having been spared when the six million were foully destroyed, there is considerable agreement among Jewish thinkers that any neat solution amounts to a callous unawareness of the magnitude of the disaster and that, for example, it would be an insufferable insult to the memory of the six million to dare even to try to see their sufferings within a tidy scheme of reward and punishment.

Holy Places The Jewish religion, like any other, has its holy places, locations possessing a special degree of sanctity, some to a greater extent than others. In polytheistic religions, where the earth is seen as inhabited by a multiplicity of gods, it seems natural to assume that each god has his own particular abode, the plot where he actually resides, zealously maintaining his right of possession. For Judaism and the other monotheistic religions, on the other hand, it is hard to understand how the God whose glory fills the whole earth can be said to reside in one place more than another. Why is the building in which He is worshipped more His 'house' than any other spot on earth? And what meaning can be given to the idea that there are degrees of sanctity in which one place is more holy than another? Does this mean that there is a greater degree of in-dwelling in the holier place, and if it does, how can it be said that God is located more definitely in one spot, less in another? Any attempt to deal with this kind of question from the Jewish sources is rendered difficult by the absence of anything like a systematic treatment of the topic. What exists are voluminous rules and regulations regarding the practical consequences which result from the sanctity of certain places; casual theological deliberations on the idea that God dwells in those places; observations on the psychological effects of man's confrontation with the numinous; and mystical speculations on the spiritual realm invading the secular.

There are basically two different ways within monotheism of understanding the concept of a holy place. The first is to see the divine as actually located in a quasi-physical manner in the sacred spot, or, better, as especially manifested there. The second way is to see the holy place as hallowed by experience and association. On the second view there is numinous power in the holy place, due not to any special indwelling of the divine but to the evocation of intense religious emotion resulting from the fact that the place has been the scene of divine revelation or of sustained and fervent worship. It is history that hallows the shrine.

Holy Sparks The spiritual illuminations inherent in all things. The doctrine, as found in the Kabbalistic system of Isaac *Luria, the Ari, runs that when the light of *En Sof, the Limitless Ground of Being, poured into the vessels which were to receive this light in order to produce the *Sefirot, the powers or potencies in the Godhead, the light was too strong to become limited in the vessels. As a result there are holy sparks in all things it is the task of humans to restore to the holy. When the task of restoration is complete, when all the sparks have been reclaimed for the holy, the *Messiah will come and the disharmony resulting from the breaking of the vessels will be no more and cosmic redemption will have been achieved.

The doctrine of the holy sparks occupies a prominent place in *Hasidism. Hasidism taught that it is incumbent on the Hasid to be fully engaged in worldly affairs in order to reclaim the holy sparks inherent in food, drink, and other worldly things.

Holy Spirit Inspiration or the attainment of a degree of prophecy; Heb. *ruaḥ ha-kodesh*. The books of the Hagiographa such as Psalms and Proverbs (see BIBLE) are said to have been compiled under the Holy Spirit, that is, by a degree of inspiration somewhat less than the degree of prophecy, although, on occasion, the prophetic vision itself is also said to be by means of the Holy Spirit.

Homosexuality Homosexual conduct between males (putting it bluntly, anal intercourse) is mentioned much more frequently and is more heavily condemned in the traditional Jewish sources than homosexual practices between females. There is no reference to a homosexual tendency or mental condition. It is the act itself that is forbidden, as in Leviticus 19: 22: 'Thou shalt not lie with mankind, as with womankind; it is an abomination'; and in Leviticus 20: 13: 'And if a man lie with mankind, as with womankind, both of them have committed abomination; they shall surely be put to death; their blood shall be upon them.'

The sources are far less clear on the question of lesbianism. The Talmud (*Yevamot* 76a) rules that women who perform sex acts with one another are not treated as harlots but only as indulging in lewd practices.

It is clear from the above sources that homosexual practices are severely frowned upon but that female homosexuality is treated far less severely than male homosexuality. Why this should be so is not stated in the sources but would appear to be because it is in the nature of the case that full sexual contact is not possible for two females. The sources, moreover, do not seem to recognize either male homosexuals or lesbians as distinct groups, or in any event there is reference only to practices, not to some men and some women having homosexual tendencies.

Orthodox Judaism continues to maintain that homosexual acts are sinful although many Orthodox Jews might accept the view that since, nowadays, homosexuality is seen to be a condition, it should be left to God to determine whether a homosexual can or cannot help himself. Orthodox Jews certainly do not countenance 'gay synagogues'. The Reform movement in the USA has allowed gay synagogues to be affiliated to the movement but would not ordain a gay man or a lesbian as a Rabbi. Only a very few Reform Rabbis would agree to officiate at a 'marriage' of two males or two females.

Horowitz, Isaiah Polish Rabbi, Kabbalist, and author (1570–1630). Horowitz was born in Prague but studied in Poland under distinguished Talmudists. After serving as Rabbi in Frankfurt-on-Main, Horowitz returned to Prague in 1614 to become Rabbi there. In 1621 he journeyed to Palestine where he became Rabbi of Jerusalem. Horowitz died in Tiberias where he was buried near to the tomb of Maimonides.

Horowitz's major work is his *Sheney Luhot Ha-Berit*, 'The Two Tablets of Stone', published in Amsterdam in 1649. The title of this book was abbreviated, after its initial letters, to *Shelah* and Horowitz himself is usually referred to as 'the Holy Shelah'. The work, encyclopaedic in range, consists of biblical commentaries, Kabbalistic discourses, explanations of the precepts and rituals of Judaism, ethical teachings, liturgical notes, and a treatment of Talmudic methodology. The work had a great influence on Jewish pietists, especially in *Hasidism.

Hosea The prophet whose book is the first and largest of the books of the Twelve Prophets. From the superscription of the book and later passages, we learn that Hosea prophesied during the reigns of Uzziah (769–733 BCE), Jotham, Ahaz, and Hezekiah, kings of Judah (727–698 BCE) and Jeroboam and Menahem, kings of Israel (784–737 BCE). The only details of his life recorded in the

book are that he received a command to marry a harlot in order to symbolize Israel's faithlessness to God and God's love nevertheless. He did marry a harlot named Gomer and had three children by her. The medieval Jewish commentators are divided on whether this incident actually took place or whether the story is part of Hosea's prophetic vision. Many modern biblical scholars believe that the consolatory portions of the book of Hosea come from a different prophet.

While the prophet *Amos places the stress on justice, Hosea speaks of lovingkindness (*hesed*). God loves His people but they have repaid that love by going a-whoring after Baal, the Phoenician god. The concluding portion of the book of Hosea, beginning with: 'Return O Israel, unto the Lord thy God' (Hosea 14: 4), is read as the *Haftarah for the Sabbath which falls during the *Ten Days of Penitence between *Rosh Ha-Shanah and *Yom Kippur. This Sabbath is consequently known as *Shabbat Shuvah* ('Sabbath of Return').

Hoshanah Rabbah 'Great Hoshanah', the seventh day of the festival of *Tabernacles. According to the Mishnah (*Sukkah* 4: 5), in Temple times, on the festival of Tabernacles, huge willow branches were placed around the altar and a circuit was made around the altar while the worshippers recited: 'Hoshanah' ('O Lord, deliver us') (Psalms 118: 25). On the basis of this Temple practice, it became the custom on Tabernacles for the worshippers to hold the four species (the palm-branch, the etrog, the willows, and the myrtles), and make a circuit around the *Bimah, while reciting Hoshanah hymns in which God is entreated to deliver His people, especially from famine and drought, since Tabernacles is the festival on which the divine judgement for rain is made. On the seventh day of the festival, there are seven circuits, at each of which a special Hoshanah hymn is recited; hence the name, Hoshanah Rabbah. After the seven circuits, the four species are put aside and bunches of willows are taken in the hand and these are beaten on the ground three times so that the leaves fall off. The usual explanation of this rite is that it is a symbolic representation either of the rain, required at this season, which beats on the leaves, or of the leaves which fall from the trees until these are revived by the rain.

Hospitality Offering hospitality to guests, *hakhnasat orehim* ('bringing in guests') in Hebrew, is considered to be a *mitzvah*, a high religious obligation. The prototype is the patriarch *Abraham who sits at the door of his tent ready to welcome hungry and thirsty travellers (Genesis 18: 18). Since the narrative states that the Lord appeared to Abraham and yet Abraham ran to welcome his guests, a Rabbinic comment has it that to welcome guests is greater than to welcome the Divine Presence, the *Shekhinah. Another Rabbinic comment is that Abraham's tent had an opening on all four sides so that he could run to welcome guests from whichever direction they came.

Humility In the Jewish tradition, humility is among the greatest of the virtues, as its opposite, pride, is among the worst of the vices. Moses, the greatest of men, is described as the most humble: 'Now the man Moses was very meek, above all the men that were on the face of the earth' (Numbers 12: 3). The patriarch *Abraham protests to God: 'Behold now, I have taken upon me to speak unto the Lord, who am but dust and ashes' (Genesis 18: 27). When Saul was chosen as Israel's first king, he was discovered 'hid among the baggage' (1 Samuel 10: 22), a phrase which became current among Jews for the man who shuns the limelight. The Hebrew king was to write a copy of the law and read therein all the days of his life,

'that his heart be not lifted above his brethren' (Deuteronomy 17: 20).

The Jewish moralists are fully aware that any conscious attempt to attain to humility is always self-defeating and that pride can masquerade as humility. Crude vanity and self-glorification are easily recognized for what they are. Mock modesty is less easy to detect. It is not unusual for a man to take pride in his humility; nor is it unknown for a man to indulge in the more subtle form of self-deception in which he prides himself that he is not a victim of false modesty.

Humour It is often said that the biblical authors took their activities too seriously to indulge in jest. There is some truth in this contention yet there is humour in the Bible, as when the prophet *Elijah mocks the prophets of Baal: 'And it came to pass at noon, that Elijah mocked them, and said: "Cry aloud, for he is a god, either he is musing or he has gone aside, or he is on a journey, or peradventure he sleepeth, and must be awakened"' (1 Kings 18: 27). There is similar irony in the prophet's mocking of the idolater who carves a god for himself, out of part of a block of wood, while using the other half for fuel (Isaiah 44: 13–17). That the Rabbis had a keen sense of humour, sufficiently close to ours for us to appreciate it, is evident from numerous witty sayings in the Talmudic and Midrashic literature. A fourth-century Babylonian teacher, we are told (*Shabbat* 30b), would always preface his lectures with a joke or a witticism in the belief that by making his pupils smile he would help prepare them for the difficult theme he was about to expound to them. Many later Rabbis were renowned for their humour. A number of collections have been made of humorous Rabbinic tales and sayings. The folk-humour of Eastern European Jews is well known—some of it sick humour in which Jews poke fun at their misfortunes and stupidity. The psychological value is fairly obvious. If Jews had lacked the courage to laugh at themselves, the crushing burden of poverty and alienation would have become intolerable. To the question: 'Why does the Jew always answer a question with a question?' the traditional answer is either: 'Does he?' or 'Why not?'

Hunting The Bible refers to hunting for food (in Leviticus 17: 13 for example) and sees no objection to this. The principle, as established by the Rabbis, is that while wanton cruelty to *animals is strictly forbidden, it is permitted to kill animals for food or for their skins and the same would apply to hunting animals for this purpose. Nevertheless, the only two persons mentioned in the Bible as hunters are Nimrod (Genesis 10: 9) and Esau (Genesis 25: 27), neither of whom is admired in the Jewish tradition. There is no reference at all in the biblical and Rabbinic literature to hunting for sport. Walter Rathenau's remark has often been quoted in this connection: "When a Jew says he's going hunting to amuse himself, he lies.' There are Jews, of course, who do enjoy taking part in the hunt, advancing the usual arguments for why this is thought to be desirable. Yet there is no record of Rabbis in any age hunting animals for sport.

There is no logical reason for distinguishing between hunting animals and catching fish, apart from the question of risk to human life, yet some Jews who would not hunt animals see no harm in angling as a hobby. Perhaps they hold that the fish caught will be eaten and fishing is not purely for sport, or perhaps they believe that fish feel less pain than animals.

Ḥuppah The wedding-canopy under which bride and groom stand during the *marriage. The *ḥuppah* represents symbolically the groom's dwelling into which the bride is escorted but from ancient times it was the custom for the marriage ceremony to be conducted under an actual canopy and this is the universal practice to the present day. There are no rules about the materials from which the ḥuppah is made. The usual form is of a canopy stretched over four posts. In many communities it is the custom to have four post-holders, one at each corner of the ḥuppah. Eventually the name 'ḥuppah' became synonymous with the marriage ceremony itself. At a *circumcision, for instance, the parents of the infant are given the blessing that they should have the joy of escorting the child under the ḥuppah when he grows up.

Hypnotism Rabbi Zevi Hirsch Spira (d. 1913), in his compendium, *Darkhey Teshuvah* (179. 6), discusses whether resort by a physician to hypnotism constitutes a natural and hence legitimate form of healing or whether it is supernatural and hence might fall under the heading of *magic and superstition. Spira quotes a Responsum, dated 1852, by Rabbi Jakob Ettlinger (1798–1871). A pious Jew had fallen ill and was advised by his physician to resort to a hypnotic cure (more specifically, to 'magnetism'). Ettlinger replies that he consulted the experts and received contradictory answers. Some dismissed the whole method as charlatanism but others were less sceptical. Ettlinger permits it on the grounds that those who practise it do believe that it is a perfectly natural form of healing. Since Ettlinger, hypnotism has been widely used by reputable physicians, especially in treating various kinds of mental illness, and it is agreed that there is no reason to forbid a pious patient from submitting to hypnotism. More recent authorities have discussed whether an act performed by a person who has been hypnotized can be held to be an intentional act in Jewish law.

Ibn Atar, Hayyim Rabbi and Kabbalist, born Morocco, 1696, died Jerusalem, 1743. Ibn Atar studied with his grandfather, also called Hayyim Ibn Atar (Oriental Jews often gave their children the names of living relatives), and acquired even in his youth a reputation for advanced Talmudic learning and, through his ascetic life, for saintliness (see SAINTS). A strong believer that Messianic redemption was at hand, he saw his destiny in helping to hasten the redemption by living in the Holy Land.

Ibn Atar is renowned chiefly for his mystical commentary to the Torah, entitled *The Light of Life* (*Or Ha-Hayyim*, a pun on his name, Hayyim). This work was published in Venice in 1742 together with the text of the *Pentateuch, a sure sign of the high regard in which he was held even while he was still alive. After the fashion of calling Rabbinic authors after the title of their major work, Ibn Atar is, in fact, known as 'The *Or Ha-Hayyim*' or, among Hasidim, 'The Holy *Or Ha-Hayyim*'.

Ibn Ezra, Abraham Poet, philosopher, grammarian, and biblical exegete (1089–1164). Ibn Ezra was born in Tudela, Spain, where he lived until he left in 1140 to wander to other lands. His life is consequently divided by historians into two periods, that of his residence in Spain, where he wrote many of his poems, and that of his sojourn in various Jewish communities outside Spain in which his other works were compiled. Few details of his personal life in Spain are known, or why he left that country. It has been conjectured that the reason for his 'troubled spirit', as he puts it, in Spain was that his son, Isaac, was converted to Islam, though the son later returned to Judaism. His wife seems to have died after he had left Spain. Details of Ibn Ezra's wanderings are, however, known from the names of the places he recorded in his works. Through these it is known that he lived for a time in Italy, France, and England. He appears to have earned his living in these places by teaching the sons of wealthy Jews and, though of a fiercely independent temperament, he allowed himself also to be supported by a number of patrons of learning. Ibn Ezra is chiefly important for his commentary to the Bible, chief of which is his commentary to the *Pentateuch.

Ibn Gabirol, Solomon Poet and philosopher (1020–57). Few details of Ibn Gabirol's life are known. He was born in Malaga, Spain, where a modern statue of him is to be found near the sea-shore. But the statue depicts him as a tall, venerable old sage, whereas, in fact, he died before reaching the age of 40. It is known that while Malaga was his native city (he signs some of his poems as Malki, meaning 'from Malaga'), he was taken as a child to Saragossa where he received a sound education and acquired a reputation as a scholar. Ibn Gabirol's poems, together with those of *Judah Halevi, are considered to be the choicest of medieval Hebrew poetry. Some of his poems were composed when he was no more than 16 years of age.

Ibn Gabirol's philosophical poem, *Keter Malkhut* (*The Kingly Crown*) is still recited by Sephardi Jews at the Neilah service on *Yom Kippur. This poem is in three parts: 1. a hymn celebrating the divine attributes; 2. a description of the wonders of creation, rising from contemplation of the sun, moon, stars, and planets to the ultimate mystery of the Godhead; 3. confession, penitence, and supplication.

Ibn Gabirol's philosophical work, *Mekor Hayyim* (*Source of Life*), composed under the influence of Neoplatonic thought, was written in Arabic and translated into Latin as *Fons Vitae*. This work, treating of the relationship between form and matter, makes no reference to the Bible or to the Rabbinic literature and is so universalistic in character that it was attributed by Christian writers to an unknown Christian or Muslim philosopher operating solely in philosophical categories.

An oft-quoted stanza in *The Kingly Crown* sees all men as worshipping God without knowing the object of their worship; the act of worship itself is sufficient evidence that this is so:

Thou art God, and all creatures are
    Thy slaves and worshippers,
and Thy glory is not diminished by
    those who worship others
than Thee, for the goal of all of
    them is to attain to Thee.

Idolatry The worship of any being other than God; Heb. *avodah zarah* ('strange worship'). The Hebrew prophets fought against the worship of Baal and the other foreign gods but nowhere in the Bible are the other nations condemned for worshipping their gods, only for the 'abominations' attendant on that worship. However, in the Rabbinic doctrine of the *Noahide laws, the Torah for all mankind so to speak, idolatry is as serious an offence for *Gentiles as it is for Jews, although, in the nature of the case, this was purely academic. It was unlikely in the extreme in Rabbinic times that a Gentile would ask a Rabbi whether or not he was allowed by the Torah to worship his gods. A whole tractate of the Talmud, tractate *Avodah Zarah*, is devoted to the laws against idolatry and idolatrous practices. Hardly any attempt is made in the classical Jewish sources to distin-

guish between different kinds of pagan or primitive worship such as animism, fetishism, and polytheism. All forms of worship that are not purely monotheistic are treated together as idolatry and severely condemned. Not only idolatry itself was treated with the greatest severity by the Rabbis, but anything appertaining to it was strictly prohibited. It was forbidden to use the leaves of an idolatrous grove, even for their medicinal properties, because leaves from another place could serve the same purpose (*Pesahim* 25a). No use might be had of an idol, but if it had been desecrated by its worshipper, by being defaced, for example, it was permitted to have use of it. This only applied to an idol belonging to a non-Jewish idolater. An idol worshipped by a Jew was permanently forbidden even after its defacement by the owner (*Avodah Zarah* 52a).

In the post-Talmudic period, there was no longer any threat to Judaism from the pagan religions and a certain relaxation was granted of some of the stricter rules against relations with idolaters. The discussion among the Jewish teachers then centred on whether *Islam and *Christianity, the two daughter religions of Judaism, as they were called, and the new rivals to the Jewish religion, were to be treated as idolatrous religions. Islam was seen as a purely monotheistic religion but opinions differed with regard to Christianity. Eventually, the consensus emerged that while Christianity did not constitute idolatry 'for them', that is, a Gentile Christian did not offend against the Noahide laws, it did constitute idolatry 'for us'. Many Jews suffered martyrdom rather than embrace the Christian faith. To worship the gods of the Far Eastern religions is, of course, held to be idolatrous by all Jewish authorities.

Image of God The idea that all human beings, whether male or female, are created in a form that in some way resembles the Creator: 'So God created man in His own image; in the image of God created He him; male and female created He them' (Genesis 1: 25). In a saying attributed to Rabbi *Akiba in Ethics of the Fathers (3. 15) the doctrine is elaborated on: 'Beloved is man for he was created in the image [of God]; still greater was the love in that it was made known to him that he was created in the image of God.' It should be noted that here and else-where, and in the clear implications of the verse, all human beings are said to have been created in God's image (see CHOSEN PEOPLE). In the biblical narrative, man is distinguished from all other creatures in being created in God's image.

The Jewish commentators differ as to the meaning of the image of God in which man has been created. The concept is not normally taken literally, since God has no 'image', though there are exceptions to this in the Middle Ages, when Talmudists like Moses of Tachau did understand the anthropomorphic expressions in the Bible and Talmud as suggesting a correspondence in some way to a corporeal conception of the divine nature. The medieval philosophers sought to combat such notions, Maimonides going so far as to state that a Jew who believes that God is corporeal in any way is a heretic and has no share in the *World to Come. There is no evidence that Jews ever actually made an image of God for the purpose of worship (but see GOLDEN CALF).

Imitatio Dei Latin for the imitation of God, the doctrine that man can and should be godlike in his conduct. The Rabbinic Midrash known as the Sifre (see MIDRASH) to the verse in Deuteronomy (11: 22) which speaks of 'walking in God's ways' (in the context, walking in the ways laid down by God) takes 'walking in God's ways' to mean: 'Just as He

is called "Merciful" be thou merciful; just as He is called "Compassionate" be thou compassionate.'

Incense A mixture of aromatic herbs burnt twice daily on the golden altar in the Temple; Heb. *ketoret*, from a root meaning 'to smoke'. The burning of the incense also formed an important part of the ritual performed by the *High Priest when he entered the Holy of Holies on *Yom Kippur (Leviticus 16: 12–13). The biblical instructions for the preparation of the incense are found in Exodus 30: 34, where four ingredients are mentioned—stacte, onycha, galbanum, and pure frankincense. But the Talmud (*Keritot* 6a) records an ancient tradition according to which there were eleven ingredients in the incense.

Incense is found in the worship of most ancient societies, no doubt because of the pleasant aroma ascending upwards towards heaven and as a symbol of purification.

Incense, however, is never used in the synagogue, probably in order to distinguish the synagogue from the Temple, although synagogues have been known to spray the building with aromatic herbs, not as any kind of ritual but solely for aesthetic reasons. Some of the Hasidic masters used to smoke a pipe of fragrant *tobacco when they meditated before their prayers.

Individual Although it is often said that the emphasis on Judaism is on the group rather than the individual, on the *Chosen People rather than on particular Jews, this glib generalization is not supported by the evidence. Where the emphasis lies in a religious tradition is notoriously difficult to determine. The possibility always exists that some ideas are rarely mentioned not because they are considered unimportant but, on the contrary, because their importance is taken for granted. Yet even if the yardstick of frequency of mention is applied, it becomes clear from the classical Jewish sources that, while there are numerous passages centred on the role of the people, passages are certainly not lacking in which the role of the individual is stressed. In any balanced picture of the Jewish religion, what the individual does with his life has eternal significance for him or her, not only for the Jewish people, which is itself made up of individuals.

In the Talmudic and Midrashic literature, the emphasis is generally on peoplehood but statements regarding individual duties, responsibilities, and needs are found throughout this literature. Each of the Rabbis is an individual with his own particular virtues and failings, so much so that it has been possible, with a fair degree of success, to reconstruct Rabbinic biographies from the hints scattered in this vast literature.

In the philosophical tradition in the Middle Ages, especially in Maimonides, Judaism is so interpreted that the aim of the religion is ultimately for the individual, the social thrust of Judaism being regarded as a means to an end; a sound social order helps the individual to rise towards perfection. Maimonides' *principles of faith are directed towards the individual Jew.

Moreover, in every version of Jewish *eschatology, it is the individual who lives for ever, whether in the doctrine of the *resurrection or of the immortality of the soul. In the other-worldly Judaism that was the norm until modern times, the whole of life upon earth was seen as a preparation by the individual for his life in the Hereafter and all the precepts of the Torah have this as their ultimate purpose.

Insanity Mental instability, of which state a number of instances are recorded in the Bible. Among the curses threatened for faithlessness to the covenant is 'so that thou shalt be mad [*meshugga*] for the sake of thine eyes which thou shalt see' (Deuteronomy 28:

34). King Saul was terrified by an evil spirit and David was invited to play the harp so that Saul could find relief (1 Samuel 16: 14–23). David feigned madness when he fled to the court of Achish the king of Gath (1 Samuel 21: 13–16; Psalms 31: 1). A Midrashic comment on this is that David questioned why God should have created such a purposeless state as insanity. But when he saved his life by pretending to be mad, David came to see that madness also has a purpose. In one passage (Hosea 9: 7), the prophet is described as 'mad', though it is clear from the context that this term is used ironically. Some moderns have understood the biblical record here and elsewhere to imply that a man who has received a vision from on high is bound to have had a profound disturbance of his mental equilibrium. In the Rabbinic literature madness or melancholia is often attributed to an evil spirit, *ruah raah*.

It is axiomatic in Jewish law that an imbecile, *shoteh* in Hebrew, is held responsible for his actions neither by a human court nor by the divine judgement. But there is considerable uncertainty about the degree of mental instability required for a person to be considered a *shoteh*. The classical definition stated in the Talmud (*Ḥagigah* 3b) is one who goes out alone at night, stays overnight in the cemetery, and rends his garments. The Talmud discusses this further but the definition remains more than a little opaque. Maimonides, in his Code (*Edut*, 9.9–10), after stating that a *shoteh* is disqualified from acting as a witness in a court of law, observes that in this context a *shoteh* is not only one who walks about naked or breaks vessels or throws stones but whoever is mentally disturbed. Evidently, Maimonides understands the Talmudic definition to be in the nature of a broad, general assessment so that for practical purposes the term denotes anyone whose mind is disturbed with regard to any one matter, and Maimonides proceeds to extend the scope of the law as follows: 'Those especially stupid in that they cannot note contradictions and cannot understand any matter in the way normal people do, and so, too, those who are confused and hasty in their minds and behave in an excessively crazy fashion, these are embraced by the term *shoteh*. This matter must depend on the assessment of the judge since it is impossible to record in writing an adequate definition of insanity.' Thus Maimonides, perhaps because of his knowledge of medicine, finds the notion of insanity too complicated and too vague to be recorded in a precise legal definition, so that the decision must be left to the discretion of the judge in each particular case.

In everyday parlance, when it is said of someone that he is *meshuggu* or a *shoteh*, these terms are used very loosely and resemble the English use of 'barmy' or 'daft'.

Inspiration Enlargement of the human psyche so as to produce an increase in vision and knowledge of the will of God. Though the actual word 'inspiration' is never used in the traditional sources, the idea that God endows spiritually gifted persons with insights that are not available to ordinary mortals is found frequently throughout the Bible, the Rabbinic literature, and among the standard Jewish thinkers. According to the tradition there are various degrees of inspiration: *prophecy; the *Holy Spirit; the heavenly voice (*Bat Kol); the appearance of *Elijah; and *dreams. Some modernists, influenced by the scientific picture of the universe, have abandoned the concept of *God as a transcendental being and have understood inspiration in purely naturalistic terms—that, for instance, the Bible is inspired in the way that Shakespeare or Mozart are said to be 'inspired'. But, while critical investigation (see BIBLICAL CRITICISM) has succeeded in raising pow-

erful objections to traditional views, and while there is a greater acknowledgement of the human element, there is no valid reason for rejecting the idea of inspiration itself. It can be put in this way: modern Jews are far less certain that works considered to be the result of divine inspiration are really so, yet a belief in God surely cannot rule out that human beings have encountered God in the special manner implied by the idea of inspiration.

Insurance In the medieval and Renaissance world, the question was widely discussed of whether taking out insurance on ships' cargoes and the like involved any infringement of the laws against *usury. Legal arguments were advanced by the authorities to allow merchants to secure their goods against risk while avoiding the prohibitions, treating insurance like any other commercial transaction but not like a loan on interest where the borrower gives back the lender more than the amount he borrowed purely in return for the loan itself. On the theological level, no one seems to have imagined that to take out insurance was to lack faith in God's power to provide. It was not until the late twentieth century that Rabbi Moshe *Feinstein raised the question, coming to the obvious conclusion that according to sound Jewish teaching God only provides when human beings play their part.

Intermarriage Marriage between a Jew and a non-Jew. In Jewish law there is no validity whatsoever to a marriage between a Jew and a non-Jew so that no *get (bill of divorce) is required to dissolve the union. The Jewish status of the children depends on the status of the mother, not the father. If a non-Jewish man marries a Jewish woman, the children are Jews; but if a Jewish man marries a non-Jewish woman, the children are not Jewish. However it evolved, this became the traditional position from early Rabbinic times. This principle of matrilineal descent, as it is termed in contemporary discussions, is still adhered to strictly by Orthodox and Conservative Jews, as well as by many Reform Jews. But, in recent years, some Reform Rabbis in the USA (and this is the position of the Liberal movement in the UK) have adopted the rule that, provided the intention of the parents is to bring the child up as Jewish, the child of a Jewish father and a non-Jewish mother also has Jewish status.

All Jewish groups frown on intermarriage, not only because of the law which forbids such unions, but primarily because intermarriage poses a severe threat to Jewish survival. There is hardly any intermarriage between Jews and non-Jews in the State of Israel, for obvious reasons, but in the *Diaspora intermarriage is the most acute problem facing Jews. A large proportion of Jews do fall in love with non-Jews and do 'marry out'. Attitudes to Jews who have married out differ widely. Every effort is made by Rabbis to discourage intermarriage and, when it happens, to encourage the non-Jewish spouse to convert to Judaism. Nevertheless, where these efforts fail, the Jewish spouse is treated as a full member of the Jewish people and is accepted as a member of the synagogue, even in many Orthodox communities.

Isaac The second of the three *patriarchs, son of Abraham and father of Jacob, whose story is told in the book of Genesis. The Hebrew name Yitzhak, from *tzahak*, 'to laugh', was apparently given to him because his mother Sarah laughed when it was foretold that she would give birth at her advanced age (Genesis 18: 12). Abraham was 100 years old at Isaac's birth and Sarah 90 years (Genesis 21: 5). The traditional commentators take this literally but the suggestion has been made that by 'years' in the narrative only half-years are meant, so that Abraham was 50 and Sarah 45. It

is extremely unlikely, however, that years should mean half-years since that meaning is found nowhere else in the Bible. The story of the *Akedah, the binding of Isaac, is told in Genesis 19. Isaac married Rebecca when he was 40 years of age and she bore him twin boys, Jacob and Esau, when he was 60 years of age (Genesis 25: 19–26). Isaac died at the age of 180 and was buried by his sons in the Cave of *Machpelah (Genesis 35: 27–9). The chronological details of Isaac's life are confusing and difficult to put together as a coherent whole. On the critical view, the narratives stem from different sources, though hardly any biblical scholars fail to treat Isaac as a historical figure.

Isaiah Prophet of the eighth century BCE during the reigns of four kings of Judah, Uzziah, Jotham, Ahaz, and Hezekiah. Although the book of Isaiah begins with the prophet's vision of the future, in which he foretells the catastrophes that will befall his people if they practise injustice and fail to put their trust in God, Isaiah's first prophetic vision is recounted in chapter 6 of the book: 'In the year that King Uzziah died, I beheld the Lord seated on a high and lofty throne and the skirts of His robe filled the Temple' (6: 1). In this vision the prophet sees the Seraphim proclaiming one to the other: 'Holy, holy, holy! The Lord of Hosts! His presence fills all the earth' (6: 3). This verse constitutes the main section of the *Kedushah recited in the synagogue. In the same chapter (6: 13) the prophet declares that a remnant of the faithful will remain come what may, an idea that was to prove influential in Jewish thought. No matter how far the Jewish people have strayed from the true path, a faithful remnant will always be found to preserve the covenant with God.

Abraham *Ibn Ezra in the Middle Ages and the majority of biblical scholars today believe that the second part of the book of Isaiah (from ch. 40 onwards) could not have been composed by the prophet Isaiah since this section of the book speaks, as if it were actually taking place, of the return from the Babylonian exile. Cyrus, the king of Persia who defeated the Babylonians in 53 BCE and issued his edict to permit the Jews to return to Jerusalem, is mentioned twice by name (44: 28; 45: 1). Diehards such as S. D. *Luzzatto remained unconvinced and even went so far as to say that anyone who denies that the second part of Isaiah was composed by the prophet Isaiah, denies altogether the power of a prophet to gaze into the future. The consensus of scholarly opinion is that the second part of Isaiah, 'Deutero-Isaiah', makes no claim to foretell events of the remote future and was compiled by an unknown prophet or prophets. As for the strong resemblance in style between the two halves of the book, scholars have suggested that a kind of Isaianic school persisted long after the death of Isaiah himself.

Ishmael Son of Abraham and his concubine Hagar (Genesis 16) and half-brother of Isaac. To some extent in the Pentateuchal narrative itself, and especially in the Rabbinic literature, Ishmael is seen in a very unfavourable light, but eventually, according to the Midrash, he repented of his evil deeds. In Islam, Ishmael is the ancestor of Muhammad and is venerated as a prophet and the true son of Abraham. In the Koran (*Sura*, 37) it is Ishmael, not Isaac, who was bound on the altar at the *Akedah*. Later Muslims accused the Jews of falsifying the Torah by substituting Isaac for Ishmael. Many of the Rabbinic Midrashim which speak of the life and conduct of Ishmael have, in fact, the Muslims in mind. This fact has helped scholars in dating some literary works. When, for instance, the Zohar states that the time will come when Edom (the name for Rome and later for

Christians) and Ishmael will fight over the Holy Land, the reference is fairly obviously to the Crusades. In the *Targum attributed to Jonathan ben Uziel, the names of Ishmael's two wives are given as Ayesha and Fatima, the names of Muhammad's wife and daughter, thus demonstrating that the work could not possibly have been compiled by Jonathan ben Uziel who lived in the first century BCE and could not have known these names.

Ishmael, Rabbi Tanna (see TANNAIM AND AMORAIM) who lived in the first half of the second century CE and contemporary of Rabbi *Akiba, with whom he often engaged in debate. He is sometimes referred to as Rabbi Ishmael ben Elisha but usually simply as Rabbi Ishmael. That a Rabbi should have the name of a biblical villain is probably to be explained on the grounds that since it was believed that eventually *Ishmael repented and was, after all, the son of Abraham, Jewish parents saw no objection to giving this name to their sons. There are references to the 'school' or 'house' of Rabbi Ishmael, meaning no doubt a group of disciples who followed his teachings. Unlike Rabbi Akiba, who held that every word of the legal passages in the Torah must be interpreted to convey its own nuances, Rabbi Ishmael held that some words have a purely stylistic significance because 'The Torah speaks in the language of men'.

Islam The religion whose prophet is Muhammad. Islam and Christianity are sometimes referred to as the 'daughter religions' of Judaism because both affirm that God did reveal His will to the Jews and many of their ideas are adopted from Judaism, although the term 'daughter religions' is never found in any of the standard Jewish sources. The accepted view among the medieval thinkers is that Islam, though false from the standpoint of Judaism, is a pure monotheistic faith so that a non-Jew who is a Muslim does not offend against the *Noahide laws, one of which is the prohibition of idolatry. Maimonides goes so far as to rule that if a Jew is ordered to embrace Islam or be killed, he is not obliged to suffer martyrdom. Others disagree. It is true, they argue, that a convert to Islam is not an idolater but, by becoming a Muslim, he rejects the *Torah and to avoid this act of apostasy, too, martyrdom is demanded.

While there is a good deal of Jewish–Christian *dialogue on the contemporary scene there is hardly any Jewish–Islamic dialogue, no doubt because of the strained relations between Jews and Muslims after the establishment of the State of Israel.

Israel, State of The literature on the State of Israel is vast. The *Encyclopedia Judaica* alone has over a thousand pages and an extensive bibliography on Israel, to say nothing of books and newspaper articles published all over the world on what, on any showing, is one of the most momentous creations in all human history. From the days of *Herzl and the rise of political *Zionism, this new movement was hailed by many as the only solution to the Jewish problem and attacked by others as an attempted substitution of nationalism for religion. With the establishment of the State of Israel, these debates became academic and, with the exception of a few religious anti-Zionists, there has been a wholehearted acceptance of the State not only as a refuge for Jews but as being in some way of the highest significance for the future of Judaism.

There are a number of political parties in the State of Israel representing religious Jews, with a variety of religious affiliations. The Aggudat Israel party, anti-Zionist in pre-State days, now accepts, somewhat uneasily, that the State of Israel is at the centre of Jewish life everywhere and is repre-

sented in the Israeli Parliament, the Knesset, and sometimes even in the government. Aggudat Israel has established its own independent religious school system. To the left of Aggudat Israel is the Mafdal, the National Religious Party, formerly the Mizrachi movement of religious Zionism. This party is totally committed to the Zionist ideal. An offshoot of Mafdal is the Gush Emunim movement. This is not a political party but a tendency among religious Zionists to try to make sure that the land promised to Abraham, as the members often say, will never be surrendered; so that trading land for peace with the Arabs, even if this is feasible, is ruled out by divine fiat. The religious parties are generally opposed to the extremist and hawkish attitudes of the Gush Emunim. Sephardi religious Jews, believing Aggudat Israel to be too dominated by the Ashkenazim, have formed themselves into the Sephardi Torah Guardians' Party (Shas). The Degel Ha-Torah party represents Ashkenazi Jews sympathetic to the Aggudat Israel philosophy but who believe that Aggudat Israel is too dominated by Hasidic Jews. Reform and Conservative Jews are not organized on party-political lines but have their own organizations and synagogues in Israel. Conservative Judaism in Israel is known as Masorti ('Traditional').

Of non-Jewish religions in Israel there are the Druzes, with a secret religion, Muslims, and Christians of many denominations, all of whom are given complete freedom to worship in accordance with their own beliefs and to further their own institutions.

The Chief Rabbinate of Israel, with two heads, a Sephardi Chief Rabbi and an Ashkenazi Chief Rabbi, goes back to the days of the British Mandate for Palestine and is modelled, in fact, on the British Chief Rabbinate, itself owing much to the office of Archbishop in the Anglican Church. The ultra-Orthodox, known as the Haredim

('God-fearing') do not recognize the Chief Rabbinate and have their own Rabbinic authorities. Since there is no doctrinal significance to the office of Chief Rabbi, voices are raised from time to time to abolish the whole institution of two Chief Rabbis, irreverently called by Israelis 'the Heavenly Twins'.

Isserles, Moses Polish authority, Rabbi in Cracow (d.1572). Isserles had a good knowledge of philosophy, Kabbalah, and history. He was the author of *Responsa and other Halakhic works but his chief claim to fame rests on his glosses to the *Shulhan Arukh of Joseph *Karo. Karo's work, meaning 'Arranged Table', was intended to provide a clear ruling on all matters of *Halakhah. But since Karo generally followed the Sephardi rulings, Isserles resolved to compile glosses in which Ashkenazi opinions and customs would be recorded. Isserles gave his work, which appeared together with the *Shulhan Arukh* in 1569-71, the name *Mappah*, 'Tablecloth' (i.e. to Karo's 'Table'). Since that time every edition of the *Shulhan Arukh* contains the glosses of Isserles, and the two, Karo and Isserles, are referred to as the authors of the *Shulhan Arukh*. Isserles is generally known, after the initial letters of his name, as Rema—Rabbi Moshe Isserles. It is thanks to Isserles that numerous Jewish *customs have been preserved; he believed that, as the old maxim has it, 'The *minhag* ["custom"] of Israel is Torah.'

J

Jacob The third patriarch of the Jewish people, son of Isaac and Rebecca, grandson of Abraham, whose story is told in the book of Genesis (25: 19 to the end of the book). On the critical view (see BIBLICAL CRITICISM), the Jacob saga in Genesis is an amalgam of various sources and traditions. For all that, most critics believe that there is a core of historical fact to all the traditions; only a very few accept the notion that Jacob and the other two *patriarchs are fictitious persons. From the point of view of the Jewish tradition, it is not, in any event, the historical Jacob who matters most but Jacob as he appears in Genesis as the progenitor of the twelve tribes constituting the 'children of Israel'. In the Genesis narrative, Jacob, Yaakov in Hebrew, is so called because at his birth he seized hold of the heel (*akev*) of his twin brother, *Esau (Genesis 25: 25), while the name Israel was given to him by the angel with whom he wrestled (Genesis 32: 25–33).

Among the salient features in Jacob's life, as told in Genesis, are that Esau sold him his birthright for a 'mess of pottage' (24: 27–34); that, at the instigation of his mother, Rebecca, he tricked his father, Isaac, into giving him, instead of Esau, the blessing (ch. 27); that he fled from Esau's wrath to his uncle Laban whose two daughters, Rachel and Leah, he married and by them, and by the two concubines Bilhah and Zilpah, he had twelve sons in all (chs. 29 and 30); that he came to sojourn in the land of Egypt (chs. 45 and 46); and that he was taken after his death to be buried in the land of his fathers ('the land of Israel') in the Cave of *Machpelah (ch. 50).

In the Rabbinic literature in particular, the figure of Jacob is made to represent the people as a whole, the conflict between Jacob and Esau being seen as a reflection of the love–hate relationship between Rome and the Jews—fierce enemies and yet, after all, brothers. Later, this conflict is interpreted as the struggle for supremacy between Christianity = Esau and Judaism = Jacob. The description of Jacob as a man who dwells in tents, in contradistinction to Esau, the skilful hunter, the man of outdoors (Genesis 25: 27), is made to signify that while the Roman ideal is to get things done in the world at large the Jewish ideal is to remain apart from the world to study God's words in the 'tents of Torah'. Much of the same is behind the Rabbinic identification of the angel who wrestled with Jacob as the guardian angel of Esau, that is, the narrative represents the struggle between the different spiritual ideals of Rome and Judaea.

Jacob ben Asher German Halakhist (d. 1340), son of Asher ben Jehiel, the outstanding authority in German and later Spanish Jewry, known as the Rosh (after the initial letters of his name, Rabbi Asher). Under threat of persecution, Jacob with his father left Germany for Spain in 1303. The Rosh became Rabbi of Toledo but Jacob refused to take up a Rabbinic appointment and lived a life of poverty, only partly relieved by money he received from time to time from patrons of learning.

Jacob is chiefly renowned for his great Code of Jewish law (first published in Piove di Sacco in 1475 and thus one of the very earliest Jewish works to be printed), known as *Arbaah Turim* ('Four Rows'). The name is based on the four rows of precious stones in the breastplate of the High Priest (Exodus 28: 17), usually abbreviated to *Tur*, so that in Halakhic literature both Jacob himself and his Code are called 'the Tur'. The work consists of four sections, hence the 'four rows'. These are: 1. *Orah Hayyim*, 'Path of Life' (after Psalms 16: 11), dealing with prayer, the Sabbath, and festivals, and with general religious duties; 2. *Yoreh Deah*, 'Teaching Knowledge' (after Isaiah 28: 9), dealing with the *dietary laws and other topics required chiefly for Rabbinic decisions on more complex matters; 3. *Even Ha-Ezer*, 'Stone of Help' (after 1 Samuel 5: 1 and Genesis 2: 20, where woman is the 'help' meet for man), dealing with the laws of marriage and divorce; 4. *Hoshen Mishpat*, 'Breastplate of Judgement' (after Exodus 28: 15), dealing with civil law and jurisprudence in general.

Jacob also compiled a commentary to the Torah in which, as in his Code, he draws on earlier teachers to give what he calls 'the plain meaning' of the text. In the introductions to each section of the Torah, Jacob playfully adds, partly for the reader's amusement, ingenious asides in which *gematria and other plays on words are utilised in an admittedly fanciful manner. It is ironical that while the commentary itself was largely ignored (it was not published until the nineteenth century) these playful comments were printed together with the text in many editions of the Torah, under the title *Baal Ha-Turim* (*Author of the Turim*). These became exceedingly popular among students who resorted to them for intellectual relaxation from their more arduous studies.

Jacob Joseph of Polonnoye

Disciple of the *Baal Shem Tov and foremost Hasidic author. Jacob Joseph (d. c. 1784), when serving as the Rabbi of Shargorod, came under the influence of the Baal Shem Tov whose doctrines he began to disseminate to the consternation of his congregation; he was obliged to relinquish his post, eventually becoming a Maggid, 'Preacher', in the town of Polonnoye. Jacob Joseph's work

Toledot Yaakov Yosef (*The Generations of Jacob Joseph*), based on Genesis 37: 2, was the first Hasidic work to be published (in Koretz, 1780) and as such set the tone and style for subsequent Hasidic publications as well as bearing the brunt of the attacks on Hasidism by opponents of the new movement, the *Mitnaggedim. The scorn Jacob Joseph poured out on Rabbinic scholars who studied with impure motives and his statement that one should not be over-scrupulous in observing the precepts because this diverted the mind from true devotion to God, were seen as a special cause of offence. Jacob Joseph is known among the Hasidim as 'the Toledot', after his first work.

Jacob Joseph stresses that God is omnipresent. The Hasid should not lead an ascetic life. He should eat and drink and participate in social life but always with his mind on God. The masses, too, can be brought nearer to God through their attachment to the *Zaddik, the holy master, who is, in turn, attached to God; as the Talmud states 'the fear of God was but a small thing' to the people in the wilderness who were closely attached to Moses. The Zaddik is, moreover, the channel through which the divine grace and blessing flows.

It appears that Jacob Joseph had hoped to be the Baal Shem Tov's successor but it was the other chief disciple of the master, *Dov Baer of Mezhirech, who became the acknowledged leader. Jacob Joseph retreated into himself to some extent and established no Hasidic following of his own. Yet his *Toledot Yaakov Yosef* is seen by all later Hasidim as the main record of the authentic teachings of the Baal Shem Tov, whose sayings Jacob Joseph quotes repeatedly with the formula: 'I have heard from my master.'

Jacob's Ladder

The dream Jacob had when he left Beer-sheba to set out for Haran (Genesis 28: 10–27) has exercised a powerful fascination over all readers of the Bible. In his dream, Jacob sees a ladder or stairway (Heb. *sulam*) set on the ground with its top reaching to heaven, and angels of God going up and down on it. In the context, the dream is of Jacob's own future: a divine promise that God will be with him, and send His angels to protect him. A Rabbinic comment notes that the angels first ascend and then descend, although the angels come from on high and the descent should have preceded the ascent. But the angels who attended Jacob in the Holy Land, the land of his fathers, ascend to be replaced by different angels who come down to guide him outside the Holy Land. Yet, in Jewish exegesis and homiletics, the dream is chiefly interpreted as a vision in which Jacob gazes into the future of his seed, the children of Israel.

In one Midrashic interpretation, for instance, the ladder symbolizes Mount *Sinai, on which the Torah was given, the angels representing Moses and Aaron who go up on the mountain (see Exodus 19). In another Midrashic interpretation, the vision is of the guardian angels of the empires of Babylon, Media, Greece, and Rome, which are destined to have successive dominion over the people of Israel. These will be in the ascendancy for a time but will later suffer decline, the permanent survival of Israel alone being assured.

The moralists have an individualistic interpretation. Angels are created by good deeds. But a man must first send these angels upwards and only then do the angels, representing God's help, descend from on high. God assists man in his spiritual efforts but the divine help depends on man's own prior attempt to lead a good life.

Jeremiah The prophet born in Anathoth, about 3 miles north of Jerusalem, whose ministry began in the thirteenth year of Josiah king of Judah (i.e. 627 BCE), and extended for a period of over forty years. The book of Jeremiah contains much biographical and autobiographical material, so that more is known about Jeremiah's life than about any other of the great literary prophets. Little is told of Jeremiah's activity during the reign of Josiah, whose grandfather Manasseh, during a reign of forty years, had led the people astray from monotheism to idolatrous worship on the 'high places'. Josiah's reformation consisted of the restoration of monotheism and the centralization of worship in the Temple. Many of the people, however, continued to follow the ways to which they had been accustomed during the reign of Manasseh and against them were directed Jeremiah's castigations. From the beginning Jeremiah witnessed the downfall of the Assyrian Empire in 606 BCE; the death of Josiah in 605 BCE; the destruction of the Jewish State by the Babylonians in 586 BCE; and the carrying-away of most of the people in captivity to Babylon. Jeremiah himself was taken to Egypt by fugitive Judaeans, where he died, according to the legend, a martyr's death.

In English a 'Jeremiah' is a person given to woeful complaining but, in fact, for all the denunciations of his people, Jeremiah sounds a note of encouragement and of hope. God, he says, remembers the loyalty of their ancestors and He will restore the exiled people to their land in the future. 'And the word of the Lord came to me saying: Go, and cry in the ears of Jerusalem, saying: Thus saith the Lord: I remember for thee the affection of thy youth, the love of thine espousals; how thou wentest after Me in the wilderness; in a land that was not sown' (2: 1–2). 'But fear not thou, O Jacob My servant, neither be dismayed, O Israel; For, lo I will save thee from afar, and thy seed from the land of their captivity; and Jacob shall again be quiet and at ease, and none shall make him afraid' (46: 27).

Jeremiah preaches not only to the nation but to the individual who is acceptable to God when he repents of his evil deeds. Even while addressing the nation as a whole, he breaks off to address himself to the individual whose temptations he recognizes: 'The heart is deceitful above all things, And it is exceeding weak—who can know it? I the Lord search the heart, I try the reins, Even to give every man according to his ways, According to the fruit of his doings' (17: 9–10).

Jeroboam Son of Nebat, first king of the Northern Kingdom after the death of Solomon, reigning for twenty-two years until around 907 BCE. When Rehoboam, Solomon's successor, refused to release the people from excessive taxation, the tribes, apart from Judah and Benjamin, broke away from the House of David to establish their own kingdom with Jeroboam as king. In order to encourage the people to worship outside Jerusalem, in the territory of the House of David, Jeroboam set up two golden calves, one at Dan and another at Bethel. The resemblance between this episode and that of the *golden calf in the wilderness has often been discussed. In the Rabbinic tradition, Jeroboam is the most grievous of sinners because he caused many others to sin by setting up the calves (Ethics of the Fathers, 5. 18): 'Jeroboam the son of Nebat sinned and caused others to sin; the sin of the many is ascribed to him, as it is said "The sin of Jeroboam who sinned and made Israel to sin" [1 Kings 14: 16].' In the Mishnah (Sanhedrin 10: 2) Jeroboam is listed as one of the three kings who have no share in the *World to Come. The Rabbis use the figure of Jeroboam to depict the highly gifted man who in his pride can never take second place to anyone, even when it is to his advantage so to do. When God said to Jeroboam: 'Repent and I, you and David will walk together in the Garden of Eden,' Jeroboam asked: 'Who will go in front?' and when God said: 'David will go in front,' Jeroboam retorted: 'In that case I do not want it.'

Jerusalem The holy city, Heb. *ir ha-kodesh*; sacred in itself and in that it contained the site of the *Temple (see HOLY PLACES). There is no explicit reference to Jerusalem in the *Pentateuch but the city Salem of which Melchizedek, priest of God Most High, was king (Genesis 14: 18), is identified by the tradition with Jerusalem, of which Salem is said to be an abbreviated or earlier form. The 'land of Moriah' (Genesis 22: 2), at which the *Akedah took place, is also traditionally identified with Jerusalem. After King David had reigned in Hebron for seven years he moved his capital to Jerusalem (2 Samuel 5: 1–13), so that another name for Jerusalem is 'the city of David' (2 Samuel 6: 12). David planned to build the Temple in Jerusalem but it was David's son, Solomon, who actually built and dedicated the Temple there (1 Kings 7 and 8). Jerusalem remained the holiest of cities during the period of the First and Second Temples. Even after the destruction of both the Temple and Jerusalem the city remained the focus of Jewish prayers, a special benediction being added to the *grace after meals in which God is entreated to rebuild Jerusalem.

Later passages in the Bible are full of the praises of Jerusalem as God's city. The Songs of Ascents in the Psalms are generally considered to have been originally the songs of the pilgrims who went up to Jerusalem. 'Our feet stood inside your gates, O Jerusalem, Jerusalem built up, a city knit together, to which tribes would make pilgrimage . . . Pray for the peace of Jerusalem, may those who love you be at peace' (Psalm 122). 'Jerusalem, hills unfold it, and the Lord enfolds His people now and for ever' (Psalms 125: 2). Zion is largely synonymous with Jerusalem but refers specifically to the Temple Mount – Mount Zion. 'Blessed is the Lord from Zion, He that dwells in Jerusalem, Hallelujah' (Psalms 137: 21). The Psalmist's oath was often repeated throughout Jewish history: 'If I forget thee, O Jerusalem, let my right hand forget its cunning; let my tongue cleave to my palate if I cease to think of thee, if I do not keep Jerusalem in memory even at my happiest hour' (Psalms 137: 5–6). The prophet, witnessing the exiles returning from the Babylonian captivity, declares: 'Rejoice with Jerusalem and be glad for her, all you who love her. Join in her jubilation all who mourned over her' (Isaiah 66: 10). In the prophetic vision of the time to come (later thought of in Messianic terms) the verse occurs, used in the liturgy when the Scroll of the Torah is taken from the Ark: 'For Torah will go out from Zion and the word of the Lord from Jerusalem' (Isaiah 2: 3).

Jerusalem is now acknowledged as occupying a special place in the heart and mind of every Jew. In the nineteenth century, the marked tendency among Reform Jews was to see Jerusalem as a spiritual ideal rather than in spatial terms. With Reform advocacy of Jewish accommodation to Western society and with its universalistic thrust, Jerusalem tended to be thought of much along the lines of Blake's 'Till we have built Jerusalem in England's green and pleasant land'. With the establishment of the State of Israel and the rebuilding of Jerusalem, such attitudes are exceedingly rare. Reform, like Orthodoxy, though to varying degrees, sees Jerusalem as a, if not the, spiritual centre of Judaism.

Jesus There is comparatively little in the Talmudic literature on Jesus of Nazareth. Uncensored editions of the Babylonian Talmud do contain a few allusions to Jesus and his disciples but these are of a clearly legendary nature; the Babylonian Jews had only a very hazy picture of Jesus or, for that matter, of Christianity as whole. Their religious challenge was presented chiefly by Persian dualism, which they attacked whenever they had the opportunity to do so. Palestinian sources are less vague but still not really informative. From the few Talmudic references we have, it would seem as if the figure of Jesus was of very little interest to the Rabbis and could largely be ignored. The suggestion by some scholars that *Balaam in the Talmudic literature is a veiled name for Jesus has largely been discounted, as has the suggestion that the word Peloni, meaning So-and-so, is sometimes a reference to Jesus, the circumlocution being used because there was a reluctance to use the real name. Followers of Jesus, on the few occasions when these are mentioned in the Talmud, are called Minim, 'sectarians', a general term applying to all sectarians, not only to believers in the Christian heresy. A direct attack on the Christian dogma such as the homily of the third-century teacher Rabbi Abbahu is rare and it must be remembered that this Rabbi lived in Caesarea where he came into regular contact with Christians. Rabbi Abbahu comments on the verse: 'I am the first, and I am the last, and beside Me there is no God' (Isaiah 44: 6); ' "I am the first" since I have no father; "And I am the last" since I have no son; "And beside Me there is no God" since I have no brother', the last phrase referring to the doctrine of dualism.

It was not until the Middle Ages, when the Church had become triumphant, that the figure of Jesus was widely discussed in the medieval Jewish–Christian *disputations and in polemical works produced by Jews in defence against Christian attacks, such as the *Toledot Jeshu* (*The History of Jesus*). In this work it is accepted that Jesus did perform miracles, but drew on the black arts for the purpose.

It is obvious that the Christian belief in Jesus as the Son of God (see CHRISTIANITY) is incompatible with Judaism, as is the belief that Jesus was the Messiah. The claims of the American 'Jews for Jesus' movement, that one can believe in Jesus and still remain a Jew, are rightly rejected by all religious Jews, who see the new movement as no more than a thinly disguised Christian mission seeking to mislead the unwary. Beyond that, attitudes towards the personality of Jesus, and on how Jews should view Jesus from the point of view of Judaism, vary from the belief that Jesus is not a historical figure at all to the acceptance of Jesus as an ancient Jewish 'Rabbi' or profound ethical teacher, a view rejected by all Orthodox Jews and by many Reform Jews. The whole question is befogged by the impossibility of disentangling the historical Jesus from the Jesus of Paul and the Synoptic Gospels, and by the central role that Jesus occupies in the Christian religion. Among the majority of Jews, the fear exists that to acknowledge in any way, however this is qualified, that Jesus has something of value to say to Jews, is to open the door to apostasy to a religion which Jews have given up their lives rather than embrace.

Jew The English word 'Jew' is derived from the Latin which, in turn, is based on the Hebrew word Yehudi, meaning 'from the tribe of Judah' (Judah = Yehudah). From the time of *Jeroboam's revolt, the division came about between the Northern Kingdom, called 'Israel', and the Southern Kingdom of the House of David. The latter was located in Judaea, the territory of the tribe of Judah. After the conquest of the Northern Kingdom by the Assyrians, the *ten tribes were carried away and all the members of the people, wherever they were found and whatever their origin, adopted the name 'Judah', hence the name 'the Jews'. In the book of *Esther (2: 5) *Mordecai is described as a 'Jew' (Yehudi) even though he belonged to the tribe of Benjamin. A Talmudic comment on this (*Megillah* 13a) has it that Mordecai was called a Yehudi because anyone who rejects idolatry is called a Yehudi. This homily became in later times a means of Jewish self-identifica-

tion, as if to say, no matter how far a Jew has gone along the road to assimilation, provided he does not worship idols and retains his belief in the One God, he is still a Jew; although, from the point of view of the *Halakhah, a Jew retains his Jewish status even if he has been converted to another religion (see CONVERSION), and the principle obtains: 'Once a Jew always a Jew'.

The Law of Return of the State of Israel gave the right to every Jew to become a citizen of the State. The problem arose of defining the term 'Jew' in this context. According to the traditional Halakhah, Jewish status depends either on the status of the mother or on conversion to Judaism. Thus the child of a Jewish mother and a non-Jewish father is Jewish, but not the child of a non-Jewish mother and a Jewish father. A non-Jew who has been converted by the due processes of Halakhah is a Jew. Furthermore, as above, a Jew never loses his Jewish status even if he has been converted to another religion. This gave rise to certain problems with regard to the Law of Return. Father Daniel, a Christian priest, born a Jew, who has been converted to Christianity, claimed Israeli citizenship as a Jew (non-Jews can, of course, be granted Israeli citizenship, but Father Daniel claimed the right by the Law of Return). By a majority decision, the Israeli court denied Father Daniel this right, arguing that it is not a question of what the Halakhah says but what was in the minds of those who framed the Law of Return. These, it can be presumed, never intended the Law of Return to apply to Jews converted to another faith. And what is the position of a Jew converted by Reform Rabbis where the Halakhic procedures have not been carried out in the proper manner? In this case, it could be argued that, while the Halakhah does not consider that person to be a Jew, those who framed the Law of Return presumably did consider such a person to qualify as a Jew. All this gave rise to the 'Who is a Jew?' controversy, as it has been called, although the persons affected were very few in number. On the whole this problem had been dealt with adequately, although voices are still raised protesting that the Law of Return must be interpreted in accordance with Halakhic categories.

Another problem arose for Jews everywhere, not only in the State of Israel, when a number of Reform Rabbis in the USA introduced the new category of patrilineal descent, ruling that as long as one of the parents of a child is Jewish, whether the mother or the father, the child has Jewish status. Here again, Halakhically the child is not Jewish if only the father is Jewish and the mother is not Jewish. Orthodox Rabbis obviously refuse to depart from the Halakhah in this matter and would require the child of a Jewish father and non-Jewish mother to be converted to Judaism by the due Halakhic processes.

Job Heb. Iyov, the central figure in the book of Job, the third book of the Hagiographa in the Hebrew Bible. Job is a good man, blessed with a wife and children and with great wealth. *Satan seeks permission of God to test Job by bringing sufferings on him to see whether he will relinquish his good way, since it may be that he is only righteous because it pays him so to be. Job loses his children and his wealth and is afflicted with a loathsome illness. Job's friends come to visit him and they imply that God has visited the torments on him because, despite outward appearances, he is not really a good man but a sinner who deserves to suffer. Job protests that his sufferings are undeserved. Eventually God appears to Job 'out of the whirlwind' to demonstrate the impossibility of humans grasping the mysterious ways of God. Job bows to the divine will and accepts his fate. The book concludes with Job's prosperity being restored to him and he is

blessed with beautiful daughters. All this is presented in exquisite poetic style, except for the prologue and the ending which are in prose, to make the story of Job one of the greatest masterpieces of world literature. Many scholars have felt that the 'happy ending' is too much like the 'and they all lived happily ever after' of the fairy story, spoiling the effect of the great drama, and must have been added at a later date by an unsophisticated pietist.

Joel The prophet whose book is the second of the book of the Twelve Prophets in the Hebrew Bible, placed between the books of Hosea and Amos who lived in the eighth century BCE. Beyond the prophet's name, Joel son of Pethuel, the book gives no indication of who the prophet was and when he prophesied. Scholars differ widely on the matter. The suggestion that he lived at the time of Hosea and Amos is based on the placing of his book between the books of these two prophets but this is no indication at all, since the placing of the books in this order is very late and has no significance for dating purposes. Many scholars prefer the much later date of the fifth century BCE. All this is, in any event, pure conjecture.

Johanan Ben Zakkai First-century CE disciple of *Hillel. Johanan took a prominent part in the controversies between the *Pharisees, of which group he was leader, and the *Sadducees. He is said to have been responsible for a number of new enactments and to have abolished the ordeal of the wife suspected of adultery (Numbers 5: 11–31) and the rite of the beheaded heifer (Deuteronomy 21: 1–9). Although not of the Princely House, Johanan was given the title usually reserved for the Nasi (the Prince), Rabban, 'Our Master', in contradistinction to the simple title 'Rabbi'. 'Master' Johanan's two outstanding disciples, Rabbi *Eliezer and

Rabbi *Joshua, succeeded him in the leadership of the Pharisaic party and, together with him, belong to the early teachers known as the *Tannaim, who developed what later came to be known as Rabbinic Judaism.

As with other early Rabbinic figures it is difficult to disentangle fact from pious legend when trying to reconstruct Johanan's history. For instance, when it is said of him, Hillel, and *Akiba that each lived for 120 years, it is as clear as can be that this is simply a device for calling attention to the significance of the teacher for later Judaism. Each lived for the lifespan of Moses, the first great leader and lawgiver. The same applies to the legend for which Johanan is especially known. According to this very late legend, during the siege of Jerusalem in 70 CE, Johanan was smuggled out of Jerusalem to meet Vespasian, then a general but greeted by Johanan as the emperor he was destined to become. Johanan requested Vespasian to spare the city of Yavneh as a home for scholars and to preserve the House of the Nasi by affording protection to the young *Gamaliel, later to become the Nasi, Rabban Gamaliel II. Apart from the fact that this story is told in the language of the Babylonian Talmud compiled centuries after Johanan, its legendary nature is obvious. But the legend is extremely significant in suggesting Johanan's importance in contributing to the continuing study of the Torah and protecting the legislative body, the *Sanhedrin, and thus assuring the survival of Judaism.

Jonah Son of Amittai; a prophet whose story is told in the book of Jonah, the fifth book of the book of the Twelve Prophets. Elsewhere in the Bible (2 Kings 14: 25) there is a reference to a prophet of the eighth century BCE named Jonah son of Amittai but even if this prophet is the same person as the Jonah of the book of Jonah this leads in no way to the conclusion that he is the author of the book. The book, quite different in form from any other prophetic book, seems to be a short story, composed much later, of which the historical Jonah is the hero, not the author. Traditionally, however, the events recorded in the book are not seen as fictitious. The religious value of the book and its message are not affected either way, any more than by (a question still discussed by fundamentalists) whether a 'big fish' (not a whale) can swallow a man. Most moderns prefer to read the book as a profound tale with the most significant religious message, from which message the attention is only diverted when the book is taken literally. As someone has remarked: 'The fish that swallowed Jonah was a red herring.'

The story of the book of Jonah has passed into world literature. The prophet receives a summons from God to go to Nineveh, the capital city of Assyria, to preach that unless its king and citizens repent of their evil deeds the city will be overthrown. Jonah is reluctant to obey the summons because he fears that the people of Nineveh may repent and this will be to the detriment of the prophet's own people of whom Assyria was the sworn enemy. Jonah seeks to flee from before the Lord. He embarks at the port of Jaffa on a ship bound for Tarshish, located in an exactly opposite direction from that of Nineveh. A terrible storm rages at sea and the God-fearing sailors cast lots to determine which of the passengers is responsible for God's wrath. The lot falls on Jonah who urges the sailors to cast him into the sea, which they do reluctantly. Jonah is swallowed by a big fish and he cries out to God in the belly of the fish. The fish spews out Jonah and he makes his way to Nineveh where he preaches his message of repentance. The king and his people fast and pray to God and God spares the city. Jonah departs from the city to take refuge under a gourd but this is smitten by a sultry east wind and Jonah, fainting in the heat, asks God to let him die. God asks Jonah whether he is deeply grieved about the plant and Jonah replies that he is so grieved that he wishes to die. The book concludes with God's reply: 'You cared about the plant, which you did not work for and which you did not grow, which appeared overnight and perished overnight. And should not I care about Nineveh, that great city, in which there are more than a hundred and twenty thousand persons who do not yet know their right hand from their left, and many beasts as well!'

Throughout the ages the book has been read as containing a twofold message: first, that it is impossible for a man to escape from doing God's will; and secondly, perhaps more significantly, that God is concerned with all His creatures, even if they are heathen, whose sincere repentance He accepts. By a stroke of religious genius, the tradition has set aside the book of Jonah, with its universalistic message, for reading as the *Haftarah on the afternoon of *Yom Kippur, the special Day of Atonement when the Jewish people becomes reconciled with its God.

Joseph Son of Jacob and Rachel; his story is told in the book of Genesis (chs. 37–50). Joseph, Jacob's favourite son, is hated by his brothers because of his dreams that one day they will all bow and pay homage to him. The brothers plot to kill Joseph but he is saved by passing merchants who sell him in Egypt where he becomes the slave of Potiphar, a high-ranking Egyptian. Potiphar's wife tries to seduce Joseph but he resists her blandishments. As a result Joseph is put in prison where he interprets successfully the dreams of two Egyptian officials who are imprisoned with him. Pharaoh has a disturbing dream which no one can interpret until Joseph is brought from prison for

the purpose. According to Joseph's interpretation, there will be seven years of plenty in Egypt followed by seven lean years. Pharaoh, impressed by Joseph's interpretation, appoints him vice-regent to prepare the country for the ordeal of the seven lean years and Joseph rises to a position of great power. Joseph's brothers come to buy corn in Egypt where they are brought into Joseph's presence without recognizing that he is their long-lost brother. On a second visit, the youngest son of Jacob, Benjamin, is accused of stealing Joseph's magic cup. *Judah, Joseph's older brother, protests vehemently and Joseph is eventually moved to disclose his identity and urges his brothers to bring Jacob and all his family down to Egypt. Jacob settles in Egypt, dies there, but is buried in the Cave of *Machpelah in Canaan, the land of his fathers. Before his death, Joseph requests that when God redeems His people from Egypt, his bones should also be taken to be buried in Canaan.

The story of Joseph is thus the prologue to the story of the children of Israel's sojourn in Egypt and the subsequent Egyptian bondage from which they were redeemed by Moses, as told in the book of Exodus. Biblical scholars have discussed at length how far the events in the Joseph saga are historical and how far they are a reading-back of the events of later times. But from the point of view of the tradition, the Joseph episode is seen as part of the divine plan for the children of Israel to be refined by their sufferings in Egypt in order to merit the land of Canaan promised to the *patriarchs. Joseph is seen as the man of destiny, the instrument of divine providence. Joseph's resistance to temptation in the affair of Potiphar's wife is seen as the supreme example of chastity, no matter how strong the allure of sex. Joseph is consequently called the 'righteous' in the Rabbinic tradition.

Josephus, Flavius Historian, soldier, and political figure (first century CE). Josephus, born to a priestly Palestinian family, was learned in the Torah but was also at home in the Roman culture of his day. While still quite young he visited Rome to intercede with the authorities on behalf of some Judaean priests who had been taken prisoner. In Rome Josephus was captivated by the rich cultural life he witnessed but while acquiring a typical Roman outlook on life he remained true to his own people and completely faithful to Judaism. During the Jewish War against Rome, which culminated in the destruction of the Temple in 70 CE, Josephus was at first commander of the Jewish forces in Galilee but, saving his own life by trickery when his colleagues killed themselves rather than give in to Rome, accompanied Titus and Vespasian on the Roman side and advocated that the Jews abandon as futile their resistance to Rome. Josephus ended his days in Rome close to the circle of the emperor. In addition to his autobiography, Josephus wrote *The Jewish War*, *Antiquities of the Jews*, and *Against Apion*.

Attitudes to Josephus vary. Some consider him a traitor to the Jewish cause in his support of Rome. Others defend Josephus as taking what he saw as the only possible course if the Jewish people were to survive and he personally to live proudly to tell the tale. Josephus naturally presents himself in a favourable light and he is not always too careful to get his facts right. For this reason, historians treat his works with caution. Nevertheless, together with the New Testament writers, Josephus is important for the true picture he presents of life as it was lived in first-century Palestine.

Joshua Disciple and successor of Moses whose story is told in the Pentateuch and in the book of Joshua. Joshua is described as the assistant of Moses

(Exodus 24: 13) and as the lad 'who would not stir out of the Tent' (Exodus 33: 11). When Moses, before his death, entreats God to appoint a leader in his stead, God replies: 'Single out Joshua, son of Nun, an inspired man, and place your hand upon him' (Numbers 27: 18) and when Moses dies it is recorded: 'Now Joshua son of Nun was filled with the spirit of wisdom because Moses had laid his hands upon him; and the Israelites heeded him, doing as the Lord had commanded Moses' (Deuteronomy 34: 9). The book of Joshua takes up the story, God saying to Joshua: 'My servant Moses is dead. Prepare to cross the Jordan, together with all this people, into the land which I am giving to the Israelites' (Joshua 1: 2). Modern biblical scholarship generally sees the book as a later compilation. In any event Joshua belongs, according to the tradition, in the line of the transmission of the Torah. Ethics of the Fathers (I. 1) begins: 'Moses received the Torah at Sinai and handed it over to Joshua who handed it over to the elders.'

Joshua, Rabbi First to second centuries CE, one of the most distinguished of the early Rabbinic teachers known as the *Tannaim. Rabbi Joshua was a disciple of Rabban *Johanan ben Zakkai and a colleague of Rabbi *Eliezer; the debates between these two teachers are found throughout the Talmud. Rabbi Joshua appears to have had a somewhat conciliatory attitude towards the Romans after the destruction of the Temple in 70 CE. When some zealots wished to give expression to their mourning over the destruction of the Temple by abstaining from wine and from marriage, Rabbi Joshua is said to have advocated less severe tokens of mourning, since one does not impose on the community regulations impossible for the majority to follow (*Bava Batra* 60b). On a number of occasions Rabban *Gamaliel is said to have behaved in an autocratic manner towards Rabbi

Joshua, as a result of which Rabban Gamaliel was deposed for a time from his position as Nasi and head of the San-hedrin. As with Rabbinic biography generally, these and similar statements about Rabbi Joshua's life and career have to be treated with a degree of caution since they are not eyewitness accounts but stories told much later. Nevertheless, the stories do reflect the high regard in which Rabbi Joshua was held by later generations as a foremost teacher of the Torah.

Joy Joy, Heb. *simḥah*, is a term used in Jewish literature to denote both the sense of physical well-being and various states of religious feeling from simple happiness in carrying out the will of God to *ecstasy and intense rapture. The Psalmist urges: 'Serve the Lord in gladness; come into His presence with shouts of joy' (Psalms 100: 2) and speaks of the precepts of the Lord as 'rejoicing the heart' (Psalms 19: 9). A notable passage in the Talmud (*Shabbat* 30b) contrasts two verses in the book of Ecclesiastes. One verse states: 'I said of laughter, it is mad: and of mirth, what doeth it?' (2: 2) while another verse states: 'Then I commended mirth' (8: 15). This is, in fact, one of the many inconsistencies in Ecclesiastes but the Talmud uses the apparent contradiction to postulate that there are two kinds of joy, religious and secular, the one advocated by the Preacher, the other denigrated. This leads to the typical Rabbinic idea of *simḥah shel mitzvah*, 'joy in the precepts', that is, taking delight in obeying God's will by carrying out His laws.

Jubilee The institution described in the book of Leviticus (25: 8–24) where it is stated that forty-nine years were to be counted (there is considerable uncertainty as to the date from when the counting is to begin, but traditionally it is from the creation of the world) and every fiftieth year declared a special year during which there was to be no agricultural work; all landed property was to revert to its original owner; and slaves were to be set free. The name Jubilee is from the Hebrew word *yovel*, 'ram's horn', the year being so called because a ram's horn was sounded when it was proclaimed (Leviticus 25: 9). Since this verse says: 'throughout the land for all its inhabitants', the Talmudic view is that the Jubilee was not observed during the Second Temple period because the majority of Jews no longer lived in the land of Israel.

The celebration as a Jubilee of such events as a special wedding anniversary or the anniversary of the founding of a synagogue is modern and has no basis in the Jewish tradition. On the other hand, there is nothing in the tradition to reject an innovation in which people give thanks for a special landmark in their lives.

Judah Fourth son of the patriarch Jacob from his wife Leah and the progenitor of the tribe of Judah which gave its name to the territory known as the 'land of Judah' or Judaea, hence the name *Jew. The story of Judah and Tamar is told in chapter 38 of the book of Genesis, where the name of Judah's son is given as Perez (v. 29). In the book of Ruth (4: 18–21), King David's ancestry is traced back to Perez. Since the *Messiah is a descendant of David, the story of Judah was often read as conveying hints of Messianic expectations.

Judah Halevi Spanish poet and religious philosopher (d. 1141). Judah Halevi's poems, secular and religious, are recognized as belonging to the foremost examples of Hebrew poetry. His Songs of Zion, giving expression to the poet's yearning for the land of Israel, are still used in synagogues during the Ninth of *Av service to introduce a note of consolation after the recital of the dirges on this day of mourning for the destruction of the Temple and for other calamities of the Jewish past. Obedient to the call of the Holy Land, Halevi, at the age of 60, resolved to leave Spain in order to settle in the country of his dreams. Legend has it that he did arrive in the Holy Land only to be murdered there but recent research has established that, in fact, on his way he stayed in Egypt, where he died.

In addition to his poems, Halevi is renowned for his very influential philosophical treatise, the *Kuzari*, originally written in Arabic but later translated into Hebrew. Halevi structured this work around the accounts of a heathen tribe, the *Khazars, whose king and people became converted to Judaism; the *Kuzari* consisting of a dialogue between a Jewish sage and the king of the Khazars.

On revelation, Halevi remarks that Judaism, unlike Christianity and Islam, affirms that God revealed Himself not to a single person but to the 600,000 Israelites who came out of Egypt. He implies that an event witnessed by so many people must be true, whereas a claim by an individual to have received a divine revelation can easily be the result of sheer delusion. That Halevi did not see that he was begging the question, since we are informed that the 600,000 were present only in the Torah itself, is to be explained on the grounds that Christianity and Islam, Judaism's rivals, admitted that the original revelation to Israel took place, but, they claimed, it had been superseded by the revelation to Jesus or Muhammad.

Judah the Prince Nasi ('Prince') of the Palestinian community (d. *c.*217 CE), known simply as Rabbi, that is, Rabbi *par excellence*. Rabbi Judah the Prince was the son of Rabban Simeon ben *Gamaliel II. Many tales are told in the Talmudic literature of his close friendship with the Roman emperor Antoninus, but the legendary nature of these

tales is so blatant that attempts by some scholars to identify him with this emperor seem utterly pointless. The tales are obviously intended to illustrate the comparatively less strained relationships between the Jewish community and the Roman government in Rabbi Judah's time. Rabbi Judah the Prince was evidently a man of great wealth and position. As the Talmud puts it, he possessed both Torah and 'greatness', in other words, he enjoyed both religious and political authority. This dual function enabled him to embark on compiling the authoritative digest of Jewish law and practice, the *Mishnah, containing the teachings of the earlier Tannaim, which became the standard source for the Oral Torah, upon which the Amoraim commented in both Palestine and Babylonia (see TANNAIM AND AMORAIM).

Judah the Saint Mystical teacher and moralist of Regensburg (d. 1217), prominent leader of the *Saints of Germany, and main author of the *Sefer Hasidim*. Judah's system is a blend of the homely and the austere and in it the ideal of suffering martyrdom for the faith occupies a prominent place.

Judges See BET DIN.

Judges, Book of The biblical book that records the history of the 'Judges', the leaders of the people, after Joshua down to the prophet *Samuel, who, according to the Talmud (*Bava Batra* 14b) is the author of the book. Modern scholarship is divided on the question of date and is uncertain about the authorship. Some scholars follow more or less the Talmudic view that the book is early, though not that it was compiled by Samuel. Others believe that the final editing of the book dates from the period after the Babylonian exile in 586 BCE. Although one of the Judges, *Deborah, functioned as a judge in the usual sense of the term, she and the others were chiefly political and military leaders. The superscription to the book of *Ruth has it that the events recorded there took place in the days of the Judges.

Jüdische Wissenschaft 'Jewish Science', the German name for the historical–critical school which arose in the first half of the nineteenth century and whose main practitioners were *Zunz, *Geiger, and *Frankel in Germany; *Luzzatto in Italy; *Krochmal and *Rapoport in Galicia (see HASKALAH and HISTORY). Jüdische Wissenschaft was not a consciously organized movement. Rather, a number of traditionally educated Jews who became familiar with the languages of Western European culture resolved independently, though in close communication with one another, to investigate by these new methods the classical sources of Judaism. The aim of Jüdische Wissenschaft was to demonstrate how the Jewish religion, literature, and philosophy had developed in response to the different civilizations with which Jews had come into contact through the ages. A prior aim of the movement was to establish correct texts by comparing current texts with those found in libraries open to Jews for the first time. Instead of the piecemeal treatment typical of the older approach, texts were studied as a whole and set in their proper period. The Greek and Latin classics were studied for comparative purposes in order to shed light on the Talmudic sources; Arabic and Islamic thought for the better understanding of the medieval Jewish works; the ancient Semitic tongues for a keener appreciation of the Bible and its background; and, above all, world history for the purpose of showing how Jewish history formed part of general historical trends. Indeed, the whole movement called attention to the fact that Judaism, like all human institutions, has had a history and did not simply drop down from heaven to be transmitted without change from generation to generation. New questions were asked. What does the text really mean? Why does it say what it says and why just at that particular time? Does the text represent normative Jewish thinking or is it peripheral or contradicted by other texts and if so, what has caused the difference?

The movement had in part an apologetic aim, as the Wissenschaft scholars sought to show that Judaism, too, is normal and 'respectable' in having a history, a literature, and a philosophy like other cultures and that the great men of the Jewish past were not mere cyphers or irrational isolationists but creatures of flesh and blood responsive to the world around them. Yet the followers of the movement did try to study their sources as objectively as possible, paving the way for the use of the new methodology in higher institutions of Jewish learning and in learned journals in which articles of impeccable scholarship appeared.

Justice The biblical injunction: 'Justice, justice shall you pursue' (Deuteronomy 16: 20), addressed originally to judges and those who appoint them, became a key text in Judaism for the pursuit of justice by all in daily living. The repetition of the word denotes a passion for justice, as if the cry is: 'Justice, only justice, shall you pursue.' The pursuit of justice is urged throughout the Bible. Of the prophets, *Amos in particular calls on his own people and the surrounding nations to practise justice. Amos declares: 'Let justice well up like water, righteousness like an unfailing stream' (Amos 5: 24). The patriarch Abraham, when pleading on behalf of Sodom, challenges God Himself to practise justice: 'Shall not the judge of all the earth deal justly?' (Genesis 18: 25).

Kabbalah The mystical, theosophical system developed in the eleventh and twelfth centuries, culminating in the *Zohar, and later reinterpreted and recast by Isaac *Luria, the Ari, in sixteenth-century Safed. Essentially, there are two distinct Kabbalistic systems, the Zoharic and the Lurianic, though the latter sees itself as no more than an elaboration of the former. The word Kabbalah means 'tradition'. This term was used in the earlier Jewish sources for the Jewish tradition as a whole but was appropriated by the Kabbalists to denote their own secret doctrine, believed to be preserved by the initiates as the true, inner meaning of the Torah reaching back to Moses and even, in some versions, to Adam. Another name for the Kabbalah is, in fact, *Ḥokhmah Nistarah*, 'Secret Science'.

The Kabbalah as found in the Zohar had its origin in twelfth-century Provence in the circle of Isaac the Blind, though various, much earlier, philosophical and mystical trends, Gnostic and Neoplatonic in particular, found their way into the system. From Provence, the doctrine spread to Spain where in Gerona, around the person of the great Halakhist *Nahmanides, who gave it a respectability it might not otherwise have won for itself, the Kabbalah became known to wider circles. At the end of the thirteenth century, the Zohar was compiled, eventually taking its place as the supreme depository of the secret lore and, for many, as the sacred book of Judaism together with the Bible and the Talmud. According to the Kabbalah, there are two aspects of Deity: God as He is in Himself and God in manifestation. God as He is in Himself is known as *En Sof, the Limitless, the Infinite, the ineffable Ground of Being, so far removed from all human apprehension that of It (the impersonal term is sometimes used) nothing can be said at all. En Sof becomes manifest through a process of emanation in the ten *Sefirot, the powers and potencies in the Godhead, from which all creation stems. All worship of En Sof is directed through the Sefirot. These descend through all creation to become manifest in the human psyche so that man is the final link in the great chain of being which he can influence by his deeds. When man is virtuous, he sends beneficent impulses on high to promote harmony among the Sefirot and then the divine grace can flow freely to all creation. When man is vicious he sends baneful impulses on high to disturb the harmony of the Sefirot and then the flow of divine grace is impeded. It has convincingly been argued that, despite its strangeness and seeming incompatibility with pure monotheism, the Kabbalah won acceptance among Jews because of this idea, typical of Judaism, though not in the Kabbalistic form, that man is at the centre of God's world with a role to play given to no other creatures. For the Kabbalists, man literally holds up the heavens.

Attitudes towards the Kabbalah differ among religious Jews. In the nineteenth century, many shared the view of the historian Heinrich *Graetz that the Kabbalah was a foreign importation into Judaism, a resurrection of the old pagan gods, and that the idea of God as both male and female amounted to sheer blasphemy. *Hasidism adapted the Kabbalah to its own philosophy, though believing in the Kabbalah as divinely revealed truth. After the débâcle of *Shabbetai Zevi, the false Messiah whose ideas were based on the Kabbalah, the study of the Kabbalah was discouraged in most Orthodox circles except for those who had amassed a good deal of Talmudic and Halakhic learning and who had reached at least the age of 40, considered to be the age of complete maturity. Many a Jewish teacher, accepting the Kabbalah as true, still recoiled from actual study of the Kabbalah texts. Although, to some extent, *Halakhah and Kabbalah were rivals for the attention of students of the Torah, a number of customs and practices based on the Kabbalah found their way into the standard Codes and are followed by Orthodox Jews even if they are non-Kabbalists or anti-Kabbalists. Reform Judaism in the nineteenth century tended to see the Kabbalah as nothing more than superstition and irrationalism but, nowadays, many Reformers acknowledge that the Kabbalah contains a wealth of insights still of value for the cultivation of Jewish spirituality.

Kaddish 'Sanctification', the doxology in Aramaic in which the hope is expressed that God's great name will be sanctified in the whole world He has created and the *Kingdom of Heaven be established on earth. Originally the Kaddish was recited after an Aggadic homily was delivered by a teacher, since the *Aggadah generally sounds a note of consolation and hope for the future. From the period of the *Geonim the Kaddish was introduced into the *liturgy of the synagogue to mark the end of a section or subsection of the prayers. The subsections conclude with what is known as half-Kaddish, that is, a shorter form containing only the first half of the doxology, and the larger sections with the full Kaddish which contains a prayer for the supplications of Israel to be acceptable to God. After the section in the liturgy that is in the form of a brief Rabbinic discourse, the older, school version of the Kaddish is recited. This contains a prayer for the well-being of students of the Torah and hence is known as Kaddish De-Rab-

banan ('Kaddish of the Rabbis'). At a funeral the sons of the deceased recite an even longer version of the Kaddish in which reference is made to the *resurrection.

In the Middle Ages in Germany Kaddish Yatom ('Mourner's Kaddish') was introduced and this has been adopted by Jews everywhere. A son (in some communities a daughter as well) recites this special Kaddish for eleven months after the death of a parent and on the anniversary (*Yahrzeit) of the death. The principle behind the Mourner's Kaddish is that when the child sanctifies God's name in public by reciting the doxology, merit is accrued to the parent's soul. Very many Jews, otherwise not particularly observant of the rituals, observe meticulously 'saying Kaddish', as it is called, attending services for the purpose each morning and evening since, according to Orthodox practice, Kaddish can only be recited in a *minyan, the quorum of ten males (in Conservative synagogues females count as well).

Kaplan, Mordecai M. Rabbi and influential religious thinker and teacher (1881–1983). Kaplan was born in Svencianys, Lithuania, but emigrated at the age of 9 with his parents to the USA. Kaplan's father, a Rabbi and renowned Talmudist, saw to it that his son received a sound, traditional Jewish education. Young Kaplan also attended general schools in New York and studied at Columbia University and at the Conservative Jewish Theological Seminary in New York, where he received Rabbinic ordination.

As a religious thinker, Kaplan adopted a naturalistic philosophy. His somewhat mechanistic view of science did not allow him to think of God as a Person or Being outside and beyond the universe. God, Kaplan maintained, is best understood by modern Jews as the power that makes for righteousness, that which is present in the universe and in the human psyche which guarantees that righteousness will eventually win out. Prayer, thought of as an appeal to a divine being whom one can influence, belongs, according to Kaplan, to a pre-scientific age. Prayer is rather, for him, reaching towards the highest in the universe and in oneself. The precepts of Judaism are commanded, according to Kaplan, not by the God of tradition but by the God within the Jewish soul, that is, by the ability Jews have to enrich their lives by drawing on all the sources of their glorious past. In Kaplan's famous work, *Judaism as a Civilization*, published in New York in 1934, Judaism is depicted as more than a religion in the narrow sense. Judaism is a whole civilization, at the heart of which, to be sure, is the Jewish religion, but which embraces art, literature, music, folk-ways, in all of which the Jewish spirit finds its fulfilment.

Kapparot 'Atonements', 'expiations'; the rite in which a live cock is waved around the head on the eve of *Yom Kippur and the words recited: 'This is my substitute, this is my vicarious offering, this is my atonement. This cock will go to its death, but I shall have a long and pleasant life of peace.' The superstitious and even pagan elements in the rite were recognized as early as the thirteenth century, when it was opposed by such outstanding Halakhic authorities as *Nahmanides and Solomon Ibn *Adret. *Karo, in the *Shulḥan Arukh* (*Oraḥ Ḥayyim*, 605), follows Ibn Adret in declaring that the rite should be abolished but *Isserles, in his gloss, records the rite as a worthy custom and provides the details of its observance. As a result, the rite is still performed by the more strictly Orthodox Jews, although some now substitute a sum of money, later given to charity, for the cock and alter the wording accordingly. Where a cock is used, it is slaughtered and given to the poor or its value given to the poor. The rite of Kapparot features

strongly in discussions of which Jewish *customs should be retained and which abolished.

Karaites The sect which arose in the eighth century CE; Heb. *Keraim*, from the root *kara*, 'to read', and so called because they relied on the 'reading' of Scripture in itself, rejecting the Rabbinic interpretations of Scripture found in the Talmud. The story that the sect was founded by Anan ben David when he was passed over for the position of *exilarch in Babylonia, is viewed with a degree of scepticism by modern scholars while they acknowledge that Anan was a prominent Karaite leader. The Karaites themselves trace their origin back to much earlier times. Maimonides identifies the Karaite *heresy with that of the *Sadducees. This view is not accepted by scholars in the field although certain Sadducean ideas appeared to have enjoyed a subterranean existence until they emerged among the Karaites.

The Karaites were treated as full, though heretical, Jews in the Middle Ages; many Rabbinic authorities permitted marriages between Rabbinites and Karaites. But eventually the breach between the two communities so widened that neither saw the other as belonging to the same religion. It has been estimated that there are around 20,000 Karaites in the State of Israel, organized as a separate religious community with its own religious authorities.

Karet 'Excision', 'cutting off', the biblical penalty, for certain offences, of being 'cut off from the people'; for example, for failing to be circumcised (Genesis 17: 14); for eating leaven on Passover (Exodus 12: 19); and for committing incest (Leviticus 20: 17). The Mishnah (*Keritot* 1: 1) lists thirty-six offences for which the penalty is *karet*. The chief problem here is the meaning of *karet*. Josephus (*Antiquities of the Jews* 3. 12: 1) remarks: 'To those who were guilty of such insolent behaviour, he [Moses] ordered death for his punishment', implying that *karet* is identical with other death penalties in the Pentateuch. This view is accepted by many biblical scholars but fails to explain why this term is used instead of 'he shall be put to death', that is, by the hands of the court. Other modern scholars hold that *karet* denotes some kind of exclusion from the community, the offender being 'cut off', that is, excluded from the community. But the penalty of *karet* is limited to purely religious offences and is never enjoined for offences such as murder, the penalty for which is judicial execution. Consequently, the unanimous Rabbinic view, as stated in the Talmud, has much to commend it, that *karet* is a form not of human but of divine punishment, though it is unclear how *karet* differs from the other divine penalty mentioned in the sources, 'death by the hand of Heaven'. In one view, *karet* means a divine punishment of death before the age of 60, which is why a Talmudic Rabbi had a party on his sixtieth *birthday. In another version *karet* means that the offender will die childless. This whole area is very obscure and is largely ignored in present-day Jewish theology.

Karo, Joseph Outstanding lawyer and mystic (1488–1575). Karo was probably born in Toledo but, after the expulsion of the Jews from Spain in 1492, his family settled in Turkey where Karo lived for around forty years, acquiring a great reputation as an authority on Jewish law. In 1536 he left Turkey for Safed, serving there until his death as a Rabbi and Head of a *Yeshivah. In Safed he became closely associated with the mystical circle that flourished there.

Karo wrote a commentary, entitled *Kesef Mishneh*, to Maimonides' Code and another commentary, his greatest work, on the Tur of *Jacob ben Asher, to which he gave the title *Bet Yosef*

(*House of Joseph*), because in it he provided a home for all the legal opinions held by the jurists of the past. In his introduction to the *Bet Yosef*, Karo remarks that he was moved to compile it because there was so much uncertainty about the actual law in practice, each Jewish community seeming to have its own 'Torah'. The Tur, he thought, is the best starting-point for the task he had set himself, since in this work, too, many different opinions are recorded. But Karo seeks to go further than the Tur in an analysis of the law as it developed from Talmudic times down to his own day. The *Bet Yosef* is probably the keenest work of legal analysis in the history of Jewish law.

Karo recorded the decisions in every branch of practical law at which he had arrived in his digest, the *Shulḥan Arukh*, which, together with the glosses of *Isserles, became the standard Code for all Orthodox Jews.

Kavvanah 'Intention', 'concentration', directing the mind to the meaning of words uttered or acts performed. The question of Kavvanah is discussed with regard to prayer and with regard to the performance of the *precepts. In connection with the precepts, the Talmud, in a number of places, records a debate among the teachers about whether Kavvanah is essential. All agree that the ideal is to have the intention of carrying out a precept, *mitzvah, when one is about to carry it out to demonstrate that the act is not a mechanical one but is carried out in order to do God's will. The debate is with regard to the *de facto* situation where the *mitzvah* has been carried out unwittingly. An example, referred to in the Mishnah (*Rosh Ha-Shanah*, 3. 7), is where a man passing by outside the synagogue on *Rosh Ha-Shanah at a time when the *shofar* was being sounded, heard the *shofar* sounds but did not listen to them with the intention of carrying out the *mitzvah*. Is he obliged to hear the *shofar* sounds again with full intention to carry out the *mitzvah* or does it suffice that he has heard the *shofar* sounds after all, albeit without intention? In other words, is a *mitzvah* carried out without the intention to carry it out, no *mitzvah* at all or, *de facto* at least, is the act counted as a *mitzvah* since it is the act in itself which ultimately counts? The Codes are divided on the question and the usual advice given is that the *mitzvah* should be carried out again but without the prior benediction: 'Who has commanded us to . . .'. It would seem, indeed, that the main purpose of the *benedictions recited before the performance of the *mitzvot* is to direct the mind to the act by stating beforehand that it is done in obedience to the divine command.

Kavvanah in prayer involves chiefly proper concentration on the meaning of the words uttered. A saying of *Bahya, Ibn Pakudah has often been quoted: 'Prayer without Kavvanah is like a body without a soul.' But here, too, the ideal is one thing, its realization in practice quite another. The medieval thinkers were fully aware of how difficult it is, especially since the prayers are in Hebrew, to concentrate adequately all or even most of the time. Although, strictly speaking, where Kavvanah was absent the prayers have to be recited again with Kavvanah, this stringency was relaxed so as to apply only to the first verse of the *Shema and the first paragraph of the Amidah (see EIGHTEEN BENEDICTIONS).

Later religious teachers continued to grapple with the problem of Kavvanah in prayer. *Hasidism in particular is much concerned with the techniques of Kavvanah in prayer and with how to cope with distracting thoughts. A main reason why early Reform Judaism preferred that many of the prayers should be recited in the vernacular, rather than in the traditional Hebrew, was because of the conviction that proper concentration is only possible when prayers are recited in a language with which one is familiar from birth.

Kedushah Sanctification of God's name during the Reader's repetition of the Amidah (see EIGHTEEN BENEDICTIONS). During the Reader's repetition, when he reaches the third paragraph, the theme of which is God's holiness, he declares: 'We will sanctify Thy name in the world even as they sanctify it in the highest heavens, as it is written by the hand of Thy prophet: "And they called one unto the other and said, Holy, holy, holy is the Lord of hosts; the whole earth is full of His glory" [Isaiah 63].' From 'Holy, holy, holy' onwards is chanted by the congregation. The Reader continues: 'Those over against them say, Blessed', to which the congregation responds: 'Blessed be the glory of the Lord from His place' (Ezekiel 3: 12). The Reader continues: 'And in Thy holy words it is written, saying', to which the congregation responds: 'The Lord shall reign for ever, thy God, O Zion, unto all generations. Hallelujah' (Psalms 146: 10).

The Kedushah is thus a re-enactment by the congregation on earth of the angelic praising of God on high. In one Talmudic passage it is stated that the *angels do not begin their song until Israel has recited the *Shema on earth and that, moreover, the divine name occurs in the Shema after only two words ('Hear' and 'Israel') whereas the angelic hosts are only permitted to give utterance to the divine name after three words ('Holy, holy, holy').

Ketubah The marriage contract by which a bridegroom obligates himself to provide a settlement for his wife if he divorces her, or his heir if he predeceases her. *Ketubah*, from the root *katav*, 'to write', is the name for both the written contract itself and for the amount the husband is obliged to settle on his wife. The main purpose of the *ketubah* is to prevent a husband divorcing his wife against her will, which, in Talmudic times, he had the right to do (see DIVORCE). The knowledge that he had to pay his wife her *ketubah* would serve as a check against hasty divorce. In addition to the basic settlement, the husband undertakes in the *ketubah* to protect his wife, work for her, provide her with her marital rights and with all that is necessary for her due sustenance. Since it was a legal document and had to be understood by both parties the *ketubah* was written in Aramaic, the vernacular in Talmudic times. This form is still preserved in the traditional *ketubah*, though in Anglo-Jewry and elsewhere there is an English translation on the back of the document.

The *ketubah* is essentially a statement of the husband's obligations. The obligations of the wife to her husband are not recorded in the *ketubah*. Most Reform Jews today, therefore, prefer a different version of the *ketubah* which is more egalitarian. It has long been the practice in many communities to have illuminated *ketubot*, with paintings of birds, flowers, and other ornamental features. Illuminated *ketubot* from the nineteenth century and earlier are now collector's items.

Khazars A Turkish people whose kingdom endured from the seventh to the eleventh centuries. There is a solid basis in fact behind the stories circulating in the Middle Ages that a king of the Khazars and his people with him converted to Judaism. The mere fact that such a kingdom of Jews had existed provided medieval Jewry with hope for the future. *Judah Halevi's *Kuzari* consists of an imaginary dialogue between the king of the Khazars and a Jewish sage after which the king is moved to accept the Jewish religion in its Rabbinic formulation. Arthur Koestler's attempt (*The Thirteenth Tribe*, London, 1976) to show that all *Ashkenazi Jews are descended from the Khazars is purely speculative, has nothing to

commend it, and is repudiated by all Khazar scholars.

Kibbutz 'Gathering', the collective, socialistic settlement in the State of Israel which had its origins in the early years of the twentieth century. The kibbutz movement believed that the establishment of kibbutzim was the best method of reclaiming the land of Israel. The influence of the highly idealistic kibbutzniks was enormous and their important contribution was acknowledged from the days of early Zionism. It has to be appreciated that the kibbutz was a secular movement, though obviously based on Jewish ideals, especially the ethical norms of Judaism. Most of the kibbutzim were and are largely unobservant of the Jewish rituals or, rather, they sought to develop a secular, nationalistic form of some observances and ritual, in the celebration of the festivals, for example, in a new form, and in the creation of new festivals based on the land. However, the Kibbutz Ha-Dati is an organization of religious kibbutzim, the slogan of which is 'Torah Va-Avodah' ('Torah and Work on the Land'), implying the socialist ideal wedded to full observance of Jewish law.

Kiddush Sanctification of the Sabbath. On Friday night, when the Sabbath begins, the Kiddush ceremony is carried out before sitting down to the Sabbath meal. A cup of wine is filled and held in the hand by the person presiding, usually but not necessarily the father of the house, and the benediction over wine recited (see BENEDICTIONS). Then the Kiddush proper is recited:

'Blessed art Thou, O Lord our God, King of the universe, who hath hallowed us by Thy commandments and hast taken pleasure in us, and in love and favour hast given us Thy holy Sabbath as an inheritance, a memorial of the creation—that day being also the first day of the holy convocations, in remembrance of the departure from Egypt. For Thou hast chosen us and hallowed us above all nations, and in love and favour hast given us Thy holy Sabbath as an inheritance. Blessed art Thou, O Lord, who hallowest the Sabbath.'

As a prelude to the Kiddush the verses of the creation narrative which speak of the Sabbath (Genesis 2: 1–3) are recited. After the drinking of the wine, the benediction over bread is recited and the family partakes of the Sabbath meal.

Kiddush Ha-Shem Sanctification of the name (of God), the opposite of Hillul Ha-Shem, the profanation of the name (of God). These two concepts, prominent in Jewish thought from Talmudic times, are based by the Rabbis on the verse: 'You shall not profane My holy name, that I may be sanctified in the midst of the children of Israel—I am the Lord who sanctify you' (Leviticus 22: 32). In the Rabbinic interpretation, the verse implies that a Jew must so conduct himself that his actions increase reverence for God's name and that none of them should bring the divine name into disrepute. Israel must be a holy people because Israel has been sanctified by God (see CHOSEN PEOPLE) and bears His holy name. The stress is placed on the words 'in the midst of the children of Israel', that is, on public conduct. Not every sin constitutes Hillul Ha-Shem and not every virtuous act Kiddush Ha-Shem but only deeds, whether good or bad, that are carried out in public and thus either decrease or increase respect for Judaism. To suffer *martyrdom rather than be faithless to the Jewish religion is the supreme example of Kiddush Ha-Shem. If a man is ready to die in public for his faith, there can be no more powerful attestation to its truth. But to suffer martyrdom is obviously quite extraordinary and is only demanded by Jewish law in extremely rare instances. Numerous examples are given in the sources of Kiddush Ha-Shem and Hillul Ha-Shem in ordinary living by the light of Judaism.

Kiddush Ha-Shem in the daily round involves actions, not necessarily enjoined by strict law, which bring credit to Jews and through them to the Jewish religion given by God. The idea behind this is that a religion that can inspire men to act so justly and so sympathetically is a noble religion. An illustration given in the Jerusalem Talmud is of the early teacher Simeon ben Shatah, a poor man who earned his living by selling flax. His pupils, desiring to spare him from too much hard work, bought him a donkey from a Saracen and found that a pearl was attached to it. They told him that he would no longer have to work so hard because his sorry financial situation would be eased by his acquisition of a pearl of such great value. But Simeon insisted that the pearl be returned to its rightful owner, even though a case could have been made in strict law for Simeon to keep the pearl. Simeon declared that he would rather hear the heathen say: 'Blessed be the God of the Jews' than have any reward this world has to offer.

The deeper theological meaning of Kiddush Ha-Shem is that God as He is in Himself is unknown and unknowable. God only becomes manifest in human life when human beings acknowledge Him by acting in such a way that His being is relevant to and influences their daily life. Professor Hugo Bergmann's famous essay entitled *Kiddush Ha-Shem* (translated into English in *Commentary* (March, 1952), 271 ff.) is rightly given the subtitle: *God Depends on Man, as Man on God.*

Kimhi, David Biblical exegete of Narbonne in Provence (*c.*1160–*c.*1235), known, after the initial letters of his name (Rabbi David Kimhi) as Radak. Kimhi was renowned as a philosopher and grammarian but his permanent claim to fame rests on his biblical commentaries, printed together with the text in many editions of the Hebrew Bible. These commentaries were so highly regarded by later generations that the saying in Ethics of the Fathers: 'Where there is no flour [*kemah*, i.e. no means of earning one's bread] there is no Torah' was adapted as: 'Where there is no Kimhi there is no Torah', that is, without Kimhi's commentaries the Bible is a closed book. The English translators of the King James Version relied heavily on Kimhi's insights.

Kingdom of Heaven Heb. *Malkhut Shamayyim*, the Rabbinic expression for the sovereignty of God as acknowledged by human beings; hence the frequent expression: 'acceptance of the yoke of the Kingdom of Heaven'. The Mishnah (*Berakhot* 2: 2) understands the reading of the *Shema to be the 'acceptance of the yoke of the Kingdom of Heaven'. The kingly metaphor is found in the Bible in the verse: 'The Lord shall reign for ever and ever' (Exodus 15: 18) and in the verse: 'And the Lord shall be king over all the earth: in that day shall the Lord be One and His name one' (Zechariah 14: 9). Both these verses are recited at the end of the Alenu prayer which looks forward to the day 'when the world will be perfected under the kingdom of the Almighty, and all the children of flesh will call upon Thy name'.

Solomon *Schechter rightly detects three aspects of the Kingdom of God: 1. the personalistic and individualistic, the acceptance of the yoke, as when reading the Shema; 2. the universalistic, in which the establishment of the Kingdom over all is the hoped-for Messianic event; and 3. the nationalistic, in which the people of Israel is redeemed from subservience to earthly rulers to worship God in freedom. In the Kabbalistic doctrine of the *Sefirot, the lowest of the Sefirot is *Malkhut*, 'Sovereignty', the divine principle by which the world is governed.

Kings, Book of The book in the Bible in which are related the histories of the kings of Judah and Israel from David and Solomon down to the last of the kings of Judah. In present editions of the Bible Kings is divided into two books, and this division has become the accepted one, although in the Jewish tradition the two form a single book. According to the Talmud (*Bava Batra* 15a) the author of the book is the prophet *Jeremiah. Modern biblical scholarship prefers a later date, since events recorded in the book took place after Jeremiah's death. The book itself states explicitly that some of its contents are derived from early histories such as 'the book of the acts of Solomon', 'the book of the chronicles of the kings of Judah', and 'the book of the chronicles of the kings of Israel'.

Kittel From the German word meaning a 'smock'; a long white shirt worn over the outer garments. The kittel is one of the shrouds in which the corpse is dressed (see DEATH AND BURIAL). The kittel is also worn by the Reader, and by many congregants, during the service on *Rosh Ha-Shanah and *Yom Kippur, as a reminder of death on these penitential occasions; as a symbol of purity; and in order to resemble the *angels who are 'clothed in white'. For similar reasons, it is the custom in some communities for the bridegroom to wear the kittel during the marriage service. Some Jews also wear the kittel at the *Seder on *Passover. The wearing of the kittel on these occasions arose among German Jews and is still largely restricted to the *Ashkenazim.

Kohen 'Priest', a descendant of *Aaron the priest, plural Kohamin. The priestly caste officiated in the Temple and have certain functions to perform even after the destruction of the Temple. The Jewish family name, Cohen, usually denotes that its members were *priests. In Temple times no one was admitted to the priesthood unless he could prove his priestly descent. In later times rigorous proof was no longer possible, so that Kohanim today act as such on the basis of presumptive status—the mere fact that a family tradition believes that it is formed of Kohanim is sufficient to establish its status as such. A Kohen may not come into contact with a corpse unless it is of a near relative (Leviticus 21: 1–4); and he may not marry a divorcee (Leviticus 21: 7). It is the Kohen's privilege to be the first of the persons called to the *reading of the Torah. Where a Kohen is present at the table he has the right to recite the *grace after Meals, though he can waive this right if he chooses. Kohanim also recite the priestly *blessing in the synagogue. These rules are followed by all Orthodox Jews. Reform Jews reject the laws concerning Kohanim in the rather fanciful belief that they tend to perpetuate a caste system in Judaism. Conservative Jews are less categorical in the matter but many Conservative Rabbis also hold that the laws about the Kohanim are in abeyance today, especially since, nowadays, those who claim to be Kohanim only enjoy their privilege by presumptive status.

Kol Nidre 'All vows', the opening words of the declaration, largely in Aramaic, at the beginning of the evening service on *Yom Kippur in which all *vows that will be uttered in the coming year are declared null and void. The declaration applies only to religious vows and has no effect on *oaths taken in a court of law. If a person makes a vow, say, to deny himself wine for a certain period, perhaps as a penance, he must keep his promise, which is thought of as a promise to God. But this applies only if the vow is uttered with full intent. A person's declaration beforehand that all vows he will take in

the year ahead are null and void means that any vow he will make is held to be without sufficient intention and hence without binding power. Because it was falsely assumed that Kol Nidre does apply to oaths taken in the court, Jews were suspected of unreliability in this matter and in a number of countries the infamous More Judaica, a special humiliating form of oath, was introduced when a Jew had to swear in court. Zechariah *Frankel and others in nineteenth-century Germany exposed the falsehood and explained the true meaning of Kol Nidre. In the Middle Ages a number of Rabbinic authorities were opposed to the Kol Nidre on the grounds that its effectiveness to nullify vows was very questionable. Yet the Kol Nidre is still recited in the majority of congregations, the night of Yom Kippur being referred to as 'Kol Nidre Night'. There is no doubt that it is the famous traditional melody, with its note of remorse, contrition, hope, and triumph, that has saved the Kol Nidre. Reform congregations often substitute a Psalm for the Kol Nidre formulation but retain the melody.

Kook, Abraham Isaac Rabbi, Kabbalist, and religious thinker, first Chief Rabbi of the Land of Israel (1865–1935). Kook was born in the small town of Greiva in Latvia. He studied at the famous Yeshivah of *Volozhyn. In 1904 Kook was appointed Rabbi of Jaffa. A strong religious Zionist, Kook travelled to Europe in the hope of persuading the recently formed ultra-Orthodox Agudat Israel organization to adopt a more positive Zionist stance. Caught in Europe by the outbreak of World War I in 1914 he stayed in Switzerland until 1916 when he was appointed Rabbi of the Machzikei Ha-Dat synagogue in London. Despite brushes with the Jewish establishment in England, Kook was widely respected by all circles in Anglo-Jewry for his great learning and piety. It is reported that he mastered the English language by reading Rodkinson's (very poor) English translation of the Babylonian Talmud. In 1917 Kook published in London the little work *Rosh Milin (First Words)* on the letters, vowels, and notes for *cantillation of the Hebrew alphabet. Years later, Kook remarked in an aside that he believed he was gifted with the *Holy Spirit when he compiled the work. In this and in his other works Kook's style is obscure, inevitably so since he was searching for new forms of expression to give to old ideas. Fascinated by the paintings of Rembrandt, in which he saw traces of the Kabbalistic idea of the 'hidden light', Kook would go frequently to the National Gallery to study the works of the great master. In 1919 Kook was appointed Ashkenazi Chief Rabbi of Jerusalem and in 1921 Ashkenazi Chief Rabbi of Palestine as a whole.

Kosher

Ashkenazi pronunciation of the Hebrew world *kasher* meaning 'fit' or 'suitable', as in the verse: 'The thing seems right [*kasher*] in the eyes of the king' (Esther 8: 5). The most frequent use of the term kosher is in connection with the *dietary laws. A food that it is permitted for a Jew to eat is called kosher, hence the abstract name kashrut for the dietary laws. The term *glatt* ('smooth') kosher originally denoted that when the lungs of an animal had been examined they were found to be 'smooth', that is, without adhesions that might render the animal forbidden. But in recent years the term *glatt* kosher has come to refer to extreme punctiliousness in the preparation of food for Jews to eat, as when an establishment prides itself that it provides only *glatt* kosher food. The term kosher is applied to other matters as well, as when a Scroll of the Torah, *Sefer Torah, is declared to be kosher, that is, properly written. In modern slang the term is applied to anything that is right and above-board, as, for example, when a business deal is said to be kosher. An upright Jew is often described as a kosher Jew.

Kotsk, Menahem Mendel of

Hasidic master (1787–1859), also known as 'the Seraph' because of his holy life and fiery temperament. In his youth Menahem Mendel was a follower of Simhah Bunem of Przysucha. The Przysucha branch of Hasidism placed the emphasis on intellectual ability, inwardness, and sincerity. When Simhah Bunem died, Menahem Mendel was elected by his colleagues to the leadership of the group. Menahem Mendel was a stern master, having little truck with the ordinary Hasidim who came to ask him to pray on their behalf for children, health, and prosperity. His appeal was chiefly to the select few, the sincere God-seekers willing to sacrifice everything to the quest. He once declared that his ambition was to raise 200 chosen disciples who would go onto the roofs loudly to proclaim: 'The Lord, He is God.' The Kotsker Hasidim were notorious for their disdain of outward religiosity and moral pretence. It was said of the Kotsker group that, unlike others who sinned in private and were virtuous in public, they were sinful in public and virtuous in private. Some Kotsker Hasidim would often sit up all night playing cards and then meet together in stealth to recite the morning prayers. Such a parade of apparent impiety was anathema to the staid, even in the Hasidic camp. The rigours of Menahem Mendel's tormented life and his total disregard for the opinion of others (he is similar in this respect to the Danish thinker Kierkegaard) seem to have produced in him severe traumas. The Kotsker regime, with all its severities, seemed doomed to failure but was saved through the activities of the Kotsker's brother-in-law, Isaac Meir Alter (1789–1866), who functioned as Hasidic master in the little town of Gora Kalwaria, known to the Hasidim as Ger. The Gerer dynasty, still very powerful, considers itself to be in the traditions of Kotsk but with a more humane face.

Krochmal, Nachman Philosopher, scholar, and leading figure (1785–1840) in the *Haskalah and *Jüdische Wissenschaft movements. Krochmal's father, a wealthy merchant in the Galician town of Brody, saw to it that his son received a traditional Jewish education in Bible, Talmud, and the Codes. At the early age of 14 Krochmal was married and, supported by his father-in-law after the fashion of those days, he continued his studies, acquiring a knowledge of German and German literature and philosophy, especially the works of Kant, Herder, and Hegel. Krochmal was entirely self-educated in general learning but his erudition was both extensive and profound. He would often bemoan the fact, however, that he never had an opportunity of studying at a university. In Brody, Lvov, and Zolkiew, Krochmal gathered around him a small group of earnest seekers after the new knowledge; some of these young men later followed in his footsteps as thinkers and historians of Judaism. Krochmal's *Moreh Nevukhey Ha-Zeman* (*Guide for the Perplexed of the Time*) was based on Maimonides' *Guide of the Perplexed*, although the title was given by *Zunz, who published the work in 1851 after Krochmal's death. What Zunz rightly saw as the difference between the two *Guides* lay in the very different challenges to which the authors responded. Maimonides' 'perplexed' were concerned with trying to reconcile Judaism with the Aristotelian philosophy dominant in the Middle Ages. No one was at all perplexed in this way in Krochmal's day when the source of confusion was the problem of 'Time', caused by the increasing awareness that Judaism, like all other religions and cultures, has had a history. Krochmal's intention was to show how Judaism had developed historically, contrary to the traditional view held in his day by his co-religionists in Galicia, that the Jewish religion was simply transmitted more or less intact from generation to generation.

Although Krochmal was a strictly observant Jew, his ideas were viewed with disfavour by the Orthodox Rabbis of his day, who were suspicious of any attempt to see Judaism in terms of historical development because this suggested a degree of relativism. Krochmal believed that the modern Jew was bound by his sense of integrity to acknowledge the developing nature of his religion without surrendering his loyalty to traditional forms, especially those of the *Halakhah; although, in Krochmal's view, Halakhah, too, has had a history. Krochmal, at the beginning of his *Guide*, quotes a passage from the Jerusalem Talmud in which it is stated that the Jew is confronted with two paths in life, one of fire, the other of ice. If he proceeds along the path of fire he will be burnt. If he proceeds along the path of ice he will be frozen. What should the wise man do? He should walk in the middle. This became Krochmal's slogan. The path of fire, of uncritical and unreasoning enthusiasm typical of Hasidism, a movement of which Krochmal was less than enamoured, encourages ignorance and leads to all kinds of vagaries and superstitions. The path of ice, on the other hand, the path of cold reason uninspired by true religious feeling, leads to a rejection of Judaism and total assimilation. The wise man, for Krochmal the informed Maskil, follower of the Haskalah, knows how to walk in the middle. Such a Jew allows both his reason and his emotions to control his life.

Ladino From Latino (Latin), the Judaeo-Spanish language spoken by Sephardi Jews, comparable to *Yiddish, spoken by Ashkenazi Jews.

Lag Ba-Omer The thirty-third day of (the counting of) the *Omer, the minor festival that falls on 18 Iyyar. Lag is formed from the combination of the Hebrew letters *lamed*, with the numerical value of thirty, and *gimmel*, with the numerical value of three. This minor festival goes back to the Geonic (see GEONIM) period but its origin is rather obscure. The traditional explanation is that the disciples of Rabbi *Akiba died in a plague during the Omer period and this ceased on the thirty-third day of the Omer. Some scholars understand the 'plague' to be a veiled reference to the war against Rome but there is no firm evidence for such a contention. Yet it is interesting that the folk-custom developed of teachers going out into the fields with their pupils on this day to play shooting-matches with bows and arrows.

According to the Kabbalah, Rabbi *Simeon ben Yohai, the reputed author of the Zohar, died on this day, his death being referred to as the 'marriage' of Rabbi Simeon, because his soul was reunited with its Source. From the seventeenth century pilgrimages were made to the grave of Rabbi Simeon in Meron near Safed on Lag Ba-Omer and these are still observed today. Various ceremonies take place at Meron, some of them bizarre, such as burning costly garments in honour of the saint. Bonfires are lit in other places in Israel on this day and the devotees dance around the fire while chanting hymns in Rabbi Simeon's honour. Prominent Rabbis in the last century looked askance at these practices but they were defended by the Rabbi of Safed. Little boys in Meron have their first haircut on Lag Ba-Omer. Although marriages do not take place during the Omer period, they are permitted on this day.

Lamedvovniks Literally, 'thirty-sixers', from the Hebrew letters *lamed*, thirty, and *vav* (in Yiddish pronunciation, *vov*), six, together with the Russian ending 'nik', 'belonging to', popular in Yiddish. The notion of the Lamedvovniks goes back to the Talmud (*Sukkah* 45b) where it is said that there are never less than thirty-six *saints in each generation who are given a sight of the *Shekhinah daily. In the Talmud and other early sources there is no attempt to identify these saints. They are simply individual good men without any necessary relation to one another. But in later Jewish legend, from the eighteenth century, the idea took root that the Lamedvovniks are hidden saints, seemingly ordinary people, usually artisans living in little villages, who do not know the identity of the other thirty-five and may not even know that they themselves belong to the charmed circle and, if they do know, will deny it when questioned.

Lamentations, Book of The biblical book consisting of elegies over the fall of Jerusalem and the destruction of the First Temple in 586 BCE; Heb., after the opening word, *Ekhah*, 'How'. In chapters 1, 2, and 4, each verse begins with a letter of the alphabet from *alef* to *tav* and in chapter 3 there are three verses for each letter of the alphabet. Chapter 5, the final chapter of the book, is not in the form of an alphabetic acrostic but contains twenty-two verses, the number of the letters of the alphabet. It can readily be seen, therefore, that the book is in contrived form, despite its sombre theme. Poetry is 'emotion recollected in tranquillity'. The traditional author of Lamentations is none other than the prophet *Jeremiah, who witnessed the destruction of the Temple. Modern scholars have found no support for the traditional view but largely agree that internal evidence does show that the book was composed by a contemporary or contemporaries of the events of which it tells. The book of Lamentations is chanted in the synagogue to a melancholy tune on the night of the fast of Tisha Be-Av, the Ninth of *Av.

Landau, Ezekiel Prominent Rabbinic leader and authority (1713–93). Landau was born in Poland but in 1755 was invited to become Rabbi of Prague, a position he occupied until his death. Landau, although he had studied Kabbalah in his youth, was opposed to its study except by the most erudite because of the danger of Shabbateanism (see SHABBETAI ZEVI), a movement which relied on the Kabbalah for its heretical approach to Judaism. He disliked the use of Kabbalistic terminology in *Hasidism and had little regard for the unlearned Hasidim whom he accused of spiritual arrogance in adopting the mystic way reserved for the initiates.

Landau's fame rests chiefly on his *Noda Biyhudah* ('Known in Judah'), a voluminous collection of *Responsa in which he replied to Rabbis and other scholars from many parts of the Jewish world. Landau's legal decisions still enjoy great authority for Orthodox Jews.

Law The Greek translation of Torah as *nomos* is followed in the English versions of the Bible in which Torah is rendered as 'the Law' with the result that Judaism is often described as a religion of law and, contrasted by some authors with Christianity, said to be a religion of love. While there is a degree of truth in this characterization, it is far too sweeping both with regard to Judaism and to Christianity. A passion for *justice, and respect and even love for the laws of the Torah, are remote from the legalism in which only actions count (see KAVVANAH). The charge of legalism is hotly denied by the majority of Jews. *Halakhah does occupy a prominent place in Judaism in the belief that there is a right and wrong way of doing things exemplified in the Halakhah. But Halakhah, the legal side of Judaism, is complemented by the *Aggadah, comprising the non-legal aspects of the Jewish religion. Judaism has its detailed laws but it also has its history, philosophy, ethics, and mysticism to redeem the religion from narrowness and rigidity. Moreover, discussions of the Halakhah itself are often conducted in a poetic spirit known to every student of the Talmud, the great depository of Jewish law. As Rabbi A. I. *Kook has remarked: 'Just as there are laws of poetry there is poetry in laws.'

Some of the greatest legal minds in Jewry had powerful interests beyond the Halakhah. Maimonides, author of the great Code, the *Mishneh Torah*, is also the author of the probing philosophical work, *Guide of the Perplexed*. The notable exponent of the Halakhah, *Nahmanides, was a Kabbalist and author of a comprehensive biblical commentary. Joseph *Karo, author of the standard Code of Jewish Law, the *Shulḥan Arukh*, kept a mystical diary for forty years in which he recorded his soul-searchings and his visions. This does not mean that Judaism has never known scholars and pietists who emphasized the legal aspect to the virtual exclusion of any other. But the Aggadah, too, has had its one-sided enthusiasts with little taste for law. Both Halakhah and Aggadah have their place in normal expressions of Judaism.

Law, Rabbinic Religious laws introduced by the Talmudic Rabbis and other early sages in order to create, as it is put in Ethics of the Fathers (1. 1), a 'fence around the Torah', that is, to add restrictions, over and above those found in the Bible, so as to keep people away from any risk of infringing biblical law. For instance, according to biblical law, it is forbidden to saw wood on the Sabbath but there is no prohibition against handling a saw or other such tools. This is forbidden by Rabbinic law on the principle that if one is not allowed even to handle tools on the Sabbath, there is less risk that the tools will be used.

There is considerable discussion in the sources on the right of the Rabbis to introduce laws not found in the Bible. Authorities like Maimonides believe that the Bible itself provides the sanction for the sages of Israel to promulgate such laws. *Nahmanides, on the other hand, defends the right of the Rabbis on the grounds that their intention is to preserve the Torah. Nevertheless, Rabbinic law is treated less severely than biblical law. Doubt in cases of Rabbinic law is treated leniently while doubt in cases of biblical law is treated strictly. In any event, the principle of consensus of the Jewish community comes into operation and Rabbinic law is binding ultimately because Jews have accepted it as part of their religion (see AUTHORITY).

Leah The biblical matriarch, wife of Jacob, whose story is told in the book of Genesis (29–31). Leah is one of the four *matriarchs of the Jewish people.

Leibowitz, Yeshayahu Israeli scientist and controversial religious thinker (1903–94). Leibowitz's contribution to chemistry, biochemistry, and neurophysiology is immense. But his main claim to fame, others would say to notoriety, are his severe criticisms of Israeli policy. He believed that the sole advantage, a very considerable one to be sure, of the emergence of the State of Israel is that it has provided Jews with a homeland in which, as he was fond of saying, they no longer have to be bossed around by goyyim. For him, to see a deeper religious significance in the emergence of Israel verges on State-worship.

Leibowitz was a strictly observant Jew, believing the *Halakhah to be the sole guiding principle for Jews. Yet he accepted the findings of *biblical criticism in his conviction that the origin of the commandments is irrelevant to their binding force. Attempts at refuting Darwin and the Bible critics, he remarks, are to see God as a superior Professor of Biology or Semitics. For Leibowitz, a *mitzvah*, a precept of the Torah, constitutes an opportunity to serve God and any attempt to see it in terms of human betterment, even of a spiritual nature, is to prefer self-worship to worship of the Creator. He takes strong issue with the attempts of Maimonides and other medieval thinkers to give 'reasons' for the commandments. Religion is not *for* anything else but is an aim in itself.

'Lekhah Dodi' Heb. for 'Come my friend'; the hymn, of which these are the opening words, sung during the synagogue service on Friday night to welcome the Sabbath. The opening stanza reads: 'Come my friend, to meet the bride; let us welcome the presence of the Sabbath'; and the other stanzas are in praise of the Sabbath and expressions of hope for the restoration of Zion and the Messianic redemption. The practice of welcoming the Sabbath as Israel's bride is mentioned in the Talmud, and on the basis of this the sixteenth-century Kabbalists in *Safed developed an elaborate ritual in which they would go out into the fields dressed in white garments to welcome the Sabbath, identified by them with the *Shekhinah. Solomon Alkabetz, the author of the 'Lekhah Dodi', was a member of this mystic brotherhood and composed the hymn especially for the ritual. The consecutive stanzas begin with the letters of his name to form the nominal acrostic, Shelomo Ha-Levi, 'Solomon the Levite'. 'Lekhah Dodi' is now recited in all Jewish congregations and various melodies have been composed with which to accompany it. The final stanza reads: 'Come in peace, thou crown of thy husband, with rejoicing and with cheerfulness, in the midst of the faithful of the chosen people; come, O bride, come, O bride.'

Leon Da Modena Italian Rabbi, prolific author, poet, and preacher (1571–1648). Da Modena, a typical Renaissance figure, was a man of many parts and contradictions. He was a staunch traditionalist and equally fervent modernist; having written, in his early youth, a treatise against gambling, he was addicted to the vice, which reduced him to penury, during his adult life. He acquired renown as a preacher in Venice, attracting Christians to his sermons as well as Jews. Da Modena had a thorough knowledge of the Talmud and wrote *Responsa, although these were not published from manuscript until as late as the twentieth century. His anti-Christian polemic, *Magen Va-Ḥerev* (*Shield and Sword*) also remained unpublished until the twentieth century. In this work he makes the observation that it is chiefly the doctrine of the Incarnation, which implies that there are three persons in the Godhead, that makes the Christian dogma highly offensive to Jews. The idea that there are three powers in the Godhead is found, in a sense, in the Kabbalah.

Lesbianism See HOMOSEXUALITY.

Leviathan Mythological sea-monster which will struggle with another monster, the Wild Ox, in the Hereafter. Both will be killed in the conflict and God will make a canopy of the skin of Leviathan under which the saints will sit to enjoy the meat of the Wild Ox. The general tendency is to interpret all this metaphorically.

Levirate Marriage The marriage of a widow to a brother of her husband from the same father. According to Leviticus (18: 16) it is forbidden for a man to marry his brother's widow (the verse must be referring to a widow; if the brother is still alive he is forbidden to marry her in any event since she is a married woman). The exception as stated in Deuteronomy (25: 5–10) is where the brother dies without issue. Then one of his brothers is obliged either to take his place by marrying the widow or to release her to marry another by the rite of *Halitzah. There are two opinions in the Talmud as to whether levirate marriage is to be preferred over the release of the widow by the rite of Halitzah. But with the ban on a man having more than one wife (see Rabbenu *Gershom), Halitzah is the only option where the brother is already married and, nowadays, levirate marriage is no longer the rule in all circumstances, even when the brother has no wife. This is the law in the State of Israel. A whole tractate in the Talmud, tractate *Yevamot* ('sisters-in-law'), is devoted to the complicated laws of levirate marriage.

Levites Members of the tribe of Levi, the third son of the patriarch Jacob. Members of the tribe are either *priests, Kohanim (see KOHEN), or Levites, their status being established by family tradition. The family name Levi or Levine generally denotes that the members of the family are Levites. In Temple times the offering of the *sacrifices was the function of the priests. The function of the Levites was to provide the musical accompaniment to the sacrifices, vocally and with musical instruments, and to act as gatekeepers and general guards. Nowadays, a Levite is given the privilege of being called, second to the Kohen, to the reading of the Torah in the synagogue and a Levite washes the hands of the Kohanim before the latter deliver the priestly *blessing.

Leviticus, Book of
The third book of the *Pentateuch, called in Hebrew va-yikra ('And He called'), after the word with which the book begins. Another name is Torat Kohanim ('Priestly Torah') since the majority of the laws in the book have to do with the *sacrifices and other laws appertaining to the *priests. The current title, Leviticus, is derived from the *Septuagint and means 'of the *Levites'. There is very little in the book about the Levites but the name is not inappropriate since the priests also belonged to the tribe of Levi and were 'Levites' as well as Kohanim (see KOHEN). The book also contains laws and exhortations addressed to the people as a whole, including chapter 19, which contains the verse (18): 'Love thy neighbour as thyself' and other directions for holy living, which led the Talmudic Rabbis to declare that this chapter contains the main principles of the Torah. It was customary for school children to begin their studies with the book of Leviticus; as the Rabbis put it, 'Let the pure [the innocent children] busy themselves with purities' (the Levitical laws governing the sacrifices and other purities). This custom of starting off little children with Leviticus has now largely been abandoned except in ultra-Orthodox circles.

The book of Leviticus, in particular, was at the centre of the fierce debates between traditionalists and the critics (see BIBLICAL CRITICISM). The traditional view is that Leviticus, like the rest of the Pentateuch, was written by Moses at the 'dictation' of God. Defenders of the traditional belief point to the fact that throughout the book the words occur: 'And the Lord spoke to Moses.'

Many of the laws are addressed to the situation in the wilderness: the sacrifices, for example, are offered in the Tabernacle, not in the Temple (chapters 1–17). And where the laws are addressed to the people when they will be settled in its land, this is stated explicitly (Leviticus 14: 34; 18: 3; 23: 10; 25: 2). The priests themselves are referred to as 'Aaron and his sons', the priests in the wilderness, not in the Temple. Moreover the book of *Ezekiel quotes or alludes to Leviticus, which shows, at least, that the book, if not Mosaic, is pre-exilic.

On the older critical view, the laws in Leviticus are too complex to have been compiled in the days of Moses; but this argument has been considerably weakened by archaeological evidence that extremely complex rituals were the norm among ancient peoples in the days of Moses. There is thus nothing in the book of Leviticus which automatically rules out Moses as the author. Nevertheless, the standard critical view is that Leviticus and parts of Genesis, Exodus, and Numbers belong to a post-exilic work which the critics refer to as 'P' (standing for the Priestly Document). On the critical view the laws of Leviticus reflect the priestly system, with its hierarchy of Levites, priests, and a *High Priest, read back into the wilderness period. When the book of *Chronicles, the critics argue, is compared with the book of *Kings, the latter probably composed around the year 550 BCE, the former possibly two hundred years later, it can be seen that while Kings says little about worship in *Jerusalem, Chronicles describes a very elaborate cult with features akin to 'P'. The Israeli scholar Ezekiel Kaufmann has argued very plausibly for the view that 'P' is not post-exilic and is earlier than the book of *Deuteronomy, although Kaufmann and his school admit that 'P' is discernible as a unit in the Pentateuch different from other units.

Levi Yitzhak of Berditchev Rabbi and Hasidic master (d. 1810); Levi Yitzhak became a disciple of *Dov Baer the Maggid of Mezhirech in 1766, later becoming a foremost exponent of Hasidism in his writings and through his life. Levi Yitzhak, the most lovable figure among the Hasidic masters, belongs to the folklore of all Jews, not only the Hasidim, in his eloquent pleadings to the Almighty to look with favour on His people. A typical story told in this connection is that when Levi Yitzhak witnessed a Jewish coach-driver greasing the wheels of his carriage while wearing his *tefillin, instead of upbraiding the man, the saint lifted his eyes heavenwards to proclaim: 'See how wonderful Jews are. Even while greasing the wheels of their carriages they wear *tefillin.*'

Levi Yitzhak's work, *Kedushat Levi (Holiness of Levi)* is a commentary in the Hasidic vein to the *Pentateuch and other sacred books. The first part of the work was published in Slavita in 1798, the second part in Berditchev in 1816, since when it has gone into a number of editions and is acknowledged as a supreme Hasidic classic.

Liberal Judaism The English branch of Reform Judaism founded by C. G. *Montefiore. Liberal Judaism in England corresponds to American Reform Judaism and is to the left of both Reform Judaism in England and what used to be called Liberal Judaism in Germany, the last two being closer to left-wing Conservative Judaism in the USA. Such are the complexities of religious labels in contemporary Jewish life.

Life, Book of There is a reference to the Book of Life in Psalms (69: 29) where the Psalmist pleads that wicked men 'be erased from the Book of Life, and not be inscribed with the righteous'. During the *Ten Days of Penitence from *Rosh Ha-Shanah to *Yom Kippur prayers to be inscribed in the Book of Life are added to the Amidah and on the eve of Rosh Ha-Shanah people bless one another that they be inscribed in the Book of Life. Very few Jews think of the Book of Life as a kind of huge ledger in which God inscribes the names of the righteous and from which He erases the names of the wicked. It is widely acknowledged that inscribing in the Book of Life is a powerful metaphor for God's judgement at the beginning of the New Year.

Life, Saving of Judaism places the highest value on the preservation of life. In order to save life the precepts of the Torah must be set aside (except for the offences of murder, idolatry, incest, and adultery). If, for example, the doctors order a man to eat on *Yom Kippur, otherwise his life may be endangered, he is obliged to eat on this sacred fast day. Every effort must be made to save life. The Talmudic Rabbis interpret the verse: 'Neither shalt thou stand idly by the blood of thy neighbour' (Leviticus 19: 16) to mean that if a man is in danger of drowning it is the duty of all who can swim to dive in to save him and the same applies to a man held to ransom by bandits or attacked by wild beasts. Included in the obligation to save life is to take adequate care of one's *health.

Light Light (and *fire) as a symbol for the divine is ubiquitous in the religious literature of Judaism. To refer only to the Psalms: 'light is sown for the righteous' (97: 11); 'the Lord is my light and my salvation' (27: 1); 'at the brightness before Him' (18: 23); 'the commandment of the Lord is pure, enlightening the eyes' (19: 9); 'thy word is a lamp unto my feet, and a light unto my path' (119: 105). In the vision of the divine *Chariot seen by the prophet Ezekiel (ch. 1) the divine is described in terms of flashing lights and the colours of the rainbow. The command to kindle the lights of the *menorah (Exodus 27: 20–1; Numbers 8: 1–4) was interpreted early on in the history of Judaism as symbolic of the need to bring the illumination of the Torah into human life. In the *Havdalah prayer, recited at the termination of the Sabbath, the benediction over light reads: 'Blessed art Thou, O Lord our God, King of the universe, who makest a distinction between holy and profane, between light and darkness, between Israel and other nations, between the seventh day and the six working days.' In an oft-quoted passage in the Talmud (*Berakhot* 17a) the saints in the *World to Come are said to bask in the radiance of the *Shekhinah.

Lilith Queen of the demons, consort of Samael, the demon king. The word *lilith* occurs in the verse: 'Wildcats shall meet hyenas, goat-demons shall greet each other, there too the lilith shall repose and find herself a resting place' (Isaiah 34: 14). In the context Lilith seems to be the Assyrian Lilitu, a wind-spirit with long hair and wings. But in the Talmud the name is connected with the Hebrew word *lailah* ('night') and Lilith is a demon who is abroad at night. Later still, especially in the Kabbalah, Lilith becomes the demonic queen. In legends found in the later Midrashim Lilith is associated with Adam, either as Adam's demonic wife or as his original wife, created, like him but unlike Eve, from the dust of the ground. Lilith has designs on Eve's children and *amulets were written for women in childbirth to protect them from her evil designs. Some Jewish *feminists have adopted Lilith, the more aggressive and less docile wife of Adam, as their heroine and have published a magazine called *Lilith*.

Literature, Religious The *Pentateuch and the other books of the *Bible are the sacred books *par excellence* for the Jewish religion although, traditionally, the Pentateuch was not treated as

a human composition at all and the other biblical books were also acknowledged as being the product, in varying degrees, of divine *inspiration. Yet while the Bible was studied chiefly for its religious message and was not held to be like any other literature, the medieval biblical commentators, Abraham *Ibn Ezra, *Kimhi, and *Abravanel point to the stylistic elements in the Bible, treating it, to some extent at least, as if it were a literary work and adapting for this purpose the Rabbinic saying: 'The Torah speaks in the language of men.' The books of the *Apocrypha, on the other hand, whatever their literary value, were excluded from the canon of sacred Scripture because they were not held to be inspired works. The consensus at work in the Jewish community of believers decided that these books and works such as those of *Philo of Alexandria were undoubtedly religious works, in the sense that they were composed by religious men with a religious aim, but they were not held to belong to sacred, inspired literature. These works were never used as part of the synagogue *liturgy and Philo was not even mentioned at all in Jewish writings until the sixteenth century. The clear distinction between form and content in a book was continued throughout Jewish history. A book was judged by what its author had to say, rarely by the way he said it.

The *Septuagint, the Greek translation of the Bible, was largely unknown to Jews until modern times. The *Targum, the Aramaic translation (Targumim, 'translations', would be better, since there are more than one), took its place early on as a companion to Scripture and is printed together with the text in most editions of the Hebrew Bible. Among the standard commentators to the Bible, in addition to those mentioned above, are: *Rashi, *Rashbam, *Nahmanides, *Bahya *Ibn Asher, *Gersonides, and Sforno in the pre-modern period, *Mendelssohn and his Biur, S. D. *Luzzatto, Samson Raphael *Hirsch, and J. H. *Hertz in the modern period. All these, in greater or lesser degree, belong in the traditional camp. From the nineteenth century onwards, the Bible had been studied objectively and a host of scholarly works on it have been produced by Jews. It is a moot point whether these many works can be said to be religious literature, since their authors claim, rightly or wrongly, that they engage in their task without any religious bias, simply studying the Bible as they would any other great literary work. These works of modern scholarship do, however, have important implications for the Jewish religion (see BIBLICAL CRITICISM).

Liturgy The order of the daily, Sabbath, and festival services. Scholarly investigation into the historical development of the liturgy began with the *Jüdische Wissenschaft school, especially by Leopold *Zunz and the early Reformers, the latter with an axe to grind. The Reformers wished to build their new orders of service around the traditional liturgy, rejecting whatever they considered to be outmoded, such as prayers for the restoration of the sacrifices and Israel's return to the Holy Land, and retaining some of the older forms while adapting them to what they saw as the new requirements.

At the core of the synagogue liturgy, dating from Talmudic times, are the *Eighteen Benedictions, the *Shema and its special benedictions, and the *reading of the Torah and the *Haftarah. Other prayers and *benedictions, some found in the Talmud but often only as individual songs and petitions, were added until the first *prayer books were compiled in the Geonic period. Other prayers and hymns and even passages from the Halakhah of the Talmud were added from time to time. The *Lekhah Dodi' poem, for instance, was composed by Solomon Alka-

betz in the sixteenth century. The growth of the liturgy was never determined by anything as official as a synod of Rabbis but grew organically out of the customs of the various praying communities, so that a number of liturgies developed around the essential core as found in the Talmud. The Ashkenazi and Sephardi rites are the best known, but there are also Italian, Yemenite, and other rites. As noted above, Reform Judaism created its own forms of worship as did Conservative Judaism, the latter with only a very few departures from the traditional Prayer Book.

Longevity Long life is the blessing promised in a number of biblical passages (e.g. Exodus 20: 12; Deuteronomy 11: 21; 22: 7). Moses is said to have been 120 years of age when he died (Deuteronomy 34: 7) and the common, jocular Jewish blessing is: 'May you live for 120 years.' Another common blessing is to live long enough to see children and grandchildren engaging in the study and practice of the Torah. Statistics are not available of how long people lived in ancient times but, according to the Psalmist (Psalms 90: 10) the normal span of life was 70 years and, by reason of special strength, 80 years. Abraham *Ibn Ezra has an interesting comment on the verse which states that a priest may not come into contact with a corpse unless it is of his mother or his father (Leviticus 21: 1–2). Ibn Ezra remarks that the mother is mentioned before the father because females usually do not live as long as males. Whatever the situation in twelfth-century Spain, statistics now show that women generally have a longer life span than men.

Love and Fear of God In Jewish thought the love and fear of God are often understood as complementing one another. Fear without love can easily result in a too rigorous and ultimately stultifying approach to the religious life. Love without fear can just as easily degenerate into sheer sentimentalism.

There is no single Jewish understanding of the concept of the love of God. On the whole, two distinct tendencies emerge. On the one hand, there are Jewish teachers, represented particularly in the Rabbinic tradition, who prefer to speak of the love of God in terms of the practical details of the religious life. For them, to study the Torah and keep its precepts is the love of God. On the other hand, there are those who understand the love of God in its mystical sense of intense longing for the nearness of God and for communion with Him. But even this latter group of teachers emphasize the great difficulties in the way of attainment of their ideal and teach that in its highest reaches it is only for a few very rare souls.

In medieval Jewish thought a distinction is drawn between two kinds of fear: fear of punishment and fear in the presence of the exalted majesty of God. The latter comes very close to the feelings of awe and dread described in Rudolf Otto's phrase as the 'numinous'.

Love of Neighbour The biblical injunction to love the neighbour occurs in the Holiness Code in the book of Leviticus. Readers of the Bible in English are familiar with the rendering of the King James Version: 'Thou shalt not avenge, nor bear any grudge against the children of thy people, but thou shalt love thy neighbour as thyself' (Leviticus 19: 18). The latter part of the verse has often been detached from the beginning as well as the 'but', so that among both Jews and Christians the injunction is read simply as 'love thy neighbour as thyself', meaning, so it has been understood, that man is obliged to love a neighbour as much as he loves himself, with the result that countless worthy people have been pos-

sessed with powerful guilt-feelings for failing to live up to this unrealistic expectation. Is it really possible to love a neighbour as one loves oneself? Is not the whole concept of 'love', by definition, directed to another, and do people, except those with split personalities, love themselves? Moreover, can love, an emotional condition, be coerced by divine command?

To appreciate what the verse actually says, the end should not be detached from the beginning and the 'but' should not be ignored. When the verse is read as a whole the meaning is clear: it states that instead of taking vengeance against the neighbour and bearing him a grudge, one should act lovingly to him. In spite of the fact, the verse is saying, that he has behaved badly towards you, you should not be tempted to retaliate but should behave decently towards him. Furthermore, the Hebrew *le-reakha* means not simply 'thy neighbour' but 'to thy neighbour', And the Hebrew *kamokha* means 'who is like thyself', the meaning being: behave lovingly towards him because he is like yourself, that is, with the same rights and feelings that you have. Thus in the original context the verse means: even when someone has behaved badly towards you, try to overcome your desire for revenge but rather behave lovingly towards him because, after all, he, too, is a human being and a member of the covenant people as you are and therefore entitled to be treated as you yourself wish to be treated.

As in other areas, however, the plain, original meaning of the text is not necessarily the meaning it bears in the long tradition of Jewish life and thought. In that tradition, the second clause is taken on its own as a command to love the neighbour as the self, even though it is the outcome of the love in deeds that is stressed rather than the loving feelings and emotions.

Lubavitch The branch of the *Habad

tendency in Hasidism with many thousands of followers all over the Jewish world. The second Rebbe of Habad, *Dov Baer, settled in the Russian town of Lubavitch, after which this group of Hasidim is called. The sixth master, Rabbi Joseph Isaac Schneerson (1880–1950), settled in Brooklyn, USA, in 1940, where he was succeeded by his son-in-law, Rabbi Menahem Mendel Schneerson (1902–94), the seventh Lubavitcher Rebbe, who established a worldwide network of educational institutions and a major publishing house. Many of Rabbi Menahem Mendel's followers hailed him as the *Messiah, and went about singing in public places: 'We want the Messiah now', in the hope that God would reveal to the Rebbe his true identity as the hoped-for redeemer, to the consternation of most of the other Hasidim and traditional Orthodox Rabbis. The latter were not slow to point out the dangers of unbridled Messianic fervour, especially when the Messiah is identified with a particular known leader. Even after the Rebbe's death many of his followers still retained belief in his Messianic role.

Lulav see TABERNACLES.

Luria, Isaac The foremost Kabbalist after the Zoharic authors (see ZOHAR), founder of the Lurianic *Kabbalah (1534–72), known as the Ari ('the Lion') and his disciples as Gurey Ha-Ari ('the Lion's Cubs'). Legendary biographies of Luria convey little reliable information about his life. It seems that he was born in Jerusalem but, orphaned from his father at an early age, he was brought up in Cairo by his mother's brother, Mordecai Francis, a wealthy tax farmer. Luria received a good Talmudic education and also studied the Zohar which had recently been printed (Mantua, 1558–60; Cremona, 1560). At the age of 15 he married his cousin, Mordecai Francis's daughter. It is said

that for seven years he lived in a little cottage on the banks of the Nile, where he meditated on Kabbalistic themes, returning to his home only for the Sabbath. The Kabbalists, aware of the unconventional and in some respects radical nature of Luria's ideas, believed that he was visited by the prophet *Elijah who imparted to him new Kabbalistic mysteries, linking in this way the Lurianic system to the Zoharic. In the year 1569, Luria went to Safed where he became a member of the mystic circle around *Cordovero and soon after became the leading light among the Safed Kabbalists, attracting a small number of chosen disciples, of whom the chief was Hayyim *Vital. Luria wrote very little himself (a few of his poems were incorporated into Kabbalistic prayer books) but his teachings were recorded by his disciples, especially Vital, and the Lurianic scheme is described in elaborate detail in the various works known as 'the Writings of the Ari'.

Luzzatto, Moses Hayyim Italian Kabbalist, poet, and religious thinker (1707–47). Luzzatto was born in Padua. His father, a wealthy merchant, saw to it that his son received a good traditional Jewish education and a sound grounding in Latin, Italian, and the general culture of his day. In all his writings there is a remarkable blending of the two cultures. He composed, for example, allegorical dramas in the Italian style but in elegant Hebrew and has often been hailed as the father of modern Hebrew literature. A mystic, who claimed to have received, like Joseph *Karo, a heavenly mentor, he attracted around him a group of young enthusiasts with whom he studied the Kabbalah. These followers, and, possibly, Luzzatto himself, believed that he would be the longed-for Messiah. His activities were viewed with suspicion by the Rabbinic authorities and he was compelled to hide his Kabbalistic writings and to move to Amsterdam, where he earned his living as a diamond-polisher. He journeyed to the land of Israel in 1743 and died there at the early age of 40. His grave can still be seen in Tiberias.

Luzzatto was a prolific author, compiling works on theology, the Kabbalah, and Talmudic methodology. His Kabbalistic works are in the rationalistic vein in which the the Kabbalistic concepts are demythologized, to some extent at least. Luzzatto's major work is the *Mesillat Yesharim (Path of the Upright)*. In this work Luzzatto provides a step-by-step account of how the ladder of saintliness is to be scaled until the devotee attains to the *holy spirit. Luzzatto was held in the highest esteem by both the Hasidim and the *Mitnaggedim. The *Path of the Upright* became one of the most popular works of Jewish devotional literature, especially among the adherents of the *Musar movement. Luzzatto states in the introduction to the *Path of the Upright* that his aim is to demonstrate that saintliness is a science that can only be appreciated by the learned.

Luzzatto, Samuel David Italian historian, theologian, and biblical exegete (1800–65), known, after the initial letters of his Hebrew name, as Shadal. Shadal was one of the pioneers of the *Jüdische Wissenschaft movement, contributing many studies in Jewish history to learned periodicals and producing a critical edition of the Italian Prayer Book. An opponent of the *Kabbalah, he wrote a critique of this mystical lore in which he argued against the traditional ascription of the Zohar to the second-century teacher, Rabbi *Simeon ben Yohai. Shadal was also critical of Maimonides' attempt to interpret Judaism in the light of Aristotelian philosophy, which he dubbed Atticism. He was particularly severe on Maimonides' espousal of the Greek golden mean. The disciples of Abraham are required to go to extremes in generosity. In 1829 Shadal was appointed Principal of the Rabbinic College in Padua where he influenced more than one generation of Italian Rabbis.

Although Shadal's work on the Bible is not uncritical, he was not averse to *textual* criticism, for example, he believed that Moses was the author of the Pentateuch (see BIBLICAL CRITICISM) and that the whole of the book of *Isaiah was the work of the prophet whose name it bears. He believed that to deny that a prophet can foretell events that would take place long after his time was to deny prophecy altogether. He was not bothered by the command to exterminate the Canaanites, including the little children, since it was God's will, and God does sometimes allow the death of little children. In Shadal's understanding of divine *providence, each human being is given an equal degree of happiness and frustration, which should all be accepted in faith and trust. In his personal life, Shadal was an observant Jew but with reservations regarding some of the details of observance as laid down in the Rabbinic tradition. Shadal's religious philosophy has had virtually no influence on Jewish life and thought but his scholarly works are still acknowledged to be of much value.

M

Maccabees The military heroes, the leader of whom was Judah the Maccabee, in the struggle against the Syrian king Antiochus Epiphanes in 168 BCE; their victory is celebrated on the festival of *Hanukkah. The story of these heroes is told in the first and second books of the Maccabees in the *Apocrypha. The meaning of the name Maccabees, first given to Judah and then applied to the whole group, is uncertain. The popular explanation is that the name is derived from a Hebrew word meaning a hammer, hence: 'the Hammerers'. The Maccabees were also called the Hasmoneans, a name of similar uncertain meaning but possibly from a word meaning 'chieftain'. From a number of indications in the Rabbinic literature, it would seem that the ancient Rabbis had an ambivalent, not to say hostile, attitude to the Hasmonean dynasty because of the Hellenizing tendencies (see HELLENISM) of its members. With the rise of *Zionism and the establishment of the State of Israel the Maccabees regained their popularity as the prototype of those who battle against the loss of Jewish identity.

Machpelah, Cave of The burial place acquired by the patriarch Abraham from Ephron the Hittite (Genesis 23). According to the biblical record, Abraham buried his wife Sarah in the Cave of Machpelah and eventually Abraham himself, Isaac and Rebecca, Jacob and Leah were buried there. According to legend, Adam and Eve are also buried in the Cave of Machpelah. The Cave of Machpelah in Hebron is still a place of pilgrimage for both Jews and Muslims: for the latter because of the central place Abraham occupies in *Islam (see ISHMAEL).

Magen David 'Shield of David', the familiar six-pointed star, consisting of two interlocking triangles, said to be the shape of King David's shield and now serving as the most popular Jewish symbol. From the historical point of view, while the device itself is very ancient, as one among other magical symbols, and while it features occasionally in some earlier Jewish records and on some very few communal buildings, it did not begin to assume universal significance as a typical Jewish symbol until as late as the nineteenth century when it began to be used on synagogue buildings in Western lands on the analogy of a cross on a church building; nor was it called the Shield of David before this time. Jewish *objets d'art* claimed by dealers to be older than the nineteenth century should, consequently, be viewed with a strong degree of suspicion if they have a Magen David. There is no doubt at all that the popularity of the Magen David in the twentieth century is due to its adoption by *Zionism as a symbol of Jewish nationality. The device is depicted on the blue and white Israeli flag. In late Kabbalistic sources, the supposed Shield of David is the *menorah, the true, ancient, specifically Jewish symbol. Nevertheless, the Magen David has been interpreted to suggest various philosophical ideas; for example, the two interlocking triangles, the one pointing upwards, the other downwards, are supposed to represent the divine reaching downwards and the human response upwards.

Magic and Superstition There are numerous references to magical practices in the Torah. At the beginning of Moses' confrontation with Pharaoh, he engages in a conflict with Pharaoh's sorcerers in which he performs greater acts of magic than they are able to do (Exodus 7: 8–13). It is commanded that a witch be put to death (Exodus 22: 17). Israel is enjoined that when the people enter their land they are to reject all magical practices: 'Let no one be found among you who consigns his son or daughter to the fire, or who is an augur, a soothsayer, a diviner, a sorcerer, one who casts spells, or one who consults ghosts or familiar spirits, or one who inquires of the dead. For anyone who does such things is abhorrent to the Lord and it is because of these abhorrent things that the Lord your God is dispossessing them before you' (Deuteronomy 18: 9–12). There are discussions in the Talmud on the precise meaning of these examples of magic and divination and various additional superstitious practices are added to the list by the Talmudic Rabbis under the heading 'The Ways of the Amorites', the Amorites being one of the seven nations referred to in the verse.

The medieval Jewish thinkers discussed the question of whether magic really works, the majority of them holding that from the biblical references it appears that witchcraft and similar practices do have a real effect. Magic works and is a real danger and that is why the Torah is so strict in banning it. Moreover, it is clear that the Talmudic Rabbis believed in the existence of *demons, the power of witches to do harm by spells, incantations to ward off evil, and the *evil eye. Maimonides and some few other rationalists, on the other hand, believe that magic has no power to do harm and has no effect other than a psychological one. Maimonides remarks that the Torah does not forbid magic because it is true but because it is false.

Maharal of Prague Acronym for Morenu Harav Rabbi Laib, 'Our Teacher Rabbi Leow', Talmudist, theologian,

Rabbi of Prague (d. 1609). It is unfortunate that the Maharal is known chiefly as the creator of the *golem and that his grave is one of the tourist attractions in the city, since he was an original and influential thinker who deserves better than a reputation as a vulgar miracle-worker. In his thought Maharal was influenced by the Renaissance and the emerging new scientific picture of the universe. A prominent theme in his writings is, consequently, the role of man in the creation. Following Rabbinic teachings on this theme, the Maharal develops the idea that God created an incomplete universe which it is the task of humans to bring to completion. This applies even to the Torah, which is incomplete and requires to be applied by the sages of Israel through their deliberations.

There is a strong mystical tinge to Maharal's thought. He was obviously influenced by the Kabbalah but formulates his thought in such a way that his theories are presented in his own style without any direct reference to Kabbalistic terminology. His presentation in his voluminous works is far from systematic and it is often difficult to see the wood for the trees. This probably accounts for the comparative neglect of this original thinker.

Mahzor See PRAYER BOOK.

Maimonides Known, after the initial letters of his name (Rabbi Moshe Ben Maimon, 'Rabbi Moses son of Maimon') as Rambam, generally acknowledged to be the greatest Jewish thinker, Talmudist, and codifier in the Middle Ages (1135–1204). Maimonides was born in Cordoba where his father was a Dayyan, a judge. Maimonides was later proud to trace his descent from judge to judge back through many generations. When Maimonides was 13 years of age he left Spain together with his parents under threat of religious persecution to wander in various places, but eventually he settled in Fostat near Cairo in Egypt. There he became the leader of the Jewish community and in 1183, by which time he had acquired skills in medicine and had practised as a physician, he was appointed physician to Saladin's vizier (not to Saladin himself as is often thought). He lived all his life in an Islamic society and had little knowledge of Christian life and thought. Maimonides died in Egypt but his body was taken to be buried in the land of Israel, where his grave in Tiberias is still a place of pilgrimage.

Maimonides was a prolific author. Among his published works are: letters, *Responsa*, medical treatises, and works on *Halakhah*. But his three major works are: his commentary to the Mishnah, compiled in his youth; his gigantic Code of law, the *Mishneh Torah*, compiled in his middle age; and, his best-known work among non-Halakhists, the *Guide of the Perplexed*, compiled in his old age. There is an astonishing consistency about Maimonides: the works of his old age depart hardly at all from his youthful works. Medieval authors rarely changed their minds—a pity, perhaps.

The Guide of the Perplexed

The 'Perplexed' in the title of this three-part work are the students of Aristotelian philosophy puzzled and confused by the many apparent contradictions between philosophy (= human reasoning) and certain statements, especially about the nature of God, in the Bible and Talmud. The basic thrust of the *Guide* is to demonstrate that all truth is one so that the Bible, containing the revealed will of God, has to be interpreted not to be in conflict but to be in harmony with reason. In an oft-quoted passage in the *Guide*, Maimonides declares that he rejects the Aristotelian view that matter is eternal on the grounds of reason, not of faith. Had he been convinced that the Aristotelian view is correct he would

have had no difficulty in interpreting the biblical narrative of *creation to accord with this view. As it is, there is no 'reason' for rejecting the traditional Jewish view of *creatio ex nihilo*. The first part of the *Guide* deals similarly with the question of the biblical anthropomorphisms. It is true that the Bible describes God in human terms but these are not to be taken literally. In the third part of the *Guide*, Maimonides proceeds to give 'reasons' for those commands in the Torah which seem unreasonable at first glance such as the *dietary laws (see MITZVAH).

For all his reliance on reason Maimonides is not, however, a rationalist in the conventional sense. He believes beyond question in the Torah as divine revelation. Moreover, there is a strong mystical element in Maimonides' thought. In the remarkable account in the *Guide* (3. 51) of the man whose thoughts are always on God (see DEVEKUT), such a rare individual is said to be beyond the normal mishaps of nature. He can walk through fire without being burned and pass through water without being drowned.

The *Guide* is a very difficult work not only because of its subject-matter but also because Maimonides presents his thoughts, contrary to the precision he employs in his other works, unsystematically, evidently in his desire to prevent those incapable of following abstruse arguments from venturing into the dangerous field that might easily lead to loss of faith. He has even been accused of planting false clues for this purpose, so that it is often impossible to grasp what he is really saying. The commentators to the *Guide* often leave the student in a greater state of perplexity than he was when he began the study.

Malachi The post-exilic prophet whose book of three chapters is the final book of the Twelve Prophets. It is uncertain whether Malachi is the actual name of the prophet, since the Hebrew word *Malakhi* can mean 'my messenger' and chapter 3 of the book begins with the words: 'Behold, I send My messenger [*malakhi*], and he shall clear the way before me.' In a Rabbinic legend Malachi is identified with none other than *Ezra. According to the Talmud (*Megillah* 15a) Malachi and his contemporaries *Haggai and *Zechariah were the last of the prophets, *prophecy coming to an end when they died. The book concludes with two verses which speak of God sending his prophet *Elijah to turn the heart of the fathers to the children—the earliest reference to the view that Elijah is the herald of the *Messiah. Malachi 1: 11 reads: 'For from the rising of the sun even unto the going down of the same My name is great among the nations; and in every place offerings are presented unto My name, even pure oblations; for My name is great among the nations, saith the Lord of hosts.' One Rabbinic interpretation has it that this verse refers to the *Jewish* scholars among the nations who offer the 'pure oblations' of Torah study. But the other interpretation which takes the verse literally and is thus universalistic is obviously the more probable. The meaning is then said to be that for all their worship of other gods the nations acknowledge a Supreme God, the one God worshipped by the people of Israel.

Malbim Acronym of Meir Laib Ben Yehiel Michal, Russian Rabbi and biblical exegete (1809–79). The Malbim occupied a number of Rabbinic positions including the Rabbinate of Bucharest, which post he was compelled to relinquish because he fell out with the lay leaders of the community owing to his strict views concerning the *dietary laws and other observances, which were not to the taste of people with standards that fell far short of his own. Malbim's commentary to the whole of the Bible became one of the most popular commentaries for Orthodox Jews because its aim is to show, chiefly by philological investigation, that the teachings of the *Oral Torah, as found in the Talmud, are contained in the *Written Torah, the Pentateuch. Very few modern biblical scholars are at all enamoured of Malbim's methodology but acknowledge the many insights into the meaning of the biblical texts found in his commentary.

Malbim was well acquainted with the scientific and philosophical theories of his day which, he claims, are in no way in opposition to the Bible if the latter is correctly understood and interpreted. For instance, in his comment on the command to *love the neighbour, he points out that this cannot mean that a man is obliged literally to love others as he loves himself, but that the command means that others should be treated in the way one wishes to be treated oneself. Moreover, he maintains, the command does not only apply to other Jews but to all human beings. Malbim's commentary is completely in the traditional mode. He has no use for the theories of *biblical criticism, though he does seem to accept the modern view that Psalm 137 was not composed by King David but by someone who lived through the events with which it deals, during the Babylonian exile.

Mamzer A child that is the issue of an adulterous or incestuous union. The law of the mamzer is stated in the verse: 'A mamzer shall not enter into the congregation of the Lord; even to his tenth generation shall he not enter into the congregation of the Lord' (Deuteronomy 23: 3). Whatever the original meaning of the word *mamzer*, in the Rabbinic tradition, as finally recorded after much discussion, the mamzer is the offspring of an adulterous or incestuous relationship, for example, of a man and a married woman or of a brother and sister, and 'entering the congregation of the Lord' is understood to mean that the mamzer (or mamzeret, for a female) is forbidden to marry a Jew. Since the verse states 'even to his tenth generation', this is taken to mean that the taint is transmitted over all the mamzer's generations so that the child of a mamzer, his grandchildren, and great-grandchildren may not marry into the Jewish community.

The fact that an innocent child is penalized in this way through no fault of its own has always presented a severe theological and ethical problem. On the practical level, any proliferation of mamzerim could result in the Jewish community being split into two groups, the members of one being disallowed from marrying the members of the other. Because of these problems there is a distinct tendency throughout the history of Jewish *marriage law to discover legal remedies to prevent the mamzer being exposed or declared as such. Isserles in his gloss to the *Shulhan Arukh* (*Even Ha-Ezer*, 2. 15) states, on the basis of Talmudic rulings: 'If one who is unfit has become mixed in a particular family, then once it has become mixed it has become mixed and whoever knows of the disqualification is not permitted to disclose it and must leave well alone since all families in which there has been an admixture will become pure in the future.' The last remark refers to a Talmudic statement that in the Messianic age the taint of mamzerut (the abstract term for the mamzer situation) will be removed. Reform Judaism rejects the whole concept of mamzerut. Many Conservative and all Orthodox Rabbis do accept the traditional law in this matter but generally follow the Talmudic precedence of adopting various legal remedies in order to avoid the taint of mamzerut, and the ruling of Isserles is also followed that no investigation is to be made in order to expose mamzerut. It is certainly contrary to the tradition to compile, as unfortunately some few Orthodox Rabbis do, a register of mamzerim.

Manna The 'bread from heaven' with which the children of Israel were miraculously fed during their forty years in the wilderness (Exodus 16: 4–36; Numbers 11: 7–9). Some modern scholars, noting that the Arabs give the name *man* to a sweet, sticky, honey-like juice, exuding in heavy drops from a shrub found in the Sinai peninsula, understand the manna to have been a similar, natural substance. But it is obvious that the biblical account sees the manna as a miraculous substance dropping down from heaven. In a Rabbinic legend the manna had whatever taste those who ate it desired to experience but in the mystical lore the manna is the ethereal bread by which the angels in heaven are sustained. In the later tradition the manna became the symbol of man's need to trust in God for his sustenance. Devout Jews read the account of the manna in Exodus before going out to engage in their business activities and for this reason the account is printed after the morning service in a number of prayer books. The manna did not fall on the Sabbath but a double portion fell on the eve of the Sabbath (Exodus 16: 22). On the basis of this it is the universal custom to break bread for the Sabbath meals over two loaves. These are covered with a cloth while the Kiddush is recited over the wine, just as the manna in the wilderness was covered with dew (v. 13–14).

'Maoz Tzur' 'Fortress, Rock of my salvation', the hymn, of which these are the opening words, sung on *Hanukkah to a well-known melody in celebration of the deliverance by the *Maccabees, commemorated on this festival, and other deliverances from tyranny. The hymn itself dates from the thirteenth century, the melody from the fifteenth century, both in Germany, and they were consequently used only by *Ashkenazi Jews until recently adopted by the *Sephardim as well.

Marranos The Jews of Spain and Portugal from the fifteenth century who submitted to baptism under threat of death or persecution, and many of whom kept Jewish observances in the secrecy of their homes. The Hebrew term for Jews forced to convert to another religion is *anusim* ('those who were forced'). Marranos means 'swine' in Spanish and is a term of opprobrium obviously resented by Jews even though this name is used in the history books. Many of the *anusim* later took up residence in Amsterdam where they formed a large proportion of the Jewish community (see CONVERSION).

Marriage In every interpretation of Judaism, marriage is the ideal state. The purpose of marriage is, in the first instance, for *procreation but the institution is also held in the highest regard in that it provides husband and wife with, in the language of one of the marriage benedictions, 'joy and gladness, mirth and exultation, pleasure and delight, love, peace and friendship'. Although *celibacy is not entirely unknown in Judaism, the vast majority of Jews favour marriage as the higher state. It used to be extremely rare, for instance, for the Rabbi of a community to be a bachelor. From the biblical story of *Adam and Eve and from the prophetic comparisons of the love of God and Israel to the love of husband and wife, it seems that monogamous marriage was the ideal, even though in early times a man could legally have more than one wife. From around the eleventh century CE polygamy was outlawed by the 'ban of Rabbenu *Gershom' for Ashkenazi Jews and this ban is now the norm for Sephardi Jews as well. In the State of Israel polygamy is proscribed by law for all citizens whether Ashkenazi or Sephardi.

The following is the traditional Jewish marriage ceremony, still observed in all its details by Orthodox Jews. Reform and some Conservative Jews have changed some of the details but essentially the traditional ceremony is identical with the Orthodox form. After the signing of the *ketubah, bride and bridegroom are escorted under the *huppah by their parents who stand beside them during the ceremony. In Western lands it is often the custom for the bride to be led 'down the aisle' in the synagogue by her father. Exceptionally traditionally-minded Jews do not follow this practice. Indeed, many ultra-Orthodox frown on marriages taking place in the synagogue on the grounds that this is to copy Christian practice (see GENTILES). The marriage ceremony proper begins, in many communities, with the recital of Psalm 100 and other verses from the Psalms and the blessing: 'He who is mighty, blessed and great above all, may He bless the bridegroom and the bride.' In most Western communities, the Rabbi delivers a brief address before the ceremony. This, too, is rejected by the ultra-Orthodox as a quasi-Christian practice.

The officiant is usually a Rabbi or another learned man but there is no such thing in Judaism as a priest 'marrying' people as in the sacrament of the Christian Church. The officiant takes a cup of wine and recites the benediction over wine. He then recites the benediction over the betrothal:

'Blessed art Thou, O Lord our God, King of the universe, who hast hallowed us by Thy commandments, and hast given us command concerning forbidden marriages; who hast disallowed unto us those that are betrothed, but hast sanctioned unto us such as are wedded to us by the rite of the nuptial canopy and the sacred covenant of wedlock. Blessed art Thou, O Lord, who hallowest Thy people Israel by the rite of the nuptial canopy and the sacred covenant of wedlock.'

Bride and bridegroom sip the wine and the groom then places the ring on the forefinger of the bride's right hand and declares: 'Behold thou art consecrated unto me by this ring, according to the law of Moses and Israel.' The *ketubah* is then read aloud.

The second stage consists of a further benediction over wine and the recital of the 'seven benedictions' (really six, but the benediction over the wine is also counted). In these God's blessing is called down on bride and bridegroom and a prayer for Zion is included. Bride and groom again sip the wine and the bridegroom stamps on a glass and breaks it. Whatever the origin of this custom, the official interpretation is that it is to remind bride and groom on their happy day of the destruction of the Temple (see CUSTOMS).

Marriages, Forbidden The list of marriages forbidden by Jewish law is found in the book of Leviticus (18: 16–30; 20: 9–22). The union of a sister and brother or mother and son and the other instances mentioned have no validity whatsoever, so that if such a 'marriage' has taken place no *divorce is required to dissolve it. While a nephew may not marry his aunt, a niece may marry her uncle and the marriage of first cousins to one another is allowed. A man's stepson may marry his wife's stepdaughter and his stepdaughter his wife's stepson since there is no blood relationship. The marriage of a *mamzer to a Jew is not allowed but a mamzer may marry a mamzeret. The children of such a marriage, however, would be mamzerim. A *Kohen may not marry a divorcee. A man may not marry his wife's sister while both are alive but may do so after the death of his wife.

Martyrdom Giving up life rather than being false to the Jewish religion; Heb. *Kiddush Ha-Shem, 'Sanctification of the Divine Name'. There is consider-

able discussion in the Talmudic literature on when martyrdom is demanded of the Jew and when it is not, much of it purely academic but some of it severely practical. The Mishnah (*Berakhot* 9: 5) interprets the command to love God 'with all thy soul' (Deuteronomy 6: 5) to mean 'with all thy life', that is, love Him even at the cost of your very life. But against this is the verse (Leviticus 18: 5): 'by the pursuit of which man shall live', understood in the tradition to mean live and not die, implying that martyrdom is not demanded in pursuit of the precepts of the Torah. The resolution of this apparent contradiction is that a Jew is required to give his life for some precepts but not for others. The question is then where to draw the line. Generally from the Talmudic discussions (e.g. *Sanhedrin* 74a) the rule emerges that all the other precepts of the Torah can be set aside rather than martyrdom be suffered, but a Jew is required to give up life rather than offend against three basic commandments. These offences are: idolatry, the forbidden sexual relations recorded in the book of Leviticus (see MARRIAGES, FORBIDDEN), and murder. Following the further details in the Talmudic discussion, Maimonides (*Yesodey Ha-Torah*, 5, 1–9) rules that a Jew may transgress the precepts of the Torah in order to save his life but that this does not apply to the three offences nor does it apply where the intention of heathens is to compel a Jew to commit an offence in order to demonstrate his disloyalty to the Jewish religion. Similarly, where there is a government decree against Jewish observance the Jew is obliged to suffer martyrdom rather than transgress a 'light precept' even in private. Where martyrdom is not demanded it is forbidden for a Jew to suffer martyrdom, according to Maimonides, and if he does he is guilty of the offence of suicide.

Obviously the above discussions are from the purely legal point of view. It is hard to imagine that in the actual situations in which Jews were called upon to give their lives for their religion they looked up the rules in the Talmud and the Codes. History records many examples of Jewish martyrdom in which the martyrs offered up their lives regardless of whether the law required them to do so. The converse is also true, that Jews whom the law required to be martyrs failed to be strong enough in their loyalty to their faith. Moreover, in the Middle Ages, the period of the Crusades, for example, Jews were killed for professing the Jewish religion regardless of whether they were ready to submit to the sorry fate or escape it by surrendering. The awesome drama was always worked out against the particular situation.

Marxism The economic and social doctrine propounded by Karl Marx (1818–83). Attempts have been made to see Marx's passionate concern with social justice as the heritage of the Hebrew prophets. Others have seen Marx's dialectic as derived not only from the philosopher Hegel but from the Talmudic reasoning of Marx's forebears—he was descended from Rabbinical families on both the paternal and the maternal side. These theories are purely speculative, however, and do not affect the question of the attitude taken towards Marxism by religious Jews. Marx was born a Jew but when the boy was only 6 years of age his father embraced Christianity. As soon as he grew to manhood, Marx declared himself to be an atheist. Marx's thought on religion is utterly at variance with theism. Marxism, as developed by Marx himself, by his collaborator Engels, by Lenin, and in the Communist philosophy, treats belief in God as positively harmful. Marxism declares that men adhere to theistic religion not because it is true but because it serves as a tool for the preservation of the economic and social *status quo*. This is particularly so since in the theistic faiths man's final bliss is not in this world at all but is reserved for him in the Hereafter.

Masorah 'Transmission', the establishment of the traditionally correct text of the Hebrew Bible by the group of scholars, the Masoretes, whose activity extended from the sixth to the tenth centuries CE. The Masoretes examined the many biblical manuscripts, noting divergences and seeking to determine which text is the more accurate. They noted where a traditional reading (*keri*) differs from the traditional written text (*ktiv*), for example where the written text contains a coarse or vulgar expression. Such expressions were left in the text but the euphemisms required by the tradition are noted for the benefit of the reader in the synagogue. The Masoretes also noted where the tradition requires certain letters to be larger than the others and certain letters smaller than the others. They provided notes in which they conjecture that some words should have been written differently, for example where the text has the singular form while the context seems to require the plural, but such conjectures were left in the margins and the text itself remained unchanged. A further activity of the Masoretes was to count the number of verses in each section of the Pentateuch. A list of these is now given at the end of each section. The current text of the Bible was established by the Masorete ben Asher in Tiberias in 930 CE and this is known as the Masoretic Text (abbreviated in scholarly works as MT).

Masturbation Sexual self-abuse, often connected with the story of Onan who 'spilled his seed on the ground' (Genesis 38: 9); hence the term onanism, though the usual Rabbinic term for masturbation is 'waste of seed', meaning, presumably, the unlawful emission of semen which should be produced only in the procreative act, although normal marital relations are permitted even where no procreation can follow— where, for instance, the wife is too old to conceive (see BIRTH-CONTROL, SEX, and PROCREATION). The Kabbalah is particularly severe on 'waste of seed', treating this hyperbolically as the most severe of sins. To think lustful thoughts during the day is also forbidden in that it can lead to involuntary 'waste of seed' in dreams at night. Since the main objection to masturbation is because of 'waste of seed' there are hardly any references in the sources to female masturbation and, indeed, there is no explicit condemnation of this in the Rabbinic sources. Human nature being what it is, it is hard to believe that all observant Jews avoided the practice. From the references to 'the sins of youth', for which repentance is required in adult life, it would seem that masturbation was certainly not unknown even among pious young men.

Matriarchs *Sarah, *Rebecca, *Rachel, and *Leah. These four are the matriarchs of the Jewish people, since the majority of the sons of *Jacob were the offspring of Rachel or Leah and Jacob was the son of Rebecca and the grandson of Sarah. A Talmudic saying has it that only these four are called 'matriarchs' and only *Abraham, *Isaac, and Jacob are called *patriarchs'.

Matzah The unleavened bread that the Israelites ate when they went out of Egypt (Exodus 12: 39), after which the festival of *Passover, during which leaven (*hametz) is forbidden, is called hag ha-matzot, 'Festival of Unleavened Bread' (Exodus 23: 15; Deuteronomy 16: 16). As the law is expounded in the Talmudic literature and the Codes, the obligation to eat matzah applies only to the first night of Passover, when matzah is eaten at the *Seder. During the remaining days of the festival, leaven must not be eaten but there is

no obligation to eat matzah; although some later authorities hold that it is meritorious to eat it. There are strict rules regarding the preparation of matzah; care must be taken that during the kneading and baking of the dough it is not allowed to become fermented. This care is known as shemirah ('watching over'). Most authorities hold that shemirah is only required from the time of kneading but some hold that it is required from as early as the time of reaping the grain. Many pious Jews only use on the first night of the festival matzah that has been watched over from the time of reaping, called shemurah matzah ('matzah that has been watched over'). The especially strict only eat shemurah matzah and no other during the whole of the festival. The watching over the matzah has to be done intentionally for the purpose of using it for the fulfilment of the precept (to eat it on the first night). This was one of the reasons why a fierce controversy arose in the nineteenth century over machine manufactured matzah. It was argued that a machine cannot have intention. Those who favoured machine-made matzah argued that the intention of the man operating the machine is sufficient for the purpose and this is now generally accepted. Nevertheless, very strict Jews only use matzah that has been manufactured by hand.

Mazal Tov 'Good luck', the usual greeting or congratulations for a happy event or some particular achievement. The word mazal means a planet and the word tov means good so that the expression 'Good Mazal' obviously has its origin in a belief in *astrology. Nowadays, the phrase has lost its astrological connotation and is no more than an expression of goodwill. In congratulatory telegrams the expression is usually in the form of a single word, Mazaltov. In Yiddish parlance an unfortunate person prone to mishaps is called a shlimazal ('one without luck') as in the English 'he is unlucky'.

Meat and Milk See DIETARY LAWS for the rules against eating meat and dairy dishes together and for those against using the same cooking utensils for both meat and milk.

Medicine See DOCTORS and HEALTH for physical cures. Frequently in the Rabbinic literature and in the moralistic literature there are references to the study of the Torah and the practice of its precepts as medicine for the soul.

Megillah See PURIM.

Meir, Rabbi Prominent teacher of the second century CE, the period of the later *Tannaim. Meir was one of the last disciples of Rabbi *Akiba. Like his master, he was responsible for collections of teaching that eventually found their way into the *Mishnah, a work in which Rabbi Meir often features. It was said that Rabbi Meir was so brilliant that his colleagues were incapable of fathoming the full profundity of his thoughts and for this reason where Rabbi Meir is in dispute with his colleagues, his rulings are not followed. There is something of a mystery about Rabbi Meir's background. Unlike the other Tannaim, his father's name is never given. A Talmudic legend has it that Rabbi Meir was descended from none other than the Emperor Nero; this is probably a folk-tale based on the resemblance between the name Meir, which means 'illumination', and a folk etymology of Nero from *ner*, a lamp. There are legends about Rabbi Meir's wife, *Beruriah, said to be a woman of great learning.

Meiri, Menahem Talmudist and religious thinker of Perpignan in southern France (1249–1316). Meiri is chiefly renowned for commentaries to the tractates of the Talmud, the majority of which were in manuscript until the twentieth century. Meiri has an attractive style and methodology which are all his own. For each individual tractate he first presents the framework and then comments on the tractate section by section, providing a résumé of the views of all earlier teachers of note, together with his own original observations. For contemporary students of the Talmud, Meiri is second only to *Rashi as a Talmudic commentator and is even superior to Rashi in comprehensiveness. Meiri is a religious rationalist, explaining away and occasionally ignoring completely apparently superstitious Talmudic passages such as those referring to *demons. Meiri also compiled a large work on repentance, moved, he remarks, by the accusation by a Christian friend that Judaism is weak in its treatment of *sin. Particularly important is his treatment of Christianity. As a devout Jew he was convinced that Christianity is false in its basic beliefs but he refused to treat Christians as pagans, calling Christians and Muslims, 'people whose lives are governed by religion'. Typical of both Meiri's rationalism and his tolerance is his explanation of the Talmudic saying that astrological forces have no effect on 'Israel'. A human being has been given free will and thus endowed can escape planetary influences. Since Christians and Muslims are encouraged by their religion to exercise their free will in order to live worthy lives, they, too, are immune to the fatalistic influences of the stars (see ASTROLOGY) and for this purpose are embraced by the term 'Israel'! In effect Meiri goes beyond the Talmudic division of human beings into Israelites and idolaters, creating a third category of his own in which 'peoples whose lives are governed by religion' occupy a position midway between Jews and pagans.

Memorial Prayers The main prayer for the dead is known as Yizkor ('May

He remember the soul of . . .'). Memorial prayers originated in Germany in the form of martyrologies (see MARTYRDOM) for victims of the Crusades and from these Yizkor developed as a prayer for departed parents on *Yom Kippur. Later still it became the practice to recite Yizkor on the last days of the festivals. This practice, otherwise incongruous for a festive occasion, derives from the fact that on these days the portion read from the Torah concludes with the words: 'each with his own gift, according to the blessing that the Lord your God has bestowed upon you' (Deuteronomy 16: 17), on the basis of which donations to charity were promised, offered for the repose of the souls of the departed.

Another individual memorial prayer of seventeenth-century origin is the 'El Male Rahamin' ('O God full of compassion') recited at a funeral or when visiting a grave and by the *Cantor in the synagogue on behalf of those who are observing the anniversary of the death of a near relative, the *Yahrzeit. These memorial prayers of German origin were recited until fairly recently only by Ashkenazi Jews but are now recited also by the majority of Sephardi Jews as well, though often in a slightly different form. Despite the remarks of some of the *Geonim that it is futile to offer prayers on behalf of the dead since a man can only gain merit by his deeds while he is alive, these memorial prayers are now exceedingly popular among all sections of Jewry (and see KADDISH).

Mendelssohn, Moses German Jewish philosopher (1729–86), often called the father of the *Haskalah. Mendelssohn was born in Dessau, where he received a thorough grounding in Bible, Talmud, and Codes. He accompanied his teacher to Berlin in 1743 and, acquiring a comprehensive acquaintance with German culture, became a leading figure among the German intelligentsia. The hero of Lessing's *Nathan the Wise* is a thinly disguised Mendelssohn. In collaboration with other Maskilim, Mendelssohn produced his commentary to the Pentateuch, the *Biur*, in a modern idiom, interpreting Scripture in its plain meaning and providing a German translation. Typical of Mendelssohn's thinking is his *Phaedon*, published in 1767, a philosophical exposition, in universalistic terms, of the doctrine of the immortality of the *soul, a doctrine which Mendelssohn, like his contemporary Kant, believed to be based not on dogma but on the demands of reason. Mendelssohn's general treatment of Jewish *dogmas has been much discussed. For Mendelssohn, it would seem, or at least so it has been understood by many of his exponents, Judaism is revealed law. It is the practices enjoined by *revelation that are significant for Judaism, questions of belief being left open to a large extent; though, as Mendelssohn's critics have not been slow to point out, belief in a revealed law is itself a dogma.

Mendelssohn's thought has rightly been seen as a pioneering attempt to find the correct balance between strong Jewish commitment and the necessary accommodation the modern Jew has to make in order to be at home in Western culture and civilization. Yet he has had a large number of detractors, who have viewed his approach as dangerous to Jewish faith, especially since a number of his children became converted to Christianity. In the circle of strict Orthodoxy in Hungary in the nineteenth century a ban was placed on the study of the *Biur*. It has been said with justice, none the less, that every Jew has been influenced, directly or indirectly, by the three great figures of eighteenth-century Jewry—*Elijah, Gaon of Vilna, the *Baal Shem Tov, founder of *Hasidism, and Mendelssohn.

Menorah The seven-branched candelabrum in the Tabernacle in the wilderness (Exodus 25: 31–8; 37: 17–24) and in the First and Second Temples. The *Maccabees, after their victory over the forces of Antiochus, celebrated on *Hanukkah, refashioned the menorah. The Hanukkah menorah used on the festival in Jewish homes, has, however, eight branches, one for each of the eight days of the festival. Nowadays, the Hanukkah menorah is often called a Hanukkiyah rather than a menorah. The menorah depicted on the Arch of Titus in Rome is not an accurate representation of the original. The menorah, as the symbol of spiritual light, is the most ancient and most powerful of Jewish symbols (see MAGEN DAVID). According to Jewish law it is forbidden to have a replica of the menorah outside the Temple, which is why many authorities frown on the representation of the seven-branched menorah found often in synagogues. Others see no harm in having a menorah of this kind in the synagogue, since it is never an exact replica of the Temple menorah. In a medieval interpretation, the central stem of the menorah represents the light of the Torah while the six branches represent the sciences—good to study provided the student treats them as secondary to the wisdom of the Torah.

Menstruant Hebr. *niddah* ('one set aside'). According to Jewish law, it is forbidden for husband and wife to have marital relations during the time of the wife's periods and for seven days after these have ceased. The practice is for the wife to examine herself for seven days after her flow has ended. If the examination during these seven 'clean days' shows that there is no longer any flow of blood, the wife immerses herself in the ritual bath, the *mikveh, after which marital relations may be resumed until just before the time when the next period is expected. This means that usually husband and wife can only be together for sixteen days in each month, making the laws of 'family purity' among the most difficult to observe, especially since strict observance of these laws involves no physical contact at all between husband and wife during this time. The majority of Orthodox Jews follow these laws and there is evidence that they are observed nowadays even in some Reform circles. As with the *dietary laws, the keynote in the sources for the observance of 'family purity' is holiness. The *Karaites were extremely strict in keeping a menstruant away from contact with sacred things. Against this, the Talmud states explicitly that 'the Torah cannot contaminate', so that the widespread notion that a woman in her periods should not handle a *Sefer Torah finds hardly any support in the Codes.

Messiah 'The anointed one', the person believed to be sent by God to usher in a new era in which all mankind will worship the true God, warfare will be banished from the earth, and peace will reign supreme. With the strongest antecedents in the Bible, the doctrine of the Messiah was developed, elaborated upon, and given a variety of interpretations throughout Jewish history, but its basic affirmation is that human history will find its fulfilment here on earth. The doctrine of the Messiah denotes the this-worldly aspect of Jewish *eschatology, with the *World to Come as the other-worldly aspect (see also HEAVEN AND HELL).

Modern Jewish thinkers were the heirs to all the previous notions. The fluctuating nature of the doctrine in former times; the accretion of legends and fanciful details; the debates among the sages on this or that detail; the possibility of a naturalistic as well as a supernaturalistic interpretation of the doctrine; the emphasis here on the personal Messiah and there on the Messianic age; all contributed to make this principle of the Jewish religion the one most fluid of all in its capacity for re-interpretation. Hardly any Jewish thinkers have been prepared to give up the doctrine entirely. Orthodox Jews continue to believe in the coming of a personal Messiah who will lead all mankind back to God, even while acknowledging, as did Maimonides, that the details must be left to God. Classical Reform Judaism believed that the doctrine of a personal Messiah had to be abandoned. Moreover, the early Reformers in the nineteenth century believed that the Messianic promise would be realized not in a return of the Jews to the Holy Land but in the new world they saw beginning to emerge in Europe of sound education for all, greater liberalism in theory and practice, and greater opportunities for human betterment.

Metatron A supreme angel referred to in ancient Jewish writings. Many conjectures have been made on the meaning of this name—for instance, that it is a combination of the Greek *meta* and *thronos*, 'one who serves before the Throne [of God]'—but the name remains obscure. In some sources Metatron was created at the beginning of the creation of the world, in some even before the creation of the world. In later sources Metatron is the antediluvian, Enoch, who 'was no more, for God took him' (Genesis 5: 24). The figure of Metatron in the early literature and the Talmud aroused suspicions of dualism, especially in the references to him being 'the lesser Lord'. The *Karaites attacked the Talmud on these very grounds. Although Metatron continues to appear in Jewish angeology (see AN-GELS) he occupies a very peripheral role in later Jewish thought and has no real theological significance, testifying only to the persistence of semi-dualistic tendencies even in Jewish monotheistic thought.

Methuselah Grandfather of *Noah

(Genesis 5: 21–5), who lived for 969 years, the longest lifespan of all the antediluvians. U. Cassuto has advanced the ingenious theory that in the biblical account of the fabulous ages reached by the antediluvians there is an implicit protest against the pagan notion that certain humans were admitted into the ranks of the gods. The Psalmist refers to a thousand years being as a day in God's eyes (Psalms 90: 4). Hence not even a Methuselah lives 1,000 years, thus stressing the gulf that exists between God and human beings. In Yiddish, as in English, the 'years of Methuselah' is an expression for extreme longevity.

Mezuzah Lit. 'door-post', the parchment scrip containing the two sections of Deuteronomy 6: 4–9 and 11: 13–21 and fixed to the door-posts of the house. The injunction in these two passages to write 'these words' on the door-posts (*mezuzot*) of the house was understood from early times to mean that these two should be inscribed on parchment and attached to the door-posts. The mezuzah is placed in a case (nowadays highly decorated cases that are works of art are often used) and fixed, either by nails or by glue, to the door-post of every room in the house, except the bathroom, toilet, and garage. The mezuzah is fixed to the right-hand door-post as one enters the room. It is placed about a third of the way down from the top of the door-post, slanting upwards. The reason given for the slanting positioning is that the medieval authorities are divided on whether the mezuzah is to be in a vertical or horizontal position and to place it diagonally satisfies both—an interesting illustration of the striving for compromise. Only houses in which people actually reside require a mezuzah. Synagogues, therefore, do not have a mezuzah. But the Bet Ha-Midrash, 'House of Study', does have a mezuzah since scholars sometimes eat and sleep there. A somewhat amusing debate centres on the question of whether prison cells require a mezuzah since residence there, it is hoped, is not permanent. In the State of Israel, the prison cells do have a mezuzah. The majority of Jews, Reform as well as Orthodox, take pride in the mezuzah, understand its symbolism, and have a mezuzah, if not on all the doors of the house, on the outer door facing the street at least.

Micah The prophet who prophesied during the reigns of Jotham, Ahaz, and Hezekiah (739–693 BCE) and whose book is the sixth in the book of the Twelve Prophets. The vision of the 'end of days' (see MESSIAH) in Micah 4: 1–4 has an almost exact parallel in Isaiah 2: 2–5, suggesting either that Micah is quoting from Isaiah or Isaiah from Micah or, most probably, both are quoting from a common source, which shows that some passages in prophetic writings are not necessarily the prophet's own words but can be understood as direct quotations, throwing, in turn, some light on the nature of prophetic *inspiration. Micah's famous declaration of what God requires of man, 'only to do justly, and to love mercy, and to walk humbly with thy God' (Micah 6: 8), has been described as 'the noblest definition of true religion'.

Midnight Vigil The practice, introduced by the followers of the famous Kabbalist Isaac *Luria, of rising at midnight to mourn for the destruction of the Temple and offer prayers for the exile of the *Shekhinah to come to an end; Heb. *Tikkun ḥatzot*, 'Arrangement [or Rectification] for Midnight'. The practice is still followed in some devout circles, especially among Kabbalists and Hasidim.

Midrash The method by which the ancient Rabbis investigated Scripture in order to make it yield laws and teachings not apparent in a surface reading. The word Midrash is from the root *darash*, 'to enquire', 'to investigate'. This searching of Scripture has been traced back to the book of *Ezra: 'For Ezra had set his heart to seek [*lidrosh*] the Torah of the Lord, and to do it, and to teach in Israel statutes and ordinances' (Ezra 7: 10). In any event, the Midrash method was ubiquitous throughout the period of the *Tannaim and Amoraim.

Collections of Midrash were made from time to time. These Midrashim are conventionally divided into two classes: 1. the Halakhic or Tannaitic Midrashim; 2. the Aggadic Midrashim. In the Halakhic Midrashim the Tannaim use the Midrashic method to derive laws (Halakhot) from Pentateuchal passages. Many of the debates in these works depend on the different methods used by the teachers for the elucidation of the texts. The Aggadic Midrashim (see AGGADAH) do not purport to convey the actual meaning of Scripture but usually employ the very different method of reading ideas into Scripture.

The three main Halakhic Midrashim are: Mekhilta ('The Measure') to the book of Exodus; Sifra ('The Book'), also called Torat Kohanim ('The Law of the Priests') to the book of Leviticus; and Sifre ('The Books') to the books of Numbers and Deuteronomy. There is no Halakhic Midrash to Genesis since there is hardly any legal material in that book. The Halakhic Midrashim also contain some Aggadic material but this has a much closer connection with the biblical texts than in the Aggadic Midrashim. It might also be noted that Halakhic material is sometimes introduced in passing in the Aggadic Midrashim.

Mikveh 'Gathering' of water, the ritual bath. The basic scriptural text for the mikveh is: 'Only a spring, cistern, or collection [*mikveh*] of water shall be clean' (Leviticus 11). 'Shall be clean' is understood by the Rabbis to mean 'shall be cleansing', that is, one who has suffered contamination remains unclean until he has immersed himself in the mikveh. In the context the reference is to one who has suffered contamination by coming into contact with a dead rodent or other sources of contamination mentioned in Leviticus. The law only applied in its fullness in the period of the Temple. One who had become contaminated was not allowed to enter the Temple or eat sacred food (e.g. sacrificial meat) until he had immersed himself in the mikveh. After the destruction of the Temple, the law of mikveh has had relevance chiefly to a *menstruant. After her period and after counting the seven 'clean days', a wife has to have immersion in the mikveh before she can resume marital relations with her husband.

The mikveh is constructed so that there is a tank of rain-water (ordinary water from the tap may not be used, since the water must not be poured from a container) which is connected to the waters of a small pool rather like a swimming-pool; the waters of the latter then acquire, so to speak, the purifying quality of the waters of the tank. The laws of mikveh-construction are very complex and, nowadays, the architect will consult with a Rabbi when a mikveh is being built. Orthodox Jews observe the laws of mikveh very strictly and every sizeable Jewish community has one or more mikvaot. Some Jews who observe the laws regarding menstruation use the bath in the house for the purpose of the ritual cleansing but, as stated, this is not allowed by Orthodox law. The laws of mikveh and menstruation are called the laws of 'family purity'. It is the custom for some pious Jews to have immersion in the mikveh on the eve of *Yom Kippur in readiness for the prayers of the sacred day. In Hasidism, the mikveh is a very important means of cultivating purity of body and soul. All Hasidim immerse themselves in the mikveh on the eve of the Sabbath.

Minyan 'Number', the quorum of ten males over the age of 13 for communal prayer and the reading of the Torah with the benedictions. Where no minyan is present in the synagogue some of the prayers can still be recited but not the *Kaddish, the *Kedushah and the *Cantor's repetition of the Amidah (see EIGHTEEN BENEDICTIONS). The Torah may be read even where no minyan is present but the benedictions over the reading must not then be recited. From Talmudic times it was considered especially meritorious to be among the first ten in the synagogue for the daily prayers. Some synagogues hire poor men to come there in order to make up the minyan. These are known as 'minyan men'. Many Reform Jews ignore altogether the need for a minyan and recite the prayers no matter how few are present. Conservative Rabbis now rule that women can be counted in the minyan as well as men.

Miracles In the Bible, the Talmud, and all other ancient and medieval Jewish writings it is taken for granted that miracles can and do occur, although a miracle was not thought of as a suspension of natural law since, before the rise of modern science, there was no such concept as a natural law that required to be suspended. A miracle was an extraordinary event which, precisely because it was so different from the normal course of events, provided evidence of God's direct intervention; hence the biblical term *nes*, 'sign', for a miracle. The miracle is an indication of divine intervention in particular circumstances. The whole question of miracles involves the doctrine of divine *providence, how the transcendent God can be said to become manifest in the particular events of the world, although this way of looking at the problem did not emerge in Jewish thought until the age of the medieval philosophers.

Despite the tensions in this matter,

the power of holy men to work miracles is recognized in the Bible, the Talmud, and Midrash, and in subsequent Jewish hagiography down to the Hasidic tales of the miracles performed by the Hasidic *Zaddik.

The real question for moderns is not *can* miracles happen, but did they and do they happen. As Hume recognized, the question is one of evidence. Many events that were seen in the past as miracles can now be understood as due to the operation of natural laws, even though Hume himself is less than categorical about the absolute necessity of cause A always to produce the effect B it usually seems to produce. Undoubtedly, a modern Jewish believer will be far less prone to attribute extraordinary events to a supernatural intervention, but his belief in God's power will not allow him to deny the very possibility of miracles occurring. A Hasidic saying has it that a Hasid who believes that all the miracles said to have been performed by the Hasidic masters actually happened is a fool. But anyone who believes that they could not have happened is an unbeliever. The same can be be said of miracles in general.

Miriam Sister of *Moses and *Aaron, who, together with them, led the people of Israel through the wilderness (Micah 6: 4). Traditionally, the sister who watched over the infant Moses when he was placed in the Nile (Exodus 2: 2–8), although her name is not given, is Miriam. Miriam is described as a prophetess who led the women in a song of victory after the crossing of the sea (Exodus 13: 20–1). Miriam spoke ill of Moses, for which offence she became leprous until Moses prayed for her to be cured (Numbers 12). After stating that Miriam died at Kadesh and was buried there, Scripture goes on to say that the community was without water (Numbers 20: 1–2). On the basis of this juxtaposition of the verses, there is a popular legend, mentioned in

Midrashic sources, that through the merit of Miriam a miraculous well accompanied the Israelites in their journeys but ceased when Miriam died. In a Talmudic passage (*Bava Batra* 17a) it is said that Miriam, like her two brothers and the *patriarchs, died by a 'divine kiss'.

Mishnah 'Teaching', the digest of the *Oral Torah compiled by Rabbi *Judah the Prince around the end of the second and the beginning of the third century CE. Rabbi Judah is best described not as the author of the Mishnah but as its editor, since he used earlier collections and other early material, often leaving these in their original form in his compilation. The Mishnah is in Hebrew, the scholarly language of the *Tannaim.

The Mishnah is divided into six orders:

1. *Zeraim*, 'Seeds' (agricultural laws).
2. *Moed*, 'Appointed Time' (Sabbath, festival and fast-day laws).
3. *Nashim*, 'Women' (laws of marriage and divorce).
4. *Nezikin*, 'Damages' (torts, buying and selling, jurisprudence in general).
5. *Kodashim*, 'Sanctities' (laws of the sacrificial system in the Temple).
6. *Tohorot* (the laws of ritual contamination and the means of purification, though the title may be a euphemism for 'impurities').

The titles of the six orders are not given in the Mishnah itself but by later teachers, and the titles do not all necessarily refer to the contents. The title of the fourth order, for example, seems to have been given after one of the opening words and is not descriptive of the order as a whole, just as the title of the first book of the Pentateuch is called *Bereshit* ('In the Beginning'), after its opening word. Similarly, the title *Nashim* may have been given after one of the order's opening words, since this order is primarily about marriage and divorce and not about all the laws appertaining to women found in other orders.

The six orders of the Mishnah are divided into tractates (*masekhtot*) and these are divided into chapters. Each chapter (*perek*) is made up of smaller units called *mishnayot* (plural of *mishnah*; see also MIDRASH). Thus the term Mishnah is used of the work as a whole and of its smallest unit; each of the units is a 'teaching', and the work as a whole is the teaching of Rabbi Judah the Prince. While many attempts have been made to discover why the tractates of the various orders are arranged in the 'order' in which these are found, *Geiger has noted that the arrangement is largely an artificial one, determined by the respective lengths of the tractates in that order, the lengthier ones coming first and the others in descending rank.

Once the Mishnah had been compiled, it assumed the character of a canonical text upon which the Amoraim, the post-Mishnaic teachers in Palestine and Babylon, based their own teachings. Both the Palestinian (or Jerusalem) Talmud and the Babylonian Talmud are in the form of a running commentary to the Mishnah.

The Mishnah contains Aggadic (see AGGADAH) as well as Halakhic (see HALAKHAH) material. Tractate *'Ethics of the Fathers', for example, is a purely Aggadic tractate of the Mishnah and there are Aggadic asides in many other sections. The description of the Mishnah as a Code of law is consequently imprecise.

Mitnaggedim 'Opponents' or 'Protestants', the traditionalist Rabbis and communal leaders who opposed the ideas and practices of *Hasidism in the eighteenth century and beyond. It speaks volumes for the success of the Hasidic movement that, despite the fact that the movement was new, it was their foes, not the Hasidim, who were called, and called themselves, Mitnaggedim. The most prominent of the Mitnaggedim was *Elijah, Gaon of Vilna. The controversy between the Hasidim and the Mitnaggedim was at first conducted with vehemence and even violence but eventually the two groups made common cause against the inroads into traditional Jewish life made by the *Haskalah.

Mitzvah 'Command', the Hebrew for a precept of the Torah (pl. *mitzvot*). On the basis of a homily dating from the third century CE there are said to be 613 *precepts, 365 negative ('do not do this') and 248 positive ('do this') but this numbering of the precepts did not really come into prominence until the medieval period. The distinction, however, between positive and negative precepts is found throughout the Rabbinic literature. In that literature the term *mitzvah* is used for a negative precept as well as a positive but the *mitzvah* is more usually reserved for a positive precept, while the more usual term to denote a negative precept is *averah* ('transgression'); as when, for instance, it is said that a stolen palm-branch must not be used on the festival of *Tabernacles because it is a *mitzvah* that is the result of an *averah*.

A further classification of the precepts is that of 'between man and God' and 'between man and his neighbour', that is, religious and social obligations, although both are seen as ultimately as having their sanction in a divine command. Another classification distinguishes positive precepts that depend for their performance on time (i.e. the precept of *tefillin* which is only obligatory during daytime) and precepts that are binding whatever the time in which they are carried out (love of the neighbour, for instance). Women are exempt from carrying out the former. Still another classification is between light and heavy precepts, that is, those that can easily be carried out and those that require much effort and are costly to carry out.

For the Talmudic Rabbis the fact that God commanded the positive and negative precepts is sufficient reason for the Jew to keep them. But the medieval philosophers seek to provide reasons for those precepts such as the *dietary laws for which no reason is stated in the Torah. Maimonides devotes a large section of the third part of his *Guide of the Perplexed* to reasons for those precepts which seem on the surface to be irrational. Some thinkers were opposed to the whole attempt to discover reasons for the precepts, arguing that, apart from the Rabbinic stress on pure obedience, if reasons are suggested this could easily lead to neglect where it is assumed the reasons do not apply. If, for example, the dietary laws are explained on hygienic grounds, this could lead to Jews saying that the laws need not be kept where improved methods of food-production and the advance of medicine have made the risk to health more remote than it was in ancient times. On the other hand, those thinkers who did seek for reasons believed that unless it can be shown that the observance of the *mitzvot* is reasonable, Gentiles will taunt Jews as owing allegiance to an irrational faith in which God tends to be seen as a tyrannical ruler imposing arbitrary laws on His subjects. Many modern Jews are far less bothered about the reasons for the precepts or, for that matter, about the question of the origin of the precepts as suggested in biblical scholarship. What matters for such Jews is the opportunity the precepts afford for worshipping God (see CONSERVATIVE JUDAISM and FRANKEL).

Mizrachi Religious Zionist movement founded in 1902. The name Mizrachi is a shortened form of the Hebrew words *merkaz ruḥani*, 'spiritual centre,' and signifies that the aim of *Zionism to es-

tablish a Jewish State is highly laudable but this State should serve not only as a political focus but also as a spiritual centre for world Jewry. The Mizrachi maxim gives expression to the movement's special emphasis: 'The Land of Israel for the people of Israel in accordance with the Torah of Israel.' The essential problem for the Mizrachi is posed by the obscurity of the final statement of its programme. How was a modern democratic State, comprising both religious and non-religious Jews, to be conducted in accordance with 'the Torah of Israel'? With the establishment of the State of Israel, the Mizrachi became the National Religious party (Mafdal) and still grapples, not very successfully, with this severe problem.

Mizraḥ 'East', the direction Jews living to the west of Jerusalem face in their prayers, the prayers speeding to heaven, so to speak, through the former site of the *Temple. Wherever possible synagogues in Western lands are built with the Ark containing the Torah Scrolls in the east, the *mizraḥ* of the building. Seats in the *mizraḥ* section of the synagogue are the most prized seats. Private homes sometimes have a plaque with the word *mizraḥ* in Hebrew on an eastern wall so that worshippers in the privacy of their homes can recognize the direction they should face.

Molech A god to whom there are a number of references in the Bible (Leviticus 18: 21; 20: 2–4; Deuteronomy 18: 10; 2 Kings 16: 3; 17: 17; 21: 6; 23: 10). In some of these references the worship of Molech consists of passing children through the fire. Whatever the original meaning of 'giving his seed to Molech', the Mishnah (*Sanhedrin* 7: 7) defines the offence of Molech-worship on the basis of the biblical verses in which passing through fire is mentioned.

Montefiore, Claude Modernist Jewish theologian and author (1858–1938). Montefiore, a great-nephew of the famous philanthropist, Sir Moses Montefiore, studied at Balliol College, Oxford, where he came under the influence of the liberal Christian thinker, Benjamin Jowett, the Master of the College. From Oxford, Montefiore, resolving to increase his Jewish knowledge, went to study Judaism at the Hochschule in Berlin. There he met Solomon *Schechter, whom he brought to England to act as his private tutor. In 1902, Montefiore founded the radical Reform organization the Jewish Religious Union, which led to the establishment, in 1911, of the Liberal Jewish Synagogue, of which he became the President. Together with Herbert Loewe, an Orthodox Jewish scholar, Montefiore published *A Rabbinic Anthology*, a collection of Rabbinic teachings to which he and Loewe added notes in which the teachings were assessed, respectively, from the Liberal/Reform and the Orthodox point of view.

Montefiore accepted the findings of *biblical criticism, which, he believed, had demonstrated that the Pentateuch was a composite work, produced at different periods in Israel's history. A convinced theist, Montefiore believed that Judaism's main contribution consisted in keeping pure monotheism alive.

Moon, Blessing over Heb. *Birkat Levanah*, 'Blessing over the Moon' or *Kiddush Levanah*, 'Sanctification of the Moon'; the ceremony, still observed by many Jews, in which God is praised, at the beginning of the month, for having created the moon, especially significant since the Jewish calendar is a lunar calendar.

Mordecai The hero of the book of *Esther who refused to bow to Haman, as a result of which Haman sought to persuade the king to destroy the Jews. The deliverance of the Jews is celebrated on the festival of *Purim. A degree of ambiguity is present among the Talmudic Rabbis about Mordecai's refusal to bow before Haman as the king had requested, thus endangering the life of his people. One excuse advanced for Mordecai's refusal is that Haman had set himself up as a god. In any event, in subsequent Jewish lore Mordecai is the prototype of the proud Jew who refuses to bow to tyranny.

Moses The most important figure in Judaism, the leader of the children of Israel from Egyptian bondage and, particularly, the great teacher of the Torah he received from God; hence the Torah is often called 'the Torah of Moses'. As told in the *Pentateuch from the beginning of Exodus to the end of Deuteronomy, the story of Moses begins with his birth to Amram and Jochebed in Egypt. When his mother had hidden him in the reeds of the Nile in order to save his life, because he was threatened by Pharaoh's decree that every Hebrew male be put to death, Pharaoh's daughter took pity on the infant and adopted him as her son. When Moses grew to manhood he went out of the royal palace, where he had been brought up as an Egyptian prince, to see the afflictions of his Hebrew brethren toiling under the lash of the Egyptian taskmasters. Witnessing an Egyptian seeking to kill an Israelite, Moses slew the Egyptian, as a result of which he was obliged to flee for his life. Escaping to Midian, Moses served as a shepherd to Jethro, the priest of Midian, whose daughter, Zipporah, he married. During his stay in Midian, God appeared to Moses in the burning bush and ordered him to go to Pharaoh to demand that the people be released from their bondage; eventually, God said, Moses would lead them to the land of Canaan, the land of their fathers. When, after the ten plagues, Pharaoh finally let the people go, the Egyptians pursued the escaping Israelites but were drowned in the waters of the sea, whereupon Moses led the people in a song of victory. Arriving at Mount *Sinai, the people received the *Decalogue and, during his forty days' stay on the mountain, where he neither ate nor drank, Moses received further laws and instructions which he taught to the people. Moses led the Israelites through the wilderness for forty years until they came to the borders of the Promised Land. There Moses died at the age of 120 and there he was buried.

A marked ambivalence is to be observed in the Jewish tradition with regard to the personality of Moses. On the one hand, Moses is hailed as the intermediary between God and man, as the instrument of God's revelation of the Torah and the teacher of the Torah to Israel, as the father of all the prophets, with whom God spoke 'face to face' (Exodus 33: 11). On the other hand, strenuous efforts were made to reject any notion that Moses is divine or semi-divine. Even in the Pentateuch, Moses is described as a human being with human failings. He is reluctant to be God's messenger (Exodus 3: 11); he loses his temper (Numbers 20: 9–11; 31: 14); he marries and has children (Exodus 18: 2–4); and eventually, like all human beings, he dies and is buried (Deuteronomy 34). For all his role as the intermediary, it is not Moses but God who gives the Torah to Israel. There is even a Rabbinic saying that if God had not given the Torah to Moses, He could have given it, with the same effect, to *Ezra. Judaism is in no way 'Mosaism'. It is the religion of the Jewish people. In the Middle Ages, there were a number of Jewish thinkers who, evidently in response to the claims made for *Jesus by Christians and for *Muhammad by Muslims, so elevated the role of Moses that the Jewish religion was made to centre on him. But the opposite tendency is also clearly to be observed. Precisely because Christianity and, to a lesser degree, Islam centre on an indi-vidual, these thinkers declared that Judaism, on the contrary, singles out no individual, not even a Moses, as belonging to the heart of the faith. The stresses in the matter vary in proportion to the particular challenge in the period in which the role of Moses is considered. Throughout, the tension exists between an affirmation that Moses is supremely significant and the need to play down the role of Moses.

From Talmudic times the usual appellation of Moses is Moshe Rabbenu, 'Moses our Teacher'. A passage in the Talmud (*Yevamot* 49b) states that the difference between Moses and all the other *prophets is that they saw through a dim glass while Moses saw through a clear glass. Moses was chosen to be Israel's leader because he was so considerate to his flock when shepherding for Jethro (Midrash Exodus Rabbah 2: 2). In another passage (*Nedarim* 38a) Moses is said to have been wealthy, strong, and meek since the Holy One, blessed be He, only causes His spirit to rest on a person who has these endowments. Moses and his brother *Aaron are frequently mentioned together as the leaders of the people, Moses being the stern man of law, brooking no compromise, while Aaron is the leader who loves peace and pursues it. Moses died through a kiss of God (*Bava Batra* 17a) and God Himself buried him (*Sotah* 14a) in a grave that had been prepared for him since the eve of the Sabbath of creation (*Pesaḥim* 54a).

There is thus no official Jewish attitude to Moses. What matters for Judaism is the role Moses plays in bringing the Torah to Israel and in interpreting the Torah for them. In this sense every teacher of the Torah follows in Moses' footsteps and adds something to the Torah of Moses.

Moses de Leon Spanish Kabbalist (d. 1305). De Leon was the author of a number of Kabbalistic works but these pale into insignificance when compared to his major work, the *Zohar, or, at least, to the major portions of this work. There is hardly any doubt that Moses de Leon introduced the Zohar to the world of the Kabbalists but he is reported as saying that he copied the work from an ancient manuscript and that the true author was the second-century teacher Rabbi *Simeon ben Yohai. It is, however, the virtually unanimous view of modern scholarship, especially thanks to Gershom Scholem, that de Leon was the author of the bulk of the Zohar. De Leon obviously used earlier material but he compiled the Zohar in an Aramaic of his own and in this sense the work is highly original. The later additions were made by other hands and efforts have been made by scholars to point to the differences between these and the body of the Zohar.

Mountains Mountains feature very frequently in the biblical narratives, the best known in the Jewish tradition being *Sinai, upon which the Torah was given, Moriah, upon which the *Akedah took place (later identified with Mount Zion, upon which the *Temple was built); and Carmel, upon which *Elijah struggled with the prophets of Baal. Clearly to be observed in the biblical record is the attempt to wean the people away from the ancient practice of worshipping the gods on the mountains. 'You must destroy all the sites at which the nations you are to dispossess worshipped their gods, whether on lofty mountains and on hills or under any luxuriant tree' (Deuteronomy 12: 2). The mountains are invoked to describe God's love for His people. 'The mountains are round about Jerusalem, and the Lord is round about His people, from this time forth and for evermore' (Psalms 125: 2). 'For the mountains may depart, and the hills be removed; but My kindness shall not depart from thee' (Isaiah 54: 10). Implied in these verses and in other parts of the Bible is that God is the Lord of creation, in which the mountains are the most awe-inspiring evidence of His mighty acts. A special *benediction on seeing lofty mountains was introduced by the Rabbis: 'Blessed art thou, O Lord our God, King of the universe, who hast made the creation.' The Talmud (*Horayot* 14a) describes a scholar familiar with all the teachings of the Torah as a Sinai, while a scholar not so well versed but keener is called 'one who uproots mountains'.

Mourning, Laws of Jewish tradition enjoins that when a near relative dies mourning rites are to be observed (see DEATH AND BURIAL). A near relative is defined in this connection as: father, mother, son, daughter, brother, sister, husband, wife. The periods of mourning are closely defined.

There are three periods of mourning: 1. the Shivah (seven days); 2. the Sheloshim (thirty days); and 3. the first year. The first two are observed by all relatives; the third only by sons and daughters on the death of their parents. The Shivah period is counted from the burial but a part of the day is counted as a day for the purpose. If, for example, the relative was buried on Tuesday afternoon, the rest of Tuesday is counted as the first day and the Shivah ends after one hour on the next Monday morning. During the Shivah the mourners sit on low stools (hence the expression 'sitting Shivah'); they do not bathe, shave, or have a haircut, they do not have marital relations; they do not study the Torah (because the latter is a great delight for the Jew); and they do not work or attend to their business affairs. If, however, the mourners are poor a dispensation is generally given them to go to work after the first three days of the Shivah. Mourners do not leave their homes during the Shivah but they may do so to go to the synagogue in order to recite the *Kaddish. It is the universal custom, however, wherever possible, to arrange for a *minyan to be present in the home of the mourners to obviate the need to leave the home. It is considered a high religious duty to visit mourners during the Shivah to offer them words of comfort and consolation. The manner of greeting mourners during the Shivah is: 'May the Omnipresent comfort you in the midst of all other mourners over Zion and Jerusalem' (referring to Jewish mourning in general over the destruction of the *Temple). Since public expressions of grief are proscribed on the Sabbath the mourners attend the synagogue on the Sabbath but they are not called to the reading of the Torah and do not have marital relations. If a festival falls during the Shivah, the festival rejoicing overrides the Shivah. For example, if the burial took place two days before Passover, the Shivah period would last for only two, not seven, days. On the principle that, in these matters, any part of the day counts as a day, even if the burial took place on the eve of the festival, the hours until the festival count as the Shivah, which ends as soon as the festival comes in. It is customary to have a candle burning during the Shivah on the basis of the verse: 'The soul of a man is lamp of the Lord' (Proverbs 20: 27).

The Sheloshim period extends for thirty days but here, too, a part of the first day and a part of the thirtieth are counted in the total. During the Sheloshim mourners do not shave or have a haircut and do not listen to music, nor do they attend weddings or go to parties. At the end of the Sheloshim the period of mourning is over and there are no further restrictions, except for those who mourn the passing of parents, for whom the restrictions of the Sheloshim apply for a whole year. It seemed extremely onerous even in Talmudic times for people to go without a haircut for a whole year and the Talmud permits this if the appearance of the mourner is so unkempt that his friends rebuke him for his untidiness. Many people, nowadays, shave after the Shivah since it is the present custom to shave daily so that the 'rebuke' occurs as soon as the beard has a few days' growth.

Orthodox Jews observe the laws of mourning very strictly, as do the majority of Conservative Jews. Reform Jews, too, observe some of the laws but generally do not see all the mourning rituals as binding, believing that they should be adopted by free choice where they are psychologically helpful.

Muhammad The prophet and founder of the religion of *Islam (d. 612). After the rise of Islam, many Jewish thinkers reacted to the claims made for Muhammad by elevating the role and personality of Moses. Maimonides, for example, lays down as one of the *principles of the Jewish faith that no prophet has ever arisen, even in Israel, greater than Moses, and thinkers like *Bahya, Ibn Pakudah tend to speak of Moses as 'the Prophet', adapting this form from the Islamic designation of Muhammad.

Muktzah 'Set aside'; an object that must not be handled on the Sabbath and festivals. The basic principle behind the laws of muktzah is that a fence is made around the Sabbath and festivals to prevent any infringement of the law. If, for instance, it had been permitted on the Sabbath to handle working implements such as a saw or a chisel or to handle money or a pen, it would have been far easier to forget that the day is sacred and actually use the saw to saw wood or the money to buy and sell or the pen to write with it, all acts forbidden on the Sabbath. It is, however, permitted to touch muktzah objects, the prohibition extending only to handling them.

Musar Movement The movement was founded by Israel *Salanter in nineteenth-century Lithuania with the aim of promoting greater inwardness, religious piety, and ethical conduct among traditionally minded Jews. There can be little doubt that the impetus for the movement was given by the inroads the *Haskalah had made among Russian Jews as well as the success of the Hasidic movement (see HASIDISM) which taught that the traditional study of the Talmud and Codes, while highly significant, did not in itself suffice to promote a sound religious outlook on life. At first the movement sought to influence small circles of businessmen but it soon became a much more élitist movement, attracting, especially, the students in the Lithuanian Yeshivot.

The word *musar* means 'reproof' or 'instruction', as in the verse: 'Hear, my son, the instruction [*musar*] of thy father' (Proverbs 1: 8). There developed in the Middle Ages and later, side by side with works on Talmud, Halakhah, Kabbalah, and philosophy, a Musar literature with the specific aim of encouraging religious awareness and character-formation. Classics of this genre are: *Bahya, Ibn Pakudah's *Duties of the Heart*, *Cordovero's *Palm Tree of Deborah*, and Moses Hayyim *Luzzatto's *Path of the Upright*. What was novel in Israel Salanter's approach, and that of his disciples, was the contention that the mere study of the Musar works was inadequate. In order for the ideas found in these works to penetrate the heart it was essential to reflect deeply on their implication. The new Musar movement encouraged the reading of a few texts over and over again, attended by a melancholy tune. Anticipating Freud, to some extent, Salanter and his followers believed that the subconscious mind has to be moved by severe introspection, as a result of which ethical and religious conduct becomes second nature. Salanter pointed out that observant Jews who would never dream of offending against the *dietary laws could still be unscrupulous in their dealings with others. This can only be, he maintained, because generations of Jews had become so accustomed to observance of the dietary laws that it was literally unthinkable for them to conduct themselves otherwise, whereas there had been no such habit-forming training in the ethical sphere.

There is only one full-scale history of the Musar movement, that of Dov Katz, in Hebrew, in five volumes with an additional volume on the polemics surrounding the movement. The Musarists themselves wrote very little but in recent years a number of collections of Musar teachings have been published. The novels of the Yiddish writer Hayyim Grade contain heroes and anti-heroes taken from the Musar movement.

Music Music has been associated with religion in Judaism from the beginning. The word *shirah* ('song') is often used in the Bible simply to denote a poem but there is enough evidence that it frequently refers to a chant or song, sometimes accompanied by musical instruments, as when *Miriam leads the women in the great song of victory at the sea with a tambourine (Exodus 15: 20). Especially noteworthy in this connection is the singing and playing of the *Levites in the *Temple. It is generally understood that the *Psalms were chanted by the Levites accompanied by the playing of instruments and this may be the meaning of Psalm 150 in which various instruments are mentioned. Biblical scholars see the superscriptions to the Psalms as indications of the various melodies to which they were sung.

Instrumental music was not used in the traditional synagogue but the prayers and hymns were usually chanted (see CANTOR; CHOIRS) and the reading of the Torah was done in a special chant (see CANTILLATION).

There are numerous Hasidic sayings about the significance of melody in, as the Zohar puts it, opening those heavenly gates that firmly shut except to song and tears. The Habad master, Rabbi Solomon Zalman of Kopust (1830–1900), wrote a great deal on the philosophy of melody in prayer. He suggests, for instance, that the three colours of white, red, and green can be expressed in prayer. When the worshipper arrives in his prayer to the section in which God's mercies are related, he should sing a 'white' song, the colour of the divine mercy. When he arrives at more solemn passages, he should sing a 'red' melody, the colour of the divine judgement. A 'green' melody is suitable for the harmonizing principle between judgement and mercy, which, in the Kabbalistic scheme of the *Sefirot, is represented by this colour.

Mysticism The difficulties encountered in attempting to define mysticism are well known. Dean Inge, in his *Mysticism in Religion*, quotes no fewer than twenty-six different definitions of mysticism to which he adds others. All of these refer to religious experience, more specifically to communion with God, of an intense and direct nature. Jewish mysticism can be defined, therefore, as that aspect of Jewish religious experience in which the mind encounters God directly. The *Kabbalah is often identified with Jewish mysticism but, while undoubtedly the Kabbalistic doctrines were formulated by men who reflected profoundly on the divine and who were in this sense mystics, there were Jewish mystics before the rise of the Kabbalah and the Kabbalah itself is not limited to purely mystical speculations. Gershom Scholem, the great master of Jewish mystical historiography, attributes the reticence of Jewish mystics about their personal experiences, and the lack of mystical testimonies in Jewish literature, to the fact that Jews have always retained a sense of the incongruity between mystical experience and the idea of God as Creator, King, and Lawgiver. But personal mystical testimonies, though extremely rare in Judaism, do exist. Scholem also tends to deny that Jewish mystics know of the *unio mystica*, in which the soul of the mystic is absorbed in God. Here again, as Moshe Idel and others have recently pointed out, Scholem's generalization is too sweeping. The *unio mystica* is not entirely unknown even in a religion like Judaism which stresses the vast gulf between God and the individual soul.

Nahmanides Spanish Talmudist, Kabbalist, and biblical exegete (1194–1270), known, after the initial letters of his name, as Ramban (Rabbi Moshe ben Nahman). Nahmanides was born in Gerona, Spain, where he lived for most of his life. An outstanding Talmudist, his work in this field still enjoys the highest esteem among students of the Talmud. As a Halakhic authority, he exercised a great influence on the *Codes of Jewish law, especially through the *Responsa of his most distinguished disciple, Solomon Ibn *Adret. Nahmanides was also the leading figure in the Gerona circle of Kabbalists. Indeed, it was through his renown as a Talmudist that respectability was won for the Spanish Kabbalah; though he was very circumspect in sharing his Kabbalistic insights, referring to them, for instance, in his Commentary to the Pentateuch, only by hint. Nahmanides was on very good terms with Christian notables, including King James I of Aragon. In the famous *disputation in Barcelona with the convert to Christianity, Pablo Christiani, in the presence of the king, Nahmanides emerged the victor and was rewarded by the king. But this victory aroused the ire of the Dominicans with the result that Nahmanides, at the age of 70, was forced to leave Spain for the land of Israel, where he settled in Acre, compiling there his great Commentary. During a stay in Jerusalem, Nahmanides worshipped in a synagogue that has recently been excavated and partially rebuilt and is now a tourist attraction in the Old City.

In his Commentary, one of the standard biblical commentaries which took its place side by side with that of *Rashi, Nahmanides tries, wherever possible, to arrive at the plain meaning of the text. At the same time, he believes that the Torah has a deeper, inner meaning as a mystical text. For instance, he accepts the Kabbalistic view that on one level the Torah is a series of combinations of divine names and goes far beyond the actual narratives, which is why, for him, the Torah, in this mystical sense, preceded the events of Moses' life, even though the book of Genesis, dealing with events before Moses was born, was also given by God to Moses. The mystical Torah actually preceded the creation of the world. Even on the level of the plain meaning, Nahmanides rejects the rationalizations of Maimonides. According to Maimonides all biblical references to angels appearing to men refer to their appearances in dreams. Nahmanides finds such a notion contrary to the meaning of the texts which clearly speak of actual appearances, as in Genesis 18: 1–15 and the continuation of the narrative.

Nahman of Bratslav Hasidic master and religious thinker (1772–1811). Nahman, a great-grandson of the founder of *Hasidism, the *Baal Shem Tov, sought to reinvigorate the movement which he saw as having lost its original impetus. He gathered around him a small number of chosen disciples, among them Nahman of Tcherin and Nathan Sternhartz, the latter acting as his faithful Boswell, recording his life and teachings. Nahman undertook a hazardous journey to the land of Israel (1798–9). A year or two after his return he settled in Bratslav where he remained unto 1810. The last year of his life was spent in the town of Uman in the Ukraine where he died of tuberculosis at the early age of 39. In Uman, Nahman became friendly with followers of the *Haskalah movement of enlightenment. Although he is extremely critical of all secular learning, some of the ideas he seems to have obtained from these Maskilim do occasionally surface in his own works. Nahman's grave in Uman is a place of pilgrimage for his Hasidim to this day.

Nahman encouraged his followers to practise 'solitude'. Solitude is defined by Nahman to mean that a man sets aside at least an hour or more during which he is alone in a room or in the field so that he can converse with his Maker in secret, entreating God to bring him nearer to His service. This pouring-out of the heart in solitude should be in Yiddish, the ordinary language of conversation. Nahman also stressed the value of worshipping God in man's present circumstances. Too much planning for the morrow is inadvisable even in spiritual matters. 'For all man has in the world is the day and the hour where he is, for the morrow is an entirely different world.'

Nahman's famous *Tales* (published by Sternhartz in 1815) are unique in Hasidic literature. The historian of Hasidism, Simon *Dubnow, dismisses these as 'fairy-tales' and certainly on the surface that is what they are: 'The Loss of the Princess'; 'The King Who Fought Major Wars'; 'The King's Son and the Maidservant's Son Who Were Switched', and so forth. Naturally, Nahman's followers read all kinds of mystical ideas into the *Tales*. Whatever their meaning, the *Tales* are admired for their literary merit.

Nahum Prophet whose book of three chapters is seventh in the book of the Twelve Prophets. The superscription to the book reads: 'The burden of Nineveh. The book of Nahum the Elkoshite' (of Elkosh, a town mentioned nowhere else in the Bible). Nineveh fell to the Babylonians in 612 BCE and Nahum's prophecy is devoted entirely to this theme.

Names From biblical times, much significance has been attached to the names given by parents to their children. The form of the name given to a boy is: 'X son of [ben] Y'; to a daughter: 'X daughter of [bat] Y'. The name is given to a boy at his *circumcision; to a girl in the synagogue when her father is called up to the *reading of the Torah soon after her birth. According to *Nahmanides, the father has the right to choose the name for the firstborn child, the mother for the second child, but the custom is the opposite, the mother having the right to choose a name for the first-born, the father for the second child. Names are often given after relatives; among the *Ashkenazim only after deceased relatives, among the *Sephardim, even after living relatives. Thus a name like David ben David denotes for the Ashkenazim that the father died before the child was born. A child may have two or more names after different relatives. A number of Rabbis have advised against giving a child an unusual name that will invite ridicule and cause the child embarrassment. Although disapproval is also expressed against giving children Gentile names, some of the Rabbis had such names; Antigonus or Symmachus, for example. In Western lands, Jews often have a Gentile name in addition to the Hebrew name, and this is often a form of the Hebrew: Arnold for Abraham or Maurice for Moshe (Moses). Hasidic children are often named after the particular *Zaddik to whom the family owes its allegiance. Except for a few families, family names were unknown until comparatively modern times.

Names of God The two divine names occurring most frequently in the Bible are the *Tetragrammaton—the four-letter name YHVH, and Elohim; the former is used of God in His special relationship to Israel, the latter in His relationship to the world and to human beings in general, as in the opening verse of Genesis: 'In the beginning God [Elohim] created the heavens and the earth.' In the Rabbinic literature, the Tetragrammaton denotes God in His attribute of mercy, Elohim in His attribute of justice. Other biblical names for God are: Adonai ('Lord'); El ('the Strong'); Shaddai ('the Almighty'); Elyon ('the Most High'); Yah (a shorter form of the Tetragrammaton); and Ehyeh ('I Am'). The Tetragrammaton occurs 6,823 times in the present text of the Bible. The book of *Esther is the only biblical book without any mention of a divine name.

In his study of the divine names in the Rabbinic literature, Marmorstein lists over ninety names for God in the literature. The most frequent names used by the ancient Rabbis are: Ha-Makom ('the Place' of the world, i.e. the Omnipresent); Shamayyim ('Heaven', as in the expression: 'The fear of Heaven'); Ha-Kadosh Baruch Hu ('The Holy One, blessed be He', used in indirect speech); Ribbono Shel Olam ('Master of the universe', used in direct speech); *Shekhinah ('Divine Presence', used of God's particular manifestations and His immanence); Avinu ('Our Father'); Malkenu ('Our King'); and Gevurah ('Power').

The medieval philosophers have a coinage of their own in accordance with their general fondness for abstraction when speaking of God. The more frequent terms used in the philosophical literature are: First Cause; Prime Being; Cause of causes; Beginning of beginnings; Creator; and Ha-Shem yitbarakh' ('The Name, blessed be he'), a name often used by contemporary Orthodox Jews, sometimes shortened simply to Ha-Shem.

The practice of some Orthodox Jews, writing today in English, to spell the word God as G-d is based on Rabbinic teachings about the need for reverence for the divine name. But many Orthodox Jews considered this pernickety, since there is no particular significance to the letter 'o' in English and G-d stands as much for God as the actual word God.

Nature The idea of a natural order and natural laws is unknown in the Bible. The nearest reference to nature in the Rabbinic literature is the expression: 'The world follows its own habit', that is, events occur normally in an established pattern, though there is nothing of necessity in this and *miracles are possible as abnormal events under divine *providence. In the Middle Ages, however, the word teva ('implant' or 'impression') was coined for the idea of nature. Nature is the order imposed by God on His creation. At a later date the word ha-teva (literally 'the nature') was noted as having a numerical value (see GEMATRIA) equivalent to that of the word Elohim, God, thus identifying nature with God. On 20 November 1708, the Rabbi of the Sephardi congregation in London, David Nieto, preached an antideist sermon which aroused the ire of some members of the congregation. In opposition to the deists, who taught that God, after having created the universe, left it to its own devices, so to speak, much as a watchmaker, after having manufactured his watches, does not intervene in their subsequent operations, Nieto declared that Judaism, on the contrary, teaches that God is involved directly in the workings of nature. It is God who causes the rain to fall and the crops to grow. As a result, Nieto was accused of being a follower of *Spinoza in identifying nature with God. The congregation applied for guidance to Rabbi Zevi Ashkenazi (1660–1718), the famed Rabbinic leader in Amsterdam. Ashkenazi, in a Responsum, springs to the defence of Nieto. Far from it being heresy to affirm, as Nieto did, that God works directly in the world, using nature as His instrument, the heretical view is that of the deists who see nature as existing independently of God.

Nazirite A man or woman who had vowed to be in a state of separation (from the root *nazar*, 'to separate'). The Nazirite vow was binding for as long as the one making it decided, but it could not be less than thirty days. The laws of the Nazirite are stated in the book of Numbers (6: 1–21) from which it emerges that the Nazirite was not allowed to drink wine or even eat grapes; he had to let his hair grow long; and he was not to come into contact with a corpse. Elaborate rituals are recorded for the termination of the Nazirite state. Once his term had been completed the Nazirite was obliged to bring to the Sanctuary a male lamb for a burnt-offering, a ewe lamb for a sin-offering, a ram for a peace-offering, and a basket of unleavened cakes and wafers spread with oil. It follows that the whole institution could only be in operation in the Temple period. Nevertheless, some few Jews, even after the destruction of the Temple, still undertook Nazirite vows, although this was then of the order of any other vow and did not fall under the heading of the Nazirite. David Cohen, a disciple of Rabbi A. I. *Kook, was a modern Nazirite in this sense, taking upon himself, in addition, an obligation never to leave Jerusalem.

Nehemiah The Jewish governor of Judah in the fifth century BCE as told in the book of Nehemiah. Nehemiah is usually spoken of in the Jewish tradition together with the other great leader, *Ezra. In this tradition, Ezra's main role was to teach the Torah while Nehemiah was the political leader. Indeed, the Talmud (*Bava Batra* 15a) suggests that Ezra was the author of the book of Nehemiah as well as his own book, the book of Ezra. Modern scholarship tends to see the book as a much later compilation, from around 300 BCE.

After the return from the Babylonian exile, Nehemiah is said to have built the walls of Jerusalem despite opposition on the part of the *Samaritans.

New Testament The second part of the Christian Bible, of which the first part is the *Old Testament. The expression is based on Jeremiah 31: 30 where the prophet speaks of a *berit ḥadashah*, 'new covenant', that God will make with Israel. In early Christian interpretation, the verse was read as a prophetic foretelling of the rise of *Christianity. Many modern Christians no longer understand prophecy quite in the sense that a prophet could see into the remote future and tell in detail what would happen then. In any event, the books of the New Testament are sacred for Christians. Jews, of course, accept neither the term Old Testament nor New Testament. As for attitudes towards the New Testament, no Jew accepts these books as in any way sacred and many see in some of them a strong anti-Jewish sentiment. Yet they were produced by Jews and constitute an important source for historians of first-century Jewry and Jewish life. Jewish as well as Christian scholars have studied the New Testament not as sacred literature but in the spirit of general scholarly investigation.

Nishmat 'The breath of', the opening word of an ancient hymn, after which the hymn itself is called. The hymn begins: 'The breath of every living being shall bless Thy Name, O Lord our God, and the spirit of all flesh shall ever extol and exalt Thy fame, O our King', and continues with the praises of God. Thanksgiving for God's mercies is expressed with typical oriental hyperbole: 'Were our mouths full of song as the sea, and our tongues of exultation as the multitude of its waves, and our lips of praise as the wide-extended skies; were our eyes shining with light like the sun and the moon, and our hands were spread forth like the eagles of the air, and our feet were swift as the wild deer; we should still be unable to thank Thee and to bless Thy Name, O Lord our God and God of our fathers, for one-thousandth or one ten-thousandth part of the bounties which Thou hast bestowed upon our fathers and upon us.'

The hymn continues further with thanks for God's past deliverances from the time of the Exodus from Egypt, which is why the hymn is recited at the *Seder on Passover. Nishmat is recited in all rites during the morning service on Sabbaths and festivals. Parts of the hymn may go back to Temple times; other parts are later additions. By the Middle Ages, the whole hymn was known in its present form.

Noah The biblical hero saved from the *Flood as told in the book of Genesis (5: 28–9: 28). Noah is described as 'a right-eous man in his generation' (Genesis 6: 9). Some of the Rabbis understand this to mean that Noah was a good man even in his generation of evil-doers. But others understand it to mean that Noah's goodness was only relative. Compared with his evil generation Noah was a good man but had he lived in the time of Abraham he would not have amounted to much when compared with the great patriarch. In the table of nations (Genesis 10) all the seventy nations are descended from Noah's sons, Shem, Ham, and Japheth. Thus, after the Flood, Noah takes the place of Adam as the father of all mankind. The Rabbinic tradition has it that seven laws were given by God to Adam and then to Noah. These are the seven *Noahide laws which constitute, as it were, the Torah for a 'son of Noah' (Gentile) in contradistinction to the full Torah given to Israel.

Noahide Laws The seven laws given to *Noah, the father of all mankind after the *Flood. The doctrine of the Noahide laws is Rabbinic but is based on the constant appeals in the Bible to *Gentiles to behave justly and practise righteousness, implying that all human beings know either instinctively or by tradition what constitutes justice and righteousness. These seven laws seem to be basic rules by which all humans are expected to live. They constitute the Torah for the Gentile world. Opinions are divided in the Rabbinic literature on the precise formulation of these seven principles but the accepted view of the seven is that they consist of the prohibition of *idolatry, *blasphemy, murder (see DECALOGUE), adultery and incest (counted as one, see MARRIAGES, FORBIDDEN), robbery (see DECALOGUE); the need to establish a proper system of *justice; and the prohibition against eating flesh torn from a living animal (see ANIMALS). A 'son of Noah' (ben noah) is the name given to a Gentile. He is obliged to keep the Noahide laws and if he does he belongs among 'the right-eous of the nations of the world' who have a share in the *World to Come.

Nudism The modern movement which believes that the wearing of clothes is unnatural and that it is healthier for men and women to move about unrestricted by garments, allowing the beneficial rays of the sun to get to the body. Nudists or naturists have special camps in which their ideal can be followed without upsetting other people and there are special sections of beaches in some seaside resorts for nude bathing. Nudism conflicts with the Jewish ideal of tzeniut, 'modesty', in dress and comportment. No representative Jewish religious teacher, whether Orthodox or Reform, has ever advocated nudism. In the Genesis narrative (Genesis 2: 25) it is only in the pristine innocence of the Garden of Eden that *Adam and Eve are naked without feeling shame. After they had sinned 'the eyes of both of them were opened and they knew that they were naked' (Genesis 3: 7). Judaism does not frown on nudism because Judaism holds the body in contempt and therefore teaches that it should be concealed. On the contrary, the reason why Judaism would be opposed to nudism is that Judaism insists on human dignity. It befits a human being to be clothed and the wearing of clothes is one of the ways in which humans differ from animals.

Numbers, Book of The fourth book of the Pentateuch, usually called in Hebrew *bemidbar* ('in the wilderness') after one of its opening words. The English 'Numbers' is based on the Latin *numeri*, since the book records the musterings of the children of Israel. According to the traditional view the book of Numbers, like the rest of the *Pentateuch, was 'dictated' by God to Moses. On the critical view (see BIBLICAL CRITICISM) the book is a composite work with its sections deriving from different periods in the history of Israel. More recent scholarship, while acknowledging the composite nature of the book, tends to treat it as the unit it has become, that is the book is seen as a work of art, albeit one that has been reworked, so to speak, by an editorial process. The book describes the journey of the Israelites from Mount *Sinai to the borders of the land of Canaan, a journey that took forty years,

O

Oaths Jewish law recognizes two different types of oath: 1. the oath taken in a court of law; 2. the purely religious oath in which a solemn promise is made to do or not to do something. The judicial oath is imposed in civil cases on one of the parties to a dispute, usually on the defendant. The word of two witnesses is accepted on its own and they do not have to take an oath. The testimonial oath is unknown in Jewish law. Examples of the judicial oath are: where the defendant admits the truth of a part of the plaintiff's claim but denies part of the claim; where a bailee declares that the object deposited with him has been stolen; where the plaintiff has only one witness. The judicial oath involves holding a *Sefer Torah and swearing by God that the statement is true. To take a false oath is a serious offence. The third commandment (see DECALOGUE) is directed against taking God's name in vain by swearing falsely. Some pious Jews never take an oath and are prepared to lose the case rather than invoke God's name for their own purposes. Others, however, see no value in this self-imposed prohibition since the Torah explicitly permits the taking of an oath in support of a true statement.

The second type of oath, the religious oath, is really a form of *vow. The technical difference between an oath (*she-vuah*) and a vow (*neder*) is that the former is imposed on the person, the latter on the object. For instance, an oath is where a person swears that he will not drink wine. A vow is where he places a ban on wine. The key text in this connection is: 'If a man makes a vow to the Lord or takes an oath imposing a prohibition on himself, he shall not break his pledge; he must carry out all that has crossed his lips' (Numbers 30: 3). Oaths and vows of this kind are a form of religious offering.

Obadiah The book of Obadiah, fourth in the book of the Twelve Prophets, contains only one chapter of twenty-one verses and is thus the shortest book in the Bible. The first sixteen verses consist of an oracle against the kingdom of Edom, a fierce and violent people constantly at war with Israel. Verses 17–24 foretell the victory of Israel over Edom. Some scholars see these two sections as coming from different hands but there is no real reason for departing from the traditional view that the book forms a unit. While the book opens with the words 'The vision of Obadiah', no indication is given of the identity of this prophet. According to a Rabbinic Midrash, Obadiah was an Edomite convert to Judaism. This Midrash obviously comes from a time when Edom was identified with *Rome. A prophecy, also against Edom, in the book of *Jeremiah (49: 9, 14–16) is expressed in virtually the same words as Obadiah, verses 1–5. This can either mean that Jeremiah was quoting from Obadiah or Obadiah from Jeremiah or, possibly, both prophets are quoting from the same source, demonstrating, in any event, that some prophetic utterances are in the form of quotations.

Old Testament The term used by Christians to denote the Hebrew Bible in contradistinction to the *New Testament. Jews do not normally use either of these terms because of their Christian significance and their implication that the Old Testament has been superseded by the New. Nevertheless, Jewish biblical scholars do use these conventional expressions purely as a matter of scholarship while rejecting anything in them of doctrinal significance.

Omer, Counting of

The Omer ('sheaf') was a harvest-offering brought to the Temple on the second day of *Passover (Leviticus 23: 9–14). There is a further command that, from the day when the Omer was brought, seven weeks were to be counted and on the fiftieth day a festival was to be celebrated (Leviticus 23: 15–21). This festival was later called *Shavuot, 'the Feast of Weeks' (because it falls on the day after the seven weeks have been counted). In the Rabbinic tradition, all this was understood to mean that, even after the destruction of the Temple, each individual should actually count these days, by saying each day: 'This is the X day of the Omer.' Among the many interpretations given to counting the Omer is that Shavuot celebrates the giving of the Torah while Passover celebrates the Exodus from Egypt. The free man, as he reminds himself of the bondage in Egypt, counts each day towards the even greater freedom enjoyed by those who live by the Torah.

In the Middle Ages the Omer period became one of sadness and mourning. Various conjectures have been made about why what was presumably a joyous period in Temple times (see LAG BA-OMER) was transformed in this way. Orthodox Jews do not have a haircut during this period and weddings do not take place. There are, however, different customs regarding the duration of the mourning period. Some observe it from the end of Passover to Lag Ba-Omer (the thirty-third day), others from the end of Passover until Shavuot or until three days before Shavuot, and there are other variations.

Oral Torah

In the scheme developed in Rabbinic Judaism there is a *Written Torah, the *Pentateuch, and an Oral Torah. The doctrine runs that *Moses received at *Sinai a detailed elaboration of the laws and doctrines contained in the Written Torah and this is the Oral Torah. But the term denotes much more than the original revelation. All the later teachings of the sages and teachers of Israel are embraced by the Oral Torah, seen as a continuous process. The *Mishnah and the Talmud are thus the great depositories of the Oral Torah (see AUTHORITY, HALAKHAH, and TANNAIM AND AMORAIM).

Ordination

The appointment of a disciple as a teacher of the Torah; Heb, semikhah, based on the verse: 'And he laid his hands [va-yismokh] upon him, and gave him a charge, as the Lord spoke by the hand of Moses' (Numbers 27: 23). In the verse, Moses, at the command of God, lays his hands on his disciple Joshua so that the latter can function in Moses' stead as the spiritual leader. In the early Rabbinic period only scholars who had received ordination, in the chain reaching back to Joshua, could act as judges and this was reserved for scholars in the land of Israel, the Babylonian scholars being given a minor form of authority as agents of the Palestinian scholars. After the close of the Talmud full ordination came to an end. Although the term semikhah is still used for the ordination of *Rabbis, this is not the full ordination but is only convention by which a scholar does not render decisions in Jewish law unless he has been authorized so to do by a competent Halakhic authority who has himself been ordained. Modern seminaries train their students in many disciplines other than that of pure Jewish law, so that ordination in these seminaries is a matter of attesting to the proficiency of the graduates to carry out all the other functions of a modern Rabbi such as preaching, counselling, and pastoral work, and there is often a service of ordination and a celebration with pomp and ceremony, rather like a university graduation ceremony, from which, in fact, it seems to have been copied.

Organ The use of the organ to accompany the prayers in the synagogue was the subject of a fierce conflict between the traditional Rabbis and the early Reformers in the nineteenth century. Orthodox Rabbis to this day object to the organ in the synagogue service on the grounds that it constitutes a breach of the Sabbath laws when played on the sacred day, and even when played at a weekday service it is an example of aping Christian worship. Reform congregations use the organ and, nowadays, many Conservative synagogues see no objection to it. Some Conservative synagogues which do use the organ on the Sabbath have it played by a non-Jew. Some Orthodox Jews, who do not tolerate an organ in an ordinary service, do accept the use of this instrument in an occasional service—a wedding service, for example.

Original Sin The doctrine that, as a result of Adam's fall, all human beings are tainted with sinfulness. It is often said that Judaism does not know of the doctrine, believing that man does not sin because he is a sinner but is a sinner because he sins, as it has been neatly but inaccurately put. The truth is that, while the notion of original sin does not feature at all prominently in conventional Jewish theology, a similar doctrine is found in the Kabbalah and even in the thought of some moderns. Of course, even in those versions of Judaism in which the idea of original sin is accepted, it differs from Christian dogma in that God alone, not a saviour like Jesus, helps man to overcome his sinful nature (see YETZER HA-TOV and YETZER HA-RA).

Orthodox Judaism The trend in Jewish life and thought which accepts without reservation and in its literal sense the doctrine: 'The Torah is from Heaven.' The actual term Orthodox is derived from Christian theology and was, at first, a term of reproach hurled against the traditionalists by the early Reformers at the beginning of the nineteenth century to imply that those who failed to respond to the modernist challenge were hidebound. Eventually, however, the term was used by the traditionalists themselves as a convenient shorthand for the attitude of complete loyalty to the Jewish past, although some traditionalists prefer the term 'Torah-true' to describe their religious position. In any event, Orthodoxy came to mean for Jews faithfulness to the practices of Judaism, to the *Halakhah in its traditional formulation. Orthodoxy is none the less much more than Orthopraxy. It is far removed from the attitude: believe what you like as long you keep the laws. For all that, though the dogmatic assumptions are never ignored, the emphasis is on practice. A popular definition of the Orthodox Jew is a Jew who obeys the rules laid down in the standard Code of Jewish law, the *Shulḥan Arukh. The Orthodox Jew is a Shulḥan Arukh Jew, which is not to say that all innovations introduced after the Shulḥan Arukh are never countenanced. These are allowed, and even encouraged, provided that the Halakhic process by which the Shulḥan Arukh itself was produced is faithfully observed.

Orthodox Judaism rejects the notion introduced by Reform that, in the light of modern thought and life in Western society, Judaism requires to be 'reformed'. Granted that the Torah is of divine origin, as the Orthodox affirm, to attempt to reform it is to imply that God can change His mind, to put it somewhat crudely. Orthodoxy also takes issue with Conservative Judaism which, unlike Reform, does accept the Halakhah but perceives it in a more dynamic fashion, according to which changes are legitimate if they are in the spirit of the Halakhah. Naturally, the Orthodox disagree with the notion that there is a Halakhic spirit in obedience to which the letter of the law can be set aside where it is considered necessary. Ultimately, the difference between the Orthodox and the Conservative approach depends on whether or not there is a human element in the Torah.

There are, in fact, a variety of Orthodox approaches from the ultra-Orthodox to neo-Orthodoxy and it by no means follows that every Jew who belongs to an Orthodox synagogue is fully Orthodox in theory and practice. Yet all who subscribe, at least nominally, to Orthodoxy, have it in common that they believe the Torah is unchanging, so that while, here and there, minor changes do take place in the wake of new social and economic conditions, for the Orthodox these are not really 'changes' at all, but simply the application of the traditional law in new situations. On the dogmatic side, Orthodoxy rejects totally the view of *biblical criticism that the *Pentateuch is a composite work and was not 'dictated by' God to Moses, although some Orthodox Jews are prepared to use the scholarly methodology in determining the dates of the other books of the Bible. For Orthodoxy, too, the Talmud, as the depository of the *Oral Torah, is the infallible source for Jewish practice and, to a large extent, for what Jews are expected to believe.

Orthodoxy is less an organized movement than a reaction to other groups. There is much internecine feuding, for example, among the Orthodox and

there is nothing like any official world organization for Orthodox Judaism. While *Hasidism is now accepted by the *Mitnaggedim as a legitimate expression of traditional Judaism and while, in the Council of Sages, the spiritual leaders of Aggudat Israel, there are Hasidic Rebbes as well as non-Hasidic Rabbis of the old school, the old conflict is not entirely a thing of the past. Ashkenazi Rabbis still tend to view their Sephardi opposite numbers as somewhat inferior in learning and Sephardi Rabbis often tend to see their Yiddish-speaking colleagues as uncouth and insufficiently flexible. Modern Orthodox Rabbis often have difficulties in matters of Halakhic interpretation with Rabbis of the pre-modern type. For instance, a number of Yeshivah heads placed a ban, which largely went unheeded, on participation by modern Orthodox Rabbis in organizations of which Reform and Conservative Rabbis are members. It is probably true to say that, for most of its adherents, Orthodoxy means simply that one's own religious traditions are followed, whether Hasidic or Mitnaggedic, Ashkenazi or Sephardi. The real issue on the level of practice between the Orthodox and the non-Orthodox is whether the tradition needs to be revised in some respects. The Orthodox rightly claim that theirs is the Judaism of tradition as followed in the pre-modern era. But this is precisely the question. Is the pre-modern tradition true to the tradition as it is now required to be interpreted? To what extent, in other words, is 'traditional Judaism' traditional?

Palestine The non-Jewish name for the land of Israel, so called after the ancient Philistines who lived on the sea coast. Jews normally refer to the land as Eretz Yisrael, 'Land of Israel', When the State of Israel was established it shortened the name to 'Israel'.

Panentheism 'All is in God', the doctrine that all creation is embraced by God. Panentheism is quite distinct from pantheism (see SPINOZA) or monism. According to pantheistic or monistic theory, God is the name given to the universe as a whole. The 'all' is identified with God, so that it is meaningless to speak of God as distinct from the universe. Pantheism means that all is God and monism (the theory of 'oneness') that God is a synonym for the 'stuff' or 'substance' of the universe. In panentheism, on the other hand, the 'all' *is* in God. The Being of God is both transcendent and immanent in relation to the universe, so that while it is inconceivable for there to be a universe without God it is not inconceivable for God to exist without the universe. The panentheistic doctrine is Jewishly unconventional but traces of it are found in some Jewish sources. The Zohar speaks of God both 'filling all worlds' and 'surrounding all worlds'.

Parapet The small wall that has to be erected around a flat roof as a protection against people falling off. The law of the parapet is stated in the verse: 'When you build a new house, you shall make a parapet for your roof, so that you do not bring bloodguilt on your house if anyone should fall from it' (Deuteronomy 22: 8). The parapet had to have a minimum size of 10 handbreadths. The law of the parapet ap-

plies only to flat roofs on which people can walk. The Talmud (*Bava Kama* 15b) records that the second-century teacher, Rabbi Nathan, extended the law of the parapet to prohibit keeping a vicious dog or a precarious ladder in the home. Obviously, it would apply today to the need to keep away from children medicines that could cause them harm or to failure to repair faulty electrical appliances. Another instance would be failing to check the brakes of an automobile.

Parveh A word of uncertain etymology to denote food that is neither meat nor milk. According to the *dietary laws, meat and milk foods must not be eaten when mixed and the two must not even be eaten together. *Parveh* food such as eggs, fish, vegetables, and fruit, can be eaten together with either meat or milk. In Yiddish parlance the term *parveh* is often applied to an in-between person, as in the English expression 'neither fish nor fowl'.

Passover The spring festival, celebrating the Exodus from Egypt, beginning on 15 Nisan and lasting for seven days (eight for Jews outside the land of Israel). The Hebrew word, *Pesaḥ*, means the Paschal lamb offered on the eve of the festival in Temple times (Exodus 12: 1–28; 12: 43–9; Deuteronomy 16: 1–8) and is so called because God passed over (*pasaḥ*) the houses of the children of Israel when He slew the Egyptian firstborn (Exodus 12: 23). Later on the festival itself came to be called Passover, although the usual biblical name is *Ḥag Ha-Matzot*, 'the Festival of Unleavened Bread', because of the command to eat only *matzah* ('unleavened bread') and to refrain from eating *ḥametz* ('leavened bread') during these seven days (Exodus 23: 15; Leviticus 23: 6; Deuteronomy 16: 16). After the destruction of the Temple the Paschal lamb could not be offered and the Passover rituals centred entirely on the avoidance of leaven and the celebration of the *Seder on the first night (and the second outside Israel) during which the *Haggadah is recited.

In the synagogue liturgy for Passover the festival is referred to as: 'the season of our freedom', freedom from bondage being the keynote of the celebrations. The readings from the Torah and the prophetic readings are from passages dealing with the Exodus. On the seventh day, traditionally the anniversary of the parting of the sea, the passage dealing with this event (Exodus 14: 17–15: 26) is read. Some pious Jews, on the eve of the seventh day, used to pour water on the floor in the home and walk through it as a symbolic reenactment of the ancient crossing of the sea, but this ritual is carried out nowadays by only a very few super-traditionalists. On the Sabbath in the middle of the festival, Ezekiel's vision of the dry bones (Ezekiel 37: 1–14) forms the prophetic reading (the *Haftarah), appropriate because of the theme of renewal and the final redemption in the Messianic age (see MESSIAH). It is customary in many synagogues to read the *Song of Songs on this Sabbath since there is a reference in the book to the spring (2: 11–13) and to the Exodus (1: 9). On the first day a prayer for dew is recited. The rainy season being over, supplication is made for the more gentle dew to assist the growth of produce in the fields.

Patriarchs The three fathers of the Jewish people, *Abraham, *Isaac, and *Jacob, who, together with the *matriarchs, are acknowledged as the ancestors of all Jews born to a Jewish mother. Proselytes, however, are called son or daughter of Abraham (see CON-

VERSION) because Abraham and his wife *Sarah, who taught the monotheistic faith, are the spiritual ancestors of all who embrace the Jewish religion even though converts are not the physical descendants of the patriarchs. The first benediction of the Amidah is called *Avot* ('Fathers') because in it God is described as the God of Abraham, Isaac, and Jacob. Jewish feminists (see FEMINISM) add the names of the matriarchs, *Sarah, *Rebecca, *Rachel, and *Leah.

Peace Heb. *shalom*. From the earliest times, Jews have considered peace to be among the highest values. The Talmudic Rabbis refer to peace as the vessel in which all blessings are contained. The traditional Jewish greeting is: 'Shalom alekhem' ('Peace to you'), to which the response is: 'Alekhem Shalom' ('To you Peace'). Nowadays, this is often shortened simply to Shalom. Typical of the high regard Jews have for peace is the ruling that Jews must not use the Shalom greeting in the public bathhouse because Shalom is one of the *names of God. Although Judaism does not advocate total pacifism, the Messianic vision (see MESSIAH) looks forward to the time when *warfare will be banished from earth.

Among the acts of benevolence listed by the Talmudic Rabbis is making peace between husband and wife, parents and children, man and his neighbour. For all the value set on *truth, a white lie can be told for the sake of peace. Peace, for the Rabbis, is not a mere absence of strife but a positive, harmonizing principle in which opposites are reconciled. The verse: 'he maketh peace in His high places' (Job 25: 2), repeated at the end of the Amidah and the *Kaddish prayers, is interpreted in the Midrash as referring to the high *angels Michael and Gabriel. Michael is the angel of mercy, Gabriel the angel of justice, yet God 'makes peace in His high places' by combining the aspects of both Michael and Gabriel, mercy and justice.

Peace also means that the individual character is not pulled too much in opposite directions. A Hasidic master observed: 'You cannot find peace anywhere save in your own self.' Cantankerousness is often a manifestation of inner feelings of instability and inferiority for which compensation is sought in combat with others. Another Hasidic saying notes that the verse says: 'The Lord will give strength to His people; the Lord will bless His people with peace' (Psalms 29: 11). Peace is the fruit of inner strength.

Pentateuch The five books of Moses—*Genesis, *Exodus, *Leviticus, *Numbers, and *Deuteronomy—called, in the Jewish tradition, the Torah, as distinct from the other two divisions of the *Bible, the Prophets and the Writings. On the traditional view, the Pentateuch is a single book, 'dictated' by God to Moses, with the exception, according to one opinion in the Talmud, of the last eight verses of Deuteronomy which describe the death of Moses. The still prevailing theory in *biblical criticism is the documentary hypothesis, according to which the Pentateuch stems from different periods in the history of Israel. On this hypothesis there are four 'documents' (many modern critics prefer to speak of oral 'strands' rather than actual 'documents')—J, E, D, and P—later combined by a redactor, hence the symbol 'R'. J represents the source in which the divine name used is JHVH (the *Tetragrammaton), hence, after the first letter, the symbol 'J'. E is the source which uses the divine name Elohim (see NAMES OF GOD). D represents the book of Deuteronomy; and P, the priestly strand. The documentary hypothesis purports to discover these strands throughout the Pentateuch and many critics, extending the analysis to the book of *Joshua, prefer to speak of a Hexateuch rather than a Pentateuch. Some of the critical theories tend to be unbalanced. Nevertheless, the whole

theory cannot so easily be dismissed, as traditionalists often try to do (see FUNDAMENTALISM). Even if the documentary hypothesis is completely overthrown, as it may be one day, the verdict of all modern biblical scholarship is that the Pentateuch is a composite work. That this poses problems for the tradition is undeniable. The major difference on the question of divine *revelation between Orthodox Judaism, on the one hand, and Reform and Conservative Judaism on the other, depends on whether the traditional view of the Pentateuch must yield to critical theories.

Pentecost See SHAVUOT.

Peot 'Corners', the sidelocks worn in obedience to the injunction: 'Ye shall not round the corners of your heads' (Leviticus 19: 27). The Talmudic Rabbis interpret this to mean that the hair of the head must not be removed in such a way that there is no hair between the back of the ears and the forehead. Maimonides gives as the reason for growing *peot* that the idolatrous priests used to 'round the corners of their heads' and thus the practice symbolizes rejection of idolatry. Hasidim tend to cultivate long, corkscrew *peot*, although this is not required by law. A typical description of a Hasid is 'a Jew with *beard and *peot*'.

Perpetual Light The light kept burning over the *Ark in the synagogue; Heb. *ner tamid*. The actual expression *ner tamid* is used of the *menorah in the Tabernacle (Exodus 27: 20) but the light of the menorah was not left burning all the time—it burned only during the night and was allowed to go out in the morning (v. 21)—whereas the perpetual light in the synagogue is kept burning all the time. In point of fact there is no reference at all in the sources to the perpetual light in the synagogue before the late sixteenth century. Nevertheless, it is the established practice to have this light in the synagogue. Some synagogues still use an oil lamp for the purpose but in the majority of synagogues an electric light is used.

Pharisees One of the three sects mentioned by Josephus as having flourished from the second century BCE to the early second century CE, the other two being the *Sadducees and the *Essenes. There is considerable uncertainty about the meaning of the term Pharisees, in Hebrew, *Perushim*. The Hebrew word seems to mean 'separatists', which might have meant originally 'separation' from the Sadducees or, possibly, people who led a life separate from worldly concerns. But, as Ellis Rivkin has noted, this term is often used for 'separatists' in general, so that it is precarious to assume that all the Talmudic passages about the *Perushim*, except those in which the Pharisees are mentioned together with the Sadducees, refer to the Pharisaic party. This explains why, on the one hand, the Pharisees are hailed in the Talmudic literature as the forerunners of what became Rabbinic Judaism, while there are other references to the *Perushim* as hypocrites, as in the *New Testament, although it is obvious that the New Testament does refer to the Pharisaic party. Under the influence of the New Testament accounts, the term Pharisee came to denote among Christians a person excessively scrupulous with regard to the rituals and the niceties of the law but without any real inner depths. Needless to say, the Jewish tradition, in which the Pharisees are the forerunners of Rabbinic Judaism, rejects as totally biased this picture of the Pharisees. Indeed, Christianity itself owes much to the Pharisaic background of Jesus—the Christian doctrine of the Hereafter and the *resurrection of the dead, for instance.

According to both Josephus and the Talmud the two main theological differences between the Pharisees and the Sadducees were: the Pharisaic belief that Israel was given by God an *Oral Torah, and the Pharisaic belief in the reality of the *World to Come.

Philo Of Alexandria, Jewish philosopher (d. 50 CE). Philo wrote in Greek and used, for his biblical comments, the Greek translation of the Bible, the *Septuagint. Philo's main endeavour is to reconcile the Platonic philosophy, popular in his day and place, with Judaism. His usual method is allegorical. For instance, the biblical narrative that Abraham sent away his handmaiden Hagar at the request of his wife Sarah (Genesis 21: 9–21) is interpreted as referring to the good man, Abraham, sending away (i.e. avoiding) the lure of his bodily passions, represented by Hagar, in obedience to his intellect, represented by Sarah. Generally, Philo adopts the Greek view that the body is the tomb of the soul. Only that soul is immortal which refuses to become trapped in bodily desires. Such a soul returns to its source at the death of the body. Philo quotes the Greek philosopher, Heraclitus, who says: 'We live their death, and are dead to their life', meaning that during earthly life the soul is entombed in the body as in a sepulchre but at the death of the body the soul lives its proper life released from the corpse to which it was bound. This notion is found in Rabbinic literature as well, the Rabbis saying that the righteous are alive even when their body has died but the wicked are dead even while they are alive in the body.

It is a moot point whether Philo knew Hebrew. If he did his knowledge was not at all extensive. His works were known to Christians in the Middle Ages but there was no reference to him at all in Jewish literature until the sixteenth century, when he is mentioned by Azariah de *Rossi. In his book *Maor Eynayyim* de Rossi refers to Philo by a

Hebrew translation of his name, Yedidiah.

Philosophy Although philosophical ideas are found, of course, in the Bible—monotheism itself is such an idea—philosophy proper, in the sense of a systematic examination of the teachings of the Jewish religion in the light of what was considered to be pure human reasoning (see RATIONALISM) did not emerge fully until the Middle Ages, although it was anticipated by *Philo of Alexandria. The philosophy of the medieval thinkers such as *Saadiah Gaon, *Bahya Ibn Pakudah, *Judah Halevi, *Maimonides, *Gersonides, and *Crescas, was either Aristotelian or Neoplatonic or a mixture of both. None of these thinkers were acquainted with Greek thought at first hand; they only knew it from Arabic translations, which enjoyed a wide circulation. Although the medieval thinkers employed philosophical method, their main aim was to demonstrate that the Jewish religion can be reconciled with the truth, as they saw it, of Greek philosophy. Their endeavours were not directed to the question: is Judaism true? Rather the thrust of their thinking was to show that the true religion, in which they believed and to which they subscribed without reservation, can be interpreted so as to conform with philosophical truth. In this sense, these thinkers are best described as theologians rather than philosophers. In their various ways, they tried to show that the truth conveyed through *revelation is the same truth taught by the Greek thinkers, except where the two clearly diverge. When the divergence became apparent, philosophy had to yield to revelation, since there is only one truth.

Photography The invention of photography has given rise to a number of Halakhic problems (see HALAKHAH). Can a photograph be relied on for the pur-

pose of identifying a corpse so that the wife can be permitted to remarry? (The photograph can be relied on together with other criteria, according to many authorities.) Is a photographed *mezuzah valid? In view of the opposition to representation of the human figure in *art, is it permitted to take photographs of people? While a few authorities were, at first, strict in this matter, nowadays hardly anyone takes exception to the practice. Photographs of famous Rabbis abound and presumably they allowed themselves to be photographed.

Pig The prohibition of swine-flesh is stated explicitly in the Pentateuch (Leviticus 11: 7; Deuteronomy 14: 8). According to the Rabbinic tradition the prohibition covers only the eating of pig's meat, but not other benefits from the animal. It is permitted, for instance, for a Jew to have a pigskin wallet. There is, however, a Rabbinic ban on pig-breeding. Maimonides suggests that the prohibition is on hygienic grounds; the pig is an excessively dirty animal. The prophet connects eating swine-flesh with idolatrous practices (Isaiah 66: 17). Since the time of the *Maccabees, when Jews were forced to eat pig as a sign of their disloyalty to the Torah, Jews have had a special abhorrence for the pig. Even Jews who do not observe strictly other *dietary laws usually draw the line at eating bacon or ham.

Pilgrimages The book of Deuteronomy (16: 16–17) states: 'Three times a year—on the Feast of Unleavened Bread [*Passover], on the Feast of Weeks [*Shavuot], and on the Feast of *Tabernacles—all your males shall appear before the Lord your God in the place that He will choose. They shall not appear before the Lord empty-handed, but each with his own gift, according to the blessing that the Lord your God has bestowed upon you.' In the book of

Exodus (23: 14–17) the same command is given. The Mishnah (*Ḥagigah* 1: 1) understands the words 'not appear . . . empty-handed' to mean that every male Jew is obliged, when he appears in the Temple on the pilgrim festivals, to bring two offerings, a festival offering and an 'appearance' offering. The Israeli scholar Samuel Safrai has argued convincingly that Talmudic statements which suggest that three times a year every Jew was actually obliged to make the pilgrimage and bring these offerings are purely academic, and were made long after the Temple had been destroyed. It is hard to imagine that in Temple times all Jewish males left their farms and homes to travel to Jerusalem on all three festivals. It would seem that in the Temple period, while it was certainly considered meritorious to visit the Temple on these three occasions, especially on Passover when the Paschal lamb had to be offered, there was no actual obligation so to do. It seems probable that the pilgrimage was undertaken only by those who lived near to the Temple.

Pilpul Keen argumentation, sharp-witted discussion, especially of Talmudic and Halakhic themes, probably from the word *pilpel*, 'pepper', hence a peppery argument. In Ethics of the Fathers (6. 6) the pilpul of disciples is mentioned as one of the ways in which learning is advanced. Generally speaking, the method of keen dialectics represented by pilpul is highly prized. A distinction must, however, be drawn between pilpul with the aim of arriving at the truth (by a close examination of the various moves in an argument) and pilpul for its own sake as a kind of game in which far-fetched analogies are produced by a scholar with the aim of demonstrating his skill in debate. The latter form, prevalent in the Middle Ages, met with strong opposition on the part of some teachers, although others encouraged it as a means of

sharpening the mind. The term pilpul is often used, nowadays, to denote hair-splitting.

Plagiarism While there is little about plagiarism in the sources compiled before printed books were known, the practice of passing off another's thoughts as one's own was frowned upon as a form of theft. In Ethics of the Fathers (6. 6) one of the ways of learning with which the student of the Torah is expected to be familiar is the repetition of a thing in the name of the one who said it originally. Throughout the Talmud the greatest care is taken to attribute teachings to those originally responsible for them. While there is no legal redress for stealing an author's ideas, this is certainly held to be a severe moral offence.

Pornography In the Jewish sources disapproval of pornographic literature and obscene talk is expressed largely in the moralistic rather than the legalistic literature. So far as the ancient Rabbis and later Jewish moralists are concerned, there is no doubt that they frown on lewd or foul talk and on sexual thoughts other than those relating to husband and wife.

Poverty Jewish attitudes to poverty vary. Throughout Jewish history the poor are treated with respect, and alleviation of their sufferings is strongly advocated (see CHARITY). But this does not necessarily mean that poverty is seen as something of value. There is nothing in Judaism to correspond to the Christian monastic ideal of taking poverty vows. In the Bible possessions are usually seen as a blessing. Generally speaking, much depended on the economic conditions in which Jews found themselves. In Eastern Europe, for example, where the economic conditions were on the whole very low, poverty was accepted with resignation to the will of God but with a degree of irony.

This explains the contradictory statements about poverty found in the Talmud. On the one hand, there is the saying: 'Poverty befits Israel like a red trapping on a white horse' (*Ḥagigah* 9b). On the other hand, the early third-century Babylonian teacher, Rav, used to pray that he be given 'a life of riches and honour' (*Berakhot* 16b), a prayer which, incidentally, has been incorporated in the liturgy for recital by all Jews on the Sabbath before the New Moon. It has been noted that, in the prayer, 'riches' are associated with 'honour'. Dishonourable means of acquiring wealth were severely condemned from the time of the great Hebrew prophets onwards.

Prayer The most striking difference between prayer as it is found in the Bible and prayer as developed in post-biblical Judaism is that in the Bible the prayers are of private persons in their individual needs, whereas, from the earliest Rabbinic times onwards, while there is an acknowledgement that private prayers are also essential, the emphasis is on public prayer. All the standard prayers are in the plural: 'Grant *us*'; 'We praise Thee'; '*We* give thanks unto Thee', and so forth. Some prayers can only be recited where a quorum of ten—the *minyan*—is present.

A Talmudic comment (*Taanit* 2a) on the verse: 'And serve Him with all your heart' (Deuteronomy 11: 13) states: 'What is service of the heart? This is prayer.' Maimonides, at the beginning of the section of his Code which deals with prayer, understands this to mean that, while the actual times and forms of the prayers are Rabbinic, there is a biblical injunction for every man and woman to pray daily. Others see the whole obligation to pray to be of Rabbinic origin but no less binding for that reason.

Prayer Book Heb. *Siddur* ('Arrange-

ment'), a book containing the daily and Sabbath prayers. The book containing prayers for the festivals is known as a Mahzor (from a root meaning 'to come round', i.e. for use when the festivals arrive). All prayer books have the same basic features (see LITURGY) but each rite has its own additions and version, for example, the Ashkenazi Siddur, the Sephardi Siddur, the Italian Siddur, in modern times the Reform and Conservative Siddurim (plural of Siddur), and others, each in conformity with the ideological stance of the compilers and users.

In Talmudic times the prayers were recited by heart and there were no written orders of service at all. The first Prayer Book was compiled in the ninth century by Amram Gaon (see GEONIM), and is known as the Seder Rav Amram Gaon. This was followed in the tenth century by the Siddur of *Saadiah Gaon. Since then, especially after the invention of printing, numerous prayer books have been published. The Kabbalists have their own Prayer Book, of which there are a number of different versions. In these the special 'intentions', *kavvanot* (see KAVVANAH), of the Kabbalah are given to allow the worshipper to concentrate on them in his prayers. There are also a number of Hasidic prayer books, usually with comments offering guidance to the particular branch of Hasidism for which they are intended. Material was added to the Prayer Book from time to time, often at the mere whim of the printers.

Preaching That sermons were delivered in the synagogue, especially on Sabbaths and the festivals, from early Rabbinic times, is attested in numerous Midrashim (see MIDRASH). It would seem that the later Midrashim had their origin in sermons, although the Midrashim themselves bear all the marks of literary productions in their own right. The usual preaching method, until the modern period, was to take scriptural verses out of context and to apply them to the religious and ethical questions of the preacher's time. This method of scriptural application became known as *derush* (from a root meaning 'to search' or 'to enquire') and the sermon became known as a *derashah* (from the same root, as is the word Midrash itself). Preachers were known as Darshanim or Maggidim ('Speakers' or 'Tellers'). Again until modern times, the function of preaching belonged not to the *Rabbi of a town but to the special class of preachers, usually learned men but not necessarily well versed in the practical *Halakah. In Eastern Europe, Maggidim would wander from town to town to preach in the synagogue, attracting the masses by their popular, homely expositions liberally sprinkled with proverbs, folk-tales, and illustrations from the daily life of their audiences. Collections were published of the sermons of the more renowned preachers and these were used as guides for preachers everywhere.

Although the historian Leopold *Zunz, in his famous work, *Gottesdienstliche Vortraeger der Juden*, published in 1832, sought to demonstrate, when challenged by the Prussian government (under the influence of Orthodox groups who saw sermons in the vernacular as the beginnings of Reform), that preaching is an ancient Jewish institution, the traditional *derashah* took, in Germany, the new form of the *Predigt*, as it was called. The new type of sermon was more formal and in the vernacular, and it became a regular part of the service. The modern sermon is also based on a scriptural verse, usually taken from the portion of the weekly Torah reading, but treats a particular theme in systematic fashion and its aim is more one of edification rather than instruction.

In modern Rabbinical seminaries, Orthodox, Reform, and Conservative,

homiletics is an important subject in the curriculum. For the modern Rabbi, preaching is an important part, perhaps the most important part, of his Rabbinic activity.

Precepts, 613 A precept of the Torah, a *mitzvah*, is a divine command contained in the *Pentateuch and can be either a positive precept—a command to do something—or a negative precept—a command to refrain from doing something. The command to give charity, for example, is a positive precept. The command not to steal is a negative precept. The idea that there are 613 precepts is first found in a homily delivered, according to the Talmud (*Makkot* 23b), by the third-century Palestinian preacher, Rabbi Simlai. This teacher states that there are 613 precepts: 365 negative precepts, corresponding to the days of the solar year, and 248 positive precepts, corresponding to the 'limbs' of the body. 'Limbs' here denotes parts of the body, such as the joints of the fingers, and the concept of 248 parts in this sense is ancient and found in the Mishnah (*Ohalot* 1: 8). It is as clear as can be that all this belongs to the *Aggadah. It is an instance of sermonizing in which the preacher used concepts that predated his observation, applying them to convey a moral lesson, as preachers do. The homiletical nature is apparent in the Midrashic comment that each 'limb' says to man: 'Perform a *mitzvah* with me' and each day of the solar year says: 'Do not commit a sin on me.' Louis Ginzberg has noted that in the ancient Aggadah, referred to by *Philo among others, the *Decalogue is said to contain 613 letters. It was only at a later date that these 'letters' become 'precepts'.

Pride Pride is, in the Jewish tradition, among the most serious of the vices, as *humility is among the highest of the virtues. The Talmudic Rabbis, perhaps because of their awareness that scholars are easily tempted to lord it over the ignorant, denigrate pride in the most caustic terms. God and the proud man, a Talmudic saying has it, cannot reside together in the same world. Pride is an abomination akin to idolatry and the self-sufficiently proud deny the basic principle of Judaism that God is the Lord of creation. The Torah, say the Rabbis, is compared to water which flows only downwards, never upwards. The proud man can never truly assimilate the teachings of the Torah. Yet one Rabbi declared (*Sotah* 5a) that a scholar should have an 'eighth of an eighth' of pride out of respect for his own learning. His colleague remonstrated: 'He should not possess it [pride] or part of it', quoting the verse: 'Every one that is proud in heart is an abomination to the Lord' (Proverbs 16: 5).

The Jewish moralists stress that avoidance of pride is not to be confused with self-deception. If a man has a good mind and worthy qualities he is not expected to try to ignore them, only not to take credit for them. Whatever talents a man possesses should be seen as God's gifts to him, undeserving though he is of them.

Priestly Blessing The blessing recited by the *priests (see KOHEN) in ancient times in the Temple and nowadays in the synagogue. The biblical source is Numbers 6: 22-7: 'The Lord spoke to Moses: Speak to Aaron and his sons: Thus shall you bless the people of Israel. Say to them: The Lord bless you and protect you! The Lord deal kindly and graciously with you! The Lord bestow His favour upon you and grant you peace! Thus they shall link My name with the people of Israel, and I will bless them.' The blessing is in three parts and is called 'the threefold blessing'. In the Hebrew the first section consists of three words, the second of five, and the third of seven. In the Temple the priests recited the blessing twice daily, in the morning and afternoon, while they stood on a special platform, known as the *dukhan* ('platform'). In the synagogue the blessing is recited by the priests while standing in front of the *Ark. To this day, the recital of the priestly blessing is called in Yiddish *dukhenen*, literally, 'platforming', after the Temple procedures.

Priests In Temple times the chief function of the priesthood was to offer the sacrifices in the Temple. The priestly families served in a weekly rotation. The priests received no fees for officiating in the Temple but they were given generous portions of meat from the sacrificial animals and a proportion of all wheat, wine, and oil. The priest (see KOHEN) is described as holy. The people of Israel were to be 'a kingdom of priests and a holy nation' (Exodus 19: 6), but the special sanctity of the priest depended on his having been born as a descendant of *Aaron. Although a priest was not intrinsically holy or spiritually superior to ordinary Israelites, there is no doubt that priests in ancient times saw themselves as the aristocrats of the Jewish people.

Since the destruction of the Temple, those believed to be Kohanim because of a family tradition have the privilege of being called first to the Torah, of delivering the priestly *blessing, and of being invited to say *grace after meals. A Kohen may not come into contact with the dead except for his near relatives and he may not marry a divorcee. Reform accepts neither the privileges nor the restrictions of priesthood because it sees the whole institution as having lapsed with the destruction of the Temple. Still to maintain it, the Reformers hold, is to perpetuate a caste system. Orthodoxy retorts that it is absurd to see the very few laws concerning the Kohanim as perpetuating any kind of caste system.

Principles of Faith The essential beliefs on which the Jewish religion is founded; the basic Jewish *dogmas from which all else in the religion follows. The thirteen principles of the faith as laid down by Maimonides are implied attacks on ideas the sage believed were foreign to Judaism. It is these thirteen that are significant for Maimonides because it was in the areas covered by them that the struggle between Judaism and rival faiths took place.

Maimonides' thirteen principles are:

1. Belief in the existence of God.
2. Belief in God's unity.
3. Belief in God's incorporeality.
4. Belief in God's eternity.
5. Belief that God alone is to be worshipped.
6. Belief in *prophecy.
7. Belief in Moses as the greatest of the prophets.
8. Belief that the Torah was given by God to Moses.
9. Belief that the Torah is immutable.
10. Belief that God knows the thoughts and deeds of human beings.
11. Belief that God rewards and punishes.
12. Belief in the coming of the *Messiah.
13. Belief in the resurrection of the dead.

Maimonides adds a very dogmatic note. Even a complete transgressor, though he will be punished for his sins, has a share in the World to Come if he believes in these principles. But anyone who denies one of these principles is an unbeliever and no longer belongs to the community of Israel. Maimonides here makes correct belief the supreme value. The believing sinner is included in the 'general body of Israel'. The unbeliever, even though he is not guilty of serious sin, is excluded from 'the general body of Israel' and, Maimonides continues, 'we are obliged to hate him

and cause him to perish'. (This final statement may be sheer hyperbole but is indicative of Maimonides' severely dogmatic cast of mind.) For Maimonides a Jew is defined not by what he does but by what he believes.

Printing The invention of printing had an enormous influence on Jewish religious life, in which the study of the Torah is paramount. In the Middle Ages few were able to afford to have a good library, even when enough patrons of learning were found to pay skilful copyists to produce books for the use of scholars. In the Geonic period, there were so few copies of the Talmud in Jewish communities that the *Geonim were often consulted not about the meaning of the texts but about what the texts actually said. With printing all this changed. Books of all kinds were published and widely disseminated. Editions of the Talmud, the Midrashim, the Codes, the commentaries, the works of the philosophers and the Kabbalists, and, of course, the Bible and the Prayer Book, placed all the sacred Jewish classics within the reach of everyone, if not in private homes at least in synagogue and communal libraries. The first complete edition of the Babylonian Talmud was printed by the non-Jewish publisher, Daniel Bomberg, in Venice in the years 1500–23. Not only did Bomberg's pagination become universally accepted, thus facilitating easy reference, but the placing in this edition of the *Tosafot together with Rashi's Commentary beside the text caused scholars to look upon these commentaries as part of the text itself, as it were, widening immensely the scope of Jewish learning.

Procreation According to the Rabbis, the first *mitzvah* of the Torah is the command to engage in procreation (Genesis 1: 28; 9: 1). Procreation is, in addition to companionship, the aim of *marriage. Opposition to *birth-control .

is partly based on the duty to have children. According to the majority, and accepted, Rabbinic opinion this duty does not devolve upon women, no doubt because it was unreasonable in ancient society to demand that a woman should be obliged to attract a man to marry her.

Prophecy The *inspiration of certain individuals by the divine power, which enables them to gaze into the future and bring to other human beings a message from God (Heb. *neviim*).

Perhaps the most remarkable thing to be observed of the literary prophets is the assurance with which they speak of their message as coming directly from God. 'The lion hath roared,' declares *Amos, 'who will not fear? The Lord God hath spoken, who can but prophesy?' (Amos 3: 8). *Isaiah tells of the Lord speaking to him 'with a strong hand' (Isaiah 8: 11). *Jeremiah tells how the Lord put words into his mouth (Jeremiah 1: 9) and how God imparted to him words of fire (Jeremiah 23: 29). The message which comes to the prophet is, in the first instance, to his contemporaries and it frequently has to do with future events. It is consequently too glib to make the common distinction between 'forthtellers' and 'foretellers' and to claim that the classical prophets belonged only to the former group. There is an element of prediction in the work of the classical prophets, too, though the predictions are of a future arising out of the present rather than a distant, unrelated future, notwithstanding the views of *Fundamentalism, whether Jewish or Christian.

The position taken in classical Reform Judaism, that the prophets are more significant than the Torah—Reform has sometimes described itself as 'Prophetic Judaism'—is untraditional, as the Reformers admitted. In the Rabbinic tradition the Torah contains God's complete revelation for Jewish practice so that the Rabbis could say that if Is-

rael had not sinned, no further revelation through prophets and the sacred writings would have been required (*Nedarim* 22b). No prophet was able to make any innovations, once the revelation to Moses was complete (*Shabbat* 104a; *Megillah* 2b). This traditional attitude accounts for the fact that some ultra-Orthodox Jews (see ORTHODOX JUDAISM) devote very little time to the study of the prophets and are even somewhat easygoing in chanting the *Haftarah, the prophetic readings in the synagogue. Yet no Jew, whether Reform or Orthodox, fails to acknowledge the tremendous significance for Judaism of the prophetic books of the Bible.

Many Jews today would be prepared to argue, with plausibility, that not being prophets ourselves we cannot hope to comprehend the exact nature of the prophetic experience. What matters is that however the prophets received their revelation, their message concerning the God who demands holiness, justice, and mercy in human affairs contains the highest demands made upon man, and this is so whether the classical prophets are understood as ecstatics or, as *Heschel sees them, as men who shared the divine pathos, or on any other understanding of the phenomenon of prophecy. As Otto Eissfeldt puts it:

'With regard to the psychology of the prophets, opinions still differ widely whether, and in what degree, supernormal—or to give the usual adjective "ecstatic"—qualities, experiences and acts are to be thought of. Yet all are at one in the view that the religious and ethical value of these figures does not depend on the answer given to this question, but that they have an enduring meaning for mankind in any case, and that here lies their true significance.'

Prostitution Prostitution, 'the oldest profession', is naturally referred to frequently in the Bible (e.g. Genesis 38: 14;

Joshua 2: 1). In the famous judgement of *Solomon (1 Kings 3: 16–27) the claim to be the true mother of the infant was made by two prostitutes. A *priest was forbidden to marry a woman who had been a prostitute (Leviticus 21: 7). The book of *Proverbs (ch. 7) warns against the loose woman who entices young men to sin with her. Israel is described metaphorically as a prostitute when unfaithful to God (Numbers 25: 1–2; Jeremiah 3: 6; Hosea 4: 12). In the ancient Near East, temple prostitutes (men as well as women) offered the gain of their bodies to the gods. It appears that this practice was at times copied by the Israelites from their pagan neighbours, hence the injunctions: 'No Israelite woman shall be a cult prostitute, nor shall any Israelite man be a cult prostitute. You shall not bring the fee of a whore or the pay of a dog [usually understood to refer to a male prostitute] into the house of the Lord your God in fulfilment of any vow, for both are abhorrent to the Lord your God' (Deuteronomy 23: 18–19). The practice persisted until King Josiah suppressed it as part of his reforms (2 Kings 23: 7).

The Talmudic Rabbis not only condemned professional prostitution but also referred to any sexual contact between a man and a woman who were not married to one another as harlotry (zenut).

Proverbs, Book of The second book in the third section of the *Bible, the Ketuvim, the Sacred Writings. This book of thirty-one chapters consists of collections of proverbs and wise sayings and belongs to what scholars refer to as the wisdom literature, a type of literature that flourished over many centuries in the ancient Near East and which had a marked influence on Proverbs, *Job, and *Ecclesiastes. Wisdom in this context refers to prudent counselling for the conduct of daily life, praise of learning, and warnings against sloth, profligacy, and the like.

Hence the book of Proverbs has a strong universalistic tone but with a specific Israelite and religious thrust. Although a few sayings in the book are reminiscent of popular saws, the book contains literary forms produced by skilful writers and cannot be seen as a simple collection of examples of folk wisdom.

The book opens with the words: 'The proverbs of Solomon, the son of David, king of Israel' and Solomon is referred to in two other passages (10: 1 and 25: 1). Since it is said of Solomon that 'he spoke three thousand proverbs' (2 Kings 5: 12), the traditional view is that King Solomon is the author of the book of Proverbs. However, in a Talmudic passage (Bava Batra 15a), the book is said to have been 'written', that is, finally edited, or, possibly, committed to writing, by King Hezekiah and his associates, on the basis of the verse: 'These also are proverbs of Solomon, which the men of Hezekiah king of Judah copied out' (Proverbs 25: 1). The verdict of modern scholarship is that the book consists of a number of collections from different periods in Israel's history but all belonging to the wisdom type. There is no real reason, however, for rejecting the view that some of the material may have come from King Solomon himself or from members of his courtly circle.

Providence The Hebrew term for divine providence, hashgahah, was first used by the medieval Jewish theologians who, under the influence of Greek philosophy, preferred abstract terms to denote ideas found in concrete form in the Bible and the Rabbinic literature. But the idea that God controls and guides the world He has created permeates the Bible and the post-biblical literature. The very term hashgahah is based on the verse in Psalms (34: 14): 'From the place of His habitation He looketh intently [hishgiah] upon all the inhabitants of the earth.' The abstract discussions of the medievals were largely around the scope of divine providence. Two types of providence are considered: 1. *hashgahah kelalit*, 'general providence', God's care for the world in general and for species in general; and 2. *hashgahah peratit*, 'special providence', God's care for each individual.

The Talmudic Rabbis did not explore the question of divine providence as a philosophical problem and, generally speaking, prefer to affirm that God's care extends over all without dwelling too much on how providence operates. The result is that, as on other theological topics, a wide variety of opinions are expressed without any attempt at systematic treatment. The famous Talmudic statement regarding God's providence extending to all His creatures is the saying that God 'feeds the whole world from the horned buffalo to the brood of vermin' (*Avodah Zarah* 3b). The late second-century teacher Rabbi Hanina gave expression to the extreme view of divine providence over human beings when he said: 'No man bruises his finger here on earth unless it was so decreed against him from on high' (*Ḥullin* 7b). For Hasidism, as for the Islamic Ashariyah centuries before, divine providence extends over everything; nothing moves without direct divine control, no stone lies where it does unless God wills it so. The early Hasidic master Phineas of Koretz remarks: 'A man should believe that even a piece of straw that lies on the ground does so at the decree of God. He decrees that it should lie there with one end facing this way and the other end the other way.' The later master, Hayyim Halberstam, similarly states: 'It is impossible for any creature to enjoy existence without the Creator of all worlds sustaining it and keeping it in being, and it is all through divine providence. Although the Rambam [Maimonides] has a different opinion in this matter, the truth is that not even a bird is snared without providence from above.'

There are tales of Hasidic masters rebuking disciples who idly plucked grass as they walked along, since each blade of grass has its own particular place in the divine scheme.

Contemporary theologians, Jewish and non-Jewish, have grappled with the problem for divine providence posed by the greater realization, through scientific research, that everything proceeds by cause and effect. If God's providence extends to particulars, what precisely is the relationship of this type of providence to the perceived (and predictable) natural processes? Some have argued that scientific explanation employs probabilities in place of certainties. There is still a random element, even in the picture of nature provided by scientific theories and it is in this area of 'chance' that divine providence comes into operation. Others have approached the subject from the point of view of *existentialism. For the religious existentialist, God's providence does not consist in affecting the outcome of natural processes but in the way we relate to them (see MIRACLES). The problem is acute but then so is the problem, of which it is a part, of how God can be both transcendent and immanent (see PANENTHEISM).

Psalms, Book of Heb. *Tehillim* ('Praises'), the first book of the third section of the *Bible, the *Ketuvim*, Sacred Writings, comprising 150 psalms. Many of the psalms have superscriptions, describing their contents, their author, and, it is generally assumed, in some cases, the melodies to which they were sung in the Temple. In the Jewish tradition, but not in the King James Version, these superscriptions are counted as separate verses. Many of the psalms are obviously liturgical compositions. The Levites sang a psalm for each day of the week and on the Sabbaths and festivals, accompanying the song with instrumental music.

The Rabbinic *Midrash to Psalms

states that *David composed his Psalms in five books just as Moses wrote the five books of the *Pentateuch. In this Midrash, and very frequently in the Rabbinic literature, David is assumed to be the author of the book of Psalms. This view of Davidic authorship was not left unquestioned in the Middle Ages and is rejected by all modern biblical scholars (see BIBLICAL CRITICISM and FUNDAMENTALISM) as anachronistic. The book of Psalms is now seen rather as a collection or anthology of psalms compiled at different periods, though there is no real reason to deny that some of them may go back to David himself, with psalms or groups of psalms added later to the collection. There is no agreement on the dating of the various psalms. The older view that the whole book dates from as late as the period of the *Maccabees is now rejected by the majority of scholars, some holding, on the analogy of ancient Near Eastern texts unearthed fairly recently, that psalm-making, even with the employment of the same terms and language-patterns, was a feature of the surrounding culture long before Israel came on to the scene. Needless to say, the question of dating and authorship is totally irrelevant to the value of the book of Psalms as religious outpourings of the highest order, recognized as such by the millions of worshippers, Jews, Christians, and others, who have used the Psalms to express the deepest emotions of their own heart. Many Psalms have been incorporated into the liturgy of the synagogue.

Psychology The study of psychological states is prominent throughout Jewish thought even though there is nothing like a systematic treatment of the subject in the classical sources. The Talmudic literature is especially rich in psychological observation. In the Rabbinic doctrine of the *yetzer ha-tov and the yetzer ha-ra, the good and evil inclinations, the Rabbis, like Freud, see

man's internal struggle in terms of a tripartite division—the man himself, the good inclination, and the evil inclination. Man, in this doctrine, has the two inclinations, each pulling him in a different direction. The Jewish moralists, too, often probe human psychology. *Bahya, Ibn Pakudah's Duties of the Heart, as its name implies, is a call to the Jew to purify his inner thoughts and refuse to be satisfied with mere outward observances, the 'duties of the limbs'. While the demands of the moralists are severe, often too severe for a healthy approach to the moral life, they are usually tempered by a realism in which the individual is encouraged not to aim too high. The *Musar movement is based firmly on severe introspection, too much so according to opponents of the movement.

Any discussion of Judaism and psychology is bound to take into account the views of Freud, both because Freud himself was a Jew and because of the impact which psychoanalytic theory has had on modern thought. The parallel between the Rabbinic doctrine of the good and evil inclination has been noted above, though it is purely coincidental. Despite claims to the contrary, Freud was not familiar with Rabbinic or Kabbalistic literature and they certainly had no influence on his work. For all that, it is interesting to note that a close approximation to the Freudian idea of sublimation occurs in the Talmudic saying (Kiddushin 30b): 'My son, if this repulsive wretch [the evil inclination] attacks you, pull him into the House of Learning. If he is stone, he will dissolve. If he is iron, he will shatter into fragments.' Freud's idea that religion is a 'collective neurosis' is hardly acceptable to any branch of Judaism. Among religious Jews there are neurotic personalities who are constantly in fear that they have not carried out the rituals properly. This is not the fault of the rituals. Non-observant neurotics find their own means of catering to their neurosis. The Freudian critique of religion as wishful thinking does hit home, since religion is sometimes based on irrational desires and needs. But antireligious attitudes can similarly be the fruit of irrational desires and this applies to Freudian views as well. When the Jewish religion declares itself true, this does not necessarily mean that the truth is always arrived at by rational investigation and reflection. Religious Jews will acknowledge that they believe because they have a need for God but would go on to say that the need is generated by the truth, not the truth by the need. If human beings have a hunger for God, Judaism affirms, this is because there is a God to satisfy that hunger, just as hunger for food arises because there really is food to satisfy the hunger.

Purim The minor festival (on which it is permitted to work, unlike on the major festivals) which falls on 14 Adar. Purim is celebrated in commemoration of the deliverance of the Jews from the designs of Haman who cast lots in order to determine the date of their destruction, as related in the book of *Esther. 'For Haman son of Hammedatha the Agagite, the foe of all the Jews, had plotted to destroy the Jews, and had cast *pur*—that is, the lot—with intent to crush and exterminate them. . . . For that reason these days were called Purim, after *pur*' (Esther 9: 24–6). Modern biblical scholars (see BIBLICAL CRITICISM) have questioned the historicity of the events told in the book of Esther and have tried to discover the origins of Purim in a Babylonian festival, later adapted by Jews. But there is evidence that Jews celebrated Purim as early as the first century BCE. Classical Reform Judaism tended to look askance at the festival of Purim both because of the lack of evidence that the events really happened and because the festival was seen as too nationalistic and vindictive for Western taste. Orthodox, Conserva-

tive, and now some Reform Jews do celebrate Purim, as representing God's deliverances through the ages.

The central feature of Purim is the reading of the Megillah ('Scroll'), as the book of Esther is called, on the night of Purim and on the next morning. Although the Megillah is normally read on these two occasions during the synagogue service, where synagogue attendance is not possible it can be read in the home.

Since the book of Esther speaks of sending portions to friends and gifts to the poor on Purim (Esther 9: 22), the rule, as stated in the Talmud (tractate *Megillah* is devoted to the laws of Purim), is that each person must send a gift of at least two items of food to a friend (some, today, prefer to send books instead) and give at least one donation to two poor men. From the reference to 'days of feasting and joy' (Esther 9: 17) the Talmudic Rabbis ordained that a special Purim meal be partaken of in the home, at which much wine is imbibed. The Talmudic statement in this connection (*Megillah* 7b) that a man is obliged to become so drunk on Purim that he is no longer aware whether he is blessing *Mordecai or cursing Haman, is still taken literally by some ultra-Orthodox Jews, although many Rabbis understand it as hyperbole and advise against taking drinking to the extreme of drunkenness, even on Purim.

Undoubtedly influenced by the Italian carnival, people dress up and, children especially, perform Purim plays in which they take on the characters mentioned in the Megillah. In learned circles, it is often the practice to give fanciful interpretations of the Bible and Talmud and frivolously manipulate sacred texts. Scholars have seen in this 'Purim Torah', as it is called, a means of obtaining psychological relief, on one day in the year, from what otherwise might have become a burden too hard to bear.

Quest Although the Torah is traditionally conceived of as a 'given', conveyed by God to Moses in all its fullness, Jews are expected to enquire into its meaning and, in the process, receive new insights that have been left opaque—intentionally so, many Jewish theologians have held. The *Maharal of Prague (*Tiferet Yisrael*, ch. 2) goes so far as to say that just as God created an unfinished world for human beings to bring to perfection, He created an incomplete Torah to be brought to completion through diligent application on the part of its students over the ages. The problem for the modernist Jew is that if he is a follower of the Torah, there are whole areas in which the quest must be in response to the challenges presented by modern thought. The modernist quest, in these areas, is a quest for the Torah itself (see FUNDA-MENTALISM). Nevertheless, it is not too difficult for the modernist to base his particular quest on the idea stressed by the Maharal and others. The quest for the Torah is itself part of what is meant by Torah, so that it is not so much a question of seeking in order to find as one of finding in the very quest.

Questions Jews have been fond of asking questions, even of answering a question with a question (see HUMOUR). The Talmud is full of questions being raised in discussions on the Torah. Nothing is taken for granted. Even when answers are propounded, these too are questioned in turn as the argument proceeds. The *Responsa literature consists entirely of questions and answers. The Zohar (i. 1b–2a) states that there is a stage in the divine unfolding (see EN SOF and SEFIROT) of which one can ask the question: 'What is it?' without expecting any answer to be forthcoming, so elevated is that stage beyond human comprehension. It is permitted to ask but futile to expect an answer. The Zohar calls this stage 'Who' and ingeniously interprets the verse: 'Lift up your eyes and see who created these' (Isaiah 40: 20) to mean that 'Who' created, that is, brought into manifestation, the lower stages, called 'These' because they can be perceived by human thought. It is possible to point to them: God's mercy and compassion, for instance. The Zohar adds that of an even higher stage of the divine unfolding one cannot ask the question, so elevated is this above all human thought. Even to ask of this stage—what it is—is an absurd attempt to extend thought beyond its legitimate boundaries. Behind all this is the idea that the truths about God and His relationship to the universe cannot be delivered in a neat package and that in making the attempt to probe, deeper and unanswerable questions are bound to arise.

Quietism The doctrine, found in some versions of Christian thought, that men of faith should sit back and leave everything to God. Quietism is rarely found in Jewish thought, which believes in human co-operation with the divine. *Saadiah Gaon (*Beliefs and Opinions*, x. 15), while admiring those who say that the highest endeavour of the servant of God in this world ought to be to dedicate himself exclusively to the service of his Lord, believes that it is contrary to Jewish teaching to take this to the extreme that a person ought not to take care of himself and make the effort for his affairs to prosper.

The difference between trust in God and quietism is that trust involves the belief that God helps human effort, while quietism believes that no human effort is required at all and everything can be left to God.

Qumran The site on the north-west shore of the Dead Sea at which the *Dead Sea Scrolls were discovered. Ruined buildings, the Khirbet Qumran, had been discovered much earlier. At Khirbet Qumran there is much evidence of more than one occupation from Roman times. It is generally seen by scholars as most plausible to assume that the people of the Scrolls discovered in the nearby caves had their community at Khirbet Qumran.

Rabbi Teacher of Judaism qualified to render decisions in Jewish law. The term is derived from *rav*, meaning 'great man' or 'teacher'; Moses is called Moshe Rabbenu ('Moses our teacher'). The suffix 'i', meaning 'my', is somewhat strange. Why '*my* teacher'? It has been suggested that the letters RBI should be vocalized, as they are among Sephardi Jews, as 'Ribbi', 'great one', and that the 'i' is not, in fact, a suffix at all. It has also been conjectured that the term Ribbi originally denoted a fully ordained teacher, one who received the *ordination reaching back to Joshua on whom Moses laid his hands. When full ordination came to an end (in the fourth century CE) the title Rabbi was given to every teacher of the Torah and was a purely honorific one.

In the traditional pattern, the Rabbi is a scholar-saint, devoting himself entirely to learning (the study of the Torah is a never-ending occupation from which no one ever graduates), to guiding the community in spiritual affairs, and, especially, to acting as judge in civil cases and rendering decisions in matters of religious law. Some Rabbis were more powerful and more autocratic than others. There are many recorded instances of Rabbis at loggerheads with the lay leaders of the community. Although in modern times the English expression 'laymen' is often used, the term is basically inappropriate. The Rabbi is also a 'layman', occupying no sacerdotal role. It is consequently quite erroneous, as is often done by non-Jews, to describe the Rabbi as a Jewish *priest.

After the *Emancipation and the emergence of the Jew in Western society, the need was increasingly felt for a new type of Rabbi, one able to guide his congregation in the new situation in which they had to face challenges hitherto unknown. Even Orthodox congregations, in Germany for instance, required their Rabbi to be proficient in general learning, to be a cultured man able to represent his people to the non-Jewish world, and, where possible, to have a university degree. Seminaries were founded for the training of modern Rabbis, in which such subjects as homiletics, philosophy, ethics, history, and psychology were included in the curriculum as well as pure Rabbinics. So many roles are demanded of the modern Rabbi that it is impossible for even the most gifted to fill them all successfully. He has to be preacher, pastor, counsellor, fund-raiser, politician, and popular after-dinner speaker, so that he has little time and energy left for what used to be the Rabbi's main occupation, the study of the Torah. The old-fashioned Rabbi was also called upon from time to time to defend Judaism against attack but the modern Rabbi, Orthodox, Reform, or Conservative, has to defend his own group's understanding of what Judaism means. The problems of the modern Rabbinate are regularly discussed in the various Rabbinic and general Jewish journals.

There is little objection in Jewish law to the appointment of a woman as a Rabbi (see FEMINISM and WOMEN) and, in any event, the modern Rabbinate itself is an innovation not envisioned in the traditional sources. The voice of tradition is somewhat muted since the office of modern Rabbi is itself untraditional. To date there are no women Rabbis in Orthodox Judaism. Reform and Conservative Judaism decided years ago to ordain women as Rabbis and women serve in this capacity in Reform and Conservative congregations. Nevertheless, a considerable minority of Conservative

Rabbis in the USA are opposed to the ordination of women as Rabbis and some have broken away from the main Conservative Rabbinic movement in protest.

Rabbis, the Talmudic The Rabbis who flourished in Palestine and Babylon in the first five centuries CE, the Tannaim and Amoraim, the sages who produced and appear in the Talmud and the *Midrash. These ancient teachers are usually referred to simply as 'the Rabbis' *par excellence*. The Rabbis are seen as spiritual supermen, bearers not only of the tradition, the *Oral Torah, but of truths revealed to them by divine inspiration through the '*Holy Spirit'. Orthodox thinkers are prepared to say, on occasion, that some of the views of the Rabbis are difficult to accept in their plain meaning and require to be reinterpreted. Some would follow the line of the *Tosafot in medieval France that *nature has changed so that, in scientific matters, the Rabbis were speaking of the nature that obtained in their day. Modern scholarship, even when engaged in by the Orthodox, tries to study the lives of the Rabbis as objectively as any other biographies. No Orthodox scholar today would fail to applaud David Hoffmann's attempt in the nineteenth century to write a biography of the third-century teacher Samuel (see RAV AND SAMUEL), and would totally disregard Hoffmann's Orthodox critics who contended that such an enterprise is heretical in its implication that a Talmudic sage can have a 'biography' compiled about him, as if he were an ordinary human being. For all that, on the theological level, no Orthodox thinker will ever allow himself to say that the Rabbis were wrong, any more than he would dare to say that the Bible was wrong. Even Reform theologians are usually hesitant in using expressions like right and wrong when speaking of the Rabbis since, after all, Rabbinic teachings belong to the evolu-

tion of Jewish thought. Even for Reform Judaism, the Rabbis are 'our' Rabbis, and the radical Reformer *Holdheim expressed himself circumspectly when he declared: 'The Talmud was right in its day and I am right in mine.'

Rachel The biblical heroine, one of the four *matriarchs, wife of *Jacob and mother of *Joseph and Benjamin, whose story is told in the book of *Genesis (chs. 29–50). Rachel died as she gave birth to Benjamin, and she was buried 'on the road to Ephrath—now Bethlehem' (Genesis 35: 19). The prophet Jeremiah (31: 15) speaks of Rachel weeping for her children in exile. This passage from Jeremiah is read as the *Haftarah on the second day of *Rosh Ha-Shanah. When Boaz married Ruth the people blessed him that Ruth would be like Rachel and Leah, 'both of whom built up the House of Israel' (Ruth 4: 11). When parents bless their daughters on the eve of the Sabbath, the form of the blessing is: 'May God make you like Sarah, Rebecca, Rachel and Leah.' From as early as the tenth century CE the tomb of Rachel was identified as existing on its present site just outside Bethlehem. The tomb is a place of pilgrimage for the pious, who pray to God to help them in the merit of 'mother Rachel'.

Racial Discrimination A major source for the Jewish view on racial discrimination is the prosaic account of the family of nations (Genesis 10), where all the peoples then believed to be on earth are described as one huge family descended from the three sons of *Noah, the father of mankind after the *Flood. It is irrelevant to the issue that few believe nowadays that all men are descended from Noah and that races such as the Chinese are not mentioned at all, since the Jewish view is based on the passage as it stands in the Bible and its moral and religious truth does not depend on the account being factual. No people is declared to be in any way subhuman because of its colour or race. However the doctrine of Israel as the *Chosen People is understood, Israel's superiority is not seen to be established on racial grounds, except by a very few theologians. Any human being, if he so wishes, can be admitted as a convert (see CONVERSION) to Judaism and, in any event, the notion of a 'pure' Jewish race has long been exploded by biological science.

Rainbow After the *Flood and the deliverance of *Noah and his family, God shows Noah the rainbow in the clouds as a sign of His covenant with mankind that He will never again bring a deluge to destroy them (Genesis 9: 8-17). Nahmanides observes that the rainbow is a natural phenomenon, so that the narrative does not mean that God created the rainbow after the Flood, only that He declared that the already existing phenomenon would serve as the sign of His covenant from now on. The rainbow, pointing upwards, denotes, according to Nahmanides, that God's arrows would no longer shoot downwards to destroy the human race. The Talmud (*Berakhot* 59a) states that a special benediction should be recited when beholding a rainbow. The exact form of this benediction is elaborated on and now appears in the *Prayer Book as: 'Blessed art Thou, O Lord our God, King of the universe, Who remembers the covenant, is faithful to His Covenant, and keeps His word.'

Rain, Prayers for Failure of the rains to come in their proper season was the most serious calamity that could befall the Jewish community in ancient Palestine, an agricultural society which depended for its very life on a good harvest. Prayers for rain were therefore a prominent feature of congregational worship, a whole tractate of the Mishnah, tractate *Taanit*, being devoted in large measure to prayers for rain. In the *Gemara to this tractate there are tales of miracle-workers whose prayers for rain were heeded because of their saintly lives. Some of these tales, though legendary, express not only the attitude of trust in God but also the idea that the *saints have the power to coerce God to bring the rains.

On the basis of the statement in the Mishnah (*Rosh Ha-Shanah* 1: 2) that on the festival of Sukkot ('*Tabernacles') the world is judged for rain, it is the universal custom, during the Additional Service on *Shemini Atzeret, at the end of this Tabernacles festival, for the *Cantor to wear white robes as a symbol of purity and mercy and the *Geshem* ('Rain') prayer is chanted, in which God is entreated to send rain in the merits of biblical heroes about whom there are accounts concerning 'water'. On the seventh day of Tabernacles, *Hoshanah Rabbah, there is now a more elaborate service of petition for rain. A similar service to *Geshem* takes place on the first day of Passover. This is called *Tal* ('Dew') and consists of a petition for God to grant the more gentle dew now that the rainy season is over.

Rape The Jewish law on rape, as it was developed in the Talmud, is based on the biblical passages (Deuteronomy 22: 22-8) but with certain qualifications. For instance, the question of *capital punishment for a man who raped a married woman was never applied since capital punishment for any crime was not carried out in Rabbinic times. A married woman who had been raped is not forbidden to her husband (unless he is a *Kohen) but where she consented to have sex with a man she is forbidden to her husband. But even here the final ruling is that her consent once the rape had begun is not treated as consent for the purpose and she is permitted to her husband on the grounds that in such circumstances it is assumed that she cannot be said to have been able to control the urge once the sex act had been initiated by the rapist. The Rabbis further limited the application of the law that where a man rapes a virgin he is obliged to marry her in the case of a girl under the age of 12 years and 6 months. Nevertheless, in all cases of rape the rapist must compensate his victim for her ordeal and the amount is assessed by the court. Each community has the right to fix its own penalties for rape. Thus in the State of Israel rape is treated under the general laws governing physical assault.

Rapoport, Solomon Judah Galician Rabbi and scholar (1790–1867), one of the pioneers of the *Jüdische Wissenschaft movement. Rapoport held no official Rabbinic position until his appointment in 1837 as Rabbi of Tarnopol. Before that time he was supported by his father and father-in-law or engaged in business, devoting most of his time to Talmudic learning and, under the influence of *Krochmal, to the study of science and Western languages. In 1840 Rapoport was appointed Rabbi of the prestigious community of Prague where the *Haskalah had made inroads and the community felt the need for a more or less modernist Rabbi.

Rapoport acquired fame as a result of his biographies of some of the *Geonim and *Rashi in which, for the first time, the lives of spiritual giants of the past were approached critically and historically. With astonishing erudition Rapoport supplied copious notes to his articles, his keen analysis helping to pave the way for all later scholars who wished to employ the historical–critical methodology in the investigation of the Jewish past.

Rashbam French commentator to the Bible and the Talmud (d. *c*.1174), called Rashbam after the initial letters of his name, *Rabbi Shemuel ben Meir*. Rashbam's father, Rabbi Meir, married Yochebed, daughter of *Rashi. Rashbam studied with his grandfather in Troyes, France. Rashbam's commentary to the Torah has become one of the standard commentaries, taking its place beside those of Rashi and *Nahmanides. Rashbam observes that Rashi had told him that if he could have had his time over again he would have put more emphasis on the plain meaning (*peshat*) of the text. Rashbam's aim is to explain the text in its plain meaning, though not without reference to the Rabbinic *Midrash.

Rashi Foremost French commentator, called Rashi after the initial letters of his name, *Rabbi Shlomo Yitzhaki* (1040–1105). Rashi was born in Troyes in northern France and spent most of his life in this city. In his youth Rashi studied for a number of years at the great centre of Jewish learning, Mayyence in Germany, where his teachers, to whom he refers repeatedly in his commentaries, were the disciples of Rabbenu *Gershom of Mayyence, the spiritual father of Ashkenazi Jewry. Returning to his native city, Rashi taught without fee a number of chosen disciples, earning his living by means of the vineyards he owned.

Rashi's undying fame rests on his commentaries to the Bible and the Babylonian Talmud, printed together with the text in practically all editions. Rashi's commentary to the Humash (the *Pentateuch) was first printed in Reggio, Italy, in 1475 and seems to have been the first Hebrew book ever printed. Over the generations this commentary has been used as the prime guide, so that the term 'Humash and Rashi' became part of the universal Jewish vocabulary. Rashi was jocularly called the 'brother' of the Humash.

Rashi's great genius as a commentator is particularly evident in his massive running commentary to the Talmud. Rashi here rarely raises questions of his own but, with uncanny anticipation of the difficulties the student will find, supplies the required solution in a few well-chosen words. He also records variant texts he had discovered in his travels and, where necessary, suggests a plausible emendation of the text. The Tosafot and other commentators often take issue with Rashi's explanation but all students agree that without Rashi the Talmud would have remained a closed book. Rashi often explains Talmudic terms by giving the French equivalent. These *laazim* ('foreign words') have become a major source for scholars of Old French.

Rationalism The attitude in which religious faith has to justify itself at the bar of reason before it can be accepted. There is much reasoned appeal in the Bible. The Hebrew prophets seek to persuade by rational argument. The translation, in the Jewish Publication Society version, of the verse in Isaiah (1: 28): 'Come let us reach an understanding says the Lord', may not be an accurate rendering. A footnote to the translation says: 'Meaning of Hebrew uncertain.' Yet the implication that the prophets do employ reason becomes apparent from even the most casual reading of the prophetic books, even though terms like 'reason' in the abstract sense are unknown in biblical Hebrew. The Talmud consists almost entirely of reasoned arguments, although the Talmud, like the Bible, does not normally rely on human reason to support *faith. In the *Haskalah ('Enlightenment') movement, which arose in the eighteenth century, the 'Age of Reason', there is the strongest emphasis on the ability of the human mind to arrive at the basic truths of religion by unaided human reason. This rationalistic tendency in Jewish thought has been heavily assailed by the religious existentialists (see EXISTENTIALISM) in modern times. The religious existentialists argue that God must be encoun-

tered as a 'given', not reached as the end of an argument, though even the existentialists are bound to rely on reason to support their very case. The mystics, too, are suspicious of philosophical enquiry in religious matters. God, the mystics affirm, is to be known through experience. Unlike the medieval philosophers, who hold that to 'know' God is to prove by reason that He exists and that belief means only that one takes it all on trust, the mystics declare that, on the contrary, reason can only tell a little about God, but to know God means to experience His nearness. The mystics declare that there are things *higher* than reason.

Rav and Samuel The two foremost teachers of the early third century CE in Babylon, belonging to the first generation of Amoraim (see TANNAIM AND AMORAIM). Both Rav (whose personal name was Abba but who was called 'Rav' [Rabbi *par excellence*] in respect for his great learning) and Samuel were born in Babylon but studied in the land of Israel under Rabbi *Judah the Prince. On Rav's return to Babylon he settled in the town of Sura where he served as teacher of the law and spiritual guide. Samuel settled in the town of Nehardea where a centre of learning had existed from much earlier times and in which he took the leading role on his return. After Samuel's death, his pupil Rabbi Judah ben Ezekiel settled in Pumbedita. Thus the colleges of Sura and Pumbedita in the period of the *Geonim traced their descent from the early third century.

Reading of the Torah The practice of reading the Torah from a Scroll (*Sefer Torah) in the synagogue is mentioned in sources dating from the first century CE and it is evident that it had been long established. The Talmud even suggests that the reading of the Torah on Monday, Thursday, and Sabbath afternoon was introduced by *Moses so that the Israelites should not allow three days to go by without Torah. *Ezra is said to have introduced the weekly Sabbath reading on Sabbath morning. It is obvious, in any event, that the custom is ancient. To this day the custom is to read a lengthy portion of the Torah on Sabbath morning and a smaller portion of the next Sabbath reading on Sabbath afternoon and on Monday and Thursday morning. On festivals a suitable portion dealing with the particular festival is read. Although it is conventional to speak of the reading of the Torah, the Torah is, in fact, chanted (see CANTILLATION).

The Reading of the Torah as Practised Today

The *Ark is opened and the Scroll from which the reading is to be done is taken in procession around the synagogue. Many people bow to the Scroll as it passes, although some Rabbis in the Middle Ages objected to this because it might seem that the Torah was being treated as an object to be worshipped. The Scroll is then placed on the reading-desk and a number of people are called up to the reading of a portion. The term for this privilege is *aliyah* ('ascent') and the usual expression is 'given an *aliyah*' (plural *aliyot*). In Talmudic times those called to the reading chanted the portion themselves but, since not everyone is capable of reading the unvowelled texts, the universal custom is now for the chanting to be done by a special competent reader; those called up recite a benediction before and after the reading of their portion in which they thank God for having given the Torah to Israel.

On the Sabbath there are seven *aliyot*; on Yom Kippur six; on the festivals five; on *Rosh Hodesh four; on Monday, Thursday, and Sabbath afternoon three. The first *aliyah* is given to a *Kohen, the second to a *Levite, and the third and the others to *Israelites*. Some members of the congregation are specially

entitled to be given an *aliyah*: a boy celebrating his *Bar Mitzvah; a groom on the Sabbath before the wedding; the father of a new-born child; and a person on the anniversary of the death of a parent (on the *Yahrzeit). On Sabbaths and festivals a small portion of the reading is repeated as the Maftir ('Conclusion') and the person called up for this reads the prophetic portion for the day (the *Haftarah), not from the Scroll but from a printed vocalized book from which it requires no great expertise to read. It is considered a special honour to be given Maftir and to read the Haftarah. It is also considered a special honour to be called up for the reading of the third portion, the first given to an Israelite, and to the *Decalogue on the occasions when this is read. In many congregations there is much competition for the privilege of being given an *aliyah*, often paid for by a donation to the synagogue or to charity. In some congregations there is even an 'auction' of *aliyot* but this is frowned on in more staid congregations.

Rebbe, Hasidic The Hasidic master also called the *Zaddik. Unlike the formal *Rabbi, whose main function was to teach the Torah and render decisions in Jewish law, the Zaddik served his followers as a spiritual guide and mentor and offered prayers on their behalf. The term Rebbe is simply a variation of Rabbi and is used to distinguish between the two types of leader.

Rebecca Wife of Isaac and mother of Jacob and Esau; the second of the four *matriarchs, whose story is told in the book of Genesis (22: 23–28: 5). Rebecca was buried beside her husband in the Cave of *Machpelah (Genesis 49: 31). The blessing given to Rebecca by her father and brother as she set out to meet her future husband (Genesis 24: 60) is recited in traditional communities before the wedding ceremony, when the groom places the veil over the bride's face as Rebecca veiled herself when she first saw her husband to be (Genesis 24: 65).

Rebuke The source for the obligation to offer reproof to a neighbour is the verse: 'Thou shalt not hate thy brother in thine heart: thou shalt surely rebuke thy neighbour and not suffer sin because of him' (Leviticus 19: 17). The plain meaning of the verse is: if you believe that your neighbour has wronged you, do not keep silent and hate him in your heart but rebuke him for his offence and have done with it. It is as if the verse is saying: if you bear a grudge against someone get it off your chest and then forget about it, instead of bottling it up inside you and going about with hatred seething in your heart. But the Rabbis extend the obligation to offer rebuke whenever a neighbour has committed or intends to commit any offence, whether ethical or religious, as the prophets rebuked the people for their shortcomings. Rabbis and preachers, especially, were called upon to offer constant rebuke to their people, although *Hasidism was unhappy about the severe castigations indulged in by the preachers. The Rabbis were realistic enough to appreciate that a rebuke can all too easily encourage defiance, hence the Rabbinic saying: 'Just as it is meritorious to offer reproof when it is known that it will be heeded, it is meritorious not to rebuke when it is known it will not be heeded' (*Yevamot* 65b).

Reconstructionism The American movement, with branches elsewhere, founded by Mordecai *Kaplan with a view to revitalizing Judaism in the modern world. The central idea of Reconstructionism is that Judaism is more than a religion in the narrow sense but is a religious civilization, with its own art, music, literature, culture, and folk-ways. Although Reconstructionists like Milton Steinberg

were believers in the Personal God of traditional Judaism, the movement generally follows Kaplan's naturalistic interpretation in which God is 'the power that makes for salvation'. Moreover, 'salvation' in this context does not mean of the soul in the Hereafter but of the Jewish people on earth through the enrichment of Jewish life that is the result of an acceptance of Jewish values and their dynamic adaptation to the new conditions in which Jews now find themselves. At first Kaplan thought of the movement as one cutting across the usual divisions in Jewish life between Orthodoxy, Conservative, and Reform Judaism. But, while all three branches have been greatly influenced by Kaplan's ideas, their followers preferred to develop their own philosophies of Judaism. Kaplan's religious naturalism was far from being to everyone's religious taste. Reconstructionism has now developed as a fourth movement with its own seminary for the training of Reconstructionist Rabbis, the Rabbinical College in Wyncote, Pennsylvania, founded in 1957. A small number of Reconstructionist synagogues have also been established but Reconstructionist Rabbis serve in Reform and Conservative congregations as well. Founded in 1935, the journal *The Reconstructionist* is devoted to the philosophy of Reconstructionism.

Redemption Heb. *geulah*. In Judaism redemption usually denotes the saving of the Jewish people from exile and oppression. The Exodus from Egypt, for example, is called the Egyptian redemption. The final redemption will take place with the advent of the *Messiah. It is not, however, quite correct to say that Judaism, unlike Christianity, knows nothing of the idea of the redemption of the individual soul from sin. Psalm 130 certainly uses redemption in the sense of deliverance from iniquity. The difference between Judaism and Christianity with regard to personal redemption is that, in Judaism, the soul is redeemed from sin by sincere repentance and the power of the Torah to influence human conduct, and God and no other is the Saviour. Redemption, in the sense of salvation of the people as a whole, is generally discussed in Judaism under the heading of the coming of the Messiah who will bring Israel's exile to an end and establish the Kingdom of God upon earth. In the Messianic age, all mankind will be saved from war, enmity, and hatred. In the Kabbalah, God Himself is redeemed, so to speak, when the *Shekhinah is restored from exile and all the *holy sparks have been rescued from the demonic forces. In modern times, Reform Judaism interpreted the redemption as the advance of modern society towards greater freedom, tolerance, and social justice. For *Zionism, redemption meant the return of the Jewish people to its homeland.

In the traditional understanding there is both a severely practical and a numinous approach to redemption. It is God who redeems Israel and the result of the final redemption is the emergence of a new and higher type of humanity. The *Mizrachi, the party of religious Zionists, wishing to preserve both the practical and numinous aspects in the emergence of the State of Israel, coined the expression *athalta degeulah*, 'beginning of the redemption', as if to say, the State of Israel is a state like any other, with normal political, economic, and social concerns, and with the inevitable faults and shortcomings of any political state. But, for the Mizrachi thinkers, the final Messianic dream is yet to be realized and this dream is on the way, at least, to its fulfilment now that the State of Israel has been established. This is an attempt to have one's cake and eat it. Traditionally, and logically, the final redemption can be said either to have come or not to have come. There is no such concept as a semi-final, final redemption.

Red Heifer Heb. *parah adumah*, the cow the ashes of which were used in the purification rites for one who had been contaminated through having come into contact with a corpse. As described in the book of Numbers (19: 1–22), the cow had to be slaughtered outside the Israelite camp and its blood sprinkled in the direction of the holy of holies in the *Tabernacle (in *Temple times, the holy of holies in the Temple). The cow was then burned whole together with cedar wood, a crimson thread, and hyssop. The ashes were mixed in a vessel containing spring water. The person contaminated was sprinkled on the third and seventh day of his defilement and he was then allowed to enter the sanctuary. This rite was followed in the Temple. The Talmud states that the red heifer was a rarity since it had to be completely red. But Milgrom has suggested that the word *adumah*, translated as 'red', really means 'brown' and the rarity consisted in it having to be completely brown without any white or black streaks or spots. There is some evidence that ashes of a *parah adumah* were preserved for centuries after the destruction of the Temple. These ashes are no longer available and since, according to Maimonides, the site of the Temple still enjoys its sanctity and since everyone has come into contact with a corpse or with one who has, Orthodox Jews, nowadays, do not enter the Temple site and a notice appears at the entrance to warn them off. The section of the Torah dealing with the *parah adumah* is read on the Sabbath before the month of Nisan as a reminder of Temple times when this portion was read to warn those contaminated to purify themselves in readiness for the offering of the Paschal lamb on the festival of Passover. This Sabbath is called 'the Sabbath of Parah'.

Reform Judaism The religious movement which arose in early nineteenth-century Germany with the aim of reinterpreting (or 'reforming') Judaism in the light of Western thought, values, and culture where such a reinterpretation does not come into conflict with Judaism's basic principles. (Orthodox Judaism maintains that the very principle of Reform is in conflict with the basic *principle of faith that the Torah is immutable.) After the *Emancipation and the emergence of the Jew into Western society, the need for a degree of adaptation of the traditional faith to the new conditions of life was keenly felt. The *Haskalah movement of Enlightenment, of which Moses *Mendelssohn was the leading figure, grappled with this very problem but tended to leave traditional norms more or less intact. It was left to Reform to introduce various innovations in the synagogue service and in other areas of Jewish religious life. Reform, however, did not, at first, become organized as a separate movement. A number of cultured laymen in various German cities tried their hand at creating a liturgy and form of service which they believed was more in keeping with Western ideas. The first Reform congregation was established in Hamburg in 1818, in the Hamburg Temple. Reform generally came to prefer the term Temple rather than synagogue for its house of prayer in the belief that the Messianic doctrine could no longer be interpreted in terms of a personal *Messiah who would rebuild the *Temple. The new opportunities presented in the West for greater social and educational advancement and for the spirit of freedom to flourish were themselves seen as the realization of the Messianic dream and it was felt that the synagogue, standing in place of the Temple, should be known as such.

The Hamburg Rabbis enlisted a number of prominent Orthodox Rabbis to publish a stern prohibition against these reforms. Not very long after-

wards, a number of Rabbis educated in German universities met in conferences in the years 1844–6; Reform ideas were put forward and a fully fledged Reform movement became established. The leaders of Reform in Germany, Abraham *Geiger and Samuel *Holdheim, tried to develop a Reform theology in which Jewish particularism, while never entirely rejected, yielded to a far greater degree of *universalism than was envisaged at any time in the Jewish past. The European Reform movement was centred on Germany, but Reform congregations were also established in Vienna, Hungary, Holland, and Denmark. In England the Reform congregation, the West London Synagogue of British Jews, was established as early as 1840. At the beginning of the twentieth century a more radical type of Reform was established in England under the influence of Claude *Montefiore. This took the name Liberal Judaism. In Germany itself, however, the movement known as Liberal Judaism was more to the right than German Reform.

Essentially, Reform Judaism departs from Orthodox Judaism in its understanding of *revelation. For Orthodoxy the Torah is the revealed will of God and the Jew is required to observe the commands of the Torah not because they enrich his spiritual life (though Orthodoxy believes that they do have this effect) but because this is God's will. Reform, with its doctrine of 'progressive revelation', believes that in successive generations God allows for different appreciations of the truth of the Torah. Critics of Reform have accused the movement of being too much influenced by the Zeitgeist in its departure from tradition. It is in the area of revelation that Conservative Judaism seeks to understand the concept in a way that acknowledges the human element in the Torah while recognizing, at the same time, that the practical observances, as laid down in the Halakhah, are the will of God, albeit given *through*

Israel not, as in Orthodox Judaism, simply *to* Israel. The three basic ideas on which Judaism is based are God, the Torah, and Israel. There is much truth in the generalization that, of the three, Reform places the stress particularly on God, Orthodoxy on the Torah, Conservative Judaism on the peoplehood of Israel.

Reincarnation The idea that a soul now residing in a particular body may have resided in the body of another person in an earlier period of time. Theories of reincarnation or metempsychosis are found in many religions and cultures, ancient and modern, but there are no references to the idea in the Bible or the Talmud and it was unknown in Judaism until the eighth century CE, when it began to be adopted by the *Karaites (possibly, it has been suggested, under the influence of Islamic mysticism). The usual Hebrew term for reincarnation is *gilgul*, 'rolling', that is, the soul 'rolls' through time from one body to a different body.

The Kabbalists do believe in reincarnation. The Zohar refers to the doctrine in a number of passages (e.g. ii. 94a, 99b). *Nahmanides, in his commentary to the book of Job (to Job 33: 30), speaks of reincarnation as a great mystery and the key to an understanding of many biblical passages. Manasseh ben Israel (d. 1657) devotes a large portion of his *Nishmat Hayyim* ('The Soul of Life') to a defence of reincarnation. In chapter 21 Manasseh observes that the doctrine was originally taught to Adam but was later forgotten. It was revived by Pythagoras, who was a Jew (!), and he was taught the doctrine by the prophet Ezekiel. The Hasidim believe explicitly in the doctrine and tales are told of Hasidic masters who remembered their activities in a previous incarnation.

Religion As an abstract term the word religion is found in neither the Bible nor the Talmud, both of which

use concrete language. *Zangwill once said that the Rabbis, the most religious of men, had no word for religion; perhaps, one might add, precisely because they were the most religious of men they could not contain their religious attitudes in a single word or in any kind of formula. For the Rabbis, the all-embracing term, Torah, stood for what we call religion. Moreover, the Rabbis, and the biblical authors, did not see their faith as one religion among many. People who believed in many gods and worshipped them were all lumped together as idolaters (see IDOLATRY). It was not until the Middle Ages, when *Christianity and *Islam had emerged, that Jewish theologians were obliged to consider Judaism as a religion, different from these two religions but resembling them in certain respects. For purposes of discussion and debate a term for religion had to be coined. The term the medieval thinkers used, *dat*, derived from a Persian word found in late passages in the Bible, originally meant law, in the very concrete sense of a particular way of conduct, but now came to denote religion in the abstract. The *dat* of Israel came to mean the religion of Israel and the plural, *datot*, the other religions.

There is no uniform attitude among contemporary Jews on the relationship between Judaism and other religions. Many Jews adopt the attitude of the medieval thinkers that, while it is possible to learn some things of value from other religions, basically they are false and only Judaism true. Others adopt the relativistic attitude, often expressed as: it does not matter which religion you profess as long as you profess a religion or as long as your religion inspires you to lead a good life. But the fallacy here is obvious. To say that all religions are equally true is to say that all religions are equally false. Every believer in a particular religion, no matter how broad-minded he is and no matter how strong is his avoidance of triumphalism, cannot ignore the truth-claims his religion makes. For all the things they have in common, the great religions of the world affirm as basic principles ideas that are simply not compatible with one another. If certain forms of atheistic Buddhism are true, then Hinduism with its many gods and Judaism, Christianity, and Islam with their one God must be false. When Judaism denies that God can ever assume human flesh it thereby rejects the basic Christian dogma. If the 'way' of the Buddha is alone 'true' for all men, then the way of the Torah cannot be true for Jews. For all that, it is exceedingly difficult to dub all the great religions of the world simply as idolatrous faiths of which Jews can and should be tolerant but which they should declare to be totally false. The increased knowledge of the rich vein of spirituality in all the world religions militates against such a notion of total rejection. Many modern Jews, eager to avoid undue dogmatism and, at the same time, uneasy with the vagaries of relativism, prefer to adopt the attitude that, while there is truth in all religions, there is more truth in Judaism. It is obvious that such an attitude leaves many questions unanswered but for all its vagueness many modern Jews see it as the only reasonable approach to the great mystery of the God whom Judaism brought to the world and who allows other religions apart from Judaism to exist.

Responsa The answers given by authorities in Jewish law to questions put to them; Heb. *sheelot u-teshuvot*, 'questions and answers'. There are occasional references in the Talmud to letters sent by one Rabbi to another asking for information in matters of law but the Responsa activity proper dates from the period of the *Geonim, when the practice developed of scholars addressing questions to the heads of the great Babylonian communities at Sura and

Pumbedita in Babylonia, the foremost authorities in this period. Collections were made of the Geonic Responsa, especially those of *Sherira Gaon and his son *Hai Gaon, but while these collections were known to the medieval authorities they did not appear in print until as late as the nineteenth century. Essentially, the questions in the Responsa concern problems which arose out of new conditions, for which no direct answers could be found in the Talmud, the final *authority for Jewish *law. The leading Respondents through the ages, faced with new questions, tried to discover analogies in the Talmud and the later Codes and from time to time the replies in the Responsa served as sources for new Codes.

Responsibility Only a person who acts of his own *free will and in full knowledge of what he is doing is held responsible in Jewish law. A person of unsound mind is not held responsible for any injuries he inflicts on others nor has he any obligation to keep the precepts of the Torah. The degree of *insanity required is discussed in the Talmud and the Codes. A minor is similarly held unaccountable because his state of mind is considered to be defective. A boy loses his minor status to become fully responsible for his actions at the age of 13, a girl at the age of 12, hence *Bar Mitzvah and *Bat Mitzvah. A person is not held responsible, even if he knows what he is doing, where he is forced by others to commit an offence. The Talmud states that if a man is threatened with death if he does not kill someone, it is his duty to allow himself to be killed rather than kill. Nevertheless, Maimonides and other codifiers rule that if he did kill in order to avoid his own death, his act is not treated as an act of murder since he did, after all, perform it under duress. While a father is not held responsible in law for acts carried out by his children, he has a responsibility to train them to lead an honourable and useful life and he has a responsibility for their education.

Resurrection The doctrine that in a future age the dead will rise from their graves to live again. This doctrine appears frequently in Jewish *eschatology, where it is associated with the doctrine of the *Messiah and the immortality of the *soul. There are only two biblical references to the resurrection of the dead, in passages generally held by biblical scholars to be of late date, so that it has been conjectured that the doctrine owes something to Persian influence. The first is: 'Thy dead shall live, my dead bodies shall arise, awake and sing, ye that dwell in the dust, for thy dew is as the dew of light, and the earth shall bring to life the shades' (Isaiah 26: 19); and the second: 'And many of them that sleep in the dust of the earth shall awake, some to everlasting life, and some to reproaches and everlasting abhorrence' (Daniel 12: 2).

Although Maimonides lists belief in the resurrection as a basic *principle of faith (the thirteenth) he refers to it in a very offhand manner. In Maimonides' *Guide of the Perplexed* there is no reference at all to the doctrine. There are one or two stray references to the resurrection in Maimonides' Code but, on the whole, he seems to identify the Rabbinic *World to Come not with the resurrection but with the immortality of the soul, or, rather, he seems to believe that the resurrection itself is of the soul, not the body. Maimonides' critics accused him, in fact, of denying the doctrine of the resurrection. These critics point out that his virtual silence on the fate of the body in the Hereafter certainly contradicts Rabbinic teachings on the subject. There are found in the Rabbinic literatures such statements as that the dead will be resurrected wearing their clothes (*Ketubot* 111b) and that the righteous whom God

will resurrect will not return to their dust (*Sanhedrin* 72a), obviously pointing to a belief in bodily resurrection.

On this subject the great debate took place between Maimonides and *Nahmanides. Writing after Maimonides' death, Nahmanides, in *The Gate of Recompense* devoted to the subject, takes strong issue with Maimonides' view that the bodies of the resurrected dead will also die eventually, although he does believe that these bodies will be exceedingly refined and ethereal. Crescas in *The Light of the Lord* (iii. 4) agrees with Nahmanides and discusses how the decomposed body will be reconstituted. It is not necessarily the case, say Crescas, that the same body the soul inhabited during its lifetime on earth will be given to it at the resurrection, but one that will have the same purpose. The identity of the individual will not be affected by this, since even during a person's life in this world the body suffers changes all the time. *Albo (*Ikkarim*, iv. 35) also agrees with Nahmanides and offers his speculations on how the new bodies will take form and shape. But Albo discourages too much speculation on what is by all accounts a miracle and a mystery. He quotes with approval the Talmudic saying: 'We will consider the matter when they come to life again' (*Niddah* 70b). As one might have expected, no perfectly coherent doctrine of the resurrection emerges from the medieval thinkers any more than it does from the Rabbinic literature.

The tendency among some of the medieval thinkers to play down the doctrine of the resurrection is evident in the modern period in even greater measure. *Mendelssohn believed in the immortality of the soul and wrote his treatise, *Phaedon*, on the topic but did not seem to believe in a physical resurrection. Among many contemporary Jewish theologians there is a marked tendency to leave the whole question of eschatology without discussion, either because they do not believe in the Hereafter at all or because they believe that the finite mind of man is incapable of piercing the veil and it is best to leave the subject severely alone. Orthodox theologians still maintain the belief in the resurrection and refer to it, as did their forebears, in their daily prayers and at funerals. One of the Orthodox objections to *cremation is on the grounds that it involves a denial of the doctrine of the resurrection. Reform Judaism in the nineteenth century went the whole way in rejecting the doctrine of the resurrection in favour of that of the immortality of the soul. In Reform prayer books passages in the traditional Prayer Book on the resurrection have either been deleted or interpreted as referring to immortality of the soul.

Revelation The appearance of God to the prophets and, especially at *Sinai, to the people as a whole. The form of revelation most discussed in Judaism is that of God's will as revealed in the Torah. In the Rabbinic formulation this is always referred to as the doctrine: 'Torah from Heaven.' While the manner of revelation in this sense is seen as beyond the human mind to grasp there is no ambiguity about the content of the revelation. This traditional view, still adhered to in Orthodoxy, is based on the theophany at Sinai (Exodus 19, 20) but the scope of revelation is widened to include the whole of the Torah, both the *Written Torah and the *Oral Torah, together conceived as the complete communication of God's will. On this view God conveyed the *Pentateuch, the five books of Moses, directly and in its entirety to Moses (with the possible exception of the final verses in Deuteronomy, which speak of Moses' death) during the forty years in which the Israelites journeyed through the wilderness. The Torah is the very word of God—the teachings, laws, doctrines, and rules for the conduct of life as re-

vealed by the Author of life. To study the Torah is to think God's thoughts after Him. To practise the precepts, the *mitzvot* (see MITZVAH), of the Torah is to obey God's revealed will. And this Torah has remained unchanged throughout the ages, conveyed, through the chain of tradition, from Moses to Joshua, from Joshua to the Elders, from the Elders to the prophets and from the prophets to the Men of the *Great Synagogue, as stated in the opening passage of Ethics of the Fathers, and then by father to son, teacher to disciple, through 3,000 years of Jewish history.

How do contemporary Jews cope with the problem of revelation in the light of modern biblical and Rabbinic scholarship? Secularists hold that the new picture has succeeded in demolishing completely the whole idea of the Torah as God's revelation. For them the Torah has now to be seen as a series of purely human documents or traditions and for the secularist there is, in any event, no Revealer. *Fundamentalism, on the other hand, preserves the traditional picture intact and either rejects all modern thought or interprets the Bible in such a way that it is in accord with the scientific picture—a 'day' in the creation narrative in Genesis, for example, meaning a vast period of time. While many Orthodox Jews accept the critical method when applied to the prophetic books and the Rabbinic literature and rightly resent being dubbed fundamentalists, there is still a definite recoil from any acknowledgement of a human element in the Pentateuch itself. Reform Judaism accepts the findings of modern criticism and generally shifts the idea of divine revelation from the Torah to the prophets. Moreover, Reform believes in the doctrine of 'progressive revelation' according to which revelation was not a once and for all event of the remote past but an ongoing process. Conservative Judaism (although there are differing emphases in the movement on this topic) accepts the idea of revelation of the whole of the Torah but sees this in dynamic terms and recognizes a human element in the process. God revealed the Torah, on this view, not only to the people of Israel but through them. (See CONSERVATIVE JUDAISM, ORTHODOX JUDAISM, and REFORM JUDAISM.)

Revenge The biblical verse in which it is stated that it is wrong to take revenge is the same verse in which 'love thy neighbour' occurs: 'Thou shalt not take vengeance, nor bear any grudge against the children of thy people, but thou shalt love thy neighbour as thyself: I am the Lord' (Leviticus 19: 18). The plain meaning of the verse is that *love of the neighbour is to be expressed by refusing to take revenge because the neighbour is like the self. The Jerusalem Talmud (Nedarim 9: 4) gives the illustration, in this connection, of the man who cuts his hand while cutting meat. He will not be so foolish as to cut out of spite the hand which did the damage. Evidently, the Jerusalem Talmud is stressing that man and his neighbour are one. To harm the neighbour is to harm the self. In the English version of the saying, it is cutting off the nose to spite the face.

Reward and Punishment The idea that God rewards those who keep His commandments and punishes those who transgress them is one that runs through the whole of the Bible.

The biblical references are all to divine recompense and retribution in this world, in terms of material prosperity and suffering here on earth. But a remarkable shift of emphasis took place, it is generally held, at the time of the *Maccabees, when righteous men and women were being slaughtered because of their loyalty to their faith. In the face of such direct contradiction to the notion of reward and punishment in the here and now, faith could only be maintained by affirming that recom-

pense and retribution were to be the fate of humans in the Hereafter, in the *World to Come, as it is called by the Rabbis. In the Rabbinic literature, while this-worldly formulations are not unknown, it is in the World to Come that the doctrine is made to receive its chief application (see GARDEN OF EDEN and GEHINNOM).

Because of all these factors the doctrine of reward and punishment is frequently interpreted by modern Jews in terms of natural progress rather than in terms of tit-for-tat. The emphasis among contemporary religious thought is on wickedness as carrying the seeds of its own destruction. The details can be left to God, while humans so conduct themselves that all the ancient teachings on reward and punishment are relevant to their lives. The doctrine as interpreted by moderns means that it is *ultimately* better to live the good life and reject an evil life.

Righteousness The carrying-out of religious and especially ethical obligation. The usual Hebrew word for 'righteousness', tzedek or tzedakah, has the root meaning of 'straightness', as in the English expression 'straight as a die', and is often used in the Bible in apposition to the word mishpat, '*justice', from a root meaning 'to judge'. But righteousness often has a somewhat wider connotation than justice in that the practice of righteousness is advocated even beyond the claims of strict justice. The righteous man is called the tzaddik. In the Bible generally the tzaddik is not a saintly individual, a man of extraordinary piety and moral worth, but simply the ordinary good man and this is the meaning of the term in the Rabbinic literature, except for a few passages in which the term tzaddik is used of the saint, as in the famous statement (Sukkah 45b) that there are never less than thirty-six tzaddikim who welcome the countenance of the *Shekhinah daily (see LAMEDVOVNIKS).

Rituals See MITZVAH and PRECEPTS, 613.

Rome That Palestine was a Roman colony; that the Jews fought against Roman dominion (see BAR KOCHBA and JOSEPHUS); that the Romans destroyed the Temple in 70 CE; that the emperor Hadrian persecuted the Jews for adherence to their religion; and that, on the other hand, Jews were bound to acknowledge that the Roman occupation had brought considerable benefits in its wake; all these factors help to explain the love–hate relationship between the Jews and the Romans.

Roman influence is pervasive in the Rabbinic literature. The Mishnah and the Jerusalem Talmud were compiled when the Jews were under Roman rule and expressions taken from Roman life and culture abound in these works. Even the Babylonian Talmud, compiled by Jews under Persian rule, has numerous references to the Romans, reflecting not only conditions in Palestine but the impact of Roman civilization on Babylonian Jewry.

Generally on the question of Roman influence on Jewish religious life, it has to be noted that the ubiquitous references in the Rabbinic literature to God as King of the universe owe much to the Roman background. Numerous are the Rabbinic comparisons between the conduct of earthly kings (i.e. the Roman emperors) and the King of the universe. The Rabbis introduced a special *benediction to be recited when beholding a 'Gentile king': 'Blessed art Thou, who hath imparted of Thy glory to Thy creatures.' Nevertheless, the Rabbis warned against attempts to curry favour with the Roman officials. Two statements in Ethics of the Fathers are relevant. The first (1. 10) reads: 'Love work, hate lordship, and seek no intimacy with the ruling power.' The other (2. 3) says: 'Be on your guard against the ruling power; for they who exercise it draw no man near to them except for their own interests; appearing as friends when it is to their own advantage, they stand not by a man in the hour of his need.'

It has to be added, that statements about Jewish attitudes to Roman rule in the Rabbinic literature come from different periods so that it is not historically permissible to speak of any official Jewish attitude. Yet running through all the Rabbinic sources is the ambivalence mentioned above. The Romans are both hated conquerors and brothers; both foes of the Jewish religion and helpful in making Jewish life easier; both immoral idolaters and people of noble bearing from whom Jews could profitably learn regarding the conduct of life.

Rosenzweig, Franz Influential German Jewish existentialist thinker (1886–1929). Rosenzweig's parents belonged to an assimilated Jewish family with little attachment to Judaism or Jewish life. He himself, although extremely well educated in general German culture and especially proficient in the classics and philosophy, had, at first, hardly any Jewish knowledge. A cousin who had become a Christian urged Rosenzweig to take the same step. The story has often been told of how Rosenzweig felt that if he was to be converted to Christianity he ought to do so as a Jew, moving, as he saw it at the time, from a lower to a higher form of religion. While contemplating his conversion, he attended an Orthodox synagogue in Berlin on *Yom Kippur. There he was so profoundly overcome by the devotion of the worshippers as they sought forgiveness from the God of their fathers that he realized there was no need for him to find his salvation outside his ancestral faith. As he was later to put it, the Christian claim that no man can come to the Father except through Jesus was true for all others but not for the Jew, since Jews, being already with the Father, had no need to 'come' to Him.

Rosenzweig's major work, *The Star of Redemption*, was written, in part, on postcards he sent home from the trenches when he was serving in the German army at the end of World War I. In this work, God, the World, and Man are described as interrelated through a process of Creation, Revelation, and Redemption. God created the world and revealed His will for man to find redemption. This theme is represented by two interlocking triangles. At the three points of one triangle, pointing downwards, are Creation, Revelation, and Redemption. At the three points of the other triangle, pointing upwards, are Man, the World, and God. Man relates to the world and through the world to God. God relates to the world through creation and after creation from revelation through to redemption. The two interlocking triangles form the Star of Redemption (see MAGEN DAVID). Rosenzweig claimed to be giving expression to a new (i.e. existentialist) type of thinking. His work, therefore, as he himself states, is heavy-going in parts. It is nevertheless seminal for twentieth-century Jews, though hardly to everyone's literary and philosophical taste.

Rosh Ha-Shanah 'Head of the year', the New Year festival. This festival is mentioned in the Bible as falling on the first day of the seventh month (counting from the spring month, the month of the Exodus, see CALENDAR) and is described as a day of blowing the horn (Leviticus 23: 23–5; Numbers 19: 1 6). The name Rosh Ha-Shanah stems from Talmudic teachings that on this day all mankind is judged for its fate in the coming year. For this reason the festival is also called: Yom Ha-Din, 'Judgement Day'. In the book of *Nehemiah there is a vivid description of the dramatic occasion when the Jews who had returned from the Babylonian captivity renewed their covenant with God (Nehemiah 8: 1–8). Ezra read from the

Torah on this first day of the seventh month; the people, conscious of their shortcomings, were distressed at hearing the demands of the law, but Nehemiah reassured them: 'Go your way, eat the fat, and drink the sweet and send portions unto him for whom nothing is prepared; for this day is holy unto our Lord; neither be you grieved for the joy of the Lord is your strength' (Nehemiah 8: 10).

Rosh Ha-Shanah is associated with *Yom Kippur which falls on 10 Tishri. Rosh Ha-Shanah and Yom Kippur, because of the judgement theme and the numinous quality of these days, are called 'Days of Awe'. The ten days from Rosh Ha-Shanah to Yom Kippur are the *Ten Days of Penitence, the special penitential season of the year. Rosh Ha-Shanah itself is thus a day of both joy and solemnity, joy in that it is a festival, solemnity in that it is the day of judgement. The themes of God as King and Judge feature prominently in the Rosh Ha-Shanah liturgy. The Musaf ('Additional Prayer') on Rosh Ha-Shanah consists of three groups of scriptural verses and prayers: 1. Malkhuyot ('Sovereignties'), in which God is hailed as King; 2. Zikhronot ('Remembrances') , in which God is said to remember His creatures; 3. Shofarot ('Trumpets'), referring to the blowing of the horn. Among the many interpretations that have been given to these three groups, is that they represent the three basic *principles of the Jewish faith: belief in God, belief in *reward and punishment (God remembers man's deeds), and belief in *revelation (the horn was sounded when the Torah was given at *Sinai; Exodus 19: 16). Another prayer of the day looks forward to the Messianic age (see MESSIAH) when the *Kingdom of Heaven will be established and all wickedness will vanish from the earth. At various stages in the liturgy there are prayers with the entreaty: 'Inscribe us in the Book of Life.' This is based on a Talmudic passage stating that the average person whose fate is in the balance has the opportunity to 'avert the evil decree' by repentance, prayer, and charity. Among the more sophisticated, this is interpreted in terms of self-criticism and the resolve to lead a better life in the year ahead rather than in terms of pleading before an undecided God. Many a Jewish thinker, especially in modern times, has said that the Jew should inscribe *himself* in the Book of Life.

The central feature of Rosh Ha-Shanah is the blowing of the horn, the *shofar*. The nature of the *shofar*, the elaborate rituals, and the numerous interpretations of the rite are discussed at length in the Talmud and the Codes.

Rosh Hodesh 'Head of month', the first day of the month (see CALENDAR). In Bible times Rosh Hodesh was an important festival, being compared to the Sabbath in a number of passages (2 Kings 4: 23; Isaiah 1: 13; Amos 8: 5), but it is now only a minor festival (see FESTIVALS) on which it is forbidden to fast but on which work is permitted. There is an ancient tradition, however, that women do not work on Rosh Hodesh, perhaps an echo from the biblical period. There is an old Midrashic idea that because women refused to paricipate in the making and worshipping of the *golden calf they were given Rosh Hodesh as a reward for their steadfastness.

Rossi, Azariah de Italian scholar, physician, and historian (c.1511–c.1578). Rossi is chiefly renowned for his *Meor Eynayim*, a study of aspects of Jewish *history in which the author, a typical Renaissance man, used Greek and Latin sources in his research. In addition to his numerous references to traditional Jewish literature, Rossi quotes extensively from *Philo, *Josephus, Plato, Cicero, Aquinas, and even the Church Fathers. The work is rightly seen, therefore, as the first attempt by a Jewish

scholar to study the Jewish past 'scientifically' by using comparative critical methods, a pioneering effort to write real Jewish *history as distinct from the mere chronologies compiled before Rossi's time. It is no accident that scholars of the *Jüdische Wissenschaft school, such as *Zunz, utilized the *Meor Eynayim* extensively in their objective studies of the Jewish past. Among other original contributions, the work offers a correction of errors in Jewish chronology. Included in the work is a translation into Hebrew of the Latin version of the *Letter of Aristeas*, which tells how the *Septuagint came to be written.

Rossi was also the first Jewish scholar to point out that some statements in the Talmud about historical personages cannot be accepted as factual since they contradict known historical records. For instance, the Talmud (*Gittin* 56b) says that the emperor Titus who destroyed the Temple was punished by a gnat which entered his nose and grew in his head into a bird of brass with claws of iron. We know, Rossi observes, that Titus died a normal death. What the Talmud is saying is that a tiny gnat of remorse pecked away at Titus' conscience because he had destroyed the Temple, growing ever stronger until he could no longer live with his guilt. Rossi, in other words, recognizes that Talmudic and Midrashic legends are just that, legends told not as sober history but as pious tales intended to convey moral lessons. But Rossi goes further, following some earlier teachers who held that while the Talmudic Rabbis are to be accepted as authorities in matters of law and tradition, in scientific and historical matters they had only the scientific and historical knowledge of their day and could have been mistaken in these areas (see AUTHORITY and RABBIS, THE TALMUDIC).

Roth, Aaron Mystical teacher and Hasidic master (1894–1944). Roth was born in Ungvar, Hungary. He studied the Talmud under Rabbi Isaiah Silverstein and Moses Forhand and came under the influence of various Hasidic masters, especially Rabbi Issachar Dov of *Belz and Rabbi Zevi Elimelech of Blazowa. The latter urged Roth to become a Hasidic master himself. A group of young followers gathered around Roth in the town of Beregszasz (Beregovo) and towards the end of his life a similar group was formed around him in Jerusalem. This was a departure in *Hasidism from the principle of hereditary succession. When Roth died the principle was restablished. He was succeeded by his son and son-in-law who were rival candidates for the succession: each inherited his own group of Roth's Hasidim.

Ruth Biblical heroine whose story is told in the book that bears her name. Ruth's marriage to Boaz, the kinsman of her first husband, is the central theme of the book of Ruth, at the end of which King *David's ancestry is traced back to the child born to Ruth and Boaz. In the famous passage in the Talmud on the authorship of the biblical books (*Bava Batra*, 14b) the author of the book of Ruth is said to be the prophet *Samuel. Modern scholarship is generally uncertain about the authorship and the date of the book, some scholars postulating a date as early as the time of David, others as late as the time of *Ezra and *Nehemiah. On this latter theory, the book of Ruth is a gentle protest against Ezra's opposition to intermarriage, Ruth being a Moabite woman. There is no evidence, however, to enable a clear answer to be given on the question of date and authorship. The Rabbis too were puzzled by Ruth's marriage to Boaz. The usual reply is that Ruth was first converted to Judaism and, in fact, Ruth serves in the Rabbinic tradition as the supreme example of the sincere proselyte (see CONVERSION).

Saadiah Gaon Foremost medieval spiritual leader, Talmudist, biblical exegete, and philosopher (882–942). Saadiah was born in Egypt, and lived for a time in Tiberias, after which he was appointed by the *exilarch, David ben Zakkai, to be the head of the college at Sura in Babylon, hence the title Saadiah Gaon (see GEONIM). But rulers seem to have a habit of falling out with their protégés and David soon deposed Saadiah. The quarrel between the two lasted for seven years, remaining unresolved until Saadiah was reinstated. Saadiah, responding to the *Karaite interest in the Bible, wrote a translation of the Bible into Arabic, in which he displays his virtuosity as a grammarian and philologist as well as his vast knowledge of the Jewish traditional sources. His *Prayer Book was one of the earliest to be compiled and is more comprehensive than those of his very few predecessors. But Saadiah's fame rests on his philosophical work, *Emunot Ve-Deot* (*Beliefs and Opinions*), written in Arabic and translated into Hebrew by Judah Ibn Tibbon. This work is the first systematic Jewish theology. It has a special significance as a philosophical defence of Rabbinic Judaism by the leading representative of that Judaism of his day.

The 'beliefs' in the title are the postulates of the Jewish religion, while 'opinions' are the truths arrived at by empirical investigation and rational reflection. Saadiah takes issue with those who see philosophy as harmful to faith. On the contrary, faith is strengthened when supported by reason. Influenced strongly by the thought of the Arabic thinkers who sought in similar fashion to reconcile Islam with philosophical enquiry, Saadiah holds that there are two ways to religious truth, reason (see RATIONALISM) and *revelation (of the Torah, for Saadiah). Both ways are essential: reason because without it superstitious ideas will proliferate; revelation because not everyone can arrive at the truth by speculation. Saadiah's famous illustration is of the man who is told that a heap of coins contains a certain number of coins. He may not have the time to count them and will then have to rely on those who have told him the number of the coins. But, if he counts the coins, he will know how many there are with a certainty he would not otherwise have had. Saadiah thus proceeds to prove by reason the existence of God, relying chiefly on the cosmological proof. The world could not have created itself since it is a logical absurdity for anything to cause itself. God is the uncaused Cause of the universe but His nature is beyond human comprehension.

Sabbath The weekly day of rest, Heb. *Shabbat* (from the root *shavat*, 'to rest'), which begins on Friday at sunset and lasts until nightfall on Saturday (in the Jewish *calendar day follows night). The Sabbath is connected with God's creation of the world: 'On the seventh day God finished the work which He had been doing, and He rested on the seventh day from all the work which He had done. and God blessed the seventh day and declared it holy because on it God ceased from all the work of creation which He had done' (Genesis 2: 2–3). Although the actual word *Shabbat* is not used in this narrative the verbal form *shavat* is used to describe God's resting or ceasing from work. The Hebrew text can mean that God created also on the seventh day, which leads to the beautiful Rabbinic idea that rest from work is itself a creation. The command to keep the Sabbath is stated, as the fourth commandment, in both versions of the *Decalogue (Exodus 20: 8–11; Deuteronomy 5: 14–15). In the Exodus version the reason of the creation is given. In the Deuteronomic version a social reason is given, that the purpose of the Sabbath is to provide rest for all, including slaves, who are also entitled to a day of rest. The Israelites who were slaves in Egypt should know how rest from labour is needed both for themselves and for their slaves. In the Sabbath liturgy the Sabbath is said to be both 'a remembrance of the work of creation' and 'a remembrance of the Exodus from Egypt'.

At least two candles are kindled before the advent of the Sabbath. Originally the Rabbinic rules of the Sabbath lamp were intended for the purpose of having a well-lit home in order to further what the Rabbis call 'peace in the home', that is, the avoidance of the strife and contention in the family that might easily result from meals being partaken of in a dark room. Probably in reaction to the *Karaites, who forbade the burning of lamps on the Sabbath even if kindled before the Sabbath, the Rabbinic authorities in the Middle Ages introduced this practice of kindling two special lights even if the room is otherwise well lit. The kindling of the Sabbath candles is usually performed by the mother of the family, who offers a silent prayer for the well-being of her husband and children. The practice of waving the hands to and fro in front of the candles probably represents the summoning of the spiritual light of the Sabbath into the home.

Before the Sabbath meal on Friday night and Saturday morning, the *Kiddush is recited over a cup of wine, in which God is praised and thanked for giving the Sabbath to His people. At the termination of the Sabbath, the *Havdalah is recited over a cup of wine and God is praised for distinguishing be-

tween the Sabbath and the weekdays. According to the Rabbis, three meals have to be partaken of on the Sabbath, one more than the usual two meals a day in Rabbinic times. At these meals special songs (*Zemirot) are sung to joyous melodies.

According to the *Halakhah, Jews are not permitted to discuss their business affairs on the Sabbath; they must not handle money; they must not carry anything in the street (but see ERUV); they must not ride in an automobile, even if driven by a non-Jew, and they do not switch on electric lights or use any electrical appliances (see ELECTRICITY). Since cooking food is forbidden on the Sabbath, food is cooked before the Sabbath and kept hot on the stove until it is required. Similarly, it is permitted to have a time-switch fixed to the electric lights before the Sabbath so that they go on and off when required. All these rules have been seen as bothersome to critics of Orthodoxy but, for Orthodox Jews, they are not seen as a burden at all but as providing welcome opportunities of doing God's will and cultivating the special Sabbath atmosphere through which their lives are elevated far above the mundane. Reform Jews seek to preserve the Sabbath as the holy day while remaining largely indifferent to the precise rules and regulations. Conservative Jews accept the provisions of the Halakhah with regard to the Sabbath, as they do with regard to the Halakhah generally. But many, perhaps the majority of, Conservative Rabbis favour a more lenient interpretation of the Sabbath laws so as to permit, for example, the switching-on of electric lights and riding in a car to the synagogue where this is not within walking distance of home.

Sabbatical Year The seventh year, during which the fields were to be left fallow (Leviticus 25: 1–7) and debts released (Deuteronomy 15: 1–11); Heb. *Shemittah* ('Release'). The seven years are counted in the cycle of fifty culminating in the *Jubilee and are known by tradition. The year 2000/1, for instance, will be a Sabbatical year. In order to avoid the cancellation of all debts, a serious hardship in our commercial society, the device was introduced even in Talmudic times of handing the debts over before the end of the Sabbatical year, to a temporary court consisting of three persons, the debts then being considered to have been paid to the court beforehand. The problem of agricultural work in the Sabbatical year did not arise in modern times until, under the impact of *Zionism, colonies were established in Palestine; it is a severe difficulty now that the State of Israel has been established. The more Orthodox do observe the laws of the Sabbatical year, using only agricultural products bought from Arabs. But other Orthodox Rabbis have tried to find a dispensation by noting that according to many authorities the Sabbatical year is, like the Jubilee year, binding by biblical law only when the majority of Jews live in the land of Israel. (These laws do not apply to Jewish-owned farms outside Israel.) The laws are now Rabbinic, so that it is easier to find a dispensation. Moreover, there is considerable doubt whether the present identification of Sabbatical years is correct and whether the count begins again on the Jubilee year, the fiftieth, or on the next year, the fifty-first after the previous cycle. Because of all this and the great difficulty in keeping the law, the official Rabbinate in Israel adopts the legal fiction of selling the land to a Gentile. Many have felt, however, that, while legal fictions have their place in Jewish law, it seems more than a little absurd to effect a merely formal sale of all Jewish land to a Gentile. Some religious kibbutzim resort to the new scientific method of hydroponics to avoid the prohibition and they donate a share of their proceeds during the Sabbatical year to charity. In any event, non-agri-cultural work is allowed in the Sabbatical year, which is called 'the Sabbath of the land'.

Sacrifices Animal sacrifices are described in detail in the book of Leviticus and were offered throughout the period of the First and Second Temples. That Gentiles as well as Jews brought sacrifices to the Temple is implied in the prayer of Solomon when he dedicated the Temple (1 Kings 8: 41–3) and in the declaration by the prophet that the Temple will be a house of prayer for all peoples (Isaiah 56: 7). The Rabbis say (Ḥullin 13b): 'Sacrifices are to be accepted from Gentiles as they are from Jews', although this saying dates from after the destruction of the Temple. The significance of the role of the sacrifice in the Temple period is expressed in the saying in Ethics of the Fathers (1. 3) that the world stands on three things, the Torah, the service in the Temple, and benevolence. That occasionally the prophets seem to decry the offering of sacrifices (e.g. Amos 5: 21–4; Isaiah 1: 11–13) is explained in the Jewish tradition, and this might well be the case, that the prophets only object to sacrifices used as an attempt to buy off God while practising iniquities. The ancients did not have the scruples of many moderns about offering up 'poor defenceless animals'. People did and still do kill animals for food and, apart from the wholly consumed burnt-offering, the meat of all the other sacrifices was eaten either by the priests or by those who brought the sacrifices.

Although, in the nineteenth century, suggestions were put forward for the Temple to be rebuilt and sacrifices offered there once again, these were not taken seriously since, among other objections, the actual site of the altar is now unknown; corpse contamination cannot now be removed in the absence of the *red heifer; and there are no means of establishing the claim of the *priests that they really are such (see

KOHEN). Thus the restoration of the sacrificial system was left to the *Messiah. There was even an opinion in the Middle Ages, quoted by *Rashi, that the Third Temple would drop ready-made from heaven. The Orthodox position today is that the offering of sacrifices will be carried out only when the Messianic age dawns and their restoration is not a matter of practical concern in the here and now, although there is a *Yeshivah in Jerusalem in which the laws of the sacrifices are studied assiduously so that scholars will be able to advise on how the sacrifices are to be offered when the Messiah does come.

Sadducees Heb. *Tzaddukim*, one of three main parties in the late Second Temple period, the others being the *Pharisees and the *Essenes. The Mishnah and *Josephus record the differences between the Sadducees and the Pharisees. From all accounts it would appear that the members of the Sadducean party were the aristocratic priests and the wealthy landowners. The meaning of the word *Tzaddukim* is uncertain. In the Talmud the Sadducees are said to be followers of a certain Zadok who rejected, as did the Sadducees according to both the Mishnah and Josephus, belief in the *World to Come. Modern scholarship suggests that the Sadducees were descended from Zadok, the priest who lived in the time of King David (1 Kings 1). The prophet Ezekiel declares that only the priests who are the sons of Zadok will be worthy to serve in the Temple (Ezekiel 44: 15–16) and it is plausible to suggest that the Sadducees identified themselves with this family of priests. With the victory of the Pharisees the Sadducean party vanished from the Jewish scene but some of their ideas enjoyed a subterranean existence until they resurfaced among the *Karaites.

Safed City in Upper Galilee. The economic life of Safed was strengthened by the influx of Jewish immigrants after the expulsion from Spain in 1492. Perhaps because of its elevation, nearly 3,000 feet above sea-level, its wide panoramic views, and its pure air, Safed was considered to be one of the four holy cities in the land of Israel, the others being Jerusalem, Hebron, and Tiberias. In the sixteenth century Safed was the home of some of the great luminaries in Jewish spiritual history, among them Joseph *Karo, Moses *Cordovero, and Isaac *Luria. All three are buried in Safed and their graves are still visited in *pilgrimage. The circle of Kabbalists in Safed pursued a mystic and ascetic way of life that became a model for later Jewish pietists. In modern Israel an artists' colony has been established in Safed.

Saints Like other religions, Judaism knows of individuals noted for their extraordinary piety and goodness. The usual term for this kind of individual is *hasid*, probably from a root meaning of 'abundance', that is, the *love of God and humanity of such intensity that it is almost about to burst its bonds. The Hasid is perceived as an identifiable type in the Bible, the Rabbinic literature and through to the *hasidey Ashkenaz*, 'the *Saints of Germany' and the followers of the *Baal Shem Tov, known as the Hasidim (see HASIDISM). The term *tzaddik* is often used in the earlier literature to denote simply a good man (see RIGHTEOUSNESS) but is also used to denote the especially saintly individual (see LAMEDVOVNIKS). This is not to say that there is anything in Judaism like the Catholic idea of official acknowledgement of people as 'saints' and there is nothing like the Catholic process of canonization. What happens in Judaism is that certain persons renowned for their holy life are afforded the title Hasid by a kind of consensus of the faithful.

William James, in the chapters on 'Saintliness' in his *The Varieties of Reli-*

gious Experience, gives examples of the extravagant behaviour of some of the Christian saints. It is a gross error to view Judaism as too rational to tolerate such excesses, too 'sane' to permit its adherents to be 'fools of God'. In the literature of Jewish piety there are enough examples of extreme, not to say bizarre, conduct on the part of the saints. The Saints of Germany would engage in severe mortification of the flesh, rolling naked in snow and ice in winter and smeared with honey to be stung by the bees in summer. A number of the Jewish saints were fond of meditating, whenever they recited the Shema, on the theme of *martyrdom, allowing their minds to dwell on the tortures they would suffer rather than be faithless to God and His Torah. They would reflect in gruesome detail on the cruel fate that awaited them. The Hasidic master Aaron *Roth practised and urged his followers to practise various forms of self-torment including flagellation (albeit with a 'small strap') and refraining from ever scratching an itch.

Saints of Germany Heb. *Ḥasidey Ashkenaz*, a group of pietists in twelfth- and thirteenth-century Germany. The German Saints were not organized as a movement but flourished as individual followers of a particular saintly path in the towns of Regensburg, Speyer, Worms, and Mayyence. The main leaders of this tendency were Samuel He-Hasid (second half of the twelfth century); his son, Judah He-Hasid (d. 1217); and Judah's disciple, Eleazar of Worms (d. *c*.1230). The major works produced in this circle are the *Sefer Hasidim* and the *Rokeaḥ* of Eleazar of Worms. In these works the novel ideas of the group, influenced to some extent by the Christian monasticism of the period, are given expression. Naturally in the period of the Crusades, there is particular emphasis on *martyrdom for the sanctification of God's name. The

Hasidim were ready at all times to suffer martyrdom if need be (see HASIDISM). Repentance for these Saints was not reserved for extreme sinners but was an essential ingredient in the life of piety. The Saints were ever conscious of their sinfulness and engaged in self-mortification both as a penance and as a means of overcoming the temptations of the flesh. The Hasid was expected to be exceedingly generous in relieving the fate of the poor. *Confession of sin, usually in Judaism a purely private matter between the individual and his God, was made to a spiritual mentor who advised the 'sinner' on how to rectify his faults. The tension between saintliness and learning (see SAINTS) is particularly evident among the Ḥasidey Ashkenaz. Many of these men were learned in the Torah but the ideal of saintliness in the circle was quite independent of learning. It was possible for a simple Jew, with only a bare knowledge of the Bible, let alone the Talmud, to become a Hasid. The influence of the Christian background on the Hasidim is evident too in the superstitions (see MAGIC AND SUPERSTITION) referred to in the works of the *Ḥasidey Ashkenaz*. In their whole activity there is to be observed a remarkable blend of popular religion and mystical thought of the highest order.

Salanter, Israel Lithuanian Talmudist and religious thinker (1810–83), founder of the *Musar movement. Israel's family name was Lipkin, but he is known as Israel Salanter after the town of Salant in which he grew up and where he studied to become an outstanding Talmudic scholar (although he sought, wherever possible, to conceal his great learning). It appears that Salanter did not originally intend that his Musar approach should be élitist but that it should promote greater inwardness in the lives of Jewish artisans and businessmen. However, eventually Salanter's ideas were appreciated only by Yeshivah students, and Salanter's disciples, encouraged by him, established Musar Yeshivot of their own. At first there was determined opposition by traditional Rabbis to the introduction of Musar into the Yeshivah curriculum. The Torah itself, these Rabbis argued, was balm for the soul and there was no need to supplement study of the Torah with Musar. But Salanter's ideas prevailed, so that the majority of the Lithuanian type Yeshivot became Musar Yeshivot.

Samaritans The descendants of the people settled in Samaria, in the Northern Kingdom, after the ten tribes had been deported by the king of Assyria in 722 BCE. The verse in the book of 2 Kings (17: 24) states: 'The king of Assyria brought [people] from Babylon, Cuthah, Avva, Hamath and Sepharvim, and he settled them in the towns of Samaria in place of the Israelites; they took possession of Samaria and dwelt in its towns.' The passage continues that these foreign peoples worshipped their own gods but God let loose lions among them, as result of which the king of Assyria ordered a priest to be sent to teach them the worship of the true God. After the name Cuthah, one of the places from which these people came, the Samaritans are called Cuthim (Kutim) in the Rabbinic sources. The Rabbis understood the story in the book of Kings to mean that the Cuthim were eventually converted to Judaism, the only question being whether they were true converts or only 'lion converts', that is, never really converted to the true faith but only pretending to have been converted out of their fear of the lions. The conclusion in the Talmud is that their descendants are fully Jewish even though they do not keep all the precepts. Nevertheless, according to the Talmud (Hullin 6a), Rabbi Meir, hearing that some Samaritans had worshipped a dove on Mount Gerizim, declared that all Samaritans must henceforth be treated as if they were

idolaters. The story of the dove is, of course, legendary. The Samaritans were monotheists and worshipped God on Mount Gerizim. Behind all this are echoes of the conflict in ancient times between the Samaritans and the Jews, the Samaritans claiming, in fact, that they were the descendants of the ancient Israelites and that the story in the book of Kings is a false account of their origins. The book of Nehemiah (ch 4) relates how the Samaritans sought to prevent the Jews rebuilding Jerusalem after the return from the Babylonian exile.

For the Samaritans the central holy place is not Jerusalem but Mount Gerizim in Samaria. For them, too, only the *Pentateuch, of which they have their own version, is sacred and they reject the prophetic and the other books of the Bible.

Samuel Prophet in the eleventh century BCE who anointed Saul as king and, when God rejected Saul, anointed *David. According to the famous Talmudic passage (Bava Batra 14b) on the authorship of the biblical books, the book of Samuel was written by Samuel himself up to the account of his death, and was completed by others. Modern scholarship views the book as a later work in which the author used oral traditions and written chronicles. In the Jewish tradition there is only a single book of Samuel. The division into two books, 1 and 2 Samuel, is based on Christian versions of the *Bible, though it has come to be accepted by Jews when quoting the Bible. Legend locates the burial place of the prophet in the Arab village, near Jerusalem, called Nebi Samwil.

Sanhedrin From the Greek sunedrion ('sitting in counsel'), the supreme court composed of seventy (or seventy-one) members which sat in the 'chamber of hewn stone' in Jerusalem until the destruction of the Temple in 70 CE, after which it was located in various other cities. Such is the picture of the Sanhedrin which emerges from the Mishnah, tractate *Sanhedrin*, and other Rabbinic sources. The references to the Sanhedrin in the *New Testament present a different picture. Here the High Priest, in his palace, presides over the Sanhedrin (e.g. in the trial of Jesus (Matthew 26: 57–68)), rather than a Nasi ('Prince') as in the Rabbinic sources. The older view among Christian scholars was that the New Testament account is correct and that of the Mishnah incorrect. Among Jewish scholars the opposite was said to be true: the Mishnaic account is the reliable one, the Christian account has been altered for doctrinal purposes. Some later Jewish scholars suggested that there were two Sanhedrins: one a political body, a kind of parliament, the other a body to decide matters of Jewish law. This suggestion is now seen to be untenable. Both sources no doubt preserve ancient traditions of a supreme legislative assembly that existed in former times but each has read ideas of its own into the ancient institution. When the Roman government abolished the office of Nasi, the Sanhedrin came to an end. There was no longer any central *authority for Jews, although the Babylonian *Geonim did enjoy a measure of authority for Jews in other parts of the world. In any event, the Sanhedrin plays no role in later Jewish life. The attempt, soon after the establishment of the State of Israel, to revive the Sanhedrin for the purpose of introducing new legislation was doomed from the outset. There were those who held that Jewish law changes automatically whenever the need arises and those who denied that Jewish law can be changed even by a Sanhedrin. Both succeeded in quashing the idea that the Sanhedrin be revived. Nowadays, it was seen, a Sanhedrin would be either superfluous or ineffective.

Sarah Wife of Abraham and mother of Isaac, the first of the four *matriarchs. In Rabbinic legend, Sarah was one of the most beautiful women who ever lived and she had a greater degree of prophetic insight even than her husband. The story of Sarah is told in the book of Genesis (11: 29–23: 20). Abraham purchased the *Cave of Machpelah from Ephron the Hittite as a burial place for Sarah (Genesis 23) and Abraham himself was buried there by his sons.

Satan The Devil, the prosecuting angel. The word Satan simply means an 'adversary' and is used in the Bible of any opponent or enemy, the root meaning of the word being 'to oppose', with no supernatural overtones. In the opening chapters of the book of Job, however, 'the Satan' (with the definite article, so the meaning is 'the Adversary' and Satan here is not a proper name) is an angel who appears in the council of the angels in order to challenge God to put Job to the test. Similarly, in the book of Zechariah (3: 1–2) the angel whom God rebukes for his evil designs upon Jerusalem is 'the Satan'. In the book of 1 Chronicles (21: 1) 'Satan' (without the definite article) is used as a proper name. Interestingly, in the parallel story in the book of Samuel (2 Samuel 24: 1) it is God, not Satan, who entices David to count the people. The later book of Chronicles, reluctant to ascribe the temptation to God, substitutes Satan. In subsequent Jewish literature Satan is the personification of both a demonic power outside man and the urge to do evil in the human psyche. Very revealing of the demythologizing tendency in Rabbinic thought is the saying (*Bava Batra* 16a) that Satan, the *yetzer ha-ra* ('evil inclination', see YETZER HA-TOV AND YETZER HA-RA) and the Angel of Death are one and the same. On the whole, it can be said that the figure of Satan does not occupy any prominent role in Jewish theology, though it would be incorrect to say that Satan is entirely ignored. In modern Jewish theology, even among the Orthodox, Satan, as a baneful force outside man, is relegated to the background if he is considered at all.

Schechter, Solomon Scholar, theologian, leading thinker of Conservative Judaism (1847–1915). Schechter was born in Fascani, Romania. His father, a *Habad Hasid, was a *shohet* (see SHEHITAH), hence the family name, Schechter. Schechter received a thorough grounding in traditional Jewish learning but, in his early twenties, went to Vienna to study at the Rabbinical College, where his main tutor was Meir Friedmann, a renowned Talmudist in the modern idiom. Later Schechter took courses at the University of Berlin and the Berlin Hochschule, where a fellow-student was Claude *Montefiore. Montefiore brought Schechter to England to be his private tutor. In England, Schechter cultivated the exquisite English style of writing (by reading numerous English novels, it is reported) which has made his *Studies in Judaism* and his *Aspects of Rabbinic Theology* classics of English literature as well as of modern Jewish thought, though, to his dying day, he spoke English with a strong foreign accent.

Schechter's philosophy of Judaism is based on the ideas of Zechariah *Frankel. Both Reform and Orthodoxy fail, in this view, to understand 'positive historical' Judaism. Reform, according to Schechter, fails to appreciate the positive elements in traditional Judaism, while Orthodoxy fails to grasp the dynamic aspects of the tradition itself. Schechter thus sought to encourage a marriage between the old learning and the critical methodology adopted in the *Jüdische Wissenschaft school.

Scholem, Gershom World-renowned German Jewish scholar of Jewish mysticism (1897–1982). Scholem was born in Berlin, in an assimilated Jewish family, but became attracted to Jewish studies, eventually specializing in the study of Jewish mysticism. From 1925 until his retirement in 1965 Scholem taught as lecturer and later as Professor of Jewish Mysticism at the Hebrew University in Jerusalem. There he founded a school and succeeded in creating an entirely new scholarly discipline. It is not true to say that no scholarly work had been done in the field of Jewish mysticism prior to Scholem and his school, but the subject had been relegated to a remote corner of scholarly interest. Scholem examined the mystical texts by the best methods of modern critical and historical scholarship, demonstrating in the process that Judaism had not infrequently expressed itself in terms of the non-rational and the mythical.

Scholem's pioneering work, *Major Trends in Jewish Mysticism*, examines Jewish mystical tendencies from the Merkavah (*Chariot) mystics down to the latest manifestation in *Hasidism. His study of the false Messiah *Shabbetai Zevi uncovered the irrational forces, latent in the Jewish soul, which erupted when the time was ripe. This is not to say that Scholem approved of the bizarre events connected with Shabbetai Zevi. Scholem has described the reticence of the Jewish mystics in describing their own experiences, which is why, according to Scholem, there are so few personal Jewish mystical testimonies available. The same reticence can be observed in Scholem himself. He worked as an objective scholar and was usually very reserved about his own personal attitude to mysticism. He was certainly no mystic himself but seems to have been a religious, though not an Orthodox, Jew. There was an element of antinomianism in Scholem, an element he detected in some Jewish mystical texts, although in his scholarly work he showed that the Kabbalah, which invested every detail of the precepts with cosmic significance, saved Judaism as a religion of law.

Science and Religion The struggle between science and religion in the nineteenth century, although largely engaged in, on the religious side, by Christians, was naturally of equal concern to religious Jews. With regard to the basic problem of the scientific approach to the discovery of truth versus religious faith, Jewish thinkers, believing that all truth comes from the One God, generally refused to adopt the 'two-truth' theory, according to which religion is in conflict with science but each is 'true' in its own sphere. Relying on the medieval discussions of faith versus reason (see RATIONALISM), the majority of Jewish thinkers who grappled with the problem held that religion has to do with life's values and with a reaching-out to the transcendent and is therefore fully compatible with scientific views about the composition and workings of the world perceived by the senses. While Judaism views with favour investigation into the nature of the physical universe—from the religious point of view this increases human perception of the glory of God as manifest in His *creation—such investigations are irrelevant to the question of religious faith. As C. S. Lewis puts it, the scientist, in his field, knows, whereas the religious person believes. In other words, scientific explanation is of the way in which the universe works as it does, while religion seeks to explain the purpose of the universe and man's place within it. The one is a matter of knowledge, the other a matter of belief. Very few Jewish thinkers, for instance, felt themselves compelled by their religious faith to hold fast, despite all the new evidence, to the geocentric view of the universe. Far from the new picture of the immense size of the universe (with our whole solar system a mere speck in the vastness of space) destroying faith, it helps to increase man's sense of wonder at the divine wisdom.

Where science does come into conflict with the tradition is when scientific method is employed to examine the documents of the Jewish religion and to discover how religion itself came to be. *Biblical criticism, and sociological and psychological theories about the nature of society and the human personality, do present a challenge to the doctrine of divine *revelation. Some Jewish thinkers have argued that biblical criticism is only conjectural, and sociology and psychology are not exact sciences to reject which is to reject reason. Orthodox thinkers still pursue this line, at least so far as criticism applied to the *Pentateuch, the very word of God, is concerned. Reform and Conservative thinkers hold that, indeed, the application of scientific method in these areas has to be accepted even if the conclusions reached demand a new approach to the whole question of revelation. As in many other areas, Reform and Orthodoxy have their differences, Reform allowing greater weight to modern thought when this is in conflict with the tradition than Orthodoxy is willing to do. Yet Orthodoxy, too, seeks an accommodation with science wherever possible—by a new interpretation of the tradition, for example.

Secularism Although Judaism makes a distinction, as in the *Havdalah benediction, between the sacred and profane, it acknowledges that secular life is good in itself, for which God is to be thanked; hence the various benedictions over food, drink, and other physical and material pleasures. Usually the Jew is encouraged by his religion to live firmly in the 'secular city', provided life's spiritual side is also given its due. The Jew is not presented with the stark choice of either gaining the world and losing his soul or gaining his soul and losing the world. He can have both.

In modern times, some Jews, who

have lost their belief in God and the Jewish religion while still attached to what is called 'the Jewish way of life', have tried to develop a form of 'secular Judaism', in which Jewish observances and even prayer are cultivated not in obedience to the will of God but as colourful Jewish folk-ways. A good case can be made for a non-believing Jew to follow the Jewish way of life as a means, perhaps the only means, for the enrichment of life. From the religious point of view it might even be said that such a Jew is doing God's will without knowing it. Yet, when all is said and done, 'secular Judaism' is a contradiction in terms since Judaism is a religion not a secular philosophy.

Seder 'Order', the festive meal and service held in the home on the first night of *Passover (and on the second night as well in the *Diaspora) at which various rituals commemorating the *Exodus are carried out and the *Haggadah recited, all in obedience to the injunction to parents to tell their children of God's mighty deeds in delivering the people of Israel from Egyptian bondage (Exodus 13: 8). The Seder is a re-enactment of the lives of the slaves and their joy when given their freedom. The keynote is sounded in the statement in the Haggadah that everyone is obliged to imagine that he or she has personally been delivered from Egypt. The essential features of the order (Seder) of procedure on this night are described in the Mishnah (final chapter of tractate Pesaḥim) but many additions have been made through the ages. The following is a brief description of what happens at the Seder in Jewish homes today.

The table is covered with a white tablecloth upon which the festival candles are placed. A decorative plate (exquisite Seder plates have been produced by Jewish craftsmen) is placed on the Seder table upon which rest the symbolic foods required for the rituals.

These are: three *matzot* (plural of *matzah*, unleavened bread); *maror*, 'bitter herbs', serving as a reminder of the embitterment of the lives of the Hebrew slaves by their Egyptian taskmasters (Exodus 1: 14); ḥaroset, a paste made of almonds, apples, and wine, symbolic both of the mortar used by the slaves in building and of the sweetness of *redemption; a bowl of salt water, symbolizing the tears of the oppressed; parsley for a symbolic dipping in the salt water; a roasted bone as a reminder of the Paschal lamb; and a roasted egg as a reminder of the festival offering brought in Temple times in addition to the Paschal lamb. These last two are not eaten during the meal but left on the plate. During the Seder all the participants drink four cups of wine, representing the four different expressions for redemption found in the Exodus narrative.

The Seder begins with the *Kiddush, the festival benediction over the first cup of wine. The middle *matzah* is then broken in two, one piece being set aside to be eaten later as the *afikoman* ('dessert'), the last thing eaten before *grace after meals is recited, so that the taste of the *matzah* of freedom might linger in the mouth. It is customary for the grown-ups to hide the *afikoman*, rewarding the lucky child who finds it with a present. A cheeky child might bargain for the size of the present before handing over the *afikoman*. Some frown on this practice because it might encourage mendacity on the part of the children but most Jews ignore these spoilsports and see it as a harmless bit of fun that succeeds in holding the interest of the children. The parsley is dipped in the salt water and eaten. The youngest child present then asks the Four Questions, a standard formula beginning with the words: 'Why is this night different from all other nights?' The head of the house and the other adults present at the Seder then proceed to reply to the child's questions by reciting (more usually by chanting) the *Haggadah, in which the answers are given in terms of God's deliverances.

The celebrants then proceed to partake of the festive meal. Grace before meals is recited over two of the three *matzot* and, in addition to the benediction over bread (unleavened bread is still bread), the benediction is recited: 'Blessed art Thou, O Lord our God, King of the universe, who hath sanctified us with thy commandments and hath commanded us to eat *matzah*.' The bitter herbs (usually horseradish) are then dipped in the *ḥaroset* and eaten.

At the end of the meal the *afikoman* is 'found', surrendered, and eaten and grace after meals is recited over the third cup of wine. The *Hallel (Psalms 113–18) and other hymns of thanksgiving are recited over the fourth cup of wine. Before the recital of the Hallel, a cup is filled for the prophet *Elijah, the herald of the *Messiah, who, legend states, visits every Jewish home on this night. The door of the house is opened to let Elijah in and the children watch eagerly to see if they can notice any diminution in Elijah's cup as the prophet quickly sips the wine and speeds on his way to visit all the other homes.

Sefer Ḥasidim 'Book of Saints', the major work produced in the circle of the *Saints of Germany. Although Judah the Saint of Regensburg (d. 1217) is considered to be the author of *Sefer Ḥasidim* there are a number of passages which come from other hands. The book in its present form also contains the Ethical Will of Judah the Saint. The *Sefer Ḥasidim* is not a systematic work of religion and ethics but consists of moral tales, ethical maxims, short treatises on various religious themes, all describing the ideal life of the *Hasid, not necessarily a scholar, who strives to lead a life of extraordinary piety.

The *Sefer Ḥasidim* is insistent that Jews must be completely honest in their dealings with Gentiles and this against the background of the Crusades when Christian–Jewish relations were strained, to say the least. 'If a Gentile cheats himself in accounts, the Jew must return the additional amount, and if a Jew is poor, it is better for him that he beg than cheat a Gentile' (no. 661). It appears that, even in this period, it was not unknown for Christians to become converts to Judaism. The *Sefer Ḥasidim* says: 'If a Jew who is kind-hearted marries a kind-hearted proselyte woman, it is better for other Jews to marry their descendants rather than the descendants of pure Jews who lack their virtue' (no. 377).

Together with the lofty maxims, the *Sefer Ḥasidim* contains many medieval superstitions (see MAGIC AND SUPERSTITION), the common property of both Jews and Christians of the time. There are ghost stories, tales of werewolves and vampires who prowl at night, and advice on how to forestall the evil designs of witches. Some of these ideas, under the influence of the *Sefer Ḥasidim*, reappear in later Jewish works. But it is for its piety and sincere love of humanity that the book is admired as a classic of Jewish moralistic literature.

Sefer Torah 'Scroll of the Torah', the *Pentateuch, written by hand on parchment, from which the reading of the *Torah is carried out in the synagogue. The parchment on which the Sefer Torah is written must come from a *kosher animal. There are detailed rules on how the Sefer Torah has to be written by the *sofer* ('scribe'), the expert skilled in the rules and in writing. The writing is done with a quill pen and black ink. Before the *sofer* writes he uses a ruler and stylus to make forty-two lines underneath which the letters are to be written and two vertical lines at the sides, so that the written text will have wide margins and be straight and uniform. The writing is done on strips of parchment, four columns of writing to each strip. The strips are then sewn together to form the complete Scroll. The sewing-together of the sections is done with material from the tendons of a kosher animal. A space is left between the letters and the words and at the end of the paragraphs. A space equal to four lines of text is left between the books of Genesis, Exodus, Leviticus, and Numbers. There is a tradition that some letters have to be written larger than the others and some smaller. The seven letters *shin, ayin, tet, nun, zayin, gimmel,* and *tzaddi* have little crown-like designs on the left-hand corner. Before writing, the *sofer* declares that he is doing it for the sake of the sanctification of the Sefer Torah. Some pious scribes immerse themselves in the *mikveh before they begin to write.

In order to avoid touching the sacred Scroll with the bare hand, the Sefer Torah is mounted on wooden handles by which it is held when reciting the benediction over the Torah and when elevating the Scroll. Sephardim do not have these handles but instead have the Scroll wrapped in silk and placed in a kind of open box. The Sefer Torah, when it is not in use, is covered with an embroidered mantle over which are placed silver adornments consisting of two bells, a breastplate, and a pointer. The last is for the use of the Reader, who points to the words as he reads so as not to miss out any. Some Scrolls have a crown at the top of the handles instead of the bells. The breastplate is based on the breastplate worn by the *High Priest which contained twelve precious stones on which the names of the twelve tribes were engraved (Exodus 28: 15–21). Some breastplates of the Sefer Torah have a representation of these stones. The bells are called *rimmonim,* 'pomegranates', after the bells and pomegranates attached to the coat of the High Priest (Exodus 28: 33–4). Most *rimmonim* today are in the shape

of a tower. This has no significance and was introduced by eighteenth-century silversmiths who used the towers in Amsterdam for their model.

Sefer Yetzirah 'Book of Creation', mystical work in Hebrew, containing less than 2,000 words, probably compiled between the third and sixth centuries CE. As its name implies, the *Sefer Yetzirah* consists of brief speculations on the creation. According to this work, God created the world by means of the twenty-two letters of the Hebrew alphabet and the numbers one to ten, that is to say, by the spiritual forces represented by these letters and numbers. The total of the numbers and the letters are called 'the thirty-two paths of wisdom'. The numbers (Sefirot) in the *Sefer Yetzirah* may simply have meant the numbers one to ten, though it is probable that the idea of cosmic entities is also implied. In any event, the work was understood by the Kabbalists as referring to their doctrine of the *Sefirot, the powers or potencies in the Godhead. The Talmud (*Sanhedrin* 65b) tells of third- and fourth-century teachers who created a 'man' and a calf by means of the *Sefer Yetzirah,* though it is uncertain whether this refers to our *Sefer Yetzirah.* Implied in the book itself is the notion that man, as a microcosm, can repeat, if he knows the secret, the creative processes by means of which God brought the world, the macrocosm, into being (see GOLEM).

Sefirot The powers or potencies in the Godhead as taught by the Kabbalah. The doctrine features prominently in the Zohar, although the Zohar does not actually use the word Sefirot, preferring terms such as 'stages' or 'crowns', probably because the Zohar is a pseudepigraphic work set in the second century CE and it would have given the game away to use a near-contemporary term like Sefirot. The doctrine runs that the *En Sof, the unfathomable

Ground of Being, produces, by a process of emanation, ten powers in which It (En Sof is sometimes referred to in impersonal terms) becomes manifest. These ten Sefirot are the source of all cosmic energy and vitality. Ethics of the Fathers (5. 1) speaks of ten words by means of which God created the world. In the context these are the ten 'sayings' mentioned in the creation narrative at the beginning of Genesis but are identified by the Kabbalists with the Sefirot.

The ten Sefirot, in the usual Kabbalistic terminology, are:

1. *Keter* ('Crown').
2. *Hokhmah* ('Wisdom').
3. *Binah* ('Understanding').
4. *Hesed* ('Loving-kindness').
5. *Gevurah* ('Power' or 'Judgement').
6. *Tiferet* ('Beauty').
7. *Netzah* ('Victory').
8. *Hod* ('Splendour').
9. *Yesod* ('Foundation').
10. *Malkhut* ('Sovereignty').

Selihot Prayers for pardon, from the root *salaḥ*, 'to forgive'. These supplications, composed during the Middle Ages, are recited a few days before *Rosh Ha-Shanah and during the days between Rosh Ha-Shanah and *Yom Kippur. God is described as 'good and ready to pardon' (Psalms 86: 5) and the Psalmist prays: 'Pardon my iniquity for it is great' (Psalms 25: 11), making the Selihot prayers especially appropriate for the penitential season. Selihot are recited on Yom Kippur itself at every service, on the other days only during the morning service. The *confession of sin on Yom Kippur is recited privately but also by the whole congregation during the Selihot. In many communities on the first day of the week in which Rosh Ha-Shanah falls, Selihot are recited at midnight. The *Sephardim recite Selihot from 1 *Elul, the month before Rosh Ha-Shanah, with which the fuller penitential sea-

son begins. In addition to these days, Selihot are recited on all fast days and on Mondays and Thursdays throughout the year (except on festive occasions) since these days are seen as judgement days on the analogy of the human courts which sat, in Talmudic times, on Mondays and Thursdays. The central feature of every Selihot service is the recital of the verse containing, in the Rabbinic expression, the thirteen attributes of mercy: 'The Lord, the Lord, merciful and gracious, long-suffering, and abundant in goodness and truth; keeping mercy unto the thousandth generation, forgiving iniquity' (Exodus 34: 6–7, but with the omission of the words 'but that will by no means clear the guilty'). The Talmud (*Rosh Ha-Shanah* 17b) states: 'A covenant has been established that whenever the thirteen attributes are invoked in prayer, that prayer will not be in vain.'

Sephardim The descendants of Spanish Jewry, as distinct from the *Ashkenazim, who are descended from German Jewry. The names Sepharad and Ashkenaz are found in the Bible but were used in the Middle Ages to denote, respectively, Spain and Germany. Spain was the land in which Jewry reached its Golden Age, as this has been called; an age which saw the flowering of Jewish culture and produced such eminent figures as *Maimonides, *Nahmanides, *Judah Halevi, *Ibn Gabirol, *Abravanel, and many others. After the expulsion from Spain in 1492, Spanish Jews resettled themselves in the land of Israel (see SAFED), the Ottoman Empire, and North Africa and later in America, in Amsterdam, and in other European cities. Sephardim and Ashkenazim are not divided on doctrinal lines and should not be considered as two distinct Jewish sects. The differences, of which there are many, between the two groups are the result of different cultural conditions, local customs, and, especially, the different Halakhic authorities favoured by each group. The rivalry between the two groups was often intense in former times, but is less so nowadays. Located, in the nineteenth century, outside Germany, the Sephardim were far less influenced by the *Haskalah than the Ashkenazim, which partly accounts for the absence of any organized Reform movement among the Sephardim, except for the comparatively mild form that emerged in London. The popular language of Sephardi Jews is *Ladino, as *Yiddish is of the Ashkenazi Jews. Because of the differences in law, custom, and ritual between the two groups, Sephardi Rabbis lead Sephardi communities and Ashkenazi Rabbis Ashkenazi communities.

Septuagint The ancient Greek translation of the Pentateuch produced, according to the second-century BCE *Letter of Aristeas* (see ROSSI), in Alexandria in the reign of Ptolemy II (third century BCE). The name, Septuagint, is based on the story in this letter that the translation was made, at the request of the king, by seventy-two scholars (seventy being the nearest round number). The Talmud (*Megillah* 9a) has a different version of the story, according to which the translation was made by seventy sages, sitting in different rooms, each being inspired to make the same alterations to the text where the original might prove offensive to the king. The Talmud states that it was a dark day for Israel when the translation into Greek was made, whereas the Greek-speaking Jews of Alexandria, we learn from *Philo, hailed the translation as a great event. Many scholars now hold that the translation, first of the Pentateuch, later of the whole of the Bible, was made at different times by the Alexandrian Jews themselves and that later additions were made to the text from time to time.

In biblical scholarship the Septuagint (designated as LXX) is widely used,

though with caution, for the establishment of the biblical text (see BIBLICAL CRITICISM).

Sex Naturally, with regard to such a complex topic that affects human life so powerfully, there are to be found differing attitudes among religious Jews. On the one hand, the Bible has a positive attitude to marriage (see CELIBACY) and to sex within marriage, witness the fact that the patriarchs and Moses were married, and the Rabbis declare that it is a religious obligation for a husband to satisfy his wife's needs in this respect. On the other hand, it is urged that the sex drive be severely controlled and there is a definite tendency in Rabbinic thought to curtail too much sexual indulgence even in the marital bed, as when the Rabbis warn: 'There is a small organ in man's body which when hungry is sated but when sated is hungry.' Another Rabbinic saying has it that on judgement day a man will be told the frivolous conversations he has had with his wife Maimonides (*Guide of the Perplexed*, 2. 36), though his view is Jewishly atypical, approves of Aristotle's remark that the sense of touch is 'shameful'. Risking a generalization, it might be said that the Jewish teachers welcome the sex drive as a divine gift to human beings while acknowledging, at the same time, that of all human instincts, sex is the most likely to lead people astray.

In modern Jewish thought until very recently, there have been no discussions of Jewish attitudes to sex. The reason is no doubt because of nineteenth century prudery, reflected in Jewish works of the time. Indeed, from the works of Jewish thinkers writing in European languages in the nineteenth century, one would imagine that they had no sex life at all or, if they did, they kept it very secret. It is only recently, when sex has been more frankly and openly discussed, that Jewish thinkers have begun to consider Jewish points of view. There is, in fact, no single Jewish attitude to sex except that a completely negative view of sex is not possible for thinkers in the authentic Jewish tradition.

Shaatnez A mixed garment of wool and linen. The prohibition against wearing this kind of garment is stated in Leviticus (19: 19): 'neither shall come upon thee a garment of two kinds of stuff [shaatnez] mingled together'. The word shaatnez occurs in the Bible only here and in the parallel verse in Deuteronomy and its etymology is uncertain. According to the Rabbis the meaning is explained in the verse in Deuteronomy (22: 11): 'Thou shalt not wear a mingled stuff [shaatnez], wool and linen together.' Orthodox Jews still observe the law of shaatnez as a divinely given ordinance, whatever its reason. Reform and many Conservative Jews no longer keep this law since, according to them, it has no meaning for the modern Jew.

Shabbetai Zevi Turkish scholar and mystic (1626–76) who claimed to be the *Messiah.

Shabbetai Zevi was born in the city of Smyrna, where he received a sound grounding in the Talmud. He was ordained as a Rabbi at the early age of 18. He later acquired, too, a comprehensive knowledge of the Kabbalah. Shabbetai was born on 9 *Av, the anniversary of the destruction of the Temple but also, according to tradition, the day on which the Messiah will be born. To prepare himself for his Messianic role Shabbetai consciously carried out a number of illegal acts, in the belief that in the redeemed world some of the laws of the Torah will no longer be required. In 1665 Shabbetai journeyed to the land of Israel where he was hailed as the Messiah by the young visionary Nathan of Gaza (1643–80) who claimed to be his *Elijah, the herald of the Messiah. When Shabbetai returned to Turkey his claim to be the Messiah became widely acknowledged.

The news spread rapidly throughout the Jewish world. There was even talk of Shabbetai assembling a Jewish army to reconquer the Holy Land. Jewish communities everywhere were captivated by these events which gave many their first taste of real religious enthusiasm. But when Shabbetai was given the choice of either converting to Islam or being executed, he became a Muslim, though he continued to practise the Jewish religion. Later Shabbetai was banished to Albania where he died still venerated by his loyal followers. After Shabbetai's death his followers still believed in him but kept quiet about it. These crypto-Shabbeteans behaved outwardly as learned and pious Jews but, in secret, carried out 'holy sins', sins committed for the express purpose of bringing to completion the task begun by Shabbetai. In the eighteenth century the *Frankist sect, the followers of Jacob Frank, who claimed to be a reincarnation of Shabbetai Zevi, carried out bizarre rituals which included sexual excesses such as incest. Eventually the Frankists became converted to Christianity.

Shammai Prominent teacher, together with *Hillel, of the first century BCE. In the famous story of the two proselytes (*Shabbat* 31a) the Talmud advises: 'Let a man always be as humble as Hillel and never as cantankerous as Shammai.' It is curious, therefore, that the saying is attributed to Shammai in Ethics of the Fathers (1. 15): 'Welcome every man with a cheerful countenance.' There were probably different traditions regarding Shammai's character. The numerous debates between the House of Shammai and the House of Hillel are referred to frequently in the Mishnah and the Talmud.

Shavuot The Feast of Weeks, Pentecost, the festival celebrated on 6 Sivan (and 7 Sivan in the *Diaspora). In the book of Exodus (34: 22) the festival is called the Festival of Weeks (Shavuot means 'weeks') as it is in the book of Deuteronomy (16: 16), where it is one of the three pilgrim festivals when the people visited the Temple, the others being *Passover and *Tabernacles. The name Shavuot is derived from the statement in the book of Leviticus (23: 15–16) that the festival falls after seven weeks have been counted from the day after the *Omer is brought, hence also the name Pentecost ('fifty'), though this name is not used in the Jewish sources. The Rabbinic name for the festival is Atzeret, a name used for other festivals (Leviticus 23: 26; Numbers 29: 35). The original meaning of Atzeret is not clear (the word is usually translated as 'Solemn Assembly') but the Rabbis seem to understand it as meaning 'completion' or 'adjunct' and it is used of Shavuot in the sense that it is a complement to the festival of Passover.

A remarkable transformation of this festival took place in Rabbinic times. In the Bible Shavuot is obviously a harvest festival. But, based on the verse in Exodus (19: 1) that the children of Israel came to *Sinai on the third month (the month later called Sivan), the Rabbinic understanding of the real significance of the festival is that it commemorates the giving of the Torah and Shavuot is referred to in the liturgy as 'The season of the giving of our Torah'. Over the centuries, a number of Shavuot *customs were introduced. It is the custom to eat dairy products on Shavuot. This might have been simply because Shavuot falls in the hot season when milk dishes are more acceptable fare. But various further ideas have been read into the custom: for instance, that the Torah is compared to milk since it nourishes both the very young and the very old and because, if kept in golden vessels, milk turns sour—a warning to the Torah scholar not to give in to *pride. It is the custom to adorn the synagogue with plants and flowers on Shavuot. One reason given is that this denotes the fragrance and beauty of the Torah.

Shehitah 'Slaughtering', from the root *shahat*, 'to kill'; the manner in which animals and fowl have to be killed for food if their meat is to be eaten (see DIETARY LAWS, KOSHER, and TERE-FAH). There is no explicit reference in the Pentateuch to the need for *shehitah* for animals not offered as sacrifices in the Temple nor are there any indications as to how *shehitah* is to be carried out. In the Rabbinic tradition the laws of *shehitah* were conveyed by God to Moses at *Sinai. *Shehitah* is performed by a specially trained person, the *shohet*, who has to use a finely honed knife free from the slightest notch. For an animal *shehitah* involves the cutting of the major portion of both the windpipe and the foodpipe, for a bird the major portion of either of these. Further rules are described in great detail in the sources; it is stated, for instance, that there must be no pause in the act from beginning to end. Maimonides (*Guide of the Perplexed*, 3. 48) understands the reason for the *shehitah* laws to be the avoidance of unnecessary cruelty to animals. It is permitted to kill animals and birds for food but forbidden to do this in a cruel manner. In modern times animal-welfare groups have tried to have *shehitah* banned on the grounds that it is a cruel method. Jews reply that, on the contrary, *shehitah* is the most painless method available, especially since it has to be carried out by a learned and pious man. No Jewish woman, it has been pointed out, will ever take a chicken and wring its neck. Since some defects in the lungs of an animal render the animal unfit to be eaten, the *shohet* is expected, after *shehitah*, to examine the lungs to see if they are free from these defects. Orthodox and Conservative Jews still keep the laws of *shehitah* and consider meat that comes from an animal which has not had *shehitah* to be non-kosher, as do some Reform Jews, although classical Reform saw no need to be particular about the *shehitah* laws since these are not found in the Torah.

Sheitel 'Wig', worn by married women to avoid the offence of going about with uncovered head. It was considered immodest for Jewish married women to go out into a public place with the head bare (see BARE HEAD). The usual practice was to have a head-covering, often richly embroidered. But when, in the eighteenth century, wigs came into fashion, many Jewesses preferred to wear a *sheitel* as a head-covering, despite the opposition of some Rabbis who claimed that the *sheitel* gives the appearance that the head is uncovered and hence defeats the whole purpose of the law. Some exceedingly pious women still prefer a proper head-covering but the majority of Orthodox women do wear the *sheitel*. Reform and Conservative Jews and even some Orthodox Jews do not consider the wearing of a head-covering to be necessary nowadays since women today do not insist on having their heads covered, so that failure to do so is no longer any indication of immodesty.

Shekhinah The in-dwelling presence of God, from the root *shakhan*, 'to dwell'. The verbal form is found in Scripture, for example, in the verse: 'And let them make Me a sanctuary, that I may dwell [*ve-shakhanti*] among them' (Exodus 25: 8) but Shekhinah as a noun is a Rabbinic coinage, used in the Talmudic literature and the *Targum* both for the abiding of God in a particular spot (see HOLY PLACES) and as a divine *name irrespective of spatial location.

As in other highly speculative topics it is impossible to speak of *the* Rabbinic view. Rabbinic thought is neither abstract nor systematic so that the most

that can be done is to note a few typical passages while appreciating that they are direct responses to particular situations rather than a systematic theology of the Shekhinah. A favourite Rabbinic metaphor is the *light or 'shining' (*ziv*) of the Shekhinah. A Midrashic paraphrase of the verse: 'May the Lord cause the light of His countenance to shine upon thee' (Numbers 6: 25) is: 'May He give thee of the light of the Shekhinah' (Sifre to the verse). A Midrashic homily (Numbers Rabbah 12: 4) compares the shining of the Shekhinah in the tent of meeting (Exodus 40: 35) to a cave by the sea. The sea rushes in to fill the cave, but the sea suffers no diminution of its waters. Similarly, the Shekhinah filled the tent of meeting, but it filled the world just the same. The shining of the Shekhinah is referred to in the famous statement about life in the *World to Come by the third-century teacher *Rav (*Berakhot* 17a): 'In the World to Come there is no eating nor drinking nor propagation nor business nor jealousy nor hatred nor competition, but the righteous sit with their crowns on their heads and bask in the radiance [*ziv*] of the Shekhinah.'

Shema The Jewish declaration of faith: 'Hear [*shema*] O Israel, the Lord our God, the Lord is One' (Deuteronomy 6: 4). To this basic verse of the Shema are added the whole paragraph containing the verse (Deuteronomy 6: 4–9); the paragraph beginning: 'And it shall come to pass' (Deuteronomy 11: 13-21); and the paragraph containing the law of *tzitzit (Numbers 15: 37–41). The two paragraphs in Deuteronomy state that 'these words should be spoken of when lying down and when rising up'. The Rabbis understand 'these words' to mean the words of the Shema and 'when lying down and rising up' to mean that the Shema must be recited in the evening and in the morning, so that it must be recited each night and morning, at the exact times described in detail in the Talmud and the Codes. The Mishnah in the first tractate of the Talmud, tractate *Berakhot*, rules, for instance, that the night Shema should ideally be recited before midnight but can be recited any time during the night until daybreak. The morning Shema should not be recited before daybreak or after the time when about a quarter of the day has gone by. The paragraph from Numbers was added because of the reference in it to the Exodus from Egypt, since the verse states: 'that thou mayest remember the day when thou camest forth out of the land of Egypt all the days of thy life' (Deuteronomy 16: 3). The two passages from Deuteronomy are written in the *mezuzah and are two of the four in the *tefillin*.

After the first verse of the Shema, the words: 'Blessed be the name of His glorious Kingdom for ever and ever' are recited softly, unlike the Shema itself which is recited in a loud voice. The Talmud says that this has to be recited in an undertone because it is not in Scripture. Some modern scholars hold that, under Roman dominion, it was hazardous for Jews to recite this declaration in a loud voice since it might be understood by the Roman authorities as a challenge to their rule. The original implication of the declaration may, indeed, have been that it is as if to say: 'God is our King and not the Romans now ruling over us.' These two declarations are recited by the whole congregation in unison at the solemn Neilah ('Closing') service on *Yom Kippur, the Shema once, 'Blessed be the name' three times. Contrary to the practice during the rest of the year, 'Blessed be the name' is recited in the evening and morning on Yom Kippur in a loud voice, as if to say: 'On the great Day of Atonement we fear no one in hoping for the Kingdom of Heaven to be established and we say these words aloud.'

Shemini Atzeret The festival that falls on 22 Tishri and is the eighth day of the festival of *Tabernacles. Shemini means 'eighth' and Atzeret is usually translated as 'Solemn Assembly', thus 'the Eighth Day of Solemn Assembly', although Atzeret may mean 'adjunct'; so that this festival is understood to be a complement to Tabernacles as *Shavuot is to *Passover. According to the Rabbis, Shemini Atzeret is also a festival in its own right in some respects. It is mentioned as a separate festival in the book of Leviticus (23: 36) and in the book of Numbers (29: 35) in the list of festivals. There are no special rituals for Shemini Atzeret except that on it the special prayer for *rain called *Geshem* ('Rain') is recited during the Musaf ('Additional Service') of the day. In Israel Shemini Atzeret is also the festival of *Simhat Torah but in the *Diaspora Simhat Torah is celebrated on the next day, though it is still referred to as Shemini Atzeret. As the culmination of the penitential season from *Rosh Ha-Shanah to *Yom Kippur and of the festive season of Tabernacles, Shemini Atzeret is the most joyous festival in the Jewish *calendar, though the joy is expressed in a less boisterous manner than on *Purim.

Sherira Gaon Head of the college in Pumbedita (see GEONIM). Reliable reports have it that Sherira lived for 100 years, the date of his death being given as around the year 1000. Sherira did not assume office as Gaon of Pumbedita until he was almost 70 years of age, after the Gaonite had suffered an eclipse. Thanks to Sherira's efforts, the Gaonite of Pumbedita became a central authority for Jews in other parts of the Jewish world. Because of Sherira's great age he was assisted towards the end of his life by his son, *Hai, who was officially appointed Gaon of Pumbedita when Sherira died. Sherira and Hai feature very prominently in the *Responsa of the Geonim, of which various collections have been made. Questions were addressed to these two Geonim from many parts of the Jewish world and their replies became authoritative in subsequent codifications of Jewish law.

Sherira's chief claim to fame rests on the letter he wrote in in the year 987 to Jacob ben Nissim of Kairowan in North Africa, Jacob having requested Sherira to explain in detail how the Mishnah and the Talmud had been compiled. Sherira's reply, in Aramaic, known as *The Letter of Rav Sherira Gaon*, is a major source for the history of the Talmudic period, based as it is not only on Sherira's erudition but also on the traditions preserved in the Babylonian schools. For the first time we have in the *Letter* a comprehensive account of how Rabbi *Judah the Prince compiled the Mishnah and how the Babylonian teachers compiled the Talmud. Sherira's *Letter* is, however, used by modern historians of the Talmudic period with a degree of caution since, after all, it was written hundreds of years after the events of which it tells and occasionally Sherira reads back into the Talmudic period the conditions in the Babylonian schools of his and recent ages.

Shneur Zalman of Liady Hasidic master (1745–1813), founder of the *Habad school in *Hasidism. Shneur Zalman (the name Shneur probably comes from 'Señor', suggesting that the family came originally from Spain) was born in the Belorussian town of Liozno, near Vitebsk. He married at an early age and, with the approval of his young wife but against the wishes of both his father and father-in-law who were suspicious of the new trends, he resolved to journey to *Dov Baer of Mezhirech, disciple of the *Baal Shem Tov and organizer of the Hasidic movement, in order to learn, as he said, how to pray.

Shneur Zalman's *Tanya* (so-called after its opening word in Aramaic, *Tanya*, 'It was taught') is a systematic treatment of Kabbalistic and Hasidic themes in the Habad interpretation. The work, in its complete form, was published in Shklov in 1814 since when it has gone into numerous editions. Lubavitch Hasidim often place their copy of the *Tanya* in the bag in which they keep their *tallit and treat the work with a veneration that appears to the non-Hasid to be bordering on the bizarre.

Shofar The horn sounded on the New Year festival, *Rosh Ha-Shanah. This festival is described in the *Pentateuch as a day of blowing the horn (Leviticus 23: 23–25; Numbers 19: 1–6). According to the Talmudic Rabbis, the horn of any clean animal (i.e. any *kosher animal; see DIETARY LAWS), sheep, goat, or antelope, is fit to be used on Rosh Ha-Shanah but preference is given to the ram's horn because of the substitution of a ram for Isaac at the *Akedah (Genesis 22: 13). The only exception made by the Rabbis was the horn of a cow, because Israel had once worshipped the *golden calf and it is unfitting for Israel to appear before God on the great day of judgement with something which would recall this lapse. As the Rabbis put it: 'A prosecutor cannot act as a defender.'

The Torah gives no reason for the command to blow the *shofar* on Rosh Ha-Shanah. This is one of the precepts referred to by the Rabbis as divine decrees which have to be obeyed even if the reason for them is unknown. When the Talmud (*Rosh Ha-Shanah*, 16a) asks: 'Why do we sound the *shofar* on Rosh Ha-Shanah?' the immediate retort is: 'Why do we blow [you ask]? We blow because the All-Merciful has told us to blow.' For all that, the strange, fascinating ritual has encouraged later teachers to suggest reasons of their own. David *Abudarham states that *Saadiah Gaon advanced no less than ten different 'reasons', of which the following have been particularly noted in later discussions of the rite. On Rosh Ha-Shanah

God is hailed as King and trumpets are sounded at the coronation of a king. The sound of the *shofar* was heard at *Sinai (Exodus 19: 16, 19; 20: 18), so that on Rosh Ha-Shanah Jews reaffirm their loyalty to the Torah by re-enacting the theophany at Sinai. This theme is, in fact, found in the Rabbinic rule of the Shofarot, the scriptural verses recited during the Musaf service on Rosh Ha-Shanah in which the Sinai verses are quoted. On Rosh Ha-Shanah the merits of Abraham, ready to sacrifice Isaac, are invoked and the ram's horn is a reminder, as above, of Abraham's trial. The eschatological motif is also introduced. The prophet speaks of the great *shofar* that will be blown to herald the advent of the *Messiah (Isaiah 27: 13). Centuries before Saadiah, *Philo of Alexandria noted the connection between the blowing of the *shofar* and the theophany at Sinai. Philo also suggests that since trumpets are sounded when armies go into battle, the *shofar* is a reminder of the horrors of warfare, a prayer to God to help establish peace on earth, and an expression of gratitude to Him when the precious gift of peace is given to mankind. The congregation stands while the *shofar* is sounded. In order to prevent any mistakes being made by the one who blows, a member of the congregation calls out to him each note before he sounds it. The *shofar* should be held facing towards the right with its wider end facing upwards. The *shofar* should be curved, not straight, symbolic of man's readiness to bow in submission to God.

Shulḥan Arukh 'Arranged Table', the standard Code of Jewish law compiled by Joseph *Karo in the sixteenth century with glosses by Moses *Isserles.

Orthodox Judaism accepts the *Shulḥan Arukh* as binding, although this does not mean that Orthodox Jews follow all the bare rulings of the work. The standard commentaries and later authorities are often relied on where a ruling is required which departs from that of the *Shulḥan Arukh*, especially when new conditions demand fresh rulings. Many Hasidic masters, while generally accepting the authority of the *Shulḥan Arukh*, felt themselves free to offer their prayers at different times from those laid down in the *Shulḥan Arukh*. A Hasidic saying has it that the difference between the Hasidim and the *Mitnaggedim is that Hasidim stand in awe of God while the Mitnaggedim stand in awe of the *Shulḥan Arukh*. But generally, a strictly Orthodox Jew is known as 'a *Shulḥan Arukh* Jew'. Reform Judaism in the nineteenth century had a negative attitude to the *Halakhah generally, to say nothing of the codification of the Halakhah in the *Shulḥan Arukh*. At the Reform Synod in Augsburg in 1871 a debate took place on the suggestion that a new, thoroughly revised *Shulḥan Arukh*, more in line with Reform philosophy, should be produced. Against this it was argued that any revision would imply recognition that the *Shulḥan Arukh* is an authority, which it is not for Reform, that such a *Shulḥan Arukh* would stifle further development in Judaism, and that so little would be left when the obsolete elements (from the Reform point of view) had been removed that a revision was pointless. This remains the Reform position, though there is evident, in contemporary versions of Reform, a greater awareness of the values enshrined in some, at least, of the rulings of the *Shulḥan Arukh* (see REFORM JUDAISM).

Conservative Judaism, with its stress on the developing nature of Judaism in general and Jewish law in particular, has a far more positive attitude to the *Shulḥan Arukh* as a stage in this development but feels free to employ the Halakhic machinery in order to develop the law further even though, as a result, changes may be introduced contrary to the rulings of the *Shulḥan*

Arukh: for instance, on the question of riding in an automobile to the synagogue on the Sabbath. It is also true that for all three groups the actual practice of Jews has a decisive voice, whether or not this is officially acknowledged. Even among Orthodox Rabbis, the saying is popular that there is a fifth, unwritten part of the *Shulḥan Arukh* by which the other four parts are to be interpreted. This is the part of common sense.

Siddur See PRAYER BOOK.

Simeon Ben Yohai Famous Rabbi of the second century CE, disciple of Rabbi *Akiba and colleague of Rabbi *Meir, Rabbi Judah, and Rabbi Jose. Rabbi Simeon ben Yohai's opinions in Halakhah are referred to frequently in the Talmudic records of the debates and discussions among the *Tannaim. He was also renowned as an exponent of Scripture and a miracle-worker. In the Talmudic legend, Rabbi Simeon made some adverse remarks about the Roman occupation of Judaea (see ROME) and when this was reported to the government authorities he was obliged to flee for his life. Together with his son, Eleazar, he lived in a cave for thirteen years. According to the Kabbalists, Rabbi Simeon ben Yohai is the author of the *Zohar, a work composed in the main during his forced stay in the cave and the bulk of which consists of mystical interpretations of Scripture by Rabbi Simeon and his chosen companions. Recent Zoharic scholarship has demonstrated that the true author of the major part of the Zohar was *Moses de Leon, who made Rabbi Simeon the hero of his pseudepigraphic work. An annual pilgrimage is still made on *Lag Ba-Omer, the anniversary of Rabbi Simeon's death, to his supposed tomb in Meron, near *Safed.

Simhat Torah 'Rejoicing of the Law', the festival at the end of *Tabernacles,

on the eighth day (22 Tishri) in Israel, coinciding with *Shemini Atzeret; the ninth day (23 Tishri) in the *Diaspora, the second day of Shemini Atzeret. Reform Jews do not observe the second days of the festivals and, since they only have one day of Shemini Atzeret, Simhat Torah is celebrated on this day as it is in Israel. The celebration of Simhat Torah dates from the ninth century (in the liturgy the ninth day is referred to as Shemini Atzeret, not Simhat Torah) and is based on the Babylonian custom (now universally followed) of *reading the Torah in an annual cycle, unlike the triennial cycle in which the Torah was read by Palestinian Jewry in Talmudic times. The weekly portions are so arranged that the final portion of the Torah (Deuteronomy 33 and 34) is left to be completed on this day. On the same day the cycle begins again with the reading of the first portion of Genesis. The person who has the honour of being called up to the final reading from Deuteronomy is called the Hatan Torah, 'the Bridegroom of the Torah', while the one called to the reading of the first portion of Genesis is called Hatan Bereshit 'the Bridegroom of Bereshit' ('In the beginning', the first word of Genesis and of the whole Torah). On the eve of Simhat Torah and during the day all the Scrolls (see SEFER TORAH) are taken from the *Ark and carried in procession seven times around the synagogue, accompanied by singing and dancing and general merriment. In many synagogues it is the custom to call up for the reading every member of the congregation, the portions being repeated as many times as required for the purpose, though otherwise a portion is not read more than once on the same day. All the children in the synagogue are called up together to a portion of the Torah and they are blessed by the congregation and given sweets, apples, and other treats. The children also walk in the procession holding flags on which there is a symbol of the Torah. It is customary for the two 'Bridegrooms' to give a party, or at least provide drinks and cakes, for the congregation. In some Reform congregations women are given these honours and are called 'the Bride of the Torah' and 'the Bride of Genesis'—surely a little odd, since the Torah is a 'female'.

Sin and Repentance The usual word for sin, *averah*, is from the root *avar*, 'to pass over', hence 'transgression', overriding God's will. The usual word for repentance is *teshuvah*, meaning 'turning', that is, from sin to God. In Rabbinic theology sin is caused by the evil inclination, which tempts man to disobey God's laws (see YETZER HA-TOV AND YETZER HA-RA). No human being is free from temptation but is assured that sincere repentance is always accepted.

Repentance is acceptable, the Rabbis teach, at any time but the special time for repentance is the the season from *Rosh Ha-Shanah to 'Yom Kippur, the *Ten Days of Penitence. In all the Rabbinic sources repentance involves two things: remorse at having sinned and *confession of the sin.

As in other matters, contemporary Jews interpret the classical sources on sin and repentance in accordance with their particular philosophy of Judaism and will take into account, too, modern psychological, sociological, and medical theories about the causes of criminal behaviour. Not everything considered to be a sin in the traditional sources is so considered by all Jews today. Reform Jews will hardly be moved to 'repent' for carrying out acts that, for Reform Judaism, are not sins at all. Yet no Jewish thinker has ever wished to be rid of the whole idea of sin and repentance. The need to find peace in one's soul; to shed the guilt load by constructive means, namely, by making good the harm that has been done; the renewal of one's personal life; reconciliation

with God and with other human beings; all these would be accepted by all religious Jews, whatever their particular stance, as tests of a mature religious personality. There is no Judaism, whether ancient or modern, without teachings about the evil of sin, as there is no Judaism without teachings about the high value of repentance. Both sin and repentance are religious concepts. It is before God that one sins and it is God who pardons.

Sinai The mountain on which God appeared to the people of Israel (Exodus 19, 20). It is further stated (Exodus 34: 27–32) that Moses ascended the mountain and stayed there for forty days and forty nights and then came down, with the *tablets of stone on which the *Decalogue was inscribed, to teach the people the instructions he had received there. This is the basis for the Rabbinic doctrine that at Sinai Moses received the *Oral Torah, the explanations of the laws conveyed to him during his stay on the mount. Hence, in the Rabbinic tradition, laws not stated explicitly in the *Written Torah but which have the status of biblical law are called 'laws given to Moses at Sinai'. Ethics of the Fathers opens with the statement: 'Moses received Torah from Sinai and he gave it over to Joshua.' The current expression 'Torah from Sinai' (*Torah mi-Sinai*) as synonymous with 'Torah from Heaven' (*Torah min Ha-Shamayyim*) is consequently very imprecise in describing the Rabbinic view. The latter doctrine refers to the whole of the *Pentateuch as well as to the laws given at Sinai and the Pentateuch itself records laws that were given and events that took place after the theophany at Sinai during Israel's sojourn in the wilderness. There is no warrant in the Rabbinic sources for the obviously anachronistic view that the whole of the Pentateuch was given to Moses at Sinai (and see BIBLICAL CRITICISM, CONSERVATIVE JUDAISM, and REVELATION).

Slander The strongest moral disapproval is expressed in Jewish teachings of slander in all its forms. The prohibition against going around as a tale-bearer is stated in the Holiness Code in Leviticus (Leviticus 19: 16). The prophet Jeremiah castigates those 'who go about with slanders and who speak iniquity' (Jeremiah 9: 2–4). The Psalmist declares: 'Who is the man that desireth life, and loveth days, that he may see good therein? Keep thy tongue from evil, and thy lips from speaking guile. Depart from evil and do good, seek peace and pursue it' (Psalms 34: 13–15).

Morally, the slanderer meets with the strictest condemnation. A Rabbinic saying has it that a habitual slanderer is unworthy of 'receiving the divine countenance' in the *World to Come. Whoever makes a habit of speaking slander, say the Rabbis, acts as though he denies the existence of God (*Arakhin* 15b).

The scholar who, more than anyone else in the past few hundred years, devoted his life to combating *lashon ha-ra*, 'the evil tongue', as slander is called, was Israel Meir Kagan, the *Hafetz Hayyim. Among other matters mentioned by the Hafetz Hayyim in his comprehensive works on the subject is that Jewish law makes no distinction between libel and slander, between written and verbal calumny. He demonstrates that the prohibition of 'evil talk' includes: listening to it; making libellous remarks about a competitor's merchandise; and praising a person to his enemies, who will react by speaking ill of him. According to the Hafetz Hayyim defamation of a whole group, not only of an individual, is forbidden.

Slavery Civilized societies have abolished slavery. The problem is that while campaigners against slavery, such as Wilberforce, drew their inspiration from the biblical narrative of the redemption of the Hebrew slaves from Egyptian bondage and from the biblical teaching that all men are created in the

image of God, the Bible and, for that matter, the Rabbinic literature, do tolerate the institution even though they do not positively advocate it. During the great struggle over the slavery issue in America in the nineteenth century, there were Jews as well as Christians on both sides of the debate. Rabbi David Einhorn, who risked his life to oppose slavery, declared it to be 'the greatest possible crime against God'. Rabbi Morris J. Raphael, on the opposite side, pointed to the biblical law in support of the institution. Rabbi Raphael must have known that even in the biblical law a marked tendency can be observed to limit slavery and to demand that slaves be treated humanely. The Deuteronomic law states (Deuteronomy 23: 15–16): 'Thou shalt not deliver unto his master the slave who escapes from his master unto thee; he shall dwell with thee, even among you, in that place which he shall choose in one of thy gates, where it liketh him best; thou shalt not oppress him.' But, while Rabbi Raphael and those who shared his views hardly thought highly of slavery, they felt unable honestly to condemn outright an institution that was sanctioned by Moses speaking in the name of God.

All Jews today accept that the abolition of slavery was a great step forward for mankind. Many would say that the Bible and the Rabbinic literature have to be seen against the background of the times when they were compiled, when both slavery and polygamy were part of the very fabric of ancient society. In some periods of human history society would have collapsed without these two institutions. Jews accept that there are ideas of the utmost value that could not be realized until a different form of society had emerged. The abolition of slavery in the nineteenth century, many Jews would say, was the fuller realization of principles taught by the Torah.

Sofer, Moses Foremost Hungarian Rabbi, Halakhic authority, and champion of Orthodoxy (1762–1839), known, after the title of his Responsa collection, as Hatam Sofer ('Seal of the Scribe'). Sofer was born in Frankfurt where he studied under Rabbi Phineas Horowitz, the Rabbi of the town, and Rabbi Nathan Adler, a Talmudist and Kabbalist whose esoteric leanings were not to the taste of the staid Frankfurt community, which he was forced to leave, taking his disciple, Sofer, with him. After occupying Rabbinic positions in Dresnitz and Mattersdot, Sofer was appointed Rabbi of Pressburg (Bratislava) where he served until his death. He was succeeded in this position by his son, Abraham Samuel Benjamin Wolf (1815–71), known as the Ketav Sofer ('Writing of the Scribe'), who, in turn, was succeeded by his son, Simhah Bunem (1842–1906), known as the Shevet Sofer ('Pen of the Scribe').

Sofer saw danger to traditional Judaism in the *Haskalah movement and he had a largely negative attitude towards Moses *Mendelssohn and his followers. Yet it is a mistake to see him as obscurantist in his attitude. It has to be appreciated that the Jewish communities in central Europe were attracted to the Reform movement, then growing in influence, in nearby Germany. In Pressburg itself there were strong Reformist tendencies which Sofer successfully overcame in his belief that Reform threatened the very foundations of Judaism. When the Hamburg Reform Temple was established, the Hamburg Rabbinate issued, in 1818, the document *Eleh Divre Ha-Berit* ('These are the Words of the Covenant'), attacking Reform innovations. Sofer and his father-in-law, the famed Talmudist, Rabbi Akiba Eger, contributed to this protest well-reasoned essays in defence of total adherence to traditional forms.

Sofer's strong opposition to the Reform movement was continued by his son and grandson and their disciples.

Every practice that seemed to have been influenced by Reform or by Christian practices was declared taboo, for instance, to have the *bimah at the end of the synagogue near the *Ark, or to have weddings in the synagogue with an address by the preacher to bride and bridegroom, or for the Rabbi and Cantor to wear canonicals.

Solomon King of Israel, tenth century BCE, son of *David; his story is told in the book of Kings (1 Kings 1–12). Solomon built the *Temple in Jerusalem, offering at its dedication his famous prayer (1 Kings 8). The two episodes in Solomon's reign that have become famous in world literature are the visit to him of the queen of Sheba (1 Kings 10: 1–13) and his famous judgement (1 Kings 3: 16–28). In the Rabbinic tradition Solomon is the author of the *Song of Songs, *Proverbs, and *Ecclesiastes and he is called, after the scriptural verse, 'the wisest of all men' (1 Kings 5: 11). Legends abound of Solomon's skill in interpreting the speech of animals and birds, of his power over the spirits, and of the way the demon *Ashmedai usurped Solomon's throne.

Soloveitchik Family Lithuanian Rabbinic family of which the four most influential members were: Joseph Baer (1820–92); his son Hayyim (1853–1918); Hayyim's son, Isaac Zeev (1886–1960); and Hayyim's grandson, Joseph Baer (1903–93). The first Joseph Baer served as one of the heads of the famed Yeshivah of *Volozhyn and then as Rabbi of Brest-Litovsk (Brisk). Hayyim also served as a teacher in Volozhyn and then succeeded his father as Rabbi of Brisk, becoming known as Reb Hayyim Brisker. Isaac (Reb Velvel) succeeded his father as Rabbi of Brisk but settled in Israel in 1941, where he became the acknowledged leader of the ultra-Orthodox party. The second Joseph Baer studied philosophy at Berlin University and, in 1941, became head of the Talmud faculty at Yeshivah University in New York, where he influenced generations of modern Orthodox Rabbis. Because of his expertise in Talmudic learning and because of his ancestry, Joseph Baer was acknowledged as a teacher even by the ultra-Orthodox but in recent years, especially after his death, his views and those of his school have come under fire from the extreme right wing.

Song of Songs Heb. *Shir Ha-Shirim*, the book of eight chapters in the third section of the *Bible, the *Ketuvim*, first of the five Megillot, 'Scrolls' (the others are: *Ruth, *Lamentations, *Ecclesiastes, and *Esther). According to the Rabbinic tradition generally, the author of the book is King *Solomon (based on the heading: 'The Song of Songs by Solomon', though this can also mean 'about Solomon') but in the famous Talmudic passage (*Bava Batra* 15a) on the authorship of the biblical books it is stated that the book was actually written down by King Hezekiah and his associates (based on Proverbs 25: 1). Modern scholarship is unanimous in fixing a much later date for the book than the time of Solomon, though opinions vary regarding the actual date. On the surface, the book is a secular love-poem or a collection of such poems and is considered so to be by the majority of modern biblical scholars. No doubt because of this surface meaning, the ancient Rabbis, while accepting the Solomonic authorship, debated whether the book should be considered part of the sacred Scriptures. The Mishnah (*Yadaim* 3: 5), after recording this debate, gives the view of Rabbi *Akiba, eventually adopted by all the Rabbis, that no one ever debated that the Song of Songs is sacred: 'for all the ages are not worth the day on which the Song of Songs was given to Israel; for all the *Ketuvim* are holy, but the Song of Songs is the Holy of Holies'. In the liturgy of the synagogue, the Song of Songs is recited during the morning service on the intermediate Sabbath of *Passover. Under the influence of the Kabbalah the custom arose in some circles, especially in *Hasidism, of reciting the Song of Songs on the eve of the Sabbath.

That the Rabbis in the second century CE could debate whether Song of Songs belongs to sacred Scripture is evidence enough that in this period there were some who took it all literally as a dialogue of love between a man and a woman, sexual desire expressed exquisitely but with the utmost frankness. One or two Orthodox Jews in the twentieth century did try to suggest that even on the literal level the book can be seen as sacred literature, since love between husband and wife is holy and divinely ordained. But, while there is no explicit rejection of such a literal interpretation in Rabbinic literature, the standard Rabbinic view, and the reason why Rabbi Akiba declared the book to be 'the Holy of Holies', is that the Rabbis saw the 'lover' as God and the 'beloved' as the community of Israel.

Soul, Immortality of the The doctrine that the soul lives on for ever after the death of the body. Originally there were two distinct doctrines with regard to the Hereafter, namely, the immortality of the soul and the resurrection of the dead. According to the latter doctrine, in its original meaning, when the individual died he was truly dead and there was no separate soul to live on in *heaven after the death of the body. The resurrection of the dead was explicitly what that name implies. Later in Judaism, however, the two doctrines were combined and this helps to explain the tensions in this matter in the Rabbinic literature and the ambiguities in the Rabbinic term 'the *World to Come'. Once the two doctrines were combined, the three beliefs contributed to the Jewish eschatological scheme. In this, the individual does not lose his soul at death. The soul lives on in heaven. Some time after the coming of the Messiah the body is resurrected and the soul returns to it here on earth. Obviously, this bald description can serve as no more than an extremely abbreviated picture of a very complicated scheme.

Philo seems to know nothing of the doctrine of the physical resurrection of the dead but believes strongly in the immortality of the soul, understanding the doctrine of the resurrection as referring to this.

The most powerful influence on subsequent Jewish thought on this topic is obviously the Talmudic literature and here both ideas, that of the resurrection and that of immortality of the soul, are found, but with most of the emphasis on the former. The usual Talmudic term for the immortality of the soul is the *Garden of Eden (and see GEHINNOM).

Orthodox Jews accept the whole traditional, eschatological scheme, believing in the coming of the Messiah, the resurrection of the dead, and the immortality of the soul, though most would admit that the details cannot be grasped by the finite mind of man and must be left to God. The Orthodox often quote Maimonides' saying that to seek, while in the body, to grasp the nature of pure spiritual bliss in the Hereafter is as impossible as for a man born blind to grasp the nature of colour. The rites attending *death and burial are all based on belief in the resurrection but in the *memorial prayers reference is made to the soul 'resting under the wings of the Shekhinah'. Hasidim, when commemorating a parent's death at the *Yahrzeit, invite their companions to a drink and the toast is: 'May the soul ascend higher.' Reform Judaism in the nineteenth century abandoned the belief in a personal Messiah and in the resurrection of the dead but Reform retained prayers for the dead and believed in the immortality of the soul.

Space Spatial *symbolism for the spiritual abounds in classical Jewish sources. One of the *names of God in the Rabbinic literature is Ha-Makom, 'the Place', explained as: 'He is the place of the universe but the universe is not His place', meaning God is both transcendent and immanent (see GOD and HOLY PLACES), although such abstract terms are unknown in this literature. The *angels are referred to as 'those on high' in contradistinction to human beings, 'those who are beneath', although, originally, this kind of terminology may well have been used literally, to indicate that the angelic hosts are somehow 'up there' around the heavenly throne. The medieval thinkers certainly understood all this as purely symbolic. Maimonides (*Guide of the Perplexed*, 1. 8), for example, understands the verse: 'Blessed be the Lord from His place' (Ezekiel 3: 12) to refer to the distinguished degree and exalted nature of His existence, as when it is said of a dispute in law to which no conclusion is reached that 'it stands in its place' or when it is said that a man occupies the place of his ancestors in wisdom and piety. Often an originally spatial expression is adapted for a spiritual purpose. An example of this is the interpretation given in many moralistic works to the verses: 'Who may ascend the mountain of the Lord? And who may stand in His holy place? He that hath clean hands and a pure heart; who hath not set his desire upon vanity and hath not sworn deceitfully' (Psalms 24: 3–4). The Psalmist in all probability was thinking of an ascent to the Temple built on a hill. But 'ascending the mountain of the Lord' is frequently understood in terms of ascent in stages towards spiritual perfection (see HEIGHT). The Psalmist's plea: 'Out of the depths have I cried unto thee, O Lord' (Psalms 130: 1) seems to mean out of the psychological depths of sin and distress, as the Psalm continues (v. 3): 'If Thou, Lord, shouldst mark iniquities, O Lord, who could stand?' In Hebrew, as in English, a deep subject is one that is difficult to comprehend and a wide knowledge of a subject denotes a comprehensive acquaintance with it. This whole matter is extremely complicated by the fact that Hebrew is a very concrete language, so that abstractions are bound to be expressed in language that is normally reserved for things perceived by the senses.

Spinoza, Benedict One of the most significant figures in the history of general philosophy (1632–77). Spinoza was born in Amsterdam to Mikael and Hanna Deborah, Mikael's second wife who died when Spinoza was a little boy of 6. The family were *Marranos who had fled from Portugal in order to return to Judaism. The details of Spinoza's Jewish education are still unclear but he seems to have been taught by Rabbi Saul Morteira, teacher of Talmud at the Etz Hayyim school, and later taught himself, becoming especially proficient in medieval Jewish philosophy and general philosophy and science. He seems to have also acquired a knowledge of the Kabbalah, and the philosophical system he developed in his own original way owes something to the *Safed Kabbalist, Moses *Cordovero. There are echoes in Spinoza's thought of Cordovero's summary of the relationship of the universe to God: 'God is the all but the all is not God', although, according to the majority of his interpreters, Spinoza's pantheism goes much beyond Cordovero in actually identifying the universe with God, as in his famous maxim: *Deus sive natura* ('God or nature'), that is, God is the name given to the universe as a whole, monotheism becoming, for Spinoza, monism. Spinoza's approach and his general independent attitude to religion awakened the suspicions of both the Calvinists and the Jewish community in Amsterdam. On 27 July 1656, Spinoza was placed under the ban (*herem) by the Amsterdam community. The ban, written in Portuguese, is still preserved in the archives of the Amsterdam community. Spinoza's ideas about God seem to suggest that there is no God as the Supreme Being, only as a philosophical idea, God corresponding to the universe in totality. Spinoza's tight and carefully worked-out scheme is deterministic with no apparent room for the doctrine of free will and, for him, there is no longer any need for Jews to remain a separate people who worship God in a special way. For Spinoza God did not create *nature but is nature and neither intellect nor will can be ascribed to God. This, at least, is the usual understanding of Spinoza's pantheism, although a few scholars have interpreted his thought as rather more in accordance with traditional theism.

From time to time attempts have been made to reclaim Spinoza for Judaism. If this means that Spinoza was a Jew and an admirable person who did not deserve to have been placed under the ban, many Jews would go along with it. But if it means that Spinoza's philosophy is compatible with Judaism, Spinoza himself would have rejected totally any such claim. Spinoza is generally seen by Jews as outside the religion and as therefore posing no threat to the religion. That is why nowadays religious Jews usually view the whole Spinoza question in a detached way and even feel proud of Spinoza's influence on world philosophy—one of 'us' extending such a great influence on 'them'. In a Hasidic tale, a Rebbe was told by one of his followers that, in Spinoza's view, there is no basic difference between humans and animals. The Rebbe replied: in that case, why have animals never produced a Spinoza?

Spiritualism The attempt to get in

touch with the spirits of the dead. Spiritualism as a modern religion, with its own doctrines, hymns, Christian references, and the like, is obviously at variance with Judaism and no Jew can, at one and the same time, be a Spiritualist in this religious sense any more than he can be a Christian, a Muslim, or a Buddhist (see RELIGION). But what of attending seances and other attempts at contacting the dead, and what of psychical research?

On the face of it there is a clear biblical injunction against any attempt at contacting the dead.

The Halakhic position is, however, rather ambiguous. The Talmudic interpretation of the passage in Deuteronomy is that enquiring of the dead is only forbidden when the wizard does this by starving himself and spending the night in the cemetery that an 'unclean spirit might rest upon him' (Sanhedrin 65b). The Shulḥan Arukh (Yoreh Deah, 179. 14) states the position in this way: 'It is permitted to make a dying person swear to return after his death in order to convey some information he will be asked. And some permit an attempt to do this even after the person has died provided that he does not conjure the actual corpse but only the ghost of the dead man.' The point here is that in the first instance there is no offence, since when the promise is made the man is still alive. The second opinion goes further and understands the whole prohibition as referring only to an attempt somehow to conjure up the actual corpse (like the zombi of horror films and fiction) and not the spirit or ghost of the dead.

It would appear, then, that nowhere is there a clearly stated Halakhic ruling that attendance at a seance or staying in a house reputed to be haunted for purposes of psychical research or even out of sheer curiosity is forbidden.

Spirituality The attitude in which the emphasis in life is placed on spiritual rather than material things. In the Bible and Talmud, while the idea behind spirituality is found throughout, it is never expressed in abstract terms. In the Middle Ages, under the impact of Greek thought, the term ruḥaniyut (from ruaḥ, 'spirit') was coined to denote spirituality and the term gashmiyut (from geshem, 'a bodily substance') to denote its opposite. For instance, concern with the religious life of prayer, worship, and the study of the Torah is said to be a concern with ruḥaniyut while a concern with eating, drinking, and the other needs of the body is said to be a concern with gashmiyut. But the two ideas are never kept in two separate compartments. It is possible, when engaging in ruḥaniyut, to have the mind on the material advantages that will result from the engagement—studying the Torah, for instance, in order to win wealth and fame—and then ruḥaniyut is converted into gashmiyut. Conversely, *Hasidism stresses the idea of avodah be-gashmiyut, 'worship through corporeality', and there is the Rabbinic saying in Ethics of the Fathers (2. 12), attributed to Rabbi Jose the Priest who is described as a Hasid 'saint': 'Let all your deeds be for the sake of Heaven.' In this gashmiyut is converted into ruḥaniyut. Jewish saintliness (see SAINTS) does not normally involve living in an ivory tower of spirituality remote from the daily life of normal human beings with physical and material needs, hence the stress on *charity as an essential ingredient in the life of piety and the numerous tales of saintly men who prayed for rain, and for health and sustenance, if not for themselves, for others who were in distress.

The tendency among modern religious Jews is to feel themselves less bound to the medieval notion of the powerful dichotomy that exists between body and soul, a dichotomy expressed in the medieval maxim: the construction of the soul is in direct proportion to the destruction of the body.

Sport There are not many references to sport in the classical Jewish sources but this does not necessarily denote any lack of interest in the subject. Archery was practised as a sport as well as in warfare, as seems evident from the story of David and Jonathan (1 Samuel 20: 21–2). Jeremiah's reference to 'contending with horses' (Jeremiah 12: 5) has been understood to mean a kind of athletic contest, but this is very uncertain. The Psalmist's reference to the strong man running his course (Psalms 19: 6) is much clearer, though here, too, the reference is not necessarily to sport. The Mishnah (*Sukkah* 5. 4) and the Talmudic comments on it refer to the pious men ('Hasidim and men of good deeds') in Temple times on the festival of *Tabernacles dancing and juggling lighted torches. Ball games were played in Talmudic times. The Midrash (Lamentations Rabbah 2: 4) gives as one of the reasons for the destruction of Jerusalem that ball games were played on the Sabbath. However, the *Tosafot (*Betzah* 12a) state that ball games were permitted on the Sabbath in medieval France in private, though not in the public domain. The *Shulḥan Arukh (*Orah Ḥayyim*, 308. 45) records two opinions on the permissibility of playing ball games on the Sabbath.

The values promoted by sporting activities—health, the team spirit, refreshment of mind and body—are acceptable to Judaism. But it can be argued that sports such as boxing and wrestling, in which violence is consciously done to the person (unlike football and cricket, where any injury to the players is incidental and not intended) are hardly in keeping with the spirit of Judaism, although it might be going too far to suggest that these sports are forbidden by Jewish law.

Steinberg, Milton American Con-
servative Rabbi and theologian (1903–50). Steinberg studied philosophy at City College in New York and took the Rabbinical course at the Jewish Theological Seminary, where he was ordained in 1928. Steinberg first served as a Rabbi in Indianopolis but in 1933 he became Rabbi of the prestigious Park Avenue Synagogue in New York, in which capacity he served until his death at the early age of 47. At the Park Avenue Synagogue Steinberg became renowned for his thought-provoking sermons, some of which have been published in the form of sermon notes (*From the Sermons of Milton Steinberg*, ed. Bernard Mandelbaum (New York, 1954)). Steinberg's preaching methods have become models for modern Rabbis in their apt quotations from world literature and in their application of philosophical ideas to the traditional Jewish texts without distorting either the philosophical ideas or the texts themselves.

Sterilization The use of artificial means to render persons or animals incapable of producing offspring. According to biblical law (Leviticus 21: 20) a priest who 'has his stones crushed' may not serve in the Sanctuary because he has a 'blemish'. He is compared in the verse to other persons with blemishes such as a hunchback or a dwarf. There is a further biblical law (Deuteronomy 23: 2) that one who is 'crushed or maimed in his privy parts' may not enter into the assembly of the Lord, understood by the Rabbis to mean that he must not marry. The prohibition against castrating *animals is stated, according to the Rabbis, in the verse (Leviticus 22: 24): 'That which hath its stones bruised or crushed, or torn, or cut, ye shall not offer unto the Lord; neither shall ye do thus in your land', the last clause being understood by the Rabbis to mean that it is prohibited to castrate human beings and animals. Does all this mean that sterilization is categorically forbidden in all circumstances? The Mishnah (*Shabbat* 14: 3) rules that since it is forbidden to take medicine on the Sabbath (provided there is no danger if it is not taken) it is forbidden to drink a 'cup of roots', evidently a certain herbal compound possessing healing powers. Commenting on this Mishnah, the Talmud notes that the 'cup of roots', while efficacious in curing jaundice, causes the sufferer to become impotent so that it is forbidden for a man to drink this since it is a form of self-castration. With regard to a woman the matter is rather more complicated since, in the Rabbinic ruling, the duty of *procreation devolves only on men, not on women, although it is religiously meritorious, but not a full obligation, for a woman, too, to marry and have children. Elsewhere in the Talmud (*Yevamot* 85b) the conclusion is that since a woman has no actual obligation to have children she may drink the potion. In fact, the Talmud states that the wife of Rabbi Hiyya, who had had severe pain in giving birth to two sets of twins, resolved to drink the 'cup of roots' in order to prevent further pregnancies. On the basis of all this the ruling is that any interference with the organs of generation by a direct act is forbidden but that a woman may drink the 'cup of roots', since this is indirect. According to some authorities she may only drink it where, like the wife of Rabbi Hiyya, she has severe pains in childbirth but other authorities permit it in any event for a woman. These are the principles as laid down in the Talmud and the Codes. We no longer know what exactly is meant by the 'cup of roots' and modern medicine does not know of any sterilizing agent taken by mouth, but this does not affect the *principles*.

Streimel The fur hat worn by Hasidic Jews on the Sabbath, festivals, and other festive occasions. This kind of fur hat was worn by the Polish aristocracy when the Hasidic movement grew in the eighteenth century, as can be seen from prints of Polish noblemen, and was adopted by the Hasidim as a dignified head-covering suitable for wear on special occasions. Eventually the *streimel* became the specific Hasidic form of head-gear and various mystical ideas were read into it, for example, that the thirteen tails of which it is composed represent the thirteen attributes of divine mercy. The majority of the Hasidim do not don the *streimel* until their marriage, when the father-in-law gives it as a present to the young bridegroom, but among some groups even small boys wear it. Some groups wear the *spodek*, a high fur hat, instead of the *streimel*.

Strikes It cannot be expected that there should be references to strikes in the classical Jewish sources since, before the industrial age, the economic forms of society were quite different from those obtaining today. Among other differences, in biblical and Rabbinic times workmen did not hire themselves out as more or less permanent employees of a particular employer, nor was there much organized labour in those days. Nevertheless, important principles are laid down governing the rights of workmen and these can be applied to the contemporary situation. Attempts have been made by Rabbis in the State of Israel to find some guidance in the ancient sources on the question of strikes in the modern sense.

In biblical law (Leviticus 19: 13; Deuteronomy 24: 14–15) there are stern injunctions against keeping back the wages of a workman. The Rabbinic Midrash, the Sifre, comments on this: 'Why does this workman ascend the highest scaffolding and risk his life if you do not pay him his wages as soon as they are due?' Among other Rabbinic rulings regarding the rights of workmen is the rule that a workman hired for a day can break the contract in the middle of the day if he so wishes (Bava Metzia 10a), though in the Talmudic discussion this right is somewhat qualified. Following Talmudic statements Maimonides records (Shekalim 4: 7):

'Those who kept the scrolls in order in Jerusalem and the judges who decided in cases of robbery in Jerusalem received their wages from the Temple treasury. How much did they receive? Ninety manehs a month. If this amount was insufficient, the wages should be increased, even if they objected to the increase, so as to be adequate for their own provisions and for those of their wives and families.'

The Talmud (Sukkah 51b; Bava Kama 116b) speaks with approval of craftsmen organizing themselves in guilds for their own protection. Similarly, the Talmud (Bava Batra 8b–9a) rules that the people of each locality are entitled to determine democratically such matters as prices and wages.

None of this amounts to a clear statement about strikes in the modern sense and in any event Jews do not simply consult the Talmud with regard to social and economic problems but rely on their social conscience, knowledge of the conditions, and sheer common sense in trying to work them out. Yet there can be no doubt that the sentiments expressed in the Talmudic sources would justify, if such justification were needed, the organization of workers into trade unions with the perfectly legitimate right to strike. Naturally, Judaism encourages its adherents to avoid industrial as well as other forms of strife wherever possible. The ideal social order is one where fair wages and conditions of employment can be negotiated favourably without recourse to strikes and lock-outs.

Study From early Rabbinic times the study of the Torah was seen as a supreme religious obligation. In the opening passage of Ethics of the Fathers the Men of the *Great Synagogue are quoted as advocating the raising of many disciples. The opening Mishnah of tractate Peah states that the 'things which have no fixed measure' are deeds of loving-kindness and the study of the Torah (talmud torah). The Mishnah continues: 'These are the things whose fruit a man enjoys in this world while the capital is laid up for him in the *World to Come: honouring father and mother, deeds of loving-kindness, making peace between a man and his fellow; and the study of the Torah is equal to them all.'

In the addition to the chapter of Ethics of the Fathers (now ch. 6) entitled Kinyan Torah ('The Acquisition of Torah') the qualifications for study are carefully mapped out, forty-eight 'excellences' by which the Torah is acquired being listed (Ethics of the Fathers, 6. 6):

'By the hearing of the ear, by the ordering of the lips, by the understanding of the heart, by the discernment of the heart, by awe, by reverence, by humility, by cheerfulness; by attendance on the Sages, by consorting with fellow-students, by close argument *[pilpul] with disciples; by assiduity, by knowledge of Scripture and Mishnah; by moderation in business, in wordly occupation, pleasure, sleep, conversation, and eating; by long-suffering, by a good heart, by faith in the Sages, by submission to sorrows; by being one that recognizes his place and that rejoices in his lot and that makes a fence around his words and claims no merit for himself; by being one that is beloved, that loves God, that loves mankind, that loves well-doing, that loves rectitude, that loves reproof, that shuns honour and boasts not of his learning and delights not in rendering decisions; that helps his fellow to bear his yoke, and that judges him favourably, and that establishes him in the truth and establishes him in peace; and that occupies himself assiduously in his study; by being one that asks and makes answer, that hearkens and adds thereto; that learns in order to teach and that learns in order to practise; that makes his teacher wiser; that retells exactly what he has heard, and reports a thing in the name of him that said it.'

In the same treatise (Ethics of the Fathers, 6. 4) this advice is given to the student of the Torah: 'This is the way of the Torah: a morsel of bread with salt to eat, water by measure to drink; thou shalt sleep on the ground, and live a life of hardship, while thou toilest in the Torah. If thou doest thus, happy shalt thou be, and it shall be well with thee; happy shalt thou be—in this world, and it shall be well with thee—in the world to come.' This total dedication to the study of the Torah can be observed throughout the history of Jewish learning. There were, of course, rich students but the majority of students who journeyed long distances to sit at the feet of a master were poor and denied themselves for many years the luxuries and often even the necessities of life, going hungry and thirsty in order to 'toil in the Torah'.

This kind of devotion was not limited to the Talmudic period. Indeed, after the close of the Talmud, this work itself became the sacred text most studied and in the process even heavier demands were made on the student. To 'know Shas [the Talmud]' was the ideal. Numerous scholars were found who knew the whole Talmud by heart. But the ideal of Torah study was not only for scholars. Following Talmudic statements Maimonides (*Talmud Torah*, 1. 8) rules:

'Every man in Israel is obliged to study the Torah, whether he is firm of body or a sufferer from ill-health, whether a young man or of advanced age with his strength abated. Even a poor man who is supported by charity and who is obliged to beg at doors and even one with a wife and children is obliged to set aside a period for Torah study by day and by night, as it is said: "Thou shalt meditate therein day and night" [Joshua 1: 8].'

To be sure, all the passages quoted present an idealistic picture and the temptation to idolize or idealize the past has to be resisted. Not all Jews engaged so assiduously in their studies and the mental horizons of many who did were, at times, exceedingly narrow *Schechter was being unfair when he spoke of the Eastern European scholars of his day as mere 'study machines' but the phenomenon of students merely getting through huge chunks of texts without any serious reflection is certainly not unknown. The numerous references in the literature of Jewish piety about the importance of studying so many hours a day and of the sin of wasting a moment that could be spent in study of the Torah do sometimes suggest an attitude of mind where the act of sitting before the open book and piously mouthing its words mattered more than the assimilation of its contents. But the ideal of Torah study, like any other ideal, has to be seen in the light of its best representatives.

Subjectivity The theological attitude, especially prevalent in *mysticism and in religious *existentialism, according to which the experiences of the person rather than *history or *revelation determine the truths of religion. Naturally there are different emphases in this matter among religious thinkers, ranging from very rare complete subjectivity to acceptance of revelation in enabling the person to make subjective judgements. The actual term 'subjectivity' is not found in Jewish religious thought, nor is the idea behind it found very frequently. The medieval Jewish philosophers, for example, all believed that they were investigating truths already conveyed in the Torah, which truths they tried to understand and explicate in terms of the similarly objective truths they saw in the Greek–Arabic philosophy of their day. Yet the personal subjective element in the religious life seems to be recognized in the Talmudic saying (*Yoma* 86b) that if a man commits a sin and repeats it, it becomes for him as if it were permitted.

An appreciation of the subjective element in religious faith, that not all men have the same capacity for faith and that apprehension of the divine is arrived at in many different ways, is expressed in a Midrashic passage (Exodus Rabbah 5: 9) on the theme of revelation. Psalm 29: 4 is translated as 'The voice of the Lord is with power', taking 'power' as referring not to God but to the power of the individual to hear the divine voice. The voice of God, says the Midrash, was heard by the men according to their capacity, by the women according to theirs. Young men heard it differently from old men. Each individual heard it according to his own capacity. It is not a distortion of the meaning of this passage to paraphrase it as: human nature and individual temperament have a role to play if the divine voice is to be heard.

On the ethical level, Judaism holds fast to the belief that the moral law is objectively grounded in the will of God and therefore takes issue with ethical theories such as hedonism and eudaemonism in which the good is defined in terms of subjective pleasure and happiness, whether of the individual or of the greatest number of persons. This is not to say that individual happiness does not result from obedience to God's law. It does, but only as a by-product; it is not the aim of the religious life, and is not necessarily promised in this life at any rate (see REWARD AND PUNISHMENT and SOUL, IMMORTALITY OF THE).

Sublimation The transmutation of less worthy or unworthy instincts and thoughts into something more elevated; in psychoanalysis (see PSYCHOLOGY), the direction of energy, especially sexual energy, into more socially acceptable channels. The actual term 'sublimation' is not found in Jewish sources but the idea is implied in a number of Talmudic passages as well as in subsequent Jewish teaching. For instance, the Mishnah (*Berakhot* 9: 5) understands the injunction to love God with all the heart (Deuteronomy 6: 2) to mean with both impulses, the *yetzer ha-tov* and the *yetzer ha-ra*, the good and the evil inclination. Some of the classical commentaries understand this simply to mean that man should overcome the temptations of the evil impulse, but others take it to mean that evil traits of character can be used in the service of God. Anger, for example, is bad in itself but when used in righteous indignation at wrongdoing, becomes good. Similarly, envy is an unworthy trait but, in the language of the Talmud, 'the envy of scholars increases wisdom'.

Submission Surrender of the individual to the will of God or to teachers of the Torah. For all the significance it attaches to the *individual, Judaism demands that personal will and opinions be abandoned in certain circumstances. Submission is obviously required to the will of God and the laws of the Torah in which this will is reflected. The Rabbis describe the first paragraph of the *Shema as 'the acceptance of the yoke of the Kingdom of Heaven' and the second paragraph as 'the acceptance of the yoke of the commandments'.

Concerning acceptance of the discipline of the Torah there is the hard saying of the third-century teacher, Resh Lakish (*Berakhot* 63b): 'The words of the Torah become established only for one who kills himself for it.' Yet the oft-repeated claim that in the 'Old Testament' and in Rabbinic Judaism God is conceived of as a tyrannical king imposing His arbitrary will on unwilling subjects is a complete canard. Against the apparently harsher passages in the literature which dwell on submission there should be placed the many in which God is spoken of as a loving Father who desires only the good of His creatures and whose demands are never for more than lies in the capacity of His creatures to undertake. A typical Rabbinic saying is: 'The Holy One, blessed be He, does not deal imperiously with His creatures' (*Avodah Zarah* 3a). Another saying in the same vein is: 'The Torah was not given to the ministering angels' (*Berakhot* 25b).

Substitution The idea that one thing can be substituted for another is found especially in connection with objects dedicated to the Temple. The rules of substitution or *pidyon* ('redemption') are in brief as follows. If, for example, a man dedicates his house to the Temple, it becomes sacred from that moment and no profane use may be made of it. But since the Temple has no need for the house but does need money for the repairs and general upkeep of the sacred building, the Temple treasurer can sell the house and its sanctity is then transferred to the money for which it is purchased. The man who dedicated the house can redeem it himself but when he does he is obliged to add a fifth to the value of the house, the whole becoming sacred (Leviticus 27: 14–15). Maimonides explains the addition of a fifth of the value where the redemption is done by the man himself on the grounds that he may undervalue the house, so the additional fifth makes up for any undervaluation. An animal dedicated as an offering to the Temple can only be redeemed if the animal develops a blemish that disqualifies it as an offering. If a man, having dedicated an animal as an offering, seeks to exchange it for another animal, declaring that this animal is the substitute (*temurah*) of the animal that has been dedicated, the rule is that both animals become sacred. 'One may not exchange

or substitute another for it, either good for bad or bad for good; if one does substitute one animal for another, the thing vowed and its substitute shall both be holy' (Leviticus 27: 10). Tractate *Temurah* in the Mishnah is devoted largely to the details of this law.

Success In Jewish life success, Hebrew *hatzlahah*, whether in material or in spiritual matters, is seen as a blessing; a popular Jewish wish is: 'May you have blessing and success in your undertaking.' In the *Hallel the verse is repeated by the Reader and the congregation: 'O Lord, deliver us! O Lord, let us prosper!' (Psalms 118: 25). Of Joseph it is said: 'The Lord was with Joseph, and he was a successful man' (Genesis 39: 2). And of David: 'David was successful in all his undertakings, for the Lord was with him' (1 Samuel 18: 14). In these verses success is made to depend on God. Similarly, Moses warns the people not to say: 'My own power and the might of my own hand have won this wealth for me' (Deuteronomy 8: 17). The normal Jewish attitude is neither to see failure as a sign of virtue nor success as somehow unworthy. Success is a good, provided it is not seen as self-made but as God-made, and is not attained through disregard for the interests of others.

Succession The order of priority of near relatives to inherit the estate of a deceased person. (For the right or lack of it to inherit an office or a position, see DYNASTIC SUCCESSION.) The order of succession as stated in the Pentateuch (Numbers 27: 8–11) is: son, daughter, brothers, father's brothers, kinsman (i.e. next nearest relative on the father's side). There is no mention here of a father inheriting his son's estate but the Mishnah (*Bava Batra* 8: 2) fills in the gap by ruling that a father takes precedence over all his offspring (i.e. that the order is: son, daughter, father, brothers, father's brothers). Even if a son is born out of wedlock and even if he is a *mamzer, he inherits the estate of his natural father, so that the concept of an illegitimate child in this connection is unknown in Jewish law. A husband inherits the estate of his wife. A wife does not inherit the estate of her husband but she is entitled, of course, to claim her *ketubah out of the estate. A wife's ketubah has to include a clause that any daughters she bears to her husband will be maintained out of his estate when he dies. If a son dies before his father and leaves children, whether sons or daughters, they take precedence in inheriting their grandfather's estate over their aunt, their grandfather's daughter.

A first-born son inherits a double portion of his father's estate (Deuteronomy 21: 17). As understood by the Rabbis, a 'double portion' means not two-thirds of the whole estate but a portion double that received by his brothers.

Suffering The biblical authors and the Talmudic Rabbis, unlike the later Jewish philosophers, do not consider the general problem of evil in the universe, of why the benevolent Creator should have brought evil into being (see GOD). The earlier writers seem to have accepted the existence of evil as a 'given', seeing this, in so far as they gave any thought to it, as belonging, like questions on the true nature of God, to an area which it is beyond the capacity of the human mind to grasp. Their difficulty was not with the problem of evil per se but rather with the apparently random way in which sufferings are visited on creatures. In a Talmudic passage (Berakhot 7a) Moses is said to have asked God why one righteous man enjoys prosperity while another righteous man is afflicted with adversity; why one wicked man enjoys prosperity and another wicked man is afflicted with adversity. If all righteous men suffered and all wicked men were prosperous some kind of pattern might have emerged, perhaps on the lines that the righteous suffer for their sins here on earth while the wicked are rewarded here on earth so as to be punished by being deprived of bliss in the Hereafter. This notion of divine reward and retribution as accounting for suffering is found frequently in the Talmudic literature but, in the passage quoted, it is implied that such solutions fall short of the truth because of the sheer arbitrariness evident in the way afflictions and prosperity are apportioned. The book of *Job is directed explicitly to the rejection of the idea that suffering can be easily explained on the grounds of *reward and punishment. Job is a good man and yet he suffers greatly and he cannot accept the 'comforts' of his friends that his sufferings are the result of his sins. He cannot believe that any sins he may have committed are commensurate with the torment inflicted on him. In the twentieth century, the unparalleled horrors of the *Holocaust have presented Jewish theologians with the most acute and agonizing problem of suffering Jews have ever had to contemplate, one which it seems to be obscene to attempt to explain in terms of reward and punishment.

That some of the Rabbis believed that the problem of suffering does not bear discussion at all can be seen from the Talmudic legend (Menahot 29b) in which God transports Moses through time to witness Rabbi *Akiba teaching the Torah. Moses asks God to show him what Akiba's fate will be and God shows him Akiba being tortured to death for teaching the Torah and his flesh sold by weight. Moses is moved to cry out: 'Sovereign of the universe, such Torah and such a reward!' to which God replies: 'Be silent, for such is My decree.'

Suffering Servant The servant of the Lord referred to in the second part of the book of *Isaiah (Deutero-Isaiah), especially in chapter 53 but also in chapters 42: 1–4; 49: 1–6; 52: 13–15. In Christian theology the 'suffering servant' used to be identified with Jesus but modern Christian scholarship no longer reads the prophetic books as foretelling events of the remote future. The Jewish commentators understand the 'servant' to be the God-fearing Jews who were in exile, the people of Israel in general, and so forth, although, occasionally, the passages are read as referring to the *Messiah. It is interesting that, while the Haftarot (see HAFTARAH) for the seven weeks of consolation between the Ninth of *Av and *Rosh Ha-Shanah are all taken from Deutero-Isaiah, they do not include any of the 'servant' passages, probably in conscious reaction to the Christological interpretation. It can safely be said that the whole concept of the 'suffering servant' and, indeed, the detachment of the passages from the rest of the book, is a Christian invention of no relevance to Jewish theology and is only discussed by Jewish theologians in response to the Christian claim.

Sufism The Islamic ascetic and mystical movement which, it has been conjectured, was partly influenced by the Jewish Midrashic literature but which certainly, in turn, exercised considerable influence on Jewish mystical and ethical literature. But the most marked influence of Sufism on Jewish thought is found in *Bahya, Ibn Pakudah's *Duties of the Heart*, where the very title and the ideas behind it belong to Sufism. Bahya gives examples of Hasidim who are not Jews and are probably Sufi saints. The arrangement of the material in the form of Ten Gates in Bahya's work also owes much to Sufi treatises. Some of the titles of these 'Gates' to piety are the titles used in Sufic works. In Gate Nine, on the theme of abstinence, Bahya quotes sayings of the Sufis whom he calls Perushim

('Separatists' or 'Abstainers') in the sense of ascetics, although he takes issue with the extreme *asceticism followed by the Sufis.

Suicide In Jewish teaching the prohibition of suicide is not contained in the sixth commandment: 'Thou shalt not kill' (Exodus 20: 13 and Deuteronomy 5: 17). Obviously it does not follow from the fact that a man may not take the life of another that he may not take his own life. There is, in fact, no direct prohibition of suicide in the Bible. In the Talmud (*Bava Kama* 91b), however, the prohibition is arrived at by a process of exegesis on the verse: 'and surely your blood of your lives will I require' (Genesis 9: 5), interpreted as: 'I will require your blood if you yourselves shed it.' It is possible that there is no direct prohibition because very few people of sound mind would be inclined to commit suicide in any event.

It follows from this that suicide and murder are two separate offences in the Jewish tradition, as they are in most cultures. Suicide is not homicide and is not covered in the *Decalogue.

Suicide is considered to be a grave sin both because it is a denial that human life is a divine gift and because it constitutes a total defiance of God's will for the individual to live the life span allotted to him. The suicide, more than any other offender, literally takes his life into his own hands. Yet there are exceptional circumstances when a man is permitted to take his own life or allow it to be taken, of which martyrdom is the supreme example. The general tendency among the later authorities is to extend the idea of mitigating circumstances so that the law, recorded in the *Shulḥan Arukh (Yoreh Deah*, 345), that there are to be no rites of mourning over a suicide is usually set aside wherever it can reasonably be assessed that the act was committed while the suicide was 'of unsound mind'. Saul's suicide (1 Samuel 31: 4–5) is defended on the grounds that he feared torture if he were captured by the Philistines and would have died in any event as a result of the torture. Similarly, Samson's suicide (Judges 16: 30), in which he destroyed himself together with his Philistine tormentors, is defended on the grounds that it constituted an act of *Kiddush Ha-Shem, 'sanctification of the divine name', in the face of heathen mockery of the God of Israel.

Sukkah The booth in which Jews are commanded to dwell during the festival of *Tabernacles, as stated in the book of Leviticus (23: 42–5): 'You shall live in booths [*sukkot*] seven days; all citizens in Israel shall live in booths, in order that future generations may know that I made the Israelite people live in booths when I brought them out of the land of Egypt, I am the Lord your God.' According to the Talmudic Rabbis, a sukkah has to have at least three walls (though the third need not be a complete wall) and a covering. It has to be at least 4 square cubits in size, but this does not necessarily mean that it has to have a square or oblong shape. A circular sukkah, for instance, is valid provided it covers an area of at least 4 square cubits (a cubit is approximately 18 inches). The covering must be of things that grow from the soil (e.g. straw or leaves of trees) but it must be detached from the soil, so that it is not valid to use the leaves of a tree still growing from the soil as a sukkah covering. The covering has to have more shade than light, that is, there must be more covered than uncovered space. The covering can be quite thick, although it is customary to make the covering sufficiently sparse for the stars to be seen through it. The sukkah has to be outdoors. A sukkah under a roof is not a valid sukkah, nor is it valid to have a sukkah underneath, say, the overhang of a balcony.

All full meals should be eaten in the sukkah, that is, meals at which bread is partaken of, although some pious Jews do not eat or drink anything outside the sukkah. In Talmudic times people slept in the sukkah, treating it as their abode for the duration of the festival. In Western lands the majority of Jews do not sleep in the sukkah (some of the more pious still do, however). The rationale for this is that where to stay in the sukkah is uncomfortable, the obligation is set aside and in colder climes it is certainly uncomfortable in autumn to sleep outside in the sukkah. For the same reason there is no obligation to eat in the sukkah when it is raining and the rain comes through the covering. According to the authorities, it is undesirable for a man to stay in the sukkah even when the rain comes in, on the grounds that to persist in carrying out a religious precept when the law does not demand it suggests an attitude of religious superiority, of trying to be more pious than the Torah demands. Nowadays, many sukkahs are built with a roof on pulleys so that, after the meal, the roof can be lowered so as to prevent rain coming into the sukkah during the times it is not used. When the time comes to use the sukkah the roof is raised and the sukkah is once again open to the sky. The raising and lowering of the roof does not constitute forbidden 'work' and can, therefore, be done on the Sabbath and the festival days. Synagogues often have an adjacent sukkah to which the congregation repairs for *Kiddush after the service. In some Reform congregations the Sukkah is erected in the synagogue itself but, according to the Orthodox law, such a sukkah is invalid since it is covered by the roof of the synagogue.

On the principle of adorning the precepts (i.e. carrying out the precepts of the Torah in as beautiful and elegant a manner as possible), it is the practice to decorate the sukkah and to hang fruit and fragrant plants from the covering.

These must be left in place until the festival has come to an end.

Sun The sun and the *moon are compared with one another in Jewish symbolism. The nations of the world, say the Rabbis, have a solar *calendar but Israel has a lunar calendar because the fortunes of Israel, unlike those of other nations, wax and wane like the moon. The face of Moses is said to have been like that of the sun with its own light while the face of Joshua, Moses' disciple, was like the face of the moon, enjoying only reflected light. In opposition to the sunworshippers the Bible throughout speaks of the sun itself as worshipping its Creator, bowing to Him as its moves joyfully from east to west, in the words of the Psalmist, like a groom coming forth from his chamber (Psalms 19: 6).

Sun, Moon, and Stars The worship of the heavenly bodies, so prevalent in ancient religions, is severely condemned throughout the Bible, which demonstrates incidentally that the Israelites, too, were prone to idolatrous worship. In the creation narrative at the beginning of the book of Genesis, God creates 'the two great lights, the greater light to dominate the day and the lesser light to dominate the night, and the stars' (Genesis 1: 16). The Deuteronomist declares: 'And when you look up to the sky and behold the sun and the moon and the stars, the whole heavenly host, you must not be lured into bowing down to them or serving them' (Deuteronomy 4: 19). The Mishnah (*Avodah Zarah* 4: 7) records that the Jewish elders on a visit to Rome were asked why God, if He had no pleasure in idols, did not make an end of them? The elders replied that, for the sake of fools, God does not wish to destroy the sun, moon and stars of which the world has benefit. The Romans said: 'If so, let Him destroy that which the world does not need and leave that which the world needs.' The elders replied: 'We should but confirm them that worship them, for they would say: Know that these are gods, for they have not been brought to an end.'

Supernatural The ancients had no word for the supernatural any more than they had for *nature. All events proceeded from God; some of these events were so contrary to the perceived order of things that they were seen as *miracles. In modern Jewish thought, however, the distinction is often made between the natural order as perceived by the senses and the supernatural invasion of that order by spiritual forces (see KAPLAN, SPINOZA, and SPIRITUALISM).

Supplication The offering of petitionary prayers in the mood of entreaty. The attitude to supplication is summarized in a saying attributed to the second-century teacher, Rabbi *Simeon ben Yohai, in Ethics of the Fathers (2. 13): 'When you pray do not make your *prayer a fixed form but supplications before God.' Similarly, the earlier teacher, Rabbi Eliezer, is recorded in the Mishnah (*Berakhot* 4: 4) as saying: 'He who makes his prayer a fixed task, his prayer is no supplication.' In the Jewish literature of prayer there is a constant demand that prayer should be expressed from the heart and not as a mere fixed duty. The majority of the prayers of supplication in the traditional Prayer Book are in the plural: 'Grant us', 'Help us', and so forth. This form of request was evidently considered to be less self-serving than prayers for the individual solely on his own behalf. There is, of course, no objection to an individual offering up his own private supplications and the special prayer for protection against suffering known as Tahanun ('Supplication') consists entirely of individual supplications taken from the book of Psalms. In the Psalms it is often difficult to know whether the first person is used of the Psalmist or of the people as a whole conceived of as an individual person. A distinction is drawn in the Mishnah (*Berakhot* 2: 4) between the recital of the *Shema and prayer. Workmen at the top of a tree or scaffolding may recite the Shema where they are but for their prayers they must descend. The Shema involves a bare recital, whereas prayer requires a supplicatory mood impossible to sustain while precariously balanced high up in the air. Some Jewish teachers say that in prayers of supplication a man should see himself as a beggar asking humbly for his needs out of the bitterness of his heart.

Sura and Pumbedita The two great seats of learning in Babylonia which enjoyed, with few interruptions, a continuous existence from the third to the tenth century CE. In the period of the *Geonim the colleges of Sura and Pumbedita each had its own head, the Gaon of Sura enjoying a greater degree of authority than the Gaon of Pumbedita, which is why Sura is usually mentioned first in the literature. *Saadiah was Gaon of Sura, *Sherira and his son *Hai were Geonim in Pumbedita. Sura and Pumbedita were the prototypes of *Yeshivah learning throughout the ages.

Surrogate Mother The following question has recently been discussed in Jewish legal literature: where a naturally fertilized ovum has been removed from the womb of a pregnant woman and reimplanted in the uterus of another woman, which of the two is considered to be the 'mother' in Jewish law? To date the problem has not been solved; some authorities hold that the donor is the true mother, others that the woman who actually gives birth to the child is the true mother, and others again that the child will have two 'mothers'. There has also been a discussion on whether the practice would be approved of according to the Jewish tradition. The whole problem is too recent to allow any kind of consensus to emerge.

Suspicion The general attitude in the Jewish ethical sources is that people should be encouraged to give those whose conduct is not above suspicion the benefit of the doubt. The earliest saying in this connection in the Rabbinic literature is: 'Judge every man in the scale of merit' (Ethics of the Fathers, 1. 7). A hyperbolic statement in the Talmud (*Shabbat* 97a) has it that whoever entertains a suspicion about a worthy man will be bodily afflicted, as was Moses when he suspected that the children of Israel would not believe him (Exodus 4: 1–6). In another Talmudic saying (*Shabbat* 127b), whoever judges others in the scale of merit will himself be so judged. When Eli, who had imagined Hannah to be drunk, discovered his error, he apologized and blessed her (1 Samuel 1: 12–17), from which the Rabbis conclude (*Berakhot* 31b) that such is the proper form when a person has been unjustly suspected of wrongdoing. Those guilty of the suspicion should apologize and offer a blessing.

Swastika The cross consisting of four L shapes placed at right angles to one another and used as a magic symbol in many ancient civilizations. Archaeological discoveries of swastikas on ancient synagogues show that these were used by Jews, too, albeit only as decorations. The swastika had as little significance in Judaism as any other form of decoration. It was neither favoured nor denigrated and there was no mention of the swastika in Jewish literature until the Nazis adopted it as their emblem, when it became the most abhorrent symbol for Jews as well as for many others as a reminder of the *Holocaust and the other atrocities of Nazism. Jews today recoil with horror from any use of the swastika. To the consternation of decent people everywhere, vandals have been known to daub swastikas on Jewish tombstones.

Swaying The movement of the body during prayer and the study of the Torah, still practised by many Jews (see GESTURES). The earliest references to swaying in Jewish literature are in connection with the study of the Torah. *Judah Halevi, in his *Kuzari* (ii. 79–80), gives a rational explanation for the custom of swaying to and fro when studying the Torah. It often happened that ten or more people read from a single volume so that each was obliged to bend down in turn to read a passage and then turn back again. Thus swaying became a habit through constant seeing, observing, and imitating, which is human nature. The Zohar (iii. 218b–219a) gives a mystical reason for why Jews sway when they study the Torah. The souls of Israel, says the Zohar, have been hewn from the Holy Lamp, as it is written: 'The spirit of man is the lamp of the Lord' (Proverbs 20: 27). 'Now once this lamp has been kindled from the supernal Torah, the light upon it never ceases for an instant, like the flame of a wick which is never still for an instant. So when an Israelite has uttered a single word of the Torah, a light is kindled and he cannot keep still but sways to and fro like the flame of a wick.' Evidently, some time during the late Middle Ages, the custom arose of swaying during prayer as well as during study.

*Isserles, in his gloss to the *Shulhan Arukh* (Orah Hayyim, 48: 1), quotes earlier authorities who advocate swaying during prayer on the basis of the verse: 'All my bones shall say, Lord who is like unto Thee?' (Psalms 35: 10), the verse being taken literally to mean that all the bones should be involved in prayer by a swaying motion of the body.

In his note to the passage in the *Shulhan Arukh*, Abraham Gumbiner, a standard commentator to the work, after quoting authorities who favour swaying during prayer and others who denigrate it, concludes: 'It is correct to prefer either of these opinions provided that it assists concentration' (see KAVVANAH).

Reform Judaism generally frowns on swaying in prayer as falling short of Western standards of decorum and this attitude is often shared by the Orthodox in Western lands. But at least a gentle swaying is often the norm among many Jews when praying or when studying the Torah.

Swedenborg, Emanuel Swedish author, scientist, and mystic (1688–1772). Some of Swedenborg's ideas have certain affinities with Jewish *mysticism. There is some evidence that Swedenborg was influenced by the Zohar but none, however, of any influence of Swedenborg on later Jewish mystical ideas.

Swimming Among the duties of a father to his children listed in the Talmud (*Kiddushin* 29a) is teaching them how to swim, because their lives may depend on it. The verse: 'neither shalt thou stand idly by the blood of thy neighbour' (Leviticus 19: 16) is interpreted by the Rabbis to mean that if a man is in danger of drowning, a man who can swim is obliged to save him. An example of a 'foolish pietist' is given as a man who can swim but refuses to save a woman in danger of drowning because he does not wish to touch a female. Swimming was adopted as a metaphor for immersion in the 'sea of the Talmud' and skilful Talmudists were given the title of 'great swimmers'. Of the scholar who adduces a proof that leads nowhere it was said (*Bava Kama* 91a) that he has dived into deep waters only to bring up an oyster shell without the pearl. The Talmud (*Rosh Ha-Shanah* 23a) incidentally has a vivid description of divers bringing up coral in the Persian Gulf. Swimming in the river was a favourite pastime among *Yeshivah students in Eastern Europe.

Sword Although *warfare is not banned entirely in the Bible, hatred is often expressed of the sword as the symbol of warfare (see PEACE). That 'no sword shall cross your land' is stated as a supreme blessing (Leviticus 26: 6), just as the unsheathing of the sword is the worst of curses (Leviticus 26: 33). Esau, later identified with *Rome, was 'blessed' that he would live by the sword (Genesis 27: 40). However, there are plenty of examples in the Bible in which killing by the sword is justified. Psalm 149 speaks of the battling saints who sing the high praises of the Lord while holding a two-edged sword in their hands. Execution by the sword for certain offences was, according to the Mishnah (*Sanhedrin* 7: 1–3), one of the four methods of execution meted out by the *Sanhedrin, although this statement is purely theoretical as, in the time of the Mishnah, there was no *capital punishment. From Rabbinic times onwards Jews thought of the sword as, at the most, a necessary evil. All weapons of destruction came to be designated as the 'sword'. In a very revealing passage in the Mishnah (*Shabbat* 6: 4) it is said that Rabbi Eliezer permitted a man to go out on the Sabbath wearing a sword, since this could be seen not as carrying in the public domain (forbidden on the Sabbath) but as simply having an item of dress, an adornment. But the sages retorted that a sword can never be considered to be anything but a reproach and they quoted the verse: 'And they shall beat their swords into plowshares' (Isaiah 2: 4).

Symbolism The use of concrete things to denote abstract ideas. Judaism does not tolerate the making of plastic images of God (see GOLDEN CALF, IDOLATRY, and IMAGE OF GOD). The idea behind the prohibition of image-making appears to be that while an image of God is bound to be present in the mind, otherwise it would be impossible to think about God, to give this any kind of permanence in a concrete and lasting image is to attempt to perceive as the reality that which is beyond all human perception. Symbolism for the divine is either purely verbal, calling attention to natural phenomena, as when the prophet *Ezekiel uses the *rainbow in his vision of the *Chariot: 'Like the appearance of the bow which shines in the clouds on a day of rain, such was the appearance of the surrounding radiance' (Ezekiel 1: 28). It is noteworthy that in the whole of this account the prophet speaks of 'what looked like', as if to distance the symbol from the Reality.

In the Bible the Sabbath is a 'sign', that is, a symbol, of God's covenant with Israel (Exodus 31: 16–17). The fringes (*tzitzit) at the corners of the garment are reminders of God's commandments (Numbers 15: 38–40). The *tefillin are described in the *Shema as a 'sign' as, it is implied, is the mezuzah (Deuteronomy 6: 8–9). The *sukkah is a symbol of the 'booths' in which the children of Israel lived during their journey through the wilderness (Leviticus 23: 42-3). The *shofar sounded on *Rosh Ha-Shanah has received many symbolic interpretations, for example that it is a call to alertness to God's will, or symbolic of the crowning of God as King since trumpets are sounded at a coronation. The four species of *Tabernacles (Leviticus 23: 40) have been given various symbolic interpretations, for example, the upright palm branch represents the human spine; the heart-shaped citron, the etrog, the heart; the willows of the brook, the mouth; and the myrtle the eye, all of which are called upon to play their part in the worship of God. From early times Judaism itself was symbolized by the *menorah, itself the symbol of spiritual light, and by the *tablets of stone. The symbol of the *Magen David is, however, very late and was not used as a symbol for Judaism until the nineteenth century.

Symmachus Translator of the Bible into Greek. Symmachus lived towards the end of the second century CE. Some have suggested that Symmachus was a *Samaritan converted to the Judaism of the Rabbis and there was even an ancient report that he was not a Jew but a Christian. These are pure conjectures, since no details of his life are available. It is curious that the Talmud speaks of a teacher called Symmachus who was a disciple of Rabbi *Meir, and he, too, lived at the end of the second century. *Geiger's suggestion that the two are one and the same is not generally accepted, because the Symmachus mentioned in the Talmud is renowned for his acumen in Halakhic debate and decision, and there is no mention of him being a translator.

Sympathy The need for fellow-feeling with those who suffer is a constant theme in Judaism, finding its expression in practical acts of benevolence and *charity. The many biblical injunctions to care for and show *compassion to widows, orphans, and strangers and not to oppress them, all imply that the key to such care and consideration is sympathy with their lot. In *Hasidism, when a man prays for his needs, his motivation should be not for his own needs to be satisfied but for the lack in the *Shekhinah to be made good, since the divine presence is affected whenever creatures are in want. This idea goes back, in fact, to the Mishnah (*Sanhedrin* 6: 5) in a saying attributed to Rabbi *Meir.

Rabbi Meir comments that God suffers in sympathy even with the criminal who is executed for his crimes: 'When a man is sore troubled, what does the Shekhinah say? My head is ill at ease, my arm is ill at ease [some texts add here the words, "if it is permitted to say this"]. If God is sore troubled at the blood of the wicked that is shed, how much more at the blood of the righteous?'

*Heschel's well-known study of the Hebrew prophets depicts the prophet as a person who sees the world with the eyes of God and who suffers with God when human beings suffer. According to Heschel's understanding, the consciousness of the prophet is in such sympathetic union with the *pathos* of God that he can bring that union to bear in any given set of circumstances.

Synagogue The building in which Jews worship and offer their prayers. The word synagogue, from the Greek word meaning assembly, corresponds to the Hebrew name *bet ha-keneset*, 'house of assembly', that is, the place in which Jews come together.

For all its importance in Jewish life, little is known of the origins of the synagogue. There are no explicit references to anything like a synagogue anywhere in the Bible. Many scholars have suggested that the synagogue originated in the period of the Babylonian exile, which followed the destruction of the first Temple in 586 BCE. On this theory the earliest synagogues were small meeting-places in which the exiles gathered together for prayer. The prophet *Ezekiel, in Babylon, states in one of his addresses: 'Thus saith the Lord God. Although I have cast them afar off among the heathen, and although I have scattered them among the countries, yet will I be to them a small sanctuary in the countries where they shall come' (Ezekiel 11: 16). What the prophet means by God becoming for them a small sanctuary is unclear, but the Talmud (*Megillah* 29a) identifies the 'small sanctuary' with the synagogue. The reference in the book of Psalms to the enemy destroying 'all the meeting-places of God in the land' (Psalms 74: 8) has also been understood as applying to the synagogues. However, if synagogues did exist in this early period it is astonishing that there is no explicit reference to them. All that can be stated with certainty on the question of origins is that by the first century CE the synagogue had long been an established institution. The Mishnah (*Tamid* 5: 1; *Yoma* 7: 1) refers to a synagogue in the Temple itself. Philo refers to a synagogue in Rome and, as evidence from the Talmud and the *Septuagint shows, there were synagogues in ancient Alexandria. In the New Testament, Jesus is said to have preached in the synagogues of Galilee (Matthew 4: 23) and, according to Acts, Paul preached in synagogues in Damascus, Asia Minor, and Cyprus. Archaeologists have uncovered the remains of synagogues in Palestine and elsewhere dating from this early period.

There are no rules in Judaism regarding the architectural form of the synagogue building. Jews have adopted the styles of the countries in which they lived (see ARCHITECTURE). The famous Altneu synagogue in Prague, for instance, is in the Gothic style in which churches were built at the time. On the other hand, in Western lands during the nineteenth century, it was far from unusual to build synagogues in the oriental style, in the belief that this best represented the 'oriental' origins of Judaism: a romantic lapse from the Westernization that was proceeding apace. But many synagogues in the West were also influenced by church buildings, although, of course, the cruciform mode was never adopted. Orthodox Rabbis were opposed, too, to a synagogue having a spire like a church, and their advice was generally followed by the non-Orthodox as well.

Jewish teachers, legalists and moralists never tired of stressing that strict decorum and reverence are to be observed by worshippers in the synagogue. There must be no idle conversation in the synagogue and the worshippers must always be aware of the fact that they are in the presence of God. These constant appeals for decorum in the synagogue demonstrate that the problem was acute, naturally so since for many Jews the synagogue was the main place for social intercourse, often serving, whether or not the Rabbis approved, as a kind of club. The Mishnaic rule (*Berakhot* 9: 1) that one must not use the Temple Mount as a short-cut is applied in the Talmud (*Berakhot* 62b) to the synagogue as well. This together with other rules is recorded in the *Shulḥan Arukh* (*Oraḥ Ḥayyim* 151) under the heading: 'The Laws With Regard to the Sanctity of the Synagogue'.

The question of selling a synagogue that is no longer used has been much discussed. As stated above, the question is discussed in the Mishnah (*Megillah* 3) and in the Talmudic elaboration of the Mishnah. The final ruling is that when a synagogue can no longer be used it may be sold on the grounds that synagogues are sanctified on condition that they are used as such, so that once the synagogue is no longer used it loses its sanctity and may be sold. The Talmud does make a distinction between a synagogue in a village and one in a large city. A synagogue in a village belongs to the villagers and can be sold by them. But a synagogue in a large city does not belong solely to the citizens, since the frequent visitors from other towns have presumably contributed to the building and are thus part-owners, so that the town council has no right to dispose of their share. Later authorities, however, hold that since, nowadays, each synagogue has its own members who contribute to its upkeep these members are the sole owners and the synagogue may be sold when it is no longer used as such even where it is in a large town. For this reason a synagogue may be sold to be used as a church or a mosque, although here it is common practice to sell the synagogue indirectly through a third party. The accepted opinion among the authorities is that, conversely, it is permitted to buy a mosque or a church to be used as a synagogue, though, in the case of the church, the building must not contain any symbols of the Christian faith, built-in crosses for example.

The main function of the synagogue is for public worship but there is, of course, no objection to a person entering the synagogue for private meditation at other times than those of public worship. The advice is given in the sources to proceed hurriedly when going to the synagogue but to depart from the synagogue with unhurried steps, to indicate eagerness to be there and reluctance to leave. The verse homiletically interpreted in this connection is: 'We shall run to know the Lord' (Hosea 6: 3). The verse does not, of course, refer to the synagogue but is made to yield the meaning that it is right 'to run' to know God and to go to the synagogue is to proceed to a greater knowledge of the divine.

While all Jews have a reverential attitude towards the synagogue, some no doubt finding much significance even in the mystical understanding of the synagogue as the abode of the Shekhinah, a degree of resistance has come about in modern times, as it did in former times, to the idea that Judaism is synagogue-oriented. Rabbis are fond of preaching that Judaism demands far more than regular worship in the synagogue and that, for example, many of the highest ideals of the Jewish religion are realized in the Jewish home rather than in the synagogue. Worship in the synagogue is a sublime end in itself but it is also a means of inspiring Jews to lead a full Jewish life and much of life has its place outside the synagogue. For all that, the majority of Jews, nowadays, still view the synagogue as the best means of retaining loyalty to Judaism and preserving Jewish identity.

As with regard to other particular aspects of Judaism, synagogal life is both an end in itself and a means to the ultimate end of Jewish life, the worship of God in every one of life's situations: 'In all thy ways acknowledge Him, and He will direct thy paths' (Proverbs 3: 6). Contemporary Rabbis thus find themselves in a dilemma. On the one hand they feel obliged to urge Jews to attend synagogue services regularly but, on the other hand, they cannot countenance the view that synagogue attendance is the be-all and end-all of Judaism. It is hard to determine how many Jews are regular attenders at the synagogue during the rest of the year, but a majority of Jews are found there on *Yom Kippur, which exercises a powerful fascination over Jews as the great day of reconciliation with their God.

Syncretism The assimilation by Judaism of elements stemming from other religions and civilizations. The process of syncretism in Judaism is rarely conscious or intentional, but as Jews came into contact with the ideas and institutions of the various peoples among whom they resided, their language and thought-patterns were naturally and automatically affected, so that Judaism itself came to absorb these ideas into its own theology. This does not mean that Jews simply adopted uncritically the beliefs and practices of their neighbours. A kind of consensus has been at work in the history of the Jewish religion by virtue of which those elements that could be adapted to Judaism without in any way coming into conflict with essential Jewish beliefs (see DOGMAS) were not totally rejected but given a Jewish interpretation. Where ideas from without were seen to be incompatible with the Jewish religion they were rejected without any attempt at compromise. Naturally, considerable tensions arose in these matters.

When Western civilization posed a threat to the survival of Judaism, the diverse ways in which Jews responded to the challenge resulted in a degree of syncretism. The *Haskalah, Reform and Conservative Judaism, and Samson Raphael *Hirsch's neo-Orthodoxy are all examples of adaptation of the old to the new. In the area of scientific theory, many Jewish thinkers accepted the view that the universe is not geocentric, that life has been on earth for a vast period of time and that human beings have evolved from lower forms (see EVOLUTION) and they reinterpreted the biblical record so that it could be understood in accordance with the new picture of the universe. Thus, while the actual term 'syncretism' is not found in any of the Jewish sources, and while Jewish fundamentalists (see FUNDAMENTALISM) deny that any form of syncretism ever took place in Judaism, the idea denoted by this term is clearly evident to Jews with any sense of history, although this recognition does not interfere with their belief in the basic truths of the religion. On the contrary, the evidence for syncretism is evidence of the Jewish genius that has made Judaism an undying faith.

Synods, Rabbinical Assemblies or conferences of Rabbinic leaders at which rulings were given governing the social life of Jews under their jurisdiction. In the Middle Ages the synod was known as the *asifah* ('assembly'). The Rabbinical synods differed in two respects from the synods of the Church. First, the Christian synods were convened largely for the purpose of defining complicated issues of dogma, whereas the Rabbinical synods were chiefly concerned with practical legislation. Secondly, the Christian synods enjoyed an international authority, whereas the Rabbinical synods in the Middle Ages were confined to particular communities or districts. Once the period of the *Geonim had come to an

end there was no central *authority for Jews. The main activity of the Rabbinical synods was to establish *takkanot* ('enactments'). A *takkanah* (a 'putting right') consists of new legislation to cover situations for which the standard laws are inadequate or on which they are silent. The principle behind the *takkanah* is that locally accepted authorities have power, granted to them by the community itself, just as members of Parliament act on behalf of the country. A synod had the power to issue new financial and social regulations, at first binding only on those under the particular Rabbinic jurisdiction but often finding their way into the Codes of law, when they thus became binding on Jews outside the original communities in which the *takkanot* were promulgated.

Synonymous Parallelism The feature of biblical poetry, described by modern scholars, who were anticipated by Abraham *Ibn Ezra and *Kimhi in the Middle Ages, in which the same idea is repeated for effect in different words. For example: 'For fire went out from Heshbon, flame from the city of Sihon' (Numbers 21: 28). Sihon was the king of Heshbon, so that the second clause simply repeats in different words the statement in the first clause. 'My doctrine shall drip as the rain, my speech shall distil as the dew; as the small rain upon the tender grass, and as the showers upon the herb' (Deuteronomy 32: 2). In Psalm 23, in which the Lord is described as the Shepherd, the Psalmist declares: 'He maketh me to lie down in green pastures; he leadeth me beside the still waters' (v. 2); the second clause, although referring to a different form of pastoral care from the first, is a parallel to the first in that both are examples of that care. Many biblical commentators try to discover subtle differences between the two clauses wherever this phenomenon occurs but, while their comments can be valuable as homiletics, they are far removed from the plain meaning of the verses. Other forms of poetic parallelism in the Bible are antithetic and synthetic, that is, the second clause is contrasted with the first and elaborates on it. All this provides an excellent illustration of how the Bible can be understood at the level of its plain meaning without detriment to the homiletical insights (see MIDRASH). On the plain meaning biblical poetry is just poetry plain and simple, the poet expressing his thoughts in the form of parallelism to produce an effect.

Syriac A dialect of eastern *Aramaic. The Talmud (*Bava Kama* 83a–b) implies that Syriac was used by Palestinian Jews while Aramaic was used by Babylonian Jews. Rabbi *Judah the Prince is reported as saying: 'Why use the Syriac language in the Land of Israel where either the Holy Tongue [Hebrew] or the Greek language could be used?' Rabbi Jose is reported as saying: 'Why use the Aramaic language in Babylon where the Holy Tongue or the Persian language could be used?' In point of fact scholars have noted that the Aramaic of the Babylonian Talmud is a Jewish modification of Syriac. Syriac is so called because it was the Aramaic dialect of the people who lived in Syria and has no special connection with that country any more than Babylonian Aramaic had any special connection, other than that of dialect, to the country of Babylon. The written documents in Syriac, in a script different from that of Hebrew and Aramaic, come from the Christians in Syria in the early centuries CE.

Syriac is important for comparative purposes in the study of biblical philology but is especially significant because of the Syriac translation of the Bible known as the Peshitta ('The Simple', i.e. the simple translation of the Bible), made by the Syriac Church of Edessa probably at the beginning or middle of the second century CE. The Peshitta, like the *Septuagint and other ancient versions, is used by biblical scholars for their investigations into the original biblical text, but they warn that great caution has to be exercised in relying on the Peshitta to emend the Masoretic Text (see MASORAH), since it is far from evident that the Syriac translation is necessarily based on an authentic version of the text. Nevertheless, where a text different from the Masoretic is found also in other versions, it is less precarious to use the Peshitta for a suggested emendation (and see BIBLICAL CRITICISM).

Systematic Thinking The type of thinking in which diverse ideas and concepts are brought together to form a coherent whole. It is obvious to even the most casual reader that biblical thought is not of this order. The Hebrew prophets, for example, urge their people, in the name of God, to practise *justice and show *compassion but Socratic analysis of the concepts of justice and compassion are completely foreign to the biblical way of thinking in which it is taken for granted that these and similar values are good without having to use any abstract term such as 'values' for them to be substantiated. Even in the book of Proverbs, which does form a unit and was intended as such, there is no attempt at systematization. The proverbs are precisely that, a series of dynamic responses to various situations and, since human life is full of variety, hope, and frustration, it is pointless to attempt to find consistency in the book. Contradictory advice is offered in Proverbs because what is called for in one situation is unhelpful in a different situation. The book of Job is a tremendous poem on the sufferings of a righteous man but one will look in vain there for an examination of why evil and suffering should exist at all.

It was under the influence of Greek *philosophy, which came to them in

Arabic garb, that the medieval thinkers tried to present their thoughts systematically and, since a good deal of their thinking had to do with the teachings of the Bible and the Talmud, they were bound to cast the ideas found in these works into a form essentially alien to their nature. The very systematization of biblical and Rabbinic thought, even when that thought was conveyed accurately (this was not always the case), was a distortion. Nevertheless, once Jewish thinkers had become accustomed to systematic thinking, there could be no turning back. This kind of thinking had become endemic to the Jewish mind as it had to the human mind in general.

Szold, Henrietta American Zionist leader and philanthropist (1860–1945). Henrietta was born in Baltimore where her father Benjamin Szold served as the Rabbi of Congregation Oheb Shalom. She was educated by her father and in private schools, became a schoolteacher, and wrote articles for the Jewish Press. Under her father's influence and that of Russian refugees who had settled in Baltimore, she became a fervent Zionist. She was the co-founder of Hadassah, the Women's Zionist organization, served on the Executive of the Jewish Agency, and in her last years was active in Youth Aliyah, the movement engaged in saving young Jews from Nazi persecution.

T

Tabernacle The portable structure erected by the Israelites at the command of God to accompany them in their journeys through the wilderness, as told in the book of Exodus (25: 1–31; 17; 35: 1–40: 38). The Tabernacle consisted of an outer courtyard, oblong in shape, 100 cubits by 50 cubits. This enclosure consisted of all-round hangings with an opening, the entrance, at the east side. These hangings were the means of separating the sacred spot from the profane realm outside it but did not form a cover to the area within it, which was open to the sky. The hangings of the courtyard were supported by upright pillars of acacia wood, overlain with gold, secured by sockets of copper. This oblong consisted of two squares, each 50 by 50 cubits. The western square contained the Holy Place, the Sanctuary proper, at the western end of which was situated the holy of holies, divided off from the Holy Place by a curtain. A screen was placed at the entrance to the Holy Place to divide it off from the rest of the courtyard and another screen at the entrance to the courtyard. There were thus three separate entrances, each leading to a more sacred spot: the entrance to the courtyard, with a screen in front, the entrance to the Holy Place, with a screen in front, and the entrance to the Holy of Holies, with the curtain in front. Only the *priests were allowed to enter the Holy Place and no one was allowed to enter the Holy of Holies, except the *High Priest on *Yom Kippur.

The *Ark was placed in the holy of holies behind the curtain. In the Holy Place there was a table in the north, the *menorah in the south, and a golden altar, the altar of incense, placed in front of the curtain in front of the Ark at the entrance to the Holy of Holies.

The table and the altar were made of wood overlain with gold but the menorah was of solid gold. In the eastern square of the courtyard were placed the wooden altar covered with copper, upon which the sacrifices were burnt and their blood sprinkled, and a laver for the washing of the hands and feet of the priests. The Holy Place and the Holy of Holies were draped with hangings which completely covered the whole area. There were four separate layers of hangings, one on top of the other. The innermost hanging, the one that could be seen by whoever came into the Sanctuary, was made of fine linen decorated with figures of *cherubim, as was the curtain in front of the Ark. Over the hanging of fine linen was placed a coarser hanging made of goat's hair and over this a hanging of tanned rams' skins and over this a hanging of the skins of tehashim, a word of uncertain meaning, often translated as 'dolphins'. The outer hangings of leather seem to have been intended as a protection from the elements. These hangings were supported by gilded pillars of acacia wood set in silver sockets. On each of the three walls (the fourth, at the eastern side, had an opening to form the entrance) there were five gilded crossbars of acacia wood placed into ring-like holders in the uprights in order to secure the structure. The whole structure was designed to be dismantled whenever the Israelites journeyed onwards and to be set up again wherever they encamped.

Tabernacles The autumn festival which begins on 15 Tishri and lasts for seven days, followed by the festival of *Shemini Atzeret on the eighth day in Israel (and on the ninth in the *Diaspora). The ninth day in the Diaspora is called *Simhat Torah but in Israel Simhat Torah and Shemini Atzeret are celebrated on the same day, the eighth. Thus, the Rabbis say, there are really two festivals, one following on the other, Tabernacles and Shemini Atzeret, but both came to be named as Tabernacles. The Hebrew name for Tabernacles is sukkot, and is so called after the command to dwell for seven days in the *sukkah (singular of sukkot), as a reminder of the 'booths' or 'tabernacles' in which the Israelites dwelt during their forty years' journey through the wilderness (Leviticus 23: 32–44). Since Tabernacles falls at harvest time and is also the last of the three pilgrim festivals, it is the especially joyous festival (Deuteronomy 16: 13–17). In the liturgy Tabernacles is referred to as 'the season of our joy'.

In addition to the sukkah, the precept of the 'four species' is carried out on Tabernacles (i.e. on the seven days of Tabernacles proper but not on Shemini Atzeret.) This command is given as: 'And ye shall take you on the first day the fruit of goodly trees, branches of palm-trees, and boughs of thick trees, and willows of the brook, and ye shall rejoice before the Lord your God seven days' (Leviticus 23: 40). The Rabbinic understanding of the verse, still followed universally by Jews, is that 'ye shall take' means to hold in the hand these four species. From early times the 'fruit of goodly trees' was understood to mean the etrog (citron), the 'boughs of thick trees' the myrtle. The other two species are, as stated explicitly in the verse, the palm branch (the lulav) and the willow. These four species are held in the hands, the lulav, together with three sprigs of myrtle and two of willow, in the right hand and the etrog in the left hand. These four are waved upwards and downwards and in the four directions of the compass during the recital of the *Hallel. One reason given for this waving is that it is for the purpose of dispelling harmful winds. Another reason is that it is to acknowledge God as Lord of all that is above and below and on all sides. The four species are also taken in a circuit around the synagogue while the petition Hoshanah ('Save now') is recited for a good harvest. On the seventh day seven circuits are made and hence this day is called *Hoshanah Rabbah, the 'Great Hoshnanah'.

Tablets of Stone The two tablets upon which the Ten Commandments were inscribed. The book of Exodus (31: 18; 32: 15–16) tells of Moses receiving from God the 'tablets of the testimony' inscribed by 'the finger of God'. When Moses came down from the mount and saw his people worshipping the *golden calf he cast the tablets from his hands and broke them (Exodus 32: 19). Moses pleads with God to pardon the people and God tells him to hew out two further tablets upon which God will write the words that were on the first tablets (Exodus 34: 1). In an interesting homily the Rabbis observe that the theophany at *Sinai which resulted in the inscribing of the first tablets was attended by thunder and lightning (Exodus 20: 15), whereas the inscribing of the second tablets was a quiet affair, from which they conclude that the Torah, symbolized by the tablets, is more likely to find lodgement in an atmosphere of quietude and serenity than among the more spectacular events of human life. Nevertheless, the tablets of stone do not appear in Jewish *art as a symbol of the Torah until the Middle Ages. Moreover, the conventional picture of the two tablets as joined together with a copula at the top is not a traditional Jewish picture but was adopted from representations in Christian illuminated manuscripts (see DECALOGUE).

Tallit The robe with which the worshipper is wrapped during prayer and hence often referred to as a 'prayer shawl', though this is not the traditional Jewish name for the garment, which was not originally associated particularly with prayer. In the book of Numbers (15: 37–40), the Israelites are commanded to put *tzitzit ('fringes') on their garments in order to remind them of God's laws. But in the book of Deuteronomy (22: 12) it is stated that these fringes have to be placed on the four corners of the garment, from which the Rabbis conclude that only four-cornered garments have to have tzitzit affixed to them. In Talmudic times people wore four-cornered garments and to these tzitzit were attached. In fact, the word tallit, of uncertain etymology, simply means a robe or a cloak (some connect the word with the Latin *stola*). The sole significance of the tallit was in the tzitzit. The tallit itself had no religious significance. The result was that in Europe in the Middle Ages, where people did not wear four-cornered garments, the precept of tzitzit was in danger of being forgotten. To prevent this Jews took it upon themselves to wear a four-cornered garment to which they would be obliged to attach the tzitzit and thus restore a precept that was in danger of vanishing from Jewish life. This special four-cornered garment was given the name tallit on the analogy of the four-cornered garments worn in ancient times. Strictly speaking, the precept of tzitzit has to be carried out for the whole of the day but since Jews could hardly go about wearing such an unusual garment as the tallit all day, the wearing of the tallit was limited to the time of the morning prayers.

The ultra-Orthodox wear the tallit over the head when they recite the more important prayers. The earlier authorities are divided on the question of covering the head. Some are none too happy with a practice that might be seen as showing off, since the essential idea of covering the head in this way is for the worshipper to be lost in concentration, on his own before God, as it were. Religious one-upmanship is generally frowned upon. Some hold that only a *Talmid Hakham, a man learned in the Torah, should cover his head with the tallit. The final ruling is that one should follow whatever is the local custom.

Talmid Ḥakham 'Disciple of the wise', the name given to the scholar, especially one proficient in Talmudic and Halakhic studies since these were the main subjects of Torah *study in the traditional scheme. There is no clear evidence as to when the term Talmid Hakham was first used. The suggestion that Jewish sages, in their humility, have always spoken of themselves as 'disciples' is no doubt homiletically inspiring but it is historically unsound. The facts are that the term is not met before the second century CE. Before that time scholars were called Hakhamim, 'sages', not disciples, a term reserved for the students who had not as yet attained to great learning. But from around the second century the term is applied to the mature scholar.

The rise of the *Jüdische Wissenschaft movement and the development of modern Jewish scholarship from the nineteenth century brought about a complete reassessment of the role of the Talmid Hakham. Even those modern scholars who have acquired expertise in Talmudic studies adopt a 'scientific' approach to their studies—a critical stance towards the sources, one that is at variance with the attitude of total acceptance typical of the traditional Talmid Hakham. The modern Talmudist is generally known as a 'scholar' rather than a Talmid Hakham, though some modern scholars refuse to give up the traditional title and, of course, the traditional attitude is still preserved in the world of the *Yeshivah, where every student has the ambition to become a Talmid Hakham in the old sense.

Talmud The work containing the teachings of the Amoraim (see TANNAIM AND AMORAIM) of Palestine and Babylon, presented in the form of a running commentary to the Mishnah. The term Talmud is from the root *limmed*, 'to learn', and means 'teaching' or 'study'. In the Middle Ages the substitute term *Gemara was used for Talmud. There are, in reality, two Talmuds: the Palestinian and the Babylonian. The former is often called the Yerushalmi or Jerusalem Talmud, although there were no schools in Jerusalem itself. The Babylonian Talmud is referred to as the Bavli ('of Babylon').

As noted under *Mishnah, this digest of Tannaitic teachings, edited by Rabbi *Judah the Prince at the end of the second and beginning of the third century CE, is divided into six orders.

In addition to the Mishnah, other works containing Tannaitic teachings are quoted extensively in the two Talmuds. These works are: the *Tosefta ('Supplement' to the Mishnah); the Mekhilta ('Measure'), on the biblical book of Exodus; Sifra ('The Book'), on Leviticus, also called Torat Kohanim ('The Law of the Priests'); and Sifre ('The Books') on Numbers and Deuteronomy. The last three are known as the Halakhic Midrashim or the Tannaitic Midrashim (see MIDRASH). There are also other Tannaitic teachings quoted in the Talmud and these, as well as the aforementioned, are all known as Baraitot (singular: Baraita; the word means 'outside', i.e. teachings not found in the Mishnah but which come from without).

Once the Mishnah had won acceptance as a canonical text, the teachers in both Palestine and Babylon devoted much of their efforts to its elucidation; hence the name Amoraim, 'Expounders' of the Mishnah and the other Tannaitic texts. The scholarly debates and discussion of the Amoraim were largely conducted in *Aramaic, although, naturally, many of the legal maxims and quotes from earlier sources were in Hebrew. The Palestinian Amoraim used the western Aramaic dialect, the Babylonians the eastern dialect, and these are the two dialects used in the Yerushalmi and the Bavli, respectively.

Around the year 400 CE the teachings, debates, and discussions that took place among the Palestinian Amoraim were drawn on to form the Palestinian Talmud, the Yerushalmi. There has been much discussion on the question of who the editors of the Yerushalmi were. There is evidence, stylistic and historical, that some sections of the Yerushalmi were edited earlier, and in a different centre, from others. The style of the Yerushalmi is, in any event, terse, even 'choppy', so that some scholars have suggested that the work never received any final redaction at all and is an incomplete, unfinished work.

A similar process is to be observed in the Babylonian Talmud, the Bavli, compiled some time around the year 500 CE (the date is very approximate). The style of the Bavli is, however, much more elaborate than that of the Yerushalmi. Apart from five tractates, the style of the Bavli is uniform, suggesting that the same editors were responsible for the whole work, with the exception of these tractates. Yet even these five tractates differ only slightly from the rest in style and vocabulary, so the impression is gained of a co-ordinated editorial activity, though one carried out in at least two different Babylonian centres. Although Palestinian Amoraim are frequently mentioned in the Bavli and Babylonian Amoraim in the Yerushalmi (naturally so, since some of the sages of each country visited the other from time to time, carrying the teachings with them), the weight of scholarly opinion is that the editors of the Bavli did not have before them the actual text of the Yerushalmi, nor did the Palestinian editors have anything like a proto-Bavli. If the editors of either had had access to an actual text of the other, it is inconceivable that they would not have mentioned this. Here the argument from silence is very convincing.

Christian denunciations of the Talmud in the Middle Ages were based on the supposedly adverse comments found in the work on Christianity and Christians. In Paris in the year 1242, it is reliably reported, twenty-four wagonloads of books, among them many copies of the Talmud, were confiscated and later destroyed and there were burnings of the Talmud in other places, which explains why only a single manuscript of the complete Bavli, the Munich Codex, is extant. In point of fact the references to Christianity in the Talmud are scanty and pure fancy, since the Babylonian Jews had no contacts with Christians and they obtained their information only at second and third hand and even then in vague form. But Christian accusations, justified or not, caused Jewish copyists and later printers to exercise their own *censorship of the Talmud, omitting the few references to Christianity (these were later collected and published as a separate small volume) and substituting such 'innocent' terms as 'Egyptian' or 'Sadducee' for the original goy, 'Gentile'.

The *Karaites rejected the Talmud as they did the doctrine of the *Oral Torah on which it is based. The Geonim were much concerned with refuting the accusations of the Karaites that, for instance, the Talmud contains grossly anthropomorphic and other inferior conceptions of God. Reform Judaism, in the early days of the movement, had a similar negative attitude towards the Talmud, one that was softened to a considerable degree in the later history of Reform. It was not that the Talmud was considered to be valueless in itself, only that the Reformers no longer saw the Talmud as the source of authority for Jewish practice.

Within the Rabbinic camp the Tal-

mud was the main subject of *study, the supreme religious duty to study the Torah being expressed by scholars without number in the mastery of the Talmudic texts. Probably in reaction to the Karaite rejection of the Talmud, the Talmudic *Rabbis came to be designated as Ḥazal (an abbreviation of the Hebrew for 'Our Sages of blessed memory') and, in many circles, came to be regarded as infallible authorities on every topic which they considered. Maimonides' statement was accepted that the Babylonian Talmud has been adopted by the whole of Jewry as the supreme *authority in Jewish law so that 'to it [the Talmud] one must not add and from it one must not diminish'. For all that, many teachers in the Middle Ages, while accepting that the Talmud is the final court of appeal in Jewish law, did not feel themselves bound by every statement in the Talmud on such matters as medicine, astronomy, and even Jewish history (see ROSSI). Maimonides' categorical statement only applied to the laws of the Talmud and he rejected the *magic and superstition found there as well as the belief in *astrology. Some Jewish commentators to the Bible like Abraham *Ibn Ezra often preferred what they considered the plain meaning of the text over the Midrashic interpretations found in the Talmud and the Midrash except where issues of Jewish practice were involved.

The Talmud has been studied by modern scholars, Jewish and non-Jewish, for the light it throws on the customs, dress, architecture, languages, philosophy, religion, and ethics of the Hellenistic world. As Marcus Jastrow remarks in the preface to his great dictionary of the Talmud and kindred literature:

'The subjects of this literature are as unlimited as are the interests of the human mind. Religion and ethics, exegesis and homiletics, jurisprudence and ceremonial laws, ritual and liturgy, philosophy and science, medicine and magic, astronomy and astrology, history and geography, commerce and trade, politics and social problems, all are represented there, and reflect the mental condition of the Jewish world in its seclusion from the outer world, as well as in its contact with the same whether in agreement or in opposition.'

Tam, Rabbenu The name given to Jacob ben Meir (1100–71), the foremost French authority of the Middle Ages. The name is based on Genesis 25: 27: 'Jacob was a mild man [ish tam], dwelling in tents', interpreted in the Rabbinic tradition to mean that Jacob was a 'perfect' man, dwelling in the tents of the Torah; hence this famous teacher is known universally as Rabbenu Tam, 'Our Teacher the Perfect One'. A daughter of the great French sage, *Rashi, married Rabbi Meir of Ramerupt and Tam was the youngest of their three sons; the other two were Rabbi Samuel ben Meir (*Rashbam) and Rabbi Isaac ben Meir (Ribam). Tam studied under his father, his much older brother Rashbam, and Jacob ben Samson, a pupil of Rashi, eventually to become the acknowledged spiritual leader of French Jewry and the most outstanding contributor to the *Tosafot glosses to the Talmud.

Tam established a *Yeshivah in Ramerupt, teaching the Torah to scores of distinguished Talmudists. (The report that each of Tam's students was a particular expert in a chosen tractate of the Talmud is now seen to be legendary.) Tam's fame spread beyond France. Questions were addressed to him from other parts of the Jewish world and he was known as far as Spain as a great Halakhist, teacher, and liturgical poet, corresponding with Abraham *Ibn Ezra, who visited Tam during his stay in France.

Tammuz, Fast of The public fast on 17 Tammuz. The Mishnah (*Taanit* 4: 6)

lists five calamities which took place on this date as a result of which the fast was ordained. On this day Moses broke the *tablets of stone; the daily offering ceased; the walls of Jerusalem were breached; a general named Apostomus (exact identity unknown) burnt the Torah; and an idol was set up in the Sanctuary. There is considerable doubt about the meaning of these events, but clearly most of them have to do with the destruction of the Temple. The three weeks from the Fast of Tammuz to the Ninth of *Av (Tisha Be-Av) are weeks of mourning during which no marriages are celebrated and observant Jews do not listen to music. According to the sources, the Fast of Tammuz (see FAST DAYS) lasts only from early morning until sunset, unlike the fasts of Tisha Be-Av and *Yom Kippur which last from sunset to sunset. With the establishment of the State of Israel some (even Orthodox) Jews do not observe the Fast of Tammuz, but many Orthodox Jews retain the tradition.

Tannaim and Amoraim The Talmudic *Rabbis, the teachers whose views are recorded in the Talmudic literature. Both these terms are also found in the Talmud in connection with learning activity. In this context, a Tanna ('rehearser' or 'teacher') was a functionary who rehearsed opinions and statements of the teachers of the first two centuries CE; an Amora ('expounder') was a different functionary, whose job it was to explain to the assembly the words of a contemporary sage, the latter making only a series of brief rulings which the Amora would then explain in detail. But, in the later passages of the Talmud, both these names were adopted for the two sets of teachers mentioned in the first sense above. The name Tanna was given to the teachers who flourished in Palestine in the first two centuries CE and whose views appear in the Mishnah and other literature from this period. The name

Amora was given to the expounders of the Tannaitic teachings. The Amoraim belong both to Palestine and Babylon down to the end of the fifth century CE. Thus, in the most common usage, the Tannaim are the Palestinian teachers of the first two centuries and the Amoraim the Palestinian and Babylonian teachers from the third to the fifth centuries CE. In the discussions of the Babylonian Talmud, for example, where two different teachers are referred to in the Mishnah, the first is called the Tanna Kama ('the first Tanna').

The general principle followed in the Talmudic arguments is that an Amora is not at liberty to disagree in matters of law with a Tanna unless he can quote another Tanna in support. This principle was no doubt established after the Mishnah had acquired canonical status, so that teachers belonging to the Mishnaic period, whether or not their opinions were actually recorded in the Mishnah, came to enjoy a much greater degree of *authority. Thus one finds frequently in the Talmud an objection of the sort: how can Amora A say such-and-such, since a Tanna has said otherwise? The reply is either that the Tanna said no such thing, his statement being reinterpreted, or that the Amora can produce the opinion of another Tanna who takes issue with the first.

Although the Tannaim enjoy greater authority than the Amoraim, the actual decisions in Jewish law are not rendered on the basis of Tannaitic statement in themselves but on these statements as expounded by the Amoraim.

Of the many Tannaim and Amoraim it is possible here to list only some of the more prominent, those whose names occur very frequently in the literature.

Tannaim

The members of the schools of *Hillel and *Shammai; Rabban *Johanan ben Zakkai; Rabban *Gamaliel I and II; Rabbi *Eliezer; Rabbi *Joshua; Rabbi *Ishmael; Rabbi *Akiba and his disciples: Rabbi *Meir, Rabbi Judah, Rabbi Jose, and Rabbi *Simeon ben Yohai; Rabbi *Judah the Prince, editor of the Mishnah, and his disciples: Rabbi Hiyya, Rabbi Hoshayah, and Rabbi Hanina.

Palestinian Amoraim

Rabbi Joshua ben Levi; Rabbi Johanan; Rabbi Simeon ben Lakish (usually referred to as Resh Lakish); Rabbi Eleazar ben Pedat; Rabbi Simlai; Rabbi Abbahu; Rabbi Ammi; Rabbi Assi; Rabbi Zera; Rabbi Jeremiah.

Babylonian Amoraim

*Rav and Samuel; Rav Huna (the Babylonians did not have the full title 'Rabbi'); Rav Hisda; Rav Judah ben Ezekiel; Rav Nahman; Rav Sheshet; *Abbaye and Rava; Rav Pappa; Rav Ashi and Ravina. The last two are said (in the *Letter* of *Sherira Gaon) to have been the editors of the Babylonian Talmud but this cannot be taken too literally since both feature as 'heroes' of the work and are mentioned in the third person, apart from the fact that there are clearly to be detected Talmudic passages that obviously derive from a later period.

The problem of dating the various Tannaim and Amoraim is notoriously difficult, given the paucity of biographical detail and the legendary nature of some of the details that are given.

Targum 'Translation', of the Bible from the Hebrew into other languages, especially *Aramaic. In the ancient synagogue during the *reading of the Torah, there was a verse-by-verse translation into Aramaic by a Meturgeman ('dragoman', 'interpreter'). From the warnings that the Meturgeman had to keep to the text and not introduce into it meanings of his own, it would seem that, at first, the Meturgeman supplied his own translation. Eventually, however, standard, official Targumim came to be used. One of these, the Targum Onkelos, was considered to be the most authentic and is now printed together with the original Hebrew text in most editions of the *Pentateuch. (Two other Targumim, that of Pseudo-Jonathan and Targum Yerushalmi (of Jerusalem) are also printed in the better editions, as are Targumim to the rest of the Bible.)

Targum Onkelos is largely a literal translation of the text, although its tendency is to paraphrase anthropomorphic statements so as to make them more acceptable, for example, by using expressions like 'the word of God' instead of 'God'. For instance, the verse: 'the God of thy father, who shall help thee' (Genesis 29: 25) is rendered by Onkelos: 'the word of the God of thy father, shall be thy help'. The verse: 'And the Lord came down to see the city' (Genesis 11: 5) is rendered by Onkelos as: 'The Lord revealed Himself to punish those who built the city.' Similarly, the verse: 'I will go down now and see' (Genesis 18: 21) is rendered: 'I will reveal Myself and judge.' Occasionally, Onkelos gives a Midrashic explanation to the text. For instance in the verse: 'the voice of thy brother's blood crieth unto Me' (Genesis 4: 10) the word for 'blood' is in the plural, literally 'bloods'. This leads Onkelos to paraphrase the verse as: 'the voice of the blood of the seed that would have come from thy brother crieth unto Me'. Rashi, in the commentary to the verse, quotes a Rabbinic Midrash to the same effect. *Rashi often quotes the Targum Onkelos in his commentary to the Torah.

Once Jews in Western lands had little or no knowledge of Aramaic the institution of the Meturgeman came to an end. Nowadays, everywhere in the Jewish world, the reading of the Torah consists of the Hebrew text alone. Yet the Targum Onkelos has acquired a great sanctity of its own. On the basis of a Talmudic statement (*Berakhot* 8a–b)

that a man is obliged to read for himself twice during the week together with the Targum the weekly portion read in the synagogue, it is still the practice of pious Jews to read twice in their homes each week the sidra ('portion') of the week, together with Targum Onkelos.

Tashlikh The ceremony in which sins are symbolically cast into water, after the verse: 'Thou wilt cast [ve-tashlikh] their sins into the depths of the sea' (Micah 7: 19). Tashlikh is observed on the first day of *Rosh Ha-Shanah (the second if the first day falls on the Sabbath). Jews repair to a river or the sea to cast therein their sins, while reciting scriptural verses (Micah 7: 18–20; Psalms 118: 5–8 and 130; Isaiah 11: 9). In some rites Kabbalistic passages and prayers are also recited. A further custom is for the garments to be shaken as a token of total cleansing by casting away every vestige of sin.

The tashlikh ceremony is not found in any of the ancient sources, although *Isserles (*Shulhan Arukh, Orah Hayyim*, 584: 2) records it as a custom to be followed. The earliest reference is by Jacob Moellin, the Maharil (d. 1425), in his compendium of customs observed by German Jews.

Tattoo The prohibition of tattooing is stated in the verse: 'You shall not make gashes in your flesh for the dead, or incise any marks on yourselves, I am the Lord' (Leviticus 19: 28). Commentators explain the prohibition on the grounds that it was an idolatrous practice of the ancient pagans to incise in the skin the name of their god. In the Hebrew of the verse a tattoo is called ketovet kaaka, literally, 'writing of kaaka'. The last word is not found anywhere else in the Bible but clearly some kind of tattoo is meant. Since the verse speaks of 'writing', the Mishnah (*Makkot* 3: 6) states that the law only applies when words or letters are incised. Another opinion in the Mishnah is that the prohibition refers only to the tattooing of the name of a pagan god. Nevertheless, according to Rabbinic law, every form of tattooing is forbidden and very few Jews have tattoos of any description.

Tefillin The cube-shaped black leather boxes, containing four scriptural passages, attached to the head and arm and worn during the morning prayers. It is purely coincidental that the word *tefillin* so closely resembles the word for prayer, *tefilluh*, since, although eventually the *tefillin* were only worn for the morning prayer, in Talmudic times they were worn all day and had no special association with prayer.

In four Pentateuchal passages it is stated that certain words should be on the hand and between the eyes. Many commentators, including *Rashbam, hold that the plain meaning of these passages is that the words of the Torah should be constantly in mind, as in the verses: 'Set them as a seal upon thy heart, as a seal upon thine arm' (Song of Songs 8: 6) and 'Let not kindness and truth forsake thee; bind them about thy neck, write them on the table of thy heart' (Proverbs 3: 3). The *Karaites understood the passages in this figurative way and did not wear *tefillin*. But very early on Jews understood the passages in a literal sense and wore these four sections on the head and the arm, the words being those in the sections themselves. These are the *tefillin*, although, undoubtedly, they have developed over the years to assume the form they now have. The following is a brief description of what *tefillin* are now and how they are worn.

The *tefillin* consist of two cube-shaped leather boxes, one worn on the head, the other on the arm, with leather straps fixed to them for attaching them to the head and the arm. Into these boxes, known as *batim*, 'houses', the four passages, written by hand, are inserted. The hand *tefillin* (in the Rabbinic tradition the 'hand' here means the arm) contains all four sections written on a single strip of parchment. In the head *tefillin* there are four separate compartments, one for each of the four. The four sections are: 1. Exodus 13: 1–10; 2. Exodus 13: 11–16; 3. Deuteronomy 6: 4–9; 4. Deuteronomy 11: 12–21. Although the box (*bayit*, 'house', singular of *batim*) of the head *tefillin* has to be in the form of an exact square (in the part into which the sections are inserted; this part rests on a larger base), it is divided into four compartments for the insertion of the sections, care being taken that these should not be separated from one another in such a way as to interfere with the square shape. The box of the hand *tefillin* consists of a single compartment into which all four sections, written on a single strip, are inserted. The boxes have to be completely black as well as square-shaped. Black straps are inserted into each of the *batim*.

The procedure for putting on the *tefillin* is as follows. The hand *tefillin* is taken out of the bag in which the *tefillin* are reverentially kept, and placed on the upper part of the left arm, and the benediction recited: 'Blessed art Thou, O Lord our God, King of the universe, who hast hallowed us by Thy commandments, and hast commanded us to put on the *tefillin*.' The knot is then tightened and the strap wound seven times around the arm. The head *tefillin* is then taken out of the bag, placed loosely on the head, and the further benediction recited: 'Blessed art Thou, O Lord our God, King of the universe, who hast hallowed us by Thy commandments and hast given us command concerning the precept of *tefillin*.' The head *tefillin* are then tightened round the head so that the *bayit* rest in the middle of the head above the forehead and where the hair begins. The strap of the hand *tefillin* is then wound thrice around the middle finger while the verses (from Hosea 2: 21–2) are recited: 'And I will betroth thee unto me for ever; yea, I will betroth thee unto me in righteousness, and in judgement, and in loving-kindness, and in mercy: I will even betroth thee unto me in faithfulness: and thou shalt know the Lord.'

The Talmudic Rabbis wax eloquent on the value of *tefillin*. The Talmud (*Rosh Ha-Shanah* 17a) defines a 'sinner in Israel with his body' as 'a skull that does not wear *tefillin*'. Yet, even in the Geonic period, there was a certain laxity in the observance of *tefillin*. Some of the *Geonim, and they were followed by the *Tosafot (to the passage), observed that the Talmudic denunciation applies only to those who refuse to wear *tefillin* out of irreligious reasons, but if a man does not wear *tefillin* because he believes he has not attained to the purity of body and mind required for them to be worn, he is no sinner at all. It is known that Rabbi Moses of Coucy travelled through Spain and France in the year 1237 on a preaching mission in which he urged the Jews of these lands to wear *tefillin*, arguing that sinners require all the more this 'sign' of allegiance to the divine law. The result has been that Orthodox Jews, although they no longer wear *tefillin* all day, since they do not believe they have the degree of purity so to do, do wear them for prayer, and *tefillin* have become one of the indications of Orthodoxy. The majority of Reform Jews, however, do not wear *tefillin*, interpreting, as did the Karaites, the references to binding on the arm and head as purely figurative. Conservative Jews do wear *tefillin*, like the Orthodox.

Teitelbaum Family Hungarian family, the members of which served as town Rabbis as well as Hasidic masters. The founder of this Hasidic dynasty, Moses Teitelbaum (1750–1841), Rabbi of Ujhely and author of Halakhic *Responsa, although distant from *Hasidism at first, became a disciple of the Hasidic master known as the 'Seer' of Lublin. His work in the Hasidic vein, *Yismaḥ Moshe* ('Let Moses Rejoice') is acknowledged by all Hasidic groups as a classical work in the *genre*.

Moses Teitelbaum's grandson, Jekutiel Judah Teitelbaum (1808–83), was Rabbi of Sziget, also writing Responsa and a number of works in the Hasidic vein. He was succeeded in the Rabbinate of Sziget by his son Hananiah Yom Tov Lipa Teitelbaum (d. 1904). These two Rabbis were influential in setting the tone of fiery opposition in Hungary to anything that smacks of Reform, following the stand taken by Rabbi Moses *Sofer. Their zeal was inherited by Hananiah Yom Tov Lipa's son, Joel Teitel-baum (1888–1979), Rabbi of Sotmar. After Rabbi Joel's arrival in the USA, he established his 'court' in Williamsburg, New York, and became the Zaddik of virtually a new dynasty, his followers being known as the Sotmarer Hasidim.

Telz Yeshivah The world famous *Yeshivah that flourished in the town of Telz in Lithuania from 1875 to 1941. The first principal of the Yeshivah was the Rabbi of Telz, Eliezer Gordon, a disciple of Israel *Salanter, founder of the *Musar movement. Gordon's efforts to introduce Musar into the curriculum of the Yeshivah met with opposition on the part of the students. Eventually, a somewhat different and more philosophical form of Musar was introduced under Gordon's son-in-law, Joseph Laib Bloch (d. 1930). This variant was called Daat ('Knowledge') rather than Musar. In Bloch's published *Lectures on Knowledge* (*Sheurey Daat*) such philosophical issues are discussed as the old problem of how divine foreknowledge can be reconciled with human freedom of choice. After World War II, Joseph Laib's son, Elijah Meir Bloch, and his son-in-law, Hayyim Katz, re-established the Telz Yeshivah in Cleveland, Ohio, where it became one of the outstanding Yeshivot in the world. Bloch and Katz were succeeded in the principalship of the Yeshivah by the American-born Rabbi Mordecai Gifter, who had studied as a young man in Telz in Lithuania. A branch of the Yeshivah was established in Telstone, near Jerusalem.

Temple The great building on Mount Moriah in Jerusalem, the place in which sacrifices were offered to God by the people of Israel. The First Temple, built by King Solomon, as told in the first book of Kings, was destroyed by the armies of Nebuchadnezzar in 586 BCE. When the Babylonian exiles returned, the building of the Second Temple began around the year 515 BCE. This Second Temple was reconstructed by Herod from the year 20 BCE and stood until it was destroyed by the Romans in the year 70 CE.

According to the Mishnah tractate *Middot* ('Measures'), the Temple stood on an area 500 cubits square known as the Temple Mount (a cubit measures approximately 18 inches). Within the northern part of this square and bearing to the west there was a rectangle of 135 cubits on its east and west sides and 322 cubits on its north and south sides. The space in the main square of the Temple Mount that was outside the rectangle was known as the 'Court of the Gentiles' since Gentiles were allowed to enter this area. At the eastern end of the rectangle there was a square of 135 cubits known as the 'Court of the Women', divided from the Court of the Gentiles by the *Ḥel*, a rampart, which ran right round the whole large rectangle. There remained in the larger rectangle a smaller rectangle (187 cubits east to west and 135 cubits north to south) and this was known as the Temple Court, the *Azarah* ('courtyard'). The easternmost strip of the Temple Court, measuring 11 cubits east to west, was known as the Court of the Israelites. West of this was a strip of equal length

known as the Court of the Priests. Fifteen semicircular steps led into the middle, from the Court of the Women to the Court of the Israelites, and opposite these steps between the Court of the Israelites and the Court of the Priests there was a platform upon which the *Levites stood. To the west of the Court of the Priests stood, to the south, the altar with the ramp leading up to it. West of the Altar stood the *Hekhal*, the Sanctuary, the actual Temple building. Twelve steps led from the Inner Court, the *Azarah*, into the porch which led into the *Hekhal* proper. The Holy of Holies was situated at the western end of the *Hekhal*, hence the Rabbinic saying: 'The *Shekhinah was in the west.' Around the court there were chambers for special purposes, among them the Chamber of Hewn Stones, where the *Sanhedrin sat in judgement.

In addition to the mourning rites of the Ninth of *Av, Tisha Be-Av, the anniversary of the destruction of the Temple, other practices were introduced in remembrance of the destruction. Although not widely observed, there is the rule that a portion of the house near the door should be left undecorated. One of the reasons for the breaking of a glass by the bridegroom under the *ḥuppah is that it is a reminder of the destruction of the Temple. A few pious bridegrooms still follow the Talmudic rule that a groom should have ashes on his head during the marriage ceremony. They do this by placing a little cigarette ash in tissue paper which they wear under the hat. Pious Jews, too, still follow the Talmudic rule of rending the garments when first seeing the site of the Temple, although only a token tear of a garment is made.

Throughout the ages the hope was kept alive that with the advent of the *Messiah the ancient glories would be restored through the building of the Third Temple that would never be destroyed. This hope was expressed in hymns and prayers.

Given the conditions that existed in the Middle Ages, it is hardly surprising that no attempt to rebuild the Temple in anticipation of the Messianic age was ever thought of. Now that such a project has become feasible with the establishment of the State of Israel, only a tiny fringe group has tried to plan the rebuilding of the Temple. The vast majority of the Orthodox find insuperable Halakhic obstacles to such a plan. The site of the sacred places is not known with anything like certainty, for example, and the status of people who claim to be Kohanim ('priests') is in doubt, so that a prophet is awaited who will show what has to be done. The whole matter is left to the Messiah. An ancient tradition, recorded by *Rashi, has it that the Third Temple will not be built at all by human hands but will drop ready-formed from heaven. This has not prevented some of the Orthodox from making a diligent study of the laws of the Temple and the sacrificial system in order to be prepared when the hoped-for event takes place. Reform Judaism has long reinterpreted the Messianic hope in terms of a Messianic age of universal peace and does not believe that one day the Third Temple will be built. Conservative Judaism is similarly very uneasy abut the belief in the restoration of the Temple. However, Conservative Jews, unlike the Reformers, still retain the references to the sacrifices in the Prayer Book but change the words so as to read 'and there our fathers offered the sacrifices' instead of 'and there we will offer the sacrifices'.

Ten Days of Penitence The ten days from *Rosh Ha-Shanah to *Yom Kippur during which repentance is especially acceptable to God. The Rabbis comment on the verse: 'Seek the Lord while He can be found' (Isaiah 55: 6) that these ten days are the time referred to by the prophet, the special period in which God can be found. In an oft-quoted passage in the Babylonian Talmud (*Rosh Ha-Shanah* 16b) a saying of the third-century Palestinian teacher, Rabbi Johanan, is quoted. Three books are open on Rosh Ha-Shanah, the beginning of the new year and the day of judgement. One is the book of the righteous, another the book of the wicked, and the third the book of the average persons, those who are neither completely righteous nor completely wicked. The righteous are recorded at once in the book of life, the wicked in the book of death. The fate of the average is left in abeyance during the days until Yom Kippur (the actual expression 'The Ten Days of Penitence' is found in the parallel passage in the Jerusalem Talmud). If they repent of their misdeeds they are written and sealed in the book of the righteous, otherwise they are written and sealed in the book of the wicked.

Rabbi Johanan's homily is far removed, of course, from anything like a precise theological statement. Wicked people do live on during the coming year and righteous people die during the year. But the Jewish theologians treat the saying as factual, explaining it on such grounds as that when the wicked live on it is because they have significant good deeds to their credit and the righteous die because they have some evil deeds which require expiation. As a result of the discussion and the insertion of prayers in the liturgy to be recorded in the book of life, it was all taken very seriously as demanding a special effort to repent during these ten days. Jews otherwise not particularly observant of the precepts try to mend their ways and be more scrupulous in these days in their religious and ethical conduct. Many modern Jews understand the whole matter more as a reminder to do better in the year ahead rather than as an attempt to persuade an undecided God to decide in their favour.

Ten Martyrs The ten teachers, among them Rabbi *Akiba, Rabbi *Ishmael, and Rabban Simeon ben *Gamaliel, who suffered a *martyr's death at the hands of the Romans. The story of the ten martyrs is told in a late Midrash and poetic versions of it are part of the *liturgy for the Ninth of *Av, Tisha Be-Av, and *Yom Kippur. According to this legend, the Roman emperor wished to put to death ten of the foremost scholars in expiation of the sin of Joseph's brethren who had sold him (Genesis 37) since the Torah states: 'He that stealeth a man and selleth him . . . shall be put to death' (Exodus 21: 16). These ten were selected to atone for the sin of their ancestors. Rabbi Ishmael purified himself and ascended on high, where he was informed that the decree of death had indeed been pronounced, and the ten submitted to their fate. Scholars have found the whole legend puzzling on a number of counts. While there are references in the Talmud to Rabbi Akiba and one or two of the others suffering a martyr's death, they could not all have been executed, as in the legend, on the same day, since they did not all live at the same time. And it is certainly contrary to Jewish theological thought that innocent men should die for a sin committed by their forebears, to say nothing of the fact that it is the emperor who is determined to obey the laws of the Torah.

Terefah Food which it is forbidden for the Jew to eat, so termed after the verse: 'And ye shall not eat any flesh that is torn [terefah] of beasts in the field; ye shall cast it to the dogs' (Exodus 27: 30). The Rabbis understand terefah as applying to any animal or fowl with a serious defect in one of its vital organs. Although the term was originally used in this sense only, it came to be used for anything forbidden by the

*dietary laws, the opposite, in fact, of the term *kosher. The term is often shortened to treif.

Tetragrammaton The four-letter name of God formed from the letters yod, hey, vav, and hey, hence YHVH in the usual English rendering. The older form JHVH is based on the rendering of yod as jod. This name is usually translated in English as 'the Lord', following the Greek translation as kyrios. All this goes back to the Jewish practice of never pronouncing the name as it is written but as Adonai, 'the Lord'. In printed texts the vowels of this word are placed under the letters of the Tetragrammaton. (Hence the name was read erroneously by Christians as 'Jehovah', a name completely unknown in the Jewish tradition.) The original pronunciation of the Tetragrammaton has been lost, owing to the strong Jewish disapproval of pronouncing the name. The pronunciation Yahveh or Yahweh is based on that used by some of the Church Fathers but there is no certainty at all in this matter. Most biblical scholars, nowadays, prefer to render it simply as YHWH or JHVH without the vowels. This name occurs 6,823 times in the present text of the Hebrew Bible.

What does the name mean? In Exodus 3: 14–15 the name is associated with the idea of 'being', and hence some have understood the original meaning to be 'He-Who-Is', or 'He who brings being into being'. Generally, as Cassuto and others have noted, the name Elohim ('God', see NAMES OF GOD) is used in the Bible of God in His universalistic aspect, the God of the whole universe, while the Tetragrammaton is used of God in His special relationship with the people of Israel.

Generally in the Rabbinic literature, the Tetragrammaton is interpreted as referring to God in His attribute of mercy and Elohim to God in His attribute of judgement. Thus a Midrash explains why the Tetragrammaton is used together with Elohim in the second chapter of Genesis while Elohim on its own is used in the first chapter, on the grounds that God created the world with His attribute of strict justice but added the attribute of mercy so that the world could endure. Similarly, the verse: 'God [Elohim] is gone up amidst shouting, The Lord [the Tetragrammaton] amidst the sound of the horn' (Psalms 47: 6) is interpreted to mean that when the *shofar is sounded on *Rosh Ha-Shanah God rises from His throne of judgement to sit on His throne of mercy.

Tevet, Fast of One of the public *fast days, falling on the tenth day of the month of Tevet. This fast is in commemoration of the day on which the siege of Jerusalem by the armies of Nebuchadnezzar began (1 Kings 25: 1), an event which led to the destruction of the *Temple in 586 BCE. Like the other minor fasts, this one lasts only from dawn to dusk and does not begin on the previous night like Tisha Be-av (see AV, NINTH OF) and *Yom Kippur.

Thanksgiving In Temple times, in order to express his gratitude to God for having dealt bountifully with him, a man would bring a thanksgiving offering (todah), the details of which are found in the book of Leviticus (7: 12–15). To this day, 'Thank you' in modern Hebrew is 'Todah' and 'Many thanks', 'Todah Rabbah'. It is a general principle in Judaism that gratitude is to be shown not alone to God but to human beings who have been gracious and bountiful, and ingratitude is held to be a serious defect. From Talmudic times onwards a special benediction of thanksgiving was introduced based on Psalm 107. In this Psalm deliverances from severe danger to life are mentioned: 1. travellers who reach their destination after a hazardous journey (vv. 4–9.); 2. prisoners who regain their free-dom (vv. 10–16); 3. sick persons who have been restored to health (vv. 17–22); 4. sailors who reach land in safety (vv. 23–32). After each of these the Psalmist concludes: 'Let them give thanks unto the Lord for His goodness, and for His wonderful works to the children of men.' Thus in the Talmud (Berakhot 54b) it is stated: 'Four types of person must offer thanksgiving: those who go down to the sea, who journey in the desert, the invalid who recovers and the prisoner who has been set free.' The Talmud supplies the details of this *benediction, and further details and later *customs are supplied in the *Shulḥan Arukh (Oraḥ Ḥayyim, 219). The general tendency is not to restrict the benediction to the instances recorded in the Talmud but to extend it to all cases of deliverance from danger, after an escape from a bombing or a mugging, for example. Nowadays, when air travel is much safer than it used to be, there is some doubt whether the benediction should be recited after a safe return from travel in a plane. The benediction is not recited after a journey in a car or a train unless there has been a serious accident.

Theft According to the Talmudic Rabbis, the eighth commandment (see DECALOGUE): 'Thou shalt not steal' (Exodus 20: 15) refers to kidnapping, a capital offence (like that of murder in the sixth commandment), though it is sometimes made to include other types of theft. The prohibition of theft in general, that is, theft of property, is derived from the verse: 'Ye shall not steal' (Leviticus 19: 11). In the book of Exodus two different penalties are recorded for theft. In one verse (Exodus 21: 37) it is stated that if a man steals an ox or a sheep, and then kills it or sells it, he is obliged to pay (to the victim) five oxen for an ox and four sheep for a sheep. But in another verse (Exodus 22: 3) the penalty is stated that the thief must pay double (i.e. only twice as much) to the victim. These verses are understood to mean that one who steals any object has to pay double to the victim, whereas in the case of the ox or the sheep he is obliged to pay four or five times over, but only if, after he has stolen it, he either kills the animal or sells it. This law applies only to the theft of an ox or a sheep, not of any other animal. A distinction is also drawn between a thief, who steals by stealth, and a robber, who takes something directly from his victim despite the victim's protest. The laws of paying double or four or five times over only apply to the thief. The robber has simply to make restitution by either giving back that which he has stolen, if the object is still in his hands, or compensating the victim to the value of the stolen object. The payment of double or four or five times over is held to be in the nature of a fine, and admission to an offence involving a fine exonerates the perpetrator from payment of that fine. Thus if the thief admits to the court, before he has been charged, that he is guilty he pays only the object he has stolen or its value.

The Talmud (*Bava Kama* 79b) offers this rationale for the distinction between the thief and the robber. At first glance, the thief's offence is less than that of the robber and yet the thief has to pay double and the robber only has to compensate his victim to the value of that which he has stolen. But the thief, unlike the robber, hides from people when he steals and yet disregards the fact that God sees him, whereas the robber has regard neither for God nor man and simply does not care who sees him. The illustration is given of two people in a town who make a banquet. One invites the townspeople but fails to invite the members of the royal family while the other invites neither the townspeople nor the royal family. The former commits a greater offence in that he offers a slight to the royal family.

In the same passage a rationale is given for why there is a payment of five oxen for an ox and only four sheep for a sheep. Two reasons are given. The first is that in the case of the ox the thief has deprived the owner of the labour of his ox, whereas a sheep does not work for its owner. The second reason is that one who steals an ox simply leads it away, whereas the thief has to suffer the indignity of carrying the sheep away on his shoulder. The first reason offers a homily on the value of productive labour, the second a homily on human dignity.

Theology Theology, as defined by Richard Hooker, the Renaissance theologian, is 'the science of things divine'. Theology (from the Greek *theos*, 'God', and *logos*, 'word', 'doctrine') involves the systematic treatment of what belief in God entails and Jewish theology can therefore be defined as an attempt to think through consistently the implications of the Jewish religion as the way to God.

The kind of questions the theologian asks and seeks to answer are chiefly concerned, by definition, with *God. The Jewish theologian deals with questions such as: what is the Jewish concept of God? Is there a Jewish concept of God? What does Judaism teach about the nature of God? Does God reveal Himself to mankind and if so how? How is God to be worshipped? But as soon as questions of this nature are raised the element of absurdity in the whole theological enterprise becomes overwhelming. The best religious thinkers have been unanimous in declaring that God is unknowable.

Judging by the experience of the most subtle of religious thinkers, the more one reflects on the tremendous theme the more one is inclined to reject all faltering human attempts to grasp the divine. The question has consequently been put with regard to both general and Jewish theology, does all this not mean that the whole exercise is futile? The theologian replies that he follows respectable antecedents when he draws a distinction between God as He is in Himself, which indeed cannot be discussed at all, and God in manifestation, that is, in relationship with mankind. The latter can be discussed unless theistic faith is itself ruled out of court.

It has been argued that the whole notion of a Jewish theology is a contradiction in terms and that there is no warrant for theology in the Jewish tradition. This position has been advanced on two grounds. The first of these is that Jewish thinking in its classical and formative periods—those of the Bible and the Rabbinic literature—was 'organic' rather than systematic, a response to particular concrete situations rather than a comprehensive account of what religious belief entails (see SYSTEMATIC THINKING). Secondly, the emphasis in Judaism is on the *Halakhah, on action, on doing the will of God, not on defining it.

While there is some truth in both these contentions, it is far from the whole truth. A concern with systematic thinking about Judaism did not emerge until Greek modes had made their impact on the Jewish teachers. Once this happened, however, sustained reflection on the nature of the Jewish faith was seen as an imperative, at least in those circles which experienced the full force of the collision.

Unless *Philo of Alexandria, *Saadiah, *Bahya Ibn Pakudah, *Maimonides, *Gersonides, *Crescas, and *Albo among the ancient and medieval thinkers; *Cordovero, Isaac *Luria, *Shneur Zalman of Liady among the Kabbalists; and, in modern times, Moses *Mendelssohn, *Krochmal, *Schechter, *Kook, *Rosenzweig, and *Baeck are to be read out of Judaism, theology is a legitimate pursuit for Jews.

Therapeutae The order of contemplatives who settled in the first century CE on the shores of a lake called Mareotis near Alexandria in Egypt and were described by *Philo in his *On the Contemplative Life*. Philo understands the name Therapeutae either as 'Healers' (of the soul) or as 'Worshippers'. Philo's is the only contemporary account of this group. Although some scholars have questioned the ascription of the work to Philo and have argued that it was fathered on him by a Christian writer who wished to describe Christian monasticism as existing in that early period, the scholarly consensus is not only that the account is Philo's own but that there really existed such a Jewish sect since Philo, who lived in Alexandria, would hardly have invented the circumstantial details he supplies, although it is probable that he does present an over-idealized picture in accordance with his own philosophical leanings.

Thirteen The number thirteen, far from being 'unlucky', features in the Jewish tradition as a highly significant number. There are thirteen attributes (Heb. *middot*, lit. 'measures') of divine mercy. These thirteen attributes are found by the Talmudic Rabbis (*Rosh Ha-Shanah* 17b) in the verses in the book of Exodus (34: 6–7) in which God assures Moses that He will pardon the people for worshipping the *golden calf. In the Talmudic passage it is said that whenever Jews are in trouble they should recite these verses and God will have mercy on them; following which these thirteen are recited from time to time during the *Yom Kippur services, on other *fast days, and as part of the *Selihot prayers. They are also recited as part of the special prayer offered when the *Ark is opened on the *festival before the *reading of the Torah.

The number thirteen also features in the thirteen principles (also called *middot* in Hebrew) by means of which the Torah is expounded. These principles of *hermeneutics, attributed to Rabbi *Ishmael, are now incorporated into the daily liturgy and have become part of the mental furniture of ordinary Jews, far removed from any real understanding of these intricate rules.

Still another famous instance of the number thirteen occurs in the thirteen *principles of faith laid down by Maimonides. There has been much discussion around the question of why Maimonides should have laid down thirteen principles in particular, but he may have chosen this number on the analogy of the other two thirteens.

Three Weeks The weeks of mourning between 17 *Tammuz and the Ninth of *Av. These three weeks correspond to the three-week siege of Jerusalem before it was destroyed. During this period marriages are not celebrated and observant Jews do not listen to music or have their hair cut. There is a curious custom according to which this period is particularly open to risk of harm so that schoolteachers must not beat their charges even when they are unruly. *Corporal punishment in Jewish schools is in any event rare nowadays. With the establishment of the State of Israel even many Orthodox Jews favour a degree of relaxation of the laws of mourning over the destruction of the *Temple, but no marriages are celebrated during the three weeks in Orthodox synagogues.

Throne of God The great throne upon which God is seated, seen by the prophet Isaiah: 'I saw the Lord seated on a high and lofty throne' (Isaiah 6: 1). In the vision of the prophet *Ezekiel, who, unlike Isaiah, lived outside the Holy Land, the throne is carried to him on a chariot (Ezekiel 1). Ezekiel's vision is the subject of contemplation by the mystics described as Riders of the *Chariot. The book of Kings (1 Kings 22: 19) tells of the vision of the prophet Micaiah (not to be confused with the

prophet *Micah) who spoke of God seated upon His throne, with all the host of heaven standing in attendance to the right and left of Him. A particularly anthropomorphic description of the throne is found in the late book of *Daniel (Daniel 7: 9): 'Thrones were set in place, and the Ancient of Days took His seat, His garment was like white snow, and the hair of His head was like clean wool. His throne was tongues of flame; its wheels were blazing fire.' Against these visions, in which God is located on a special throne, the prophet of exile declares: 'Thus saith the Lord, The heaven is My throne, and the earth My footstool' (Isaiah 66: 1). The Talmudic Rabbis often speak of God leaving His throne of judgement to sit on His throne of mercy, when, for example, the *shofar is sounded on *Rosh Ha-Shanah.

In all the biblical instances the throne is seen in a vision so that, with the exception of the thirteenth-century German Talmudist, Moses of Tachau, the medieval thinkers interpret the throne as a metaphor. Moses of Tachau really believes that God is seated on a throne on high surrounded by the heavenly hosts, or, rather, that God occasionally assumes this form. *Saadiah Gaon (Beliefs and Opinions, ii. 10) holds that the throne was created by God out of fire for the purpose of assuring His prophet that it was He and no other that had revealed His word to him. For Maimonides (Guide of the Perplexed, 1. 9) the throne is a metaphor for God's greatness and sublimity.

Time and eternity Maimonides' fourth *principle of faith, that God is eternal, having neither beginning nor end, is no more than a restatement of that which is axiomatic in every version of Judaism.

The word most frequently used in the Bible to denote eternity is olam (possibly from a root meaning 'to be concealed'). This word is used in some biblical contexts to denote simply an extremely long duration of time, particularly ancient time, that is, the days of old. But when used of God, the word (usually translated as 'for ever') does refer to God's eternity, though such an abstract term as 'eternity' is foreign to the concrete nature of biblical language and thought-pattern.

The Talmudic Rabbis has quite literally a down-to-earth attitude in this matter. God is eternal but it is not given to man to explore the full meaning of this idea. Aimed at contemporary attempts to pierce the veil is the famous statement in the Mishnah (Ḥagigah 2: 1): 'Whoever reflects on four things it were better for him that he had not come into the world: What is above? What is beneath? What is before? And what is after?' No doubt there are echoes here of Gnostic ideas about *creation and it is even possible that 'before' and 'after' do not refer to time at all but to space, that is, what is in one direction beyond the earth and what in another direction. One cannot therefore expect to find in the Rabbinic literature anything like a detailed examination of what is involved in the doctrine of divine eternity. The medieval thinkers, on the other hand, were much concerned with philosophical questions regarding time and eternity and their relationship to God.

Maimonides (*Guide*, 2. 13) believes that time itself is created, so that expressions such as that God *was before* He created the world (suggesting a time-span 'before' time was created) are to be understood as a supposition regarding time or an imagining of time and are not to be understood as referring to the true reality of time. However, Maimonides (*Guide*, 2. 27–9) also argues for the indestructibility of the universe, which implies endless duration in time. Maimonides' view would seem, therefore to be that 'once' time has been created it endures for ever. Ideas such as these go back to Plato's *Timaeus*, in

which time is distinguished from what is in time, though the difficulty has often been noted in the idea of time as a kind of box into which is placed that which is in time. *Albo (*Ikkarim*, ii. 18–19) observes that the concepts of priority and perpetuity can only be applied to God in a negative sense. When, in speaking of God, terms are used such as 'before' or 'after' some period, this means no more than that He was not non-existent before or after that period but, in reality, terms life 'before' or 'after', indicating a time-span, cannot be applied to the Eternal One. Albo, following Maimonides, makes a distinction between two kinds of time. The first is measured time, which depends on motion and to which the terms prior and posterior can be applied. The second is not measured or numbered but is a duration existing prior to the 'sphere' (in the medieval view the entity into which the planets are fixed). This time in the abstract is possibly eternal. Consequently, the difficulty of whether or not time originates in time is avoided. The second kind of time has no origin. It is only the 'order of time', the first kind, that originates in time in the other sense. It is, indeed, difficult, if not impossible, to conceive of a 'duration' before the creation of the world, but, says Albo, it is similarly difficult to think of God as 'outside' space. This is why, Albo concludes, the Rabbis of the Mishnah (mentioned above) declare that one must not ask what is above, what is below, what is before, and what is behind. (Albo obviously understands these terms as applying to space and time.)

In all this the medieval thinkers are grappling with the insurmountable problem of the relationship between the eternity of God and time as humans perceive it. The Jewish mystics draw in this connection on the Neoplatonic idea of the 'Eternal Now', though they do not attribute this idea to non-Jewish sources.

Present-day philosophical discussion

of eternity as timelessness are concerned with the question of whether this notion can be 'cashed' (as linguistic philosophers would put it): does the notion have any meaning? Yet the Jewish discussions still try to say something on the subject. The twentieth-century *Musar teacher, Rabbi E. E. *Dessler, reflects on the idea of spiritual progress in the Hereafter since the *World to Come is beyond time and progress implies a time-sequence. His solution is that the soul is endowed with the capacity to experience time when it has left the material world behind. This capacity, as well as that of comprehension, both of which prevent the soul from becoming absorbed in the divine (see UNIO MYSTICA) and hence incapable of spiritual progress, belong to the 'bodily element' of the soul, the *guf* ('body') which the soul inhabits even in eternal life.

The problem of time is one of the great mysteries. The mind reels at the thought of time flowing endlessly along. The notion of eternity has been understood by many religious thinkers as conveying the thought of existence beyond or outside time. An illustration sometimes given is of fictitious two-dimensional creatures who may be able with difficulty to imagine a third dimension but who would be obliged to think of it in terms of the two dimensions they know and would be incapable of grasping the nature of the third dimension. In whatever way time is thought of, the only recourse is to fall back on the insoluble. Even if time is thought of as duration alone, the human mind is presented with the alternatives of either postulating that time will eventually come to an end or that it will last for ever. As Kant has noted, whenever we think of time as coming to an end we find ourselves asking: and what will happen *then*? Endless duration in time is similarly quite beyond our imagination. The attitude of religious Jews to the whole question of time and eternity is that to try to gain knowledge in this area is as futile as to try to grasp the nature of God. Jews generally prefer to speak of God as the 'Timeless' or 'Eternal' and leave it at that.

Tisha be-av See AV, NINTH OF.

Tithing The main biblical passages regarding the tithing of produce are: Numbers 18: 21–32 and Deuteronomy 14: 22–7 and 26: 12. Biblical scholars (see BIBLICAL CRITICISM) have seen the differences in these sources concerning the recipients of the tithe as due to the social background of two separate sources, each having its own applications. Throughout the Rabbinic literature, however, the sources are harmonized and the following system emerges. The tithes have to be given from corn, wine, and oil by biblical law and from fruit and vegetables by Rabbinic law. The farmer first separates from the yield a portion (a sixtieth, fiftieth, or fortieth at the farmer's discretion), known as *terumah* ('heave offering' or 'gift'). This is given to a *Kohen (*priest) and is treated as sacred food in that it must not be eaten when the priest is in a state of ritual contamination or when the *terumah* itself has suffered contamination. Nor may it be eaten by a non-Kohen. A tenth of the remainder of the yield, known as *maaser rishon*, 'the first tithe', is then separated and given to a *Levite. The Levite, in turn, separates a tenth of his tithe and this, known as *terumat maaser*, is given to a Kohen to be treated with the same degree of sanctity as the original *terumah*. The portion given to the Levite has no sanctity and may be eaten by an ordinary Israelite. The farmer separates a tenth of the reminder of his yield, known as *maaser sheni*, 'the second tithe'. This has to be taken to Jerusalem and consumed there in a spirit of sanctity. However, every third and sixth year of the cycle culminating in the *Sabbatical year, the second tithe is given to the poor and is known as maaser ani, 'poor man's tithe'. After the destruction of the *Temple, maaser sheni was redeemed for a small amount and this tithe could then be consumed by the farmer wherever he happened to live. Produce from which the tithes had not been separated was strictly forbidden but once the tithes had been separated their actual distribution could be postponed. The farmer could please himself as to which Kohen or Levite he gave his tithes. Not everyone was scrupulous in separating the tithes. A whole tractate of the Mishnah, tractate Demai ('Doubtful Produce') is devoted to the need for tithing the produce bought from an *am ha-aretz suspected of laxity in the matter.

According to the Rabbis, the laws of tithing only apply to the land of Israel, and farmers in the *Diaspora have no obligation to give tithes, although there is some evidence of communities outside Israel, in Egypt for example, having a system of tithing. Again according to the Rabbis, the full tithing laws apply only when the majority of Jews live in the land of Israel and since, in the absence of the purification rites of the *red heifer, everyone today suffers from corpse-contamination, the terumah is inoperative in any event. Moreover the purpose of tithing, for the upkeep of the priests and Levites, has no meaning nowadays. The present practice in the State of Israel is to have only a token separation of the tithes.

Some Rabbinic sources make reference to a tithe of money as well as of produce, although it is not too clear whether this was seen as a voluntary contribution rather than an obligation. Nevertheless, many observant Jews today do donate a tenth of their annual income to *charity. This is known as maaser kesafim, 'the money tithe' or 'wealth tax'.

Titles In the Rabbinic tradition each of the more famous biblical characters is given a title suitable to his or her life's work. The *patriarchs are known as the 'fathers' and the *matriarchs as the 'mothers', for example: 'Abraham our father', 'Sarah our mother'. Moses (except for one reference in the Mishnah) is always called 'Moshe Rabbenu' ('Moses our Teacher'), although, obviously under the influence of Islam, medieval thinkers sometimes refer to Moses as 'the Prophet'. Joseph is usually called 'Joseph the Righteous' because he resisted the advances of the wife of Potiphar (Genesis 39). Miriam is known as 'Miriam the Prophetess' (Ha-Neviah), after Exodus 15: 20; David is 'David Ha-Melekh' (King David) and his descendant, the *Messiah, is 'Ha-Melekh Ha-Mashiah'. The *High Priest is naturally given this title to distinguish him from the ordinary *priests. The Vice-High Priest was called 'the Segan' ('Deputy'). The President of the *Sanhedrin is known as the Nasi ('Prince') and the Vice-President of this body as 'Av Bet Din' ('Father of the Court'). The head of the Jewish community in the land of Israel is also known as the Nasi, as in *Judah the Prince. The bearer of this office is also called 'the Parnas' (literally: 'the Sustainer', in the sense of the person responsible for the government of the community).

Tobacco When tobacco first began to be used in Europe there was considerable objection to it on the part of the Church. Rabbis, on the whole, saw no objection to tobacco per se, but its use has been widely discussed by Jewish teachers from various other aspects of the law.

One of the questions discussed was whether a benediction has to be recited over the use of tobacco. The Talmudic Rabbis coined *benedictions for eating and drinking in obedience to the principle that God should be praised and thanked for His gifts. The Rabbis had no knowledge of tobacco but once this new means of enjoyment became available the question of a benediction arose. It is now the universal practice not to require a benediction over tobacco.

In more recent years, when medical research has demonstrated that there is a causal relationship between smoking cigarettes and lung cancer (and heart disease), a number of Rabbis, especially Conservative Rabbis, have suggested that the *Halakhah now be invoked to forbid smoking as injurious to health. Undoubtedly, the Jewish tradition is emphatic that *health should be preserved but it is somewhat questionable whether the Halakhah can be invoked in this area. There is a risk as well as advantages in smoking, as there is in imbibing alcohol and in failing to have a sensible diet, and, indeed, in driving a motor car. Each individual should at his own discretion balance the risks against the advantages. To be sure most people will probably decide that the risk is not worth taking and this outweighs any advantages, but such decisions cannot be made a matter of Jewish law. Or, in any event, this seems to be the attitude of law-abiding Jews who do smoke.

Tolerance Religious tolerance is, in the main, a modern idea advanced by thinkers such as *Spinoza, John Locke, and John Stuart Mill, who broke consciously with tradition in this matter. Pre-modern Judaism, like pre-modern Christianity and Islam, held that there could be no toleration of religious viewpoints other than its own. Jews with a historical sense appreciate that certain ideas acceptable in a pluralistic society are simply not found in the classical sources but are none the worse for that.

The most striking fact which emerges from the biblical writings in the matter of tolerance is that the prophets of ancient Israel were totally uncompromising with apostasy and *idolatry among their own people but tolerant of the idolatry of their pagan neighbours who had no opportunity to know the God of Israel. The prophets do castigate the neighbouring peoples for the atrocities they commit in the furtherance of their cult—*Molech-worship is a case in point—but nowhere is there found in the Bible the idea that the worship of the pagan gods by the nations is to be condemned in itself. So far as the internal life of the people was concerned, the Hebrew prophets had to be ruthless if the long struggle against idolatry was to be successful. The cry of *Elijah (1 Kings 18: 21) was echoed by all the prophets: 'How long halt ye between two opinions? If the Lord be God, follow Him: but if Baal, follow him.' Similarly, while the Deuteronomist declares that the gods of the nations were 'allotted' to them by God Himself (Deuteronomy 4: 19), he is altogether ruthless when it comes to Israel worshipping strange gods. In the book of Deuteronomy (13: 13–19), the doom of the city that has gone astray to worship strange gods is pronounced in the most virulent terms: 'Thou shalt surely smite the inhabitants of that city with the edge of the sword, destroying it utterly, and all that is therein and the cattle thereof, with the edge of the sword.' It should none the less be noted that, as the Talmudic Rabbis remark, this passage is academic. There is no record of this kind of procedure ever having been carried out.

Among the Talmudic Rabbis, too, there appears the distinction between tolerance to those outside and those within. The Rabbis teach everywhere that converts to Judaism can only be accepted if they come of their own free will. But so far as Jews are concerned there are numerous instances in Rabbinic literature of coercion in matters of belief and practice; the *herem is only one example of religious coercion of Jews by Jews. According to Maimonides (*Edut*, 11. 10) the **epikoros* has to be destroyed (this, too, is academic, since Jews in Maimonides' day did not have any such powers) and has no share in the **World to Come. For all that, two outstanding twentieth-century Orthodox authorities declare that these ancient regulations are no longer operative. Rabbi A. I. **Kook argued that present-day unbelievers are quite different from the defiant *epikoros* of whom the Rabbis speak, while Rabbi Abraham Isaiah Karelitz (1878–1953), known as the 'Hazon Ish', declared that nowadays we must try so far as we can to bring them back to the truth by means of the cords of love and to help them see the light.

Tombstone Heb. *matzevah* (from a root meaning 'to stand', hence 'pillar'). When his wife died the patriarch Jacob marked her grave: 'And Jacob set up a pillar [*matzevah*] upon her grave; the same is the pillar of Rachel's grave unto this day' (Genesis 35: 20). Historically speaking, Jews in ancient times did have tombstones, as the archaeological evidence shows, but in the Jerusalem Talmud (*Shekalim* 2: 5) there is a saying that tombstones should not be erected over the graves of the righteous, since their deeds are their memorial. This saying has puzzled the commentators in view of the verse regarding Rachel. In any event, it is now the universal custom to erect a tombstone, especially under the influence of the Kabbalah in which great importance is attached to the custom. In Hasidic practice it is even the custom to erect a mausoleum over the grave of a **Zaddik, to which **pilgrimages are made. Among the **Sephardim the tombstone is placed horizontally on the grave but the **Ashkenazim have a vertical stone. In these matters all depends on local **custom, as does the time for the 'tombstone setting', as it is called. The usual practice in the State of Israel nowadays is to set the stone thirty days after the burial but in other communities it is

set either during the eleven months after the burial or after twelve months (see DEATH AND BURIAL).

Torah 'The Teaching'. In the **Pentateuch the word *torah* is used frequently to denote a particular law or ritual, for example, the *torah* of the burnt-offering (Leviticus 6: 2). But once the Pentateuch itself was seen as the revealed will of God in its entirety (see REVELATION) it became known as 'the Torah of Moses' or 'the Torah' without qualification, so that the Hebrew **Bible is divided into the three sections of Torah (= the Pentateuch), the Prophets, and the Hagiographa. All three came to be subsumed under the heading of the **Written Torah. In addition, the expositions and derivations from Scripture found in the Rabbinic literature were also thought of as revealed, that is, as given verbally in the first instance to Moses and then handed down from generation to generation, with provision for various additions and adaptations to new circumstances as they arose. This whole process is called by the Rabbis the **Oral Torah. Both these *torot* are thought of as one complete *torah* so that, in the tradition, the term Torah denotes: 1. the Pentateuch; 2. the whole of Jewish teaching as revealed by God in the Written and the Oral Torah; 3. the later applications and deeper understanding of these down to the present day, so that the Torah is synonymous with the Jewish religion.

This is the traditional view, in which the Torah is the same always. It is the will of God for the Jewish people and in a wider sense for all mankind (see NOAHIDE LAWS). The Jew is obliged to **study the Torah and to observe the **precepts, the *mitzvot* (see MITZVAH). This static view of Torah has been challenged in modern times and attempts have been made to interpret the doctrine 'The Torah is from Heaven', in the Rabbinic formulation, in a manner that takes into account the findings of historical research into the origins of Judaism (see BIBLICAL CRITICISM; CONSERVATIVE JUDAISM; FUNDAMENTALISM; HISTORY; and JÜDISCHE WISSENSCHAFT).

Throughout Jewish history the Torah has been hailed as Israel's supreme and most precious gift, given by God as His own special benefaction to His people. In the Midrash the Torah is said to have been created before the creation of the world, God using the Torah as the architect uses his blueprint. When God wished to give the Torah to Israel, the Midrash observes, the angels objected, wishing to retain the Torah for themselves. Moses managed to convince the angels that the Torah, containing as it does such teachings as 'Thou shalt not steal'; 'Thou shalt not commit adultery'; 'Thou shalt not kill', could only have meaning for creatures of flesh and blood who are sorely tempted by envy, lust, and hatred. In this vein, the Talmudic Rabbis declare that the Torah does not make too heavy demands on humans since 'The Torah was not given to the ministering angels'. In many a psalm the praises of the Torah are sung. The first Psalm praises the man who avoids the counsel of the wicked for whom the Torah is his delight. In Psalm 19 (v. 8) the Torah of the Lord is said to be perfect, renewing life. The whole of Psalm 119, the Pharisaic Psalm, as this has been called by Christian scholars, utilizes each letter of the alphabet eight times in praise of the Torah: 'Oh, how I love Thy Torah! All day long it is my study' (v. 97).

Yet for all the supreme significance of the Torah it is never an object of worship. God alone is to be worshipped, the Torah being the means of coming to God. The usual expression in Jewish piety is 'love of the Torah and the fear of Heaven'. The term 'fear', denoting worship, is never applied to the Torah. Some authorities even object to bowing to the Torah since this might suggest that the Torah is being worshipped. The custom, however, is to bow to the Torah just as one bows to a person one wishes to honour without the slightest suggestion that he is being worshipped.

It is axiomatic in Judaism that the Torah is immutable. God does not change His mind and no other religion can ever take the place of Judaism. On this all religious Jews are agreed. But the doctrine of the immutability of the Torah has also been taken to mean that its laws are binding for all eternity, although the view is to be found that in the Messianic age the precepts of the Torah will be abrogated as no longer essential to the new, perfected world that will emerge. Maimonides' ninth *principle of faith puts the matter in this way: 'The ninth principle of faith. The abrogation of the Torah. This implies that this Torah of Moses will not be abrogated and that no other Torah will come from before God. Nothing is to be added to it nor taken away from it, neither in the Written Torah nor in the Oral Torah, as it is said: "Thou shalt not add to it nor diminish from it" [Deuteronomy 13; 1].' Thus Maimonides, by quoting the Deuteronomic verse, adds to the doctrine that the Torah cannot be abrogated the idea that its laws can never be changed.

Among the many medieval discussions on this doctrine, the most comprehensive is that of *Albo in his *Sefer Ha-Ikkarim* (iii. 13–23). Albo begins by giving three reasons why it seems to many that there can be no change in the Torah. The first is that God who gave the Torah does not change and it should follow that the Torah which stems from God does not change. Secondly, the Torah was given to the whole people of Israel and, unlike an individual, a people does not change. Thirdly, since the Torah is truth it cannot suffer change, for truth is eternal. If it is true, for instance, that there is only One God it is inconceivable that there should come a time when this will no longer be true and there will be many gods. For all that, Albo believes that there is no a priori reason why a divine law should not change, since it is directed to recipients whose conditions in life are not always the same and who require, therefore, different rules of conduct for their different situations. A physician may prescribe a certain regimen for one period and a different one at a later stage of his patient's cure. It is not that the physician has changed his mind but that there are stages in the patient's restoration to health. Moreover there are examples in the Torah itself of a divine law being changed. Adam was only permitted vegetable food (Genesis 1: 29), Noah was permitted animal food (Genesis 9: 3). Abraham was given the additional precept of *circumcision and many new precepts were revealed to Moses. But from Moses onwards there have been no changes in the divine law. According to Maimonides, then, the Torah of Moses will never change and since, as Albo has demonstrated, a divine law can change, this must mean that the Torah of Moses is the sole exception to the rule.

After showing that changes in practice did take place after the time of Moses—*Ezra, for example, introduced the square Hebrew script in which the Torah is written in place of older cursive script—Albo concludes, contra Maimonides, that a law can be changed by a *prophet who orders this at the command of God, but the change will only be temporary so far as the last eight laws of the Decalogue are concerned. (The first two, that there is one God and that no other gods are to be worshipped, cannot be abrogated by a prophet even for a time.) As for other laws of the Torah, these can be changed even permanently provided that the change is made by a prophet speaking in God's name, just as Ezra arranged for the introduction of the square script.

From the whole medieval discussion of the doctrine, it emerges that the question of the Torah's immutability

has to do with the question of whether a law promulgated by God will ever be repealed and from Albo's further discussion it emerges that Maimonides' ninth principle stands only in connection with the claims of Christianity and Islam that a new religion has superseded the Jewish religion. That modern historical studies have demonstrated conclusively that the *Halakhah has developed over the ages in response to changed conditions does not therefore really pose a challenge to the doctrine of the immutability of the Torah. Many modern Jews, accepting that Judaism has developed historically, have found refuge in the distinction between the abrogation of the Torah as a whole and the element of change evident in the Halakhic system.

While it is true that some statements in the Rabbinic literature do suggest that, as in the passage quoted above, everything was given by God to Moses at Sinai so that there can be no change at all in the Halakhah, and while some Orthodox authorities have roundly declared that, in the famous saying of Rabbi Moses *Sofer, 'Anything new is forbidden by the Torah', it is extremely doubtful whether such views were really taken too seriously even in the pre-modern era. Yom Tov Lippmann Heller (1579–1654), in the introduction to his commentary to the Mishnah, gives a profound and original interpretation of the ancient Rabbinic saying that God showed to Moses all the interpretations of later generations of scholars. This should not be taken to mean, says Heller, that the ancient Rabbis believed that each generation received a complete Halakhic tradition from its predecessors. He writes:

'Although there existed a complete interpretation of the Torah and its commands there is no generation in which something new is not added and which is without its own legal problems. Do not contradict me by pointing to the Rabbinic saying that God showed

Moses the minutiae of the Torah and the minutiae of the Scribes and the innovations that would be introduced by the Scribes, for I say that this was not handed down by Moses to anyone else. A careful examination of the Rabbinic saying shows that they spoke of God "showing" Moses, not "teaching" or "handing down" . . . By using the word "showing" they meant that these teachings were revealed to Moses but not "given" to him, like a man who "shows" his friend an object but does not give it to him.'

Modern Jews, more aware than Heller could have been of development in the Halakhah, would no doubt word it differently but the basic principle is there in Heller. Internal changes in the Halakhah have taken place in the past and are taking place in the present and this is acknowledged by the Orthodox, although the Orthodox generally make a distinction between the Halakhah itself, which is unchanging, and the changing conditions to which the Halakhah addresses itself. The extent to which changes from within are allowed is the essential feature of the ongoing debate between Orthodoxy and Reform (and Conservative Judaism). Each of these movements understands the Torah in its own way. Yet all agree that the Torah, however conceived of in that movement, will never be abrogated by God. Except for purposes of reference, no Jew, no matter to which denomination he belongs, will speak of the Hebrew Bible as 'Old Testament' since he does not believe that there has been a 'New Testament'.

Tosafot 'Additions' to the Babylonian Talmud; the glosses, now printed together with the text in practically all editions, produced by the French and German scholars during the twelfth to the fourteenth centuries. The Tosafot activity, in which the Talmud was examined minutely and in such a manner as to further the debates and discus-sions found in that work, began among the members of the family and pupils of *Rashi. The Tosafists flourished in northern France, England, and Germany, the two best-known of the three hundred or so practitioners being Rashi's grandson, Rabbenu *Tam, and the latter's nephew, Isaac of Dampierre. There are various collections of Tosafot, the printers of the Talmud selecting from those they had to hand in order to incorporate these into the published work. There is also a collection of Tosafot to the Pentateuch, known as *Daat Zekenim (Opinion of The Elders)* but this work is far less influential than the glosses to the Talmud.

Tosefta 'Addition' to the Mishnah. The Tosefta contains the rulings, sayings, and debates of the *Tannaim and is arranged on the same pattern as the Mishnah in six orders and with the same tractates within the orders. The name Tosefta would seem to suggest that the work is a supplement to the Mishnah but the problem of the relationship between the two works is far more complicated in that the Tosefta contains material not found in the Mishnah at all and it gives throughout the impression that it is a separate work standing on its own. The problem is further complicated by the fact that while the Babylonian Talmud frequently quotes Baraitot (Tannaitic teachings not found in the Mishnah) from the Tosefta it only has one reference to a Tosefta and it is by no means certain that this is to our present Tosefta, which, scholars have suggested, is a post-Tannaitic compilation, although it undoubtedly is of Tannaitic origin. Passages found in our Tosefta are often quoted in the Talmud in a paraphrased form for the purpose of the Talmudic discussion. The Tosefta is printed in sections in many editions of the Babylonian Talmud at the back of each tractate. M. S. Zuckermandel published what is now the standard edition of the Tosefta (Pasewalk, 1880). Saul Lieberman has published an edition comprising three orders of the Tosefta, *Zeraim, Moed,* and *Nashim* (New York, 1955–73). The study of the Tosefta was engaged in far less than that of the Mishnah and the Talmud, receiving only very few commentaries. But modern scholars have utilized the Tosefta to shed much light on the whole Talmudic period.

Tower of Babel The great tower built by 'the children of men', with its top reaching to the heavens, as told in Genesis 11: 1–9. God was displeased with the attempt to build the tower, as a result of which He confounded human language so that each nation would have its own language, unintelligible to the others, and He 'scattered them abroad upon the face of all the earth'. The generation which built the tower is called in the Rabbinic literature 'the Generation of the Dispersion'.

Trees, New Year for The minor festival that falls on 15 Shevat, known as Tu Bi-Shevat (from the letters *tet* (9) and *vav* (6) = 15). In the Mishnah (*Rosh Ha-Shanah* 1: 1), 15 Shevat is said to be, according to the House of *Hillel, the New Year for Trees. This means that the tithes for fruit of the tree had to be given from each year's growth separately and it was consequently necessary to determine when the new year begins for this purpose. Most of the rains had fallen before this date so that fruit that blossomed after the date belonged to the next year for tithing purposes. In the Mishnah the New Year for Trees is not a festival at all, but it became a minor festival chiefly under the influence of the mystics of Safed in the sixteenth century. In the State of Israel, especially in the kibbutzim, Tu Bi-Shevat is celebrated as an agricultural festival. Generally, nowadays, the festival is taken as an opportunity for encouraging children to give thanks to God for the growth of trees and flowers.

Tribes, Lost Ten The tribes of Reuben, Simeon, Dan, Naphtali, Gad, Asher, Issachar, Zebulan, Ephraim, and the half-tribe of Manasseh, who belonged to the Northern Kingdom in ancient Israel and who were exiled when the Northern Kingdom fell to the Assyrians in 722 BCE, as told in the book of Kings (2 Kings 17, 18). Many legends circulated according to which the lost ten tribes established a new kingdom, across the mysterious River Sambation in some versions, and one day they will be returned. Travellers' tales in the Middle Ages told of people who had managed to reach the lost tribes, returning with reports of their military prowess.

Truth Generally speaking, while Judaism obviously attaches great significance to intellectual honesty, as evidenced, for example, in the constant quest for the truth in the Talmudic debates and among the medieval philosophers, the main thrust in the appeals for Jews to be truthful is in the direction of moral truth and integrity. An oft-quoted Rabbinic saying (*Shabbat* 55a) is: 'Truth is the seal of the Holy One, blessed be He.' In *Rashi's explanation this saying refers to the Hebrew word for truth, *emet*, formed from the first letter of the *alphabet, *alef*, the middle letter, *mem*, and the final letter, *tav*. The God of truth is found wherever there is truth and His absence felt where there is falsehood. The prophet similarly declares: 'The Lord God is truth' (Jeremiah 10: 10) and the Psalmist declares: 'Thy Torah is truth' (Psalms 119: 142). Of the verse in Psalms: 'And speaketh the truth in his heart' (Psalms 15: 2) one explanation by the Jewish moralists is that the God-fearing man should keep his promise even if he only made it in his heart, even if it was no more than a promise he had kept to himself without revealing it to the one to whom he made it.

Yet, for all the high value it attaches to truthfulness, the Jewish tradition is sufficiently realistic to acknowledge that there are occasions when the telling of a 'white lie' can be in order; for instance, where the intention is to promote peace and harmony (*Yevamot* 85b) The Talmud (*Bava Metzia* 23b–24a) observes that a scholar will never tell a lie except in the three instances of 'tractate', *purya*, and 'hospitality'. The commentators explain 'tractate' to mean that a modest scholar is allowed to declare that he is unfamiliar with a tractate of the Mishnah in order not to parade his learning. Rashi translates *purya* as 'bed' and understands it to mean that if a scholar is asked intimate questions regarding his marital life he need not answer truthfully. The *Tosafot find it hard to believe that such questions would be addressed to the scholar or to anyone else and they understand *purya* to be connected with the festival of *Purim*. If the scholar is asked whether he was drunk on Purim he is allowed to tell a lie about it. 'Hospitality' is understood to mean that a man who has been treated generously by his host may decide not to tell the truth about his reception if he fears that as a result the host will be embarrassed by unwelcome guests.

Tzitzit The fringes the Israelites were commanded to put in the corners of their garments: 'Speak unto the children of Israel, and bid them that they make throughout their generations fringes [*tzitzit*] in the corners of their garments' (Numbers 15: 38). The tzitzit are now placed in the special *tallit worn during prayer. The insertion of the tzitzit in the tallit is as follows. Four threads, one longer than the other three, are inserted in a hole at the corner of the tallit and then doubled over to form seven threads of equal length and one longer one at the right-hand side. The threads of the two sides are tied in a double knot. The longer thread is then wound around the others seven times and a further double knot is made. The longer thread is then wound around eight times and another double knot is made. A third winding is then made eleven times and a double knot is made, and then there is a winding of thirteen and the last of the double knots is made. It is desirable that after the windings and the knots have been made, all eight threads are of equal length. (The manufacturers of the tzitzit make the longer thread of a length sufficient for this to be done.)

The symbolism of all this has been variously interpreted. Thus, on one view, the Hebrew word *tzitzit* has the numerical value (see GEMATRIA) of 600 (*tzaddi* = 90; *yod* = 10; *tzaddi* = 90; *yod* = 10; *tav* = 400; = 600 in total). When the eight threads and the five knots are added there is a total of 613, corresponding to the 613 *precepts of the Torah. In another version, the eight threads correspond to the eight days that elapsed from the Israelites leaving Egypt until they sang the song of deliverance at the sea (Exodus 15). The five knots correspond to the five books of Moses (the *Pentateuch). The numerical value of the Hebrew for 'the Lord is One' in the *Shema is 39 and this is represented by the total of the windings (7 + 8 + 11 + 13 = 39). Since the tzitzit are on all four corners of the tallit they act as a reminder to Jews to acknowledge God and His Torah at every turn.

U

Unio Mystica The union of the mystic's soul with God. In many religious traditions the ultimate aim of man is for his soul to be absorbed in the transcendent—in theistic religious traditions, in God—and not only in the Hereafter but in this life as well, in rare moments of religious *ecstasy. The actual term *unio mystica* is not found in Jewish *mysticism, such abstract expressions being foreign to Jewish thought in general. The question, therefore, is rather whether the phenomenon itself is found there under different headings. It has been suggested that, while the Jewish mystics do speak of communion with God, they draw back from any idea that there can be a complete union of the *soul with God, in view of the strongest Jewish emphasis on the utter transcendence of the Deity.

The nearest thing to the *union mystica* in Jewish mysticism is the ideal of *devukut, 'attachment' to God, but the great authority on Jewish mysticism, Gershom Scholem, has argued that *devekut* falls short of union with the divine. As *Scholem puts it (*Kabbalah* (Jerusalem, 1974), 176): '*Devekut* results in a sense of beatitude and intimate union, yet it does not entirely eliminate the distance between the creature and its Creator, a distinction that most kabbalists, like most Hasidim, were careful not to obscure by claiming that there could be a complete unification of the soul and God.' In view of the nature of the mystical experience generally, which the mystics themselves find it virtually impossible to describe to others, it is difficult to know how Scholem's distinction is to be drawn and Scholem himself seems to admit that for some of the Jewish mystics, at least, the *unio mystica* was thought of as possible.

Universalism The question of universalism in Judaism is, and is bound to be, an extremely complicated one. The God Jews worship is the Creator of the whole world and of all peoples yet Jews believe that they are the *Chosen People, however the latter concept is understood. The balance between universalism and particularism has always been difficult for Jews to achieve. In point of fact, terms such as these are never found in Judaism, which does not usually go in for abstractions. What is found in Jewish religious literature are statements about God's watchful care for all His creatures side by side with statements expressing the supreme significance of the Jewish people, who have freely accepted the Torah and have the desire to live in obedience to the divine word. No Jew, no matter how particularistic his attitude, can dare ignore the universalistic aspects of his religion. And no Jew, no matter how universalistic his stance, can dare ignore the simple fact that there can be no Judaism without the Jews.

It is all really a matter of where the emphasis is to be placed and there have been varying emphases in this matter throughout the history of Judaism. Some Jews have spoken as if God's chief, if not total, interest, so to speak, is with 'His' people. Others, especially in modern times, have gone to the opposite extreme, preferring to stress universalism to the extent of watering down the doctrine of particularism to render it a vague notion of loyalty to a tradition in which universalism had first emerged. Few Jews will fail to admit that there are tensions between the two doctrines.

The Talmudic Rabbis coped with the problem by postulating that God did not give the Torah only to Israel but to the nations of the world as well in the form of the *Noahide laws. And while Rabbi *Eliezer held that only Israelites have a share in the World to Come, the view followed in Judaism is that of Rabbi *Joshua, who taught that all the righteous of the nations of the world have a share in the World to Come (see GENTILES). In Rabbinic thought, too, the hope is repeatedly expressed that in the Messianic age God will be hailed as King by all peoples. A section of the kingship prayers on *Rosh Ha-Shanah is now recited by Jews as the Alenu prayer at the end of every service:

'We therefore hope in Thee, O Lord our God, that we may speedily behold the glory of Thy might, when Thou wilt remove the abominations from the earth, and the idols will be utterly cut off, when the world will be perfected under the kingdom of the Almighty, and all the children of flesh will call upon Thy name, when Thou wilt turn unto Thyself all the wicked of the earth. Let all the inhabitants of the world perceive and know that unto Thee every knee must bow, every tongue must swear. Before Thee, O Lord our God, let them bow and fall; and unto Thy glorious name let them give honour; let them all accept the yoke of Thy kingdom, and do Thou reign over them speedily, and for ever and ever.'

And no discussion of Jewish universalism can afford to neglect the hymn 'And all the world shall come', of unknown authorship, for long part of the liturgy on Rosh Ha-Shanah and *Yom Kippur, the first stanza of which reads in *Zangwill's translation:

All the world shall come to serve Thee
And bless Thy glorious name,
And Thy righteousness triumphant
The islands shall proclaim
And the peoples shall go seeking
Who knew Thee not before,
And the ends of earth shall praise
  Thee,
And tell Thy greatness o'er.

The tensions persist among modern Jews, as they did in the age of the medieval Jewish philosophers and in the eighteenth-century *Haskalah, but in every variety of the Jewish religion today there is the most powerful affirmation that every human being is created in the *image of God.

Urim Ve-Thummim The oracles in the breastplate of the *High Priest: 'And thou shalt put in the breastplate of judgement the Urim and the Thummim [etymology uncertain but could mean "Lights and Perfections"]; and they shall be upon Aaron's heart, when he goeth in before the Lord; and Aaron shall bear the judgement of the children of Israel upon his heart continually' (Exodus 28: 30). That the Urim and Thummim were oracles can be seen from other biblical passages, for instance from: 'And he shall stand before Eleazar the priest, who shall inquire for him by the judgement of the Urim before the Lord; at this word shall they go out, and at his word they shall come in, both he, and all the children of Israel with him, even all the congregation' (Numbers 27: 21). A Talmudic passage (Berakhot 3b) states that King David, before deciding whether or not to go to war, would consult the *Sanhedrin on whether it was permitted and the Urim Ve-Thummim to discover whether he would win the battle if he did go.

The nature of these oracles has eluded scholars, ancient and modern. Some commentators believe that the Urim Ve-Thummim were two lots placed in the breastplate but others identify them with the breastplate itself. The Talmudic Rabbis understood the oracle to work by certain letters of the precious stones on the breastplate, upon which were inscribed the names of the twelve tribes, becoming miraculously illumined. For instance, if the answer to a query was in the negative the letters forming the world lo ('No') would shine forth. In a Talmudic pas-

USHPIZIN

286

sage (*Yoma* 73b) it is stated that the Urim Ve-Thummim are so called because they illumine (from *or*, 'light') and are complete (from *tam*, 'perfect'). The problem of the Urim Ve-Thummim still awaits its solution.

Ushpizin 'Guests', the seven celestials who visit the *sukkah on the festival of *Tabernacles. The seven Ushpizin are first mentioned in the Zohar (iii. 103b) in which it is stated that Abraham and five others, together with David, visit the sukkah. These seven correspond to the seven lower *Sefirot. The portion of the Ushpizin is to be given to the poor who have to be invited to sit in the sukkah, otherwise the Ushpizin depart. The seven Ushpizin are: Abraham, Isaac, Jacob, Moses, Aaron, Joseph, and David. As the custom developed, it became the practice to welcome Abraham (the counterpart of the Sefirah Ḥesed, 'Loving-kindness') on the first day of Tabernacles and the others with him; Isaac on the second day, and so on. The custom of inviting the Ushpizin is still observed by many pious Jews, especially by the Hasidim, with special emphasis on the injunction to care for the needy when rejoicing on the festival.

Usury The payment of interest on a loan by borrower to lender. The two biblical passages which forbid the taking of interest are: 'If thou lend money to any of My people, even to the poor with thee, thou shalt not be to him as a creditor; neither shalt thou lay upon him interest' (Exodus 22: 24). 'Thou shalt not lend upon interest to thy brother: interest of money, interest of victuals, interest of any thing that is lent upon interest. Unto a foreigner thou mayest lend upon interest; but unto thy brother thou shalt not lend upon interest; that the Lord thy God may bless thee in all that thou puttest thy hand unto, in the land whither thou goest in to possess it' (Deuteron-

omy 23: 20–1). The meaning of these verses is clear. In an agrarian society a loan to a poor man to tide him over, for instance, until the harvest or to help him buy farming instruments, was a basic act of human kindness which should be done freely without demanding any return. For the lender to take interest on the loan would be to impoverish the borrower still further. But the 'foreigner', the man who is on a visit to the land of Israel, is not bound by this law. He will take interest on any loans he makes to Israelites so that there can be no obligation for the Israelite not to reciprocate and take interest when lending to him. The Christian Church in the Middle Ages adapted the law as it stands in the Pentateuch but understood 'thy brother' as referring to other Christians and the 'foreigner' to non-Christians, hence Jews were allowed to become moneylenders, with many a sorry consequence, as Jewish history shows.

The spirit of the law against usury would not seem to be violated when money is invested in business in our advanced economy, since the money is being used to increase profits and there is no reason why *A* should invest his money in *B*'s business as a sleeping partner unless he hopes to gain as *B* hopes to gain. Nevertheless, the letter of the law was held to be violated even where the loans were of a commercial nature. From the sixteenth century, a device, known as the *hetter iska* ('dispensation for commerce'), was introduced in which money invested in a commercial arrangement is treated as 'half loan and half deposit'. Even though the principle presumably behind the original prohibition of usury, that of helping the needy, hardly applies to business investment, many observant Jews still arrange for the *hetter iska* document to be drawn up when investing money in a business.

Values The thought of the biblical authors and the Talmudic Rabbis—comprising the classical sources of Judaism—is of a concrete nature. Nowhere in these sources is there to be found an abstract term like 'value'. When modern Jews speak of such ideals (this abstract term, too, is never found in the classical sources) as *compassion, *truth, *holiness, *humility, love, and *peace as Jewish values, they are really spelling out what is implicit but never explicit in the tradition. This is not a mere semantic quibble. Even if the classical sources had known of the idea of value, it is doubtful whether they would have seen it as 'valuable', since the whole notion of value implies selectivity. Ideals such as those mentioned are ends in themselves not to be evaluated against higher or more comprehensive ends.

Vashti Persian queen, wife of King Ahasuerus. The story of Vashti, as told in the book of *Esther (1: 9–22), relates how the king, while in his cups, orders Vashti to appear before the assembled nobles wearing her royal crown in order to display her charms to them. (The Talmudic Rabbis embellish the tale by understanding the king's order to mean wearing her royal crown and nothing else.) Vashti refuses to obey the king's command, accusing him, according to the Rabbis, of not being able to hold his liquor, after which his counsellors advise him to depose her, otherwise all women will take her as an example to defy their husbands. The king deposes Vashti, thus paving the way for the eventual appointment of Esther as queen. Henceforth, the verse states, every man will be 'lord in his house'. In the Jewish tradition, Vashti is por-

trayed largely as a figure of fun but in Jewish *feminism she is the heroine of the feminists because of her refusal to submit to the extraordinary and obscene demands of her drunken husband.

Vegetarianism Vegetarians often quote two biblical passages in support of their view that it is morally wrong for human beings to kill *animals for food. In the creation narrative (Genesis 29: 30) both man and animals were given the herbs of the field for their food and they were not permitted to prey on one another. In Isaiah's vision (Isaiah 11: 7) 'the lion shall eat straw like an ox'. The first passage, however, only expresses the ideal that obtained at the beginning of creation and the second an ideal for 'the end of days', later understood as referring to the Messianic age. It is nowhere stated in the Bible that in the here and now vegetarianism is an ideal. On the contrary, when Noah and his sons emerge from the *ark the animals are given to them as food. In any event, in Judaism attitudes are not formed simply on the basis of biblical verses culled from here and there but on the way the teachers of Judaism have interpreted the religion throughout the ages.

There is, of course, no actual obligation for a man to eat meat and there are even a number of Jewish vegetarian societies. But it can be argued that for a Jew to adopt vegetarianism on the grounds that it is wrong to kill animals for food is to introduce a moral and theological idea which implies that Judaism has, in fact, been wrong all the time in not advocating vegetarianism. For this reason many traditional Jews look askance at the advocacy of vegetarianism as a way of life superior to the traditional Jewish way.

Venice There was an influx of Jews into Venice after the expulsion from Spain, among them Don Isaac *Abravanel who, in his commentary to the Pentateuch, is eloquent on the advantages of the oligarchical system of government in the Venetian Republic over the monarchical system to which he had been accustomed in Spain. It has been estimated that Venice had around 900 Jews in 1552. Shakespeare's *Merchant of Venice* is therefore a not inaccurate reflection of Jewish–Christian relationships in Venice, although the picture of Shylock who demands his 'pound of flesh' is, of course, pure invention. It was in Venice that the Jews were confined in the 'foundry' known as the *ghetto and were obliged to wear the special badge or hat to distinguish them from Christians. The old Jewish ghetto in Venice, with its highrise buildings and beautiful synagogues, is now a tourist attraction. Venice is renowned as the great nursery of Hebrew *printing. The house of Daniel Bomberg, a non-Jew, poured forth Hebrew books, printed with fine type on paper of excellent quality, which won the widest acceptance— among them the famous Rabbinic Bible, known as *Mikraot Gedolot*, and the first edition of the complete Babylonian Talmud, the form and pagination of which became the model for practically all subsequent editions.

Via Negativa 'The Negative Way', of speaking of God. The proponents of this way believe that God is so beyond all human comprehension that it is only possible for humans to describe what He is not, never to attempt to speak of His true nature. Prominent among the medieval Jewish philosophers who prefer the way of negation are *Bahya, Ibn Pakudah and *Maimonides, both of whom develop the theory of negative attributes. For Maimonides the attributes which are of God's essence—existence, unity, and wisdom—have to be understood solely as negating their opposites. With regard to the attributes which refer to God's activity, these can be applied to God even in positive form but that is because they are not of God's nature but only of His actions. When, for example, God is spoken of as good this is meant in a positive sense but denotes only that such action would be attributed to goodness if a human being had carried it out. The Kabbalists go further in not permitting even negative attributes of God as He is in Himself. This aspect of God is called by the Kabbalists *En Sof or Ayin ('Nothing') because nothing can be said or even thought of It. Only of God as manifest in the *Sefirot is it permitted to speak, but then one can speak in a positive sense.

Vienna The city of Vienna, capital of Austria, came to occupy an important place in the history of Jewish learning from the fourteenth century, when many German Jews emigrated to Austria. Prominent among the 'Sages of Vienna' were the renowned Isaac Or Zarua (so-called after the title of his work on Jewish law) and his son Hayyim. But it was in the nineteenth century that the Jewish community in Vienna became a centre where the new trends in Jewish life after the emergence of the Jews from the *ghetto were given a unique expression. Here European culture flourished and here the *Haskalah movement, originating in Berlin, found many advocates. In Vienna, as in Germany, the struggle over Reform was acute. Later still, it was in Vienna, the home of Theodor *Herzl and Sigmund Freud, that both *Zionism and psychoanalysis (see PSYCHOLOGY) began to exercise a powerful influence on Jewish, as well as on general, life.

Vilna Lithuanian city renowned for its

contribution to Jewish learning and piety and hence known as 'the Jerusalem of Lithuania'. The Jewish community of Vilna flourished from the seventeenth century until its destruction in the *Holocaust. Vilna was the home of many prominent Rabbis and preachers, the most notable being *Elijah, Gaon of Vilna, who occupied no official Rabbinic post but whose influence extends to this day over all Orthodox Jews. The famous printing-house of Romm in Vilna published works in every branch of Jewish learning. The splendid Romm editions of the Babylonian and Jerusalem Talmuds are highly prized and are now the current editions in photocopy. Although Vilna in the eighteenth century did not tolerate the slightest deviation from the traditional view (there was even a pillory into which 'heretics' were exposed to public derision), eventually the city became a centre of the *Haskalah movement in Lithuania. There was a *Karaite community in and around Vilna but, as in Lithuania generally, the Reform movement never gained any hold there.

Violence In Jewish law, as in other legal systems, the victim of an assault is entitled to receive adequate compensation (see DAMAGES) but, in addition, Jewish teaching is emphatic that any attack on another's person is strictly forbidden. The Hebrew word for 'violence', *ḥamas*, denotes especially robbery with violence—'grievous bodily harm' in English legal phraseology—as in the verse (Genesis 6: 11): 'And the earth was corrupt before God, and the earth was filled with violence [*ḥamas*].' In the Babylonian Talmud (*Sanhedrin* 58b) there is a list of sayings directed against physical violence in itself, even where there is no attempt at robbery. The third-century teacher, Resh Lakish, is reported as saying: 'He who only lifts his hand against his neighbour, even if

he did not actually smite him, is called a wicked man.'

Visions The Bible contains accounts of prophetic visions of various kinds. Both the prophet Isaiah (Isaiah 6: 1–7) and the prophet Ezekiel (Ezekiel 1) see a vision of the *throne of God, the latter as coming to him on a *chariot. The Talmud (*Ḥagigah* 13b), seeking to explain Ezekiel's prolixity in comparison with Isaiah's brevity, observes that Isaiah, accustomed to seeing this kind of vision, can be compared to a townsman who sees the king while Ezekiel can be compared to a villager who sees the king and on whom the sight makes a greater impression. In another Talmudic passage (*Yevamot* 49b) it is said that King Manasseh had Isaiah slain because he claimed to have seen God whereas his teacher, Moses, had said: 'For man shall not see Me and live' (Exodus 33: 20). The Talmud seeks to resolve the contradiction by making a distinction between seeing through a clear glass and seeing through a dim glass. As *Rashi understands this distinction, Moses, whose visions generally were through clear glass, had the insight that God cannot be seen, whereas Isaiah, whose general visions were through a dim glass, imagined that his vision of God reflected the true Reality. Another explanation of the passage is that when Moses declared that no man can see God, he referred to seeing through a clear glass, implying that He could be seen through a dim glass as Isaiah in fact saw Him. In any event the use of the glass simile suggests that it is impossible to see God directly, even in the most intense prophetic vision. This remained the Rabbinic and medieval attitude, that the true 'beatific vision' is only possible after death: 'For man shall not see Me *and live*.'

Visiting the Sick Among the acts of benevolence enjoined by the Torah, visiting the sick is especially significant.

The Rabbis depict God Himself as a visitor of the sick when He appeared to Abraham just after he was recovering from his *circumcision (Genesis 18: 1), and they give this as an example of man pursuing the ideal of *Imitatio Dei. For the Rabbis and in subsequent Jewish teaching it is not the simple visit that counts, though this is also important. The main purpose of the visit is to see if the sick person's needs have been attended to and to help him obtain whatever extra help he requires over and above his medical requirements to which his doctor attends. Among the instructions for visiting the sick are that people who do not belong to the sick person's immediate family should wait a while before visiting him in order not to call attention to the fact that he is sick; that the sick person should be visited often but not where this imposes a burden on him and his family; that a sick enemy should not be visited because it may appear as gloating over his discomfiture. A sick visitor should be tactful, neither giving the impression that the sick person is beyond human help nor giving false hopes of recovery. The general principle in the sources is that it is not necessary to inform a seriously ill person that his illness is incurable; some hold that, unless there is a real need for it, he should not, in fact, be told that the doctors have given him up. Prayers for the sick are recited during the synagogue services and at other times. In Hasidic and many other circles it is customary when praying for the sick to use the patient's mother's name rather than the father's, for example: Moses son of Sarah not Moses son of Abraham. Every Jewish community of any size has a special society devoted to visiting the sick.

Vital, Hayyim *Safed Kabbalist (1542–1620), chief disciple of Isaac *Luria, the Ari, whose teachings Vital propagated through his voluminous writings. In his youth Vital studied Talmud and Codes under the guidance of Moses Alsheikh who ordained him as a Rabbi. Vital began to study Kabbalah in 1562. At first Vital followed the Kabbalistic system of Moses *Cordovero but when Luria arrived in Safed he studied the Lurianic system with Luria until the latter's death in 1572.

Vital's major work, Etz Hayyim ('Tree of Life', a pun on his name Hayyim) is a huge compendium in which he presents the Lurianic teachings or, rather, his own understanding of them.

Volozhyn Russian town famed for its Rabbi, Hayyim of Volozhyn (1749–1821), and for the *Yeshivah he established there in 1803. Hayyim of Volozhyn was the foremost disciple of *Elijah, Gaon of Vilna. Like his master, Hayyim preferred the analytical approach to Talmudic studies in which excessive casuistry (*pilpul) is avoided and an attempt is made to discover what the Talmudic texts are actually saying rather than what ingenious but far-fetched exegesis makes them say. Moreover, the *Codes should not be relied on themselves but only the Codes as based on the Talmud.

Despite attempts by the Russian authorities to interfere with the curriculum of the Yeshivah and despite its complete closure in 1892 (to be reopened surreptitiously), it functioned, albeit in severe decline, until the *Holocaust. The Yeshivah reached its zenith in the nineteenth century under Naftali Zvi Judah Berlin, known, after the initial letters of his name, as the Netziv. Hundreds of keen students flocked to the Yeshivah, some even from America. Contributions to the upkeep of the Yeshivah, which had a building of its own, were solicited from Jews in all the European communities. Emissaries, Meshulahim, went out to elicit support which was usually given willingly.

Yet while on the surface traditional faith was unchallenged at Volozhyn, the *Haskalah and secular philosophies found their way into the Yeshivah. A number of the students read Haskalah and scientific works hidden between the pages of the Talmud they were supposed to be studying. The official teachers at the Yeshivah were either unaware of these trends or turned a blind eye to them. But even those students who later deserted traditional Judaism still retained their admiration of this 'factory in which the soul of the people is manufactured', as the Hebrew poet Bialik, a former student at the Yeshivah, described it.

Vows The basic text regarding the taking of vows is: 'When a man voweth a vow unto the Lord, or sweareth an oath to bind his soul with a bond, he shall not break his word; he shall do according to all that proceedeth out of his mouth' (Numbers 30: 3). In the traditional understanding of this verse the reference is to a vow or an oath to refrain from some enjoyment as a kind of sacrifice to God. (The term 'oath' is also used to refer to *oaths taken in a court of law, but both vows and oaths in this text denote only personal declarations of a religious nature.) According to the Rabbis, the vow refers to the object, the oath to the person. For instance, a man may place a ban on wine for a given period, perhaps as a means of controlling his drinking habits that seem to be getting out of control. This ban on the object, the wine, is said to constitute a vow. If, on the other hand, he swears that he will not drink wine, this constitutes an oath. In both instances for the man to break his word is a religious rather than an ethical offence. The idea behind it all is that the man has given to God his word, which he must not break. It is only a verbal declaration that constitutes a vow. A vow 'taken in the heart', as the Rabbis call it, a mental resolve, has no binding force.

The Talmudic Rabbis are divided on whether the taking of vows and oaths is desirable; some of them see no harm in the practice, others frown on it even when the promise is in a good cause, a promise to give to *charity for example. The general tendency is to frown in principle on vow-taking but to leave room for a personal decision as to whether the circumstances demand it. For instance, if a man promises to study a portion of the Torah in order not to surrender to indolence in his studies this, while not ideal, would be tolerated and perhaps even advocated. A whole tractate of the Talmud, tractate *Nedarim*, is devoted to the subject of vows.

Warfare Although Judaism sets the highest store on *peace, it does not adopt the completely pacifist stand according to which warfare can never be justified, no matter what the circumstances. At the most, Judaism treats warfare, when it has to be engaged in, as a necessary evil but an evil none the less, or at any rate this has been the way Jewish teaching on the subject has developed. There are numerous references to the biblical heroes, including King David, engaging in warfare. But the Chronicler (1 Chronicles 22: 8) implies that, even if his wars were justified, David's plan to build the *Temple had to be frustrated because a warrior is not a suitable person to build a House of God: 'But the word of the Lord came to me saying, Thou hast shed blood abundantly, and thou hast made great wars: thou shalt not build an house unto My name, because thou hast shed much blood upon the earth in my sight.' It is possible, indeed, that the Chronicler, reflecting on David's career, denies that all David's wars were justified. In the Rabbinic literature there is a definite tendency to downgrade David's prowess as a warrior and anachronistically to turn him into a scholar whose fights were in the battles of the Torah, as the Rabbis call debates among scholars.

The truth of the matter is that, as in other extremely complicated matters of great moral concern, there is no single, official view in Judaism on the legitimacy of warfare. The fact is that in the post-biblical period Jews did not have any opportunity to engage in warfare, since, until the establishment of the State of Israel, no Jewish State existed to which the terrible question could be addressed. Every Jewish discussion on what Christian theology calls the 'just war' could only have been purely academic. The general principle laid down in the Talmud (*Sanhedrin* 72a) is: 'If someone intends to kill you, get in first and kill him' (i.e. to kill another in self-defence does not constitute an act of murder). Even then the rule is stated that if you can save your life by only maiming the attacker, to kill him does constitute murder. It is obviously difficult to extrapolate from this principle (which refers to an individual would-be murderer and an individual defender of his life) rules about a whole people engaging in warfare where the issue is always far from clear-cut. For that matter, it is rarely clear-cut even with regard to individuals. Once a whole nation has resolved to make war in self-defence the result is bound to be the killing of innocents, and yet for a nation simply to sit back and let an attacking nation take over can also result in great suffering and severe loss of life. A further question is whether a preemptive strike comes under the heading of self-defence. There are all sorts of questions which arise in modern warfare that are unenvisaged in the classical sources of Judaism—the use of highly developed technical weapons, for instance, which bring about mass destruction and which can surely only be contemplated as a last resort. Moreover, the question of war and defence in the State of Israel is decided not by Rabbis, who have no voice in the matter, but, as among other nations, by generals and politicians, and the whole question of diplomacy arises, to say nothing of the authority or otherwise of the United Nations. Nevertheless, Rabbis have not been inhibited from stating what appears to them to be the attitude the Torah would have Jews adopt. With hardly any exceptions, Jewish teachers have held that the wars engaged in by Israel when attacked or threatened by attack by the Arab nations were completely justified as wars of self-defence. On the war in Lebanon alone opinion was divided.

Wasserman, Elhanan Foremost Lithuanian Talmudist (1875–1941). Wasserman studied in his youth in the Yeshivah of *Telz and for several years in the house of his father-in-law, Rabbi Meir Atlas. He later spent some years in the town of Radin, the home of the famous *Hafetz Hayyim, whom Wasserman considered to be his chief mentor in his religious approach to the Jewish problems of the day. His main official position was as principal of the Yeshivah in the town of Baranowitz in Poland, to which students flocked from many parts of the Jewish world. Wasserman was active in the ultra-Orthodox Aggudat Israel movement. Essentially a kind and gentle man, Wasserman was none the less fearless and outspoken in his struggle against Reform, Zionism, and secularism, all of which, he believed, were preventing the coming of the *Messiah by attempting to take Jewish destiny into their own hands instead of relying on God to save His people.

Water-Drawing Ceremony The ceremony that took place in the *Temple during the seven days of the festival of *Tabernacles. The usual libation on the altar was of wine but after the Tamid, the perpetual offering, had been offered in the morning of each of these seven days there was a libation of water, the festival of Tabernacles being the season when prayers for *rain were offered. The whole ceremony was rejected by the *Sadducees as having no basis in the Bible. But the *Pharisees declared it to be a 'law given to Moses at *Sinai' and they set the greatest store by it. A verse quoted in this connection

was: 'Joyfully shall you draw water from the fountains of triumph' (Isaiah 12: 3). The Mishnah (Sukkah 5: 1–5) describes the great celebration that took place in honour of the water-drawing from the night after the first day of Tabernacles and on the subsequent nights of the festival. The Mishnah states: 'He that has never seen the joy of the Bet Ha-Shoevah ["the joy of the House of the Drawing"] has never in his life seen joy.'

Wayfarer's Prayer The prayer recited before setting out on a journey. The source for this prayer is in the Talmud (Berakhot 29b), where the prayer for the journey (tefillat ha-derekh) is referred to as taking counsel with the Creator before setting out. The Talmud gives the following version of this prayer: 'May it be Thy will, O Lord my God, to conduct me in peace, to direct my steps in peace, to uphold me in peace and to deliver me from every enemy and ambush by the way. Send a blessing upon the work of my hands and let me obtain grace, loving-kindness and mercy in Thine eyes and in the eyes of all who behold me. Blessed art Thou, O Lord, Who hearkeneth unto prayer.' However, Abbaye says in the passage that prayers should be offered in the plural in order for the individual to associate himself with the community, so that the wording should be: 'May it be Thy will, O Lord our God, to conduct us in peace', and so on. The practice, therefore, is to follow Abbaye and in most versions of the prayer the plural is used. In the *Hertz Siddur, for some reason, the prayer is in the singular and a number of scriptural verses have been added, based on earlier prayer books. It is customary nowadays to recite the wayfarer's prayer before travelling in a plane, even though the hazards are far less than they would have been when journeying in a caravan in Talmudic times.

Western Wall Part of the wall around the *Temple Mount built by Herod in the first century BCE. Five rows of the original huge stones, each weighing many tons, are now seen above ground; the lower, original stones are below ground. The smaller stones that can now be seen were added at various periods. This wall, called Ha-Kotel ('the wall') is not the actual wall of the Temple, as some imagine, but of the Temple Mount. The reference in the Midrash to the 'Western Wall from which the *Shekhinah will never depart' may originally have been to the actual western wall of the Temple, since the Holy of Holies was situated in the west. But pilgrims to Jerusalem increasingly understood the Midrash as referring to this wall with the result that, at least from the sixteenth century, the wall was held to be a specially sacred spot from which prayers offered there ascended directly to heaven. Some pious Jews still insert written petitions in the crevices of the wall. Because Jews have mourned there over the destruction of the Temple, the wall came to be known, by non-Jews, as the 'Wailing Wall', but this name is unknown in the Jewish tradition.

After the Six Day War, when east Jerusalem came into Jewish hands once again, a large space was cleared in front of the wall to form a plaza and, nowadays, constant services are held there, men and women being separated in accordance with the Orthodox view. Some Jews, especially those of Oriental extraction, celebrate a boy's *Bar Mitzvah at the wall accompanied by singing and dancing (and see HOLY PLACES).

Widows and Orphans There are numerous injunctions in the Bible to care for widows and orphans and to avoid taking advantage of their situation of having no husband or father to protect them. The underprivileged to whom the poor man's tithe (see TITHING) was to be given include 'the orphan,

and the widow' (Deuteronomy 26: 12). The warning not to oppress a widow or an orphan is stated with full rigour: 'You shall not ill-treat any widow or orphan. If you do mistreat them, I will heed their cry as soon as they cry out to Me, and My anger shall blaze forth and I will put you to the sword, and your own wives shall become widows and your children orphans' (Exodus 22: 21–3). The Midrash stresses the word 'any' in the verse to include 'the widow of a king' and in the Jewish tradition generally concern for the feelings of the widow and orphan applies even to wealthy widows and orphans, not only to the poor and disadvantaged. From Talmudic times onwards the courts appointed a guardian for orphans, a trustworthy man who would administer faithfully and voluntarily the estate they had inherited from their father. The prophet Isaiah urges his people: 'Uphold the rights of the orphan; defend the cause of the widow' (Isaiah 1: 17). Similarly, the prophet Jeremiah declares: 'No, if you really mend your ways and your actions; if you execute justice between one man and another; if you do not oppress the stranger, the orphan and the widow' (Jeremiah 7: 5–6). Job, protesting his innocence, says: 'For I saved the poor man who cried out, the orphan who had none to help him. I received the blessing of the lost, I gladdened the heart of the widow' (Job 29: 12–13).

In Jewish law as developed by the Rabbis, while orphans inherit their father's estate, a widow does not inherit her husband's estate. But the *ketubah consists of a settlement on the estate from which the widow is entitled to maintenance until she remarries. Many Jewish communities had an orphanage in which the young charges were cared for, not always as kindly as they should have been judging by the frequent complaints found in Jewish literature. A teacher was allowed to chastise an orphan 'for his own good' but orphans should otherwise be treated with special tenderness and consideration. Unfortunately, some teachers appear to have interpreted 'for his own good' in a less than generous way.

Wills The chief religious problem with regard to a will, in which a person declares how his estate is to be distributed after his death, is that, on the face of it, any disposition that is not in accord with the laws of *succession, as stated in the Torah (Numbers 27: 8-11; Deuteronomy 21: 16-17), is contrary to the laws of the Torah. According to the Talmudic sources, however, the laws of succession only apply where the testator states that the deposition of his property is in the form of an inheritance. The laws of succession do not apply if the deposition is given as a gift, that is, if the estate is distributed while the man is still alive, with the stipulation taking place immediately but the distribution only when he dies, since a man is allowed to give away that which he owns to whomsoever he pleases. The key passage in this connection is the Mishnah (Bava Batra 8: 5) which states: 'If a person gives his estate, in writing, to strangers, and leaves out his children, his arrangements are legally valid [literally, what he has done is done], but the spirit of the Sages finds no delight in him. Rabban Simeon ben Gamaliel said: If his children did not conduct themselves in a proper manner he will be remembered for good.' Most authorities, consequently, see no harm in a man making a will in favour of whomsoever he wishes, provided it is in the form of a gift not an inheritance, since the will is precisely that—a gift given in his lifetime to come into operation 'from now until after his death', as this is formulated in the Mishnah in the same tractate. Nevertheless, he should leave a substantial amount to his children in order to satisfy the 'spirit of the Sages'.

Wills, Ethical Instructions given in writing by a father to his children in anticipation of his death. The term 'ethical will', now widely used to describe published works in this genre, seems to have originated with Israel Abrahams, who called his famous collection *Hebrew Ethical Wills*. But the term is very imprecise in that the concerns of the writers of these documents were religious as well as ethical and they often give instructions regarding such matters as the procedures to be followed at the writer's burial. The Hebrew term is simply *tzavvah* ('testament'), the term used for *wills in general.

Wine There are differing attitudes in the classical sources of Judaism towards the drinking of wine. The Psalmist declares that wine gladdens the heart of man (Psalms 104: 15) and the Rabbis introduced a special *benediction over wine as well as ruling that other important benedictions such as the *Kiddush and *Havdalah have to be recited over a cup of wine. At the *marriage ceremony the benedictions are recited over a cup of wine from which bride and bridegroom drink. Libations of wine were offered on the altar as an accompaniment to the *sacrifices. The practice developed of giving mourners wine to drink to assuage their grief on the basis of the verse which enjoins giving wine to 'the bitter in spirit' (Proverbs 31: 4). A Talmudic saying (Eruvin 65a) has it that wine was only created for the purpose of comforting mourners. On the other hand, according to one view in the Midrash, the fruit of the tree from which *Adam and Eve partook was the grape which 'brought a curse to mankind'. The *Nazirite, whose vow includes abstention from wine, is praised by one Rabbi in the Talmud as a 'holy man', although according to another opinion, the Nazirite is a sinner in that he rejects God's gift of wine (see ASCETICISM and HOLINESS). There is a biblical reference to a family which abstained from wine as well as from building houses and cultivating the soil. These men, the Rechabites (the descendants of Jonadab son of Rechab) were held up as an example of loyalty and obedience by the prophet Jeremiah (Jeremiah 35) but there is no suggestion in the chapter that it was advisable for others to follow the ways of the Rechabites.

The general principle that emerges from all the debates and discussions on the subject is that the drinking of wine, and other intoxicating drinks, is harmless and can even be desirable except where it can lead to drunkenness. Only on the festival of *Purim is intoxication allowed. A Rabbi is forbidden to render decisions after he has partaken of wine since his mind will then be clouded, just as the *priests in the *Temple were forbidden to drink wine immediately before they carried out their services (Leviticus 10: 9-11). In *Hasidism the drinking of wine and alcoholic beverages in general was held to be conducive to the joy a Jew should experience as a worshipper of God, but the *Mitnaggedim were not slow to accuse Hasidim of drunkenness and frivolity because of their addiction to wine. Since wine was used in idolatrous worship the Talmudic Rabbis imposed a ban on all wine manufactured by *Gentiles. Orthodox Jews and some Conservative Jews still abstain from drinking 'Gentile wine'.

Wisdom The Hebrew word ḥokhmah, usually translated as 'wisdom', is used in Jewish literature, in a variety of ways, to denote mental processes and intellectual attitudes. In the Bible the word often means 'skill'. Bezalel, the architect of the *Tabernacle, and his co-workers are said (Exodus 36: 2) to have been gifted with ḥokhmah, meaning here the skills which enabled them to carry out their tasks successfully. Similarly, the Talmudic Rabbis say that to blow the *shofar on the Sabbath does not fall under the heading of 'work' but of ḥokhmah, that is, it is a skilled performance, for which one has to be trained, but cannot be construed as physical effort. In the books of the Bible belonging to what is known as the 'Wisdom Literature'—*Proverbs, *Job, and *Ecclesiastes—ḥokhmah acquires a more intellectual meaning. The sage, ḥakham, in this literature, and in some other late passages in the Bible, is the man who has acquired knowledge of the world and human nature, sharing his experience with others. As in the book of Proverbs, the ḥakham gives prudent advice and is the author of wise saws. Thus the prophet Jeremiah, referring to different types of people admired for their extraordinary attainments, declares: 'Let not the wise man [ḥakham] glory in his wisdom [ḥokhmah], neither let the mighty man glory in his might, let not the rich man glory in his riches' (Jeremiah 9: 23). In Rabbinic literature the 'wisdom' of the book of Proverbs is made to refer to the 'wisdom of the Torah' so that the ḥakham now becomes the scholar well versed in the Torah (see STUDY and TALMID ḤAKHAM).

Among the medieval thinkers ḥokhmah usually refers to prowess in philosophical argument and there is a marked tendency to blur the distinction made by the Rabbis between the Torah and universal knowledge, the latter itself being considered to be part of the Torah, albeit a part of Torah knowledge arrived at by purely human reasoning, not through *revelation. In modern times, ḥokhmah often denotes the sciences as well as the scientific, objective study of the Jewish sources. The Hebrew name for *Jüdische Wissenschaft is: Ḥokhmat Yisrael (literally, 'The Wisdom of Israel' or 'Jewish Wisdom') referring to the employment of the historical–critical methodology.

In everyday Jewish use ḥokhmah denotes wisdom of a deeper quality than mere cleverness. The ḥakham is not a

297

clever know-all but a man capable of penetrating into the depths of the human situation and of seeing things as a whole.

Wise, Isaac Mayer Reform Rabbi, pioneer of Reform Judaism in America (1819–1900). Although Wise received, in his native Bohemia, a good grounding in the traditional Jewish sources, he was largely self-educated in the more modern Jewish thought and the general culture of his day. In 1846 Wise left for America, serving, at first, as Rabbi to an Orthodox synagogue in Albany in which he attempted to introduce certain reforms contrary to the wishes of the congregation. Such was the opposition to Wise's reforms that the president of the congregation came to blows with him on *Yom Kippur. Wise left his post to found a synagogue on his own. In 1854 Wise became a Reform Rabbi in Cincinnati, which city, through his efforts and strong and stubborn personality, became the home of American Reform. It was the dream of Reform as suited to life in the New World that inspired Wise, unlike the Reformers in Germany whose aim it was to accommodate Judaism to Western life and civilization in general, rather than to a particular country. At one period in his career Wise became so convinced that a moderately reformed Judaism would prove attractive to all reasonable people that he forecast that in fifty years Judaism would overtake Christianity to become the religion of America as a whole—a nonsensical dream, of course, but indicative of Wise's reforming zeal and broad, though fanciful, vision.

Wise, Stephan S. Prominent Reform Rabbi, social activist, and Zionist leader (1874–1949). Wise was born in Budapest but, at the age of 2, was brought to America. He studied at Columbia University from which he later obtained a Ph.D. Wise pursued Rabbinic studies privately and was ordained as a Rabbi

by the famous preacher, Adolf Jellineck of *Vienna. In 1907 Wise founded the Free Synagogue in New York—'free' both in the sense that no fees would be demanded of the congregation and in that Wise was allowed to express his views without any interference from the governing body of the synagogue. Wise was one of the first Reform Rabbis to break with the attitude of hostility Reform had shown to *Zionism, a cause he espoused with the great oratorical power for which he was renowned.

Wissenschaft See JÜDISCHE WISSENSCHAFT.

Witchcraft The key biblical verse on the subject of witchcraft: 'Thou shalt not suffer a witch to live' (Exodus 22: 17) was understood by the Talmudic Rabbis to mean that a witch had to be executed. It is important to appreciate, however, that when this view was put forward it was purely academic, since no court in Talmudic times was empowered to impose capital *punishment (and see SANHEDRIN). Although the Hebrew uses the feminine form, the Rabbis observe that this is only because women were especially addicted to witchcraft. A wizard is as culpable as a witch. As with regard to *magic in general, opinions were divided among the Jewish teachers over whether witchcraft can work so as really to do harm. Maimonides believes that there are no supernatural magical powers, and that the Torah injunction against magic is based on a false belief that it is efficacious. Although it was not unknown for some Jews to practise witchcraft in spite of its strong condemnation, the claim in the Middle Ages that the Jew was in league with the devil to harm Christians owes everything to overheated imagination and nothing to fact (and see BLOOD LIBEL).

Witch of Endor The woman who was

consulted by King Saul and who brought up the prophet *Samuel from the dead, as told in the 1 Samuel 28. The problems connected with the story were discussed in the period of the *Geonim. Samuel ben Hophni, Gaon of Sura (d. 1013), father-in-law of *Hai Gaon, was asked whether the story was to be taken literally, and whether the witch actually succeeded in raising Samuel from the dead. Samuel ben Hophni replies that he finds it impossible to believe that God would have made a witch the instrument of raising Samuel. The true meaning of the story is that the witch, by trickery, persuaded Saul that she had succeeded in bringing up Samuel.

Witness The general rule in Jewish law is that in criminal cases and in cases involving claims on property two witnesses are required in order to establish the facts of the case. Witnesses must be perfectly reliable persons; robbers, for example, are disqualified from acting as witnesses. Witnesses must not be related to the contestants in a case nor must they be related to one another. The disqualification of a witness on the grounds of close relationship applies even where the witness testifies against his relative.

Wolfson, Harry Austryn Historian of ideas, professor for many years at Harvard University, and author of important works on the history of Jewish and general philosophy (1887–1974). In his youth Wolfson studied at the famed *Yeshivah of Slabodka in Lithuania. Arriving in the USA in 1903, he at first earned a living as a Hebrew teacher and writer but later studied philosophy at Harvard. In 1925 he was appointed Professor of Hebrew Literature and Philosophy at Harvard where he was highly admired, becoming known as 'Wolfson of Harvard'. Wolfson's works on *Philo, *Crescas, *Spinoza, and the Church Fathers won great renown. Wolfson claimed to have based his methodology on the Talmudic dialectics (*pilpul), the knowledge of which he had acquired in Slabodka, and which he applied to the study of philosophical works. This methodology has been challenged by other scholars in the field but none deny the great significance of Wolfson's work. Though not very observant of Jewish law and ritual in his private life, Wolfson had little truck with Reform Judaism. He once described himself as 'a non-practising Orthodox Jew'.

Women Any consideration of the role of women in Judaism has to reckon with the obvious: that the classical sources of the Jewish religion were all compiled by men. In the Bible, for example, while *Miriam, *Deborah, and Huldah are spoken of as prophetesses, demonstrating that in ancient Israel women, too, could enjoy the prophetic faculty, the literary prophets and those who recorded their prophetic utterances were male. Similarly, the Talmudic authors and editors and the great codifiers were all men, as were the medieval philosophers and the Kabbalists. Even when the tradition affirms that the biblical authors (and, albeit to a lesser degree, the others mentioned above) were inspired by the *Holy Spirit, the inspiration came through a male, not a female personality and this must have affected the way in which inspiration was expressed, unless the *fundamentalist view is adopted that it is God alone who 'speaks' through the inspired person in such a way as to override his personality entirely. Jewish *feminism has seized on all this to claim that there is evident in the sources a marked bias against women. Other Jews, females as well as males, do not believe that the clock of history can be turned backwards, although they, too, are naturally concerned to remove any injustices from which women suffer.

According to the *Halakhah, there

are no differences whatsoever between men and women in matters of Jewish belief, ethical obligations, and the criminal law. A Jewish woman, as well as a Jewish man, is expected to believe in the *principles of the faith, to love and care for others, to be generous and kindly, not to steal or cheat. With regard to religious law, however, women are exempt from the performance of any *precept, *mitzvah, which depends for its performance on a given time.

A more curious exemption is the study of the Torah. Women have no obligation to study the Torah and a father has no obligation to teach his daughter the Torah. The Mishnah (Sotah 3: 4) quotes the opinion of Rabbi *Eliezer that 'whosoever teaches his daughter Torah teaches her lasciviousness'. This is a minority opinion, and in any event, has to be understood in the context of the unfaithful wife with which the Mishnah deals. Nevertheless, some authorities in the Middle Ages frowned on women studying the Talmud, though not the Bible and works of devotion. Very revealing in this connection is the Talmudic observation (Berakhot 17a) that women acquire the merit of studying the Torah by participating in this indirectly in that they send their sons to study and encourage their husbands to study. The practice of the wife being the breadwinner while the husband studies is still the norm in ultra-Orthodox circles. The result was that women were not at all well versed in Jewish learning, although some few women in the earlier period did become renowned as scholars and even as Talmudists. In modern times, all circles in Jewry, with the exception of the ultra-Orthodox, not only see no harm in the study of the Torah by women but advocate it as a positive good. So far as studying the sources of Judaism by the modern historical–critical method, in Hebrew departments of universities there are many women students and several women professors and there is

no sexual discrimination in this area at all. Since women in the past did not normally study the Torah there were only a very few women competent to become Rabbis. But there is neither any Halakhic nor doctrinal reason why a learned woman should not serve as a Rabbi, although the Orthodox do not allow this on the grounds that, as they put it, 'it is against the Jewish spirit'. Reform and Conservative seminaries do ordain women as *Rabbis and, for that matter, as *Cantors. The oft-quoted section of Proverbs (31: 10–31) in praise of the capable wife is ambiguous since the wife, for all her significance to the family, is depicted as subordinate. The prophetic comparison of the love of God for Israel to the love of a husband for his wife suggests a cultural background in which women were highly respected in and in which they occupied an important place, as does the existence of prophetesses as well as male prophets and the participation of women in the choral services in the *Temple (Ezra 2: 65) in one period at least. Although the masculine pronoun is used of God and He is described as a Father, in one prophetic simile God's comfort to mourners is compared to the comfort a mother affords her child (Isaiah 66: 13).

A variety of attitudes towards women is found in the Talmudic and Midrashic literature. Too much should not be read into the wording of the benediction, recited each day, in which a man thanks God for not having made him a woman (Menaḥot 43b), whereas a woman simply thanks God for having made her 'according to His will', since it is clear from the context that the thanks are for the greater opportunities a man has for carrying out the precepts, women being exempt, as above, from carrying out those precepts dependent on time.

That the Rabbis themselves did not practise polygamy is fairly well established. Indeed, it has been convincingly argued that, while polygamy was legally sanctioned in Talmudic times, it was rarely practised by Jews. The Oriental Jews, who in the Middle Ages and later did have more than one wife, were influenced by Islamic practice rather than by Talmudic legislation.

In the Rabbinic Aggadah chivalrous statements about women alternate with sayings of a far less noble character. The reason for God creating Eve from Adam's rib is stated thus: 'God said: I will not create her from the head that she should not hold up her head too proudly; nor from the eye that she should not be a coquette, nor from the ear that she should not be an eavesdropper; nor from the mouth that she should not be too talkative; nor from the hand that she should not be too acquisitive, nor from the foot that she should not be a gadabout; but from a part of the body that is hidden, that she should be modest.' But, the Midrash ungallantly concludes, it was all to no effect (Midrash Genesis Rabbah 18: 2). In the list of tens given in a Talmudic passage (Kiddushin 49b) it is said that of the ten measures of speech that descended into the world, nine were taken by women.

Other passages in high praise of women have to be set against the above derogatory ones. A man without a wife lives without joy, blessing, and good, and a man should love his wife as himself and respect her more than himself (Yevamot 62b). When Rav Joseph heard his mother's footsteps he would say: 'Let me rise up before the approach of the *Shekhinah' (Kiddushin 31b). Israel was redeemed from Egypt by virtue of its righteous women (Sotah 11b). Women have greater powers of discernment than men (Niddah 45b). For this reason the age when a girl reaches her majority (*Bat Mitzvah) is 12 while the age for a boy is 13 (*Bar Mitzvah). The Torah is personified as a woman. She is the daughter of God and Israel's bride. It is unnecessary to multiply examples

of how different, and often contradictory, views persist among the Rabbis on the subject of women, as they do in all cultures.

Differing attitudes towards women can also be observed among the Jewish teachers in the Middle Ages. On the whole, the French and German teachers, living in a Christian society, tended to treat women more chivalrously than teachers in Islamic lands. Maimonides, in his writings, often lumps women together with children as people from whom one cannot expect too much intelligence.

Both the *Haskalah and Reform movements can claim with justice that they sought to improve the status of the Jewish woman and this tendency has been followed by Conservative Judaism and by many of the Orthodox.

Wonder The biblical authors call attention to the marvellous features of the universe in order to awaken or increase man's sense of wonder at the works of God. The prophet declares: 'Lift up your eyes on high, and see: who hath created these? He that bringeth out their host by number, He calleth them all by name; by the greatness of His might, and for that He is strong in power, not one faileth' (Isaiah 40: 26), thus anticipating Kant's famous observation: 'Two things fill the mind with ever new and increasing admiration and awe, the more often and the more steadily one reflects on them; the starry heavens above and the moral law within.'

According to Maimonides, reflection on the wonders in creation leads man to the *love and fear of God. Maimonides writes in his Code (Yesodey Ha-Torah, 2. 1–2):

'How does man come to love and fear God? No sooner does man reflect on His deeds and His great and marvellous creatures, seeing in them His incomparable and limitless wisdom, than he is moved to love and to praise and to glorify and he has an intense desire to know the great Name, as David said: "My soul thirsteth for God, for the living God" [Psalms 42: 3]. When man reflects on these very things he immediately recoils in fear and dread, aware that he is only a puny creature, dark and lowly, standing with his minute fraction of unstable thought, in the presence of the Perfect in Knowledge.'

Word In Jewish thought much is said about the power of the word, whether it be the creative word of God or the word in human speech. In *Philo the Logos represents the means by which God creates. The *Targum of Onkelos often uses the Aramaic *memra* ('word') as a means of softening the biblical anthropomorphisms so that instead of the Hebrew in which it is stated that God does this or that it is the *memra* from God that is active. Although the influence of Greek thought is evident in all this, the Hebrew prophets also trace their message to the word or oracle of God. It goes without saying that the identification of the Logos with Jesus in the Gospel of John (1: 14) introduces a notion completely foreign to any version of the Jewish religion. On the contrary, Philo and the Targum are at pains to use the Word in order to distance man from the direct action of the Deity. In Judaism the 'Word' is never 'made flesh'.

Work A high value is placed on work in the Jewish ethic. Human dignity is enhanced when man sustains himself by his own efforts. As the Psalmist says: 'When thou shalt eat the labour of thine hands, happy shalt thou be, and it shall be well with thee' (Psalms 128: 2). In a Talmudic passage (*Pesaḥim* 113a) it is said that the Babylonian teacher, Rav, urged his disciple, Rav Kahana: 'Rather skin a carcass for a fee than be supported by charity. Do not say: "I am a priest" or "I am a scholar" so that it is beneath your dignity.'

In the Jewish tradition a man's work has to be beneficial to society. One who earns his living by following an occupation which makes no constructive contribution to the well-being of others is declared by the Rabbis (*Sanhedrin* 24b) to be so unreliable that he is disqualified from acting as a witness in a court of law. Well known is the Talmudic tale (*Taanit* 23a) of the saint who saw an old man planting trees. 'Why do you plant the trees since you will never enjoy the fruit?' the saint asked, to be given the unanswerable reply (from the Jewish point of view): 'I found trees planted by my ancestors from which I enjoyed the fruit. Surely, it is my duty to plant trees that those who come after me might enjoy their fruit.'

Worlds, Four In the later passages in the Zohar there are one or two references to four worlds, one beneath the other. The doctrine of the four worlds assumes special significance in the Lurianic Kabbalah (see LURIA). The highest of these four worlds is known as 'the World of Emanation'—*Olam Ha-Atzilut* in Hebrew. The root of the word Atzilut is found in the biblical description of the spirit *spreading* from Moses to the elders (Numbers 11. 25). The names of the three lower worlds are taken from the verse: 'Every one that is called by My name, and whom I have *created* for My glory, I have formed him, yea I have *made* him' (Isaiah 43: 7). Thus the World of Emanation is the world of the *Sefirot. The World of Creation (*Olam Ha-Beriah*) evolves from the World of Emanation. Evolving from this is the World of Formation (*Olam Ha-Yetzirah*) and lower still and evolving from this is the World of Action (*Olam Ha-Asiyah*). The World of Creation contains the *throne of glory. The World of Formation is the abode of the heavenly hosts, the *angels. In some Kabbalistic schemes the World of Action is the material cosmos, but in others it is rather the spiritual counterpart and direct source of the material universe.

World to Come There is considerable ambiguity regarding the meaning of the Rabbinic doctrine of the World to Come (Heb. *Olam Ha-Ba*) and its relation to the *resurrection of the dead (see ESCHATOLOGY and HEAVEN AND HELL). In the Middle Ages Maimonides is alone in identifying the World to Come with the immortality of the *soul, while *Nahmanides is emphatic that it refers to this world, which will be renewed, after the resurrection.

The other-worldly thrust is evident in the whole of Jewish thought until the modern period. Of the numerous Rabbinic teachings about the World to Come, the following are typical of this thrust. The Mishnah (*Bava Metzia* 2: 11) rules that if a man's father and his teacher have lost something, he should first try to restore the article lost by his teacher, since a father brings his child into this world whereas a teacher of the Torah brings his students to the World to Come. In Ethics of the Fathers (4. 16) it is said that this world is like a vestibule before the World to Come. 'Prepare yourself in the vestibule, that you may enter into the hall of the palace.'

In *Hasidism and the *Musar movement, the World to Come is conceived of partly in terms of spiritual bliss of the soul after the death of the body. It is not that the doctrine of resurrection is denied in these movements, but it is treated as a mystery so far beyond human apprehension that speculation on it is futile.

Modern Jews entertain a variety of views on the World to Come. The religious naturalists, if they do not reject the whole concept, tend to see the World to Come as a metaphor for the emergence of a better world in the future here on earth. But this is to remove from the concept all its spiritual power and all sense of transcendence.

Naturalistic interpretations of this kind are sadly lacking in numinous quality. Reform Judaism, following to some extent *Philo and Maimonides, does preserve the concept but identifies the World to Come with the immortality of the soul. Conservative Judaism, too, generally follows the Reform line, though both Reform and Conservative Judaism tend to veer towards the naturalistic understanding of the doctrine. This cannot be stated too categorically, however, and many Reform and Conservative Jews still accept the doctrine of the World to Come in its traditional formulation, at least in terms of the immortality of the soul. Some few of the Orthodox as well place the emphasis on the immortality of the soul but, if it is possible to speak of the official Orthodox position in these matters, it obviously includes the resurrection of the dead after the age of the *Messiah in its doctrine of the World to Come.

Worrying For the Jewish moralists, to worry overmuch about the future betokens a lack of faith and trust in divine providence. A popular proverb in the Middle Ages was: 'The past has gone by, the future has still to reply, God's help comes in the blink of an eye, to worry why try?' In *Hasidism it is held to be wrong to worry over-much even about one's spiritual future, since this interferes with the joy the Jew should always experience at being a servant of God. Yet to worry about the future seems to be endemic to the human situation, hence the Talmud (*Yoma* 75a) advises the man who is in a state of anxiety either to put it out of his mind or to find relief by sharing his worries with sympathetic friends. Another moralist is quoted as saying that the only thing worth worrying about is why one worries.

Writing The author of the book of *Ecclesiastes may implicitly protest that there is no end to the making of many books (Ecclesiastes 12: 12) yet, from the earliest times, *books were produced; the sacred Scriptures are only one example. It is true that in Talmudic times the *study of the Torah was conducted solely by word of mouth and, with a few exceptions, the discussions were not committed to writing, but, eventually, the Talmud itself was presented as a literary work. Even in Talmudic times a scholar was advised to cultivate the art of writing for other purposes (Ḥullin 9a). The *Sefer Torah, *tefillin, and the *mezuzah had to be handwritten by a competent scribe. Such writing is called in the Talmud 'heavenly work'. With the invention of *printing there was some discussion as to whether a Sefer Torah and the others could be printed but the consensus emerged that printing does not qualify as writing for these purposes. A *get has to be written by hand. Writing is one of the types of 'work' forbidden on the Sabbath. If the *name of God had been written, it is forbidden to erase it. A recent discussion in this connection is whether the name of God in a word-processor can be erased. The general opinion here is that the words on a word-processor are no more than electrical impulses, so that they are not treated as if they were in writing and the name of God appearing on the screen can be erased—a boon to authors of religious books who work by this method! In the Responsa of Rabbi Akiba Eger (1761–1837) the interesting question is discussed whether writing qualifies as the spoken word; for example, if a man writes a letter on which he states the day of the Omer, does this qualify as counting the *Omer? The testimony of *witnesses has to be presented by them verbally and in person and written testimony is not accepted. Nevertheless, a written bond of indebtedness, duly signed by the witnesses and authorized by the court, is accepted as evidence because of the attestation of the court. The general principle be-

hind all this is that the written *word is more powerful and makes a more permanent impression than the spoken word. A key verse in this connection is: 'Let not kindness and truth forsake thee, bind them about thy neck, write them upon the table of thy heart' (Proverbs 3: 3). Similarly, verbal study is compared to writing in the Ethics of the Fathers (4. 20): 'He that learns as a child, to what is he like? To ink written on new paper. He that learns as an old man, to what is he like? To ink written on paper that has been blotted out.'

Written Torah The term Written Torah usually refers in the Talmudic literature to the *Pentateuch, the Torah of Moses, in contradistinction to the Oral Torah, the traditional explanation of the Written Torah. In a homily by the third-century teacher, Rabbi Johanan (Gittin 60b), a verse (Exodus 34: 27) is read so as to refer to both the Written and the Oral Torah: 'And the Lord said unto Moses, Write thou these words: for by the mouth of these words I have made a covenant with thee and with Israel.' Rabbi Johanan comments that God only made a covenant with Israel for the sake of the Oral Torah, meaning that Israel alone possess the true meaning of the Written Torah which is conveyed only in the Oral Torah. Usually, in the Rabbinic literature, the term Written Torah refers only to the Pentateuch, not to the other books of the *Bible, as when the same Rabbi Johanan says (Megillah 31a) that a teaching is found in the Torah, in the Prophets, and in the Sacred Writings (the Hagiographa). Teachings found in the other sections of the Bible are sometimes referred to (e.g. in Bava Kama 2b) as 'words of tradition', meaning that although these teachings are also part of the Written Torah they are stated only in the later books, the authors of which know them by tradition. Occasionally, however, a verse from other parts of the Bible is also referred to as the Torah (e.g. in *Sanhedrin* 34a). In the Talmudic passage in which is discussed proof 'from the Torah' for the doctrine of the *resurrection of the dead (*Sanhedrin* 91b), texts are quoted from the Prophets and the Hagiographa. It can be said, therefore, that the term Written Torah, at first denoting the Pentateuch, was later extended to include the other biblical books and then both the Written and the Oral Torah were referred by the embracing term '*Torah' and this eventually came to include all the teachings of Judaism. The *Samaritans, on the other hand, accepted only the Pentateuch as the Torah and the *Karaites, while applying the Written Torah to the other books of the Bible as well as the Pentateuch, rejected the doctrine that there is an Oral Torah which explains the Written Torah.

Yad Vashem The organization to commemorate the six million Jews who perished in the *Holocaust, the headquarters building of which is situated on Memorial Hill in Jerusalem. The word yad (lit. 'hand') means 'monument', vashem means 'and a memorial', following the verse: 'Even unto them will I give in My house and within My walls a monument and a memorial [yad vashem] better than sons and daughters; I will give them an everlasting memorial, that shall not be cut off' (Isaiah 56: 5). The Yad Vashem complex contains a Hall of Names (of those who perished); a synagogue; comprehensive archives; a museum of the Holocaust; and a commemoration of the 'righteous *Gentiles', non-Jews who risked their lives to save Jews from the fury of the Nazis.

Yahrzeit 'Time of the year' in Yiddish (from the German Jahrzeit), the anniversary of the death of a parent and other relatives for whom the rites of *mourning are carried out. The special observances of the Yahrzeit originated among the Ashkenazim, German Jews, in the fifteenth century, from where they spread to other Jewries. The *Sephardim generally use the term naḥalah ('inheritance') for Yahrzeit. *Karo does not refer at all to the Yahrzeit but *Isserles (Shulḥan Arukh, Yoreh Deah, 402. 12) records the Ashkenazi practice and states that it is customary for people to fast on the Yahrzeit. As early as Talmudic times there is a reference to people abstaining from eating meat and drinking wine on the anniversary of the death of a parent (Nedarim 12a). Manasseh ben Israel (1604–57), in his treatise on the immortality of the *soul (Nishmat Ḥayyim, ii. 27), gives a mystical reason for observance of the Yarhzeit. On each anniversary of the death the souls of the righteous depart from a lower world to a higher, so that each year there is a further departure, as it were, from their living relatives on earth. On the Yahrzeit the son recites the *Kaddish in the synagogue, *memorial prayers are recited, the son is called up to the *reading of the Torah on the preceding Sabbath, and *charity is distributed to the poor. Originally the Yahrzeit was observed only for parents but it is now the general custom to observe it for the other relatives for whom there is a period of mourning, namely, husband, wife, brother, sister, son, and daughter. Another custom is to keep a Yahrzeit candle burning on the day of the Yahrzeit. This custom is based on the verse: 'The soul of man is a candle of the Lord' (Proverbs 20: 27). The observance of Yahrzeit has become very widespread. Even Jews not otherwise known for their strict observance of the rituals light a Yahrzeit candle and follow the other customs of the Yahrzeit.

Yalkut 'Collection', the name given to an anthology of Midrashic homilies. There are three such anthologies, the main one being the Yalkut Shimeoni, often called simply The Yalkut. This work was compiled by Simeon the Darshan ('Preacher') in the thirteenth century and consists of verse-by-verse homilies to the whole of the Bible, culled from the Midrashim and the Talmud. The Yalkut Shimeoni became for many preachers a substitute for all the other Midrashim, since it contains so much of these. It has proved valuable to modern scholars of Midrashic literature for the variant readings it contains of the Midrashim, and for

Midrashim for which it is the only source.

Yarmulka The skull-cap worn so as not to pray or study the Torah with *bare head. The etymology of this Yiddish word is unknown. The suggestion that it is derived from *yarey malka*, 'he fears the king' (by having his head covered) has nothing to commend it. In some communities the yarmulka is called a *cappel* (small cap) and in Hebrew a *kipah* with the same meaning. The modern Orthodox in Israel wear a small knitted yarmulka known as the *kipah serugah* ('knitted'). The ultra-Orthodox, with their large black yarmulkas covering the whole head, scoff at those poor folk who only cover a very small part with the *kipah serugah*. Orthodox Jews wear the yarmulka at all times, not only for prayer and study. In recent years the wearing of the yarmulka has been taken up by many Reform Jews as well. In the Orthodox tradition only men wear a yarmulka but, nowadays, in Reform and some Conservative circles women wear it too, and women Rabbis generally officiate in the synagogue wearing a yarmulka. The yarmulka is, however, simply a convenient head-covering and has no significance as a religious object in itself.

Yemen Country in south-west Arabia, *Teman* in Hebrew. The Jewish community of the Yemen claimed to be the oldest *Diaspora community in the world, going back, according to legend, to the dispersal after the destruction of the *Temple in 586 BCE. At all events, the ancient Yemenite community lived a distinctive life remote from other Jewish communities with its own liturgical rites, its own pronunciation of Hebrew (oddly enough, similar in some respects to that of Lithuanian Jews), and its own customs. The Yemenite Jews earned their living in a variety of occupations but were renowned especially as goldsmiths and silversmiths. Generally speaking, the Yemenite Jews were treated fairly well by the Islamic rulers, although they suffered periods of adversity and, at times, religious persecution.

Yeshivah Institution of higher learning in which the *study of the Torah is pursued in an organized fashion to produce learned men (see TALMID ḤAKHAM). It would seem that the term Yeshivah (from the root *yashav*, 'to sit') referred originally to a 'sitting' of the court but, at least in the later passages of the Talmud, the term also refers to a school or college in the above sense, and it is this sense that the term became universal in Judaism. The concept of the Yeshivah in which there are lectures and keen debates in matters of the Torah was projected both into the remote past and into the Hereafter. There are Talmudic and Rabbinic references, obviously anachronistic, to the patriarch *Jacob studying for several years in 'the Yeshivah of Shem and Ever'. The Talmud (*Bava Kama* 92a; *Bava Metzia* 86a) speaks of 'the Yeshivah on High' in which the souls of the departed scholars engage in debate and discuss the Torah with God Himself; in the latter passage the scholars are daringly said even to take issue with Him in matters of Jewish law. All this reflects the actual conditions in the Talmudic Yeshivah, although it has to be said that full details are lacking about how Yeshivot functioned in Talmudic times.

After the Holocaust and the destruction of the great European Yeshivot, the few older Yeshivot were reorganized and new Yeshivot were established in the USA; the State of Israel; London, Manchester, and Gateshead in England; and in other European cities. On the contemporary scene there has been an unparalleled proliferation of Yeshivot, with far more students studying the Torah as a full-time occupation than ever before in the history of Jewish learning. The students, teachers, and graduates of the Yeshivot are today referred to as 'the Yeshivah World', which has its own particular stance in matters of learning and strict observance of the *precepts. Since the curriculum of the Yeshivot places the emphasis on theory and the students are often discouraged from taking up a career as a Rabbi, there is now evident a degree of rivalry between the Yeshivah World and the practical Rabbinate. In the ultra-Orthodox circles to which the Yeshivah World belongs, the supreme authorities are rarely Rabbis with a congregation or at the head of a community, but the Yeshivah heads and the Hasidic masters; these are both seen as spiritually superior to the Rabbi, who is said to be immersed in worldly concerns and, by virtue of his position, to be compromising the highest religious standards.

There are a few Yeshivot on the Sephardi and Hungarian pattern, in both of which the courses include the study of the Codes and practical decisions in Jewish law as well as the Talmud. There are also a very few Hasidic Yeshivot, in which the Hasidic classics are studied in addition to the Talmud, and there are one or two Yeshivot in which the Kabbalah is studied in addition to the Talmud. Mention must also be made of the Yeshivot which cater especially to the 'returners' (see BAAL TESHUVAH), young Jews from a non-Orthodox background who wish to become totally observant and who have spiritual needs of their own which the other Yeshivot cannot satisfy. But the majority of the Yeshivot today follow the Lithuanian pattern as this was set in the famous Yeshivot of Volozhyn, *Telz, Mir, Slabodka, Ponevezh, Kamenitz and many others. This Lithuanian type has several distinguishing features. The main subject of study, as in other Yeshivot, is the Talmud, but the Talmud is studied by the special methods developed by Rabbi Hayyim

*Soloveitchik and his disciples—the method of keen analysis of legal concepts.

The students, of whom there are several hundred in the larger Yeshivot (the Yeshivah of Ponevezh in Bene Berak, near Tel Aviv, has a greater number of students than any other Yeshivah in all history), are seated in the large studyhall where they prepare, either on their own or, more usually, with a companion, the section of the tractate on which the Rosh Yeshivah will lecture, lectures usually taking place twice a week. In the majority of the larger Yeshivot both the lectures and the studies in general are conducted in Yiddish as in Lithuania. Attendance at the lectures is not usually compulsory and the general tendency is to rely on the students, as mature scholars (students are not admitted until they are capable of studying the Talmud and commentaries on their own), to pursue their studies without too much interference. Nevertheless, each Yeshivah has a Mashgiah, a kind of moral tutor, who will offer guidance and, where necessary, admonition, to the students for their religious and ethical conduct. The Mashgiah is an exponent of *Musar, the moralistic trend introduced by Israel *Salanter. Once or twice a week the Mashgiah will deliver a 'Musar talk' to the assembled students. For around half an hour each night the students sit on their own reciting the classical works of Musar in a mournful tune as an exercise in self-improvement—'working on the self', as this is called in Yeshivah circles.

The majority of the students come from out of town in obedience to the Talmudic injunction: 'Exile yourself to a place of Torah.' They are accommodated in dormitories in the Yeshivah and have their meals there. The wealthier students pay for the accommodation and tuition but there are scholarships for the poorer ones, especially if they are particularly bright.

The normal age of admission into the Yeshivah is 18. Younger boys are prepared to enter the Yeshivah proper in a preparatory Yeshivah known as Yeshivah Ketanah ('Minor Yeshivah'). Students may study the Bible and other religious works but such studies, if not actually frowned upon, are not part of the curriculum. Secular learning is never allowed within the confines of the Yeshivah, although Yeshivah graduates may take courses in science or economics in order to earn a living. Talmudic learning is not normally pursued by the modern historical–critical methods used in departments of Jewish studies at universities and modern Rabbinical seminaries. The Yeshivah ideal is 'the study of the Torah for is own sake'. For this reason the students do not have a graduation ceremony at the end of the course. There is no end of the course, and the students stay for as long as their parents can support them. Some students will study for the Rabbinate but Rabbinic studies, too, are not normally part of the Yeshivah curriculum. Again on the Lithuanian pattern, however, the majority of the Yeshivot have a *kolel* (the word means 'all-embracing') in which married students and their families are supported while they study for the Rabbinate. Through the Yeshivot, ultra-Orthodoxy has acquired a powerful voice and a renewed confidence in its future.

Yetzer Ha-Tov and Yetzer Ha-Ra

'The good inclination and the evil inclination.' In the typical Rabbinic doctrine, with far-reaching consequences in Jewish religious thought, every human being has two inclinations or instincts, one pulling upwards, the other downwards. These are the 'good inclination'—*yetzer ha-tov*—and the 'evil inclination'—*yetzer ha-ra*. The 'evil inclination' is frequently identified in the Rabbinic literature and elsewhere with the sex instinct but the term also denotes physical appetites in general, aggressive emotions, and unbridled ambition. Although it is called the 'evil inclination', because it can easily lead to wrongdoing, it really denotes more the propensity towards evil rather than something evil in itself. Indeed, in the Rabbinic scheme, the 'evil inclination' provides human life with its driving power and as such is essential to human life. As a well-known Midrash (Genesis Rabbah 9: 7) puts it, were it not for the 'evil inclination' no one would build a house or have children or engage in commerce. This is why, according to the Midrash, Scripture says: 'And God saw everything that he had made and behold, it was very good' (Genesis 1: 31). 'Good' refers to the 'good inclination', 'very good' to the 'evil inclination'. It is not too far-fetched to read into this homily the idea that life without the driving force of the 'evil inclination' would no doubt still be good but it would be a colourless, uncreative, pallid kind of good. That which makes life 'very good' is the human capacity to struggle against the environment and this is impossible without egotistic as well as altruistic, aggressive as well as peaceful, instincts.

The Rabbinic view is, then, realistic. Human beings are engaged in a constant struggle against their propensity for evil but if they so desire they can keep it under control. The means of control are provided by the Torah and the precepts. One of the most remarkable Rabbinic passages in this connection states that the Torah is the antidote to the poison of the 'evil inclination' (*Kiddushin* 30b). The meaning appears to be that when the Torah is studied and when there is submission to its discipline, morbid guilt-feelings are banished and life is no longer clouded by the fear that the 'evil inclination' will bring about one's ruination. The parable told in this passage is of a king who struck his son, later urging the son to keep a plaster on the wound. While the plaster remains on the wound the prince may eat and drink whatever he desires without coming to harm. Only if the plaster is removed will the wound fester when the prince indulges his appetites. God has 'wounded' man by creating him with the 'evil inclination'. But the Torah is the plaster on the wound, which prevents it from festering and enables him to embrace life without fear.

It follows that for the Rabbis the struggle against the 'evil inclination' is never-ending in this life. Nowhere in the Rabbinic literature is there the faintest suggestion that it is possible for humans permanently to destroy the 'evil inclination' in this life. (Eschatological references to the total destruction of the 'evil inclination', and its transformation into a 'good angel', are irrelevant. The *World to Come is not the world in which humans struggle in the here and now.) For the Rabbis, the true hero is, as stated in Ethics of the Fathers (4. 1), one who 'subdues' his 'evil inclination', one who exercises severe self-control, refusing to yield to temptation. It is not given to anyone actually to slay the 'evil inclination'. Nor are there references in the Rabbinic literature to the idea, prevalent in the Jewish mystical and moralistic literatures, of 'breaking the evil inclination'.

The doctrine of the 'evil inclination' makes it precarious blithely to affirm, as is often done, that Judaism, unlike Christianity, knows nothing of the notion of original *sin. There is no doubt a difference in emphasis and, in Judaism, it is the Torah not a 'saviour' which counteracts the power of the 'evil inclination', but that human beings have a propensity for sin is not denied.

The idea that the study of the Torah is in itself sufficient to overcome the 'evil inclination' is prominent in traditional Rabbinic thought. The student of the Torah, it was held, has little need for devotional books, since the Torah he studies possesses the marvellous quality of automatically refining the character. Revealing in this connection is the story told of Hayyim of *Volozhyn, who overheard two students sitting in the study hall of the Yeshivah discussing how to combat the 'evil inclination'. The teacher said to them: 'The evil inclination is happy to see you discussing how to overcome him as long as talking about him interrupts your study of the Torah.' Yet both *Hasidism and the *Musar movement believed that other means are also required in addition to study—enthusiasm and the idea that the divine power pervades all for Hasidism, and sombre reflection on the vanities of the world for Musar. A saying of the Hasidic master, *Nahman of Bratslav, has it that the 'evil inclination' is like a man asking a high price for that which he holds in his closed fist. When the price has been paid the fist is opened and it is seen to hold nothing at all. Israel *Salanter, founder of the Musar movement, is said to have tried to analyse the doctrine of the evil inclination'. Is it to be identified with the bodily instincts, or is it a spiritual force? He replied that it is both. For if it were only a spiritual force, it should tempt all men in the same way, whereas physical temptation varies from person to person. On the other hand, if it were only to be identified with physical appetites, why is it that it entices to nonphysical faults and vices such as pride, anger, and hatred? In the Musar school generally, preoccupation with the 'evil inclination' often results in morbid introspection and a jaundiced view of human nature. Yet one of the most extreme of the Musar teachers, Rabbi Yoizel Horowitz of Navaradock, a man who, in his youth, lived the ascetic life of a hermit, could say that the doctrine of the *yetzer ha-ra* is not intended to deny the value of human inclination as such. On the contrary, the doctrine implies that for a man to be absorbed in petty, worthless things is for him to have a 'bad' inclination, bad in the sense of narrow, one that actually frustrates his wider and true inclination to enjoy a decent, moral, and worthy life, not only in order to go to *heaven but in order to enjoy life to the full in the here and now. Hasidism is far less obsessive than the Musarists, believing that joy in the service of God and the influence of the *Zaddik are sufficient, together with the balm of the Torah, to enable the Hasid to free himself from the fetters of the 'evil inclination'. Modern Jewish thought usually prefers to discuss the human situation in the abstract and is far less inclined to speak of the good and evil inclinations. Yet it is still aware, as it must be, of the contradiction in the human psyche between what is and what ought to be, and some moderns see no reason to abandon the older, powerful terminology.

Yiddish From *Jüdisch* ('Jewish') and *Deutsch* ('German'), the language spoken by Jews whose ancestors came from Germany, the *Ashkenazim. Yiddish is an amalgam of Old German, Hebrew, and Aramaic, written with Hebrew characters and reading, as in Hebrew, from right to left. At a later date Slavonic elements were introduced and later still, elements of the languages of other lands in which Jews resided. Yiddish was used in writing, until modern times, chiefly for religious purposes, for example in translations of the Bible and *Prayer Book for the benefit of Jews, especially *women, with only a scanty knowledge of the original Hebrew. In ultra-Orthodox circles Yiddish is preferred to Hebrew for everyday, secular use; Hebrew is reserved for sacred activities. The traditional *Yeshivah uses Yiddish for the exposition of the Talmud, so much so that many *Sephardim who study in the Yeshivot have been obliged to master the language. In the Yeshivah World in the USA there has been such a strong assimilation of English into Yiddish that this form is sometimes spoken of as Yinglish. There are a number of different Yiddish dialects and different forms of pronunciation. There exists now an abundance of Yiddish literature in the modern vein and a Yiddish Press still flourishes. Yiddish is also studied academically in university departments. The term Yiddishkeit ('Jewishness') is now often used as a synonym for Judaism but with a more popular and 'nationalistic' connotation. Yiddish is a homely, one might say voluptuous language and has come to be seen as the liveliest expression of the Jewish spirit, although with the rise of *Zionism and the establishment of the State of Israel a keen rivalry has developed between those who prefer Hebrew and those who prefer Yiddish; the former, naturally, win out for obvious reasons.

Yigdal 'May He be magnified', the opening word of a hymn, after which it is named. The Yigdal hymn consists of Maimonides' thirteen *principles of faith in poetic form. In the Ashkenazi version, Yigdal has thirteen lines, one for each of the principles. The Sephardi version adds: 'These thirteen principles are the foundation of Moses' Torah and his prophecy.' Yigdal is written in rhyme and metre, the rhyme consisting of a repetition at the end of each line of the same sounds. The hymn was composed in Italy at the beginning of the fourteenth century, probably by Daniel ben Judah of Rome. Yigdal is printed in Ashkenazi prayer books at the beginning of the daily service but is normally chanted only at the end of the evening service on the Sabbath and the festivals. There are a number of popular melodies for Yigdal. Some communities use a special melody for the Sabbath and a different one for each of the festivals.

Yiḥudim 'Unifications', meditations

on various combinations of the letters of the Tetragrammaton and on the various vocalizations of this name provided in the writings of Hayyim *Vital and other Kabbalists of the Lurianic school. Isaac *Luria, Vital's master, provided detailed yiḥudim to be performed at particular periods and in accordance with the special soul-root of each mystical adept. The yiḥudim were believed to be theurgic, affecting the upper worlds and the elevation of the mystic's soul. In post-Lurianic prayer books, the instruction is given to the worshipper to recite: 'For the sake of the unification of the Holy One, blessed be He, and His *Shekhinah' before carrying out a precept of the Torah. Rabbi Ezekiel *Landau took strong exception to the recital of this formula by the Hasidim, which resulted in a fierce polemic between Landau and some of the Hasidic masters. Another of the yiḥudim, printed in the Kabbalistic prayer books, is that in which the letters of the Tetragrammaton are mingled with the letters of the divine name, Adonai ('Lord'). The Kabbalists, however, sought to limit the practice of other, more esoteric, yiḥudim to initiates and, even for these, urged that it is all to be treated with great circumspection.

Yom Ha-Atzmaut 'Independence Day', celebrating the proclamation of the Israeli Declaration of Independence on 5 Iyyar 5708 (corresponding to 14 May 1948). This day was declared a public holiday by law in Israel in 1949 and is a day of rejoicing for the majority of Jews except for the anti-Zionist group Neturey Karta, which observes it as a day of mourning and fasting. In order to avoid public desecration of the Sabbath, when the day falls on a Friday or a Sabbath, the celebrations are held on the previous Thursday. In addition to a torch-lighting ceremony at the tomb of *Herzl on Mount Herzl in Jerusalem, various cultural and sporting events take place. However, the earlier prac-

tice of a parade by the armed forces of Israel has been discontinued as being too militaristic to be in accord with the Jewish spirit.

The problem of religious services to mark the day was aggravated by the reluctance of Orthodox Rabbis to introduce a new religious festival for all Jews, even though the *Halakhah advocates prayers of thanksgiving for '*miracles' through which individual communities are saved from destruction. There was a similar reluctance to introduce prayers without direct sanction in the tradition on the grounds that we 'pygmies' have no right to emulate the spiritual 'giants' of the past who created the Jewish *liturgy. Eventually, however, the Israeli Rabbinate drew up an order of service acceptable to most traditionalists.

The theological tension behind the whole question of celebrating Yom Ha-Atzmaut as a religious festival with special prayers is severe. On the one hand innovations of such a far-reaching nature have been frowned upon even by those who would not go along with Rabbi Moses *Sofer's round declaration: 'Anything new is forbidden by the Torah.' On the other hand, there is the pressing need to be grateful to God and to thank Him for one of the most tremendous events in all Jewish history. The tension is partly resolved by trying to achieve a balance between too startling an innovation and a failure to give the day any religious significance at all by treating it as a purely secular holiday. This is only another way of saying that the full theological implications of the establishment of the State of Israel have not as yet been explored.

Yom Kippur 'Day of Atonement', the great fast on 10 Tishri. The Yom Kippur ritual in *Temple times was based on the vivid description in Leviticus 16. On this day, the *High Priest was to discard his garments of splendour and, wearing only the plain linen tunic, breeches, girdle, and turban of the common priest, he was to enter the Holy of Holies, the most sacred spot in the Sanctuary, there to atone for his own sins, those of his household, and those of the whole community of Israel. Two goats were to be taken, upon which lots were to be cast, one for the Lord and one for *Azazel. The goat chosen for the Lord was to be offered as a sacrifice. The other goat was to be taken to Azazel in the wilderness. The major part of the Talmudic tractate *Yoma* is devoted to the Temple rites on Yom Kippur, even though the Temple had long been destroyed when the tractate was finally compiled.

For the Talmudic Rabbis, Yom Kippur is the great and holy day when Israel meets its God. Yom Kippur is judgement day, the culmination of the *Ten Days of Penitence which begin with *Rosh Ha-Shanah. The verse: 'Seek the Lord while He can be found, call to Him while He is near' (Isaiah 55: 6) is applied by the Rabbis to these ten days, beginning on Rosh Ha-Shanah and ending on Yom Kippur, when God is very near. It was on Yom Kippur, say the Rabbis, that Moses came down from the mount with the second *tablets of stone, bringing his people the good tidings that God had shown mercy to them and had pardoned them for the sin of worshipping the *golden calf.

The Mishnah in tractate *Yoma* (8: 9) records the accepted teaching that Yom Kippur atones only for sins committed against God, for religious offences. But for offences against a neighbour there is no atonement on Yom Kippur until the neighbour has been pacified and the wrong done righted.

Although Yom Kippur is a day of fasting and self-denial it is, for the Rabbis, a day of joy on which sin is pardoned and reconciliation achieved with God. By the Middle Ages, Yom Kippur had evolved as a day to be spent almost entirely in prayer and worship. Some Jews would not even return home on the night of Yom Kippur, preferring to spend it in the synagogue chanting hymns and singing psalms until daybreak. Although in the ordinary way it is forbidden to sleep in the synagogue, an exception was made on this day so as to enable those who spent the whole twenty-four hours in the synagogue to snatch some sleep. Most of the Rabbis, however, advised against the practice of an all-night vigil if as a result the worshipper would become drowsy during the prayers of the day.

Yom Kippur has retained its numinous appeal. Many Jews, otherwise not observant of the rites and ceremonies of the Jewish religion, make it a point of honour to be present in the synagogue on this day and to fast for the whole twenty-four hours. While Rabbis are fond of reminding their congregations that the observance of Yom Kippur is far from being the be-all and end-all of Judaism, this day seems to possess a unique appeal to Jews who are at all sensitive to the spiritual side of Jewish existence.

The name Yom Kippur is the Rabbinic version of the biblical (plural form) *Yom Ha-Kippurim. Yom* means 'day' and the root meaning of *kippur, kippurim,* and *kapparah* (the form most frequently found for 'atonement') is 'to scour', 'to cleanse thoroughly', 'to erase'. Sin is thought of as a stain to be removed if the soul is to appear pure before its Creator. Another possible meaning is 'to cover'. In atonement sin is covered; it is hidden out of sight. Yom Kippur is thus the day of cleansing from sin, the day on which Israel once again finds favour in God's eyes.

'In the seventh month, on the tenth day of the month, ye shall afflict your souls' (Leviticus 16: 29). From this verse is derived the obligation to fast on Yom Kippur. The word *nefesh*, usually translated as 'soul', means in this and other biblical passages something like the 'self', so that a more accurate translation would be: 'You shall afflict yourselves.' From the earliest times this 'affliction' was understood not in terms of positive self-torment such as flagellation, but in the negative sense of self-denial, that is, by abstaining from food and drink. It is of interest that when the prophet speaks of 'afflicting the soul' (in the portion read as the *Haftarah on Yom Kippur) he uses this expression as a synonym for fasting: 'Wherefore have we fasted, and Thou seest not? Wherefore have we afflicted our soul, and Thou takest no knowledge? Behold in the day of your fast ye pursue your business, and exact all your labours' (Isaiah 58: 3). *Fasting generally is associated with prayer and repentance (and see ASCETICISM). With regard to Yom Kippur in particular the obligation to fast is understood by the commentators as having four aims. Fasting is a penance, an exercise in self-discipline, a means of focusing the mind on the spiritual, and a means of awakening compassion. To know what it means to go hungry, even for a single day, encourages pity for the hungry, the oppressed, and the unfortunate who suffer far worse deprivations. This thought is expressed by Isaiah, which is one of the reasons why the passage above is read as the Haftarah on Yom Kippur. The prophet castigates his people for their neglect of the poor and needy. Fasting and a pretence of piety is not acceptable to God, the prophet declares, if it serves merely as a cloak for inhumanity: 'Is not this the fast that I have chosen? To loose the fetters of wickedness, to undo the bands of the yoke, and to let the oppressed go free, and that ye break every yoke? Is it not to deal thy bread to the hungry, and that thou bring the poor that are cast out to thy house? When thou seest the naked, that thou cover him, and that thou hide not thyself from thine own flesh?' The Mishnah (Yoma 8: 1) lists certain other 'afflictions' to be practised on Yom Kippur in addition to fasting. 'On the Day of Atonement, eating, drinking, bathing, anointing [the body with oil, the normal practice in Mishnaic times], putting on sandals, and marital intercourse are forbidden.' 'Putting on sandals' refers to the wearing of leather shoes only, so that many pious Jews today wear rubber shoes or felt slippers during the whole of Yom Kippur. Another reason given for not wearing shoes of leather on Yom Kippur is that these can only be obtained after an animal has been killed and since God's mercy is over all His creatures, it is not fitting to wear leather on the day when God's mercy is sought.

Yom Kippur Katan 'Minor Yom Kippur', the name given to the day before *Rosh Hodesh ('New Moon') in that this day is treated as one of fasting, repentance, and supplication on the analogy of *Yom Kippur. Yom Kippur Katan originated among the *Safed Kabbalists in the sixteenth century and is referred to by a disciple of Moses *Cordovero, Abraham Galante, who states that it was a local custom in Safed for men, women, and schoolchildren to fast on this day and to spend the whole day in penitential prayer, confession of sin, and flagellation.

Yom Tov Ishbili Spanish Talmudist and Halakhic authority (d. 1330), known as the Ritba, after the initial letters of his name, Rabbi Yom Tov ben Avraham Ishbili (Ishbili means 'of Seville'). The Ritba's teachers were Solomon Ibn *Adret and, especially, Aaron Ha-Levi of Barcelona. After Ibn Adret's death, the Ritba was acknowledged as the most prominent spiritual guide by the Jews of Spain and other lands. Ritba was a student of philosophy. His Sefer Ha-Zikkaron ('Book of Remembrance') defends Maimonides' Guide of the Perplexed against the strictures of *Nahmanides in the latter's Commentary to the Torah, although Ritba believed that Maimonides' approach was only valid from the philosophical point of view, while Nahmanides was also right from the Kabbalistic point of view; the conflict between philosophy and the Kabbalah in the time of Ritba finds echoes in his works.

York, Martyrs of Less than a year after the coronation of King Richard I (Richard the Lion-heart) in September 1189, anti-Jewish rioting broke out in the city of York, despite the king's orders that the Jews were not to be molested. The sheriff allowed the Jews to take refuge in the royal castle, Clifford's Tower, where a tablet marks the spot. Suspecting the intentions of the sheriff, the Jews expelled him from the castle which was surrounded by a mob intent on killing the Jews and plundering their possessions. The Jews of York, among whom was the famous scholar Yom Tov of Joigny, one of the Tosafists (see TOSAFOT), committed mass suicide on the Sabbath before Passover, corresponding to 6 March 1190. The few who did not give their lives pleaded that they be allowed to escape death by converting to Christianity. Being reassured, they left the castle and were massacred. In the later Halakhah the martyrdom of the Jews of York was used as proof that *suicide is permitted if it is in order to escape torture or conversion. The community of York was later reestablished and continued until the expulsion of the Jews from England in 1290. The belief is unfounded that a *herem exists against Jews living in York, and a small community has existed there since the nineteenth century.

Yose, Rabbi A number of Rabbis mentioned in the Talmud are called Yose, each with his father's name, but where the name Rabbi Yose occurs on its own the reference is to Rabbi Yose ben Halafta, a second-century Tanna (see TANNAIM AND AMORAIM). Together with Rabbi *Meir, Rabbi Judah, and Rabbi *Simeon ben Yohai, Rabbi Yose is numbered among the sages taught by Rabbi *Akiba in his old age. Rabbi Yose is quoted more than 300 times in the Mishnah and very frequently in the *Tosefta. Debates between Rabbi Yose and his colleagues are recorded, the Talmud (*Eruvin* 46b) stating that in such instances the opinion of Rabbi Yose is decisive. Rabbi *Judah the Prince, editor of the Mishnah, was a pupil of Rabbi Yose.

Zaddik The charismatic leader in *Hasidism, also known as the *Rebbe in order to distinguish him from the *Rabbi in the conventional sense. This spelling of the word in English is now the usual form but a more correct transliteration would be *tzaddik*, meaning 'righteous man'. This type of spiritual guide, renowned not for his learning but for his saintliness and ability as a religious mentor, is not entirely unknown in traditional Judaism. The model for the Zaddik was found in Hasidism in the miracle-working prophets *Elisha and *Elijah, in some of the holy men of prayer in Talmudic times, and in various saintly figures (see SAINTS) in the Middle Ages. But only in Hasidism, from the earliest days of the movement, did the figure of the Zaddik come to occupy a supreme role, with total submission to him being demanded of his followers. Later in the history of Hasidism, the Zaddik's son was believed to have acquired something of his charisma, based on the idea that the Zaddik's holy thoughts when he made love to his wife could succeed in bringing down an elevated soul into the child conceived at the time, so that the notion of dynasties of Zaddikim developed, each with its own loyal followers.

Whenever Hasidim pay a visit to the 'court' of the Zaddik (the royal metaphor is applied throughout) they present him, through his *gabbai* ('retainer' or 'overseer'), a *kvittel* ('scrap of paper') and a *pidyon nefesh* ('redemption of soul'). The *kvittel* is a written statement by the Hasid, containing his name and that of his mother, of his more pressing needs, material or spiritual. The *pidyon nefesh* is a sum of money which goes to the upkeep of the Zaddik. The usual rationale for the latter is that, while the Zaddik really needs nothing for himself, his Hasidim can only have real contact with him by contributing to his upkeep. In some versions of Hasidism the Zaddik must live in regal splendour in order for the channel of blessing which he represents to be broad and wide. Much of the money, it has also to be said, is distributed for charitable purposes.

The Hasidim were not unaware that in making the claims they did for the Zaddik they were implying that, in some measure, the Zaddik possesses powers akin to those of the biblical prophets. They defended this daring comparison of the Zaddik to the prophets or the holy men of earlier times on various grounds, one of the most popular being that in the generations before the advent of the *Messiah an abundance of new spiritual illumination has been released in anticipation of the tremendous event.

The prayer of the Zaddik for his followers to be blessed with 'children, life and sustenance' is found in many a Hasidic text. The basis in the Talmud is the saying (*Moed Katan* 28a): 'Life, children and sustenance depend not on merit but on *mazzal*.' In the context *mazzal* means 'luck'—it is not by a person's merits that he has good health, sustenance, and children but by sheer chance. But Hasidism, treating the word *mazzal* as if it came from a root meaning to flow, use the Talmudic passage for the doctrine of Zaddikism. Even if a man does not deserve to have good health, sustenance, and children on his own merits, he may be given them as a result of the special 'flow' of divine blessing through the 'channel' that is the Zaddik.

Zangwill, Israel English novelist and

playwright (1864–1926). Zangwill's writings are relevant to Jewish religious trends in the contemporary world because they express, better than most, the tensions in his soul which were typical of those suffered by thinking Jews torn between intense loyalty to the religious tradition and the allure of the wider world. Troubled, for instance, by the doctrine of the *Chosen People, Zangwill countered with his famous epigram: 'The Chosen People is a choosing people', thus shifting imperceptibly the emphasis from God to the people. Jewish peoplehood was in the forefront of Zangwill's thought and activities. When *Herzl visited England in 1895, Zangwill introduced him to a number of influential Jews, and as a result the Zionist movement took root in Great Britain with Zangwill as an influential member. Later on Zangwill, still emphasizing the significance of Jewish peoplehood, took up the idea of Jewish territorialism as a substitute for *Zionism, founding the ITO, the Jewish Territorialist Organisation, in which what mattered was not the settlement of Jews in Palestine but having them settle somewhere, anywhere in the world—wherever they could build a home as an independent people.

Zanz Town in Galicia of which Hayyim Halberstam (1793–1876) was the Rabbi; he was also the founder of the Zanzer dynasty in *Hasidism. Halberstam, a profound Talmudist, was won over to Hasidism by Shalom Rokeah of *Belz. All eight of his sons became Hasidic masters, the most famous of them being Ezekiel Shraga of Sieniwa (1811–90). A grandson founded the dynasty of Bobov, and Bobover Hasidism still flourishes in the USA. Like Hayyim himself, his descendants were noted both for their learning and their zealotry. Hayyim Halberstam, unusually for a Hasidic master, was familiar with the works of the medieval Jewish philosophers. It is said that on *Kol Nidre night he would study Maimonides' *Guide of the Perplexed*, evidently believing that many of its ideas can be accommodated within Hasidic doctrine. His *Divrey Hayyim* on the Torah was published in Munkacs in 1877 and his *Responsa, with the same title, in Lvov in 1875. A mystical note is sounded even in Halberstam's Responsa, as when he defends (no. 105) the idea that the *Holy Spirit was still at work in the writing of such later authors as Hayyim *Ibn Atar and that anyone who denies this is a heretic.

Zealots Jewish freedom-fighters in the War against Rome, 66–73 CE. *Josephus in *The Jewish War* refers to the Zealots together with other rebels against the Roman occupation. The Mishnah (*Sanhedrin* 9: 6) refers to the Zealots as *Kannaim*, a Hebrew word with the same connotation, and generally in the Rabbinic literature an ambivalent attitude emerges towards these rebels. Modern scholarship discusses at length the relationship between the Zealots, the Sicarii ('dagger men'), other rebels against Rome, and the *Qumran sectarians, a question much discussed nowadays. In later Jewish literature, the term *Kannaim* is applied to zealots of every description who use questionable means in their fight against those they consider to be enemies of God and the Jewish religion. Jacob *Emden, for example, was proud to call himself *kannai ben kannai* ('a zealot son of a zealot') in his struggle against the followers of *Shabbetai Zevi. (See also FANATICISM.)

Zechariah Prophet whose first prophecy was made in the second year of the reign of Darius, 520 BCE. The prophets Zechariah, *Haggai, and *Malachi are often mentioned together in Jewish literature as the last of the biblical prophets, after whom, the Talmud (*Yoma* 9b) states, the *Holy Spirit ceased to function in Israel. Zechariah and Haggai sought to encourage the people to continue the task of rebuilding the *Temple, begun after the return from the Babylonian exile but discontinued because of its difficulty. The book of Zechariah is the eleventh in the Book of the Twelve Prophets and is in two parts. The first eight chapters deal with the life and activity of the prophet but in the last six chapters a strong eschatological note (see ESCHATOLOGY) is sounded and came to be understood as referring to the Messianic age (see MESSIAH). The majority of modern biblical scholars consider the author of these final chapters to be an unknown prophet. The book of Zechariah is particularly noted for the vivid descriptions of various prophetic *visions, especially of *angels. The verse (Zechariah 14: 9): 'And the Lord shall be King over all the earth; in that day shall the Lord be One, and His name one' forms the conclusion of the Alenu prayer and is seen to express the supreme hope of Jews for a future in which all mankind will hail God as King and obey His laws (see CHOSEN PEOPLE and UNIVERSALISM).

Zeitlin, Hillel Religious thinker and exponent of Jewish *mysticism (1871-1942). Zeitlin belonged to a family of *Habad Hasidim, acquiring in his youth a sound knowledge in all branches of traditional Jewish learning. He was self-educated in European literature and thought and, attracted by these studies, he gave up to a large degree the practice of the Jewish religion. At a later period in his life, Zeitlin returned to his Jewish roots to become once again a strictly Orthodox Jew. Zeitlin contributed to Jewish journals essays in Hebrew and Yiddish on various themes. His writings on the Kabbalah and *Hasidism, include a key to the Zohar and an annotated translation of the introduction to the Zohar. These were collected and published in two volumes in Tel Aviv (1965 and 1975). In 1943 Zeitlin died a martyr's death when, wearing his *Tallit and *tefillin, he was shot by the Nazis on the way to the concentration camp of Treblinka to which they were taking him.

Zelophehad, Daughters of The book of Numbers (27: 1-11) tells of Zelophehad dying in the wilderness without leaving any sons to inherit his portion in the land promised to the tribes. The five daughters of Zelophehad presented to Moses their claim to the inheritance. When Moses, uncertain of the law in such a case, presented the claim of the five daughters to God, Moses was informed that, in the absence of sons, daughters do inherit. When the heads of the clan later appealed to Moses that the decision in the case of the daughters might result in a diminution of their tribal lands, since the daughters might marry into another tribe so that the land given to them would then pass over to that tribe, Moses, at the command of God, decided that the daughters of Zelophehad might only marry into their own tribe (Numbers 36). According to the Rabbis this ruling, banning intermarriage between the tribes, was rescinded in a later generation (see SUCCESSION). Together with other biblical heroines, the daughters of Zelophehad have been praised by Jewish feminists (see FEMINISM) as pioneers in the struggle for women's rights.

Zemirot 'Songs', sung at the table on the Sabbath. The Zemirot, some of them composed as Sabbath-table hymns, others as independent liturgical hymns and adapted for the purpose, date from the Middle Ages down to the sixteenth century. Each community, and even individual families, often have their own special melodies for the Zemirot with different tunes for each. The idea behind the Zemirot is the need to celebrate the Sabbath as a day of joy and gladness with a combination of spiritual and material fare, a day which, in the words of the Rabbis, is a semblance of the *World to Come. One of the most popular of the Zemirot, 'Yah Ribbon', was composed by Israel Najara (1555–1628) in Aramaic. The opening stanza of this hymn (in Israel Abraham's translation) conveys the flavour of the Zemirot: 'God of the world, eternity's sole Lord! King over kings, be now Thy name adored! Blessed are we to whom thou didst accord this gladsome time Thy wondrous ways to scan.'

Zephaniah Prophet in Jerusalem during the reign of King Josiah (640–608 BCE). According to the Rabbis, Zephaniah was a contemporary of the prophet Jeremiah and the prophetess Huldah. Since he castigates the people of Jerusalem for worshipping idols it would seem that Zephaniah's oracles were delivered before the reforms of Josiah in 621 BCE, when the king suppressed idolatry. The only detail of Zephaniah's life is provided by the superscription to the book of Zephaniah (the ninth in the Book of the Twelve Prophets): 'The word of the Lord that came to Zephaniah son of Cushi son of Gedaliah son of Amariah son of Hezekiah, during the reign of King Josiah son of Amon of Judah.' Abraham *Ibn Ezra holds that the Hezekiah referred to is King Hezekiah, since otherwise there would be no reason for tracing Zephaniah's descent particularly to him, but this view is contested since this ancestor is not called King Hezekiah. The most prominent feature in Zephaniah's prophecies is his warning that the 'day of the Lord' will dawn in which the idolaters will be severely punished for their apostasy, yet this 'day' will also usher in a new era in which Jerusalem will be saved from her oppressors and God will dwell therein (Zephaniah 3: 14–29). This final section of the book of Zephaniah features prominently in later Jewish *eschatology.

Zerubbabel Governor of Judah in the late sixth century BCE (the name means 'scion of Babylon'), to whom there are references in the books of *Ezra, *Haggai, and *Zechariah. Zerubbabel was a grandson of King Jehoiachim of Judah who was deposed by Nebuchadnezzar in 597 BCE. In Zechariah's vision (Zechariah 3 and 4), Zerubbabel and Joshua the High Priest are encouraged in their attempt to rebuild the Temple. In this section the words occur: 'This is the word of the Lord to Zerubbabel: Not by might, nor by power, but by My spirit' (Zechariah 4: 6), words that have served as an inspiration throughout Jewish history to practical leaders of the same type as Zerubbabel and as a reminder to them not to depend over-much on their own abilities. Zerubbabel remains, however, a shadowy figure, and there is considerable uncertainty about the exact role he played after the return from the Babylonian exile. In one passage in the Talmud (*Sanhedrin* 38a) he is identified with *Nehemiah. In the *'Maoz Tzur' hymn sung on *Hanukkah, the name Zerubbabel is rhymed with *ketz bavel* ('the end of Babylon').

Zevi Elimelech of Dynow Hasidic *Zaddik, Rabbi, and author (1785–1841). Extremely learned in the Talmud, Codes, Kabbalah, and the literature of early *Hasidism, Zevi Elimelech objected to Jews studying secular subjects and was a fiery opponent of the *Haskalah. Once, it is reported, carried away by his zeal, he begged God that even if Moses *Mendelssohn was in heaven, since he was a pious Jew in practice, he should be brought down to the nethermost part of *Gehinnom for the part he played in causing Israel to sin. Zevi Elimelech, a very prolific author, is best known for his *Beney Yissakhar* (*Sons of Issaachar*), a classic of Hasidic literature abounding in original ideas, though based firmly in the tradition. The tile of the book is taken

from the verse: 'And the sons of Issachar, men that had understanding of
the times' (1 Chronicles 12: 33). This
refers to the nature of the work as a
detailed commentary to the 'sacred
times' in the Jewish *calendar, the Sabbath and the *festivals.

Zimra, David Ben Egyptian Halakhic authority and Kabbalist
(1479 1573), known, after the initial letters of his name, as Radbaz (Rabbi David
Ben Zimra). Radbaz, leaving Spain,
where he was born, at the time of the
expulsion of the Jews in 1492, studied
in *Safed and then became a judge in
Cairo and eventually both the spiritual
and lay head of Egyptian Jewry. Towards the end of his long life he settled
again in Safed, where he served as a
member of Joseph *Karo's court. As a
man of great wealth Radbaz was able to
achieve a stern independence throughout his career. Radbaz is chiefly
renowned for his collection of Responsa
containing over 2,000 items. *Azulai
writes of him: 'In the light of his keen
reasoning walked those who had wan-
dered in darkness and his Responsa
went forth to every questioner from all
over the world.'

Zionism The movement that arose at
the end of the nineteenth century with
the aim of establishing a homeland for
Jews in Palestine, as it then was. The
actual term 'Zionism' was coined by
Nathan Birnbaum in 1891 to denote the
political efforts to achieve this aim, although the settlement of Jews in Palestine had begun earlier and was
represented by the *Hovevey Tzion*
('Lovers of Zion'). Zion had been a synonym for *Jerusalem from biblical
times. The Psalmist, for example, makes
the exiles in Babylon say: 'By the rivers
of Babylon, there we sat down, yea we
wept, when we remembered Zion'
(Psalms 137: 1). In the Middle Ages,
Judah *Halevi wrote his 'Songs of Zion'
in yearning for the resettlement of

Jews in Palestine, of which Zion had become the supreme symbol. Theodor
*Herzl's Zionism was thus only new in
that the opportunity was seized of attempting the settlement of Jews by political means. The full Zionist story has
been told in numerous books and pam-
phlets. Here can only be considered the
implications for the Jewish religion of
Zionism, and its implementation in the
establishment of the State of Israel.

Opposition to Zionism on the part of
some Jews came from a number of different directions. Many Reform leaders
thought of Jewish nationalism as a betrayal of *universalism. It was a divine
boon, they argued, not a calamity, that
Jews had no land of their own and so
were able to keep their religion un-
sullied by particularistic national ideas
which tend to frustrate the wider hope
of a mankind united in the service of
God. Many Orthodox thinkers shared
the Reform suspicion of a revival of
Jewish nationalism and they added the
fear that a return to the Holy Land by
human effort in the pre-Messianic age
amounts to a denial of the *Messiah
for whose coming Jews are to wait
patiently. According to the classical
scheme, the Jews, exiled from their
land because of their sins, had to wait
until God sent the Messiah to redeem
them from subservience to the nations
and bring them back to the land of Israel. It was positively impious, on this
view, to anticipate the divine intervention by human endeavour on the political level, although the religious duty of
settling in the Holy Land was still binding on individual Jews who should,
whenever possible, go to live in Palestine.

However, this opposition to Zionism
on the part of Reform Judaism eventually yielded not only to a tolerant acceptance but to strong advocacy on the
part of some of the most distinguished
and influential Reform Rabbis who became, indeed, leaders of the Zionist
movement.

Two factors have combined to make all this debate a dead letter. The *Holocaust, in which six million Jews perished, brought in its wake a fierce and completely justified resolve on the part of Jews everywhere to put an end to the kind of Jewish homelessness which had made such horror possible. The creation of the State of *Israel, a result of this resolve, made academic the whole Zionist question. The State of Israel is a reality. It has won by its achievements the goodwill of the majority of Jews everywhere. The existence of the State of Israel has so influenced Jewish thinking that it is now nonsensical to debate whether Jews are *only* the adherents of the Jewish religion. In Israel, at least, the Jews are a nation.

Zodiac An imaginary zone in the heavens determined by the twelve different positions of the full moon during the year. These twelve constellations were seen by the ancient astronomers as having the appearance of animals and other creatures, hence the name zodiac from the Greek, meaning 'little animals'. The constellations of the zodiac feature prominently in astrological calculations and are referred to by Jews who believe in *astrology, a belief rejected by Maimonides who only refers to the zodiac in an astronomical context (*Yesodey Ha-Torah*, 3. 6) without actually using the word zodiac. Nor is there any mention of the zodiac in the Talmud. In the Middle Ages, however, the constellations of the zodiac are referred to and are given in Hebrew as an exact equivalent of the Latin terms.

Zohar 'Illumination' or 'Brightness', the classical work of the Kabbalah, containing the record of revelations regarding the divine mysteries alleged to have been vouchsafed to the second-century teacher Rabbi *Simeon ben Yohai and his mystic circle. The name Zohar is based on the verse (Daniel 12: 3), commented on at the beginning of the work (as a comment on the first verse of Genesis): 'And the intelligent shall shine like the brightness [ke-zohar] of the firmament, and they that turn many to righteousness like the stars for ever and ever.' The Zohar first saw the light of day through the efforts of *Moses de Leon of Guadalajara in Spain, at the end of the thirteenth century. Modern scholarship concurs with the views of *Scholem that Moses de Leon was in fact the author of the work, which does not mean that Moses de Leon was engaged in pious fraud and that, as *Graetz puts it out of hostility to the Kabbalah, the Zohar is 'the book of lies'. The work bears all the marks of a pseudepigraphic production; that is to say, Moses de Leon used the figures of Rabbi Simeon and his associates as the vehicle for the transmission of his own ideas. It has also been noted that many of the Zoharic ideas go back to a much earlier period than that of de Leon.

The first two editions of the Zohar were published in Mantua (1558–1560) and Cremona (1559–60). A fierce debate took place on whether the Zohar should be printed at all, some Kabbalists arguing that it is forbidden to spread the Kabbalistic doctrines among the masses, the inevitable result of its publication in print. With the printing and subsequent wide dissemination of the Zohar, the process, beginning after the expulsion from Spain, continued of treating the Zohar as a sacred book and not only for the Kabbalists. Moralistic works quoted extensively from the Zohar. Laws and customs based on the Zohar found their way into the standard Codes, although there was much discussion on how far Zoharic practices should have the status of law. The followers of the *Haskalah movement denigrated the Zohar and the Kabbalah in general as a foreign shoot implanted into Judaism to encourage superstition and the irrational in religion.

In *Hasidism the Zohar became a

'canonical' book together with the Bible and the Talmud. The early Hasidic master, Pinhas of Koretz, it is said, used to thank God that he had not been created before the appearance of the Zohar for it was the Zohar that had preserved him for Judaism (gehalten bei Yiddishkeit). Of the *Baal Shem Tov it is related that he would carry a copy of the Zohar with him at all times and he would see the whole world in the Zohar. *Elijah, Gaon of *Vilna, the fierce opponent of Hasidism, also believed in the supreme sanctity of the Zohar and his attitude was shared by the majority of the *Mitnaggedim.

The Zohar, like other classical works of Judaism, has been the subject of applied study by modern scholars in the historical–critical mode. On the contemporary religious scene, many Orthodox Jews, even if they have little or no knowledge of the Zohar, still revere the work as sacred literature. But it has never become a matter of *dogma to believe that the Zohar is a sacred work and, even among the Orthodox, it is possible to be a good Jew and a true believer without accepting the Zohar as an inspired work. Reform and Conservative Judaism is normally critical of the Zohar and its influence while at the same time admiring the many beautiful ideas and numinous insights found in this remarkable work, unique in the history of religion for its mystical style and daring flights of the imagination. (See also CORDOVERO, EN SOF, KABBALAH, and SEFIROT.)

Zoroastrianism The religion founded by the Iranian prophet Zarathustra in the sixth century BCE. The third century CE, the period of stormy conflicts between Persia and Rome—between Graeco-Roman civilizations and the oriental traditions which were dominant in Persia—saw the collapse of the Parthian dynasty and the rise of the Sassanians. Ardeshir, the first of the Sassanian rulers, was

crowned at Chorossan. He became the ruler of the Persian Empire, holding sway over forty million people. One of his first acts was to restore the religion of Zarathustra and give great power to its priests, the Magi. The followers of the religion of light and darkness, of Ormuzd, the god of light, and Ahriman, the god of darkness, destroyed the Greek temples, taught that redemption was possible only through the intercession of the Magi, and began to persecute the adherents of other religions. Bitter attacks on the Jewish religion are found in Pahlavi works (of the Middle Persian period) and this bitterness was not confined, at first, to verbal attacks. The Talmud refers to the destruction of synagogues by the Magi (Yoma 10a) and to harsh decrees issued against Judaism (Yevamot 63b). Since the Magi opposed the burial of the human corpse as polluting the sacred soil, they would, at times, resurrect the Jewish dead (Bava Batra 58a). On the Persian festivals no fire was to be kindled in the home (Shabbat 45a; Gittin 17a) and fire for use in the Persian temples was taken forcibly from Jewish homes (Sanhedrin 74b). In one Talmudic passage (Kiddushin 72a) the Magi are compared to demons. The severity of this persecution, however, gradually waned and, under Shapur I (241–72), Jewish rights were restored. Shapur's edict of toleration reads: 'The Magus, the Manichaean, the Jew and the Christian, and what other sects there are, shall live in peace according to their religion.' On the whole the Jews fared far better in the Persian Empire than in Palestine under Roman rule. The *exilarch enjoyed almost the status of a Jewish king within the Persian state. The friendliest relations seem to have existed between the Jewish sages and some of the Persian rulers. Even if the Talmudic accounts of this friendship, such as that some of the Babylonian Amoraim held conversations with the Persian rulers, are legendary, the very fact that such stories were recorded in the Talmud is indicative of the situation. It was not only in Amoraic times in Babylon that Judaism came into contact with Zoroastrianism, but it was in this period that the tensions between the adherents of the two religions were particularly acute.

Zoroastrian dualism, with Ormuzd struggling against Ahriman, presented a greater challenge to Jewish monotheism than did polytheism, since the Jewish religion also acknowledges the struggle between good and evil. It has been suggested that as long ago as Deutero-Isaiah the unknown prophet preaches against Persian dualism: 'That they may know from the rising of the sun, and from the west, that there is none beside Me; I am the Lord, and there is none else; I form the light, and create darkness; I make peace, and create evil; I am the Lord, that doeth all these things' (Isaiah 45: 6–7). It is probable that Persian dualism had, in fact, an influence on Jewish thought in the emergence of the doctrine of *Satan, although, in Rabbinic thought, Satan is completely subordinate to God and is in no way a rival to Him. It is not at all surprising, therefore, to find so many passages in the Rabbinic literature in which the dualistic challenge is squarely faced.

Zugot 'Pairs', the five sets of two teachers each, whose period preceded that of the *Tannaim. The Mishnah in Ethics of the Fathers (1. 4–12), in the chain of tradition from Moses down to the Tannaim, list five pairs of teachers and their particular doctrines, although, in this source, they are not actually referred to as the Zugot. The pairs are: 1. Yose ben Yoezer and Yose ben Johanan of Jerusalem; 2. Joshua ben Perahyah and Nittai the Arebelite; 3. Judah ben Tabbai and Simeon ben Shatah; 4. Shemaiah and Avtalion; 5. Hillel and Shammai. The two teachers of the last Zug ('pair', singular of Zugot) are the founders of the two houses, Bet

Hillel and Bet Shammai, the first of the Tannaim. In another Mishnah (*Hagigah* 2: 2) it is stated (though here, too, the actual term Zugot is not used) that the first of each pair was the Nasi ('Prince') and the second the Av Bet Din ('Father of the Court'). Some modern scholars see this attribution as an anachronism on the grounds that these two offices were not known in the early period. The date of the first Zug appears to be in the Maccabean period (see MACCABEES), 174–164 BCE.

Zunz, Leopold German historian of Judaism (1794–1886). Zunz is rightly considered to be the foremost figure, if not the founder, of the *Jüdische Wissenschaft movement, in which Judaism is studied by the historical–critical method (and see HISTORY, FRANKEL, KROCHMAL, and RAPOPORT). Zunz received his early education at the Samson School in Wolfenbüttel, where the principal of the school referred to the young boy of 11 as a 'genius'. He settled in Berlin in 1815, studying at the University of Berlin and obtaining a doctorate from the University of Halle. Together with other young men, among them the poet Heinrich Heine, Zunz founded in Berlin in 1819 the *Verein für Cultur und Wissenschaft der Juden*. In 1823 Zunz became the editor of the *Zeitschrift für die Wissenschaft des Judentums*, in which he published a biography of *Rashi in the new, scientific mode.

Zunz's major achievement, published in 1832, is his *Die gottesdienstlichen Vorträge der Juden historisch entwickelt*. The work is a completely objective study of Jewish preaching throughout the ages and is, in fact, a pioneering effort of lasting significance to describe the evolution of *Midrash as a whole. Yet, typical of Zunz's lifelong concern with politics, it had the aim of convincing the German authorities not to ban Jewish preaching in the vernacular as an innovation (these authorities were always suspicious of innovations which might lead to rebellion). Zunz demonstrated not only that preaching had been an art in Judaism from the Rabbinic period but that the sermon was not infrequently in the vernacular. Zunz's *Namen der Juden* was written, at the behest of the Jewish community, when a royal decree ordered that Jews should not use German first names. Zunz demonstrated, again in a completely objective study, that Jews had used foreign names from an early period. Critics of the Jüdische Wissenschaft movement have maintained that its practitioners, with one eye on the effect of their researches on the Gentile world, were never really objective. Zunz, at least, showed that it was possible for a great scholar to pursue his researches in a completely objective manner while frankly acknowledging that he had an axe to grind in the process. Zunz was objective, too, in his biblical studies. At first these were on the later books of the Bible, but later on he espoused the full critical methodology with regard to the *Pentateuch as well (see BIBLICAL CRITICISM).

Zusya of Hanipol Hasidic master and hero of Hasidic folk-tales (d. 1800). Zusya was attracted to *Hasidism in his youth, becoming a disciple of *Dov Baer, the Maggid of Mezhirech, and encouraging his brother Elimelech to join him. Zusya was not noted for his learning, unlike his brother who became the famous *Zaddik of Lizansk and author of the Hasidic classic, *Noam Elimelekh*. Zusya's fame rests on his generous disposition and his charismatic personality.

Zweifel, Eliezer Russian author (1815–88), representative of the moderate tendency in the *Haskalah. Zweifel was born in Mogilev into a family of *Habad Hasidim, acquiring in his youth a very sound knowledge not only of the Bible and Talmud but also of the Kabbalah; he educated himself too in Russian, German, and general secular learning. He wrote extensively in a good Hebrew style but all his work is vitiated by his extreme verbosity and lack of systematic arrangement of the topics with which he deals. His copious quotes from other authors display his tremendous erudition in all branches of Jewish thought, but they often hinder rather than advance his arguments. In this respect, however, Zweifel's works can still serve as anthologies of Jewish teachings on many important subjects. In 1853 Zweifel was appointed lecturer in the Talmud at the government-sponsored Rabbinical Seminary in Zhitomir, remaining there and influencing the students towards a greater appreciation of the tradition until the seminary was closed in 1873. Both by training and temperament Zweifel, as he rightly claimed, tended to see good in everything. Though a staunch defender of Judaism and the Jewish tradition he acknowledged the value of the Haskalah's critique of strict Orthodoxy and, though viewing some aspects of *Hasidism as irrational and superstitious, he warmly espoused the cause of the movement against its enemies. His opponents accused him of lacking the ability to make up his mind. His very name, Zweifel, meaning 'doubt', they said, suited him entirely.

Reference Works

There are three multivolumed encyclopedias in English dealing with Jews and the Jewish religion. *The Jewish Encyclopedia*, edited by Isador Singer, 12 vols (New York, 1901 and various editions until 1926) has long been an indispensable work, but many of the entries are now obviously out of date. *The Universal Jewish Encyclopedia*, edited by Isaac Landman, 10 vols (New York, 1939), was published before the Holocaust and the establishment of the State of Israel and, on these grounds and on others, is now hopelessly out of date. The most up-to-date of the three is *Encyclopedia Judaica*, editors in chief Cecil Roth and Geoffrey Wigoder, 16 vols (Jerusalem, 1972). The recently published work in one large volume, *The Oxford Dictionary of The Jewish Religion*, editors R. J. Zwi Werblowsky and Geoffrey Wigoder (OUP, New York and Oxford, 1997), is a useful tool for quick reference and provides up-to-date scholarly bibliographies.

On Jewish history there can be recommended the single-volume works: *A History of the Jewish People* by Max I. Margolis and Alexander Marks (Philadelphia, 1944); *A History of the Jewish People* by H. H. Ben-Sasson (Cambridge, Mass., 1976); *Jewish People, Jewish Thought: The Jewish Experience in History* by Robert M. Seltzer (New York, 1981).

Two works on the Pentateuch are: *The Pentateuch and Haftorahs* by Chief Rabbi J. H. Hertz from the Orthodox point of view (London, 1960) and *The Torah: A Modern Commentary* by W. Gunther Plaut from the Reform point of view (New York, 1981). A more rigorous scholarly work on the Pentateuch is *The JPS Torah Commentary* under the editorship of Nahum M. Sarna (Philadelphia, New York, and Jerusalem, 1989–96).

There are three works in English in which Jewish theology is presented in systematic form: Kaufmann Kohler, *Jewish Theology Systematically and Historically Considered* (new edition, New York, 1968); Samuel Cohon, *Jewish Theology* (Assen, 1971); Louis Jacobs, *A Jewish Theology* (London and New York, 1973). The first two approach the subject from the Reform point of view, the third from the moderate Conservative point of view. On medieval Jewish philosophy and mysticism the standard works are: Isaac Husik, *A History of Mediaeval Jewish Philosophy* (New York, 1940), and Gershom G. Scholem, *Major Trends in Jewish Mysticism* (London, 1955).

Two symposia on the Jewish religion make for interesting reading: *Disciples of the Wise: The Religious and Social Opinions of American Rabbis*, edited by Joseph Zeitlin (New York, 1970), and *The Conditions of Jewish Belief: A Symposium Compiled by The Editors of Commentary Magazine* (Northvale, NJ and London, 1989). *Contemporary Jewish Religious Thought*, edited by Arthur P. Cohen and Paul Mendes-Flohr (New York, 1987), is an unusual but successful attempt at compiling a dictionary in which every shade of Jewish opinion is represented.

Appendix I: The Jewish Calendar

Nisan is the spring month corresponding to March/April and the months following *Nisan* have the same following correspondence in the solar year. The festivals and fasts of the Jewish year are listed here. For the details see the respective entries.

Nisan 15–22 (15–23 in the Diaspora): Passover (*Pesah*)

Iyyar 18: Lag Ba-Omer

Sivan 6 (6 and 7 in the Diaspora): Pentecost (*Shavuot*)

Tammuz 17: Fast of Tammuz, beginning three weeks of mourning

Av 9: Fast of Av, ending three weeks of mourning

Tishri 1–2: *Rosh Ha-Shanah*, the New Year Festival

Tishri 3: Fast of Gedaliah

Tishri 10: *Yom Kippur* (Day of Atonement)

Tishri 15–23 (15–24 in the Diaspora): Tabernacles (*Sukkot*) including:

Tishri 22: *Hoshanah Rabbah*

Tishri 23: *Shemeni Atzeret* (and *Simhat Torah* in Israel)

Tishri 24: *Simhat Torah* (in the Diaspora)

Kislev: Hanukkah begins on the 25th and lasts for eight days

Tevet 10: Fast of *Tevet*

Shevat 15: New Year for Trees

Adar 13: Fast of Esther

Adar 14: *Purim*

Adar 15: *Shushan Purim*

In recent years *Nisan* 27 has been introduced as *Yom Ha-Shoah* (Day of the Holocaust), commemorating this terrible event, and *Iyyar* 5 as *Yom Ha-Atzmaut* (Israel Independence Day).

From the Middle Ages there are: the *Omer* period of mourning from the end of Passover to just before Pentecost; the Fast of the First-Born on the eve of Passover; the month of *Elul* as a period of preparation for the penitential season in *Tishri*, the Ten Days of Penitence, the first ten days of *Tishri*, from *Rosh Ha-Shanah* to *Yom Kippur*. The Safed mystics introduced the eve of each *Rosh Hodesh* (New Moon) as a Minor Day of Atonement (*Yom Kippur Katan*).

Appendix II: Chronology

Note: dates marked with an asterisk * are uncertain.

BCE

Biblical Period and after

2000* or 1750*	Age of the patriarchs Abraham, Isaac and Jacob
1750* or 1400*	Age of sojourn in Egypt
1400* or 1250*	Moses and the Exodus
1250* or 1050*	Entry into Canaan
1000*	King David
950*	King Solomon builds the First Temple
925*	Kingdom divided into the Northern (Israel) and Southern (Judah) Kingdoms
721	Fall of Northern Kingdom
586	Fall of Southern Kingdom and exile into Babylon
520*	Second Temple built after Return from Babylonian Exile
458*	Ezra and Nehemiah
167	The Maccabees are victorious and rededicate the Temple—Hanukkah
39–34	Hillel and Shammai—Pharisees and Sadducees

CE

Period of the Tannaim 1–200*

14–37	John the Baptist and Jesus—rise of Christianity begins
70	Destruction of Second Temple
170–217*	Judah the Prince—editing of the Mishnah

Period of the Amoraim

400*	Palestinian Talmud completed
500*	Babylonian Talmud completed

Period of the Geonim 650–1038

569–632	Mohammed and rise of Islam
769	The Karaite Schism

Medieval Period

882–942	Saadiah Gaon—philosophical approach begins and grows
Eleventh to thirteenth centuries	Rashi and the Tosafot
1135–1204	Maimonides
Twelfth to thirteenth centuries	The Saints of Germany—the Kabbalah and the Zohar
Sixteenth century	The *Shulhan Arukh*—the Lurianic Kabbalah
Eighteenth century	The *Baal Shem Tov* and rise of Hasidism

Modern Period

1729–1786	Moses Mendelssohn—the Haskalah
1818	The Hamburg Reform Temple—rise of Reform begins
1762–1839	Moses Sofar—champion of Orthodoxy
1808–1888	Samson Raphael Hirsch—Neo-Orthodoxy
1860–1904	Theodor Herzl—rise of Zionism

Twentieth Century

1939–1945	World War II—the Holocaust, six million Jews exterminated
1948	State of Israel established